Marketing and Shipping
LIVE AQUATIC PRODUCTS

Proceedings of the Second International Conference and Exhibition,
November 1999, Seattle, Washington

Edited by Brian C. Paust and Allison A. Rice

Published by University of Alaska Sea Grant College Program

Report No. AK-SG-01-03

Elmer E. Rasmuson Library Cataloging in Publication Data:

Marketing and Shipping Live Aquatic Products (2nd : 1999 : Seattle, Wash.)

Marketing and shipping live aquatic products : proceedings of the second International Conference and Exhibition, November 1999, Seattle, Washington / Edited by Brian C. Paust and Allison A. Rice. – Fairbanks, Alaska : University of Alaska Sea Grant College Program, [2001].

308 p. : ill. ; cm. – (University of Alaska Sea Grant College Program ; AK-SG-01-03)

Includes bibliographical references and index.

1. Aquatic animals—Transportation—Congresses. 2. Aquatic animals—Marketing—Congresses. 3. Aquatic animals—Housing—Congresses. 4. Aquatic animals—Law and legislation—Congresses. 3. Seafood industry—Quality control—Congresses. I. Title. II. Paust, Brian C. III. Rice, Allison A. IV. Series: Alaska Sea Grant College Program report ; AK-SG-01-03.

HD9450.5 M37 1999

ISBN 1-56612-067-5

Citation for this volume is B.C. Paust and A.A. Rice (eds.). 2001. Marketing and shipping live aquatic products: Proceedings of the Second International Conference and Exhibition, November 1999, Seattle, WA. University of Alaska Sea Grant, AK-SG-01-03, Fairbanks.

CREDITS

This book is published by the University of Alaska Sea Grant College Program, which is cooperatively supported by the U.S. Department of Commerce, NOAA National Sea Grant Office, grant no. NA86RG-0050, projects A/151-01 and A/161-01; and by the University of Alaska Fairbanks with state funds. The University of Alaska is an affirmative action/equal opportunity institution.

Sea Grant is a unique partnership with public and private sectors combining research, education, and technology transfer for public service. This national network of universities meets changing environmental and economic needs of people in our coastal, ocean, and Great Lakes regions.

University of Alaska Sea Grant
P.O. Box 755040
205 O'Neill Bldg.
Fairbanks, Alaska 99775-5040
Toll free (888) 789-0090
(907) 474-6707 • Fax (907) 474-6285
http://www.uaf.edu/seagrant/

Contents

Acknowledgments vii

Physiological Characteristics of Animals Destined for Live and Ornamental Markets

Physiological Responses of Blue Crabs *(Callinectes* sp.*)* to
Procedures Used in the Soft Crab Fishery in
La Laguna de Terminos, Mexico
   Angela R. Danford, Roger F. Uglow, and Carlos Rosas 1

Effect of Long-Haul International Transport on Lobster
Hemolymph Constituents and Nitrogen Metabolism
   Angela R. Danford, Roger F. Uglow, and John Garland 9

Physiological Stress Response in Fish
   George Iwama 19

Critical Oxygen Point in Yellowleg Shrimp *(Farfantepenaeus californiensis)*: A Potential Species for the Live Seafood Trade
   Lucía Ocampo V. 23

Social, Ethical, and Humanitarian Considerations

Animal Rights Advocacy, Public Perception,
and the Trade in Live Animals
   Paul G. Olin 27

Animal Ethics and the Live Aquatic Animal Trade
   Bernard E. Rollin 35

Live Holding System Engineering and Water Quality

Holding Tank System for Reconditioning Transport
of Live Cod Recently Captured in Deep Water
   Hans-Peder Pedersen and Arnt Amble 45

Short-Term Holding and Live Transport of Aquatic Animals:
An Overview of Problems and Some Historic Solutions
   David J. Scarratt 51

Live Fish Handling Strategies from Boat to Retail Establishment
   John Seccombe 57

Ornamental Species Industry

Florida's Ornamental Marine Life Industry
   Sherry L. Larkin, Donna J. Lee, Robert L. Degner,
   J. Walter Milon, and Charles M. Adams 63

Shipping Practices in the Ornamental Fish Industry
*Brian Cole, Clyde S. Tamaru, Rich Bailey, Christopher Brown,
and Harry Ako* 73

The Ornamental Fish Industry
Craig A. Watson 87

LIVE SHIPMENT OF MARINE ALGAE AND AQUATIC PLANTS

Live Rockweed *(Ascophyllum)* used as a Shipping Medium
for the Live Transport of Marine Baitworms from Maine
Stephen E. Crawford 95

Shipping and Handling the Marine Algae *Macrocystis* in Alaska
Thea Thomas 99

LIVE SHIPMENT OF MOLLUSKS AND CRUSTACEANS

Live Transport of the Great Scallop *(Pecten maximus)*
Toril Overaa 105

Handling and Shipping of Live Northeast Pacific Scallops:
Larvae to Adults
William A. Heath 111

The Harvest and Culture of Live Freshwater
Aquatic Invertebrates
Barry Thoele 125

Optimizing Waterless Shipping Conditions for
Macrobrachium rosenbergii
John Kubaryk and Carol Harper 131

Keeping Baitfish Alive and Healthy in Holding Tanks:
Tips for Retail Outlets
Hugh Thomforde 141

What's New in Live Fish and Shellfish At-Sea Holding Systems:
High Tech and Low Tech
Mick Kronman 145

Opportunity or Threat? Implications of the Live Halibut
Fishery in British Columbia from the Harvester Perspective
Kim Mauriks 151

RESOURCE MANAGEMENT ISSUES AND THE
DEVELOPING LIVE HARVEST INDUSTRY

Resource Management and Environmental Issues Concerning
Live Halibut Landings
Bruce M. Leaman 155

Contents

Sterling Pacific Halibut: A New Approach
    Kim Mauriks 159

Resource Management Issues in California's Commercial
Nearshore Live/Premium Finfish Fishery
    Christine Pattison 163

Shipping Live Fish into British Columbia, Canada:
Basic Regulatory Requirements
    Dorothee Kieser 171

Resource Management Issues: Question and Answer Session
    Bruce M. Leaman, Kim Mauriks, and Christine Pattison 177

MARKETING LIVE SEAFOOD AND ORNAMENTAL PRODUCTS

The Live Reef Food Fish Trade in Hong Kong:
Problems and Prospects
    Yvonne Sadovy 183

Marketing Aspects of the Live Seafood Trade in
Hong Kong and the People's Republic of China
    Patrick S.W. Chan 193

Wholesale and Retail Marketing Aspects of the
Hong Kong Live Seafood Business
    Patrick S.W. Chan 201

An Overview of Irish Live Crustacean Fisheries
    Ian Lawler 207

The Construction of a Commercial Live Seafood
Transshipment Facility: Review of General Specifications
    Jon Chaiton 215

An Insight into the Shanghai Market for Imported Live Seafood
    Thomas Liu 221

REGULATORY CONCERNS ASSOCIATED WITH THE TRANSPORT OF LIVE AQUATICS

The National Seafood Hazard Analysis Critical Control Point
Program and the Live Seafood Industry
    Donald Kramer 227

Restraints to Shipping Live Product: Lessons from
the AquaSeed Corporation Experience
    Per Heggelund 231

Shipping Live Aquatic Products: Biological,
Regulatory, and Environmental Considerations
    John G. Nickum 237

NONINDIGENOUS SPECIES AND THE LIVE AQUATIC INDUSTRY: THE PROBLEM OF EXOTIC INTRODUCTIONS

Do Live Marine Products Serve as Pathways for
the Introduction of Nonindigenous Species?
    Annette M. Olson 243

Live Seafood: A Recipe for Biological and Regulatory Concern?
    Todd W. Miller, John W. Chapman, and Eugene V. Coan 249

Review of Impacts of Aquatic Exotic Species: What's at Risk?
    Paul Heimowitz 257

Impact of the Green Crab on the Washington State Shellfish
Aquaculture Industry
    Charlie Stephens 263

LIVE SHIPMENT QUALITY AND SAFETY

A New Direction for Monitoring Lobster Meat Yield,
Using Advances in Acoustic Probing
    R.J. Cawthorn, A. Battison, J. Guigné, K. Klein, Q. Liu,
    A. MacKenzie, R. MacMillan, and D. Rainnie 267

Using HACCP Principles and Physiological Studies
to Improve Marketing Practices for Live Crustaceans
    S. Gomez-Jimenez, R.F. Uglow, R. Pacheco-Aguilar and
    L.O. Noriega-Orozco 271

Live Seafood Holding Systems: Review of Systems
and Components
    John Chaiton 283

Participants 291

Index 295

Acknowledgments

The meeting "Marketing and Shipping Live Aquatic Products: Second International Conference and Exhibition" was held November 14-17, 1999 in Seattle, Washington. John Peters was conference manager. Session chairs include Donald Kramer, Roger Uglow, Allison Rice, Edward Kolbe, Paul Olin, Mike Stekoll, John Ewart, Brian Paust, John Richards, Christopher DeWees, Jodi Cassell, Skip Kemp, John Chaiton, Raymond RaLonde, Quentin Fong, Annette Olson, Scott Smith, and Charles Crapo. The meeting was sponsored by AFDF, Alaska Department of Commerce and Economic Development, Alaska Science and Technology Foundation, Alaska Seafood Marketing Institute, Anchorage International Airport, California Sea Grant, CFAB, National Sea Grant Office, Nor'westerly Food Technology Services, Oregon Sea Grant, Seafood Business, University of Alaska Sea Grant and Marine Advisory Program, University of Delaware Sea Grant, and Woods Hole Sea Grant. Julie Carpenter of the Alaska Marine Advisory Program helped make travel and financial arrangements for the meeting.

The proceedings book was published by University of Alaska Sea Grant. Sue Keller copy-edited and arranged the production of the book, Kathy Kurtenbach formatted the text pages, and Tatiana Piatanova designed the cover

Physiological Responses of Blue Crabs (*Callinectes* sp.) to Procedures Used in the Soft Crab Fishery in La Laguna de Terminos, Mexico

Angela R. Danford and Roger F. Uglow
University of Hull, Hull, U.K.

Carlos Rosas
Universidad Nacional Autónoma de México, Campeche, Mexico

Abstract

The blue crab fishery in La Laguna de Terminos, Campeche, Mexico includes *Callinectes sapidus*, *C. rathbunae*, and *C. danae*. These species are morphologically similar but differ in their physiological requirements, salinity tolerance, and distribution. They are treated identically by the local fishermen, who sell them to suppliers of soft crabs in the United States. Despite their physical similarities, the species differ in their distributions within the lagoon system and have very different physiological requirements.

Following capture, the crabs must tolerate a variety of post-harvest stresses, including periods of air exposure, temperature and/or salinity changes, handling, and interactions with other crab. At the shedding factory, they are kept at ambient temperature (range 27-35°C) and local salinity (5-10 ppt) until they molt, or, in the case of *C. danae*, probably die.

Ammonia efflux rates were used as an indicator of the severity and types of stress. At 30 minutes after handling, effluxes were 2.04±0.12, 0.18±0.13, and 2.14±0.46 µmol NH_4 per gram per hour respectively for *C. sapidus*, *C. rathbunae*, and *C. danae*. After 4 hours, these rates had dropped to 0.18±0.02, 0.21±0.03, and 0.56±0.18 µmol NH_4 per gram per hour. *Callinectes sapidus* and *C. rathbunae* did not alter ammonia efflux rates significantly on transfer to diluted seawater and were shown to be efficient osmoregulators, but *C. danae* showed large individual variability of response to dilution. Following a 4 hour period in air, all three species showed elevated ammonia excretion levels when reimmersed. After 60 minutes, the efflux rates had reverted to "normal" pre-emersion values. The findings are discussed in the context of possible procedural changes that would reduce losses, thus increasing production without the need for increased landings.

Introduction

This paper deals with the physiological responses of blue crabs, *Callinectes* sp., to procedures used in the soft crab fishery in the Laguna de Terminos, Mexico. A "soft-shell" crab is an animal that has just molted and is considered a delicacy in the restaurant market of the United States. The holding and transporting of live shellfish is now a common event in the specialized trade of crabs, lobsters, and prawns. Many current practices have arisen purely by trial and error and often without much real thought about the physiological requirements of a particular species. The natural environments of shellfish vary widely in terms of physical and chemical details such as water salinity and temperature. Hence, holding and transporting systems used for one species may not be appropriate for another. For example, the edible crab *Cancer pagurus* can be transported dry for periods up to 2 days. The velvet crab, *Necora puber*, on the other hand, inhabits a similar environment, but is much less tolerant of air exposure.

The expansion of fisheries worldwide has meant that old resource bases are becoming less reliable and more priority is being given to developing underutilized areas. The coastline of the gulf states of Mexico is one such and with the American market close by, new attempts are being made to improve communications and international trading.

The fishing industry in Mexico is still developing rapidly. Considering the abundance of commercial species there, it seems that there is much scope for further development and growth. Shellfish have been caught primarily for local consumption, and increasing amounts are being exported to the United States. This export trade has proved to be a lucrative development. The blue crab fishery of *Callinectes sapidus* in the United States is based on the gulf coast and Chesapeake Bay area and provides an annual catch of between 45,000 and 89,000 metric tons (Cameron 1984). It is thought that the harvest from the recreational fishery is almost as large. Hence, there are concerns over the sustainability of this resource due to increasing fishing effort, market demand, and the continued degradation of coastal habitats essential for the life cycle of this species. The Mexican annual catch, however, is only 6,000-9,000 metric tons (Secretaría de Pesca 1994). The Mexican fishery, however, has the advantage of being a year-round fishery.

International trade in blue crab could be particularly lucrative in Mexico if a good marketing system is developed for them (Nowak 1970). In Ciudad Del Carmen, Campeche, Mexico, blue crabs are fished by local artisanal harvesters and delivered to one of two plants that specialize in providing soft blue crab for the American restaurant market.

A description of the soft blue crab trade is presented here, as well as some preliminary physiological experiments designed to use ammonia effluxes as an indicator and identify practices that cause stress. The future success of this live and soft-shell crab industry is dependent on adequate training in holding, handling, packing, and transporting techniques. The viability of this fishery also depends on obtaining more information on the factors that cause stress and, hence, quality loss in the product.

BLUE CRABS

Blue crabs are swimming crabs (family Portunidae, order Decapoda), a worldwide group containing many species of commercial importance. "Blue crab" is actually a generic name that includes many similar species within the genus *Callinectes*. What many consider to be *Callinectes sapidus* actually comprises several species that look very much alike. In the Gulf of Mexico, at least five species are caught commercially, of which three are included in this study—*Callinectes sapidus* (Rathbun 1896), *C. rathbunae* (Rathbun 1896), and *C. danae* (Smith 1869). These species are quite similar in appearance and are identified by differences in the prominent protuberances and teeth between the eyes (Fig. 1). However, they are very different in their physiological requirements and the niches that they occupy.

These three species are caught indiscriminately by fishermen along the length of a large mangrove and lagoon system in the state of Campeche. The salinity decreases along the lagoons and estuaries from 35 parts per thousand (ppt) to levels as low as 3 ppt. *Callinectes sapidus* is an intermediate species that can tolerate varying salinities and is found most abundantly in salinity of 15 ppt. *Callinectes rathbunae* is the most tolerant to varying salinity and is caught in full seawater to as low as 5 ppt, whereas *C. danae* is a more oceanic species and has been found in salinities from 30 to 67 ppt.

THE FISHERY IN THE LAGUNA DE TERMINOS

Crabs are harvested by local fishermen from areas with salinities of approximately 35 ppt in the ocean

Figure 1. Species identification based on rostral teeth arrangement.

along mangroves to areas where the salinity can be almost zero. Once caught, the crabs are placed in large plastic containers and covered with mangrove leaves to keep humidity high. They are transported in air to the shedding plant, usually within 3-4 hours after capture. The shedding operations are non-technical and are characterized by low levels of investment and high profitability (Fig. 2).

At the plant, the crabs are sorted by molt stage and transferred to large holding tanks with a salinity of 5 to 8 ppt. Once fully molted, the crabs are dressed in the plant (removal of eyestalks, mouth-parts, and abdomen), packaged, frozen, and shipped to the United States. Crabs that do not molt are processed or made into fertilizer and animal feed, which is not as profitable as producing soft crab.

PHYSIOLOGY

Millions of years of evolution have created diverse species that are best adapted to the environment in which they live. A wild-harvested animal, such as a blue crab, is placed in an alien environment from the moment it is captured. Unless the holding and transport conditions provided are within the physiological tolerances of the animals, their deterioration and death are inevitable. The deterioration exhibited by various captive animals may be rapid or slow because certain types of stress affect each species differently. Nevertheless, the effects of abuse tend to be cumulative, and measurements of physiological changes in these captive animals can give useful information as to what is stressful. This can give an insight into the types and magnitude of stress encountered from capture to delivery—factors that can potentially delay molting. If the developing fishery is to be successful, ways must be found to mitigate these stress factors.

Stressed and unstressed shellfish normally look exactly the same but stressed animals are more likely to succumb to the rigors of marketing procedures than unstressed ones. Consequently, it appears reasonable to make practical use of physiological indicators of the animals' well being. In this study, ammonia excretion rates were measured, as they provide a reliable and sensitive indicator of general metabolism. Although other measurements of metabolism, e.g., oxygen consumption, are recognized as good indicators of physiological status and are practical means of measuring stress, other equally sensitive indicators are now available.

Figure 2. Inside of the shedding plant.

Ammonia excretion is one such indicator. Preliminary studies in our laboratory have shown that stresses such as handling caused greater changes to ammonia excretion than to oxygen consumption in several freshwater fish species (Bracewell 1999). Ammonia was measured using flow-injection analysis as developed by Hunter and Uglow (1993a).

Ammonia is the principal waste of nitrogen metabolism in aquatic organisms. It is produced continuously by the animal and excreted continuously across the gills. Ammonia exists in two forms within biological systems, the gas NH_3 and the ion NH_4^+. Ammonia gas is the most toxic of the two and the proportion of NH_3 to NH_4^+ is dependent on pH. At physiological pH (approx. 7.8) most of the ammonia exists as the least toxic NH_4^+. In these experiments total ammonia was measured, which is the combination of NH_3 and NH_4^+.

Simple investigations into the changing ammonia efflux rates of blue crabs were made in an effort to identify some of the stressful situations to which these animals are exposed with the final aim of improving some of the practices used.

IDENTIFYING THE PROBLEMS

From the point of capture to the point where they molt and are selected for final processing, the crabs are exposed to a number of stresses. With blue crabs, as with many other species, the main forms of stress involved in the harvesting, holding, and transporting are:

- Animal Interaction
- Handling
- Water quality
- Dehydration
- Temperature changes
- Air exposure

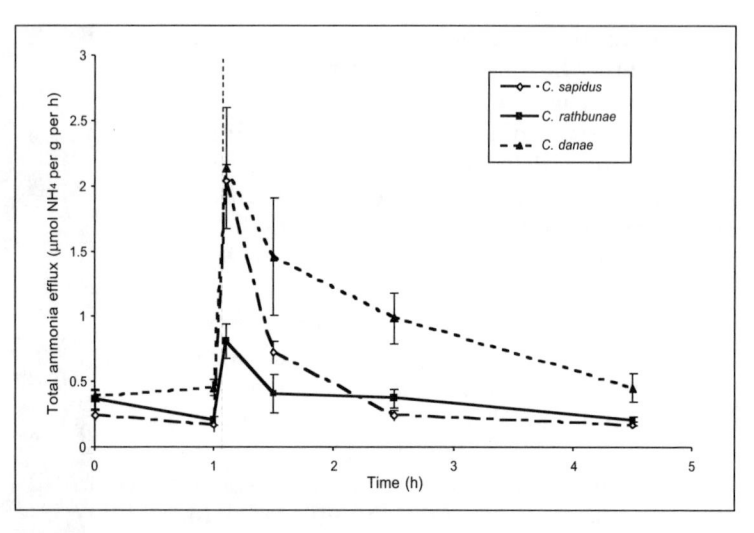

Figure 3. Total ammonia efflux rates before and after handling. Each line represents the mean of $n = 8$ with S.E. for each species. Vertical dashed line represents moment of handling.

ANIMAL INTERACTIONS AND HANDLING

Blue crabs are extremely aggressive and are especially active at tropical temperatures (30-40°C). High levels of mutual damage can occur even before crabs are landed due to fighting in the traps. Missing limbs and other forms of injury are common. This problem is not only an aesthetic point; interactions of this sort also produce stress in the animal. Regular checking of the traps should reduce the number of weakened animals.

Blue crabs are handled when removed from traps, on arrival at the plant, and a number of times at the shedding plant during transfer between tanks, weighing, and repeated examination for molt stage. Investigations were made into the changes to metabolism induced by handling on the three species of blue crabs. Figure 3 shows the change in ammonia efflux and hence the metabolic effect of a simple transfer of crabs from one container to another, an operation that lasted 1 to 2 seconds.

The ammonia excretion rate doubled in *C. rathbunae* and increased approximately 4-fold in *C. sapidus* and *C. danae*. It took a further 2-4 hours for the ammonia excretion rates to return to the pre-handling levels. Therefore, continued handling and interactions with other crabs result in a sustained higher rate of metabolism and the expenditure of valuable energy reserves. Handling-induced changes to circulating internal ammonia levels were also found to occur in the shrimp *Crangon crangon* (Hunter and Uglow 1993b).

WATER QUALITY WITH EMPHASIS ON SALINITY DIFFERENCES

Callinectes danae is entirely marine whereas *C. sapidus* and *C. rathbunae* inhabit the lagoon system in salinities which range from 5 to 35 ppt. At the shedding plant, all the crabs are placed in local water of the same salinity at between 5 and 8 ppt. This water is not monitored for quality, but is taken directly from the nearby lagoon. The effect of salinity changes on these species was investigated because it was apparent that some of these animals experienced a 30 ppt salinity change—the difference between the salinity at the capture location and that present at the shedding plant. Clearly, animals brought from regions of higher salinity are subjected to a sudden salinity change and hence, osmotic stress.

Each crab ($n = 8$) was placed individually into a plastic container holding 2 L of seawater with a salinity of 35 ppt and allowed to acclimate for 4 hours before their ammonia effluxes were measured. The crabs were then transferred to water with a salinity of 5 ppt and the procedure repeated. The salinity-dependent ammonia effluxes are shown in Fig. 4.

Hemolymph samples were taken from other individuals of each species that had been acclimated within a range of salinities in order to determine if there was any salinity dependence of blood ammonia levels (Fig. 5).

Transfer to a dilute medium (local water) produced a small but not statistically significant increase to the ammonia efflux rates of *C. sapidus* and *C. rathbunae*, but induced significant ($P < 0.05$) increases in *C. danae* efflux rates. *Callinectes danae* in a salinity of 5 ppt excreted a mean of 1.4 µmol NH_4 per gram per hour. This is the equivalent of 5.04 mmol NH_4 per day, a high rate for an animal with no food intake. Hemolymph ammonia concentrations varied widely with salinity, with the lowest hemolymph ammonia mean values at a salinity of 20 ppt. This suggests that 20 ppt may be near optimum for water used in holding systems and, in view of ammonia excretion, the least stressful salinity for *C. sapidus* and *C. rathbunae*. A lower level of ammonia in the blood is consistent with a low level of stress. *Callinectes danae*, however, did not survive long enough to acclimate in salinities below 20 ppt.

The inverse relationship between salinity and ammonia excretion, as illustrated by *C. danae*, can be related to an increased deamination of the amino acids used for cell volume regulation in dilute media (Gerard and Gilles 1972). This is energetically expensive, as is the active replacement of sodium ions with ammonium ions (Mangum et al. 1976, Pressley et al. 1981).

Salinity tolerant species, such as *C. sapidus* and *C. rathbunae*, have been shown by others to have only minor changes to blood ammonia and amino acid levels when in dilute media (Ballard and Abbott 1969, Engel et al. 1974, Findley and Stickle 1978). The only minor increases in ammonia excretion by *C. sapidus* and *C. rathbunae* demonstrate their salinity tolerance. *Callinectes danae*, however, appears to be very intolerant of transfer to diluted seawater, and attempts to do so in a commercial operation are counterproductive. Not only will this species perish at low to medium salinities, but their decomposition products are likely to foul the water and jeopardize the lives of the other species in the tanks. In this instance, it would be more sensible to cease trading in *C. danae* at the tested establishment or to invest in a better quality holding and water supply system that is capable of delivering full salinity water.

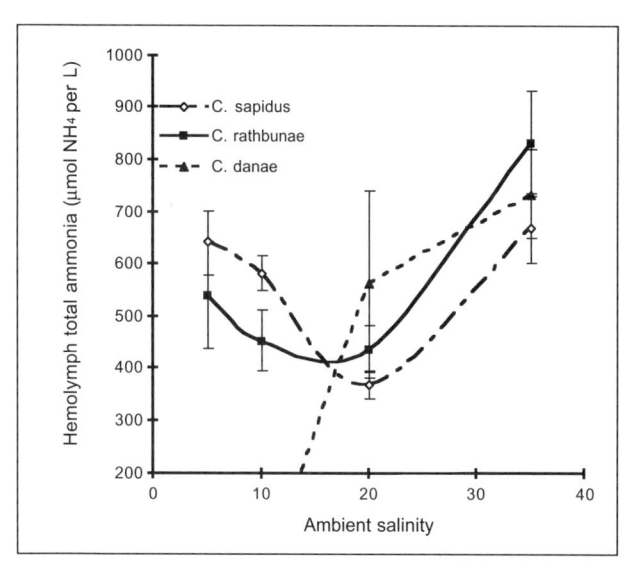

Figure 5. Salinity dependent hemolymph ammonia levels in *Callinectes* species. Values are the mean of $n = 8$ with S.E. *C. danae* died in salinities below 20 ppt.

AIR EXPOSURE (EMERSION) AND DEHYDRATION

Dehydration is a problem for these animals when transported dry. Moist gills are necessary for the continuation of respiratory gas exchange and removal of waste products. The effects of air exposure on crustacean gas exchange and blood chemistry have been studied extensively (Johnson and Uglow 1985, Burnett and McMahon 1987, DeFur 1988, DeFur et al. 1988, Burnett 1988 among others). However, studies are infrequently applied in the context of the transport of live animals.

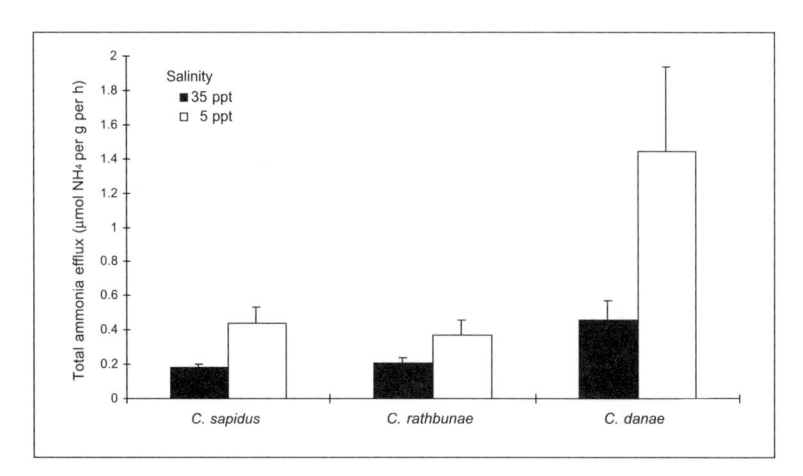

Figure 4. Total ammonia efflux rates of *Callinectes* species at salinities of 35 and 5 ppt. Values are the mean of $n = 8$ with S.E.

Out of water, an aquatic animal faces a number of physiological problems related to the functioning of their gills. Air exposure is a considerable stress because the gills are not able to function in air as efficiently as they do in water. O'Mahoney and Full (1984) found that *C. sapidus* could not maintain normal oxygen uptake levels during emersion, but is known to survive emersion for 1-3 days at low temperatures (DeFur et al. 1988).

Our observations at the shedding plant showed that *C. sapidus* could survive 2 days of emersion when held in high humidity at >30°C.

In full sunlight, mangrove leaves in the crate are unlikely to keep the relative humidity high enough to prevent dehydration. Freshly caught blue crabs may have to endure emersion for 3-4 h or more at >30°C before reaching the shedding plant.

This observation prompted a small experiment to determine the effect of 4 hour air exposure periods on the animal's metabolism. After a 4 hour air exposure at 85-90% relative humidity, eight of each species were returned to seawater (35 ppt) and their ammonia effluxes monitored. It is important to remember that the gills cannot function as efficiently when in air but ammonia is still produced continuously. A similar pattern of ammonia efflux was found in all three species (Fig. 6) even though *C. danae* was relatively intolerant of air exposure (mortalities were observed after only 4 hours in air). In all cases, a large efflux of ammonia occurred during the first 10 minutes after reimmersion which suggests ammonia had accumulated during emersion. The relationship between the amount of ammonia expected to be excreted upon reimmersion following 4 hours in air and the amount actually measured, gives the impression that either ammonia production continued at a reduced rate, or that nitrogenous wastes are excreted in some other form or by some other means. The important point is that the majority of the efflux of ammonia occurs within the first 10 minutes, and that "normal" pre-emersion rates were restored after 30-60 minutes.

The potential implications of this finding in the context of holding and transporting product is obvious. Animals that experience emersion will release large amounts of ammonia upon reimmerison.

Therefore, tanks and holding systems need to be geared to cope with such a sudden increase in ammonia concentration. The release of ammonia on reimmersion is only transient, lasting approximately ten minutes. However, the accumulation of ammonia will be more permanent in static and recirculating systems. This influx of ammonia may be accommodated in a flow-through system, but in the case of static holding systems or recirculating holding systems with biofilters, this burst of ammonia is going to present a problem.

The consequences of an overloaded system can be dire. Ambient ammonia levels in the sea and freshwater environments are usually very low (a few μmol NH_4 per L) and the ammonia excreted by animals under such circumstances rarely creates a problem for them. The accumulation of ambient ammonia ions, however, is often a problem when animals are held at high densities in holding systems. Ammonia is toxic and long-term exposure to high levels can compromise the quality of the stock.

Ammonia is highly diffusible and, when abruptly exposed to a medium with dissolved ammonia levels greater than those in the blood, an influx-induced elevation of blood ammonia levels may occur (Hosie et al. 1991, Schmitt and Uglow 1997). High ambient ammonia water levels have been found to retard growth and, in extreme cases, cause death (Wickins 1976, Armstrong et al. 1978, Chen et al. 1990).

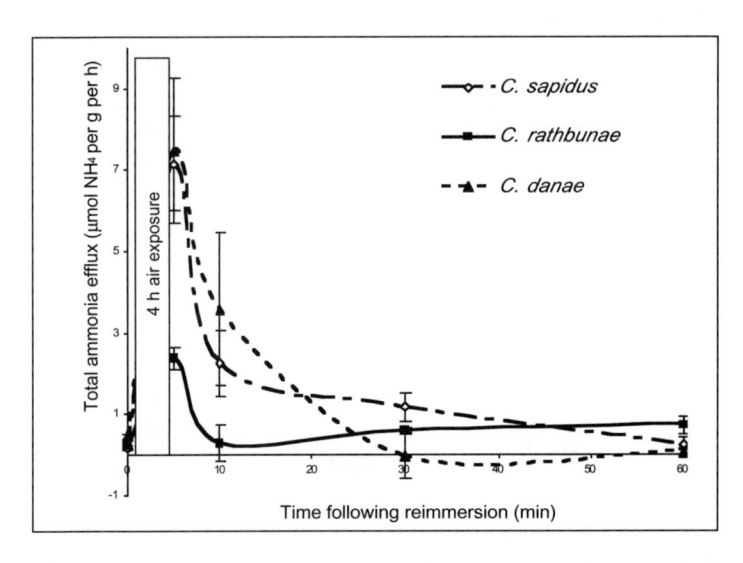

Figure 6. The effect of 4 hour air exposure on total ammonia efflux following reimmersion in *Callinectes* species. Values are the mean of $n = 8$ with S.E.

Conclusion

The measurement of ammonia proved to be a good indicator of changing metabolism in blue crabs. *Callinectes danae* was the least tolerant to salinity changes and air exposure, whereas *C. sapidus* and *C. rathbunae* could survive prolonged periods of air exposure in humid conditions and large salinity fluctuations.

At the shedding plants, the crabs are kept in large tanks filled with local water until they molt. While held, they suffer a variety of physiological stresses which probably delay ecdysis and raise the mortality rate. Providing the optimum water conditions would increase the income of the companies by promoting a quality product and would also reduce product wastage via mortalities and over-exploitation of local resources. The majority of physiological studies focus on and isolate particular stressing factors using previously unstressed and uninjured animals. It is important to consider the combined effect of several different stresses to the welfare of the animals.

There are other ways of measuring metabolism to provide stress indices. Metabolic products such as lactate, urate, glucose, and hormones are produced by crustaceans under different forms of stress, and these can also provide useful information. Investigations into such stress indices are being conducted at Hull University together with investigations into the potential detoxification mechanisms that commercial crustacean species use to combat high internal and external ammonia concentrations.

Acknowledgments

We wish to thank the researchers at the Universidad Nacional Autónoma de México (UNAM) laboratory in Ciudad Del Carmen for their help during our visit and to Consejo Nacional de Ciencia y Tecnología (CONACYT) for financial aid.

References

Armstrong, D.A., D. Chippendale, A.W. Knight, and J.E. Colt. 1978. Interaction of ionized ammonia and unionized ammonia on short-term survival and growth of prawn larvae, *Machrobrachium rosenbergii*. Biol. Bull. 154:15-31.

Ballard, B.S., and W. Abbott. 1969. Osmotic accommodation in *Callinectes sapidus* Rathbun. Comp. Biochem. Physiol. 29:671-687.

Bracewell, P. 1999. The effects of electric fishing on some freshwater cyprinid fish species. Ph.D. thesis, University of Hull, U.K. 241 pp.

Burnett, L.E. 1988. Physiological responses to air exposure: Acid-base balance and the role of branchial water stores. Amer. Zool. 28:125-135.

Burnett, L.E., and B.R. McMahon. 1987. Gas exchange, hemolymph acid-base status and the role of branchial water stores. Amer. Zool. 28:125-135.

Cameron, M.L. 1984. The paddle crab industry in New Zealand: Development of the U.S. West Coast market. Ministry of Agriculture and Fisheries, Wellington. 38 pp.

Chen, J.C., P.C. Liu, and S.C. Lei. 1990. Toxicities of ammonia and nitrite to *Penaeus monodon* adolescents. Aquaculture 89:127-137.

DeFur, P.L. 1988. Systemic respiratory adaptations to air exposure in intertidal decapod crustaceans. Amer. Zool. 28:115-124.

DeFur, P.L., A. Pease, A. Siebelink, and S. Elfers. 1988. Respiratory responses of blue crabs, *Callinectes sapidus*, to emersion. Comp. Biochem. Physiol. 89A:97-101.

Engel, D.W., E.M. Davis, D.E. Smith, and J.E. Angelovic. 1974. The effect of salinity and temperature on the ion levels in the haemolymph of the blue crab, *Callinectes sapidus*, Rathbun. Comp. Biochem. Physiol. 49A:259-266.

Findley, A.M., and W.B. Stickle. 1978. Effects of salinity fluctuation on the haemolymph composition of the blue crab *Callinectes sapidus*. Mar. Biol. 46:9-15.

Gerard, J.F., and R. Gilles. 1972. The free amino-acid pool in *Callinectes sapidus* tissues and its role in the osmotic intracellular regulation. J. Exp. Mar. Biol. Ecol. 10:125-136.

Johnson, I., and R.F Uglow. 1985. Some effects of aerial exposure on the respiratory physiology and blood chemistry of *Carcinus maenas* (L.) and *Liocarcinus puber* (L.). J. Exp. Mar. Biol. Ecol. 94:151-165.

Hosie, D.A., R.F. Uglow, L. Hagerman, T. Sondegaard, and K. Weile. 1991. Some effects of hypoxia and medium ammonia enrichment on efflux rates and circulating levels of ammonia in *Nephrops norvegicus*. Mar. Biol. 110:273-279.

Hunter, D.A., and R.F. Uglow. 1993a. A technique for the measurement of total ammonia in small volumes of seawater and haemolymph. Ophelia 37:31-40.

Hunter, D.A., and R.F. Uglow. 1993b. Handling-induced changes to haemolymph ammonia concentration and ammonia excretion rate of *Crangon crangon* (L.). Ophelia 38:137-147.

Mangum, C.P., S.U. Silverthorn, J.L. Harris, D.W. Towle, and A.R. Krall. 1976. The relationship between blood pH, ammonia excretion and adaptation to low salinity in the blue crab, *Callinectes sapidus*. J. Exp. Zool. 195:129-136.

Nowak, W.S.W. 1970. The marketing of shellfish. Fishing News (Books) Ltd. London. 263 pp.

O'Mahoney, P.M., and R.F. Full. 1984. Respiration of crabs in air and water. Comp. Biochem. Physiol. 79A:275-282.

Pressley, T.A., J.S. Graves, and A.R. Krall. 1981. Amiloride-sensitive ammonium and sodium transport in the blue crab. Am. J. Phys. 241:370-378.

Schmitt, A.S.C., and R.F. Uglow. 1997. Some effects of ambient ammonia levels on blood ammonia, ammonia excretion and heart and scaphognathite rates of *Nephrops norvegicus* (L.). Mar. Biol. 127(3):411-418.

Secretaría de Pesca. 1994. Atlas pesquero de México. Instituto National de la pesca. 234 pp.

Wickens, J.K. 1976. The tolerance of warm-water prawns to recirculated water. Aquaculture 9:19-37.

Effect of Long-Haul International Transport on Lobster Hemolymph Constituents and Nitrogen Metabolism

Angela R. Danford and Roger F. Uglow
University of Hull, Hull, U.K.

John Garland
Clearwater Fine Foods Inc., Bedford, Nova Scotia, Canada

Abstract

The American lobster, *Homarus americanus*, is a very important commercial species and is distributed alive to markets worldwide. The possible deleterious effects of long-haul consignments were investigated in terms of hemolymph constituent changes and metabolic ammonia effluxes. The study involved groups ($n = 10$) of freshly caught and 127 day stored lobsters. Lobsters were consigned with normal road and air carriers from Halifax, Canada, to Hull, U.K., and were held out of water for 48-50 hours. Journey temperature varied between 1.5 and 2.0°C. On arrival at Hull, the animals were examined, weighed, and bled to provide laboratory samples before being reimmersed, each in 6 L of 12°C seawater.

All lobsters survived the period of aerial exposure. However, three of the stored lobsters died within 4 hours of reimmersion. Hemolymph acidosis (–0.5 pH units) developed during the consignment, and hemolymph levels of metabolic end products (ammonia, lactate, and urate) increased. Blood protein levels showed a progressive decrease during consignment and recovery and had the lowest concentration in those lobsters that died. Handling and temperature produced a rise in blood glucose levels.

The initial ammonia efflux rates after the first 5 minutes of reimmersion were 5.81, and 3.82 µmol NH_4 per kg per h. These levels dropped to 0.49, and 0.29 µmol NH_4 per kg per h after 4 hours for the "fresh" and stored groups, respectively. After 18 days of storage at 12°C without feeding, the ammonia efflux rates had stabilized at 0.07 and 0.08 µmol NH_4 per kg per h for the same groups, indicating that low levels of nitrogen meta-bolism had resumed. The results are discussed in terms of the ability of *H. americanus* to cope with current holding and distribution methods and what the energy demands of such procedures are likely to be.

Introduction

The American lobster, *Homarus americanus* (H. Milne Edwards 1837) is a fully aquatic species that probably never experiences aerial exposure (also termed emersion) naturally. However, it is well known in the fishing industry that this species can survive 2-3 days out of water if kept cool and humid. This attribute helps account for the appearance of the species as a fresh product on the menus of eating establishments worldwide. Consequently, we studied the effect of long-haul international transport on hemolymph constituents and nitrogen metabolism in the lobster.

Once caught, a lobster is likely to be subjected to a number of stressors, including emersion, hypoxia, desiccation, and rapid temperature changes. All of these stressors will adversely affect the intrinsic quality of the lobsters. Such events occur more or less daily for shore or intertidal animals, which are naturally covered and uncovered by the tides. Compared to subtidal species, these intertidal species are comparatively resistant to temperature fluctuations (Newell 1970) and desiccation (Newell 1976). The subtidal lobster should be particularly vulnerable to these types of stressors during their live marketing and distribution.

The emersed lobster faces the problem of impaired gill function, which results in a reduced oxygen uptake and an impaired ability to release metabolic wastes such as carbon dioxide and ammonia. The gills are important to the proper functioning of these animals and tend to work best in water. There is a certain amount of gill collapse, almost like leaves of a wet book coming together, when the lobsters are taken out of the water.

Many decapod crustacean species switch to anaerobic metabolism when oxygen becomes limiting

(DeFur 1988). Lowered oxygen consumption during emersion has been found in the blue crab, *Callinectes sapidus* (Batterton and Cameron 1978, O'Mahoney and Full 1984, DeFur et al. 1988). Species differ in their tolerance to emersion. For example, the shore crab, *Carcinus maenas*, can survive 24 hours of emersion without recourse to anaerobic metabolism whereas the more subtidal *Necora puber* rapidly switches to anaerobiosis on emersion (Johnson and Uglow 1985).

The successful shipment of lobsters can be better assured by knowledge of the facts pertaining to their survival out of water (McLeese 1965). The fact must be pointed out that most long haul studies focus on animals that are transported by air transport—an inherently costly enterprise. It costs just as much money to transport water as it does product. Consequently, the industry is interested in the tolerance of commercial species held in air. Recent studies on the effects of commercial distribution procedures on crustaceans such as the lobster include several on respiratory gas transport and acid-base balance (Vermeer 1987; DeFur et al. 1988; Taylor and Whiteley 1989; Spicer et al. 1990; Whiteley and Taylor 1992; Morris and Oliver 1999a,b). The somewhat smaller number of studies on the effects of aerial exposure on nitrogen metabolism of commercial species includes those on the spiny lobster, *Panulirus interruptus* (Gomez-Jimenez 1998), on the brown crab, *Cancer pagurus* (Regnault 1992, 1994), and on scampi, *Nephrops norvegicus* (Schmitt and Uglow 1997).

Ammonia is the principal nitrogenous metabolic waste of aquatic animals and is excreted continuously across the gill membrane to the surrounding water at roughly the same rate as it is produced by the metabolizing tissues. When the animal is out of water less ammonia is produced, but gill function is impaired and raised levels in the hemolymph can attain harmful, even fatal, levels if emersion is prolonged.

The determination of sets of conditions under which living crustaceans can be held, immersed or emersed, with minimal accumulation of toxic wastes, such as ammonia, within their bodies is an objective that deserves to be carefully studied. Application of such knowledge would enhance the expectation of delivering quality, live product. It is usual for lobsters to be held, often for periods extending into months, between the time when they were captured until eventual final sale. In the interests of quality maintenance, it is usual to maintain the animals under a regime that keeps the metabolic rate low, so that the animals' nutritional reserves are conserved and waste products are minimized. The point of final sale is frequently far removed from the place of storage and, in order to reduce transportation costs, stored animals need to be consigned dry for journey times that may extend to 48 hours and still arrive as quality products.

This study aimed to compare stored lobsters with freshly caught ones in terms of their quality and their tolerance to long-haul distribution methods comparing hemolymph chemistry and nitrogen metabolism. An increased understanding of the physiological changes imposed on lobsters during storage and distribution protocols may lead to improvements in commercial handling methods, giving better survival, less wastage, and a more efficient utilization of a valuable sustainable resource.

MATERIALS AND METHODS

Two groups of mixed gender lobsters (*H. americanus*, 430-580 g, 10-12 cm carapace length) were sent by commercial road and air carriers from Halifax (Nova Scotia, Canada) to Hull (United Kingdom). These groups comprised freshly caught lobsters (delivered within 17 days of harvesting) and animals which had been held in a commercial storage system for 127 days at the ponds of Clearwater Lobsters, Nova Scotia. The lobsters went through the normal preparatory commercial procedures before being packed into the conventional Clearwater polystyrene boxes less than 2 hours before pickup by the courier. They were sent as if the laboratory at Hull University was a regular customer located in Yorkshire (U.K.).

The lobsters used were of the highest grade, with none in advanced stages of molt or with apparent injuries, missing limbs, or shell disease. All had been checked for the presence of ciliates and gaffkemia *(Aerococcus viridans)*. Before dispatch, the weights and lengths of a representative group were measured and a 0.5 ml hemolymph sample was collected from each animal via a hypodermic needle inserted through the arthrodial membrane at the base of a walking leg.

Lobsters ($n = 10$ from each group) were tagged and further checked for damage before being packed in polystyrene boxes ($41.0 \times 62.0 \times 32.5$ cm) provided with an outer cardboard wrap (Fig. 1). Three gel packs (Hardshell Fresh) were placed on top of the lobsters in each box and the animals were provided with seawater-soaked newsprint. The lid of each box had two holes (diam. 0.5 cm) to allow for a moderate exchange of air. A HOBO Temperature Logger (Onset Computer Corporation) with internal and external temperature sensors was placed among the lobsters (Fig. 2). The external sensor was fastened securely to the outside of the polystyrene box. The logger was programmed to measure temperature every minute for a period of 3 days.

Groups were emersed at 07:40 (Nova Scotia time = GMT – 4h). On arrival at Hull, each box was carefully opened and a relative humidity (RH) meter introduced. Each lobster was then carefully removed, measured (carapace length to the nearest mm), weighed (nearest g), and inspected for damage. A hemolymph sample (0.5 ml) was taken from each animal and measured immediately for its pH (JP pH meter and microelectrode). All blood samples were then divided into 2 aliquots, one of which was deproteinated with 6% perchloric acid (1:1, v:v) prior to being assayed for lactate (Sigma kit No. 735) and glucose (Sigma kit No. 510). The other aliquot was diluted (1:1, v:v) with ice-cold distilled water and centrifuged (2 minutes at 10,000 rpm) to reduce clotting of the sample.

All hemolymph samples were frozen until assayed and any clotted samples were gently homogenized (1-2 minutes) to liquefy. The diluted hemolymph samples were quantified for total protein (Sigma kit No. 541) and for total ammonia ($NH_4 = NH_3 + NH_4^+$) by flow injection analysis (Hunter and Uglow 1993). The time taken for handling and sampling each animal was kept to a minimum in order to reduce any hyperglycemia occurring at this time (Florkin and Duchâteau 1939; Telford 1968, 1974).

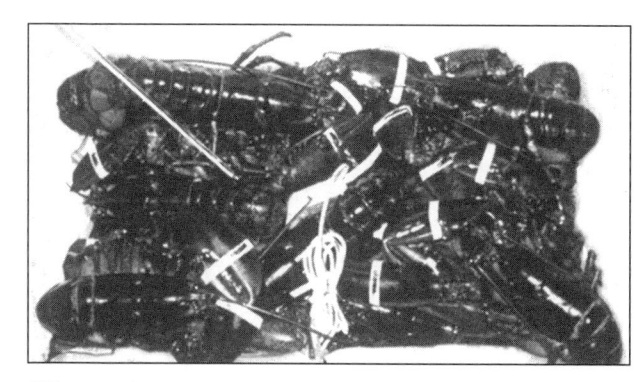

Figure 2. Inside the box, showing tagged lobsters and temperature data logger.

Hemolymph urate determinations were made spectrophotometrically at 520 nm. At this wavelength, the blood pigment haemocyanin is known to cause interference (Lallier and Truchot 1989a,b) and, consequently, test absorption measurements were corrected. For this purpose, a blank measurement was made on a sample containing the same volume of hemolymph as the test sample diluted in a phosphate buffer (pH 7.2).

Immediately after hemolymph sampling, each lobster was placed in its own plastic vessel containing 6 L of seawater (12°C and salinity 30 parts per thousand, ppt). Water samples (1.5 ml) were taken at 0, 5, 10 and 30 minutes and at 1, 2, 3, and 4 hours after reimmersion. After 4 hours, another hemolymph sample was taken from each animal and treated as described.

Following the completion of this sampling procedure, the lobsters were transferred to a recirculating aquarium (12±1°C, salinity 30 ppt). After 18 days, the lobsters were again tested in terms of their ammonia efflux rates and hemolymph constituent levels. All lobsters were starved throughout the experiments (Sokal and Rohlf 1981).

Normality was tested using Lilliefor's test and homogeneity using the Levenes' test (Zar 1999). Data that fulfilled this criterion were compared using analysis of variance (ANOVA) and the post hoc test Tukeys-HSD (Zar 1999). Significant differences wherever stated are at the 95% confidence level ($P<0.05$).

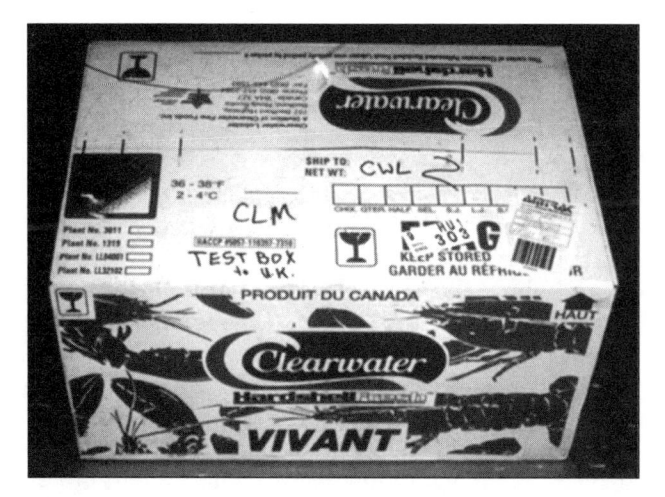

Figure 1. Conventional Clearwater polystyrene box with cardboard wrap for the packaging and transport of live lobsters.

Results

General observations

During consignment, the lobsters were emersed for 48 hours and 40 minutes. Three lobsters from the stored group died during the initial 4-hour reimmersion period and a further specimen from this group died 48 hours later. All other lobsters survived the treatments and continued to survive 6 months later. The RH on arrival at Hull varied between 85% and 90%. The internal/external temperature data are shown in Fig. 3 and reveal that the internal temperature rose just 1°C during the journey while external temperature varied between 1.6 and 14.1°C.

No significant differences between the mean weights of the two groups were found when they were first unpacked or when re-weighed 18 days later. However, both groups showed an increase in weight during that 18 day period (+1.65% = fresh group and +2.58% = stored group).

Hemolymph changes

Both groups had a mean hemolymph pH of 7.27±0.03 when first unpacked, which then rose to 7.41±0.04 at the end of 4 hours of immersion at 12°C. The pH rose to 7.69±0.01 after 18 days of storage at 12°C (Fig. 4a).

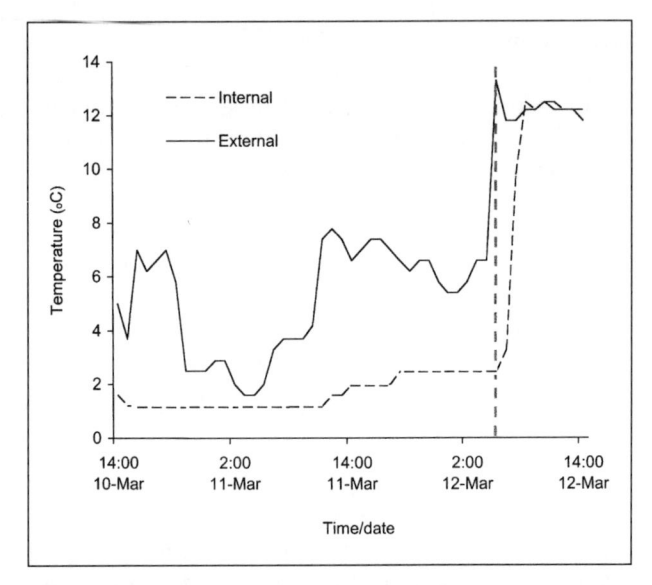

Figure 3. Internal and external temperature of the consignment of *Homarus americanus* during transportation. The vertical line indicates arrival in the laboratory and removal from packaging.

There were no significant differences between hemolymph glucose in pre-consignment and post-consignment animals in both groups (Figure 4b). However, both groups showed further significant increases in blood glucose during the 4 hour reimmersion period at 12°C ($P<0.05$ in each case). Some indication of a possible temperature-dependence of blood glucose values is also shown by the data that reveal that the initial mean blood glucose values of both groups were within the range 1-6 mg 100 ml but had increased to 8-15 mg per 100 ml after 18 days storage at 12°C despite the lobsters being denied food over this period. Although the between-group differences sometimes escaped statistical significance, the fresh group consistently showed the highest mean concentration of blood glucose.

Figure 4c shows that both groups had low initial mean values of blood lactate, but this had risen significantly on arrival and after 4 hours reimmersion at 12°C had risen significantly again ($P<0.05$ in each case). The period of 18 days storage at 12°C resulted in a significant drop to a similar circulating lactate level ($P<0.05$ in both groups) that was slightly higher than the original preconsignment value.

Blood protein levels were unaffected by the imposed treatments other than some evidence of a slow, progressive decrease over the course of the test period (Fig. 5a). The animals from the stored group that died shortly after reimmersion had a much lower mean blood protein level on arrival than the rest of the group (0.98±0.11 g per 100 ml and 5.21±0.30 g per 100 ml respectively).

Blood urate levels appeared to rise slightly during the consignment period (Fig. 5b), particularly in the case of the stored animals in which the increase was significant ($P<0.05$). The elevated levels were sustained during the post-arrival reimmersion period, but after 18 days storage at 12°C, these levels had reverted to values that were slightly higher than those initially measured.

The circulating ammonia levels measured in the fresh and stored groups are summarised in Figure 5c and show that initial levels varied within the range 400-600 µmol NH_4 per L. Consignment caused the levels to increase in both groups but, again, this attained significance for the stored group only ($P<0.05$). Blood ammonia levels rapidly reverted to initial levels during the 4 hour emersion period and, after the 18 day storage period at 12°C, had fallen to levels that were significantly lower than the initial values ($P<0.05$ for each group).

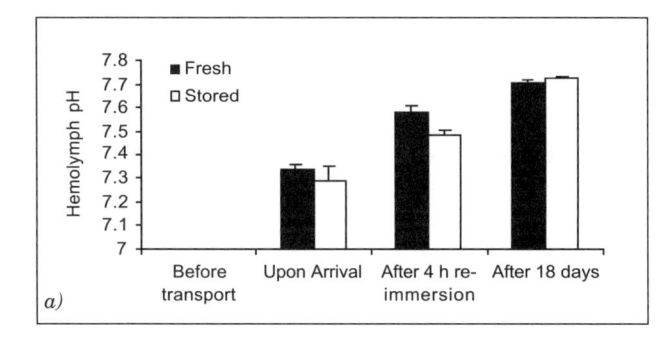

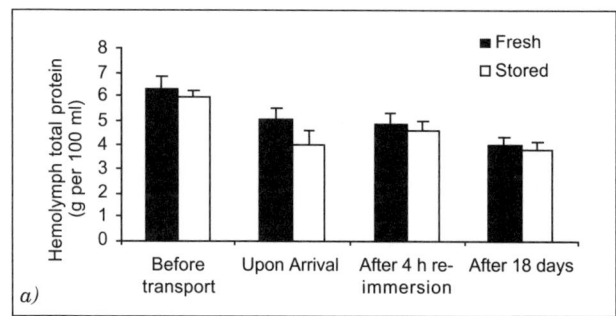

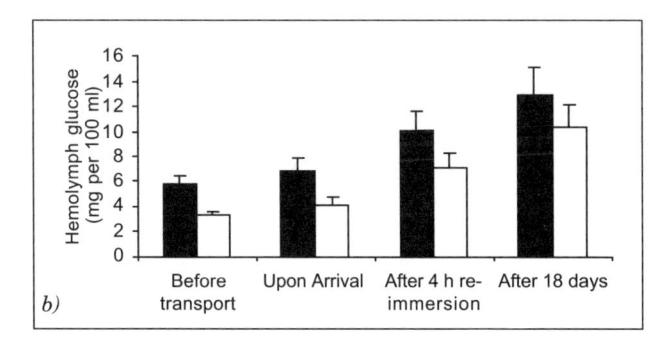

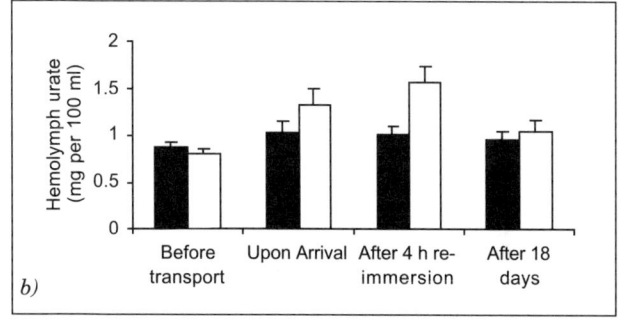

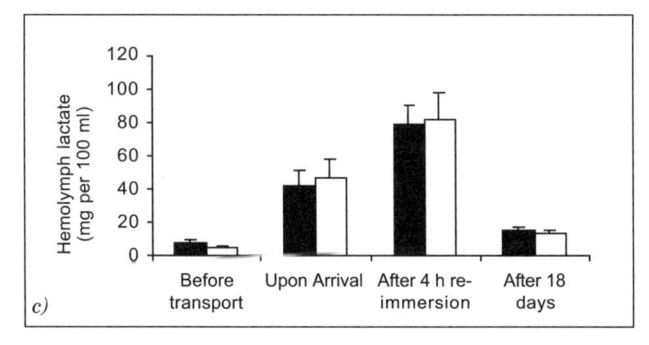

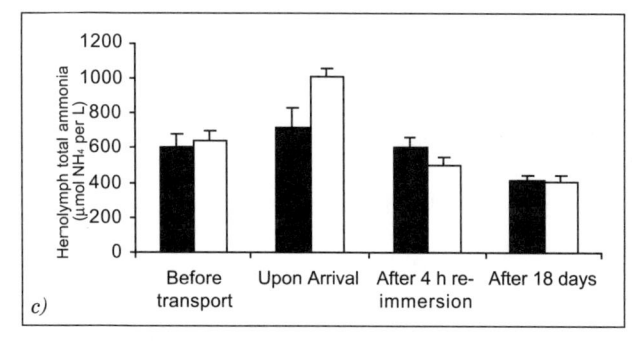

Figure 4. Changes to pH (a), glucose (b), and lactate (c) in the hemolmyph of fresh and stored groups of *Homarus americanus*. Columns show values before transportation, upon arrival, after 4 hours reimmersion, and following 18 days in the aquarium. Values are the mean of $n = 10$ in each case with S.E.

Figure 5. Changes to protein (a), urate (b), and total ammonia (c) in the haemolmyph of fresh and stored groups of *Homarus americanus*. Columns show values before transportation, upon arrival, after 4 hours reimmersion, and following 18 days in the aquarium. Values are the mean of $n = 10$ in each case with S.E.

Ammonia efflux rates

Figure 6 illustrates the data obtained for the ammonia efflux rates following reimmersion after arrival. Measurements reveal that both groups had very high efflux rates over the first 5 minutes, with the fresh group having a significantly higher rate ($P<0.05$) than the stored group. These initial rates translate to 5.81 and 3.82 mmol NH_4 per kg per h and compare with 0.49 and 0.29 μmol NH_4 per kg per h measured after 4 hours for the fresh and stored groups, respectively. Subsequently, after 18 days of storage at 12°C, the ammonia efflux rates had dropped to 0.07 and 0.08 mmol NH_4 per kg per h for the same groups. These rates are comparable with other species kept under similar conditions (Table 1).

DISCUSSION

These data refer to lobsters subjected to emersion at temperatures (ca. 2°C) which evoke a low metabolic rate. Care and attention to the provision of packaging methods, including thermal insulation, ensures the constancy of this holding temperature

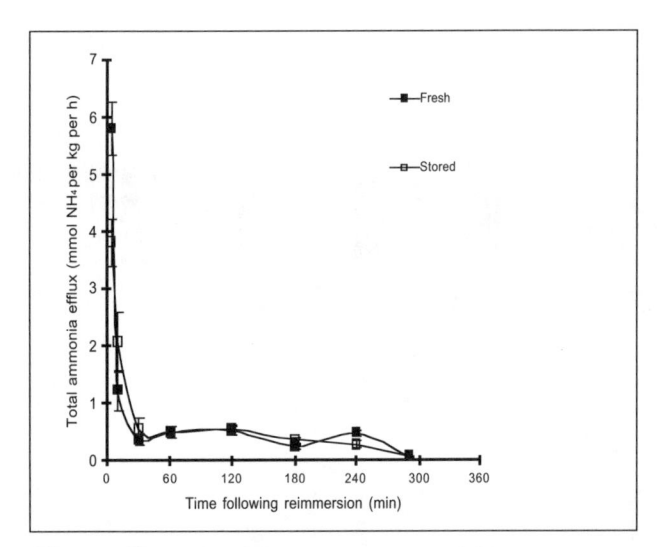

Figure 6. Total ammonia efflux rate of stored and fresh *Homarus americanus* following reimmersion after consignment, and after 18 days at 12°C. Values are the mean of $n = 10$ in each case with S.E.

during consignment. Care also needs to be taken that the immediate surroundings of the animals retain a high relative humidity. Clearly, such measures are successful in the transport of lobsters. However, lobsters were found to gain weight when reimmersed (ca. +1.5-2.5% fresh body weight) which, as they were not fed, probably indicates a recovery from *in transit* water loss. This is noteworthy in view of the functions that these small volumes of water probably serve during emersion, ensuring a moist or a very high relative humidity at the surface of the gills, thus allowing some measure of flux (gases and ions) to proceed while the animals were *in transit*. It was not possible to determine what proportion of such losses represent tissue desiccation, but losses of a similar, but slightly higher, magnitude have been noted for other species (e.g. 3.6-4.7% body weight in *Panulirus interruptus* (Vermeer 1987) and 5.0% and 5.2% body weight over 24 hours for *Carcinus maenas* and *Necora puber*, respectively (Johnson and Uglow 1985).

A hemolymph acidosis and the accumulation of metabolic end products (ammonia, lactate, and urate) in the hemolymph occurred during transit. These changes serve to emphasize the impaired function of the gills at this time and the importance of water retained in the gill chambers. Burnett and McMahon (1987) have suggested that this water also acts as a store for CO_2 and base and helps buffer against an emersion-induced acidosis event. The decrease of 0.5 pH units in the hemolymph after nearly 50 hours of emersion accords with similar findings elsewhere (e.g. a decrease in 0.23 pH units in the hemolymph of 9 hour–emersed *Carcinus maenas*, (Truchot 1975). Such decreases have been attributed to an impaired excretion of CO_2 and the buildup of lactate. Taylor and Wheatly (1981) attributed the decrease of 0.44 pH units in the blood of 3 hour–emersed crayfish, *Austropotamobius pallipes*, to a 10-fold increase in lactate and CO_2, overwhelming the buffering capacity of the hemolymph. Blood lactate, CO_2, lowered pH, and urate are each now recognized as modulators which alter (usually increase) the oxygen affinity of the respiratory pig-

Table 1. Total ammonia efflux rates of some commercial crustaceans at different temperatures.

Species	Temperature (°C)	Total ammonia efflux rate (μmol NH_4 per kg per h)	Source
Nephrops norvegicus	12	0.25	Schmitt (1995)
Nephrops norvegicus	6	0.15	Hosie et al. (1991)
Nephrops norvegicus	12	0.15	Hosie et al. (1991)
Cancer pagurus	12	0.02	Hosie (1993)
Callinectes sapidus	–	0.15	Cameron (1986)
Carcinus maenas	–	0.26-0.54	Haberfield et al. (1975)
Necora puber	12	0.03	Hosie (1993)
Panulirus interruptus	20	0.33	Gomèz-Jiménez (1998)
Homarus americanus	3	0.05	Present study
Homarus americanus	12	0.08	Present study

ment, hemocyanin, in many crustaceans (Truchot 1980; Booth et al. 1982; Graham et al. 1983; Mangum 1983a,b; Taylor et al. 1985; Morris et al. 1985, 1986).

Most of the studies made to date have been in the context of the survival of crustacean species during emersion or hypoxic periods in their natural environments. Little attention has been paid to the relevance of such work in the context of the live distribution of animals, even though such data would serve to help make sensible predictions about the ability of quality shellfish to tolerate commercial distribution practices without experiencing appreciable loss of intrinsic quality.

The practices of emersion and handling are known to evoke a hyperglycemic response in crustaceans (Kleinholtz et al. 1950, Johnson and Uglow 1985, Spicer et al. 1990, Schmitt and Uglow 1997) as a result of endocrine-mediated mobilization of glucose from stored reserves. Such reserves, of course, are extremely important to an animal that has been stored without food intake for several weeks, as was the case in this study. The implications of "kick-starting" the metabolism of an animal which has been living on its reserves for many weeks has not been fully explored. Here the effects of 50 hours in transit was to raise the circulating glucose levels from 0.16 to 0.61 µmol per L, whereas an equivalent increase occurred over the 4 hours of reimmersion at 12°C. Morris and Oliver (1999a) found that the rock lobster, *Jasus edwardsii*, increased its blood glucose levels from 0.4 to 0.85 µmol per L during >30 hours emersion at <0.5°C.

The present findings suggest that the unpacking, handling, and reimmersion procedures constituted a large and rapid stress to the animals and may explain the 4 mortalities that occurred in the stored group and the absence of any deaths among the fresh group. Certainly, post-delivery treatments, particularly temperature rises, deserve further examination in the context of intrinsic quality loss of stored product.

Dry-land pond storage treatments appear to have no adverse effects on blood protein levels as fresh and stored groups had similar mean values before consignment. The animals that died had lower protein levels than the remainder of the stored group and this may have been a significant factor in their deaths. The frequency of cases involving rapid protein loss during storage or in subsequent consignment and how such instances correlate with the pre-selection criteria used in grading lobster is an area that has still to be studied.

The rates of ammonia production decrease when lobsters are emersed, particularly at low temperatures. The data in this study show, however, that blood ammonia levels in both groups increased while the lobsters were in transit. This indicates that the rates of ammonia excretion during emersion are reduced more than are the rates of production. The decrease in hemolymph pH presumably favors the production of the less toxic, ionic (NH_4^+) form of ammonia and thus the induced acidosis at this time may actually afford some measure of protection from internal ammonia toxicity. It should be recognized that, when animals are not fed, all nitrogen losses represent a withdrawal from stored reserves. Using the oxycalorific value of ammonia, given by Brafield and Solomon (1972), the stable ammonia excretion rate of ammonia can be equated as a net loss of 0.124 kcal per kg per day or 1.575 kcal over the 127 days of storage.

Normally, any urate formed from metabolism will be oxidized by uricase to allantoin. However, during emersion, urate is formed continuously, presumably from purine catabolism (Dykens 1991), and is accumulated because of a decrease in uricase activity. Uricase requires oxygen as a cofactor and a reduced oxygen level during emersion leads to a reduction in its activity and thus the accumulation of urate (Morris et al. 1986). The studies have shown that urate increased significantly in the stored group but not in the fresh group of lobsters. This indicates a possible lessened functioning of uricase in the stored animals when under hypoxia. It is not known whether the urate accumulation comprises a means of detoxifying ammonia at such times. Clearly, the functional significance of these findings and possible commercial implications of these aspects of waste management on commercial procedures also require further study.

Conclusion

The present studies have shown that physiological and biological research can provide useful corroborative indicators of the efficacy of commercial practices for the live distribution of aquatic products. These studies also serve as indicators of procedures that require further study to determine their potential to be effective. The present findings emphasize the fact that, even with the better-studied species (e.g., lobsters), our information is still very incomplete and, for many other species with the potential for being exploited, our knowledge is almost totally lacking.

REFERENCES

Batterton, C.V., and J.N. Cameron. 1978. Characteristics of resting ventilation and response to hypoxia, hypercapnia, and emersion in the blue crab, *Callinectes sapidus* (Rathbun). J. Exp. Zool. 203:403-418.

Booth, C.E., B.R. McMahon, and A.W. Pinder. 1982. Oxygen uptake and the potentiating effects of increased blood lactate on oxygen transport during exercise in the blue crab, *Callinectes sapidus*. J. Comp. Physiol. B. 148:111-121.

Brafield, A.E., and D.J. Solomon. 1972. Oxy-calorific coefficients for animals respiring nitrogenous substrates. Comp. Biochem. Physiol. 43A:837-841.

Burnett, L.E., and B.R. McMahon. 1987. Gas exchange, hemolymph acid-base balance and the role of branchial water stores. Amer. Zool. 28:125-135.

Cameron, J.N. 1986. Responses to reversed NH_3 and NH_4^+ gradients in a teleost (*Ictalurus punctatus*), an elasmobranch (*Raja erinacea*), and a crustacean (*Callinectes sapidus*): Evidence for NH_4^+/H^+ exchange in the teleost and the elasmobranch. J. Exp. Zool. 239:183-195.

DeFur, P.L. 1988. Systemic respiratory adaptations to air exposure in intertidal decapod crustaceans. Amer. Zool. 28:115-124.

DeFur, P.L., A. Pease, A. Siebelink, and S. Elfers. 1988. Respiratory responses of blue crabs *Callinectes sapidus* to emersion. Comp. Biochem. Physiol. 89A:97-101.

Dykens, J.A. 1991. Purineolytic capacity and origin of haemolymph urate in *Carcinus maenas* during hypoxia. Comp. Biochem. Physiol. 98B:579-582.

Florkin, M., and G. Duchâteau. 1939. La glycémie de l'écrevisse aprés l'injection d'adrénaline ou d'insuline. C.R. Hebd. Soc. Biol. 132:484-486.

Gomez-Jimenez, S. 1998. Some physiological and immunological responses of the spiny lobster, *Panulirus interruptus* (Randall, 1840), to practices used in its live marketing in the Baja California fishery. Ph.D. thesis. University of Hull, U.K. 111 pp.

Graham, R.A., C.P. Mangum, and R.C. Terwilliger. 1983. The effect of organic acids on oxygen binding of haemocyanin from the crab *Cancer magister*. Comp. Biochem. Physiol. 74A:45-50.

Haberfield, E.C., L.W. Haas, and C.S. Hammen. 1975. Early ammonia release by a polychaete *Nereis virens* and a crab *Carcinus maenas* in diluted seawater. Comp. Biochem. Physiol. 52A:501-503.

Hosie, D.A. 1993. Aspects of the physiology of decapod crustaceans with particular reference to the live marketing of *Cancer pagurus* (L.) and *Necora puber* (L.). Ph.D. thesis, University of Hull, U.K. 135 pp.

Hosie, D.A., R.F. Uglow, L. Hagerman, T. Sondegaard, and K. Weile. 1991. Some effects of hypoxia and medium ammonia enrichment on efflux rates and circulating levels of ammonia in *Nephrops norvegicus*. Mar. Biol. 110:273-279.

Hunter, D.A., and R.F. Uglow. 1993. A technique for the measurement of total ammonia in small volumes of seawater and haemolymph. Ophelia 37(1):31-40.

Johnson, I., and R.F. Uglow. 1985. Some effects of aerial exposure on the respiratory physiology and blood chemistry of *Carcinus maenas* (L.) and *Liocarcinus puber* (L.). J. Exp. Mar. Biol. Ecol. 94:151-165.

Kleinholtz, L.H., V.J. Havel, and T. Reichardt. 1950. Studies in the regulation of blood sugar concentrations in crustaceans. II. Experimental hyperglycaemia and the regulatory mechanisms. Biol. Bull. (Woods Hole, Mass.) 99:454-468.

Lallier, F., and J.P. Truchot. 1989a. Modulation of haemocyanin oxygen-affinity by L-lactate and urate in the prawn *Penaeus japonicus*. J. Exp. Biol. 147:133-136.

Lallier, F., and J.P. Truchot. 1989b. Hemolymph oxygen transport during environmental hypoxia in the shore crab, *Carcinus maenas*. Respir. Physiol. 77:323-336.

Mangum, C.P. 1983a. Oxygen transport in the blood. In: D.E. Bliss (ed.), The biology of Crustacea, v. 5, L.H. Mantel (ed.), Internal anatomy and physiological regulation. Academic Press, New York, pp. 373-429.

Mangum, C.P. 1983b. On the distribution of lactate sensitivity among haemocyanins. Mar. Biol. Lett. 4:139-149.

McLeese, D.W. 1965. Survival of lobsters *Homarus gammarus* out of water. J. Fish. Res. Bd. Canada. 22(2):385-394.

Morris, S., and S. Oliver. 1999a. Circulatory, respiratory and metabolic response to emersion and low temperature of *Jasus edwardsii*: Simulation studies of commercial shipping methods. Comp. Biochem. Physiol. 122A:299-308.

Morris, S., and S. Oliver. 1999b. Respiratory gas transport, haemocyanin function and acid-base balance in *Jasus edwardsii* during emersion and chilling: Simulation studies of commercial shipping methods. Comp. Biochem. Physiol. 122:309-321.

Morris, S., C.R. Bridges, and M.K. Grieshaber. 1985. A new role for uric acid: Modulator of haemocyanin oxygen affinity in crustaceans. J. Exp. Zool. 235:135-139.

Morris, S., C.R. Bridges, and M.K. Grieshaber. 1986. The potentiating effect of purine bases and some of their derivatives on the oxygen affinity of haemocyanin from the crayfish *Austropotamobius pallipes*. J. Comp. Physiol. 156:431-440.

Newell, R.C. 1970. Biology of intertidal animals. Elsevier, New York. 555 pp.

Newell, R.C. 1976. Adaptation to environment: The physiology of marine animals. Butterworths, London. 539 pp.

O'Mahoney, P.M., and R.F. Full. 1984. Respiration of crabs in air and water. Comp. Biochem. Physiol. 79A:275-282.

Regnault, M. 1992. Effect of aerial exposure on ammonia excretion and ammonia content of branchial water of the crab *Cancer pagurus*. J. Exp. Zool. 268:208-217.

Regnault, M. 1994. Effect of air exposure on ammonia excretion and ammonia content of branchial water of the crab *Cancer pagurus*. J. Exp. Zool. 268:208-217.

Schmitt, A.S.C., and R.F. Uglow. 1995. Aspects of the physiology of some species with particular reference to their live marketing. Ph.D. thesis, University of Hull, U.K. 109 pp.

Schmitt, A.S.C., and R.F. Uglow. 1997. Haemolymph constituent levels and ammonia efflux rates of *Nephrops norvegicus* during emersion. Mar. Biol. 127:403-410.

Sokal, R.R., and F.J. Rohlf. 1981. Biometry. 2nd edn. W.H. Freeman and Company, San Francisco. 859 pp.

Spicer, J.L., A.D. Hilll, A.C. Taylor, and R.H.C. Strang. 1990. Effect of aerial exposure on concentrations of selected metabolites in the blood of the Norwegian lobster *Nephrops norvegicus* (Crustacea: Nephropidae). Mar. Biol. 105:129-135.

Taylor, E.W., and M.G. Wheatly. 1981. The effect of longterm aerial exposure on heart rate, ventilation, respiratory gas exchange and acid-base status in the crayfish *Austropotamobius pallipes*. J. Exp. Biol. 92:109-124.

Taylor, E.W., and N.M. Whiteley. 1989. Oxygen transport and acid-base balance in the haemolmyph of the lobster, *Homarus gammarus*, during aerial exposure and re-submersion. J. Exp. Biol. 144:417-436.

Taylor, E.W., S. Morris, and C.R. Bridges. 1985. Modulation of haemocyanin oxygen affinity in the prawn *Palaemon elegans* (Rathke) under environmental salinity stress. J. exp. Mar. Biol. Ecol. 94:167-180.

Telford, M. 1968. The effect of stress on blood sugar composition of the lobster, *Homarus gammarus*. Can. J. Zool. 46:819-826.Telford, M. 1974. Blood glucose in crayfish: II. Variation induced by artificial stress. Comp. Biochem. Physiol. 48A:555-560

Truchot, J.P. 1975. Blood acid-base changes during experimental emersion and re-immersion of the intertidal crab *Carcinus maenas* (L.). Respir. Physiol. 23:351-360.

Truchot, J.P. 1980. Lactate increases the oxygen affinity of crab hemocyanin. J. Exp. Zool. 214:205-208.

Vermeer, G.K. 1987. Effects of air exposure on desiccation rate, hemolmyph chemistry, and escape behaviour of the spiny lobster, *Panulirus argus*. Fish. Bull., U.S. 85(1):45-51.

Whiteley, N.M., and E.W. Taylor. 1992. Oxygen and acid-base disturbances in the haemolymph of the lobster *Homarus gammarus* during commercial transport and storage. J. Crust. Biol. 12:19-30.

Zar, J.H. 1999. Biostatistical analysis. 4th edn. Prentice Hall International, New Jersey. 663 pp.

QUESTIONS FROM THE AUDIENCE

QUESTION: Have you done any studies on phototropic responses in any crustacean species?

R. UGLOW: Phototropic responses—no. The only phototropic responses I have done in species like the lobster is some work with visual acuity many years ago. I provided test animals with bright light, darkness, et cetera, and used heart rate and ventilation rate as response mechanisms. That works perfectly well. However, I have not done it in this commercial context.

I would say more often than not these animals are kept in the dark. In fact, many of them have a natural rhythm that is lost when they are placed in storage. The natural rhythm of light and dark is lost, therefore activity will change and so will their ammonia excretion, for instance. But I have not done phototropic responses.

QUESTION: Concerning the boxes used to ship the lobsters, were they injected with oxygen?

R. UGLOW: I must ask the Clearwater people who are here, is this a normal procedure?

ANSWER: No, it is not.

QUESTION: Are there holes in the shipping boxes?

R. UGLOW: Yes, there are holes in the tops of the box. This information is in the paper.

QUESTION: How do you maintain the internal temperature of 2°C?

R. UGLOW: Primarily through the use of gel packs in the shipping containers.

QUESTION: Comment concerning the shipping boxes. The holes in the top lid are very small—about a quarter to a half inch. These holes allow sufficient ventilation.

R. UGLOW: Also, there is an outer sleeve as well.

QUESTION: You've collected a lot of data on physiological responses and I would guess this is leading to somehow improving the shipping methods or handling of the animals. What do you envision in terms of changes to handling practices to improve survivability?

R. UGLOW: How do I envision this type of work assisting in the future modification of protocols for the different species? This is only one of a long series of studies we have completed on mainly British species. As you can see, we normally would look at these reactions from the time the crustaceans are taken from the pot until final delivery. One of my other students will be giving a talk on the HACCP implications of this later in the conference involving spiny lobsters from Mexico.

We try as best we can to let the trade know what is good, what is bad, what ought to be done, and also what ought not to be done. I am afraid that this is a very, very slow process. If we do any work privately for a firm, they then do not want any of that information released elsewhere. So this transfer of information involves very slow diffusion.

What we have found from experience is that as people get succeeded in their businesses (retire), the succeeding group then abandons some of the practices that were being used. So there will be, as can certainly be seen in Europe, a gradual increase or improvement in the standards that are being used throughout the industry. I should mention here that the name of this game is a quality product at the point of final delivery. The purpose is not just an animal that is alive (unless it is being sold as fresh product) but a live product with a lot of its intrinsic quality left intact. So I envision that it will be a slow learning process, but it will gradually come about.

QUESTION: Have you or anyone else done studies on the consequences of packing in live seaweed as opposed to wet newspaper?

R. UGLOW: We have not formally studied this matter. However, I have experience with this topic. Again, have we looked at the implication of using seaweed as the agent for keeping the humidity high in the packing boxes, rather than wet newsprint? What I find is if transit times of over 24 hours are involved, you get a certain amount of fermentation when using seaweed. I would say it usually gets quite warm in seaweed rather than the newsprint (fermentation produces heat). However, people do use seaweed—quite often, I guess. Another problem is the sheer scale of the amount of packing material that is needed. In Great Britain shippers use rock wool quite a lot—rock wool and ice. Incidentally, a lot of shippers unwittingly use freshwater ice, which melts and causes osmotic problems. But I believe that it is usually the suppliers of biological specimens, rather than food items, who use seaweed.

Physiological Stress Response in Fish

George Iwama
University of British Columbia, Vancouver, British Columbia, Canada

Summary

This presentation (transcribed from a talk) describes the generalized stress response in fishes and will serve as an introduction to a range of physiological responses from the whole animal to the cellular level. Various stressors of fish will be described, as well as the positive and negative consequences of those stress responses.

Introduction

I am grateful to have this opportunity to talk to you about my work on stress. When I say "my work," please remember that I play a small role in this work. The workers in my lab, including graduate students, post doctoral fellows, and research assistants, are the people who have done all the work presented here.

This is an overview of the stress response in fish. Because I do not have sufficient time to speak in detail about any complete data set, I will provide information of basic importance to the industry. I want to define stress, give examples of stressors, and discuss the generalized stress response in fish.

Generalized stress response

We all work with stress to some extent in the animals and plants that we work with. However, what I want to discuss is a specific type of response found in fish that is common to many different stressors. That is why I call this reaction a "generalized stress response." I would like to address this response at the organismal or whole animal level, as well as at the cellular level, with particular regard to heat shock proteins. I will also discuss how to measure this stress response—not in a technical way as employed in a laboratory, but a method that can be used to measure stress in the field. I will conclude by pointing out important areas for research in the future.

What is stress? Well, as Hans Selye pointed out, "We all know what it is, but we really do not know what it is." I like to use a definition given by Dr. Roland Brett of the Canadian Department of Fisheries and Oceans who worked at the Pacific Biological Station at Nanaimo. He stated that stress is a response to an internal or external stimulus that causes the animal to extend its normal adaptive response beyond the normal range. So your heart rate, your breathing rate, or any physiological variable, has its normal rhythm and range. It has a normal maximum-minimum that varies over the time of the day and seasons of the year. But in terms of stress studies at our lab, we like to consider that a stress response has occurred when that normal maximum-minimum is exceeded. Our understanding of stress also recognizes that there is a variation in this response. This is a nice definition of stress for people involved with experimental projects because it is possible to construct experiments around this definition.

Fishes will probably try to avoid stress. However, if behavioral constraints or physical constraints are present which keep the fish in conditions that are stressful, the animal will respond with either a chronic or an acute response that can result in death or, if possible, return to its normal resting state. Examples of behavioral constraints can be seen in territorial animals that live on coral reefs that are subjected to altered conditions. Cod and other fish species that choose to stay in a given area can be exposed to a variety of potential stressors during a breeding season.

Fish are exposed to various physical and biological stressors. For example, coral reefs around the many tropical islands are exposed to suspended red earth soils that wash down to the sea during periods of heavy rainfall. Many tropical islands are being subjected to land development projects such as golf courses and hotels. Erosion can occur when deforestation occurs. In those places when it rains it usually pours, producing a suspension of solid earth washing into the coral reef environment where many of the fish are territorial. This is a routine and common occurrence at the mouths of rivers in these areas. It is common to see a plume of red earth covering the coral environment.

Closer to home, with regard to salmon culture, there are many ways to transport immature salmon from the hatcheries to the ocean cages. The smolts can be put into special buckets and airlifted to distant sites. Imagine a smolt one morning in its nice hatchery with cool fresh water and normal oxygen levels suddenly being placed into one of these buckets that has a touch of anesthetic and a touch of salt to help it osmoregulate, and then being flown by helicopter to a net cage. There the smolt is dropped back into normal oxygen, full-strength seawater, and no anesthetic. It is a wonder that they survive at all, but they seem to recover. In another example of this situation, government trucks in British Columbia take trout from a hatchery to a so-called liberation at a lake where all the coarse fish seem to know exactly when they arrive. Stress can result.

MEASURING RESPONSES

Measurement of stress depends on the physiological response. Neural and endocrine fish responses to a stressor have been well documented, particularly in salmonid fishes. Chromaffin and interrenal cells are involved which produce catacholamines, mainly adrenaline or epinephrine in the short-term. In a slow response to stress over a longer term, you see an increase in cortisol production.

This cortisol response has been well characterized and I would like to spend some time talking about it. As is well known, in the trout and similar species the kidney is the blood-covered structure you clean out after washing the guts away. In the anterior portion of this kidney, the tissue is endocrine in function as well as hematopoietic. The chromaffin cells produce adrenaline and the interrenal cells produce cortisol. Cortisol production is in response to the ACTH from the pituitary.

Resting cortisol levels can increase tenfold in response to stress. However, there is a wide range in cortisol resting conditions. My recent literature review with Bruce Barton indicates a wide range of reported values. As can be seen, it is important for you to establish the baseline values for your particular conditions and species.

The time to peak stress response is approximately five minutes in the case of adrenaline and thirty minutes to an hour for cortisol. Adrenaline is involved in various responses, including gluconeogenesis and glycogenolysis. These responses accomplish a number of changes within the affected fish including:

- Increased glucose levels in general circulation.
- Increased gill ventilation.
- Maintenance of red blood cell pH.
- Releases new red cells from the spleen.
- Increases gill surface area.
- Increases proton or hydrogen ion excretion of the gills (this will affect the species of ammonia at the gill surface).

Cortisol also increases circulating glucose levels. I repeat this because I will later need to return to this topic. However, this increase in cortisol levels can have negative effects on immune function, reproduction, and ionic and acid- base balance.

In an experiment that Bruce Barton conducted as part of his Ph.D. project, he exposed some trout to repeated netting stress. Holding a fish in a net for 30 seconds caused an increase in cortisol. The researcher did this once again after a few minutes, and in a few minutes exposed the trout to this type of stress a third time. The cortisol response was cumulative—the repeated exposure to stressors caused an accumulation of cortisol.

It is important to note that we consider the *primary stress response* to be the release of the hormones cortisol and adrenaline. The *secondary responses* are the effects of these stress hormones on the physiology and biochemistry of the animal. Many physiologists concentrate on reporting about these secondary responses. The *tertiary response* is the sum effect of these events on the individual and on the population. So stress may affect the immune system and it might affect the reproductive capacity of the animal and population. These are potential tertiary responses to stress.

In general, adrenaline levels shoot up and down very quickly. Cortisol, on the other hand, begins to rise a little later. The glucose level is quite significant because it is a variable that you can measure in the field as a secondary indicator of stress. Keep in mind that stress is adaptive. It is important to know that this physiological response is a positive one and that it does afford advantages to the animal. But under prolonged conditions of stress, it can be maladaptive.

Alan Pickering has generated some data dealing with circulating cortisol levels. His study involved confinement stress—confinement for one month using sexually mature male brown trout. His data showed that the cortisol level goes up and then the testosterone level decreases. There is equivalent data for estrodiol, estrogen, etc. for the female trout.

I would like to point out that this is the kind of data that people rely on to make the statement that stress can have negative effects on fish reproduction. Also, oxygen consumption goes up as cortisol levels rise, implying that there is an increase in metabolism. In addition, an increase in glucose is normally seen in rainbow and coho salmon. That stress response is reduced, though, when you add 100 millimoles of sodium chloride to the holding water.

When a group of fish are stressed, their survival decreases. However, if you transport them and then allow them to recover in some salt, you can increase their survival substantially. As you probably know, salt must be used with some care because it can rust out your transport trucks.

Measuring stress in the field

We conducted some experiments directed at the question—Can you measure stress in the field? The typical lab spectrophotometer is not really a portable instrument. It is possible to measure the glucose response to stress by using small glucose meters—the same meters purchased by diabetic people who measure their blood sugar. One model is literally as small as a pen. We have completed these experiments with small instruments. When you need to measure hemoglobin, etc., other small hemoglobinometers are available. Instruments like these can be taken to the field.

In our experiments, there was very good agreement between measurements taken at the lab and those taken with the field instruments. In other words, you can do these kinds of measurements quite reliably.

The cellular stress response

I also want to describe briefly the cellular stress response—primarily the production of stress proteins. The discovery of this highly conserved group of proteins is popularly attributed to giant chromosomes from the salivary glands of fruit flies. The production of stress or heat shock proteins (HSP) in response to many different stressors has been described in almost every type of cell examined. These stressors include environmental stressors such as heavy metals, many other kinds of toxicants, as well as diseases—viral, bacterial, and parasitic. It is important to know that normal cellular processes produce these proteins. They are around in constitutive levels to maintain normal cell function.

HSP-70 assists in preventing premature folding and improper aggregation of proteins. The translocation or transport of various proteins to cellular organelle compartments requires unfolding and refolding steps. In these and other ways, heat shock proteins are important to the life of a cell. In experiments conducted by Matt Vijayan in our laboratory, cells in rainbow trout exposed to a toxicant show an increase in HSP-70 production in response to this form of stress.

What can you do about stress? One topic we are currently working on is something called cross-tolerance. If you stress a fish first, it becomes somewhat resistant to subsequent stressors. Ann Todgham, working with SDS (a toxicant) exposure in our lab, has shown that fish not exposed to any previous stressor all die when exposed to SDS. If, for example, you first expose the fish to a +5° heat shock, many will survive. If the test fish are exposed to a +5° heat shock, survival is greater than with fish exposed to the toxicant alone. Thirty percent of these pre-stressed fish survive exposure to SDS.

We do not have a good understanding how this happens. We suspect that heat shock proteins are involved—that the first primary stressor induces the cellular stress response, arming the cell against subsequent stressors. This heightened state of readiness seems to work at the organismal level as well. So this is a area of research we are pursuing in the attempt to help natural stocks, as well as in cultured stocks.

Questions from the audience

QUESTION: Does the cortisol response also occur in eggs?

G. IWAMA: I do not know. There have been some experiments, but the problem with eggs, as you know, is they are a blob of protein and the yolk gets in the way. It is difficult to obtain enough sample, even in alevins or juveniles. Taking blood is out of the question and homogenizing the whole animal, all of the tissues, masks any real effects because of the volume of all the other tissues that are present. Because of these technical difficulties, there has not been reliable evidence of changes in blood cortisol in small juveniles.

QUESTION: In your pre-stressing experiment, what time elapsed between stress exposures?

G. IWAMA: About eight hours. In our work, we have infected fish and have shown that bacterial pathogens will also increase HSP level. Toxicants, temperature change, low oxygen, salinity change—they have all caused an increase in HSP levels. What has not caused an HSP-70 increase is handling. This is a great advantage when sampling fish in the field because you have about a one-hour window before handling effects begin to show up.

QUESTION: Does cold shock work as well in the development of crossed tolerance?

G. IWAMA: We do not know. We know that cold shock involves another set of proteins. These are not the same stress proteins induced with heat shock. A different type of protein is involved. Also, we have not experimented with cold shock in these specific animals. We have just completed some cold shock experiments with Amazonian species in Brazil. I am concerned that the specificity of the antibodies used in this research hinders the research—we do not have good tools. The antibody tests used in our lab work very well with rainbow trout and salmon, but they do not cross react very well with Brazilian species, such as tilapia, and other species from the tropics. So that's one thing. You've got to make good antibodies.

Critical Oxygen Point in Yellowleg Shrimp (*Farfantepenaeus californiensis*): A Potential Species for the Live Seafood Trade

Lucía Ocampo V.
Centro de Investigaciones Biológicas del Noroeste (CIBNOR)
La Paz, Mexico

INTRODUCTION

Shrimp and other crustaceans are able to either regulate their oxygen consumption independent of prevailing oxygen levels ("regulators") or they match their oxygen consumption rates to the prevailing oxygen levels ("conformers"). As conditions change, many of these species are able to switch from one strategy to the other, but may become vulnerable when conforming at low oxygen levels. The dissolved oxygen level at which a species makes the switch from acting as a regulator to a conformer is the critical oxygen level (Pcr). This point can be taken as being at, or near, the limiting level for the species. Accurate knowledge of the Pcr is particularly important for the successful commercial holding and distribution of many species.

Farfantepenaeus californiensis (Fig. 1) is a native penaeid shrimp of northwestern Mexico that spends much of the daytime in burrows in the muddy substratum. Like many burrowing species, it is tolerant of low levels of dissolved oxygen and is also tolerant of low temperatures (19-23°C). Consequently, it has the distinct potential of becoming a candidate species for culture during the Mexican winter —as an alternative to *Litopenaeus vannamei*— and also a potential candidate for the live seafood trade.

This study relates to the determination of the Pcr for *F. californiensis* and the extent by which this value is influenced by the prevailing temperature. These data are considered to be a prerequisite to any serious consideration of this species for culture or live marketing. Results indicate that the Pcr is about 1.3 mg per L within the temperature range of 19-27°C. Below Pcr, oxygen consumption decreases to approximately 10% of the value occurring during normoxic conditions when the animal is acting as a regulator.

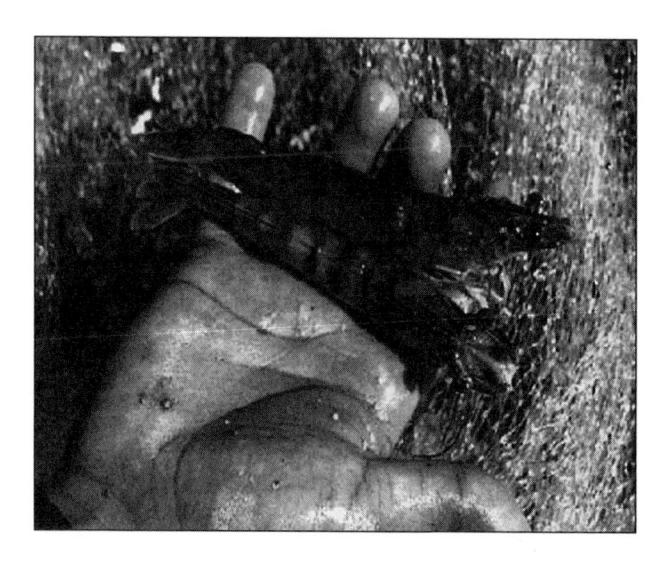

Figure 1. Yellowleg shrimp, *Farfantepenaeus californiensis*.

MATERIALS AND METHODS

F. californiensis (weight 2.5 g), obtained from the Experimental Shrimp Farm at the CIBNOR facilities, were conditioned for seven days at three different temperatures (19, 23, and 27°C) and fed ad libitum twice a day on a commercial diet.

Shrimp fasted for 24 hours were placed into an intermittent flow respirometer. Following the closed mode setting, oxygen uptake was recorded with an oxygen electrode at 10 minute intervals until dissolved oxygen depletion was sustained or the shrimp died. At the end, all shrimp were weighed.

The critical oxygen point (Pcr) was established as the point of intersection of the regression lines for consumption during normoxic and hypoxic conditions. Differences between temperatures were determined by ANOVA and the Duncan multiple range test.

RESULTS

Oxygen consumption was constant and independent of dissolved oxygen down to 1.3 mg per L for all temperatures. Consumption during hypoxic conditions decreased to approximately 10% of the consumption during normoxic conditions. The Pcr varied from 1.2 mg per L at the lowest temperature to 1.3 mg per L at the highest temperature, which leads us to conclude that the Pcr was not affected by temperature ($P > 0.05$).

DISCUSSION

The Pcr provides a good water quality variable to define the limit to which an aquaculturist should manage a species. Knowledge of this variable is critical for the management of adequate physiological status and is an important tool during live transportation.

Oxygen consumption of *F. californiensis* decreased with decreasing oxygen concentration. Subrahmanyam (1980) described the metabolic response to progressive hypoxia as a continuous hyperbolic curve. However, from the mathematical point of view, the changeover point is difficult to estimate. In our study, the definition proposed for Pcr permits different models to be fitted above and below this changeover point. Biologically, this accounts for the regulatory nature of oxygen consumption during normoxia and the conforming behavior at low oxygen levels. The distinction between organisms that conform to conditions in their external environment and those that regulate some physiological function in the face of changing environmental conditions has frequently led to confusion. It is not uncommon to find that a virtually identical set of data has been interpreted as evidence of conformity by one investigator and of regulation by another. However, a Pcr has been consistently found between 0.9 and 2.0 mg per L (Egusa 1961, Mackay 1974, Kramer 1975, Liao and Huang 1975, Armitage and Wall 1982, Llobrera 1983, Trouchot and Jouve-Duhamel 1983, Liao and Murai 1986, Villarreal 1989, Rosas et al. 1997).

Oxygen regulation capacity seems to decrease with temperature increments. A correlation between temperature and Pcr has been reported for *L. vannamei* postlarvae (Villarreal et al. 1994). In this study no effect of temperature was observed in *F. californiensis*.

The relationship between temperature and oxygen-regulation capacity in aquatic organisms seems to be related to metabolism, and particularly to increases in the metabolic rate. This relationship may also be associated with limitations involving the transport of oxygen from the environment to the cells (Fry 1957) and is strongly influenced by the activity level and the size of shrimp (Bridges and Brand 1980).

Other water quality variables such as salinity (Rosas et al. 1997), pH, and ammonia levels (Allan et al. 1990) seem to influence the tolerance to low levels of dissolved oxygen. These water quality variables also affect shrimp growth (Seidman and Lawrence 1985) and must be considered for further research. More research is required to understand the effect of these variables on the physiological capacity in *F. californiensis*.

REFERENCES

Allan, G.L., G.B. Maguire, and S.J. Hopkins. 1990. Acute and chronic toxicity of ammonia to juvenile *Metapenaeus macleayi* and *Penaeus monodon* and the influence of low dissolved-oxygen levels. Aquaculture 91:265-280.

Armitage, K.B., and T.J. Wall. 1982. The effect of body size, starvation and temperature acclimation on oxygen consumption of the crayfish *Orconectes nais*. Comp. Biochem. Physiol. 73A(1):63-68.

Bridges, C.R., and A.R. Brand. 1980. Oxygen consumption and oxygen independence in marine crustaceans. Mar. Ecol. Prog. Ser. 2:133-141.

Egusa, S. 1961. Studies on the respiration of the "kuruma" prawn, *Penaeus japonicus* Bate. II. Preliminary experiments on its oxygen consumption. Bull. Jap. Soc. Sci. Fish. 27:650-659.

Fry, F.E.J. 1947. Effects of the environment on animal activity. University of Toronto Studies for Biological Series 55. Ontario Fisheries Research Laboratory Publication 68.

Kramer, G.L. 1975. Studies on the lethal dissolved oxygen levels for young brown shrimp, *Penaeus aztecus*. Proc. World. Maric. Soc. 6:157-167.

Liao, I.C., and H.J. Huang. 1975. Studies on the respiration of economic prawns in Taiwan. Oxygen consumption and lethal dissolved oxygen of egg up to young prawn of *Penaeus monodon* Fabricius. Journal of the Fisheries Society of Taiwan 4:33-50.

Liao, I.C., and T. Murai. 1986. Effects of dissolved oxygen, temperature and salinity on the oxygen consumption of the grass shrimp, *Penaeus monodon*. In: J.L. Maclean, L.B. Dizon, and L.V. Hosillos (eds.), The First Asian Fisheries Forum, Manila, Philippines, pp. 641-646.

Llobrera, J.A., 1983. Effects of dissolved oxygen on the survival, growth and energetics of juvenile freshwater shrimp, *Machrobrachium rosenbergii*. Ph.D. dissertation, Texas A&M University, College Station. 116 pp.

Mackay, R.D. 1974. A note on minimal levels of oxygen required to maintain life in *Penaeus shmitti*. Proc. World. Maric. Soc. 5:451-452.

Rosas, C., A. Sánchez, E. Díaz-Iglesia, R. Brito, E. Martínez, and L.A. Soto. 1997. Critical dissolved oxygen level to *Penaeus setiferus* and *Penaeus shmitti* postlarvae (PL_{10-18}) exposed to salinity change. Aquaculture 152:259-272.

Seidman, E.R., and A.L. Lawrence. 1985. Growth, feed digestibility and proximate body composition of juvenile *Penaeus vannamei* and *Penaeus monodon* grown at different dissolved oxygen levels. J. Maric. Soc. 16:336-346.

Subrahmanyam, C.B. 1962. Oxygen consumption in relation to body weight and oxygen tension in the prawn *Penaeus indicus* (Milne Edwards). Proceedings Indian Academy of Sciences 55(3B):152-161.

Trouchot, J.P., and A. Jouve-Duhamel. 1983. Consommation d'oxygène de la crevette japonaise, *Penaeus japonicus*, en function de l'oxygenation du milieu: effects de la temperature et de l'acclimation a des conditions ambiantes hypoxiques. IFREMER, Actes de Colloques 1:245-254.

Villarreal, H. 1989. Feeding, growth and energetics of the freshwater crayfish *Cherax tenuimanus* (Smith) with special emphasis on its potential for commercial culture. Ph.D. thesis, University of Queensland. 249 pp.

Animal Rights Advocacy, Public Perception, and the Trade in Live Animals

Paul G. Olin
University of California Sea Grant, Santa Rosa, California

Introduction

Shipping and marketing live aquatic products is an excellent way to gain top value in the world marketplace. In order to accomplish this there are three quality issues that need to be carefully addressed:

1. The first, and most familiar of these considerations is the need to pay close attention to product quality. The consumer is paying a premium price and demands a premium quality product; fish should be healthy and not have missing scales or be marked by other defects.

2. The second consideration involves the quality of the resource from which these products are harvested and the environmental impacts associated with capture and processing. There is increasing concern about the sustainability of our fishery resources, and the public is demanding that they be protected from overharvesting.

3. The third quality issue that members of the live aquatics industry need to address is the quality of life experienced by aquatic organisms that are destined for live markets. Obviously, these are terminal markets, but there is public concern that animals should not experience pain and suffering on their way to those markets.

This paper will introduce the concepts of animal rights and animal welfare and provide some background on animal rights organizations. An overview of an animal rights controversy in San Francisco, California, will document (1) how people's concern for animal pain and suffering in the live animal trade led to an initiative to ban the sale of live food animals, and (2) how this might impact the trade in live aquatic products. Finally, some recommendations for the industry to responsibly address legitimate issues will be presented.

Animal Rights and Animal Welfare

The current concern for animal welfare developed as animal agriculture moved from a family enterprise that emphasized animal husbandry to an industrial activity involving animal production (Rollin 1996). Over the last 100 years, animal agriculture has evolved into an intensive activity made possible by expanded and efficient transportation and distribution networks, improved agricultural efficiency, intense market competition, and increasing levels of urbanization. Large agribusiness is the dominant force of agriculture in the developed world today. In terms of animals destined for human food markets, the focus is now on animal production and efficiency rather than on animal husbandry. High intensity animal culture practices are commonplace and efficient in that they provide high volume production of relatively inexpensive food. However, the public perception is increasing that animals suffer in confined production situations. Two large and diverse animal advocacy groups (animal rights and animal welfare) are now focusing their efforts on this issue.

The live aquatics industry must be aware of these concerns and understand the motivations of animal rights and animal welfare organizations and how they might come into conflict with fisheries, marketing, and ultimately meat consumption. The industry must address legitimate concerns put forward by animal rights and welfare groups and understand the significant and fundamental distinctions between their respective philosophies.

One of the largest and most prominent of animal rights groups is the People for the Ethical Treatment of Animals, better known by the acronym PETA. Animal rights groups differ from animal welfare groups which include the various societies for the prevention of cruelty to animals. Animal rights groups often focus on sensational issues and concentrate their efforts on fundraising. They spend their money to influence public opinion and government policy. Animal welfare groups, on the other hand, are concerned with the development and maintenance of programs and infrastructure to provide for animal care. They provide things like shelters for animals and low-cost spay/neuter clinics.

The developing controversy in San Francisco involves both animal rights and animal welfare groups in opposition to a group of primarily ethnic Chinese merchants who engage in the sale of live animal products to their customers. This conflict is seated in social, cultural, and religious differences that have given rise to an ethical dilemma. The dilemma stems from the fact that children learn to believe very early in life the difference between what is right or wrong. While the basics are agreed upon in most cultures, differences arise around some customs and behavior and this includes foods and the manner in which they are prepared. In San Francisco's Chinatown, for example, ethnic Chinese like to buy live animals, and they are accustomed to seeing those animals butchered at the point of purchase or after being taken home. This creates a societal dilemma between those who would champion cultural traditions, while at the same time seeking an initiative to ban the sale of live animals that interferes with some of these traditions.

The root of this controversy stems from the tendency of mainstream North American consumers to purchase packaged foods. These consumers go to supermarkets and purchase a nice clean prepared chicken that has been placed inside a plastic-wrapped package with an absorbent pad to retain any blood. There is a complete psychological disconnect between the packaged food and its living source. Most consumers never consider the history of their packaged meat products including the rearing of the animal, its slaughter, and subsequent processing into consumer-ready products.

Many Americans will not readily accept the sight of animals being killed or held in high-density confinement. In Chinatown, however, live turtles may have their shells cut off, live fish may be filleted, and frogs may be butchered in public view. This is opposed by some people and creates a basic dilemma in which society must balance members' rights to engage in certain social, ethnic, and religious practices that may upset the sensitivities of others in society.

Society has determined that animals have rights, and foremost among these is the right not to experience unnecessary pain and suffering. People also have rights, and most do not appreciate their rights being infringed upon, particularly by a group with a different social and cultural foundation. These issues are responsible for the emotionally charged nature of the controversy.

STRESS AND PAIN IN FISH

Recognizing that societal consensus confers on animals the right to avoid unnecessary pain and suffering, the question arises as to if and when animals might experience these sensations. It is evident that fish do react to stress and that different stress responses occur. What is unknown is whether these responses are indicative of pain and suffering as recognized by humans, or whether this is being anthropomorphic and attributing human emotions to animal behaviors. Fish physiologists have the opinion that pain is not a strong sensation experienced by fish (Lagler et al. 1977).

Fish and most aquatic organisms exhibit both behavioral and physiological responses to stress. Blood cortisol, blood glucose, and ammonia levels can all measurably fluctuate in fish exposed to stressors. Fish also produce endogenous opioids in response to stressful stimuli similar to the morphine-like chemicals produced in higher vertebrates. However, whether pain accompanies these measurable responses to stress is unclear. Some evidence would indicate that is the case, while other data suggest otherwise.

Fish and mammals share the same type of neurotransmitters that in mammals are used to transmit sensations perceived as pain in the neocortex of the mammalian brain. However, fish are entirely lacking a neocortex. When you go to the dentist and get a local anaesthetic to deaden pain, you can feel sensations as your teeth are drilled or pulled, but they are not painful. The local anaesthetic blocks the perception of pain in the neocortex (Harvey-Clark 1998). Furthermore, in mammals, nervous impulses triggering sensations of pain are transmitted through the spinal column in fibers of the spinothalamic tract, a structure that is entirely lacking in fish. Fish also lack nociceptors—specialized pain receptors found in higher vertebrates (Stoskopf 1993).

In summary, there is no objective scientific data to determine whether fish feel pain as experienced by humans. Pain and suffering are human intellectual constructs and science avoids anthropomorphism. That being said, most people are not scientists, and the general public perception is that fish can feel pain and suffering. Animal rights groups play upon this perception in their efforts to fundraise and recruit.

Animal rights campaigns

Animal rights organizations (AROs) often rely on sources of information other than the most reputable scientific data. One pertinent quote on a Web site reads, "The pain system in fish is virtually the same as in birds and mammals." This is simply not true. Statements on some Web sites can be found, such as "fish suffer from being impaled, thrown, crushed, or mutilated while alive, and they are often left to die slowly and painfully of suffocation." These statements conjure very graphic images which people, in many cases, tend to believe. Another quote reads, "It is unthinkable that fish do not have pain receptors. They need them in order to survive." This may be unthinkable, but there is little evidence that fish have pain receptors. It is important to keep in mind, in situations such as this, the words of U.S. Senator Daniel Patrick Moynihan: "Everyone is entitled to his own opinion, but not his own facts."

AROs and their experts have certain things to say about fish and the fishing industry as we can see from the following quote from a Web page, "Fishing is violent, bloody and cruel, fishing hurts. Please don't eat the animals." Some AROs are not as constrained as scientists about the need to rely on the best available scientific data in making determinations about pain and suffering in fish. Another Web page says, "Fishing, aquatic agony," and yet another reads, "Imagine reaching for an apple on a tree and having your hand suddenly impaled by a hook that yanks you into an environment where you cannot breathe. This is what a fish faces when hooked." Clearly this is not the case. Fish do not pick apples out of trees and neither do they have hands. But nonetheless, this is a very graphic image that engenders empathy in people and is readily available on the Internet.

In a recent ARO campaign, a human costumed as a fish is depicted as saying, "Don't be cruel to fish." In this example, they use a time-honored advertising technique by having the costumed fish accompanied by a young woman in revealing attire. Demonstrations very similar to this were observed at the Aquaculture Expo in Tampa, Florida, in 1999. The ARO protestors arrived at the convention center just before the media arrived. The camera crew quickly obtained their footage and left, followed shortly thereafter by the ARO protestors. The film clip subsequently aired on the evening news. Members of AROs are very good at what they do. They are persuasive in their advertising, and they get their message across.

Another social agenda promoted by AROs is vegetarianism, and this has obvious implications for the live seafood trade. One tack taken to forward this agenda is to attempt to denigrate the quality of meat products. Toward this end, another Web segment reads, "Like the flesh of other animals, fish flesh contains excessive amounts of protein, fat, and cholesterol." This is a ludicrous pronouncement. It is then followed by the statement that fish can accumulate toxins and that the consumption of fish can cause kidney damage, foster impaired mental development, cause cancer, and even result in death. While this statement may on rare occasions be true, it is fear mongering, and the relative risk to human health of consuming most fish is infinitesimally small, especially when weighed against the known health benefits of consuming fish with high levels of omega-3 fatty acids. Public health authorities protect consumers by issuing health advisories if particular fish, usually resident in highly urbanized estuaries, pose a health risk associated with any accumulated toxins.

AROs have outreach programs to help people organize demonstrations, including how to choose a location. They will provide stickers, leaflets, and posters. They provide instructions on how to start a campaign to ban fishing at a local lake or pond, including how to contact the regulatory authorities that have the power to manage the particular water body, how to call up the media, and, finally, how to follow up with a demonstration. Demonstrators are encouraged to use "fishing hurts" stickers in highly visible places. Another Web site op-posed to fishing is called nofishing.net

These campaigns are very persistent and have been quite successful. In 1988, for example, PETA embarked on a campaign in which they recruited 30,000 teachers (Harvey-Clark 1998). Conservatively speaking, if each PETA-indoctrinated teacher interacts with 100 students, 3,000,000 children will obtain messages promoted by the group. Keep in mind that PETA is only one of many animal rights organizations. In 1995, the top ten animal rights groups in the United States and Canada had a budget of US $410,000,000, and assets exceeding one billion dollars (Rowan and Leow 1995).

Resource sustainability

The quality of the resource supplying live aquatic products and the environmental impacts of capture and processing are also of concern to consumers and should be addressed by the industry. For example, environmental groups have had tremendous impacts on the U.S. Pacific tuna fishery and also the Atlantic swordfish industry by initiating boycotts out of concern for bycatch and declining populations. Organizations like the Monterey Bay Aquarium and the Audubon Society are recommending that farmed salmon not be consumed because of concerns with how those farming practices are impacting the environment. Protecting the environment and sustainable harvest practices is crucial to the long-term success of any live fish marketing endeavor.

Information on the Internet includes graphic images of dead and dying birds and statements that "Countless birds and other animals suffer and many die from injuries caused by swallowing or becoming entangled in discarded fishing hooks, monofilament line, and lead weights." Unfortunately, this is true, and is an issue the industry should address. While the magnitude of the mortality is unlikely to have an impact at the population level for these animals, the magnitude of negative publicity that can be generated by these graphic images is formidable. The fishing industry needs to respond by doing beach cleanups, collecting discarded nets and hooks, and becoming involved in other activities that address legitimate concerns.

Whether one agrees with groups like PETA or not, the reality is that, if the public perceives that there is pain, suffering, crowding, and close confinement associated with your business, they will react negatively. On the contrary, fish, shellfish and crustaceans that appear healthy and are being held in nice facilities with clean water will impress consumers and further the image of live seafood as a high quality and high value product. For these reasons, it is important that issues involving the handling of animals destined for the live trade be addressed in an effective and timely manner.

SAN FRANCISCO'S LIVE ANIMAL SALES DEBATE

In San Francisco, a very diverse city with many different ethnic groups, a controversy has developed over the live animal trade between some of these groups in the last ten years. There is a large Chinese and Asian community with a variety of religious traditions and cultural practices. There are also outspoken and concerned activists comprising other segments of society.

One of the strong Chinese traditions includes the purchase and preparation of live seafood and other animals in local markets. A consumer can go to many local markets in Chinatown and buy live turtles, chickens, frogs, fish, crabs, oysters, and clams. Some animal activists objected to this live animal trade as being cruel and undertook an initiative to have the Board of Supervisors ban live animal sales within the city. Allegations of cruel and inhumane treatment of animals have been countered with accusations of racial and cultural discrimination against Chinatown merchants.

Opponents of live animal sales proposed an initiative that originally would have banned the sale of all live animals in the city. The list of sales outlets originally targeted was very inclusive—from Chinatown markets to the crab houses on Fisherman's Wharf, including seafood wholesalers as well as members of the fishing industry. However, the people pushing for the ban quickly recognized that Fisherman's Wharf and a number of other businesses are visited by millions of tourists every year, and consequently, form a strong political lobby. As a result, shellfish and crabs were dropped from this initiative early on. This is not to say that the proponents lost interest in banning live shellfish and crab sales, but rather, their politically astute strategy called for dropping them in order to eliminate a strong political lobby opposed to the initiative.

At that point, Chinatown merchants felt that they were being singled out, and they cited cultural and racist motivations for the initiative. Amid a great deal of controversy, the Board of Supervisors did not pass this initiative. The animal activists then demanded legal enforcement of provisions under existing animal cruelty statutes. These statutes restrict live animal sales where food is sold and require animals be killed in a humane fashion. City officials determined that these statutes applied to restaurants, and not to markets in the Chinatown area.

Animal activists subsequently filed suit under the anti-cruelty statutes. A coalition of ten animal rights organizations sued twelve Chinatown markets. The cruelty lawsuit was rejected because the judge did not feel that the animal rights groups demonstrated that these animals were being killed in a cruel fashion. The activists then petitioned the Fish and Game Commission, which in California controls the importation of animals, to ban the importation of turtles and frogs. The Fish and Game Commission delayed action on the ban pending legislative action in the form of a bill that would mandate the permitting and monitoring of live animal markets. This bill has been temporarily deferred because of an agreement on animal treatment reached between the Society for the Prevention of Cruelty to Animals (SPCA) and a group of Chinese merchants represented by the Chinese Consolidated Benevolent Association. These two groups drafted a joint statement of principles and guidelines that effectively address important topics of concern, including the humane killing of animals, sanitary holding facilities, and related issues.

The controversy appeared resolved with implementation of the guidelines scheduled for July 2000. However, the SPCA determined that the merchants were not honoring the agreement. So the confrontation is continuing, the animal rights groups are again seeking a ban on the importation of turtles and frogs and, in addition, they are planning voter initiatives at both the local and state levels.

This animal rights coalition is also proposing a boycott of Chinatown merchants and also recommending reforms to the Fish and Game Commission. Ranking officials in a number of animal welfare associations and animal rights groups in the greater San Francisco area are positioning themselves to become members of this regulatory body.

REVIEW OF THE ISSUES

The concerns being addressed by the initiative were primarily animal suffering from lack of food and water, high-density confinement, and unsanitary conditions. These are readily dealt with by following guidelines related to other animal agriculture industries that are regulated by federal, state, and local statutes. This includes providing sanitary conditions, having available food and water, and avoiding unnecessary suffering. If the live aquatics industry avoids addressing these issues, initiatives will develop in other regions like the one in San Francisco targeting live seafood. Activists in San Francisco have stated their intentions to move into San Diego, Los Angeles, and Oakland with similar agendas.

Other valid natural resource issues are raised as justification for terminating the trade in live animals. For a variety of religious, social, and economic reasons, live aquatic animals purchased from retail outlets may be intentionally or inadvertently released alive into the wild. These animals may be exotic to the region and compete with native species, they might introduce pathogens, or they may be ill-adapted for survival in the wild. For example, public health concerns about salmonella in chickens have been raised as another argument against the live trade in chickens. The trade in live seafood has historically resulted in some exotic introductions, and this is an area that requires close management, education, and enforcement. The import permits that govern this trade require that animals be killed before leaving the retail site. The businesses involved need to make sure that happens.

There are also concerns about the live animal trade impacting the management of native wildlife. For example, the harvest of some species of frogs and turtles may be illegal in California, but not in other states. As a result, the actual origin of products in retail markets may be uncertain, leading to concerns about the intermingling of legal and illegal products and the potential for overharvesting of some California populations. Education and product identification are necessary elements of a program to ensure this does not occur.

The trade in live aquatic products will continue to grow if the industry addresses (1) the quality of the product, (2) the quality of the fishery resources being harvested and finally, and (3) the quality of life experienced by animals in the marketing chain. Product quality is the simplest factor to achieve, and this has largely been accomplished. Sustaining our fishery resources and developing a good public perception concerning capture fisheries and live marketing is a greater challenge.

First and foremost, the industry needs to address the broad range of valid public concerns with the recognition that public perception is reality. Most reasonable people feel that aquatic animals can experience pain and suffering, and practices that contribute to animal suffering or give that perception should be avoided. Traders in live aquatic products need to be willing to compromise and respect a variety of practices and deeply held convictions. This includes those of Chinese consumers who want to purchase freshly killed animals for a meal, and the convictions of animal rights and welfare groups concerned with animal suffering, and perhaps even with meat consumption itself. There may be a tendency to dismiss the animal rights people as extremists, but this strategy runs counter to good business practices as these groups have demonstrated their ability to orchestrate campaigns and sway public opinion in order to accomplish their goals.

The industry must work closely with fishery management agencies to assure that our fishery resources are stable, well managed, and productive. It is equally important to work together with natural resource agencies to ensure procedures are in place to prevent the unintentional introduction of exotic species or spread of pathogens.

The live seafood industry needs to be proactive and work toward becoming better communicators. One method to accomplish this would be the development of a Web site presenting a wide range of information about the live seafood industry—the businesses and species involved, efforts to maintain healthy animals and high water quality, and the humane practices employed in holding systems. This will serve to counter some of the information currently available on the Web about how cruel and inhumane fishing is. These and other related Web documents will help promote the industry and also serve as an open forum providing objective information about the industry and its practices.

References

Harvey-Clark, C. 1998. Live fish biology: From harvest to market. In: C. Rodgerson and C. McKenna (eds.), East Coast Live Fish Conference: A Sea of Opportunities. Nova Scotia Fisheries and Aquaculture, Halifax, Nova Scotia, pp. 33-39.

Lagler, K.F., J.E. Bardach, R.E. Miller, and D.R.M. Passino. 1977. Ichthyology. 2nd edn. John Riley and Sons, New York.

Rollin, B.E. 1996. Animal production and the new social ethic for animals. In: B. Paust and J.B. Peters (eds.), Marketing and shipping live aquatic products. Northeast Regional Agricultural Engineering Service, Cooperative Extension, 152 Riley-Robb Hall, Ithaca, New York, pp. 7-13.

Rowan, A.N., and F.M. Leow. 1995. The animal research controversy: Protest process and public policy—An analysis of strategic issues. Center for Animals and Public Policy, Tufts University, School of Veterinary Medicine, Boston, Massachusetts, pp. 22, 39, 93, 118, 124, 141, 146.

Stoskopf, M.K. 1992. Fish medicine. W.B. Saunders Company, Harcourt Brace Jovanovich Inc., pp. 82-83.

Questions from the Audience

R. UGLOW: In addition to finfish, in the United Kingdom, PETA is beginning to focus their attention on invertebrates as well. One of the consequences of all this is the negative impact on the trade. When subjected to this type of attention, you must take elaborate procedures to protect yourself. This can be hideously expensive.

QUESTION: It has occurred to me that an effective industry response to these public policy issues might be modeled after the response of the research community to confrontations with animal rights groups. Animal research has been subject to the same kinds of political pressures from animal rights groups. Animal researchers are responding with educational campaigns that inform the public about the benefits of animal research. These campaigns also indicate how animal researchers have responded as a community to the valid concerns forwarded by members of the public. Among other strategies, the research community has developed handling protocols.

It seems that this industry might look at other examples of how other workers have responded to these groups. Although the animal rights groups have not become overtly threatening, we must remember that many research institutions have heightened security because of the threat of violence from these groups.

I think that a proactive approach is definitely appropriate. I am also very troubled about the PETA outreach effort to the public schools. That seems to me to be the most critical place to respond because of the vulnerability of children to any kind of information presented by an adult.

QUESTION: How much of the PETA information is accurate?

P. OLIN: I think a very strong force behind PETA is the desire to have everyone be vegetarian. I think that this is the underlying motivation. You can see that on their Web pages. Also, there may be some good natural resource arguments that we should all be vegetarians in terms of the ecological impacts of animal protein production.

QUESTION: You mentioned the need for compromise among these groups with deeply held opinions. Do you have any successful examples from the San Francisco experience?

P. OLIN: At this point in time, I would have to say no. However, I think we will see compromises, because I think the Chinese merchants will be forced to respond and to improve their animal handling practices and their care prior to being dispatched for food.

Animal Ethics and the Live Aquatic Animal Trade

Bernard E. Rollin
Colorado State University, Fort Collins, Colorado

Summary

The last 30 years have witnessed a dramatic rise in social concern for animal treatment and animal welfare across the Western world. We demonstrate this phenomenon briefly and explain the nature and cause of these ethical concerns. Issues that could arise in aquatic food animal transport will be mentioned and a strategy explained for the industry to proactively accommodate itself to the social ethic without being forced to do so by legislation.

Background Statement

Anyone who reads a newspaper or watches television cannot have failed to notice an ever-increasing social concern with animal treatment during the past three decades in the United States, Canada, Australia, New Zealand, and Western Europe. This concern has had a major impact on all areas of animal use in society. In the United States, this concern has been operative on federal, state, and local legislative and regulatory levels.

According to the National Cattlemen's Association and the National Institutes of Health, both of whom have no vested interest in inflating the influence of this issue, since 1980 Congress has received more letters, phone calls, faxes, and personal contacts on animal welfare issues than on any other matter. Numerous locales have abolished the steel-jawed trap by statute and others, like the State of Colorado, by public referendum. Spring bear hunts have suffered similar fates, where there is a danger of shooting a lactating mother and orphaning cubs that then cannot be force-fed. In Colorado, over 70% of the public voted to abolish the hunt. An identical hunt in Ontario, Canada, was abolished by the Minister of the Environment in spite of the fact that the hunt brings a considerable amount of money into the province. In Europe, confinement agricultural practices that are the mainstay of North American animal agriculture have been swept away by public concern expressed in legislation. Sweden led the way in 1988 with what the *New York Times* called a "Bill of Rights" for farm animals.

Whereas 20 years ago one could find no U.S. federal legislative proposals pertaining to animal welfare, recent years have witnessed as many as 60 such proposals each year in Congress alone. These proposals have included attempts to protect animals in research, save marine mammals from becoming victims of tuna fishermen, and curtail the exotic bird trade. Other animal uses, such as cosmetic testing, have been changed by people voting with their pocketbook. The Body Shop, for example, became a billion dollar company by disavowing such testing. According to the executive director of the American Quarter Horse Association, their single biggest expense is tracking horse welfare legislation at all levels of government. In 1998, such proposed legislation filled a volume the size of a big-city telephone book. Last year in California, voters passed a bill making the slaughter of horses for food or shipping horses for that purpose a felony. While this law is obviously not enforceable, it is a good indicator of public sentiment.

Perhaps most indicative of the degree of U.S. public commitment to animal welfare was the passage of two pieces of federal law in 1985 aimed at regulating the use of animals in research and, particularly, at minimizing animal pain and suffering. The reason these laws are so significant is that they were vigorously opposed by the research community. This group went so far as to threaten the public with grave danger to human health, specifically to children's health, if the laws were passed. The research community even produced a less than subtle film entitled "Will I Be All Right, Doctor?," with the query coming from a sick child and the reply coming from a pediatrician who in essence affirmed, "You will be, if they leave us alone to do as we wish with our animals."

Yet despite this naked appeal to fear, the extensive research animal protection laws moved through Congress easily, even though roughly 90% of the animals used in research are rats and mice. These animals are not cute and cuddly, indeed are repulsive to most people and traditionally associated in the public mind with filth and disease. If the public can generate enough moral concern about these animals to tolerate alleged risks to children's health, it is clear that the treatment of any animal can become the focus of public concern.

It is thus quite manifest that animal welfare is a force to be reckoned with socially, more so than ever in human history. In work that I did for USDA explaining the emergence of this social phenomenon, I distinguished five reasons why it has developed so strongly during the last 30 years.

In the first place, major demographic changes have changed the paradigm for what an animal is in the social mind. A century ago, when the society was highly agricultural, if one had asked the man in the street, urban or rural, to state the first word that came to his mind when one said "animal," it would have been "horse," "cow," "food," "work," etc. With well under 1% of the public engaged in animal production agriculture (in fact, only 1.7% of the public is engaged in any agricultural production at all) coupled with increasing urbanization, this is no longer the case. The paradigm for an animal is now the companion animal with almost 100% of the pet-owning public declaring that their animals are "members of the family."

Second, the mass media, most notably newspapers and television, have discovered that "animals sell papers" (recall Animal Planet, an entire television station devoted to animals) and that exposés of animal abuse sell even more papers. Such exposure has greatly sensitized the public to animal welfare issues.

I happened to be in California during the Baby Fay incident and was besieged by a bunch of reporters because I work in ethics of genetic engineering, biotech, advances in science, and so forth. The reporters wanted me to comment on, quote, "Is it the monkey or the kid?" I said, "No, actually Baby Fay is more a human subjects issue rather than an animal issue."

There was no pain and suffering associated with taking the heart from the baboon. However, there was a failure on the part of the surgeon to notify the parents of other options.

The reporters said, "We're not interested in the human subject issue. Animals sell papers."

Another significant example occurred some years ago when the press revealed that two whales were trapped in the Arctic ice. In response to a major U.S. public outcry, the Russians sent an icebreaker to release these animals. Was this an overflowing of Russian compassion? Hardly. Rather, some clever Kremlin politicians realized that a good way to win U.S. public opinion was to help the animals. Under other circumstances the Russians might have sent a whaling boat. Suffice it to say that surveys of the general public since 1990 repeatedly reveal that at least 85% of the general public believe animals have rights!

Third, the last 50 years in the United States have seen the American citizen's moral vision expand to include a wide variety of traditionally disenfranchised human beings—black people, women, handicapped persons, children, and so on. This same "moral searchlight" has inevitably focused on the environment and on animals, especially since many animal activist leaders are veterans of other moral crusades such as civil rights, women's causes, and the labor movement.

Fourth, numerous philosophers and scientists have offered rationally based, readable, moral arguments for extending greater moral status to animals in ways that have captured the public imagination. Jane Goodall, for example, has turned the bulk of her attention to animal welfare issues. Peter Singer's book, *Animal Liberation*, has been in print constantly for 25 years. Books like *The Horse Whisperer* and *When Elephants Weep* are best-sellers. There are no less than twenty law schools in the United States that teach animal law. A substantial number of those people are working on legal modalities for elevating the legal status of animals in society.

Finally, and most important, the major changes in animal use that have occurred since World War II have called forth a demand for new and expanded ethical categories. Traditional animal use was largely agricultural—food, fiber, locomotion, and power. The essence of traditional agriculture was *husbandry* (from the Old Norse word for "bonded to the household"). Husbandry meant putting the animals into the ideal environment they were evolved for and then augmenting their natural ability to survive with protection from famine, drought, predation, disease, etc. We put square pegs into square holes, round pegs into round holes, and created as little friction as possible doing so. If we harmed the animals we harmed ourselves.

So powerfully is this "ancient contract" ingrained in the human psyche, that when the Psalmist wishes to metaphorize God's relationship to Man, he uses a paradigm case of husbandry—the shepherd: "The Lord is my shepherd, I shall not want. He leadeth me to green pastures. He maketh me to lie down beside still waters. He restoreth my soul." We want no more from God than a shepherd provides for his animals. Thus as long as husbandry was the guiding principle of agriculture, the only social ethic needed was *prohibition of overt cruelty* and to catch the few deviants who caused suffering for no reason.

The anti-cruelty ethic is almost as old as human history. It can be found in the Bible, as in the injunction not to muzzle the ox when it is threshing grain. The owner of the ox loses little by letting the ox eat the few bits of grain that fall down; the animal suffers greatly by not being permitted to enjoy a favored food. Muzzling the ox creates *unnecessary suffering* and no human benefit. The prohibition against cruelty was carried on through the Rabbinical tradition, ancient and medieval philosophy, and into modern times where it is law in virtually all civilized societies.

Traditionally, given predominantly agricultural uses of animals, the anti-cruelty ethic was designed to catch sadists and psychopaths who, as modern research has confirmed, begin with animals and move to people. The ethic was not meant to preclude all infliction of pain on animals. Some pain was taken for granted, for example in branding, castration, and dehorning cattle or trapping varmints. Such pain was perceived as necessary to "minister to the necessities of man," as one law puts it or rather to minister to normal human needs and desires. Anti-cruelty was directed against deliberate, willful, unnecessary, purposeless, sadistic, deviant infliction of pain and suffering or against outrageous neglect such as not feeding and watering.

In short, traditional agriculture was roughly a symbiotic fair contract: "we take care of the animals and they take care of us," as western ranchers still say. But this changed after World War II. With the loss of agricultural land and labor to urbanization, an industrialized view of agriculture as producer of cheap and plentiful food emerged. Thus, industry values of efficiency and productivity replaced husbandry values. Given the advent of "technological sanders" such as antibiotics and vaccines, we could now force square pegs into round holes and put the animals into situations where, though their welfare was negatively affected, profit and productivity were not.

The infliction of suffering that was not deliberate cruelty was further sanctioned by the rise of large amounts of biomedical research and testing on animals at roughly the same time. Researchers are invariably motivated not by cruelty, but by decent considerations such as curing disease and promoting health. Corporations are motivated by the desire to protect the public against toxicity of household products and themselves from lawsuits. The net result, though, was an explosion of animal suffering that inexorably called forth new ethical concepts beyond deliberate cruelty.

In fact, a moment's reflection reveals that the vast majority of animal suffering today is not the result of cruelty, but rather is the result of decently motivated activities. For example, the cases of sadistic cruelty pale in comparison to the fact that we produce 8 billion broiler chickens a year in confinement with 80% of them bruised or fractured as they go to market.

To go "beyond cruelty," then, society has looked to the ethical concepts it uses for people and applied them, appropriately modified, to animals. In summary form, the new ethic says that when we use animals, as when we use people, *we must respect their basic biological and psychological needs and natures*. Such respect for humans is encoded in *rights*. This is what I have called their "telos" following Aristotle—that is the "horseness of the horse," the "pigness of the pig." Since such respect no longer follows automatically from husbandry, this ethic demands that we legislate or otherwise impose such "fair use."

With public sensitivity to animals so intensified by all of the factors enumerated above, it is no surprise that social tolerance for animal abuse, whether the result of cruelty or not, has diminished precipitously. The new ethic of respect for animal needs and natures has, for example, abolished the old zoos that were little more than prisons for animals. The new concern for animals has also considerably broadened and expanded what counts as cruelty. It has also considerably truncated the sorts of reasons that provide valid justifications for hurting animals. In the past, society was content to interpret the prohibition against unnecessary suffering in the cruelty laws as meaning that animal suffering would be tolerated only as long as it was not sadistic, or totally purposeless, or if it was inconvenient or expensive to eliminate it. Such would be the case with castration and branding in the cattle industry.

Ever increasingly, society will accept animal suffering as necessary only if (a) the suffering occurs in the context of a use beneficial to most people and (b) it is *impossible* to alleviate. This occurs when we do biomedical research for human or animal health on animals and create disease, injury, stress, etc. in them. Even in such cases, where society sees suffering as inevitable, it will control such behavior to assure that such suffering is minimal. An example is when the laboratory animal laws mandate pharmacological control of pain and living environments that suit the animals' natures.

This new way of thinking has had and will have considerable impact on all of animal use. It will, as it has done the world over in agriculture and research, proscribe activities that significantly violate animal's natures. But, perhaps even more important, it will no longer tolerate suffering to which alternatives exist and no longer tolerate major suffering that does not benefit society in general. In other words, what is actionable under the anti-cruelty ethic and laws will be expanded. The USDA was successfully prosecuted in 1984 for mandating hot iron face-branding of dairy cows it had bought to thin the U.S. herd. A New York State judge said that USDA was indeed guilty of cruelty, for it had not attended to or considered non-painful ways of identifying these animals.

This, then, is a brief summary of the social ethical forces characterizing society's views of animals at the beginning of the new millennium. All indications point to this ethic expanding, not diminishing. And, like most other ethical movements, as its zeal increases it will claim some victims who cannot accommodate new ways of thinking.

In sum, as social concern about animals has grown in society, three responses have developed that have had or will have major impacts on those who make their living from animals. While society is not yet generally abolitionist in its view of animal use, it has shown its willingness to abolish "frivolous uses" such as horse tripping, cosmetics testing on animals, and even circuses. It will tend to try to assure that animals used by humans live full and decent lives, with their natures and basic interests met and their suffering minimized.

1. As mentioned earlier, as the restricted nature of the anti-cruelty ethic is understood, the legal system will move "beyond cruelty" in regulating animal treatment. A beautiful explanation of this move can be found in a 1985 case that animal activist attorneys brought against the New York State Department of Environmental Conservation (or land management). The lawyers were after the steel-jawed trap, but knew that previous attempts to prosecute trappers under cruelty laws were thrown out by the courts since the trap was a "standardly accepted device." This time they tried a different tack, arguing that the New York State government department was guilty of cruelty not because it allowed the use of the trap per se, but because such use was unregulated. Thus an injured animal could be held in the trap indefinitely without food, water, or medical attention, which did count as cruelty.

   The judge's response was ingenious. If it were up to him personally, he affirmed, he would ban the steel-jawed trap immediately, as it has been banned in many countries. But, he pointed out, it is not up to him. The society has not spoken against the trap for fur, pest control, or recreation. Thus, if the plaintiffs wish to end the trap use, they should change the social ethic and go not to the judiciary, but to the legislature. As we have indicated, citizens are increasingly taking this tack and hence the proliferation of laws we mentioned earlier. Laws could easily be passed limiting practices you take for granted which either cause suffering or violate animal nature.

2. Sympathetic judges and prosecutors will increasingly expand cruelty notions beyond the deviant and intentionally sadistic to anything causing pain that could be avoided, as we saw in the USDA face-branding decision. Precedent for this sort of approach exists in your industry. As early as 1911, a New York judge pointed out that what counts as cruelty changes with degree of social concern. He noted that the concept could, in principle, apply to turtles being imported for soup that were placed on their backs and tied together by a rope passing through holes in their fins, or to live codfish that were thrown in barrels of ice and sold as live cod; or to animals cooked alive. More recently, in the past two years, animal rights groups, including Chinese groups, have brought suit against merchants in San Francisco's Chinatown for cruelty for keeping live fish and other animals under conditions of pain, suffering, distress, and deprivation.

3. Campaigns can be launched to boycott animal products perceived to be produced or transported cruelly. Such campaigns have been directed against paté de foie gras produced by force-feed-

ing, tuna-fishing that uses nets imperiling dolphins, the live lobster trade, and has virtually destroyed the white veal industry.

FOCUS ON LIVE AQUATICS INDUSTRY

What areas of your industry are vulnerable? First of all, we have mentioned the furor in Chinatown of San Francisco. The same sorts of concerns could be directed against routine practices in your industry. These include the decompression associated with fishing leading to rupture of animal organs, netting practices, death by suffocation when animals are placed on ice, sorting of fish using spiked rods, and the practice wherein crabs have legs torn off and are then thrown back into the sea to regenerate the missing appendages.

It is revelatory to me about evolving social thought that some ten years ago, at an annual meeting of the fishery managers of Colorado and Wyoming, hardly radical enclaves, participants expressed major concern with catch and release fishing and the suffering it engenders. It is now far more widely accepted than ever before that fish and other aquatic animals feel pain. It is further known that fish are among the animals most susceptible to stress and stress-induced disease, which economics alone dictates you would reduce. The social ethical concerns simply increase the imperative.

Second, the transport of live fish involves much animal suffering. Some carp have their mouths sewn together for transport to prevent cannibalism. Other fish are transported with insufficient oxygen. Many are crushed; many die of heat stress or decimation. Still other sea life such as lobsters have their claws fastened shut. Many animals shipped by air die from extremes of temperature on the tarmac.

Third, the sale and boiling of live shellfish—shrimp, lobsters, and crabs—have raised serious opposition in Britain. Mainstream moderate groups such as RSPCA (Royal Society for the Prevention of Cruelty to Animals) and UFAW (Universities Federation for Animal Welfare) have supported restaurant boycotts affirming that the animals are suffering, a claim buttressed by research in the U.K. A new, humane stunner has been developed. PETA (People for the Ethical Treatment of Animals) orchestrated an effective campaign some years ago demanding that large, old lobsters be returned to the sea.

These are just a few of the issues that I, as an outsider, see as obviously placing your live aquatics industry in jeopardy in the face of the new ethic we outlined. I am sure you could greatly proliferate examples from your own specialized knowledge.

The obvious question, then, is what you should be doing proactively to avoid problems. Cruelty cases can be disastrous because even if you win, you lose. For example, if I march outside your university with a sign that says, "Dr. Johnson is not a child molester," in five years your name will be inextricably linked to child molestation. Consumer boycotts and onerous regulations devised by people who mean well but do not understand the industry can be devastating, as well.

For 25 years, I have worked to help various animal user groups stay in accord with the social ethic for animals. After five years of working with the Colorado State University Veterinary School, I was gratified to find that we were written up in *Nature* as the best animal-using campus in the United States—from an animal welfare point of view. I was also part of the group that wrote the 1985 U.S. federal laws that helped assuage public concern about the treatment of animals in research. I have also worked with U.S. cattlemen and the governments of the United States, Canada, Holland, Australia and New Zealand to achieve similar goals and am currently creating a mechanism for self-examination with the National Western Livestock Show and Rodeo.

There are two notions pivotal to the success we have enjoyed. One is to embark on a campaign of detailed and critical self examination. An industry like yours must have an inventory of practices that may be out of harmony with the emerging ethic we have described.

Second, you must continually monitor and explore the emerging social ethic and use it as a yardstick to gauge industry activities and future plans. An example of an industry that did not do this is the confinement swine industry. Now they are reaping the wind. They built too many high production units and the price of pork is radically depressed, and they are being bombarded by legislation all over the United States with impossible environmental demands. George Gaskel of the London School of Economics found that one of the biggest impediments to the acceptance of biotechnology in England and Europe is not fear of risk, but the feeling that it violates fundamental ethical norms. To my knowledge, no regulator ever paid attention to that.

Third, you must have viable action plans for rectifying and changing the problematic practices you unearth. If you tell the truth, admit your shortcomings and have a plan for correcting problem areas. The public will give you some leeway and allow you reasonable time to change established practice. If you lie or prevaricate or attempt to obfuscate, on the other hand, you will be relentlessly plagued by the media. Remember: If Nixon had told the truth, he probably would have remained President. The American public, at least, tends not to kick you when you are down and admit your problems.

I will give you an example of this effective strategy. About 12 years ago we had a massive die-off of old beagles in one of our research colonies. We were studying what effect low level radiation has on morbidity and mortality of beagles over their whole life span. We had a bunch of geriatric animals and the funding had dried up. They were in outdoor kennels and, if you know Colorado, you know that the temperature can go from 60 above to 30 below overnight and it did. We did not have any heated kennels because they were not supplying any more money. We were not allowed to change the protocol by supplying straw to insulate the animals. The result was that 30 animals died in 10 days.

We had activists coming to the university from as far away as Massachusetts. We decided in a closed meeting what we were going to do. Even though it was right before Christmas, we wrote a 30-page report telling the exact truth about what had happened—that the funding agency was no longer funding these kennels. We admitted that this did not excuse the fact that we did not have the animals under proper care. We explained that we were not allowed to change the protocol, that here is what we were doing to change it in the future, et cetera. Within minutes of release of that report, the press no longer came, the activists sent their tickets back, and we heard no more. If we had tried to cover it up, we would still be recovering from it. It is not news anymore if you admit it. That is crucial.

Toward these ends, I would recommend that you immediately plan a conference or large portion of a conference specifically focusing on animal welfare issues in your industry and on the emerging social ethic for animals. If nothing else, this shows the public you are concerned. Contrary to human nature, it would be wise to listen to and work with your moderate and rational critics. After you have explored the issues, you should set up a committee of top people from the industry to explore alternatives to morally unacceptable practices. Keep in mind that many animal welfare problems and the stress they occasion are, in any case, also costly to the industry in the form of sick, injured, or dead animals. You should also set up a timetable for implementing changes, express concern for and commitment to proper animal treatment, and publicize your plan for self-regulation.

The trick is to behave proactively and preemptively. If you wait for a crisis, it will be too late. Then it will seem as if you are being forced into making these changes, and you will be. Do not make the mistake of directing your ire against extremists. In the end, it is the general public, not the most radical activists, who must be satisfied with your commitment to animal welfare.

QUESTIONS FROM THE AUDIENCE

QUESTION: Why compare problems associated with laboratory animals with live aquatics? Why can something that someone else does harm us?

B. ROLLIN: Because you are guilty of what logicians call a "tu quoque fallacy." Let me explain why. To pursue a line like that is self-destructive. "Tu quoque" means, "you, too." If you accuse me of slapping around my child and I don't deny it, but I instead say, "you slap around your wife," that does not respond to the objection. Do you see the point? The fact that everybody is guilty of some wrong in animal use doesn't make the social searchlight any less focused on you. And if you respond by saying, "Well, what the hell are you guys saying. You treat your dogs worse than we treat our fish," I guarantee you that is just going to increase their zeal to get you. You can bet on it. That is the way human psychology works.

I know, you are just venting. But my point is you cannot afford to vent emotionally. You have to rationally address people's concerns because they are your customers. It may become socially unacceptable to order lobster—which is exactly what occurred with regard to veal. When I addressed the Agricultural Research Service at USDA, I talked to an audience of 75 people. Seventy of them said they would not eat veal even though they helped develop the production systems.

QUESTION: Do you think the traditional commercial fishery or the newly emerging live fishery is better off? It seems that those involved in the live fishery are better equipped to handle an item such as the public perception of pain. Fish are killed on commercial boats by gaffing and clubbing. Fish are dressed on many commercial boats that are still alive as compared to stunning and bleeding in a chilled tank with carbon dioxide. Do you think a live harvesting boat is better off?

B. ROLLIN: I don't know because I do not know enough about your industry. If you asked me about things in the biomedical area, the cattle area, the swine area, I can answer you. But I learned a long time ago not to talk about what I don't know.

QUESTION: Might a small industry have any advantages?

B. ROLLIN: Shooting from the hip, I would say that there are lots of complex forces operating. By and large, I think, people favor small individual industries. Do you see what I mean? And in fact, in the agricultural animal area, small usually goes with better husbandry. If you can demonstrate that small fishermen are more harmoniously connected with nature and the animals they work with in terms of sustainability and that sort of thing, I think that this will go a long way. The American public likes the little guy.

In agriculture, the corporations have been very intelligent in turning the small farmer against the animal rights people. It is only in the last five years the small farmers have begun to realize that the enemy is the big farmer. They are the ones who are putting them out of business, not the animal rights people.

QUESTION: Most of my customers are either Asian or first generation Asian-Americans living in the United States. I also export to the Asian countries. Is the animal rights attitude also found among these groups?

B. ROLLIN: No.

QUESTION: I notice that the animal rights ethic is well-developed in England as in America.

B. ROLLIN: And northern Europe as well. Yes, and it is catching on a little bit in southern Europe. For example, if any of you have been to Spain recently, you can see demonstrations against bullfights, which is incredible. Everything American spreads—good and bad. But I do not think in Asia you are going to have much of a problem. There's less animal welfare thinking in Japan.

I can tell you something about the U.S. swine industry. I have a friend who is involved in one of the big North Carolina swine production units. They figure that they have maybe six to eight years left in the United States and then they are going to move to the Orient. The Orient cares less about animal welfare and, more to the point, the Orient cares about the environmental despoliation associated with this industry. They want pig.

QUESTION: The media is important to the live industry. How can the media be more effectively used?

B. ROLLIN: There is no question. Everybody depends on the media. But, in my experience, the media is interested in any animal story. Over the years at Colorado State University, we have been able to use the media. This may serve as a model for your industry. We utilized the media, every time we made a change in established practice that the public would approve of.

Most of you will disapprove of what I am about to relate to you. In 1978 we were teaching surgery to veterinary students by using an animal eight times—cutting on them eight times. At other schools they would cut on them 20 times. We provided no after-care. At my institution, these animals were called "sub dogs" and at Purdue they were called "X dogs." The average person was shocked and horrified by this activity. What I did was to tell the public, with the permission of the institution, that we had been doing this for some time for economic reasons and that we had not thought in ethical terms. Now that we were thinking in ethical terms, we were committed to phasing this out. Do you see how this works?

The media carried this nationally and it bore far more fruit than anybody thought. When we stopped doing multiple surgery on animals and went to terminal single surgery—which, in any case, is a better model for what you are going to meet in practice—the local humane society said, "If you guys feel that strongly about animals, then we will give you the ones we are going to kill and you can do surgery on them, so it is cheaper for you."

My experience with the American public is that the American public is very fair, very open, very willing to listen to both sides, particularly if you show them that you are trying. If you just blow the issues off, they will get you.

And that is true with the media, too. The media does not only use you, you can use the media. Does that make sense? If you tell them something that is really new, that is not just propagandistic nonsense, they are going to listen. For example, if I were working for you, I would say that you hold a conference, you come up with a series of action items, and then you tell the media. "We as an industry have become conscious of moral obligation," and so on.

I was involved in saving the livestock showing industry. You may not be aware of this situation. About five years ago, there was a series of media revelations about how corrupt livestock showing was. The champion steer at a Denver show had been enhanced with the anabolic clenbuterol which enters into the human food chain and poses danger to the general public.

At the same time, a lamb in a Tulsa show had been observed by the fair manager being beaten by a kid with a two-by-four to expand the hindquarters so that it would look like muscle. In a Texas state fair, a kid shoved a hose down the throat of a pig to increase his weight. All these were well-publicized. As a consequence, we had a two-day meeting of people interested in saving livestock showing. They came from every state in the union, 500 people, and because we had to, the group agreed on 18 action items including making adulterating an animal a felony.

We adopted all of these items as an ad hoc group. Then, when the media came to me during the livestock show and said, "Tell us about some atrocities." I said, "No, I will not tell you. You know about the atrocities or you would not be coming to me. Let me tell you what is more newsworthy—the fact that 500 people from all walks of life are addressing this in a highly ethical and highly proactive fashion." And they bought it and they ran it on NPR (National Public Radio) and elsewhere. Do you see how we managed this problem?

Acting in this manner goes against your nature. It is much more natural, and I sympathize with you, to follow the "you, too" strategy mentioned earlier. The only problem is that this strategy will not work. Growing up in New York City and learning street fighting, I learned very early that the object is to win. This is not like the British where you put up the Marquis of Queensberry and do everything in a perfectly fair manner and then you get kicked in the head. Rest assured—this is a street fight.

QUESTION: This is not really a question, but a comment concerning the recent proposed Senate amendment which would have put some very onerous regulations on the shipment of all live animals in the United States by all air carriers. It was in response to animal rights activists concerned about dogs, cats, and other animals—companion animals that are being transported like luggage. The problem is that the senator who initiated the amendment had no idea about live fish, live seafood products that were going on the airplanes as well. As of late 1999, the amendment will be changed to exempt animals not covered in the Animal Welfare Act including fish, reptiles, and amphibians. It appears that the industry is going to dodge this bullet.

B. ROLLIN: Right, well said.

QUESTION: PETA and the other animal rights activists have now been put on notice that, in addition to companion animals, there are all these fish that they did not even think about. I bet you they will now go after the Animal Welfare Act to include fish, reptiles, and amphibians.

B. ROLLIN: Well, the following may interest you. The Animal Welfare Act does not cover these animals (fish, etc.), but the vast majority of animal care committees in research institutions do provide anesthesia and analgesia, in fact they demand it. It is not legally justified by either of the laws, but the committees, in interest of consistency not politics, feel that there is sufficient evidence that fish may well feel pain and also some of the higher cephalopods. So the institution committees have voluntarily said, "Let us deal with this in keeping with what we have been shown is social concern."

QUESTION: An additional comment. I direct the fish labs at the University of Florida and we have applied consistent rules. We're not required to do this, but we do.

B. ROLLIN: You do, exactly. And if people think that this does not reassure the general public, that you are now doing the right thing *not* because somebody is holding a gun at your head, believe me it does provide reassurance. That is why there have been less break-ins and that sort of thing, especially, as you know, in Florida which was a hotbed in the 1980s of people hassling and disrupting meetings and so forth. Right?

QUESTION: Still is.

B. ROLLIN: It still is? I would say, in keeping with what you said, that you should not think that you are getting away with something just because you dodged the bullet this time.

QUESTION: Precisely. My point is that it is very alarming how quickly the activists can change the entire industry.

B. ROLLIN: I worked on the federal lab animal laws with people who had 100 years of research experience, so we knew what we were talking about. And if you ever attend Congress to see how laws are passed, it would curl your hair. A senator or a congressperson who carries a piece of legislation may know nothing about it. It is put into the hands of aides who may or may not know anything about it. One version of our bill was soundly defeated because Congressman Walgren from Pennsylvania had been told that a group called AALAC (American Association for Accreditation of Laboratory Animal Care), working as an independent body under contract to NIH (National Institutes of Health), provides accreditation that assures proper animal care. Well, it doesn't.

AALAC assures that research facilities are adequate for scientific purposes. And yet, Walgren wrote this in as a provision of his bill—that you could not do animal research in the United States unless you were AALAC accredited. To make all U.S. animal research institutions AALAC accredited would have cost 500 billion dollars. This why I do not like law. That is why I much prefer encouraging you to clean up your own house. Do you understand what I mean here? If other people come to clean your house, they are going to do it with a very big vacuum cleaner.

QUESTION: In an industry where there are a lot of small operators, would you say that the associations that operators belong to should be taking proactive action? Examining your own house is difficult to do in an objective manner.

B. ROLLIN: Well, I do not mean to sound like a politician, but I am going to say yes and no and I will tell you why. First, I say yes because you are right. By this I mean a two person operation does not have the luxury of reflecting on the social ethic.

But I would also say that you should not "top down" these things because none of the rules will work unless they originate from the grassroots. Once you establish a reasonable agenda from the top, then it becomes extremely important to get people at the grassroots level to see that it is in their interest to do it, to make the adjustments. I think in the case of a lot of the problems that confront you, it is probably in your economic interest as well to proceed in this manner—for reasons of quality, dead animals, and so forth. So I think it has to be dialectical.

QUESTION: I would like to mention something similar in another industry. King County, Washington state, has a hazardous waste program that has been dealing with a lot of small individual operators. The program has actually been functioning very nicely. An anonymous information line is available where individual operators can contact hazardous waste management at the county to ask questions about their status—to assess their own status, to determine which set of regulations they fall under, and also to talk about particular practices that had not been thought about. This system opened up the process, I think. I am not an operator with hazardous materials, but I think this is a way that can open the gates to people and to provide some kind of anonymous information network.

B. ROLLIN: True, sure. Let me give you an example from the beef industry. The beef industry is a very clean industry for meat production from an animal welfare point of view compared, let us say, to swine or chicken. But there are some very public practices that people use to discredit the beef industry. These practices include knife castration, dehorning, and hot iron branding. As one cowboy in Wyoming said to me, "The castration practice does not make any sense, Doc. We cut off their testicles, and then we are dinged by the public for being inhumane. Then we put their testicles in their ears (meaning the use of replacement growth hormones) and they do not work as well and we get dinged for adulterating the food supply."

So some very smart operators now just raise young bulls. If you raise young bulls, you do not need to castrate. If you do not castrate, you do not have to use growth hormones. You can call the product "natural." Furthermore, you can market a young bull with a full month less feeding than a steer because you left the testicles on. Research at Colorado State University and Nevada has shown that these animals are indistinguishable in palatability, tenderness, or anything at an age up to about 14 months.

So there are some smart operators who are just marketing bulls. And they do not call them bulls—rather they call the product "Dakota lean." Whereas the other operators are getting perhaps a buck a pound, these smart operators are getting ten dollars a pound from exclusive restaurants on both coasts. They sure are not getting this kind of money in Wyoming, but it is not the Wyoming market they are after. Do you see my point?

So I think the smartest things to fix first are the things that also cost you money. You do not have to trumpet that, but you do not deny it either. You point out that these are welfare issues that your industry is committed to fix.

Holding Tank System for Reconditioning Transport of Live Cod Recently Captured in Deep Water

Hans-Peder Pedersen
MARINTEK (Norwegian Marine Technology Research Institute), Trondheim, Norway

Arnt Amble
SINTEF Fisheries and Aquaculture, Trondheim, Norway

Abstract

The transportation of live cod, recently caught from deep water by seine netting, has frequently resulted in high mortality, even when the fish density in the vessel holding tanks (with continuous through-flow of seawater) was restricted to 100-120 kg per m^3. In addition, a substantial mortality usually occurred after transfer from these holding tanks to floating net cages. This mortality occurred during the first few days after transport from the fishing grounds and is due to the poor condition of the fish after transport. A mortality rate of 10% has been a rather common figure and occasionally about 50% of the cod died.

Based on findings reported in H.-P. Pedersen's doctoral thesis, technology for greatly improved survival rates and transport efficiency is presented. The concept differs significantly from standard technology for live fish transport tank systems. This concept is based on the hypothesis that insufficient oxygen supply is the main cause of the high mortality rates related to transport of recently caught cod. Based on hydrodynamic analysis of the velocity and distribution of the water flow in the holding tank, a system for efficient oxygen distribution has been developed. This system allows for the avoidance of possible respiratory malfunction due to overly dense fish concentrations. The hypothesis and technical solutions are investigated theoretically and experimentally.

Through the use of this innovative system, a survival rate of practically 100% is obtainable for recently caught cod that is transported in tanks containing 400-600 kg fish per m^3 tank volume. This is about a 50:50 mixture of fish and seawater. The key to safe and efficient transport of live cod is an efficient system for circulation and distribution of the oxygen-carrying seawater. The proposed circulating system is also suitable for the "high density" live transport of other species. For certain species, the ability of this transport system to successfully handle more than 700 kg fish per m^3 tank volume is reported.

Background

The title of this report contains the phrase "reconditioning transport." By "reconditioning" we mean that the fish should be in better condition after the transport than they were when the transport started. Atlantic cod is the main topic of this presentation, but I think the results and the conclusions will be of more general interest. By "deep water" we mean depths of 100-200 meters or even more.

Fish farming based on fish derived from the fishing fleet has several advantages compared to fish farming based on juvenile fish from hatcheries. With small fish quotas in the late 1980s, Norwegian fishermen looked to the farming of cod as a way of getting added value from the limited catch. Several fish farming projects were started using live cod that originated from the coastal fishing fleet. However, mortality rates were often high (10-50%) and rather unpredictable, both during transport from the fishing grounds to near netpens and several days after vessel transportation. Without a lower and more predictable mortality rate, the future of fish farming based on the vessel transport of live cod seemed uncertain. Vessel transport and short-term storage seemed to be a risky business.

Later, people began focusing on the potential increase in income that could be gained from temporarily storing the live fish in order to "smooth out"

H.-P. Pedersen's current affiliation is Capella Technologies AS, Trondheim, Norway the fish supply during the fishing season. A variant of this idea called for storing the cod alive until after the close of the fishing season, when fish landings are smaller and prices higher.

The interest in solving the problem of high mortality rates associated with the transport of live cod gave birth to several research projects sponsored by the Research Council of Norway. These projects were the basis for a doctoral thesis dealing with "Live Fish Technology," where the live transport of wild captured cod was the main issue.

Problems and Results

As early as in 1957, Professor Gunnar Sundnes reported that live cod in good condition could be transported at high fish densities—500-600 kg per m^3 (Sundnes 1957). However, cod caught by Danish seine at depths of 100 m or more are generally not in very good shape when hauled onboard.

There was a lot of speculation about the causes of these large losses. The mortality factors considered included:

1. Condition of the cod.
2. Spawning season.
3. Feeding.
4. Rough treatment from the fishing gear.
5. Decompression from 200 meters, causing expansion of the buoyancy system to be out of balance.
6. Stress due to crowding during catching and handling of the fish.
7. The rupture of the swim bladder (a common occurrence in most of the fish).
8. Gas bubbles in the bloodstream causing damage and stress.
9. Mechanical damage onboard the fishing vessel.
10. Partial suffocation resulting from rough handling in the catching process.
11. Other holding conditions aboard the transport vessels, including water temperature variations and possible stress reactions due to the crowding of fish in the transport tanks.

A combination of a many different stress-inducing factors were possibly involved.

The various problems associated with the live harvesting and onboard transport of fish caused us to investigate several aspects of the handling process. Areas of study included:

1. Possible correlation between mortality and how the catching operation was carried out including the influence of the hauling speed of the fishing gear on the mortality rate (Pedersen 1997).

2. Laboratory tests investigating possible stress reactions due to high fish density (Staurnes et al. 1993b).

3. Stress response due to low temperature and rapid temperature drop (Staurnes et al. 1993a).

Several researchers, including myself, tried to solve the problem. We started on board the fishing vessels with observations. Many fish were cut into pieces to gain needed samples, which were taken ashore for analysis. We studied fishing gear mortality, the speed of gear hauling, and we studied the behavior of the fish in relation to the fishing gear. We recorded temperatures, oxygen levels, and so on. In the laboratory, the meat was studied. My colleagues measured stress reactions and what happens to the fish when the water temperature drops very quickly. Many aspects of this work were done at the request of the fishermen and other members of the fishing industry.

So then, what is the real problem? What could it be? None of the above tests indicated a likely reason for the high mortality rate observed in connection with full-scale transport and storage of live captured wild cod. We were having difficulty accepting the possibility that there might be a simple answer to the problem.

During the transport of live cod from the fishing grounds, it was observed that the cod had a tendency to accumulate close to the bottom of the fish tanks. In this area, oxygen levels as low as 2 mg per m^3 were measured (Pedersen 1997). In traditionally designed well vessels (live hauling vessels), seawater enters the fish holding tanks through perforations in the forward transverse bulkhead. The water leaves the tanks through the transverse aft bulkhead. This arrangement does not ensure sufficient water speed and oxygen levels near the bottom of the holding tanks.

It occurred to us that this water distribution pattern might be stressing the fish, possibly causing suffocation. In the traditional holding tank, the water will flow rather easily through the tank, but not necessarily through the fish to provide for their respiration needs. Even if the water was directly applied to the tightly grouped fish, the water would meet the resistance from this dense mass and then most of the flow would pass over the fish. The following thoughts arose from this observation: Could the reason for the high mortality rate be as simple as inferior oxygen supply? Could a better arrangement for water and oxygen distribution be the answer?

We then proposed our very simple answer to the problem—more efficient distribution of the water entering the holding tanks. Water supplied from a bottom "grid" arrangement was the proposal. We should try to take advantage of the hydrodynamic forces involved with the proper distribution of water. But now let's take a look at the principle of this upwelling arrangement. The water must pass through the tightly grouped fish, not slide over top of it.

We proposed an arrangement in which seawater is supplied through a perforated bottom in the fish tank. The bottom grid arrangement is designed to provide sufficient flow resistance to distribute the water evenly in spite of any local accumulation of fish. However, it is possible that, in spite of a very efficient distribution of water and oxygen along the bottom of the tank, the water could escape without providing a sufficient oxygen supply to all the fish in the tank. One way this could happen would be in the situation where the accumulated fish behaved like a carpet which could lift off and let the main part of the water stream escape upward along a bulkhead or a corner.

The desired water distribution would also be lost if most of the water escaped through a few randomly developing "tunnels" in the fish mass. A third pessimistic hypothesis assumed that even if there was a sufficient water and oxygen supply inside the dense "fish carpet," the pressure from neighboring fish caused by reduced buoyancy would, in turn, reduce or otherwise hinder respiratory functions.

So we started with some small calculations and studied what happens when the water stream flows from the bottom upward through the tank—vertical flow in other words. Fortunately, the laws of physics dictate that the velocity of the water will be rather low when no fish are present in the holding tank. However, when the fish are crowded together, the water flows in the small channels between the fish and the velocity of water will, of course, increase. Taking the increased vertical flow into account, we saw the possibility of some lifting forces that could lift the cod, which have completely or partially lost their buoyancy. We also realized that you do not need a large amount of extra water flow to lift cod that have lost only 5% of their buoyancy.

We commenced our study with a set of carefully considered assumptions. Assuming the presence of small openings between each fish in the rather dense fish mass, an upward water flow will reach a relatively high velocity. This high water speed will introduce lift forces on each fish and the downward pressure due to limited buoyancy will be reduced. When increasing the water supply and thus increasing the water velocity, the hydrodynamic lift forces, at some optimum level, should be able to keep each fish floating free in the water stream. Calculations indicated that some extra water supply might be needed to get cod, with no buoyancy remaining from their deflated swim bladder, to lift off the bottom in a vertical water flow. The results from the calculations seemed promising, but would it work in real life?

To further investigate our assumptions, tests were performed using cylindrical models representing fish. Three different specific gravities were tested and retested. The conclusion was rather easily drawn. The plastic fish models will separate, lift off, and will be sorted according to their specific gravity. This is, of course, not the final proof that we had arrived at a successful system, but it was a step on the way to solving the problem. The model test results indicated that fish would float individually on the water stream and fish with different specific gravities would be sorted into "gravity groups."

The next step was full-scale tests onboard the fishing vessel *Karl Wilhelm*. The fish tank arrangement is a simplified double-bottom holding tank. The adjustable bottom or "grid" provides for the proper distribution of water within the tank. Key data from two full-scale tests are given in Table 1. Results from these and other experiments and full-scale tests are summarized in Table 2.

So the real test was in practice on the fishing vessel. We made three trips. The first one was a failure caused by a rather simple fault. The flaps between the walls and the bottom were not functioning. The necessary adjustments were made and the next two trips were successful.

The results presented in Table 2 indicate that for the transport of cod captured alive, fish density in a tank with a conventional horizontal-flow water distribution system should be restricted to about 120 kg fish per m^3 tank volume. With this original

Table 1. Key data from two full-scale tests on transporting live cod from fishing grounds.

	16-17 April 1996	24-25 April 1996
Fish density	310 kg/m^3	380 kg/m^3
Transport duration	16 hours	16 hours
Number of fish	307	410
Number of dead fish after transport and two weeks storage	2	0
Mean size of fish	2.73 kg	2.50 kg
Catching depth	80 m	70-110 m
Wind and waves		L. breeze, 1 m waves
Hauling speed of fishing gear		88 m/min
Water temperature		2.8-3.6°C
Water supply		100 m^3/hour
Resistance through bottom grid		0.004-0.005 bar
Oxygen consumption		100 mg/kg/hour
Cod with ruptured swim bladder		Approx. 50%

Table 2. Fish densities achieved for safe transport of live fish.

Type of transport	Stored fish Salmon kg/m^3	Stored fish Cod kg/m^3	Stored fish Saithe kg/m^3	Newly caught transport from fishing grounds Cod kg/m^3	Newly caught transport from fishing grounds Saithe kg/m^3	Newly caught transport from fishing grounds Flounder kg/m^{2a}	Source
Well vessel Conventional, horizontal water flow	200	226	190-200		150		Interview with well vessel skippers 1994
Well vessel Water flow from bottom grids	350-400						Mads Waage, Frøya fiskeindustri
Fishing vessel							
Horizontal water flow				120	50		Isaksen and Midling 1995
Water from bottom grids				250	180		Isaksen and Midling 1995
Water from bottom grids						360	B. Isaksen 1996[b]
Water from bottom grids				380			Pedersen et al. 1996
Container Train and lorry		500-600					G. Sundnes 1957-1964
Laboratory experiments		540					MARINTEK/SINT EF 1993

[a] Storage density for flounder given in kg per square meters.
[b] Unpubl. notes

system, a mortality rate of about 10% should be expected. However, with a water distribution system using the new concept, successful transport of 380 kg fish per m³ was obtained. Mortality was practically zero. It is interesting to note that the volume actually occupied by fish, the "real density," was estimated to be about 600 kg per m³.

The new concept worked very well. Survival was close to 100%. During the second of the three trips, we had two dead cods out of about 350. However, these two fish were not very lively when they entered the system. On the third trip, about 400 cod were transported and all of them survived the 16 hours of vessel transport and storage for two weeks. Colleagues at SINTEF (Trondheim), analyzed samples for stress levels using cortisol and other indicators. They reported back that the stress level in these fish after the vessel transport period was at the same level as measured in cod stored for a long period of time. It is apparent that we have improved live holding conditions during vessel transport. The cod were in good shape at the end of transport.

For the live transport of flounder, the corresponding fish density figures are 50 kg per square meter of tank bottom area in the conventional system and 360 kg fish per square meter for a system using the new water distribution concept. We later successfully transported flounder at a density of 700 kg per m².

Conclusions

Based on our calculations, experiments, and current stage of knowledge, the following conclusions could be drawn:

1. The safe live transport of a wide range of fish species could be performed at very high holding densities through the efficient distribution of the water and oxygen supply through the bottom grid arrangement.

2. Respiratory malfunction caused by reduced or absent swim bladder buoyancy could be cured by increasing the water supply through a bottom grid arrangement, thus providing sufficient hydrodynamic lift to separate the fishes.

Comments and future developments

Fish with a high level of swimming activity will survive transport at rather high fish densities when the crew are using the proposed concept. Full-scale tests with salmon showed 100% survival at fish densities of 350-400 kg per m³ (see Table 2).

To avoid wear and tear on fish with high swimming activity, the tank geometry and water flow arrangements should be manipulated in order to allow the fish to swim in an "organized" manner, for example, in a school.

The motions of the vessel navigating in waves will introduce pressure variations and relative movements between the fish and the walls of the tank. Above certain limits of pressure variations and vessel movements, several fish species will become seasick. They will lose buoyancy and accumulate on the bottom of the fish tanks.

The rolling motions of a vessel can easily be taken care of through the use of suitable, well-known roll damping devices. Heaving and pitching motions are not adequately taken care of by conventional ship design. With a transport vessel specifically designed for live fish, however, the heaving and pitching motions of the vessel could be minimized through the use of active fins.

References

Pedersen, H.-P. 1997. Live fish technology for fishing vessel. Doctoral thesis, Norges Teknisk-naturvitenskapelige Universite. MTA-rapport 1997:119. ISBN 82-471-01424. 105 pp.

Staurnes, M., T. Sigholt, H.-P. Pedersen, and T. Rustad. 1993. Physiological effects of simulated high density transport of Atlantic cod. SINTEF, Trondheim. ISBN 82-595-7460-8.

Staurnes, M., F.R. Rainuzzo, T. Sigholt, and L. Jørgensen. 1993. Exposing of cod to cold water: Stress response, osmotic regulation and composition of lipids and Na-K-ATPase activities in gill tissue. SINTEF Report SFT21 A93015, Trondheim. ISBN 82-595-7455-1, pp. 1-26. (In Norwegian.)

Sundnes, G. 1957. On the transport of cod and coalfish. J. Cons. Cons. Int. Explor. Mer. 22(2).

Author biography

H.-P. Pedersen is a naval architect and marine engineer with more than 28 years of experience with research and development in the design of fishing vessels and equipment. Recently he completed a doctor of engineering program with a thesis on live fish handling and live fish technology for fishing vessels.

Questions from the Audience

QUESTION: What was the density of the cod when the 10% to 50% mortality was reached?

H.-P. PEDERSEN: The highest level of density was about 120 kilos per cubic meter. However, I think in most cases the density was lower than this. So you can say we have improved the process by more than three times.

E. KOLBE: How did you deal with the expanded swim bladder in the fish?

H.-P. PEDERSEN: We harvested the fish from about 100 meters depth. The experiment was performed at sea level. I think all of the cod had ruptured swim bladders. Some of the fish still had a lot of gas inside. By the way, cod are able to get rid of gas from the bladder via a small rupture in the structure. So even if the swim bladder has ruptured, the stomach or abdominal cavity could still contain a large gas volume.

QUESTION: What type of water circulation is used in the vessel live tanks—recirculation or flow-through?

H.-P. PEDERSEN: We pumped surface seawater and discharged it overboard. The oxygen consumption was about 100 milligrams per kilo per hour.

QUESTION: Did you feed the cod onboard the vessel?

H.-P. PEDERSEN: No, we did not feed the cod. They were just kept in captivity for two weeks.

QUESTION: Did the fish lose weight? Also, how much value was added to these products because they were kept in water? Did you get a higher price?

H.-P. PEDERSEN: You are asking about the loss of product weight. This was not a question for us. The big issue was "will this cod survive." I know that different species from the same family have been kept in captivity for three months without feeding. They lose weight—some from the muscle and some from the liver. I do not have any numbers for the cod in this experiment.

QUESTION: Going back to a previous question about the swim bladder, what can be done to prevent overinflation? Could you bring them up slowly? What did you do to fix the problem?

H.-P. PEDERSEN: We were much concerned about the problem of gas retained in the stomach or outside the swim bladder when the swim bladder ruptured. But it turned out to be, in fact, a problem of onboard selection. You do not retain cod that seem to keep air in the stomach. Regardless of the depth of capture, these cods will not survive. However, in the main part of the catch (about 90%), the swim bladder will rupture and most of these cod apparently are able to get rid of all of their gas. Some of the fish will have excess buoyancy. These fish tend to swim to the bottom of the tanks. They are using a lot of energy to get to and stay at the bottom. It seems that, after the passage of several hours, these cod with excess buoyancy have been able to regulate their system so that they are paddling around rather happily.

QUESTION: When you have a high density of fish at the bottom of a holding tank, not only would the oxygen concentration be of concern, but ammonia level would be high, as well. When you redirected the water flow, was the problem of ammonia buildup minimized as well?

H.-P. PEDERSEN: You are asking me about ammonia content and oxygen level. I have done some calculations of the possible problems with ammonia buildup. Very briefly, this will not occur in an open or flow-through system. However, I measured oxygen levels as low as two milligrams per liter. This is on the point of suffocation. So, it is not surprising that we observed a high level of mortality in the traditional horizontal flow systems.

Short-Term Holding and Live Transport of Aquatic Animals: An Overview of Problems and Some Historic Solutions

David J. Scarratt
Hatchery International, Bridgetown, Nova Scotia, Canada

Introduction to lobster storage and shipping

I am no longer active in scientific research, but as the editor of two aquaculture-related magazines I still have a keen interest in seafood. I believe we have a clear responsibility to comment on the industry, and it is important that scientists, engineers, equipment designers and manufacturers, and the people who are using information and equipment to grow, catch, or sell fish and shellfish, should all be talking together. My own professional history, going back to the early 1960s, began with the lobster industry, and some of my earliest field trips were to tidal lobster pounds.

Figure 1 is an aerial view of a typical Bay of Fundy lobster pound. Lobsters are still stored in these traditional pounds throughout the winter season when fishing is difficult and prices are high. The pound operators depend on the 25 ft (8 m) tides at the mouth of the Bay of Fundy to provide adequate water circulation to these holding areas. At high tide, a fresh supply of water will completely flood the pounds. The wall and fence keep the lobsters from escaping and retain a meter or so of water when the tide is out. The tides serve as a natural pump for these holding systems.

Lobsters are banded to immobilize the claws and placed in the pound. In the old days, they were simply tossed in with little regard to their condition and, as a consequence, the mortality rate was quite high. To complicate matters further, there was little in the way of record keeping. Then as now, lobsters were raked off the bottom of the pound by means of drags, and packed and shipped around the country and to more distant markets.

It is easy to forget that the transport of lobsters has gone on for many years. Before there were airplanes making rapid transcontinental journeys, the trains did a very fine job of it. Lobsters were traditionally brought to the West Coast of North America packed in wooden boxes, wrapped with seaweed,

Figure 1. Lobster pound on Deer Island, New Brunswick (Clearwater Lobsters photo).

and iced. Every two or three hundred miles, wherever the train had to stop, somebody would refresh the ice to keep the lobsters properly chilled. In this manner, they would make their way across the continent. The transport of shellfish across the continent by rail began very shortly after the last spike was driven.

On several occasions earlier in the twentieth century, lobsters were shipped by rail and introduced to several locations on the Pacific Coast in an effort to set up viable reproducing populations. Other shellfish such as oysters were also transported in this way.

Lobsters are still put into crates or boxes chilled with frozen gel packs and shipped across the country, either by truck or by airplane. The traditional standard wooden lobster crates (Fig. 2) held something in the order of 100 pounds (45 kg) of lobsters, crammed in on top of one another. Frequently the lid was put down and somebody would jump on the top to make sure that they were all firmly packed.

This same packing practice is still common in the sea urchin industry. Shippers do not realize that the skin of a sea urchin is on the outside. When

Figure 2. Traditional lobster crates still in use for short-term storage and shipping (Clearwater Lobsters photo).

they are crushed one on top of the other with their spines sticking out, and then jumped on, every urchin is going to be injured. Shippers are finally beginning to learn that product survival and low mortality rates are directly dependent on the care with which they handle their product.

REVIEW OF HOLDING SYSTEMS

Times are changing, and the cavalier disregard with which fishermen, in particular, and the industry, in general, held their lobsters is also changing. Now lobsters are genuinely perceived to be "dollars on the hoof." Although some people still need some education, most lobsters are now handled much more carefully.

Figures 3 and 4 illustrate part of Clearwater Seafood's lobster holding facility. (An extensive description of this was delivered at this conference in 1997.) Here, lobsters are handled individually, rather than in bulk, and are carefully banded. They are placed into individual compartments within trays that are then stacked on top of one another. High stacks of these trays are maintained in this state-of-the-art facility.

This system is the direct descendant of a stacking system that I first saw in the Billingsgate Market (London) in 1962. It consisted of a series of trays with a small reservoir at the bottom filled with cockleshells, and, in effect functioned as a mini-recirculation system. That innovative system was the prototype of units now seen in virtually every seafood restaurant.

Clearwater Seafoods has developed this to the nth degree. They can now store in excess of a million pounds of lobsters in a controlled environment. The operating temperature is maintained at about 2-3°C, which keeps lobsters for many months in very good condition. For the most part, these on-land pounds are located in areas where it is possible to maintain flow-through circulation systems. However, some degree of recirculation is provided because it costs money to cool water and recirculation enables energy conservation. However, recirculation may also create problems of ammonia buildup, and require the addition of a biofilter to remove it. With this compartmentalized system, it is possible to adjust the size of the compartment to suit the size of the individual lobster.

TRANSPORTATION SYSTEMS

Figure 5 shows lobsters neatly stacked vertically in a new plastic shipping container fitted with adjustable dividers. The claws are banded and the tails are tucked into the space provided—a bit like a case of wine. The totes stack for shipment, but can be nested for the return journey. This patented system is a very effective way of handling product. The Sea Hive Corporation of Halifax is now using this strategy to ship some of their product.

The lobsters are covered with wet newspaper—seaweed is no longer the standard. A layer of foil is placed on top, and then chill-packs are added. In this manner, lobsters can be transported from Halifax to Tokyo in something like 56 hours with very good survival rates.

Sea Hive is also looking at other ways to move lobsters over long distances. Figure 6 shows the inside of a 40-foot ocean-going container into which has been fitted a plastic liner and a series of sprinkler hoses. In this particular example, the liner has not yet been put on the floor. With this floor liner in place, the shippers are able to fill the container with live seafood and recirculate water through it.

The initial shipments employing this method used additional technology because the container ship's fire mains, which are used to supply seawater to irrigate the lobsters, cannot be opened until the ship is at sea. There was concern that lobster condition would deteriorate after they were removed from the pound and before they were at sea, when water circulation would be restored. Thus, Sea Hive has been experimenting with several different types of recirculation systems, each using roughly a one-to-one

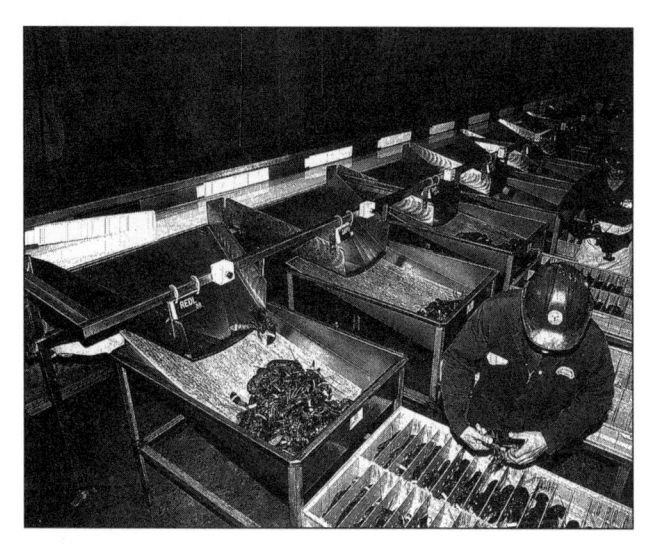

Figure 3. Lobsters are packed into individual compartments of storage trays (Clearwater Lobsters photo).

Figure 4. Stacked lobster storage trays (Clearwater Lobsters photo).

ratio of water to lobster volume built into the end of the container.

The developers of this shipping method now find that the 24-hour period at each end of the journey when ocean water is not available does not require the use of the recirculation system. They find that they can pack the lobsters in their crates inside the container, load it onto the ship, and turn the fire main on as soon as the vessel reaches oceanic water. At the end of the journey, after the fire main is turned off, the lobsters are cooled from ocean temperatures to a holding temperature of 2-3°C using a chiller system. This step is accomplished before the lobsters are off-loaded and taken to their next market destination. The lobsters must be cooled while they are still wet—they cannot be allowed to desiccate. This method is a perfectly viable way of getting bulk seafood across the Atlantic without being dependent upon an airplane.

Four shipments of shellfish have now been made from Halifax to Europe using this type of technology. It has been used not only for the shipment of lobsters, but also for mussels, American and European oysters, and scallops—all with considerable success.

SMALL SCALE LAND-BASED LIVE HOLDING SYSTEMS

Small seafood outlets and restaurants are beginning to use small-scale recirculation systems. They can hold several different species, including oysters, mussels, and lobsters. In some the animals are continuously submerged while in others they are held under a spray. Some of the small systems are chilled, and have a pump, and charcoal filter, and an ultraviolet light system to control bacteria.

Figure 8 shows a display case holding oysters, clams, and quahogs. The water enters along a channel, spills into the containers holding the product, flows into another channel across the back, and is eventually channeled to a filter, a pump, and an ultraviolet system. There is no additional reservoir in this simple system—the shellfish are in the reservoir.

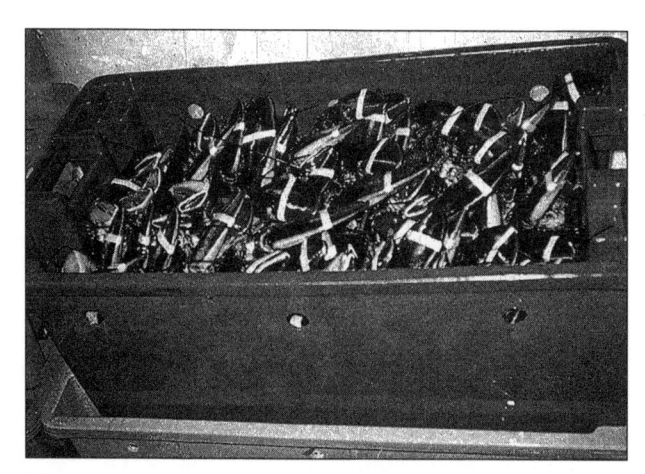

Figure 5. Sea Hive's patented lobster tote (Sea Hive Corporation photo).

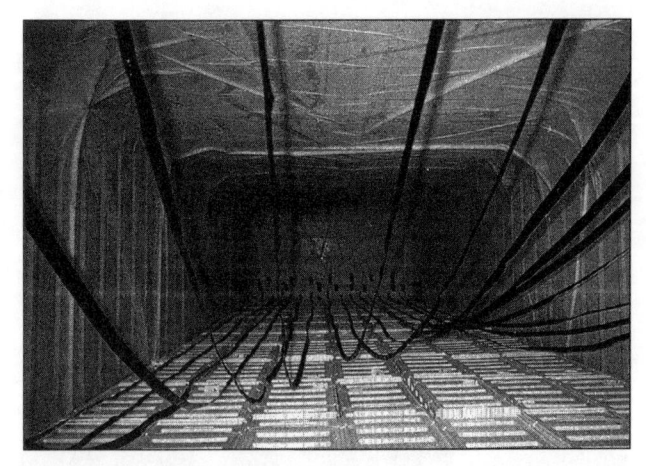

Figure 6. Ocean-going container fitted with plastic liner and sprinkler hoses (Sea Hive Corporation photo).

Figure 8 shows a much larger system currently being built in Vancouver, British Columbia. The standard tote boxes shown will each hold about 1,000 pounds of mussels. This system is being set up to accept East Coast mussels transported to British Columbia via freight truck. The journey takes just under a week. The plan is to ship cooled mussels in cool moist air from the East Coast, put them into this type of live holding system, and irrigate them with large volumes of recirculated water (Fig. 9). This is very similar to the way stored mussels are irrigated in Prince Edward Island and Nova Scotia, except that it is self-contained.

SOME BASIC CONCERNS

The advent of these and other live holding systems is an exciting development, but I am left with a few areas of unease. My concern is that we may be applying swimming pool technology without a proper understanding of the biology of the animals to be held in these systems. The lack of a biofilter on some of the systems is of concern.

I am delighted to read in Angela Danford's paper (this proceedings, Danford et al. 2001) that we are finally obtaining some numbers on ammonia and carbon dioxide production. I am aware of one lobster pound that is running into problems involving a decrease in pH of the seawater. I suspect this is probably a result of accumulating carbon dioxide produced by the animals held in the system. In the three systems I have described above, there is no indication that aeration or some other method is being used to strip carbon dioxide from the holding water. In anticipation of this talk, I spoke with Hélène Drouin, of Aquabiotech, Inc. in Quebec. She has designed biofilters for the lobster storage industry, specifically to deal with this issue in recirculating systems. She believes that her biofilter works particularly well, because it is a trickle filter that includes an aeration component which allows carbon dioxide to be blown off.

However, I am still uncertain that these "biofilters" will genuinely work effectively when the storage tanks are filled with a big load of shellfish after being semidry for a week or more. How much ammonia are the newly added animals going to dump the instant they are irrigated again, and how will the biofilter cope with this sudden spike? What will be the effects of rapid fluctuations in loading as stock is removed and replaced? It is quite different from recirculating fish culture systems where the stocking density is relatively constant. This is clearly an area for new research.

Biofilters take a long time to get up to speed, particularly at the cool temperatures that are used for storage. I am uncertain that the necessary work has been done to ensure that the biological requirements of the bacteria in these biofilters are being properly met, let alone those of the shellfish. They, too, are living organisms that require their own nutrients—the metabolic by-products that mussels, lobsters, and oysters are excreting—and also their own oxygen supply.

I would also like to comment on the National Shellfish Sanitation Program requirement for ultraviolet light sterilization systems to remove potentially harm-

Figure 7. Recirculating shellfish display case, Granville Market, Vancouver, B.C. (David Scarratt photo).

ful bacteria. We must ensure that UV sterilization does not at the same time compromise the effectiveness of the bacteria in the biofilter. If there is adequate physical separation between the two components, I think that the systems should function adequately.

Conclusion

We clearly need more research on the development of appropriate biofilters for shipping and storage systems. I am hopeful that this type of meeting will bring the people with mechanical and engineering ideas and biological backgrounds together with the people whose businesses depend on delivering product in good condition. I hope my ability to stand on the sidelines and examine the way the industry is developing, and then offer technical commentary through the medium of our newspapers and magazines will be of some value to you.

Acknowledgments

I would like to thank Ed Kolbe and the organizers of this conference for their invitation to come and address you. I would also like to thank the representatives of Clearwater Lobsters for discussing this issue and also for some of the slides: Sheridan Flynn from Sea Hive, Hélène Drouin of Aquabiotech, Inc. the proprietors of the seafood retail outlets I visited, and a number of others, for discussing the way in which this industry seems to be evolving.

Figure 8. Recirculation system in bulk mussel storage. Stacked tote boxes hold up to 10 metric tons of mussels for rewatering and short-term storage prior to distribution to retailers (David Scarratt photo).

Figure 9. Mussel storage system, Vancouver, B.C. The big reservoirs (bottom) hold water for delivery to the storage tanks in Fig. 8. Above them is a battery of filtration units. This system uses UV to help control bacteria (David Scarratt photo).

Reference

Danford, A.R., R.F. Uglow, and J. Garland. 2001. Effect of long-haul international transport on lobster hemolymph constituents and nitrogen metabolism. In: B.C. Paust and A.A. Rice (eds.), Marketing and shipping live aquatic products: Proceedings of the Second International Conference and Exhibition, November 1999, Seattle, WA. University of Alaska Sea Grant, AK-SG-01-03, Fairbanks. (This volume.)

Author biography

David Scarratt obtained his B.Sc. and Ph.D. at the University of Wales and immigrated to Canada in 1961. In 1998, having retired from a career in fisheries and aquaculture, he was appointed editor of *Recirc Today*, a magazine devoted to the use of recirculation technology and recycling in aquaculture. Scarratt is now editor of *Hatchery International,* which incorporates *Recirc Today*. His professional history with the lobster industry goes back to the early 1960s.

Questions from the audience

QUESTION: Do you know the acceptable levels of carbon dioxide for crustaceans at a given temperature, and what the critical limit for carbon dioxide might be?

D. SCARRATT: I cannot answer that offhand. I know some of the seminal work was done at the biological station at St. Andrews by a researcher named Dr. Don McCleese. In about 1964, he and Dr. Wilder published a bulletin under the old Fisheries Research Board logo titled "The care and handling of lobsters." There are copies of this publication at all of the Canadian fisheries libraries. I think this will give you some very interesting data and it is still the basic book on that subject. It will tell you the maximum temperature that a lobster can be conditioned to and will also provide you with certain survival times in air.

I ran into a problem of survival in air a few years ago when a client called to say that he had some lobsters die after they were taken out of the water. They were dead when they got to their market destination less than an hour away. The problem was that they were simply too warm when they were taken out of the water to survive in air. Throwing ice over the boxes was not enough to bring their body temperature down.

Earlier, somebody asked whether oxygen helped. McCleese found quite clearly that increasing the oxygen concentration of the air in which lobsters were being held was counterproductive. It reduced survival. This was surprising and I think that it was probably because of increased metabolic rate. He tried holding the lobsters at 30% oxygen, 40%, 50%, and 60%, and found that the higher the oxygen content the worse the survival rate was. We never followed up on this finding, but I think that it is an interesting topic of study.

QUESTION: What is involved with the preconditioning of a biofilter?

D. SCARRATT: The preconditioning of a biofilter may take up to 30 days or perhaps longer before one will accept its full design load. It is also temperature dependent. The second item I would like to mention is the advisability of using protein skimmers to take off some of the additional waste material in a live holding system and so reduce the demand on the biofilter itself.

Live Fish Handling Strategies from Boat to Retail Establishment

John Seccombe
Aquahort Ltd., Maraetai Beach, Auckland, New Zealand

INTRODUCTION

New Zealand has been exporting live lobster to Asia and Europe for approximately 15 years. Our expertise in getting lobster into these markets as a premium product is recognized worldwide. The yearly volume is about 3,000 metric tons. Significant amounts of live eels and live mussels are also exported.

Beginning in 1993, wild-caught live snapper were exported to Japan from New Zealand in a special polystyrene box transport system. After three years, however, because of price competition with farmed snapper, this business was closed down. No other live finfish were exported other than a few experimental efforts. Technical and financial complexities abound in this business. Consequently, efforts encouraging fishing companies to jump in and experiment with live fish have proven to be unproductive. A variety of risk factors are involved.

Meanwhile, a growing Asian population of 130,000 in Auckland, New Zealand's largest city (1.3 million people total population), has started to demand live finfish in the local shops and restaurants. This paper will focus on the handling and delivery of wild-caught live seafood from a fishing company, Deep Cove Fisheries Ltd., based on the South Island of New Zealand, to Auckland and into this developing restaurant trade.

THE BUSINESS OF LIVE SEAFOOD HANDLING AND TRANSPORT

Deep Cove Fisheries is faced with a number of logistical challenges servicing the Auckland live market. Product transport is just one area of overall challenge. There are basically two methods of transport to Auckland:

1. Traveling the distance of 1,200 km (750 miles) by air—a 12 hour trip in a special polystyrene box.

2. Traveling by land transport—a journey of 30 hours in a special insulated 1,000 liter bin.

Deep Cove Fisheries first developed a list of species available to be caught, handled, and sold for a profit into the domestic market. We hoped that this extensive study would also provide us with the experience to export overseas to Asian markets at a later date.

Step One: Species determination and catching methods

Our first strategy was to establish target species that were most likely to be attractive to the New Zealand Asian market. This was a problem as there were no existing preferred species originating from New Zealand. The Asian market in Hong Kong was being supplied with live fish from several countries. These fish do not have the same color or shape as ours.

We located a Chinese restaurant that would take free live samples in exchange for honest reports on product quality and the different cooking methods used to prepare the seafood. Then, without engaging scientists, we adopted a crude yet effective method of evaluating available species. One of our methods for identifying likely candidates is of particular interest. We simply asked the fisherman what species of fish they found still flopping on the deck after taking them off the hook. We also asked how long these fish survived in iced water or in chilled conditions.

From this study we found that monk fish, flounder, and cod were the strongest—the most robust species encountered by the harvesters. We have since tried about ten other species. The most popular species have been sea perch, blue cod, monk fish, trumpeter, and a strange fish we have in New Zealand known as the southern pigfish (*Congiopodus leucopaecilus*). Fortunately, the Chinese like it. The restaurant chef thinks it is ideal; he places about six of these prepared fish on a plate. We have also worked with grouper, but air bladder problems occurred when the fish were caught deeper than 30 meters. We are currently working on a means to overcome this without venting through the use of a needle.

We needed to modify the fishing vessel used in this project to accommodate the live handling and holding of fish. We made fish holding tanks using 150 liter insulated plastic bins. We plumbed in water lines to connect with the boat's deck hose and directed the water in an upwelling manner—overflowing out the top of each of the bins. The skipper also came up with the idea of a grill at the top of the bin to hold the fish under the water. When fish are affected by stress or air bladder problems or are confused by the light, they will take in air at the surface. This only worsens their buoyancy problems.

The next step was to establish the best catching methods for these species. Contrary to what I have heard or read about other live fish projects, this fishing vessel initially trawled for the live fish. I was amazed that they were getting up to a 90% success rate. They used shallow, short, slow tows, and used extreme care getting the fish onboard the fishing vessel without crushing the fish or damaging scales. The fishermen used gloves to protect the fish. However, the bycatch of school sharks, with their rough skin and thrashing about, occasionally did take their toll on the delicate fish. After carefully examining the results, the fisherman soon arrived at the understanding that catching by pots and hand lines were the preferred methods.

My ambition is to eventually have chilled seawater tanks on the boats with aeration provided to lessen the oxygen deficit incurred during the harvesting process. Also, we might eventually use an anesthetic agent to further reduce the shock accompanying harvesting.

Step Two: Receiving and holding systems

So we had all these fish species coming into the tanks located in the land-based factory. I immediately had to develop a system that could maintain them. I initially thought that I would be able to use my experience with lobster and simply transfer this carefully developed technology to the new fish live holding situation. However, this strategy did not quite work. Live fish just will not tolerate the same handling and holding protocols that we can get away with when marketing lobster. Problems like high waste levels following heavy tank loadings will not be tolerated by the fish. I would see fish darting around in a holding tank for a couple of hours and I thought that they were in good condition—just exceedingly active. Then, unfortunately, they would die. These fish had been "poisoned" by nitrite levels exceeding 0.5 ppm. Remedies had to be sought.

The receiving tank system at the plant was not ideal, but it served as a pilot or experimental system. The tanks were altered in various ways until we were able to prove that it would all work. Among other changes, I installed a foam fractionator and used natural medium in the biofilters (e.g., coral) to buffer the pH levels. I did not want the tank man to try to watch the pH and control fluctuations by adding buffering chemicals.

Another thing that I learned from the lobster industry is that, by the time the fish are brought onboard the fishing boat and transported to the holding facility, they could have built up a huge oxygen deficit. It is important to get oxygen back into their systems as quickly as possible. I put an airlift system inside the holding tanks to provide both aeration and a circular motion without too high a current. I did not want the fish to expend too much energy swimming. This also maintained a good "scrubbing" effect on released gases and gave us a backup system in case the main water pump stopped working, which it did twice over a single weekend. The water recirculation rate through the tanks was three times per hour with new seawater added once per month.

In New Zealand, the entire live industry monitors water quality parameters. In fact, this is a requirement that has been written into our "Code of Compliance for Export." We regularly measure ammonia, pH, and nitrites. If you receive a mortality claim from your overseas buyer, you must be able to produce these water quality parameter readings. In terms of the current fish holding system, the pH level is maintained around 7.8 to make the system more forgiving toward any ammonia buildup. Nitrite must be maintained as close to 0 ppm as possible with a maximum allowed level of 0.25 ppm. Ammonia is maintained in the narrow range of 0.0-0.5 ppm. We add new water about once a month or more frequently if needed in order to get rid of nitrate buildup. We try to keep the nitrate level below about 80 ppm.

A new live fish venture can have logistical problems if the fishing company has not generated large enough market volumes. Right now we are catching and moving up to 300 kg of live fish to the land-based tanks at the Deep Cove Fisheries plant. At present, one 120-seat restaurant in Auckland does between 45 and 60 kg of live fish business per week. This small volume did not currently warrant using the big transport bin that we imported from Australia. Instead, we have developed a method, much like that used in the aquarium trade, of transporting the live fish in polystyrene bins. The big difference was that we are putting up to 5 kg or about four fish into less than 15 liters of water. Some fish-to-water ratios have been as low as 1-to-1.

The secret to our handling protocol is not to use or depend on chemicals that will hide any poor fish handling problems or inadequate water quality parameters that might be present in the system. We use good purge times and grade in an aggressive manner for any weak fish. We also use an Aquahort Heat'n'Chill heat pump to gradually reduce the holding water temperature to induce a slight comatose effect. The holding temperature of some species is depressed to as low as 1°C.

We experienced a rather interesting problem with free-swimming fish. It is possible that some fish will settle down on the bottom of a holding tank in a dense school and smother each other. Solutions had to be found to resolve this difficulty. Good water circulation is a partial remedy.

Our use of water temperature to induce a comatose state in the fish before packaging for shipment is based on some simple observations. You basically observe the animal's behavior, placing your hand in the tank and carefully touching them, their eye, for example, to test their response state at different temperatures. We made use of techniques that are also used in the lobster shipping industry. We chilled the water to approximately the minimum winter temperature, less 1°. We learned that this is an optimum thing to do when handling live fish.

One additional thing about the fish that differentiates them from lobster is their inclination to regurgitate stomach contents. Some fish, for example, the monk fish, can have the digested remains of whole fish inside them for up to 2-3 weeks. I asked many scientists about this and we are still not sure whether this is an indication of stress or if it is normal for them to retain stomach contents for that length of time. In terms of our project, for that initial 3-4 days following delivery at the plant, the staff observed the fish and removed any that showed signs of weakness during the first 24 hours. They also noted the waste released by the different species over this period of time. I believe that the observed vomiting could possibly be an indication of stress in the different fish species.

We needed to incorporate a proper amount of purging time into our handling schedule. As previously mentioned, we initially had only one Chinese restaurant taking between 40 and 60 kg of live fish a week. The participating fishing vessel would come in with 300 kg of live fish and this was loaded into our small holding system of about 8,000 liters total water volume. We quickly realized that the fish needed about four days of purging time. Anything less than this and I would have the restaurant owner ringing me up to say, "John, there's a fish that's spewing a white mess into the tanks, looking unsightly...." So this has been a problem.

Most important, if fish have not been purged long enough, the stress caused by transporting them will probably induce them to vomit their stomach contents and this will pollute your transport system water.

Step Three: Transportation of live product to market

We sent the live fish to our Auckland market using an airline company that had advertised itself as being very experienced with seafood. It was a major airline. However, sometimes I would go out to the airport freight terminal to pick up the delivered fish and the freight guy would walk out holding the poly bin in a vertical position. I would say, "How would you like to be standing on your head like those poor fish?" So, we started to talk to these people about proper handling and they gradually realized what had to be done. But then the shift would change and I would have to start the education process all over again.

One night an expected delivery of live fish had not arrived, so I rang up the airline freight office and asked where they were. The lady at the desk answered "It's very good that you rang us. We're closing now at 5:30 pm at the airport. Don't worry, we'll just put them in the freezer overnight." I said, "No, you won't. I'll be straight out there." The containers had all been posted with "live fish" labels on the outside. So this is certainly something that you should not take for granted—freight people reading and responding to your labels such as "this side up" and that sort of thing. You will need to work carefully with your shippers.

Once we were able to establish good catching methods and an adequate transport method, and had educated the airline transport people not to treat our product like frozen fish, we then started using a homemade anesthetizing agent—oil of cloves. This gave us that extra performance we needed—12 hours of transport time and up to 100% survival. Some of our transport experiments lasted 19.5 hours.

Step Four: Marketing

As a marketing tool, we give our client restaurants a 24-hour grace period to notify us of problems with a shipment. Within this period they must report in writing the weight and species of fish that arrive dead. Typically, fish sell for $35.00 NZ per kilogram in live form and $3.00 NZ per kilogram for "dead" product. We are now going to adopt the Australian practice of selling "unders" (e.g., fish under 1.5 kg each) at a prevailing price per kilogram and selling "overs" (e.g., over 1.5 kg per fish) at $65.00 NZ per fish. Because of the large price differential between live and chilled fish, it is important for the live shippers to protect themselves.

The live fish trade has additional marketing challenges because it is a traditional Asian business. One must appreciate the huge cultural differences between Westerners and Asians. Neither of us can read each other's body language. I tried sending a nice live fish promotional flyer by fax machine to 30 different Japanese and Korean restaurants and did not receive a single response. Later, it was explained to me by Chinese businessperson that I must personally visit prospective customers with live fish samples. The development of a good working relationship with your client is particularly important in the live trade.

This statement highlights the next step—the procedures for transferring the live fish from the plant holding tanks to restaurant. This can mean, during peak traffic times in the inner city, a one hour delivery time for only a 15 km drive. At the plant dispatch station we need polystyrene boxes, new water to add to the plastic bags, and an oxygen bottle. The entire procedure must be carefully organized and well practiced to reduce transfer time.

Humane and ethical treatment issues will always be topics requiring careful attention. We must consider the animal rights bills being drawn up in different parts of the world. We picked up a bit of flack concerning animal rights last year in New Zealand. A member of Parliament received a cry for help from someone who had walked into a Japanese restaurant and observed a lobster that was still moving on the plate. So the New Zealand Parliament, in all of its wisdom, made the decision to include lobster, octopus, and live fish in the national Animal Rights Act. However, there were no legal requirements linked to this inclusion, just that the lawmakers were going to include these species under this act. Suddenly there were many Asian people who were not able to interpret these new regulations or how they could be applied to the live seafood industry. When I went to some Japanese restaurants, for instance, to ask if they would buy live fish, they said, "Oh, no, we don't buy live lobster—a policeman might come through the door." This was really a sad situation. I told the industry members that we would have to become proactive, that we would need to write a code of practice that would be accepted by the SPCA (Society for the Prevention of Cruelty to Animals) and so on. Obviously, the code of practice needs to include the live fish in the tanks.

Present Situation

We have now installed a 350 kg holding facility in Auckland City. We are now able to land a larger volume of live fish using the approved fish transport bin. This unit is being very successfully used in Queensland, Australia, to export live fish to Hong Kong. The unit is a fully insulated plastic Dyna bin of 1,000 liters capacity, but with only 750 liters of water actually added. The unit is fully approved by all major airlines and has a 300 hour airworthiness certificate. In terms of shipping costs, when using a small polystyrene box the freight cost is $9.50 NZ per kilogram compared to $3.50 NZ per kilogram when using the transport bin system. Incidentally, Auckland is the site of the America's Cup sailing competition. We have been gearing up to supply the participants with our product.

We shipped up some southern pigfish at the beginning of the year [1999] and I still have some samples in my office aquarium tank [11 months later]. The aquarium is provided with a chiller unit, so it is actually quite a good experiment showing that if you do it right, the fish will go on and survive for long periods of time. These particular fish are eating goldfish pellets, a food that is totally foreign to them.

We have also recently shipped sole, brill, skate, sea perch, blue cod, and monk fish. These fish have been held in the Auckland 350 kg holding system for three weeks now. We are maintaining these tanks at about 12°C, their minimum winter temperature.

FUTURE

We are quite positive about the live industry's future prospects at the moment. I am just now awaiting word from the director of Deep Cove Fisheries to say we are ready to move into export marketing. We have gained a great amount of hands-on experience working in the domestic market. Once additional markets are established, we should begin to look at the possible farming of these fish. We should also think about conducting practical scientific research on our existing transport system and determine rather precisely why it works and where it can be improved. We undoubtedly have the potential to fine-tune our working system and gain that extra distance needed when we become involved with export marketing. We have sent live fish to public aquaria and this has created still another market. As an additional benefit, this market has returned to us good technical advice.

QUESTIONS FROM THE AUDIENCE

QUESTION: Please describe what you are calling poly bins?

J. SECCOMBE: These are the small standard polystyrene insulated bins or shipping boxes that everybody packs their product in. The aquarium trade also use them.

QUESTION: How do you pack the live fish in these boxes?

J. SECCOMBE: Actually we use the IATA (International Air Transport Association) standards as prescribed by the airlines. We use "X" amount of water in double plastic bags flooded with a certain amount of oxygen. The oxygen is really not the concern. The real concern is the security of the water. Most of the major airlines will supply you with information about how to pack live fish. The secret involves educating your whole handling and freight network. There are a few other tricks that we do with the water. Initially, we try to stay away from anesthetizing agents because they will possibly camouflage some of your mistakes—poor handling, for example. We are now using an oil of clove mix. This is not a proprietary mix. There is another mix developed in New Zealand that is very successful, but we have made our own and we use a little bit of this to give us that extra mile.

QUESTION: What species is the monk fish?

J. SECCOMBE: It is a stargazer. I have also seen live monk fish in Boston. I have seen pictures of really big ones. Our variety is not quite as big as the Atlantic species. I think that they were also selling them live.

QUESTION: You mentioned a regional code of practice. Is this for the fishermen that you are working with? Is this a common issue?

J. SECCOMBE: We brought that code of practice in for the live lobster industry. I helped write the code with about six or eight other people in the industry. We drafted a copy and then obtained input from other people. It is really a set of guidelines, but occasionally people say that it is almost law. It covers everything from the biofiltration system to water testing through to cooking the product. For the lobster there are also product standards such as the acceptable number of legs that can be missing from the lobster.

The industry believes that all live fish are covered under these guidelines, but they are not. We need something special for that. I have inquired overseas on the Internet and received some information from the U.K. There is a code of practice in the U.K. dealing with live fish and fish farms. I will see if we can adapt something from this document.

QUESTION: When you put flat fish in your poly shipping containers, do you stack the fish more than one layer deep? Do you put fish on fish or do you use some method to separate them?

J. SECCOMBE: We have not quite arrived at this stage. I would not encourage stacking, although I saw fish farms in Japan working with high densities of these fish and they were basically overlapping them. You could do that, but I would like to keep them separate. We have been packing them so that they can be separated in the poly bins. We have even used a special bubble plastic to separate the other fish species from each other, especially cods and fish species that have spines. They can damage each other and also the plastic bags. Consequently, we construct this protective sleeve around them.

Florida's Ornamental Marine Life Industry

Sherry L. Larkin, Donna J. Lee, Robert L. Degner, J. Walter Milon, and Charles M. Adams
Institute of Food and Agricultural Sciences, University of Florida, Gainesville, Florida

Abstract

The United States is a net importer of live ornamental marine life products. In 1998, ornamental imports reported under the Live Ornamental Fish (LOF) code (HTS 030110) were valued at US $45 million by U.S. customs, while exports were valued at $10.6 million. The approximate $34 million trade deficit for LOF in 1998 represents a 25% increase over the deficit reported in 1994. In Florida, the increased demand for ornamental marine life has stimulated market prices and triggered an increase in the collection of certain species. Although almost 330 distinct organisms have been harvested from Florida's waters since 1990, the species harvested in the greatest numbers were anemones, sand dollars, snails, crabs, and starfishes. The species with the highest landed value included live rock and angelfish (blue, grey, queen, and rock beauty).

This paper characterizes the market for ornamental marine life collected in Florida using data from the Florida Department of Environmental Protection, which began an industry reporting system in 1990. Information was obtained on the value and harvest levels of individual species, changes in the number and location of fishing areas, and the numbers of industry participants (i.e., collectors and dealers/wholesalers). Statistics on the local industry were then compared to trends in total U.S. import and exports in the trade category LOF as reported to the U.S. International Trade Commission. These statistics were also compared to U.S. Fish and Wildlife Service trade data. Last, information from an ongoing survey of U.S. marine life wholesalers, sponsored by the Florida Sea Grant College Program, provided opinions regarding the advantages and disadvantages of Florida-caught marine life species.

Analysis of the trade data indicates that international market trends affect the market for locally harvested species. Changes in these trends are partly responsible for the large variability in harvest pressure and corresponding changes in product value since data collection began in Florida. Survey results also document the local and national importance of the supply of ornamental marine life products originating from Florida. This information is used

1. To identify species with the greatest market and, therefore, the greatest need for culture research and protection in the wild.

2. To review the likelihood of the success of existing and proposed regulatory measures in Florida.

Introduction

The State of Florida began collecting statistics on the commercial harvest of live marine species in 1990. The marine life industry in Florida—as defined by the Florida Administrative Code (F.A.C.)—pertains to the nonlethal harvest of saltwater fish, invertebrates, and plants for commercial purposes (F.A.C. Rule 46-42, recently renumbered to 68B-42). Some products, such as sand dollars, are dried and destined for the shell/curio market. The vast majority of products, however, are destined for the hobby aquarium industry.

Live ornamental aquatic products include both marine and freshwater species. In Florida, the marine component of this industry is derived almost exclusively from the capture of wild specimens and is valued at less than $5 million annually. Exceptions include the culture of clown fish and live rock. All freshwater species, on the other hand, are cultured. Florida is a leading domestic producer of freshwater fish and plants, with dockside values reaching $56 million and $13 million, respectively, in 1996 (Florida Department of Agricultural and Consumer Services). According to the Pet Industry Joint Advisory Council (1999), Florida produces and supplies 95% of the tropical fish sold in North America. For comparison, the worldwide wholesale market for marine (i.e., saltwater) ornamental products (wild and farmed) is estimated at more than $100 million (National Sea Grant College Program 1999).

In Florida, the commercial marine life industry is characterized by regulations that have been primarily enacted at the request of collectors. Commercial collectors must adhere to various gear requirements and are also constrained by a set of regulations, including daily bag limits and individual size limits (minimum and/or maximum), that specifically apply to the harvest of "restricted species." (F.A.C. 46-42). However, for many commercially harvested species, collection is essentially unregulated.

Since the official designation of a Marine Life fishery in Florida and the onset of data collection in 1990, there has yet to be a comprehensive analysis of the industry. The harvest of certain species (most notably live rock and live sand) has, however, drawn media attention to the industry. This paper attempts to synthesize the available data to provide a perspective of the industry, its trends, and its (potential) need for improved management and marketing plans. This is accomplished by first reviewing the available trade data to quantify the trade volume in the United States. Second, Florida commercial collection statistics are evaluated to determine the primary species and recent trends. Last, wholesaler information is obtained from an ongoing market survey. All information is summarized in this report to the industry.

U.S. TRADE IN LIVE ORNAMENTALS

There are two primary sources of U.S. trade data, U.S. Customs and the U.S. Fish and Wildlife Service. Customs data for LOF indicates that the trade deficit increased from US $27.6 million to $34.5 million (25%) from 1994 to 1998. As shown in Fig. 1, both imports and exports have declined since 1995 when the total trade value peaked at nearly $75 million.

Imports of LOF are primarily from Singapore (18%), Thailand (18%), and Indonesia (13%). Exports to Japan and Canada dominate the outgoing trade by accounting for 32% and 26%, respectively, of the average annual value. Since LOF includes marine and freshwater species, one way to separate these statistics is to focus on those countries known for marine production. An estimated 2% of imports originate from the Caribbean. Haiti and Trinidad and Tobago account for 68% of the value of Caribbean imports. (From our preliminary survey results, to be discussed later, we know that the majority of producers import marine products from the Caribbean.) These imports have been falling since 1995.

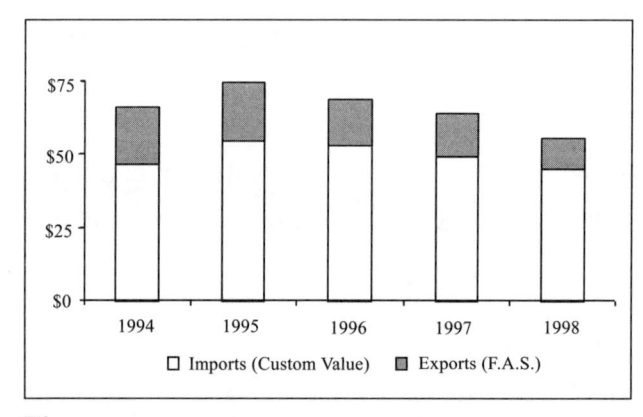

Figure 1. Live ornamental trade fish (LOF, HTS 030110, International Trade Commission) in the United States, 1994-1998, US $ millions.

No LOF were exported from the U.S. to Caribbean nations. Several survey respondents (U.S. wholesalers) have also indicated receiving larger quantities of ornamental fish from the Red Sea. These statistics have not yet been analyzed.

The U.S. Fish and Wildlife Service data for the following codes were also used in this analysis:

- TROP = all live tropical fish including goldfish.
- OLIN = other live invertebrates in tropical fish and other shipments.
- NONV = non-CITES (Convention on International Trade in Endangered Species) other invertebrates.

The above are the codes most commonly reported in Florida (J. Marquardt, Supervisory Wildlife Inspector, U.S. Fish and Wildlife Service). This data is summarized across the 170 foreign countries and 44 U.S. ports in Table 1. These statistics account for the majority, but not all, of the marine life traded. Seahorses, for example, are coded separately. However, this code is not used in all cases; seahorses are likely included in the TROP category for mixed shipments (S. Einswiler, Div. Law Enforcement, U.S. Fish and Wildlife Service, Arlington, VA, November 1999, pers. comm.).

Total trade value of TROP, OLIN, and NONV has averaged over $975 million annually from 1994 through 1998. As with LOF, the United States has experienced an overall trade deficit in TROP, OLIN, and NONV, as imports account for 62% to 77% of the total trade value. TROP trade has accounted for the vast majority of landings, averaging over 3.2 billion live tropical fish annually, worth an es-

Table 1. U.S. Fish and Wildlife Service (USFWS) average annual trade, 1994-1998.

	Quantity (millions)	Value ($ US millions)	% Value Florida	Import
NONV	7.0	2.6	63	62
OLIN	34.4	26.0	21	77
TROP	3,249.2	951.6	22	71

Data excludes shipments in January and February 1994.

timated $950 million ($0.29 each). Invertebrate categories, NONV and OLIN, collectively average approximately $29 million in annual trade. The majority of domestic NONV trade, which includes live and dead products, moves through Florida and averages 7 million invertebrates annually (each valued at approximately $0.37). Although the NONV code includes dead products and, therefore, may appear unrelated to the industry, several Florida products are harvested and reported as live catch even though they are destined for the shell/curio market. In terms of the management of the resource, all live collection is relevant.

Focusing on Florida and its 63% share of the domestic NONV (non-CITES invertebrates) trade, the 1994 through 1998 trade statistics are presented in Fig. 2 (excluding trade of unspecified direction). Since 1994, the trade deficit declined from $1.13 million to $250,000 as part of a 90% decline in the value of all imports and exports. Exports comprised nearly 40% of total trade volume in 1994, but just 25% of the trade volume in 1998. Despite a spike in NONV trade volume in 1995, overall trade volume fell 93%. It is unknown whether these observed trends are representative of the trade or a construct of the data reporting and coding process.

COMMERCIAL COLLECTION IN FLORIDA

Florida's marine life industry encompasses the harvest of live products (fishes and invertebrates) from Florida's waters that are sold in the aquarium and shell/curio trade. Information on the industry is collected by the Florida Marine Research Institute (FMRI, Florida Fish and Wildlife Conservation Commission, St. Petersburg, FL) through the Marine Information System. The Marine Information System, which began in 1990, requires licensed dealers (i.e., buyers) to report dealer and harvester (collector) license numbers, the location of harvest, the species and quantity purchased, and the value of each transaction by species. Landings that are not sold are excluded from the summary.

The total value of commercial collection in Florida increased 14% from 1990 to 1998, peaking in 1994 at approximately $4.3 million (Fig. 3). Since 1990, the commercial value of the invertebrate sector increased 91% while the value of collected fish fell 40%. Although the value of both invertebrates and fish fell between 1994 and 1998, the value of invertebrates appears to have leveled off in 1998. The decline in invertebrate value beginning in 1996 can be attributed to regulations on the collection of live rock and live sand, products that are now either cultured or require special permits to harvest.

Figure 3 depicts dockside values of marine species that are landed in Florida and destined for commercial markets. Because of the exclusion of recreational landings and the non-reporting of mortality that occurs prior to first sale, the landings statistics that follow should be considered conservative estimates of overall production in Florida. The emphasis on live commercial landings is intended to define the content of the data, not to imply any significance to the size of recreational landings or mortality rates. Generally, recreational landings (especially of high-valued fish species) are believed to be minor due to the equipment and skill needed to capture and transport these species.

Approximately 180 species of fish have been harvested in Florida over the last decade. To facilitate the evaluation of these species, this large group of harvested species was aggregated into 65 common

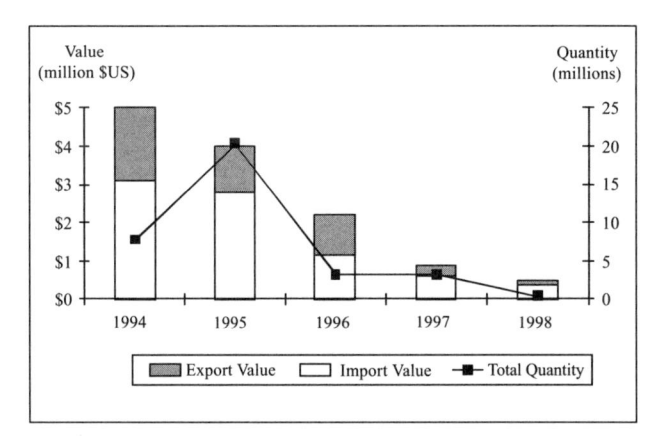

Figure 2. USFWS trade of NONV species.

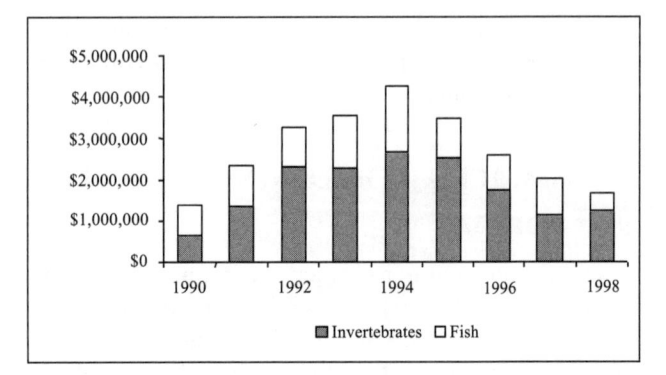

Figure 3. Dockside value of commercial marine life landings in Florida, 1990-1998.

names and then ranked by average annual value. The ten most economically important fish species groups are listed in Table 2 with the 1998 statistics and the change in landings since 1990.

Several industry trends are apparent in Table 2:

- Angelfish are the highest valued fish species group. The angelfish species group (which is primarily composed of queen, rock, and beauty angelfish) has averaged approximately 54% of the total annual value of fish landed each year. Despite the decrease in total volume landed between 1990 and 1998, the number and value of landings of angelfish remain the most economically important commercial marine fish species in Florida.

- Rankings of the economically important species have changed over time. For example, from 1990 to 1998, surgeonfish ranked ninth overall in terms of economic importance. In 1998, however, surgeonfish ranked third in economic importance. On the other hand, the economic importance of damselfish declined in 1998, falling from third overall to fourth.

- The average price of specimens within these fish species groups range from $0.80 to over $8.00 each.

- Fish landings range from approximately 3,000 to nearly 50,000 annually.

- Consideration of the change in landings from 1990 to 1998 reveals that landings of eight of the top ten fish species groups, including the top six, fell from 7% to 48%. In contrast, seahorse landings, the seventh most economically valuable fish species on average, has increased 184% while surgeonfish increased 18%.

Since 1990, approximately 150 species of invertebrates have been harvested in Florida for the aquarium or shell/curio markets. These invertebrates were grouped under 35 common names. The top ten groups by average annual value are listed in Table 3.

As with the fish species groups, the rankings of economically important invertebrates changed in 1998 with the exception of the top two species groups, namely, live rock and snails. In particular, crabs are ranked third in 1998 versus fourth overall, indicat-

Table 2. Top fish species groups by average annual value 1990-1998.

Rank by value 1990-1998	1998 Value (US $)	1998 Avg. price (US $)	1998 Landings (number)	% Change in landings 1990-1998
1. Angels	396,765	8.12	48,839	−32
2. Hogfish	62,647	8.44	7,419	−13
3. Damsels	25,298	1.19	21,225	−34
4. Jawfish	13,886	2.36	5,894	−7
5. Wrasse	22,712	1.68	13,512	−42
6. Butterflys	15,402	2.35	6,551	−48
7. Seahorses	13,664	0.80	16,977	+184
8. Parrots	17,205	5.74	2,998	−39
9. Surgeons	26,728	3.47	7,702	+18
10. Drum	14,278	2.11	6,781	−43

Table 3. Top invertebrate species by average annual value, 1990-1998.

Ranked by value 1990-1998	1998 Value (US $)	Avg. price (US $)	Landings (number)	% Change in landings 1990-1998
1. Live rock	175,580	1.93	90,975	−63
2. Snails	166,310	0.21	805,210	+791
3. Anemones	97,061	0.48	201,629	−26
4. Crabs	138,442	0.18	788,598	+755
5. Starfish	47,116	0.09	511,297	+1,824
6. Gorgonians	98,374	2.41	40,743	+129
7. Sand dollars	65,423	0.08	771,817	+203
8. Urchins	68,105	1.67	40,900	+29
9. Sponges	49,243	2.87	17,166	+1
10. Live sand	42,158	0.56	75,584	NA[a]

[a] The first live sand landings were reported in 1993.

ing that crabs are becoming more economically important to the industry. This is primarily due to an increase in the harvest of hermit crabs. Similarly, gorgonians are ranked fourth in 1998 compared to sixth overall. Anemones, on the other hand, are ranked third overall but fell to fifth in 1998. Most notable is the decline in economic importance of starfish.

The average prices for specimens within the top invertebrate groups ranged from $0.08 to $2.87, much lower than the average prices of fish species (Table 2). Conversely, invertebrate landings are much higher, ranging from 20,000 to nearly one million individuals per year. Note that these landings ignore live rock and live sand since landings of these species are measured in pounds. Overall, note the change in landings from 1990 to 1998, which are significantly greater than the landings reported for the fish species. The increase in landings for snails, crabs, and starfish ranged from 755% to 1,824%. The increase in starfish landings is notable given the decline in value relative to the other invertebrate species.

The commercial harvest of live rock and live sand has declined since restrictions were imposed in 1996. Currently, these species may be harvested only by special permit (e.g., aquaculture leases for live rock and dredge and fill permits for live sand) and thus may be removed from the marine life category if marine life endorsements are no longer required in order to sell these products.

The number of industry participants from 1990 to 1998 is summarized in Fig. 4. The number of licensed marine life dealers increased significantly in the mid-1990s, but by 1998 this number had declined to the level observed in the early 1990s. Currently, there are approximately 65 licensed dealers in Florida. These dealers are legally allowed to purchase marine life species from licensed collectors and are required to submit information regarding the transaction to FMRI. This required reporting information consists of the collectors license number, species landed (quantity and unit price), area where collection occurred, and the transaction date. Individuals can be licensed as both a collector and dealer.

To collect marine life in excess of the daily bag limit of 20 specimens and one gallon of marine plants, an individual or business needs a saltwater products license (SPL) with both a restricted species endorsement and marine life endorsement (F.A.C. 46-42.006). The marine life endorsement (MLE) is the only authority that applies exclusively to the marine life industry. The total number of MLEs increased steadily from 1990 to 1997. In 1997, approximately 800 endorsements had been issued whereas fewer than 200 were issued in 1990. The number of active marine life endorsements (i.e., endorsements with reported landings), however, has remained fewer than 230. In 1998, only 128 MLEs were active. The number of MLEs issued declined recently due to a moratorium that will remain in effect until at least 2003. However, there continues to remain a significant amount of latent effort in the fishery. It is believed that these are commercial enterprises, including individual fishermen and businesses, that are retaining permits to hedge

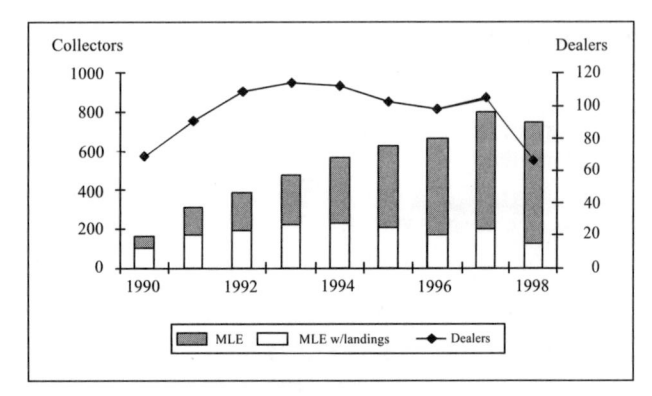

Figure 4. Number of marine life endorsement (MLE's, i.e., collectors) and dealers in Florida.

against further restrictions in other fisheries. Speculative permit holdings appear to be increasing as restrictions are imposed in other commercial fisheries in South Florida.

U.S. WHOLESALER SURVEY

We are currently interviewing U.S. wholesalers of marine life under a Florida Sea Grant project titled "Structure and Competitiveness of Florida's Tropical Ornamental Marine Species Industry." The interviews began in August 1999 and will continue through January 2000. The survey asks firms to describe their market channels (supply and demand side) and asks several open-ended questions regarding the state of the industry. Firms are also asked demographic questions that are intended to identify common answers among distinct market groups.

A sample of 183 firms were identified for inclusion in the survey. The 93 Florida firms were identified using the marine life endorsements. Only active MLEs in 1997 and 1998 were included in the survey. All firms in Florida were contacted. The non-Florida firms were identified using the *Pet Products News Buying Guide* on the recommendation of the president of the American Marine Life Dealers Association. All firms were sent a letter explaining the project and asking for cooperation in summer 1999. By November 1999, approximately a quarter of the firms had been surveyed. A quarter were eliminated as potential respondents after it discovered that their phone was disconnected or they were out of the business. The remaining half of the respondents have yet to be contacted.

One of the open-ended questions asked: "In your opinion, what is the primary advantage, if any, of a Florida caught species compared to a similar import?" The subsequent question asked: "In your opinion, what is the primary *dis*advantage, if any, of a Florida caught species compared to a similar import?" The questions were intended to assess opinions regarding industry strengths and weaknesses that could ultimately be used to aid marketing campaigns and establish consensus regarding the effectiveness of regulatory measures. The responses to these questions, to date, are summarized in Table 4.

The primary advantage of Florida-caught species, according to industry wholesalers, is that they are of a higher quality. When asked, respondents most typically defined quality in terms of higher survival rates (e.g., by packing fewer fish per box and the shorter travel time). The most frequently cited disadvantage of Florida-caught species, relative to similar imports, is the lack of sufficient quantity, both in total and seasonally. Several respondents expressed frustration at being unable to deliver the total quantities requested of them or having to procure supplies from multiple dealers.

The second most frequently cited advantage of Florida-caught species was a lower cost. This response was most prevalent among Florida wholesalers who also function as collectors. Interestingly enough, the third most frequently cited advantage of Florida-caught species was "no advantage." Uniqueness was fourth and no import paperwork was fifth. This latter advantage was most prevalent among smaller dealers in terms of annual sales. For this group the import regulations and the additional fees are major deterrents to greater participation in the international market.

The second most frequently cited opinion regarding the disadvantages of Florida-caught products was their higher price. This is an interesting view since lower cost was also cited as an advantage. The higher price (disadvantage) was from wholesalers nationwide who benefit from import competition. Weak attributes, the third response, conveyed the sentiment that Atlantic species are "uglier," perhaps less colorful, than Pacific species. The fourth was seasonality or a lack of consistent availability. Many respondents believed that the part-time nature of the collection industry results in lower supplies in the winter, as the cool water keeps divers home. The fifth response was unprofessional collectors. These wholesalers reported having not received product following payment or receiving product of such poor quality that subsequent high mortality rates made the transaction unprofitable. Those wholesalers not

Table 4. A Ranking of wholesaler's survey responses to the following question: "In your opinion, what is the primary (dis)advantage, if any, of Florida caught species compared to a similar import?"

Advantages (n = 28)	Disadvantages (n = 36)
1. "Higher quality" (36%)	1. "Low availability" (28%)
2. "Lower cost" (14%)	2. "Higher price" (19%)
3. "None" (11%)	3. "Weak attributes" (18%)
4. "Uniqueness" (7%)	4. "Seasonality" (14%)
5. "No import paperwork" (4%)	5. "Unprofessional collectors" (11%)

reporting such problems stated they only purchase from collectors they have either dealt with over time or whom they know personally.

CONCLUSIONS

National trade statistics suggest an increasing deficit as imports continue to exceed exports. The recent decline in trade of non-CITES invertebrates is likely related to the corresponding significant increase in the commercial collection of invertebrates in Florida. Regarding commercial collection in Florida, there were definite trends in both the number of fish and invertebrate species landed. In particular, landings of fish have declined while landings of invertebrates have increased. Although it is not presented, the survey has revealed that invertebrate collection has likely increased due to the following:

1. The recent popularity of live reef tanks.

2. The ease of collecting invertebrates compared to fish species.

3. The lower cost associated with collecting invertebrates versus fish, which ideally requires three individuals (two divers and a boat driver).

The overall trend is a decrease in the value of commercially landed marine life species in Florida. Domestic wholesalers distinguish Florida products from similar imports, typically citing that Florida products are of a higher quality but, unfortunately, not available in sufficient quantities. According to our survey, import competition affects the industry in terms of price, diversity, and availability.

Regulatory concerns regarding the collection industry in Florida have become increasingly visible as managers search for plans that can accommodate increasing demands on the natural resources. The Florida commercial marine life industry is just one of the many user groups including recreational harvesters and recreational observers (e.g., tourists). In addition, the commercial industry is composed of inactive, part-time, and full-time collectors with varying demands on the regulators and the resources. Currently, inactive participants outnumber active participants nearly four to one (Florida Marine Fisheries Commission 1998). The potential for an increase in observed effort and landings from previously inactive industry members raises concerns for resource sustainability and, indirectly, for the quality of resources available to non-consumptive user groups. This concern, in part, is the topic of periodic regulatory workshops designed to address the future of the industry.

In Florida, the purpose and intent of regulations are to protect and conserve the tropical marine life resources and assure the continuing health and abundance of these species (F.A.C. 46-02.001). In addition, the further intent is to assure that harvesters use nonlethal collection methods to minimize mortality and maximize economic benefits. Consequently, the significant increase in the number of MLEs resulted in the establishment of a moratorium on the issuance of new MLEs (Florida Marine Fisheries Commission 1998). Although the moratorium halts the increase in the number of speculative (i.e., inactive) permit holders, it does not restrict effort beyond current or historical levels. On the contrary, latent MLE holders may have more of an incentive to continue holding the endorsement knowing that they may be unable to obtain one in the future.

Managing the marine life industry in Florida is complicated relative to the management of traditional fisheries due to the sheer number of species involved, diverse markets supplied by these products, and the visibility of the industry. Fisheries management plans typically are defined for each species (e.g., spiny lobster) or for an assemblage of very similar species (e.g., pelagic tunas). The Florida marine life management plan includes approximately 300 species, with new species added each year. The number, variety, and similarity among species prohibits individual management and favors more aggregate policies such as daily bag limits for recreational collectors. Commercial collectors face daily bag limits on a select list of species. Improved management of the marine life collection industry in Florida is presently hampered by the cost and difficulty of enforcing collection methods and catch limits for the approximately 330 species collected by 230 active permit holders harvesting in federal and state waters along Florida's 1,350 mile coastline.

The biological status of the stocks is an important factor in any resource management plan. The stock status is, however, not available for any of the species collected in Florida. A proxy for stock status that is frequently used by fisheries biologists is the trend in catch per unit effort (CPUE). In the marine life industry, such a measure is available by using reported landings per trip over time. Examination of this data on the primary species (i.e., top species groups in terms of economic importance) revealed that *none* of the species experienced decreasing CPUE estimates. Most estimates fluctuated and many actually increased, which would be expected as the number of collectors declined. Consequently, with the data available, there is no reason to assume the industry threatens stock sustainability.

The collection statistics contain only the commercial landings of live marine species. Consequently, these statistics will underreport the number of specimens actually harvested. As reported earlier, each individual is allowed to collect 20 specimens and one gallon of plants per day for personal use. These unreported recreational landings, as well as the harvest of dead marine life used in the shell and curio industries, result in estimates of the value of the industry that are biased downward. It is also plausible that collectors selling to wholesalers in other states are not reporting their sales, which would further underestimate the overall value of the industry.

Survey results suggest that successful marketing strategies should promote the higher quality of Florida-caught products and, if possible, the availability of a consistent supply of products. The importance of this latter characteristic is likely behind the growth and success of large wholesale operations in Florida and California.

Effective regulations are the key to the success of this industry. In order to create effective regulations, the primary threats to the industry need to be identified and monitored. For example, it is unlikely that the recreational sector is a significant threat to the sustainability of the resource or the viability of the commercial industry. First, fish collection requires specialized skills, equipment, and knowledge of each species. Second, black market transactions are unlikely since dealers (wholesale and retail) must document the source of their inventory. Buying from non-licensed collectors is risky and inconsistent. In addition, in order to keep the MLE, collectors need to report at least $5,000 in annual sales. Consequently, underreporting could jeopardize a collector's claim of economic dependence on the industry. Third, the market for aquarium species is increasingly competitive, both nationally and internationally, as many products can be bought/sold over the Internet. Similar arguments apply for the latent effort in the fishery, making it an unlikely threat to the species and commercial industry.

Future regulation of this industry may need to consider more generic policies that can be easily monitored for compliance. For example, making size limits and bag limits uniform across fish species and, especially, within species, could increase the probability that the policies are enforced. The bag limits may also need to be enforceable to be effective. For example, is it possible for a marine patrol agent to accurately verify that an individual has no more than 50 Spanish hogfish or 75 butterflyfish without compromising the survival rate of the harvested animals?

For invertebrate species in particular, the marine life regulations may need to acknowledge that the shell and curio markets do not require live products. The regulations currently state that the purpose is to promote high survival rates to help sustainability and conservation (F.A.C. 46-42.001) by landing all organisms alive (F.A.C. 46-42.0035(1)). With products destined for "dead" markets, the current regulatory purpose is in-appropriate and, therefore, so are gear regulations designed to keep products alive (e.g., living well requirements) (F.A.C. 46-42.007).

Last, the purpose behind the legislation is to protect and conserve the resources and assure the continuing health and abundance of the species (F.A.C. 46-42.001). With the exception of daily bag limits, the regulations pertain to both commercial and recreational harvesters. Currently, recreational harvesters are subject to the same bag limits that apply to the capture of saltwater foodfish. The enforceability of recreational harvests is extremely limited. Given the expressed concern for the health of the resource, the lack of monitoring of the recreational sector may be crucial to the future sustainability of these resources. A more reasonable, manageable, and enforceable strategy may be to reduce the recreational harvest to a reasonable level (i.e., the number appropriate for an average-sized aquarium). To increase the effectiveness of these regulations, this information could be conveyed in the form of public service promotions. An example of the effectiveness of such a campaign is the queen conch. An extensive awareness campaign was used to alert the public (commercial collectors and tourists) that the species could no longer be harvested legally. Consequently, informational campaigns may be the most cost-effective strategy for managing this diverse industry and resource.

Acknowledgments

This article was developed under the auspices of the Florida Sea Grant College Program with support from the National Oceanic and Atmospheric Administration, Office of Sea Grant, U.S. Department of Commerce, Grant No. NA76RG-0120. The research was also supported by the Florida Agricultural Experiment Station and approved for publication as Journal Series No. R-08057. The views herein do not necessarily reflect the views of any of these organizations.

References

Florida Marine Fisheries Commission. 1998. Marine Life Staff Paper, Tallahassee, FL. September 1998.

National Sea Grant College Program. 1999. Marine aquaculture: Economic opportunities for the 21st century. Developed by the Aquaculture Task Group of the Sea Grant Association. Published by Texas Sea Grant College Program, TAMU-SG-99-603, College Station.

Pet Industry Joint Advisory Council. 1999. U.S. Ornamental Aquarium Industry. Pet Information Bureau, Washington, DC. Available at www2.pijac.org/pijac/PJF001.htm.

Shipping Practices in the Ornamental Fish Industry

Brian Cole
University of Hawaii, Kaneohe, Hawaii

Clyde S. Tamaru
University of Hawaii Sea Grant, Honolulu, Hawaii

Rich Bailey
University of Hawaii, Honolulu, Hawaii

Christopher Brown
Hawaii Institute of Marine Biology, Kaneohe, Hawaii

Harry Ako
College of Tropical Agriculture and Human Resources, Honolulu, Hawaii

Introduction

One of the most critical determinants to the financial success of tropical fish farms is the problem of delivering a quality product to distant market destinations. At times, Hawaii's geographic location offers a strategic advantage for growers. However, our islands' isolation also presents an obvious marketing constraint—the long distances to final market destinations. The location of the major markets for our ornamental products dictates that the mode of transportation must involve the various airline carriers operating out of Hawaii. The duration of transport over many of these routes ranges between 48 and 72 hours. The purpose of this report is to describe some of the critical handling and packing methods that are essential for the successful transport of live tropical fish.

In the course of a 72-hour trip from a farm to the final delivery site, the fish are confined within plastic bags charged with oxygen. During transport, the water in these closed containers may become oxygen-depleted and may accumulate excessive carbon dioxide, causing a reduction in the pH. Metabolic activity may also lead to elevated ammonia levels in the water, which can be damaging to the health of the fish or, in extreme cases, can be lethal. A densely packed shipping container further increases these risks, but also reduces the cost of transportation—a critical cost in the delivery of product at competitive prices.

The challenge confronting the shipper is to arrive at an ideal balance of handling strategies under which fish can be shipped cost-effectively, without unnecessary risk of injury or mortality. Fortunately, much of the guesswork in the handling and shipping sequence has been eliminated. This report will outline basic procedures and packing densities that, when properly applied, should get the fish to their destination in good condition.

Freight Considerations

Perhaps the most important consideration when calculating the total transport time to get a product to market is the specific airline company and its capabilities. For this reason, air freight considerations are being presented here prior to the description of the other steps in the live fish shipping sequence.

Very careful consideration must be given to the airline schedule and the procedures it uses to handle sensitive freight. These parameters vary widely from airline to airline. This analysis will be further complicated if the fish have to be transferred to another airline company before they reach the final destination. For farmers just beginning to ship fish to markets outside the state, it is suggested that they initially concentrate on markets that can be reached by direct flights from Hawaii. This will minimize the risks of lost freight and delayed shipping, which occurs most often during freight transfers from one plane to another. Hawaii has many direct flights to destinations not only in the continental United States but also other parts of the world. Check with the individual airlines to gain a list of the destinations that are served with direct flights. Also, inquire about the seasonal availability of freight space, something that can quickly change with demand and time of year.

Some important questions to consider when choosing a carrier are:

- What is the total transit time to the final destination? Be sure to calculate total transit time beginning when the bag is sealed at the farm and ending when the bag is delivered to the customer's business establishment.
- Is there a plane transfer en route? If there is a transfer, does the freight transfer facility have available climate controlled freight holding capabilities? This can be particularly important during the winter months.
- At what time does the shipment actually arrive at the final receiving airport? If the shipment arrives late in the business day, it may sit in a freight office overnight, adding considerably to total transit time.
- Do live and perishable products have first priority along the entire selected transport route? Interruptions can occur; for example, during the Christmas season mail has first priority on all U.S. carriers.
- Does the airline freight office notify the destination customer when the freight arrives?
- If container inspection is required along the selected transport route, will the shipment be delayed if it arrives at an inspection point after normal business hours?

As can be seen, the business planning process must carefully consider the entire transport route, including ground transport segments. Contingency plans should be made to further reduce risk over sections of the transport route.

Shipping methods

All farms, regardless of whether they are shipping product to a transhipper, wholesaler, or retailer, must base their stock availability list on what is presently in their holding area. This amounts to warehousing stock that is ready to be marketed in anticipation of orders that will be placed over the next two to four weeks. This practice is consistent with common business strategies used by any other distributor. Having a constant supply of fish ready to sell should be considered just another manufacturing strategy that will enable the "product supply pipeline" to remain full. In this way, new orders can be satisfied in a timely manner.

The most commonly used shipping methods are actually a variation on a single theme. The sequence is fairly basic:

1. Fish are packed in partially water-filled plastic bags.
2. Bags are inflated with pure oxygen.
3. Each bag is carefully closed with one or more rubber bands.
4. Packed bags are placed in an insulated corrugated box and the master container is sealed.
5. Necessary shipping instructions and related documents are attached to the container.
6. The box is transported to the freight facility and shipped.

The size and shape of these bags and boxes, as well as the insulation, can vary widely.

Bags

Many of the domestic producers use square bottom plastic bags, as shown in Fig. 1. The use of these pleated bags (provided with a flat bottom) is highly recommended. These bags utilize the surface area of the bottom of the shipping box more efficiently. In addition, if the bags are properly placed in the box, the problem of fish crowding into the corners of the individual bags is kept to a minimum. These bags also allow for maximum oxygen transfer through the surface of the water by expanding the air-water interface within the individual bags.

Boxes are generally packed with bags of "full" or "quarter" size. Full bags are those that occupy the entire box, half bags are packed two to a box, and quarter bags are packed four to a box. Square-bottom bags are available for custom packs down to one-eighth box size. Bag thickness ranges from 2 to 6 mls, depending on the size of the bag and the manufacturer. Some of the commonly available pleated and flat bag sizes are listed in Table 1.

Fish packers in Asia generally use bags manufactured from stock tube plastic that are heat-sealed

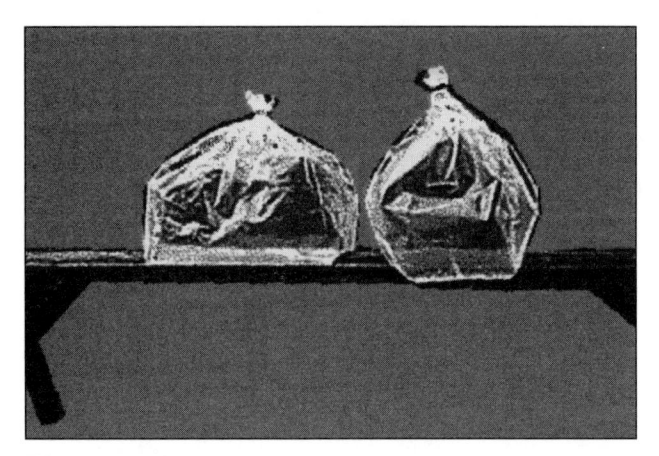

Figure 1. Half-sized (left) and full-sized pleated bags (right).

at one end so that each bag has only a single seam. Plastic shipping bags of this type are known as "pillow bags" in the industry because, when they are inflated, there is no flat surface. The air-water surface within these bags is increased by shipping the bags on their side.

Due to inexpensive manufacturing costs, there is a much wider size selection available in the pillow bag category (Table 1). Sizes range from small bags (17.5 cm × 7.5 cm), intended for the packing of individual fish to sizes as large as 65 cm × 35 cm, for the shipment of large numbers of small fish. Large bags of this type usually contain 5-7 liters total volume with a water and oxygen percents ranging from 35%

water and 65% oxygen to 20% water and 80% oxygen. The number of fish packed in this type of bag will range from 200-500. The smaller shipping bags contain proportionally fewer fish to insure survival of the fish during the typical 48-hour transport times.

Boxes

Many different styles and types of boxes are routinely used in the ornamental fish industry. Some of the most commonly used configurations are described in Table 2. Most shippers rely on boxes that they can purchase locally for most of their shipping needs. Shippers will typically send out several types of boxes as part of an effort to recycle or reuse boxes they receive. These include not only the standard types of boxes discussed below but also miscellaneous others. Some of these shipping boxes have loose panels that are used to line the box walls. Internal partitions of this sort help keep required storage space to a minimum. Other boxes are equipped with stacking molded Styrofoam compartments for use under extreme conditions.

Florida boxes

The standard box used in the domestic industry is the traditional square Florida single box (Fig. 2). In single boxes used for shipments originating from Florida, the standard insulation is constructed of molded Styrofoam that has a taper and lip about midway up the sidewall to facilitate the stacking of empty containers.

Table 1. Types and sizes of bags commonly used to ship ornamental fish.

Flat bags (pillow bags) (length cm × width cm)	Pleated bags (square bottom) (length cm × width cm × depth cm)
65 × 35 (full bag)	37.5 × 37.5 × 55 (full bag)
60 × 27.5	40 × 20 × 55 (half bag)
57.5 × 25	20 × 20 × 50 (quarter bag)
57.5 × 22.5 (half bag)	15 × 10 × 45 (eighth bag)
42.5 × 22.5	10 × 10 × 40 (sixteenth bag)
37.5 × 20	
22.5 × 17.5	
25 × 12.5 (quarter bag)	
20 ×10 (eighth bag)	
17.5 × 7.5 (individual fish)	

cm = centimeter   2.45 cm = 1.0 inch

Table 2. Styles and dimensions of common shipping boxes.

Box style	Box dimensions (length cm × width cm × depth cm)
Traditional Florida box	42.5 × 42.5 × 25
Florida double box	80 × 42.5 × 25
Asia double box	60 × 42 30
Alternate Asia box	49 × 38 × 38
Hawaii box	68 × 34 × 25

cm = centimeter   2.54 cm = 1.0 inch

In recent years, some large shippers have begun using a double-capacity version of the single box. This variation is called a "double." The doubles have been shipped with any of three different types of insulation, including:

- A molded Styrofoam box.
- Individual Styrofoam panels inserted along the inner surfaces of the shipping box.
- Sheets of fiberglass insulation lining the box.

Hawaii boxes

Ornamental fish producers in Hawaii are currently using a molded Styrofoam box that was originally designed for use in the shrimp industry (see Fig. 3). Locally, these shipping containers are called "coffin boxes." This box has approximately the same shipping capacity as the Florida box and typically involves the use of two half bags. Each half bag has the capacity to contain 3.5 liters of water and can hold half the fish listed in Table 3. An alternative means of insulating bagged ornamental fish, used in Hawaii, makes use of rectangular panels of Styrofoam rather than preformed inserts to line the shipping boxes (not shown).

Asia boxes

Ornamental fish from Asia are frequently packed in one of two size boxes, the Asia double box or the alternate Asia box (Table 2). Both sizes are packed with a minimum of four bags.

FISH PACK DENSITY

Common pack numbers used in the industry based on 48 and 72 hour transit times, along with some general guidelines for packing density are presented in Table 3. The guidelines represent a composite of packaging densities in common use in the aquarium trade. This table is based on an analysis of in-

Figure 2. Typical "Florida" single box.

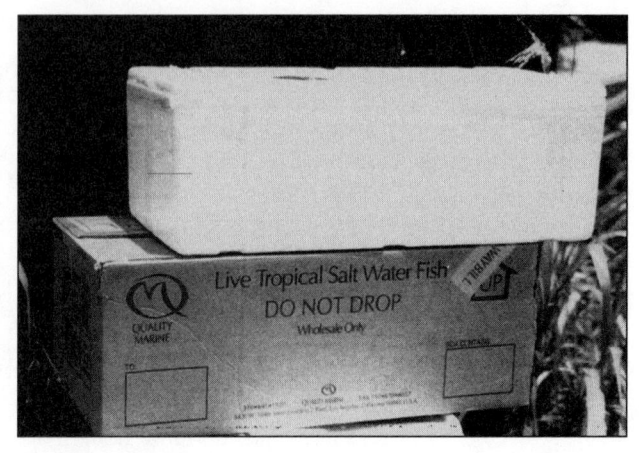

Figure 3. Typical "Hawaii" shipping box (bottom) and Styrofoam insert (top).

Table 3. Common packing densities used in the shipping of ornamental fish. The packing densities listed in this table are based on a single 7 liter capacity bag in a single Florida style box.

Species	Length (inches)	Standard Pack (48 hr)	Extended Pack (72 hr)
Swordtails	1.0	400	300
	1.5	300	250
	2.0	250	200
	2.5	200	150
	3.0	100	75
Mollies			
regular	1.5	300	225
medium	2.0	200	150
large	2.5	150	100
Platies	0.5	400	300
	1.0	300	225
	1.25	275	200
	1.5	250	175
Variatus	0.5	400	300
	1.0	300	225
	1.25	275	200
	1.5	250	175
Guppies			
(fancy)	1.25	400	300
(feeder)	1.0	1,500	1,000
Tetras			
small	0.5	300	225
medium	0.75	250	200
large	1.0	200	150
Angel fish			
regular	1.0	150	100
medium	1.5	50	35
large	2.0	20	15
Kissing gourami			
regular	2.0	125	100
medium	3.0	50	35
Blue gourami			
regular	2.0	125	100
large	2.5	100	70
Paradise gourami			
regular	2.0	125	100
large	2.5	100	70

Species	Length (inches)	Standard Pack (48 hr)	Extended Pack (72 hr)
Dwarf gourami	1.75	150	100
Tiger barbs			
small	0.75	400	325
regular	1.0	300	225
medium	1.25	200	150
large	1.5	125	100
Rosy barbs			
regular	1.5	150	100
long-fin	1.5	150	100
Danios			
small	0.75	500	400
regular	1.0	400	300
large	1.25	300	250
long-fin	1.0	300	250
Corydoras	1.0	225	175
Rainbow Sharks			
small	1.5	200	50
medium	2.0	150	100
large	2.5	100	75
x large	3.0	75	50
xx large	4.0	50	40
Cichlids			
regular	1.5	150	100
medium	1.75	100	70
large	2.0	20	10
Rainbow fish			
regular	1.5	150	100
medium	2.0	100	75
large	2.5	50	35
General guidelines			
	1.5	200	150
	2.0	150	100
	2.5	100	75
	3.0	75	50
	4.0	50	35
	5.0	20	12
	6.0	15	10

dustry price lists and the personal experience of the authors. Note that pack numbers are based on the number of pieces per 7 liters of water contained in a single bag (full pleated bag, see Table 1) packed within a Florida box. The packing densities vary depending on the size of the fish. Because of known differences in the volumes and surface areas of packing boxes, standard pack numbers for Hawaii boxes are estimated to be 1.3 times the numbers given in Table 3 for the Florida box.

Normally, egg-layers are bagged with a 5% overpack and live-bearers are bagged with a 10% overpack. For example, a box of mollies shipped at 300 pieces actually contains 330 pieces. Higher priced items, extremely delicate fish, and large fish such as cichlids are not overpacked. Large fish, and those with sharp spines or scales should be placed in double bags (one inside the other and sealed either independently or together) to reduce the possibility of a puncture and water leakage. Some buyers may require pack numbers lower or higher than those listed in Table 3. For instance, if you are selling to the retail level, the pack numbers are generally lower.

If a buyer requests pack numbers higher than normal, make it clear that the buyer assumes the risk of guaranteed live arrival. If you are shipping a fish species with which you have little experience, use the packing densities listed under "general guidelines." Fish may be packed on a trial basis using the densities given in Table 3 and held for observation up to 72 hours. The standard pack guidelines are based on 48 hour shipping time and the extended pack is based on 72 hour shipping time.

Packing procedures

A flow chart illustrating the typical processes involved in the packing and shipping of ornamental fish is presented in Fig. 4. Before harvesting and packing, it is important to have all required packaging materials available and ready for use. Any chemicals needed for pond treatment of parasites should be on hand. You should also insure that there is adequate room in holding tanks to house the harvested fish. Extra tanks for sorting by size and/or sex will be needed, as well. You will also need a comfortable sorting table in a clean, well-lit area. Suitable bags for packing should be in stock, as well as the insulated Styrofoam inserts and outer boxes. Boxes and bags can be obtained through the sources listed in Appendix 1. Other critical supplies include a full oxygen cylinder complete with regulator to inflate the bags, rubber bands to seal the bags, and tape to seal the boxes. Packing should not be attempted until the packaging area is fully operational, with none of these items missing.

Step 1. Preharvest fish should be examined for parasites and diseases at least one week prior to harvesting. This allows sufficient leadtime should any treatments be necessary.

Step 2. Post harvest fish brought into the holding tanks for sorting and sale should be checked again for parasites and diseases. Holding tanks should have adequate water and aeration. Iodine-free salt (sodium chloride) can be added to the holding tank water at 9 ppt (parts per thousand). This provides an isotonic salt solution that is effective in reducing stress and promoting the development of a natural slime coating. This helps prevent opportunistic infection caused by handling injuries.

Step 3. Feeding should be withheld for a minimum of two days and up to five days before packaging, depending on species. For example, live-bearers such as swordtails and mollies require two days without food, whereas goldfish and corydoras require four days. Any accumulation of feces in the holding tanks should be removed once or twice a day to prevent the fish from eating this material. The absence of feces in the tank is an indication that fish have had an adequate purge time prior to sorting, counting, and shipping.

Step 4. Fish are now sorted and counted into bag lot quantities and held in individual aquariums, trays, or buckets. These pre-shipment containers should have adequate water and airflow. The water exchange rate in these containers should be a minimum of four times per day. Ideally, the preshipment holding containers should have a standpipe or valves to allow the water to be drained to the correct shipping volumes. The fish and water can then be poured directly into the shipping bag. This technique saves time and minimizes handling.

Step 5. Any shipping additives are placed into the bag at this time. The bag is first purged of air and then pure oxygen is injected into the bag below the surface of the water. The

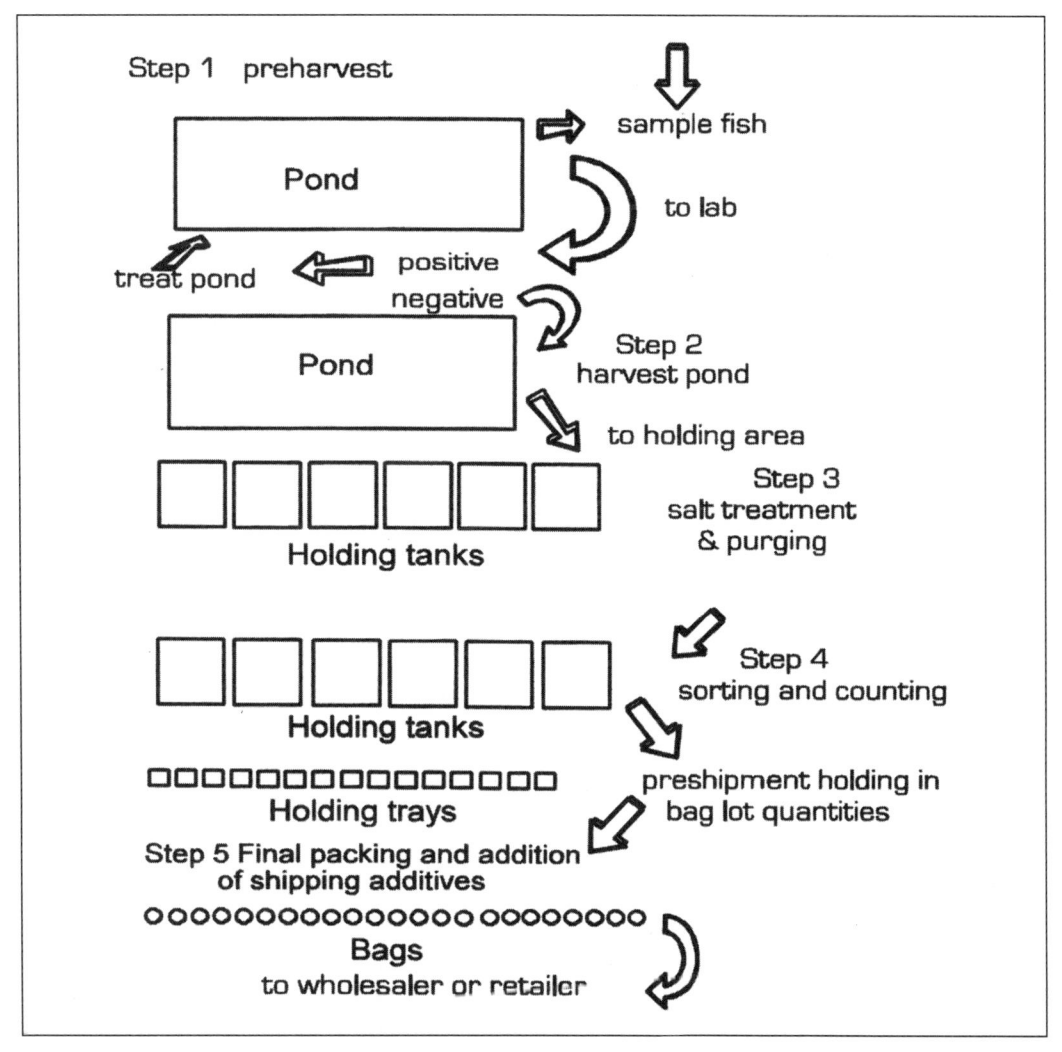

Figure 4. Flow chart of fish packing steps and procedures

bag is sealed using rubber bands or one of the commercial grade sealers or banders and placed into the shipping box. Depending on climatic conditions and species involved, ice or heat packs can be placed on top of the bag after sealing for best results.

Shipping additives

Over the last 15 years, several additives for use with shipping water have been developed to help reduce stress and increase fish survival. These products generally fall into three categories:

- Sedatives
- Water quality stabilizers
- Antibiotics

The most common sedatives are quinaldine or quinaldine sulfate and tricane methane sulfonate (MS-222). Commonly used concentrations are listed in Table 4. Quinaldine is used at 25 ppm (parts per million) in shipping water and MS-222 at 60-70 ppm, with adjustments made for sensitive species. These compounds reduce the metabolic rate of fish and can also prevent injury caused by jumping or swimming into the sides of the box.

Water quality stabilizers include pH buffers, zeolite at 20 grams per liter (effective in removing ammonia), activated carbon at 20 grams per liter, ice or heat packs to maintain temperature, and sodium chloride at 9 ppt. Other products have become available from the bait minnow industry. This group of products usually contains a combination of chelating agents, buffers, ammonia or chlorine removers, and some form of antibiotic.

Caution should be used in the application of antibiotics. These compounds are subject to regulatory controls which should be carefully considered before any application. One of the most widely used antibiotics for shipment and treatment of fish is tetracycline at 5-20 ppm. This antibiotic has been used extensively, especially with fish shipped from Asia. However, there are indications that some bacteria have developed an immunity to tetracycline due to its widespread use. This is one of the reasons why the authors do not recommend its use (J. Brock, DVM, Aquaculture Development Program, State of Hawaii, pers. comm.). Other antibiotics commonly used in shipping are furanace at 0.05-0.20 ppm, and neutral acriflavine at 3-10 ppm. Other antibiotics such as kanamycin and phenicol are used much less frequently and are primarily used as on-farm treatments for disease. Different sulfa-based drugs are being used in response to the development of bacterial resistance to antibiotics historically used in the ornamental industry.

We used tiger barbs as test animals to demonstrate the effect of packing density on total ammonia concentration during transport. The fish were packed in bags containing three liters of water and inflated with pure oxygen. Samples of the water were taken at zero, 24, 48, and 72 hours and tested for total ammonia nitrogen by the Hach colorimetric method. All readings at the level of 3 ppm were assumed to be 3 ppm and above, since this is the upper limit of accurate readings by this test method. All test results except those that were less than 3 ppm were significantly off scale. The test fish were 1.25 inches long and were either starved for 48 hours or were fed normally prior to packing. For each of the starved and fed treatment groups, there were either no additives placed in the shipping water, zeolite added at 20 grams per liter, or MS-222 at 20 milligrams per liter added to the shipping water.

Figures 5 and 6 show the increase in the concentration of total ammonia nitrogen over a 72-hour period for fish packed at two different densities with various treatments. Zeolite was the only additive that had a significant effect on ammonia concentrations. The ammonia level rose to 1.5 ppm in the first 24 hours, then leveled out for the next 24 hours as the zeolite bound with the ammonia. From hour 48 to hour 72 the ammonia started to climb again as the saturation point of the zeolite was reached. Figure 7 (200 fish per bag) shows a pattern similar to that indicated by Fig. 5 (150 fish per bag) with all treatments.

Zeolite is commonly used in bags that have been overpacked and in shipments of fish that produce large quantities of ammonia, such as *Corydoras* spp. and *Carassius auratus*. This application adds a negligible cost to each bag and may substantially reduce the risk of mortality. Shippers should check with local suppliers for current pricing. It should be noted that the group that was fed normally and was treated with MS-222 had 50% mortality by hour 48 and 100% mortality by hour 72 (Fig. 6). Survival was 100% in the lots involving the other treatments. These results suggest that the combination of MS-222 and feeding should be avoided and that zeolite may be a cost-effective shipping additive.

Receiving fish

Most farms that ship fish also receive fish, either for resale or to add to broodstock lines. A critical component of a successful farm or transshipment facility is the appropriate care and handling of incoming shipments of fish.

Arriving shipments should be inspected immediately, particularly those that have been shipped over long distances or those which have been subject to

Table 4. Common shipping additives and concentrations typically used in water for the transport of ornamental fish (adapted from Herwig 1979).

Chemical	Concentration
Quinaldine	25 ppm
Tricane methane sulfonate (MS-222)	60-70 ppm
pH buffers	As per label
Zeolite	20 gm/L
Activated carbon	20 gm/L
Salt (NaCl)	9.0 ppt
Commercial mixtures	As per label
Furnace	0.05-0.2 ppm
Neutral acriflavine	3-10 ppm

ppm = parts per million
gm/L = grams per liter
ppt = parts per thousand

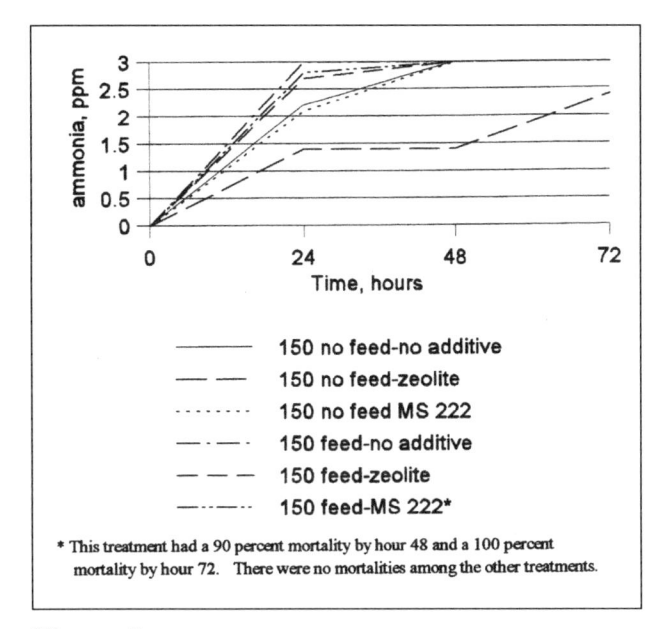

Figure 5. Changes in total ammonia nitrogen concentration over time in bags packed with 150 fish, with and without additives.

*This treatment had a 90 percent mortality by hour 48 and a 100 percent mortality by hour 72. There were no mortalities among the other treatments.

Figure 6. Changes in total ammonia nitrogen concentration over time in bags packed with 200 fish for a 48-hour transit time, with and without additives.

*This treatment had a 50 percent mortality by hour 48 and a 100 percent mortality by hour 72. There were no mortalities among the other treatments.

delays. Fish that are densely packed in bags that have taken longer than expected to arrive may be suffering from exposure to accumulations of ammonia, thermal shock, or other problems. In such cases, a quick assessment of the condition of the arriving fish can limit losses.

In order to implement a successful receiving program, you must first have a working knowledge of the chemical and physical changes that are taking place inside the shipping bag during transport. Once a bag has water, fish, and oxygen sealed inside it, certain chemical changes take place due to the metabolic activities of the fish. When fish "breathe," they absorb oxygen and excrete other gases and metabolites—primarily carbon dioxide and nitrogen in the form of ammonia.

Total ammonia nitrogen, for the purposes of this paper, consists of two forms of nitrogen that exist in a pH and temperature dependent equilibrium. These forms of nitrogen are non-ionized ammonia (NH_3) and the ammonium ion (NH_4). The non-ionized form (NH_3) is toxic to fish while the ammonium ion (NH_4) is not toxic to fish (Boyd 1979). The proportion of NH_4 (nontoxic) to NH_3 (toxic) increases with decreasing pH and decreases with increasing pH (Boyd 1979). The percentage of NH_3 also rises with increasing temperatures. Consequently, shipping conditions involving relatively high pH and elevated temperature are especially dangerous to ornamental fish. Since NH_3 cannot be measured directly, several tables have been created based on an equilibrium formula that predicts the relative percentages of non-ionized ammonia at different temperatures and pH levels. Table 5 was created for the aquaculture industry and reproduced from Boyd (1979).

Generally, when a box containing a bag of fish reaches its final destination, it has been in transit for 24-48 hours. During this period there has been enough carbon dioxide produced to reduce the pH of the water to the level of 6.5-7.0. From Table 5, using a temperature of 24°C and a pH of 7.0, the toxic fraction is only 0.52%. If the total ammonia nitrogen reading is 10.0 parts per million (ppm), the toxic fraction is only 0.052 ppm (0.0052 × 10.0 = 0.052 ppm). Long-term exposure to this concentration of toxic ammonia (NH_3) is well within the tolerable limits of most species and will not do any serious physiological damage to the fish (Post 1987). However, if the pH in this same bag of fish is 10.0 and the temperature is 24°C, the non-ionized toxic fraction of ammonia from this chart is 84.0% or 8.4 ppm (0.84 × 10.0 = 8.4 ppm). At this level, severe stress, physiological damage, and even death may occur at exposure times as short as 30 minutes or less (Post 1987).

When receiving fish, it is critical that you are aware of the temperature and pH differences between the water in the shipping bag and the receiving water at the facility. The recommended method for acclimating fish is to float the sealed bag in the receiving tank or pond for at least five minutes per degree of temperature difference, or until the temperature of the water in the bag is within two degrees of the receiving water. The bag should be kept out of direct sunlight to avoid photic shock to the fish and the elevation of water temperatures in the bag because of the greenhouse effect.

At this point in the receiving procedure, non-iodized salt may be added to reduce stress. Fish should also be inspected under the microscope for any parasites or disease and the proper treatment applied. When the bag is unsealed, the fish can be dipped out and placed directly into the receiving water. Generally, water in shipping bags is discarded rather than introduced into the culture system. This strategy limits the possible introduction of pathogens, anesthetics, etc.

If the bag is unsealed prior to this point in the receiving sequence, the carbon dioxide in the shipping water will begin to dissipate into the atmosphere. This will cause the pH of the shipping water to increase rapidly along with the toxic fraction of ammonia, potentially causing severe stress and perhaps the death of the fish. Adding water to an unsealed bag may only increase stress if the water being added has a high pH and temperature. If your water naturally has a low pH and you do choose to add water to the bag, remove and discard an equal amount of water from the bag. This will, at least, reduce the total amount of nitrogen present in the shipping water.

SUMMARY AND CONCLUSIONS

Even the most effectively run ornamental fish production facility is likely to fail if insufficient attention is paid to fish packing and shipping procedures. This is a basic problem confronting the members of the ornamental industry. Attention must be given to minimizing risk within each step of the packing and transport sequence. Appropriate adjustments need to be made without going to the costly excess of shipping underpacked bags.

Packing methods should take into account the species being shipped and the expected time in transit. Concentrating sales to destinations along well-established transport corridors and adherence

Table 5. Percentage of non-ionized ammonia (toxic) in solution at different pH values and temperatures (reproduced from Boyd 1979)

pH	\multicolumn{9}{c}{Temperature (Centigrade)}
	16	18	20	22	24	26	28	30	32
7.0	0.30	0.34	0.40	0.46	0.52	0.60	0.70	0.81	0.95
7.2	0.47	0.54	0.63	0.72	0.82	0.95	1.10	1.27	1.50
7.4	0.74	0.86	0.99	1.14	1.30	1.50	1.73	2.00	2.36
7.6	1.17	1.35	1.56	1.79	2.05	2.35	2.72	3.13	3.69
7.8	1.84	2.12	2.45	2.80	3.21	3.68	4.24	4.88	5.72
8.0	2.88	3.32	3.83	4.37	4.99	5.71	6.55	7.52	8.77
8.2	4.49	5.16	5.94	6.76	7.68	8.75	10.00	11.41	13.22
8.4	6.93	7.94	9.09	10.30	11.65	13.20	14.98	16.96	19.46
8.6	10.56	12.03	13.68	15.40	17.28	19.42	21.83	24.45	27.68
8.8	15.76	17.82	20.08	22.38	24.88	27.64	30.68	33.90	37.76
9.0	22.87	25.57	28.47	31.37	34.42	37.71	41.23	44.84	49.02
9.2	31.97	35.25	38.69	42.01	45.41	48.96	52.65	56.30	60.38
9.4	42.68	46.32	50.00	53.45	56.86	60.33	63.79	67.12	70.72
9.6	54.14	57.77	61.31	64.54	67.63	70.67	73.63	76.39	79.29
9.8	65.17	68.43	71.53	74.25	76.81	79.25	81.57	83.68	85.85
10.0	74.78	77.46	79.92	82.05	84.00	85.82	87.52	89.05	90.58
10.2	82.45	84.48	86.32	87.87	89.27	90.56	91.75	92.80	93.84

to the established packing methods, materials, and densities described in this manual will contribute to the consistent delivery of fish in excellent condition. We recommend the use of an effectively designed packing room, with harvests prepared appropriately in anticipation of shipping deadlines.

Acknowledgments

This manual is a combined effort of three institutions:

1. The United States Department of Agriculture Center for Tropical and Subtropical Aquaculture (CTSA) through a grant from the U.S. Department of Agriculture Cooperative State Research, Education and Extension Service (USDA Grant #9638500-2743).

2. The University of Hawaii Sea Grant Extension Service (SGES) through the National Oceanic and Atmospheric Administration (NOAA), project #A/AS-1 which is sponsored by the University of Hawaii Sea Grant College Program, School of Ocean Earth Science and Technology (SOEST) under Institutional Grant No. NA36RG0507 from NOAA Office of Sea Grant, Department of Commerce, UNIHI-SEAGRANT-TR-98-01.

3. The Aquaculture Development Program (ADP), Department of Agriculture, State of Hawaii, as part of the Aquaculture Extension Project with the University of Hawaii Sea Grant Extension Service, Contract 9960.

The views expressed herein are those of the authors and do not necessarily reflect the views of the funding agencies or their subagencies.

References

Boyd, C.E. 1979. Water quality in warmwater fish ponds. Auburn University/Craftmaster Printers, Auburn, AL. 359 pp.

Herwig, N. 1979. Handbook of drugs and chemicals used in the treatment of fish diseases. Charles Thomas Publishers, Springfield, IL. 272 pp.

Post, G. 1987. Textbook of fish health. TFH Publications, Inc., Ltd., Neptune City, NJ. 288 pp.

Questions from the Audience

QUESTION: If oxygen is not an issue, why do you inflate the bags with oxygen? Why not simply inflate them with air?

R. BAILEY: Good point. Some people in the industry have talked about that. Also, a few airlines have been a little bit concerned about the amount of oxygen in the hold of an airplane. I think what they're going to do is start to look at that, as a means of trying to increase the number of fish per box, and actually deflate some of the bags. Again, a lot of the bags are inflated with 80% pure oxygen. What they've found is that even after 72 hours only half of the oxygen has been consumed. It's also a function of temperature. I was just in Singapore and a farm there chills their bags of fish down to 72°, prior to boxing them.

APPENDIX 1. LIST OF SUPPLIERS IN THE AQUACULTURE INDUSTRY.

Listing in this appendix does not constitute a recommendation for, or a guarantee of, any of the products or services that the listed manufactures, suppliers or organizations may provide. For a more comprehensive listing consult your local extension agent or the buyers guide or directory editions of one of the industry related publications.

CHEMICAL PRODUCTS

Argent Chemical Laboratories
8702 152nd Ave. N.E.
Redmond, WA
ph 206 885-3777
fx 206 885-2112

Chemicals, therapeutics, speciality feeds, laboratory equipment, books and manuals

Brewer Environmental Industries Inc.
311 Pacific
Honolulu, HI 96718
ph 808 532-7400

Herbicides, insecticides, fertilizer, agriculture products

Chemaqua
P.O. Box 2457
Oxnard, CA 93033
ph 805 486-5319
fx 805 486-2491

Therapeutics, water conditioning products

Crescent Research Chemicals
4331 E. Western Star Blvd.
Phoenix, AZ 85044
ph 602 893-9234
fx 602 244-0522

Therapeutics, bacterial cultures, water conditioning products, CPE, HCG, LHRH, test kits, meters

Fritz Chemical Company
Aquaculture Division
P.O. Drawer 17040
Dallas, TX 75217

Therapeutics, water conditioning products,

Hawaiian Fertilizer Sales, Inc.
91-155 C Leowaena Street
Waipahu, HI 96797
ph 808 677-8779

Fertilizer, herbicides, agriculture products

NETTING PRODUCTS

Memphis Net and Twine Co. Inc.
2481 Matthews Ave.
P.O. Box 8331
Memphis, TN 38108
ph 901 458-2656
fx 901 458-1601

Seines, dip nets, gill nets, floats, lead, aprons, knives, rope, baskets, commercial fishing supplies

Nylon Net Co.
615 East Bodley
P.O. Box 592
Memphis, TN 38101
ph 901 774-1500
fx 901 775-5374

Seines, dip nets, gill nets, floats, lead, aprons, knives rope, baskets, commercial fishing supplies

Tenax Corporation
4800 E. Monument St.
Baltimore, MD 21205-3042
ph 410 522-7000
fx 410 522-7015

Plastic netting, liners

FISH GRADERS

Commerce Welding and Manufacturing Co.
2200 Evanston
Dallas, TX 75208
ph 214 748-8824
fx 214 761-9283

Aluminum interchangeable bar graders

Magic Valley Heli-Arc and Mfg..
P.O. Box 511
198 Freightway St.
Twin Falls, ID 83301
ph 208 733-0503
fx 208 733-0544

Aluminum adjustable bar grader

SHIPPING BAGS

Diverse Sales and Distribution   Plastic bags
935 Dillingham Bl.
Honolulu, HI 96817
ph 808 848-4852

Koolau Distributors Inc.   Plastic bags
1344 Mookaula
Honolulu, HI 96817
ph 808 848-1626

SHIPPING BOXES

Pacific Allied Products, Ltd.   Styrofoam boxes and sheet material, corrugated
91-110 Kaomi Loop Rd.   outer boxes
Kapolei, HI 96707
ph 808 682-2038

Unisource   Corrugated foam core boxes
91-210 Hanua
Wahiaw, HI 96786
ph 808 673-1300

HEAT PACKS

Grabber Warmers
205 Mason Circle
Concord, Ca 94520
ph (510) 680-0777
fx (510) 827-1161
tf (800) 990-9276

COLD PACKS

J & W Products Inc.
2931 Koapaka St.
Honolulu, Hi 96819
ph (808) 833-0755

The Ornamental Fish Industry

Craig A. Watson
Tropical Aquaculture Laboratory, University of Florida, Ruskin, Florida

INTRODUCTION

The ornamental fish industry is global in nature and relies on rapid movement of product via airfreight networks. Current technology and expertise allows for the live shipment of fish, invertebrates, and other aquatic organisms from any point of origin to any destination, provided there is space available on the commercial carrier.

Because of the need to deal with 2,000 different species and varieties of ornamental fish and various sizes of individual fish, expertise and competence in the fields of transport logistics and live handling technology are highly prized. The ability of suppliers to deliver healthy and minimally stressed animals is often the deciding factor in a company's financial success. Most suppliers provide a 24-hour, post-delivery guarantee on live animals. Factors manipulated during the packaging of ornamental fish include:

1. Amount of water.
2. Temperature.
3. Size and number of fish per pack.
4. Water additives (antibacterials, ammonia absorbers, pH stabilizers, etc.).
5. Time of packing.

On the other end of the shipment process, handling the fish at the receiving stage is of equal importance to the ultimate success of the shipment. The proper acclimation of the newly arrived animals and the timely resolution of unavoidable health problems associated with shipping stress are other specialized skills requiring extensive training and expertise.

Knowledge of airfreight practices, including schedules, layover times, and seasonal climatic conditions at all points along the shipment route is important. The development of good working relationships between shippers and the airlines enhances success during the shipping process, as well. Competition for limited cargo space may be an issue at certain locations or at certain times of the year. Other products, especially mail and certain high priority shipments, take precedence over ornamental fish. Perhaps the most important factor underlying the successful movement of ornamental fish is the unimpeded movement of live animals throughout the entire shipping process.

The development of regulatory trends involving the inspection and/or quarantine of shipments is problematic for this industry. Live aquatic animals are under unavoidable stress during shipment, and delays in the delivery of shipments can cause increased losses.

FLORIDA'S ORNAMENTAL AQUACULTURE INDUSTRY

The University of Florida has recently acquired a new research facility in Ruskin. We are currently about two years into this new program. The Ruskin facility is a laboratory specifically designed to address the needs of Florida's tropical fish industry. Our laboratory has a 6.5-acre fish farm adjacent to it. We are also building a new hatchery and nutrition lab at this site, and we maintain a small dormitory for students. The laboratory is providing us with many opportunities to assist the industry.

Every two years the State of Florida completes a survey of farmgate value in the aquaculture industry. Farmgate price is what the farmer is paid for the product. Aquaculture products pass through a number of hands before finally departing Florida. For this reason, by the time the products are transported across the Florida boundary the price usually doubles and sometimes triples. The tropical or ornamental fish sector accounted for $57 million (US) of the just over $100 million resulting from the entire aquaculture industry in 1997. The aquatic plant sector of the industry accounted for an additional $13.2 million. This particular sector deals primarily with aquatic plants destined for the aquarium trade and ornamental fish ponds; thus these two sectors are sister industries. The ornamental trade dominates Florida's aquaculture industry.

The ornamental fish industry is concentrated in the Tampa Bay region, in Hillsborough County. This is also the center of the work at our laboratory. About 95% of the U.S. ornamental fish production is in Florida and about 80% of Florida's production is cultured in Hillsborough County. One of the reasons for the concentration of farms in and around Tampa Bay is that the Tampa International Airport provides very good service to the industry. There is also a well-developed infrastructure in the county to supply essential products to the ornamental and aquatic plant industry. In addition to this, we have the benefit of occupying a region with flat, sandy soils. You can simply dig a hole and it quickly fills with water, creating a pond in the process. If you fly over Hillsborough County, you can see these farms spread out everywhere. The ornamental farms are located in the middle of a broad, flat agricultural region. The average sized farm is approximately 10-15 acres.

Progress in the Florida industry
Bigger farms
The Florida industry is moving toward bigger farms and consolidating. One farm I am familiar with illustrates a trend now gaining power in the Florida industry. The farm has recently purchased 160 acres of ponds in nearby De Soto County. Bringing these two properties together, this single company is currently farming about 1,500 ponds. In addition to production facilities, consolidation has now moved to the distribution of ornamental products. Several large retail companies are beginning to dominate the distribution of live fish to the hobby trade. Additional consolidation is expected in the Florida industry.

More fish per pond
Some of the initiatives that have been undertaken to increase the overall farmgate value of this diverse industry have not involved the construction of more ponds, but rather the placement of more fish in these ponds. We have studied ways to increase feeding rates and to increase stocking densities. Some ornamental farmers used to harvest 2,000-3,000 fish out of a typical pond. Now they are harvesting 10,000-20,000 fish out of the same pond. The use of simple production strategies such as continuous aeration and the use of automatic feeders with complete diets have allowed the industry to expand in this manner.

Covered ponds
Another innovation is the use of covered ponds. While Hillsborough County is south of the established freeze line, it does occasionally freeze in this area. We experienced a devastating freeze on Christmas Eve 1989, and lost 70% of the cultured fish in Florida overnight. Ornamental farmers are now covering 30-40% of their ponds with plastic during the winter. Although covering a pond with plastic may seem like an easy process, this represents a major cost to the farmer. However, if the farm has a profitable year because of plastic covers and other precautions, the use of these strategies will have been justified. Cost recovery usually takes only a year or two.

Bird netting
I would also like to point out that underneath the plastic cover is bird netting. The plastic cover to protect the ponds from freezing weather goes on from November to March of each year. When it comes off, the farmers cover the ponds with bird netting to ward off various species of fish-eating birds. We completed a study dealing with the problem of bird predation and found that the industry was losing up to 40% of certain species of ornamental fish. Brightly colored fish species were particularly vulnerable to bird predation.

Indoor production
We are beginning to see another trend in the industry—the movement toward the use of indoor production at all levels of the ornamental industry. The industry is getting away from the exclusive use of ponds and has now started to use recirculating water systems and related technologies.

Other changes
Among other innovations are the use of computer monitored growout systems, liquid oxygen injection, biological filters, and so on. The industry is becoming technologically advanced in order to gain the following benefits:

- Eliminate bird predation.
- Reduce the financial risks associated with cold temperatures.
- Allow for more control of the production process.

What has the spread of these various production strategies done for the industry? The adoption of these innovations has made it a lot easier to get the product to the market. It is now much easier to pick the fish out using a net and package them for the end consumer.

Transport to market

Ornamentals are the number one airfreight commodity for the Tampa International Airport. On a weekly basis, the industry now ships approximately 30,000 boxes of ornamental fish and aquatic plants from this airfreight hub. The movement of ornamental fish and associated products around the airport is quite hectic. Trucks are sometimes lined up ten deep trying to get to the cargo bays of the major airlines providing service at Tampa International. There is a huge infrastructure within Hillsborough County and other Florida regions specifically geared toward supplying shipping services. The ornamental industry is very important to the local economy—the aquaculture industry and its associated infrastructure companies are major employers. For example, local plastic bag manufacturers produce an enormous quantity of plastic bags for the industry.

Where are the markets for the ornamental fish and aquatic plant products? The answer to this question is quite simple—where is the money? Ornamental fish and aquatic plants are generally defined as luxury products, and the market for these products is largely confined to the Northern Hemisphere. It is an exotic hobby. The farther you get away from the tropics, the more interest there is in tropical aquarium fish. The times of the year when the largest numbers of tropical fish are sold generally tend to coincide with the hardest freezes in the north. When people become snowbound in their houses, they appear to find it comforting to own a little square of the tropics in their front room.

Today, the airfreight transportation network, with its speed and number of available domestic and international flights, is capable of carrying an ornamental fish from any point on the globe to any other point in the world in a very short time. The network can accomplish this task in a very efficient manner. This represents a major change from the past. In the 1930s and before, tropical fish were transported in metal cans on steamships and railroad cars. Now it is difficult to think about how hard it used to be to transport an ornamental fish from, for example, Florida to Germany. It was moved in a metal can, with someone changing the water at several points along the way.

ORNAMENTAL SOURCES WORLDWIDE

Florida and Hawaii are the major sites of ornamental production in the United States. There are smaller amounts of production in Texas, and California has several good producers. Additional production comes from southern Mexico near the Yucatan. A small amount of production takes place in Costa Rica and there is some apparently diminishing interest in Venezuela and Colombia. In Europe, the Czech Republic is generating an amazing amount of production. When the Iron Curtain fell, we found out that they were really cranking out ornamental fish. However, the major production centers of the world are Thailand, Indonesia, Malaysia, Hong Kong, Singapore, Sri Lanka, and southern India. Florida's major competition comes from Southeast Asia. Asians are producing the same kind of fish as those cultured in the United States, but with cheaper labor and "friendlier" government systems.

Wild harvesting

We need to consider ornamental fish as an international commodity. In the global marine ornamental category, we have counted 851 species that are commonly traded. The Florida industry cultures about 24 of these fish. This suggests that many marine ornamental species are harvested from the wild. We recognize that there are some real problems with this type of collection. Wild harvesting is currently being scrutinized in terms of its sustainability. Incidentally, several of us at this conference are on our way to the first international conference on the culture and conservation of marine ornamental reef species, in Hawaii, to deal with the issues associated with the wild harvesting of marine ornamental fish.

The fact remains that large numbers of marine ornamental species are being collected from the wild. The fish are brought into major wholesale centers including Jakarta, Manila, and a number of other collection points. From these centers, the fish and other species are shipped to worldwide markets. They are involved in the trading of just about anything and everything that has a little bit of color to it. For many of these tropical fish species, researchers are not even close to figuring out their complex life cycles. The proper methods to spawn them and rear their larvae are unknown.

Some fish will retail for close to $100.00 if the shipper can get it to the United States alive. You can understand why a shipper is going to spend a lot more time and money packaging and shipping this animal than other less valuable species. Where is the ornamental industry going with this type of collecting? The marine ornamental industry is moving toward aquaculture, i.e., the farming of these species.

Sherry Larkin, the first speaker in this technical session, talked about the aquarium product known as "live rock." Live rock and live sand are important items in the aquarium trade. Live sand, for instance, is frequently used as a base component in modern marine aquariums. Florida has several producers who are actively involved with the aquaculture of live rock. This is accomplished by first collecting rock from land, and then depositing this rock at various locations in the Gulf of Mexico. The rock is harvested when it has become covered with encrusting organisms, hence the name "live rock." This is a product much in demand by hobbyists. Other producers are involved with the aquaculture of various macro-algae that are also in demand by hobbyists operating reef tanks.

Most of the ornamental fish currently being cultured in Florida and elsewhere in the world are species that form strong pair bonds. The life cycles of these fish include parental care of the eggs and larvae. The larvae are quite large compared to some of the other marine ornamental species.

Small farms in the Far East

On the freshwater side of the ornamental business, a big portion of Florida's competition is from small individual producers in the Far East. These operations do not individually produce many fish, but when there are 2,000 of them in Jakarta alone, they add up. In Singapore and areas across the strait into Malaysia, this type of farming is being carried out at higher densities. Much of the culture process involves netpens and a small amount of water exchange. In this more intensive form of farming, many fish are produced in small areas. This type of operation must be highly managed because of all the small netpens.

Just like the farms in Florida, these Asian farms have an advantage over the wild-caught fish in that the fish originating from a farm are handled only once, perhaps twice, while en route to the final shipment location. In Singapore, these farms deliver their ornamental fish in bags ready to go into the box. Not many handling steps are involved. By comparison, in the Florida industry, the fish are typically delivered and then go into tanks, where they are purged and repackaged by the wholesaler.

REVIEW OF HANDLING STEPS

Following is a description of the entire handling and shipping sequence involving just one fish, the clown loach. This shows some of the complexities present in the industry. Any pet shop in the world that has a good freshwater fish section will have this fish. The clown loach probably originated from one of two islands in the southwestern Pacific—Sumatra and Borneo.

In Borneo, about 200 miles up the Kapuas River, is the Kapuas Hula Region. Moving up this river and turning a corner, you would see dozens of boats positioned against the riverbank with fishermen operating lift nets. They sit there all day long, dropping nets into the water and, at regular intervals, lifting them up. The captured fish are poured into a bucket. After sufficient fish have been harvested, the harvesters transport them back to their houses and transfer them into floating cages

Then large "collector boats," moving up and down the river, stop at the docks and transfer the fish into plastic cages that are positioned in the bilge of the boat. They flood the bilge and circulate the water by trickling water into these cages. The fish are carried 200 miles down the river to the port town at the mouth—Pontianak. One particular trader has a spacious structure enclosing glass raceways stacked two high. He claims to have approximately 5,000,000 clown loaches in inventory at this location.

It is easy to estimate the number of times that our hypothetical fish has been handled at this point and how far it still has to go. It is still in Borneo and it will probably be sold to an ornamental trader in Singapore, Los Angeles, Tampa, Miami, or some major European city before it is distributed to still another wholesaler. From this point it will be sold to a pet shop and then finally purchased by a hobbyist. Consequently, this fish may change hands as many as seven times before reaching the final market.

Pathogens

In the majority of cases, the roots of any problems associated with the shipping of fish involve the fish and the environment in which it has been placed. There are concerns about pathogens from source areas, of course, but it is typically the "environmental diseases" that flare up during shipment that cause the significant problems. The ornamental industry is faced with pathogens that can multiply rapidly during shipment, especially bacterial infections. Our laboratory and other programs work with producers, training them in disease diagnostics and treatment in an effort to eliminate disease organisms prior to shipment.

Water quality

Attention to water quality is an essential consideration when it comes to the handling of ornamental fish. If you are trying to keep alive anything that is aquatic and you do not understand the importance of water quality, then you are in for trouble. If you are involved with the shipping of ornamentals, the maintenance of proper water quality is a big issue. Many individual strategies are involved. It is important to purge the fish and to have water circulating through them during the pre-shipment holding period.

Oxygen

The provision of oxygen is a major factor when shipping fish. The reason to encourage the injection of pure oxygen on top of the water containing fish is quite simple. If you fail to inject a small volume of oxygen, the fish are going to run out. By making use of compressed oxygen for shipping, a major limiting factor can be eliminated. However, even with pure oxygen, after a period of time the fish will deplete the supply in the bags.

Ammonia

The accumulation of ammonia and other nitrogenous wastes, as well as pH alterations, present additional problems during the shipping period that need to be dealt with. It is possible to get rid of some of the ammonia produced via excretion by purging the fish prior to shipment. However, you still have excretion across the gill membranes. Although it is possible to get rid of most of the organic debris in the bag by eliminating the feed and feces, it is not possible to get rid of these things completely. The fish are going to excrete ammonia. What does ammonia do to the fish? The biggest concern about ammonia, when in the acute state, is that it can cause damage to the gills. When acute ammonia buildup occurs in the holding water, you can expect to see hemorrhagic areas on the gill filaments. Obviously, a fish suffering this type of damage will not be capable of normal respiration or other functions performed by the gills.

The use of zeolite is probably your best bet for removing ammonia during shipping. There are several other things such as Ammolock and other chemical additives, but zeolite will physically remove a certain amount of ammonia.

pH

A few words need to be mentioned about pH. The pH of the holding water will go down (become more acidic) during shipment. In some ways this is good because it pushes the ammonia into a nontoxic form. But at extremely low pH, you will start having problems. It is important in the ornamental fish trade to understand that some fish can tolerate lowered pH levels and some fish cannot. Remedies must be sought.

Corydoras adolfi, a fish being collected in the northern part of the Amazon River, is found living in pH environments as low as 5.0. On the other hand, if you go to the Rift Lake area, you will find fish living very happily in situations approaching pH 10. Thus it is important to maintain the accustomed pH during shipment. The best method to maintain proper pH is to use buffers. The alkalinity of the water is manipulated primarily using carbonates and bicarbonates. Also available are pH fixers and commercial buffer solutions that will maintain the pH of the holding water at a certain level during the shipment period.

Fish need to be acclimated to their new conditions. Many times when a shipping bag is opened right after shipment, the pH will be in the area of 6.0-6.5. In most situations, these fish will be transferred to water with a pH as high as 8.0. You need to acclimate the transported fish to this new pH. Certain fish go into a pH shock quickly if they are abruptly transferred.

Salinity

Some people add salt to their shipping bags. This is not a bad idea. The best way to look at this strategy, using the words of veterinarian Ruth Floyd, is to consider a freshwater fish to be a bag of salt sitting in a pool of freshwater. The salt content inside the fish is higher than in the surrounding water. If you poke a hole in that bag or otherwise damage or stress the bag, salt will leave the bag and freshwater will migrate in. One way to relieve the animal's osmotic stress or osmoregulatory stress is to add a little bit of salt to the surrounding pool of holding water. For proper levels of osmoregulation, Floyd recommends 0.1-0.3% salt in the shipping water.

Temperature

Temperature during shipment is another important topic. This can become a problem with shipments that are removed from a cargo plane and allowed to sit on the tarmac for a period of time. With regard to temperature, acclimation is important. This problem can go both ways. During the summer, your shipping bags may contain water that is at quite warm ambient temperatures. The recovery water in which you place these fish may be relatively cold. This is another example of the unexpected complexity present in the ornamental trade.

In terms of temperature management consider the following two fish. Koi carp can tolerate a wide temperature range. They are able to live under ice and they are also able to live during the summer in Florida in shallow ponds where the water temperatures are over 90°F. In other words, they are robust fish in terms of tolerating temperature. It is possible to chill them down before shipment, the obvious advantage of which is to lower their metabolic rate and need for oxygen. Also, less excretion will take place and less ammonia will be generated. An extreme in the other direction involves the discus fish. This fish, when taken below 70°F, will be in trouble. Consequently, it is important to know your fish in this trade.

Light

Dim light is important when opening boxes of ornamentals. Some businesses use red light since most fish do not respond to this light frequency. You and your workers can see what is going on and the fish are protected from the sudden light shock.

Questions from the Audience

QUESTION: Two years ago at this conference, there was a speaker distributing plastic bags that were supposed to be permeable to ammonia. Have you used these bags?

C. WATSON: Yes, I've seen these bags. They are permeable to ammonia. Bob Rofan with Cordon represented this product. We tried some and they actually appeared to exchange gas. Unfortunately, they had the tendency to break. The bags were thin enough to allow the gas to go across them, but they were also thin enough that they were more vulnerable to breakage.

BAILEY: A problem with these bags is the users tend to put more bags in a box. When this occurs, there is no oxygen in the box and the box is sealed.

QUESTION: What is the role of mariculture for marine ornamental species?

C. WATSON: I think that there has been a good amount of development. There is a huge amount of interest. A number of us at this gathering are going tomorrow to the first international conference on the culture and conservation of marine ornamental reef species, in Hawaii. The sponsors have a pre-registration of over 100 people from all over the world looking at this issue.

The marine ornamental aquaculture industry is in no position to provide the quantity product that the hobby demands today. We have a long way to go. We are able to culture a couple dozen fish, a dozen crustaceans, and maybe a dozen coral species. That is it. If you go into a marine aquarium shop, you will see thousands of different species available to the hobbyist.

It is important to understand that the hobby trade has been built and sustained on this level of availability. It must be like stamp collecting. A stamp collector stays interested for 10 to 20 years, because there is always a new stamp. I have been an ornamental hobbyist since I was eight years old, even now that I do this work professionally. There is still another fish to be collected. I do not think that aquaculture will ever entirely replace wild collection. However, I think that the technology is rapidly developing and this will make the culture of many species economically feasible.

QUESTION: I would like to make one comment about the stamp collecting. A stamp collector may have a stamp that is worth a whole lot of money. A fish hobbyist may purchase a fish that is worth a whole lot of money, but he is not going to purchase multiple examples of this fish. There is a considerable expense involved in raising ornamental fish.

Consequently, you do not have available a high volume market to sell your product.

QUESTION: When airplanes are in the air, they are partially depressurized. Do you have any information about fish suffering the consequences of this depressurization?

C. WATSON: No, it is not enough to cause any decompression problems. What you do need to take into account is the expansion of your bags. The physical expansion of your bags will occur and if you overfill the bags and take them to 35,000 feet, they are going to break. So, do not fill your bags up completely. Leave some space for expansion during the flight.

QUESTION: I have two comments, one relating to light in calming fish. I was a fish farmer and can report that one effective practice was to just put a large leaf in the bucket in which the fish are being held. A number of species will concentrate under this shade and they appear to be relaxed. If you take the leaf out of the bucket, the fish will begin frantically darting around the bag. That is an example of a real simple technology that is extremely effective. With regard to how much oxygen to put in a bag, another reason this strategy is important is that no carrier will guarantee a shipment of fish will arrive in an allotted amount of time. The use of oxygen is a fairly inexpensive insurance policy covering the fish that may be delayed by ten or twelve or fifteen hours.

Live Rockweed (Ascophyllum) used as a Shipping Medium for the Live Transport of Marine Baitworms from Maine

Stephen E. Crawford
International Marine Resources, Eastport, Maine

Abstract

A subspecies of rockweed (*Ascophyllum nodosum scorpioides*), locally known as "wormweed," is used as a shipping material for the live transport of marine baitworms. The baitworm industry is valued at over US $3.5 million per year and more than 400,000 pounds of wormweed was used for packing in 1998. Worms are shipped from Maine to several places around the globe, including the west coast of North America, South America, France, Italy, and Japan.

The wormweed must be very fresh (only 1-2 days old) to prevent damage to the baitworms. The wormweed is not washed; a brief survey found over 35 species of invertebrates living in the wormweed used for packing. Evidence has shown that some of these species have established themselves in San Francisco Bay. An alternative method for the packaging of baitworms is recommended to reduce the number of possible introductions of Gulf of Maine invertebrates to other places in the world.

Introduction to Wormweed

Wormweed is the common name for a form of seaweed used to pack baitworms for shipping from the Gulf of Maine. Wormweed is a subspecies of rockweed (*Ascophyllum nodosum*), the most abundant large seaweed in the Gulf of Maine. Rockweed grows to two meters long in intertidal areas attached to rocks. Small pieces break off the ends of the plant due to wave action and ice damage, and the pieces wash out into the gulf and form mats up to several hectares in size. The plants in these accumulations eventually die, releasing their nutrients into the sea.

When pieces of rockweed wash into salt marshes and come to rest among the cordgrass at the upper level of the high tide mark, a rather remarkable transformation occurs. This intertidal zone is exposed to the air for 5 of the 6 hours in a tidal cycle and is exposed to other extreme environmental conditions including desiccation, low to zero salinities during rain events, and temperature ranging from 25°C to over 35°C. In this extreme environment, the loose pieces of rockweed are able to grow vegetatively between the stems of the cordgrass. They are called wormweed.

The fronds of the offspring are not as tough as the larger rockweed and its texture is smooth to the touch. These and possibly other characteristics have allowed use of wormweed as a packing material for live baitworms.

Two species of baitworms are harvested in Maine, the sandworm (*Nereis virens*) and the bloodworm (*Glycera dibranchiata*). The sandworm is worth $0.095 to the digger (i.e., ex digger price); the bloodworm is worth $0.135 each. The diggers or "wormers" pay $43.00 per year for a license that permits them to harvest both worms and wormweed. The state requires that dealers report the number of worms shipped, but no record is kept of the amount of wormweed harvested. During 1998, 21,675,000 bloodworms were harvested and 6,704,000 sandworms. The industry is valued at over $3.5 million.

The two species of worms must be kept separate while in containers; otherwise the bloodworms will kill the sandworms. Wormers sort and count their harvest into boxes at the dealer. Each box holds 125 worms and an average of 1.67 pound of wormweed. From this data it can be calculated that 400,000 pounds of wormweed were harvested during the 1998 season. The wormers are paid $4.00 per 20 pound "bale" of wormweed. This product must be fresh. Any wormweed over three days old begins to compost or decompose and the heat generated by this decomposition literally "cooks" the worms. This presents a logistical problem to the dealer, who must have a continuous fresh supply of wormweed for shipping. This has proven to be the most satisfactory method of shipping the worms since the 1940s.

A problem exists concerning the use of fresh wormweed as packing material. When used in the baitworm industry it is not washed very well and must be very fresh. Inhabitants living in the wormweed are, consequently, shipped along with the worms. Table 1 presents a list of invertebrates found during two visits to a dealer in November 1999. Some of the observed species were quite numerous, including the green crab, *Carcinus maenus*. These animals all arrive at the shipping destination in at least as good condition as the marine worms. The worms are shipped from Maine to other locations on the East Coast and also to San Francisco, South America, France, Italy, and Japan.

A graduate student from the University of California, Berkeley, working with Dr. Andy Cohen of the San Francisco Estuary Institute (Richmond, California) surveyed anglers in the San Francisco region during 1994-1995 to determine how the anglers disposed of packages of baitworms containing wormweed. Approximately one-third of those surveyed dumped the leftover bait and seaweed into the San Francisco Bay. Between 5% and 40% left their boxes of seaweed and worms on the pier or on the shore for others to use. A substantial number of these discarded containers were washed away at high tide. The remainder was properly disposed of. Dr Cohen feels it is very likely that *Littorina saxatilis*, a small periwinkle, has been introduced into the bay by this route.

Significant dangers are involved when shipping large numbers of species and introducing them into distant waters. The zebra mussel in the U.S. Great Lakes is an infamous example of an exotic introduction and is one of many species that have caused enormous ecological damage. The green crab, originally from Europe, has decimated clam flats in the northeastern United States. A comb jelly originally from the Chesapeake Bay (U.S.) has destroyed 21 of 26 commercial species fisheries in the Black Sea by eating small food organisms formerly consumed by the juveniles of local fish populations. It is impossible to predict where or when the next introduced or exotic species might suddenly explode in numbers and destroy an ecosystem.

It would be very prudent to find alternative, ecologically safe shipping medium for packing baitworms. Because the market for this type of packaging product is rather small—worth $80,000 in 1998 for 400,000 pounds—a large company has little economic incentive to invest funds in the development of alternate packaging materials. A considerable

Table 1. Groups and species of invertebrates found in wormweed (*Ascophyllum nodosum scorpioides*) used as packaging material for shipping marine baitworms.

Group	Species or subgroup
Gastropods	*Littorina littorea*
	Littorina obtusata
	Littorina saxatalis
	Lacuna vincta
	Spirorbis planorbis
	Onchidorus bisuturalis
	Hydrobia minuta
	Thai lapillus
	Nassarius trivittatus
Bivalves	*Mytilus edulus*
	Mya arenaria
Amphipods	*Microdeutopus obtusatus*
	Microdeutopus finmarcharus
	Ampithoe rubricata
	Diastylis thea
	Gammarus angulosus
	Hyale nilssoni
	Jassa falcata
	Gammarus oceanicus
	Corophium spp.
	Orchestia spp.
Isopods	*Jaera marina*
	Idotea phosphorea
Worms	Nematoda
	Tremotoda
	Nemertina
	Polychaeta
	Oligochaeta
Insects	Chiromidae
	Turbanidae
	Collembola
Others	Halicardiae
	Harpacticoids
	Mysids
	Carcinus maenus

amount of resistance would be expected from the wormers who collect the $80,000 for harvesting the wormweed.

European researchers maintain sandworms and bloodworms for research in packing consisting of wet newspapers, charcoal, and sawdust. Such a medium could be prepared by the dealers well in advance of harvests and sales. This would eliminate the logistical problem of needing fresh packing for delivery. A decision to change the packing medium would have to originate with either the Maine Department of Marine Resources, or perhaps with the State of California if it began to refuse to accept baitworms shipped in live seaweed. Given the risks involved, finding an alternative shipping medium seems necessary.

Conclusion

The use of wormweed as a packing material for the shipping of live marine baitworms from Maine involves a significant risk of transporting and introducing a variety of invertebrate species into widely separated ecosystems. Over 35 different species were observed on a packing table at a worm shipping center in Jonesport, Maine. Several exotic species from the Gulf of Maine have been found in San Francisco Bay and may have been transported by wormweed. European researchers have used a packing medium consisting of wet newspapers, charcoal, and sawdust to culture the same species of baitworms for research. It would seem prudent to require Maine worm shippers to use the same type of packing material.

Worm diggers will continue to sell wormweed to the dealers who will pay for it. Thus to effectively eliminate wormweed shipping, all dealers must agree to change their packing material or the Maine State Legislature will need to mandate a new management regulation. One challenge associated with this problem is that no damage is being done to the Gulf of Maine. The potential for damage occurs at the locations where the worms and wormweed are shipped. As responsible global citizens, we should make every effort to raise the awareness of those involved in the marine baitworm industry. Buyers, sellers, and recreational fishermen need to be informed of the dangers involved with using wormweed. Hopefully this will help dealers to make the decision to change their shipping strategies and incorporate an alternate packing material.

Shipping and Handling the Marine Algae Macrocystis in Alaska

Thea Thomas
Cordova, Alaska

Abstract

The harvest and shipment of *Macrocystis* kelp first occurred in Alaska in 1983. *Macrocystis* kelp is used in the production of herring spawn-on-kelp, a highly prized traditional food in Japan. Large amounts of *Macrocystis* kelp are harvested from the remote bays of Southeast Alaska and shipped to the herring fishing grounds of Prince William Sound and other locations. Carefully selected portions of *Macrocystis* kelp is shipped 600 miles or more to areas where it does not naturally occur.

The logistics of harvesting and shipping this highly perishable product from one remote area of Alaska to another in a cost-effective manner are considerable. A brief history of shipping and handling methods is presented. Cost efficiency and effectiveness of present handling and shipping procedures are reviewed.

Introduction

The herring spawn-on-kelp fishery (sometimes referred to as the herring roe-on-kelp fishery) has occurred in Prince William Sound (PWS) since 1969. Pacific herring lay their adhesive eggs on marine algae and seagrass in the intertidal and upper subtidal zones. Herring spawn-on-kelp is a highly prized traditional food in Japan. Divers harvested the spawn-on-kelp in the wild until about 1979. Since this date, spawn-on-kelp has been harvested from man-made impoundments or "pounds." The pound fishery developed rapidly from 1980 to 1988 with a harvest of more than 500,000 pounds in 1992.

The Japanese buyers let it be known to the spawn-on-kelp producers that they prefer *Macrocystis* kelp to the *Laminaria* kelp growing naturally in PWS and would pay a premium for product using *Macrocystis*. The problem for the producers is that the closest *Macrocystis* beds were in the remote coastal areas of Southeast Alaska, 600 roadless miles to the south. The logistics of harvesting and shipping the kelp are considerable. *Macrocystis* kelp is highly perishable and susceptible to damage from exposure to air, wind, fresh water, freezing temperatures, and sunlight. All of these hazards are commonly encountered in Alaska during April, the time when Pacific herring return to spawn. Any damage or deterioration sustained by the kelp during harvest and shipment is quite apparent in the final product. The final product of deteriorated quality is either unusable or considerably downgraded.

Harvest methods, transport time, and the handling of the kelp is critical. Limiting the amount of time the kelp is out of seawater will reduce exposure to the elements and possible damage. Cost efficiency is also a critical factor. The spawn-on-kelp product has a limited market and if the cost of the harvested kelp going into the fishery is too high, the chance of making a profit with the final product is decreased. In the production of spawn-on-kelp, procurement of the *Macrocystis* is by far the largest single expense. Throughout the history of this PWS fishery, large amounts of kelp have been required. At the peak of the pound fishery in the early 1990s, the spawn-on-kelp producers required more than 65,000 pounds of kelp over a period of just a few days.

The kelp grows only in Southeast Alaska—just about to the latitude of Sitka or halfway up the panhandle. Keep in mind that Prince William Sound is located in southcentral Alaska, hundreds of miles north of Sitka. Also, there is now a spawn-on-kelp fishery developing in Norton Sound, part of the Bering Sea.

Methods

The herring pound fishery involves hanging individual blades of kelp on lines and stringing these lines across a rectangular floating structure in the form of a large net bag. The kelp hanging in the water is surrounded by this web enclosure. The pounds are made of aluminum, plastic floats, and lumber. They are equipped with weights to keep the web from brushing up against the kelp. Mature herring are captured in seines and transferred to the pounds. The herring are held for up to eight days in the enclosure or pound and, when they become sexually mature, will lay their adhesive eggs on the kelp. Once the herring have deposited their eggs on the kelp, they are released to continue their natural life cycle. Pacific herring will return to spawn for several years.

It is interesting to note that the main sources of herring roe for the Japanese market are the extensive sac roe fisheries that occur from California to Alaska. The roe harvested in this manner requires the harvesting of whole fish from which the egg skeins are extracted. With little or no market for the herring flesh, the carcasses, including those of the males, are treated as waste. Thus, one of the main benefits of the pound fishery is that it allows for the harvesting of the valuable roe without damaging the adult herring. Great care is taken during the capture and transfer of the herring to limit mortality caused by handling stress and descaling. The capturing of the herring requires a seine vessel, skiff, and a second vessel to transfer the herring to the kelp pound. Frequently, a spotter plane is used to locate the herring and direct the setting of the seine.

Harvesting *Macrocystis*

The initial problem for the spawn-on-kelp producer is to locate beds containing *Macrocystis* of suitable quality. The kelp that is selected must have large, thick mature blades that are free of invertebrates and damage caused by wave action. The quality of the naturally growing kelp can be highly variable depending on the location of the beds and ocean conditions. The kelp is harvested from Southeast Alaska in early April and then transported to Prince William Sound, and other locations, as fast as possible.

The window for shipping kelp is narrow due to the fact that the herring biomass may come into a given area and spawn all within the time of a few tide cycles. The major spawn rarely occurs at the same time from year to year. In PWS it can occur anytime from early April to early May. Once the *Macrocystis* is harvested, even if it is handled in the prescribed manner, it lasts for only a finite period of time, and then begins to deteriorate. Over the years, Alaska fishery managers have become concerned about the sustainability of the kelp resource. Because of the need for careful management, harvesters must obtain a permit and are allowed to harvest only a certain number of kelp blades. As a consequence, care must be taken to harvest only the highest quality kelp.

To harvest *Macrocystis*, one person cuts the kelp. The cut sections then float to the surface where another harvesting crew member, using a small skiff, pulls up these long stalks of *Macrocystis*. At this point the blades are carefully inspected to see if they are mature. Immature blades tend to quickly deteriorate. Blades that are shredded, an indication of wave damage, are also culled during this initial inspection. The kelp must also be free of invertebrates, some of which are capable of eating the blades. One type of snail, for example, is capable of producing large holes in the blades—a severe quality defect. Because of the exacting quality requirements in the spawn-on-kelp fishery, every stalk of kelp is inspected and when a suitable section of kelp is found, it is coiled down in the bottom of the skiff. A mature blade can be six feet long.

After the kelp has been picked and looked over, it is taken to the sorting and packing area. Each blade is carefully inspected to make sure it meets all of the criteria—maturity, size, free of invertebrates, absence of wave damage, etc. The harvester does not want to ship any more product than necessary because shipping is very expensive. Consequently, each blade is looked at to make sure it will work and then the kelp is packed in the shipping boxes.

Shipping *Macrocystis*

The first shipments of *Macrocystis* from Southeast Alaska to PWS for the pound fishery occurred in 1983. Since this time, a set of standard procedures has been developed. Producers will locate suitable kelp beds and then hire the boats, skiffs, and manpower needed to do the harvesting. The kelp must be handled delicately—protected from snow, rain, wind, and sun. The sorting and packing areas must remain covered, a challenge when operating a small vessel at sea.

The first shipments of kelp were transported in refrigerated seawater (RSW) in the holds of fishing vessels. The elapsed time and damage occurring during transit across the Gulf of Alaska were extensive.

The next attempted method involved placing the kelp in totes and insulated containers piped with circulating seawater aboard the fishing vessels used to transport the product. Packing in this manner offered more protection for the kelp during transport. However, once again the lengthy transit time and rough weather in the Gulf of Alaska was hard on the kelp and this method was abandoned after several years. Many problems occurred because of the huge volume of kelp required by the spawn-on-kelp fishery and because of the complexities involved with continuous and effective circulation of seawater through the totes.

First air shipments of kelp were in 1988. After being sorted and picked, the kelp was loosely packed in plastic lined Wetlok boxes of the type suitable for airfreight. Approximately 35 pounds of kelp is loosely packed in a standard 80 pound box. Airfreight was fast but expensive, and the large volumes of kelp that needed to be shipped over a relatively short period of time caused congestion within the network of commercial airfreight carriers. The kelp harvesting grounds were frequently days away from any major airport. To further complicate matters, the shipments of kelp are categorized as low priority items and the number of flights between the kelp harvesting and spawn-on-kelp production areas are limited. Quality problems quickly developed if the kelp was "bumped" from a flight and sat even one extra day out of the water. If the boxes of kelp are bumped at the airport, cargo personnel need to know that the product must be kept in coolers at 1-2°C. One day under improper holding conditions could mean the difference between acceptable and unacceptable quality.

Over the past several years, many spawn-on-kelp producers have decided that the risks associated with the use of commercial airfreight carriers were too great and have hired private air cargo companies to transport the boxes of kelp. This method is fast and efficient, but very expensive, and it is subject to another set of problems. Even with private cargo planes, the kelp must still be transported by vessel to a port within reach of a suitable airstrip. Here the product is loaded into refrigerated trucks for transport to the airstrip and flown to one of the PWS ports or other production areas. A serious effort to educate all the kelp handlers along this transport network has been necessary. Among other variables, a close watch must be maintained on ambient temperatures impacting the shipping containers.

Upon reaching PWS, the kelp is trucked to the harbor and transported by boat to the herring grounds. By this time the boxes have been handled no fewer than five times. At the spawn-on-kelp production grounds, the kelp is again sorted and graded. It is removed from the boxes and inspected to see if there has been any deterioration during shipping. Kelp fronds with any signs of deterioration are culled.

The individual blades are then broken off the stalks and individually strung on lines, and hung in the herring pounds. It is important that the blades be kept separated on these lines. If the blades are positioned too close together, some sections of the blade will be shaded by an adjacent blade resulting in uneven coverage of eggs over the kelp—a quality defect. They are separated by about 10-14 inches. This procedure is a very labor intensive—thousands of blades of kelp are involved.

Figure 1 shows the spawn-on-kelp product being removed from the water. It is sorted and graded. The processing of the spawn-on-kelp product actually begins on the fishing grounds. It is packed in salt and 100% brine before it is transported to the processing plant. Figure 2 shows the final spawn-on-kelp product.

Figure 1. The spawn-on-kelp product as it is removed from the water.

Figure 2. Spawn-on-kelp final product.

Discussion

The strategy of shipping in Wetlok® boxes by airfreight produced the strongest and freshest kelp as well as the best quality final spawn-on-kelp product. Packaging the kelp in these plastic lined boxes provided the kelp harvesters with a great advantage compared to the use of large totes. The relatively small amount of loosely packed kelp in each of the large shipping boxes helped keep the kelp cool and limited bruising caused by compression. The wax-coated boxes are, for the most part, waterproof and also offer some amount of insulation. This helps protect the kelp from exposure to fresh water, sunlight, and freezing temperatures. The plastic liners help keep the kelp moist during shipment. The boxes are also easy to handle during loading from boat to truck to plane and then back to truck and, finally, by boat to the spawn-on-kelp grounds.

Airfreight provided an obvious advantage over transport by sea—reducing transport time from seven days down to one or two days. But the logistics involved with the commercial airfreight of kelp are still substantial. An extra day was always involved and then the possibility of the freight being "bumped" was always a threat. The use of private cargo carriers has substantially increased the control the producers have over the movement of the product. This allows the harvesting and transportation times to be closely coordinated. The producers quickly realized that by pooling resources and cooperating on the use of harvest vessels and cargo flight charters, costs could be kept to a minimum. The complicated logistics of kelp harvesting and consideration of the potential costs of the spawn-on-kelp fishery necessitated this degree of cooperation. However, persuading commercial fishermen to agree on a date to harvest and ship the kelp remains a major challenge. Each group of spawn-on-kelp fishermen has a different prediction of when the herring will spawn.

Literature Sources

Morstad, S., T. Baker, and J. Brady. 1990. Pacific herring pound spawn-on-kelp fishery in Prince William Sound, Alaska. Alaska Department of Fish and Game, Regional Information Report 2A92-02.

Alaska Department of Fish and Game. 1998. Pacific herring pound spawn-on-kelp fishery in Prince William Sound, Alaska. Alaska Department of Fish and Game, Regional Information Report, Appendix H6 and H13.

Author Biography

Thea Thomas graduated from the University of Oregon in 1982 with a master's degree in biology. She then moved to Alaska where she worked as a biologist with the Prince William Sound Aquaculture Corporation and the Alaska Department of Fish and Game.

In 1985 she became a commercial fisher and has participated in the herring spawn-on-kelp pound fishery in Prince William Sound since that time. She is a specialist in the shipment of *Macrocystis* kelp for her herring group as well as for others.

Questions from the Audience

QUESTION: What is the relative value of the herring roe-on-kelp product?

THOMAS: The ex-vessel price received by the fishermen has ranged anywhere from US $10.00-30.00 per pound. By the time the product gets to the consumer in Japan, the price can easily double this ex-vessel value—$45.00-55.00 per pound. I should also mention that when the final product is brought to the processing plants in Alaska, it is repackaged and transferred into 35-pound plastic buckets. When the product arrives in Japan it is again processed and put into very small consumer containers.

QUESTION: Why was *Macrocystis* given a premium value in this market? What is value of the *Macrocystis* roe-on-kelp product as opposed to the value of *Laminaria* version?

T. THOMAS: *Macrocystis* is a stronger, firmer kelp, and a more durable kelp. *Laminaria* is fairly thin and fragile. I think *Macrocystis* is more aesthetically appealing. It has nice ridges and, when you have eggs on both sides, the product has a wavy look to it. I think that the premium value mostly involves aesthetics.

QUESTION: Is the seaweed eaten as well as the roe?

T. THOMAS: Yes—it is all eaten together, the herring eggs and kelp.

QUESTION: Can you describe the flavor of the product?

T. THOMAS: There is a very slight flavor to the product. I do not believe that the actual flavor characteristics are that important. I think that product appearance is an important factor.

QUESTION: Has there been any significant effect on the Southeast Alaska herring stocks brought about by the collection of the kelp?

T. THOMAS: No—the herring do not need the kelp for the completion of their life cycle. They will spawn on anything. Including seagrass, rocks, pretty much anything that is there. If the kelp is there in front of them, they will spawn on it, but they do not absolutely need it.

The herring have a lot of problems, but harvesting kelp is not one of them.

QUESTION: Is there a synthetic kelp product?

T. THOMAS: I am not aware of any substantial work on this. I have heard that the Japanese have worked on a manufactured product over the years. They have worked with herring that have been harvested for the eggs. There are large sac roe fisheries where the fish are harvested just for their egg masses. The Japanese researchers have attempted to take those eggs, break them apart, and then to somehow artificially reattach them to kelp. If anyone makes progress with this procedure, it would do away with this business of harvesting the kelp, putting the herring in with the kelp, and other labor intensive steps. As far as I know, none of the artificial product has been placed on the market.

QUESTION: I am aware that several groups have tried to develop an artificial product. In one case, although the product has a good appearance, it does not have the proper mouth appeal to it—cleavage and crunch—and, as a consequence, the product failed.

QUESTION: I just wanted to point out that this method of obtaining herring roe, the herring spawn-on-kelp fishery, is really fantastic. Prior to the development of this fishery, the herring were sacrificed in order to obtain the roe. Now basically we have a renewable resource with fish going into the pounds, laying their eggs, and then being released. There is the potential of the fish staying in the fishery and not being sacrificed.

T. THOMAS: This is a really good point. In traditional sac roe fisheries, the herring are seined or gillnetted, killed, laced in totes, allowed to sit and somewhat deteriorate for a few days, and then the eggs are squeezed out. In a sac roe fishery, all the herring are sacrificed. In Alaska traditionally a lot of the carcasses were just dumped. About 15 years ago the practice of dumping was stopped. Now most roe stripping takes place in the Orient. As pointed out, following the pounding, the herring are released after being held for approximately eight days until they spawn. They will come back to spawn for up to nine years in Prince William Sound.

Live Transport of the Great Scallop (Pecten maximus)

Toril Overaa
Norwegian University of Science and Technology, Trondheim, Norway

INTRODUCTION

Although Norway is one of the leading fishery nations in the world, our bivalve production is still in an early stage of development. With our long coastline and clean water, the conditions are perfect for cultivating bivalves. The coastline provides many good locations for bivalve cultivation. In addition, we have little pollution compared to other European countries. Norwegian scallops grown in this clean ocean water are of high quality.

The Gulf Stream, moving in a northeastern direction across the North Atlantic Ocean, warms our coastal surface waters. In addition, cold, nutrient-rich water is brought into the coastal zone by means of upwelling. The combination of these positive growth factors stimulates high levels of primary production in Norwegian waters. Algae is the natural food of bivalves. At present, the scallops in our coastal waters have remained free of all known diseases and parasites. One can imagine, however, that pathogens may become a problem when cultivation densities become higher.

Norway's production of scallops is estimated to reach over 1,200 tons by 2003. At the same time, the European market for Norwegian scallops is increasing. The main challenge facing Norwegian farmers has been to deliver the bivalves to the consumer in live form. Why deliver live scallops to European customers? There is a tradition in Europe of preparing dishes using live scallops. Live scallops indicate quality—the consumer or buyer knows what he is getting. A live product offers farmers the best prices, as well. Norway also exports frozen and processed scallop muscle and gonad.

Within the European market, the distance between cultivator and consumer is short. In Norway, the marketing situation is quite the opposite—the national market is small and the distance between cultivator and consumer can be long. This means that most of our scallops, oysters, and blue mussels will be consumed in other European countries. Norwegian salmon exporters are now helping the shellfish industry with their market entries and contacts on the European continent. This will increase the popularity of bivalves in the marketplace and will stimulate the more timely development of the industry.

THE GREAT SCALLOP (PECTEN MAXIMUS)

The most common scallop species in Norway is the great scallop (*Pecten maximus*). The commercial size of this bivalve ranges from 10.5 to 14 centimeters (Fig. 1). In Europe, the muscle and gonad are consumed.

There has been little research done on the live transport of scallops in Norway. The reduced level of research has occurred because the shellfish industry is not a large commercial entity in Norway. Currently, there is no sale of cultivated scallops in Norway. Scuba divers hand-pick scallops from wild populations along the coast. This makes the Norwegian scallops an exclusive product, but also more expensive than the scallops harvested by trawlers

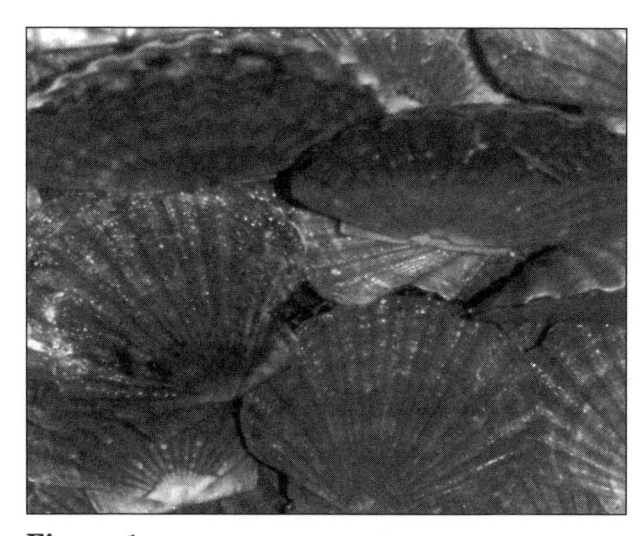

Figure 1. The great scallop (*Pecten maximus*).

in other countries. The cost of harvesting makes it difficult to compete with other European scallops.

The transport and packing methods currently used for this limited production are primarily based on the harvester's experiences. The most common method is packing the scallops in layers in Styrofoam boxes (5-12 kilos of scallops per box) with moist paper or wood fibers under and on top of the product. Some exporters use freshwater ice on top of the product to keep the temperature low. The fact needs to be pointed out that freshwater ice and scallops are not a good combination. Scallops are not able to close their shells tightly together like oysters and blue mussels. The meltwater from the freshwater ice leaks into the scallop, creating osmotic abnormalities. Because of this interaction, the scallops tend to die very fast.

There are still many challenges to overcome before the scallop industry will be able to stand on its own. This project will begin the process of resolving several of these live transport problems.

Challenges facing the Norwegian scallop industry

1. *Currently Norwegian scallops are an unknown product in Europe. Norway is faced with a significant marketing problem.* This has to do with little commercialization of the Norwegian scallop. Norway has no tradition of scallop cultivation or harvesting on a large scale. Countries like France, Italy, Spain, and Belgium are the main scallop importers. These European markets are also subject to local scallop preferences. France is the biggest scallop market, consuming 80,000-100,000 tons per year. The main supplier of this product is Great Britain. The scallop product is provided mainly in the form of frozen muscle because of the long distance between the harvesting areas and the market.

   Countries importing Norwegian scallops want to know what a Norwegian scallop is. What are the color, taste, texture, and smell of our scallops? What is so special about the Norwegian scallop that they should prefer them above, for example, Irish or British scallops?

2. *Improved cultivation and harvesting techniques must be developed.* The usual cultivation technique in Norway uses baskets to culture immature scallops from 20 mm to the size range of 50-70 mm. These maturing scallops are then planted on the ocean bed and allowed to grow until they are ready to be sold. In Norway, market-ready scallops are hand-picked by scuba divers, while in Europe scallop trawlers are used to harvest scallops. These cultivation techniques must be improved in ways that make the industry more efficient. However, a basic marketing question remains. Is it better for this developing industry to present smaller quantities of an exclusive product or large quantities of a more industrial quality product?

3. *The technical education of cultivators must be stressed.* It is crucial that the people producing and handling the scallops be thoroughly informed about scallop biology and ecology. The cultivators should also be seriously committed to this business activity. Diligent intent and close adherence to business plans is necessary for the development of a stable industry.

4. *A remedy must be sought to reduce the financial burdens associated with toxic algae testing.* Currently the cultivators and producers have to pay for these expensive tests themselves. The institutes that are qualified to conduct these tests in Norway are both understaffed and underfunded to accommodate the workload. In terms of toxic algae testing, various countries have authorized different tests. Some of these governments are willing to "see through their fingers," whereas others are strict. Norway is further challenged because our country is outside the European Union. It is important that Norwegian laws and regulations are compatible with EU trade regulations.

5. *An expanding industry needs to attract capital and investors.* The industry lost most of its financial supporters in the mid-1980s, when most of the farms went out of business. An effort must be made to rebuild trust among the Norwegian investors, many of whom saw their money end up on the ocean floor.

6. *An effort must be made to create a national market for this product.* Most Norwegians eat scallops only when they visit other European countries. A formal campaign to encourage the domestic consumption of scallop products needs to be undertaken. Many campaigns for seafood have been successful and some economists believe that seafood will eventually take over as the upper class food in place of other meat products. It would be good public relations for our scallops if Norwegians themselves can recommend them.

7. *The problem of cooler water temperatures and longer growth times in northern regions, including Norway, must be recognized.* Some observers have stated that the low water temperatures in northern aquaculture regions are a disadvantage. The average culture time for Norwegian scallops is 3-4 years to commercial size. However, other authorities state that the cold temperature may be beneficial because it decreases the spread of diseases and parasites.

8. *Norwegian scallops—live seafood or processed?* Should Norway encourage the development of the skills and transport infrastructure needed in the marketing of live product or should the industry invest in production lines so that we can process the scallops into different product forms?

Quality

If Norway is to develop a scallop industry, basic quality standards need to be developed. What is the quality of a scallop? The outward signs of bad or lesser quality in a scallop are based on rather subjective observations and, to a certain degree, depend on the experiences of the observer. What is the observer accustomed to or brought up to believe, and what are the culinary traditions in the country they live in? Essentially, people have their own preferences.

Quality varies with the smell, taste, color, harvesting season, and other variables. In addition, the taste, smell, and color of the product will vary with local growing conditions such as salinity, temperature, food access, currents, and suspended sediment. Different culture locations will produce quite different products, which may or may not suit the preferences of a given group of consumers.

The final determination of scallop quality and market suitability is dependent on the person you are asking. Preferences tend to vary. The fish dealer at the market, a gourmet cook, an experienced scallop consumer, and a scallop rookie may not be able to reach a consensus opinion.

What are indications of quality?

Various tests are currently available to objectively determine the quality of seafood products. We hope that in the future we will have available a range of portable instruments that can provide indications of meat quality, animal condition, and yield in the field. An important element in the development of the Norwegian scallop industry is the development of handling protocols. The major goal of these guidelines involves the handling of live product in a manner that produces the smallest increment of stress. As suggested, product quality is linked to stress.

A variety of tests have been proposed to observe the effects of stress. Stress is here defined as an external influence that diminishes the scallop's quality. An understanding of external conditions that promote stress and strategies for the reduction of stress are important to the development of this industry. These field tests include:

1. *Standard stress test.* Different groups of scallops are exposed to air for different periods of time. The test animals are then subdivided into groups and exposed to seawater of different salinities. The mortality in each of these different groups is observed.

2. *Condition index.* The scallop's length, width, thickness, and weight are measured before and after long periods of stress to see if there has been any impact on the growth or energy metabolism.

3. *Behavior.* How long does it take before the scallop starts to behave normally after a period of prolonged stress: Do they filtrate normally? Is their escape response intact? How long does it take before they recess into the sediments?

4. *Biochemistry.* Measurements of carbohydrate and amino acid content from different tissues can indicate if the animals are depleting energy reserves during stress situations.

5. *Physiology.* Observation and analysis of growth patterns, oxygen consumption, and the accumulation of ammonia provide hints about the impact of external forces, including handling, on scallop biology.

6. *Other.* Other observations used to monitor the impact of stress include the visual inspection of the mantle and the smell of the test animals.

Transportation methods

The main goal regarding live transport must be to deliver live scallops in good condition, every time, and without significant product loss. Is this possible?

Dry

Important factors regarding *dry holding* and transport of scallops are:

- *Temperature.* Maintaining the scallops at low temperature generates low metabolism. When scallops are held at lower metabolic states, they require less oxygen.
- *Moisture.* Adding moisture prevents the scallops from dehydrating and keeps the gills moist so that gas exchange can continue to take place.
- *Oxygen.* A high oxygen level in the transport box creates a higher oxygen gradient in the air surrounding the gills and facilitates the transport of oxygen into the scallops. A high oxygen level also helps keep the bacteria count low.
- *Pressure.* Careful placement of scallops in the shipping container places a moderate amount of pressure on the shells, which keeps them closed to help avoid excessive dehydration.

In water

Several important factors must be regarded when scallops are transported *in water*. Here the scallops are held in their natural environment, but in small water systems, even small changes can lead to major water quality imbalances. All the parameters that are listed below are interrelated, to a certain degree:

- *Oxygen.* Maintenance of dissolved oxygen within a specified range is essential to the survival of the animal and, therefore, the aeration or oxygenation of the holding water is necessary.
- *Water temperature.* Maintenance of low holding temperatures induces lower levels of metabolism, slowing the depletion of dissolved oxygen.
- *Carbon dioxide.* Usually seawater serves as a buffer for carbon dioxide produced as a result of respiration. However, in small, closed systems, the accumulation of this waste product can become a problem. One must have available compounds or biofilters that consume the carbon dioxide. Normal pH of seawater is about 8 and drastic fluctuations from this level will have negative effects on the scallops.
- *Ammonia.* This gas is also a waste product. At high concentrations, it becomes toxic and must be removed by a biofilter or other standard means.
- *Water flow.* Maintenance of water flow through the holding system creates homogeneous conditions and, in this way, prevents the development of temperature and oxygen stratification.

- *Induction of spawning.* Scallops can be induced to spawn by a sudden rise in water temperature. This can, in turn, cause oxygen depletion. In addition, spawning activity lowers product quality and the economic value.

PACKING

How can one make things better for the scallops during transport? If the intent is to develop a commercial industry, it will be necessary to optimize the packing methods in a way that takes care of the scallop's biological nature. Satisfactory solutions will have to be found for other commercial issues such as recycling the transport boxes, the preservation of product aesthetics, and close adherence to ethical treatment standards. It is crucial that the scallops, from the moment they are harvested, do not experience any form of rough treatment. Shocks can be caused in various ways and are generally not good for the scallops. Rough handling, for example, will crack shells—opening the affected animals to bacterial infections.

Repacking or reconditioning at intervals along the logistic chain may help dry-transported scallops. Regular reconditioning will supply the scallops with moisture. Dead, badly shaped, or injured scallops can be removed during the course of these inspections. It is also important to develop a system that continuously monitors water quality parameters and alerts those in charge of approaching problems. If possible, this carefully structured distribution chain should proceed unbroken from harvester to consumer.

When the scallops arrive at the retail store, restaurant, or market, it is important that they be stored in the proper manner. Keeping the product alive once it has reached the market is crucial. If the scallops are to be stored in the original transport container, it is crucial to keep them moist, at low temperature, and packed together to slow dehydration. Some establishments store the scallops in aquaria or water tanks. To some, a live product indicates quality and attracts a hungry eye. However, some people do not like to see what they are going to eat while it is still alive.

THINK QUALITY!

How does a harvester "think quality" in order to assure the world that his or her product is of good quality?

- **Quality versus quantity.** Do you want to go for quality or for quantity, or is it possible to combine the two? Often when attention is given to the preservation of quality, quantity suffers and vice versa.
- **Live transport versus processing.** Remember that live products provide an indication of high quality. The customer knows what state the scallop was in before he or she consumed it. The processing of various scallop products will require a higher level of investment, but also frozen or canned products stay fresh much longer.
- **Ethics.** How well do you treat your live scallops? Modern consumers are interested in how the products are produced and treated.
- **Aesthetics.** Here you can use your own creativity to make the live product attractive to the consumer. Arrange the scallops in ways that make the product attractive to the eye. There is a great potential for the development of niche markets, if the product is able to gain the attention of the consumer.
- **Environment.** Environmental issues must also be carefully considered. For example, is your packaging and wrapping material recyclable? Are better alternative packaging methods available?
- **Loss due to mortality and meat yield.** What level of mortality can be accepted? In addition, how can the marketer assure that the product contains an acceptable meat yield?
- **Education and information.** The quality race starts the second the scallops are taken from the sea. People occupying each segment of the marketing chain must have knowledge about the product, from scuba divers to the packers to the consumer. Should the marketer include an information sheet with each shipment about the proper care of scallops with additional tips about how to display and handle the bivalves?

Conclusion

Quality must be experienced with your senses—seeing, tasting, smelling, and touching. Scallops can be transported in different ways depending on where they are going, the quantity involved, and the quality demanded. The ultimate result of perfect live transport is that the Norwegian scallop will gain a quality trademark and establish successful market entry. This is what is needed to allow the industry to survive in Norway and, in addition, to provide valuable employment in coastal areas. Last, but definitely not the least, the marketer must respect that live animals are being dealt with and that special care must be taken.

References

Dore, I. 1984. Fresh seafood: The commercial buyer's guide. Buying, choosing, handling and using fresh fish and shellfish. Osprey Books. 375 pp.

Dore, I. 1991. Shellfish. A guide to oysters, mussels, scallops, clams and similar products for the commercial user. Osprey Books. 240 pp.

Foseide Fagerholt, A. 1999. The shell industry. Market and market entries. From oral presentation. KPMG Consulting, Trondheim, Norway. 30 pp. (In Norwegian)

Maeda-Martinez, A.N., et al. 2000. A shipment method for scallop seed. J. Shellfish Res. 19(December 2000).

Maguire, J.A. 1999. The effect of transportation on the juvenile scallop *Pecten maximus* (L.). Aquac. Res. 30:325-333.

Maguire, J.A. 1999. Some methods of quantifying quality in the scallop *Pecten maximus* (L.). J. Shellfish Res. 18:59-66.

Shumway, S.E. 1991. Scallops: Biology, ecology and aquaculture. Elsevier Science Publishing Company Inc. 1095 pp.

Marketing and Shipping Live Aquatic Products
University of Alaska Sea Grant • AK-SG-01-03, 2001

Handling and Shipping of Live Northeast Pacific Scallops: Larvae to Adults

William A. Heath
British Columbia Ministry of Fisheries, Courtenay, British Columbia, Canada

ABSTRACT

Live scallops from the Pacific Northwest have been successfully shipped as adults, juveniles, and larvae to destinations around the world by air. Juvenile and adult scallops are generally packed and shipped "dry" or exposed under cool, moist conditions since their basal metabolism is greatly lowered at temperatures of 5-8°C. Larvae and small spat can be shipped in oxygenated seawater or dry, under cool and moist conditions in an insulated box. This exposed method can be adapted for the small- and large-scale transport of all stages from spat to mature scallops. Sufficient humidity is provided by layering with seawater-moistened packing (e.g., absorbent paper or a damp, thin sponge) to prevent damage to delicate mantle and gill tissues. If there is not sufficient weight from packing materials to prevent gaping, then additional mechanical pressure should be applied to prevent valve flapping and dehydration.

Specialized handling procedures have been developed for the remote setting of scallop larvae for seed production at ocean nursery sites and for intermediate culture of seed in preparation for final growout and harvest. These methods allow even isolated coastal areas to participate in scallop farming activities and to market their products anywhere in the world that the expanding marketplace demands. Following the basic procedures for live scallop handling and shipping will pay dividends in improved survival and shelf life of the product and in business profitability.

INTRODUCTION

Scallops are highly prized as seafood for their unique flavor and appearance, especially when fresh or live. Scallop culture is expanding to meet this demand for high quality scallop products. This is, in turn, stimulating a growing trade in scallop larvae and juveniles for seed stock (Ito 1991, Walker 1993). Over 50% of world production of scallops results from culture or enhancement (Bourne et al. 1989, FAO 1999). This report reviews recommended practices for handling and shipping live commercial scallops present in the Northeast Pacific Ocean area (California to Alaska).

Although there are 23 species of scallops recorded in the Northeast Pacific Ocean (Bernard 1983), most are small or rare. Only four native species are either large enough or sufficiently abundant to be of commercial interest (Bourne 1988, 1991). These scallop species are

- *Patinopecten caurinus* (weathervane scallop)
- *Chlamys hastata* (spiny scallop)
- *Chlamys rubida* (pink scallop)
- *Crassadoma gigantea* (purple-hinge rock or rock scallop)

In addition, the Japanese weathervane scallop, *Patinopecten (Mizuhopecten) yessoensis*, is a cold water species that was first introduced from Japan to British Columbia in 1983 for its potential use in commercial culture (Bourne et al. 1989).

BACKGROUND ON COMMERCIAL SPECIES AND SCALLOP PRODUCTION IN THE PACIFIC NORTHWEST
Patinopecten caurinus

The weathervane is a large scallop (up to 25 cm; see Fig. 1) that occurs from central California to the northern Gulf of Alaska, westward along the Aleutian Islands, and into the Bering Sea. It lives in depths of 10-200 m, often on sand or mud bottom (Grau 1959, Kaiser 1986). Populations are patchy in distribution and no extensive beds occur throughout its range (Bourne 1991). In areas where commercial fisheries occur, aggregations are sporadic and local (Starr and McCrae 1983, Kaiser 1986).

In Alaska, a commercial fishery for weathervane scallops began in 1967 (Kaiser 1986, Kruse and Shirley 1994), with the catch being shucked at sea. Landings

Figure 1. Weathervane scallops. Those on the left are cultured (about 3 years old); those on the right are wild (more than 10 years old).

and ex-vessel value have varied widely (Fig. 2) as the fishery developed from a sporadic, low-intensity fishery to one prosecuted by a highly specialized fleet of large vessels capable of harvesting with greater efficiency (Shirley and Kruse 1995). Other sources of variability were the effects of exploitation of limited, patchy stocks, changes in market conditions, and the availability of more lucrative fisheries (Shirley and Kruse 1995).

From 1967 until 1991, when the use of mechanical shucking devices was first reported in Alaska scallop fisheries (Griffin and Ward 1992), weathervanes were opened manually at sea for removal of the adductor meats. Automatic shucking machines were introduced to make harvest of smaller scallops more economical, but their use in processing weathervane scallops in Alaska was prohibited in 1993 (Kruse 1994). The rule for manual shucking reduces the economic attractiveness of harvesting smaller scallops and, combined with gear and area restrictions, an observer program, and fishing season limits, will help to improve the sustainability of the Alaska scallop fishery (Shirley and Kruse 1995). The Aquatic Farm Act of 1988, which authorizes the farming of bivalve shellfish in Alaska, may also provide opportunities for farming of the weathervane scallop and other native scallop species in Alaska (RaLonde 1992). The recent development of a shellfish hatchery in Seward provides an available seed supply to Alaska scallop growers.

In British Columbia, there are two local populations of weathervane scallops, one in the southern Gulf Islands area of the Strait of Georgia and the other in Dixon Entrance off the north coast of the Queen Charlotte Islands (Bourne 1991). However, these populations are too small to support a sustained fishery. Current harvest from these areas consists only of incidental catch in other fisheries (Gulf Islands) or periodic beaching (taken by beachcombers from Masset) during ground swell events in McIntyre Bay on Dixon Entrance (R. Wylie, Fishery Committee of Village of Masset Council, B.C., pers. comm.). Hatchery and nursery methods for the weathervane scallop have been developed in British Columbia at Island Scallops Ltd. (Saunders and Heath 1994), but survival and growth of spat and juveniles have been significantly lower than for Japanese scallops. Commercial broodstock maintenance and small-scale growout of weathervane scallops is proceeding.

Chlamys hastata and *Chlamys rubida*

The spiny scallops and pink scallops are relatively small, slow-growing scallops (to 75 mm and 60 mm, respectively; Bourne and Harbo 1987). In British Columbia, they are harvested and sold live from a small dive fishery and trawl fishery (Harbo and Hobbs 1997, Lauzier and Parker 1999; Table 1).

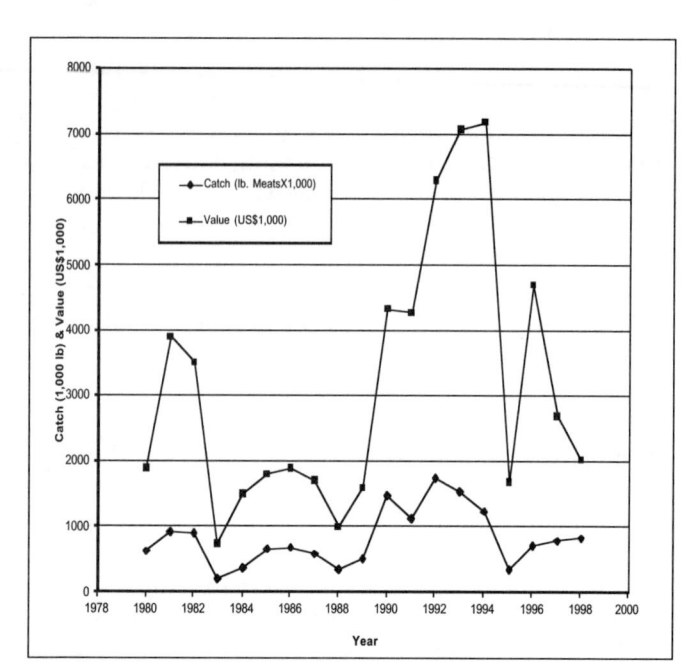

Figure 2. Alaska weathervane scallop fishery production (1980-1998).

Most of the marketed catch consists of dive-caught spiny scallops. The main harvesting areas are among the islands in the southern Strait of Georgia, relatively close to processing plants and local markets. Landings are evenly spaced throughout the year, reflecting the demand for a continuous low supply of fresh scallops (Harbo and Hobbs 1997). Spiny and pink scallops are mainly served as whole, steamed product in restaurants.

In 2000, the fishery was put under scientific license requirements as "data limited" so that it will proceed under a precautionary approach. In Washington, there is a small experimental fishery for spiny scallops (Sizemore and Palensky 1993). Only a few vessels certified by the Washington State Department of Health are permitted to fish in restricted areas. They are subject to weekly marine biotoxin monitoring. The fishery is closed between July 1 and October 1 due to consistently high biotoxin levels present in the scallops during this time.

In Alaska, there was a small fishery for *Chlamys* spp. in the early 1990s (Shirley and Kruse 1995) that used automatic shucking machines on the fishing vessels. RaLonde (1992) noted that large incidental captures of pink and spiny scallop spat by Alaska shellfish farmers has led to attempts to develop a market for whole scallops sold alive.

Crassadoma gigantea

The purple-hinge rock scallop, *Crassadoma gigantea*, is a large scallop (up to 25 cm) that usually cements its right or lower valve to rock surfaces and develops a massive shell (Fig. 3). The shell often becomes irregular during growth, conforming to the contours of the substrate. In natural populations, the shell

Figure 3. Rock scallop *(Crassadoma gigantea).*

is often pitted with holes (from boring sponge, *Cliona* sp.) or encrusted with other plants and animals (Harbo 1997). Rock scallops occur in patchy populations from Mexico to the Aleutian Islands in Alaska (Bernard 1983), from the lowest intertidal (<1 m tide level) to depths of about 80 m. They are often found in areas with strong currents or oceanic surges (Bourne 1991).

There is no commercial fishery for rock scallops due to low abundance and difficulty in harvesting, but they are prized by recreational divers. Growth in wild populations is relatively slow, but rock scallops grown in suspended culture in California reached a shell height of 12 cm in two years (Leighton 1979). Rock scallops grown in northern Strait of Georgia, B.C. reached 9 to 10 cm in three years (MacDonald et al. 1991). The economic feasibility of rock scallop farming along with oysters and without oysters in Washington State was examined by Kelly (1998). Recent research (Culver et al. 2000) has also ad-

Table 1. Production and value of spiny and pink scallop fishery in British Columbia.

Year	No. of vessels reporting Dive	Trawl	metric tons landed Dive	Trawl	Total value $ Can million
1993	9	10	82	8	0.423
1994	17	4	99	5	0.49
1995	14	8	86	10	0.476
1996	12	5	95	7	0.503
1997	13	3	70	3	0.376
1998	6	3	50	4	0.29

Fisheries and Oceans Canada statistics.

dressed the factors controlling the cementing process of *C. gigantea*, with the goal of developing methods for manipulating the attachment process for more economical culture of this intriguing species.

Patinopecten (Mizuhopecten) yessoensis

The Japanese scallop (Fig. 4) is a relatively large (up to 20 cm), cold water species distributed on sandy or gravel bottoms at 10 to 40 m in the coastal areas of northern Japan (Hokkaido and northern Honshu), the south Okhotsk Sea and the Sea of Japan. Known as "hotate-gai" or the "giant ezo-scallop," this species is the subject of a huge fishery and closely related aquaculture industry in Japan (Ventilla 1982, *Yamaha Fisheries Journal* 1990, Ito 1991). The main scallop culture areas in Japan, using natural spat collection methods, are Hokkaido and north Honshu (Aomori Prefecture). Production reached 300,000 t in Japan in 1987 (Ito 1991), valued at over ¥74 billion, making it the most productive and valuable molluscan species in Japan. In 1997, production from the Japanese scallop industry was over 500,000 t (FAO 1999).

In British Columbia, hatchery and nursery culture methods for *P. yessoensis* and the rock scallop were developed in the Canada-B.C. scallop research project conducted at the Pacific Biological Station during 1981-1988 (Bourne et al. 1989). The success of the hatchery program and subsequent commercial culture activity has produced ample cultured broodstock of Japanese scallops, so that broodstock importations into British Columbia are no longer required.

The Japanese scallop has been farmed in British Columbia coastal waters since 1989, when the culture methods developed in the Canada-B.C. scallop project were transferred to industry. Seed production was developed at the Island Scallops Ltd. hatchery at Qualicum Bay, near Nanaimo on eastern Vancouver Island. A total of six farm sites were established in the north Strait of Georgia and Baynes Sound areas and in Clayoquot Sound on the west coast of Vancouver Island (Walker 1993).

Oceanographic conditions conducive to the farming of the Japanese scallop in British Columbia (Cross and Kingzett 1992, Cross 1994) are productive waters with cool temperatures (8-16°C) and relatively high, stable salinity (>28 ppt). Cross (1994) observed reduced growth above 12.5°C and increased mortalities above 16°C.

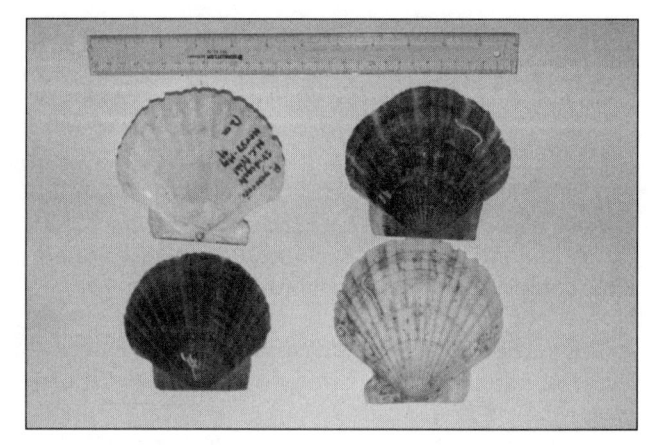

Figure 4. Japanese scallop *(Patinopecten yessoensis)*, 2 years old in culture.

Minimal motion of the culture apparatus is another important condition. If a site doesn't provide natural (geographic) protection from significant wave action and horizontal currents, anchoring and subsurface longline systems that are properly installed and maintained may mitigate these factors (Ventilla 1982, Heath and Gubbels 1993, Cross 1994).

In response to disease problems in growout at some farm sites (Bower and Meyer 1994), culturists have used strategies such as selective breeding for resistance to a protozoan parasite, *Perkinsus qugwadi* (Blackbourn et al. 1998, Bower et al. 1998) and developing viable hybrids with the weathervane scallop, *Patinopecten caurinus* (Saunders and Heath 1994, Bower et al. 1999).

In the new British Columbia industry, growout methods were initially modeled on techniques developed in Japan (Ventilla 1982, *Yamaha Fisheries Journal* 1990, Ito 1991), but have been considerably modified to adjust to faster growing conditions in the province and the challenges of disease and flatworm (*Pseudostylochus ostreophagus*) predation on scallop seed (e.g., Saunders and Heath 1994). Hatchery-produced larvae can be either set and nursery-reared at the hatchery (Island Scallops Ltd.) or transferred to an ocean nursery site for remote setting and ocean-based rearing. Techniques for handling larvae, spat, and juveniles during culture operations are described later.

Farmed scallop production has developed slowly in recent years, (Fig. 5) with a relatively small number of sites. However, this sector and the rest of the British Columbia shellfish industry appears to be poised for rapid expansion under the recently implemented provincial Shellfish Development Initiative of the British Columbia Assets and Lands Corporation and British Columbia Fisheries. This program is providing a new process for expansion of existing farms and for acceptance of applications for new sites (Osborne 2000). Its goal is to double the area (from 2,115 ha to 4,230 ha) for shellfish tenuring (or "leasing") within the next ten years.

RECOMMENDED HANDLING PRACTICES FOR LIVE MATURE SCALLOPS
Sanitary regulations and practices

There are regulations for sanitary control of bivalve shellfish harvesting, processing, and distribution under the U.S.-based National Shellfish Sanitation Program (NSSP 1993) and the related Canadian Shellfish Sanitation Program (CSSP 1996). An excellent information manual on quality assurance for shellfish producers is also available from the British Columbia Ministry of Agriculture, Fisheries and Food (Kingzett and Pirquet 1995).

Maintaining the quality of live scallops, as for other live mollusks (Kingzett and Pirquet 1995, Heath 1997), involves using common sense in managing several key factors that include the prevention of:

- Physical damage, including the avoidance of shell breakage during sorting or harvesting and subsequent handling.
- Excessive physiological stress from extremes of heat or cold, fluctuations of salinity when immersed, or exposure to desiccating agents, such as direct sunlight, wind, or prolonged air exposure at low humidity.
- Exposure to sources of contamination, such as petroleum products or other poisonous chemicals, microbial agents such as human or animal wastes, or polluted water.

The best approach is to maintain cleanliness and protection from all real or potential contamination sources.

Specific practices for harvesting live mature scallops

In general, scallops, as subtidal animals, are much more sensitive to harvest-induced stress than intertidal bivalves, such as clams or oysters. This is due to

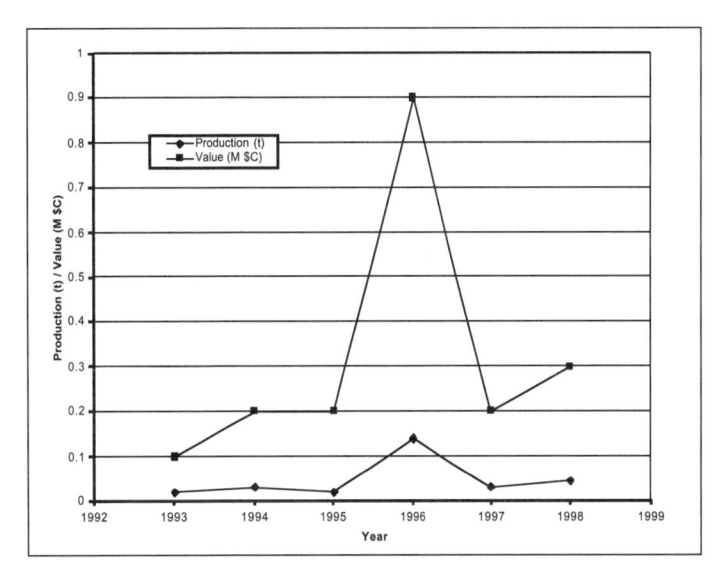

Figure 5. Farmed Japanese scallop production (t) and landed or farmgate value (Can$ millions) in British Columbia, 1993-1998. British Columbia Ministry of Fisheries statistics.

the fact that swimming scallops (weather-vane, spiny, pink, and Japanese) often have fragile shells, especially at the margins, that are prone to breakage or chipping if handled roughly. Chipping impairs the scallop's ability to retain moisture and hastens gaping. Shelf life and marketability decline sharply with breakage, so damaged product is unsuitable for live shipping.

Most scallops are prone to gaping when out of water for more than a few minutes. Once they begin to gape, the mantle and gill tissues will dry out quickly (resulting in risk of mortalities), especially if exposed to sunlight, wind, or other desiccating agents Direct sunlight on scallops will heat the shells, causing the adductor muscle to separate from the shell. This may not be immediately evident, but may show up in elevated post-harvest mortalities a few days later (Kingzett and Pirquet 1995).

Harvesting live spiny and pink scallops

The preferred method for the handling of dive-caught spiny and pink scallops (T. Harper, pers. comm.) is as follows:

- Hand-picked scallops are placed by the diver in a net bag for holding and transfer to support vessel.
- Landed scallops are placed in a live tank with flowing seawater until fishing ceases in the approved waters.

- At the dock, scallops are removed from live tank and placed in covered plastic totes for direct transport to processing plant.
- At the plant, rotary brush cleaning of fouling organisms (e.g., encrusting sponges) is performed if necessary.
- Scallops are returned to flowing chilled seawater prior to packaging for shipping to customers (see general method for scallop live shipping, below).

Harvest procedures for farmed Japanese scallops

The recommended method for harvesting farmed Japanese scallops (12-14 cm after 2 years growout; S. Scrase, Pacific Aqua Products Inc., Courtenay, B.C., pers. comm.) is as follows:

- Nets of scallops on sub-surface longlines are raised to the surface by crew on work vessel.
- Scallops are removed from nets (e.g., pearl or lantern nets), shaken into a plastic tote and with lid on, queued for cleaning and sorting.
- Culling is done if necessary to ensure that scallops for live marketing are free of major deformities of the shell margin ("conchiolin," "biting," or distorted shells; Ventilla 1982) caused by overcrowding or other environmental stress during growout.
- Biofouling organisms (barnacles, mussels, sea anemones, tube worms, etc.) are kept at a minimum so as not to detract from appearance or shelf life of the product. Manual or mechanical removal of biofouling are both viable options, but care in use of high-pressure spray is needed to prevent injury to scallops (i.e., spraying only on top or bottom surfaces, not at shell opening).
- Scallops are washed reasonably clean of sediment, detritus, or biofouling remains as soon after harvesting as feasible by vigorous rinsing or spraying. Water used in washing product must be potable (safe for drinking) or from a harvest or growing area that is classified as Approved under NSSP (state Health Department) or CSSP (Environment Canada).

If the harvest period is prolonged (several hours or more), product can be safely held in a shower system (Kingzett and Pirquet 1995) or a live holding tank (e.g., large tote with flowing seawater, Fig. 6). DO NOT wash or hold product in a harbor or other polluted area or in containers of stagnant water.

When harvest is completed, the scallops are packed into plastic tubs with lids (e.g., Rubbermaid Roughneck™, 30 L volume) for transport to the processing plant. To maintain cool conditions, the use of refrigerated trucks is best, but the use of ice on top of the totes is an effective substitute for transport in a covered, non-refrigerated truck (S. Scrase, Pacific Aqua Products Inc., pers. comm.).

SCALLOP PACKAGING AND SHIPPING

Juvenile and adult scallops are suitable for extended live shipment in insulated containers without the addition of seawater. Survival and quality are maintained if metabolic rates and other processes are depressed by cool, humid conditions. Below 8°C, Japanese scallop respiration has been found to drop sharply, therefore lowering basal metabolism (Ventilla 1982). High humidity from seawater-moistened packing materials and the application of gentle mechanical pressure on the scallops will prevent desiccation of delicate mantle and gill tissues and lessen incidence of valve flapping that can cause damage to mantle tissue. Effective transport methods for scallops will take advantage of these factors (Ventilla 1982, Overaa 2001).

General method for shipping live juvenile and adult scallops in small lots

For air cargo or other shipments of scallops that cannot be serviced economically by refrigerated ("freezer") truck or bulk freight container, the following method works well for juvenile and mature scallops:

- The most common insulated containers are styrene or Styrofoam boxes with cardboard sleeves or outer boxes, with frozen gel packs for cooling. However, other well-insulated containers (e.g., Coleman™ coolers) will serve well, but are generally more expensive.
- The frozen gel packs are placed at the bottom of the container and insulated from the scallops with a layer of packing dampened with seawater (e.g., paper toweling, thin sponge, or clean Pamper™-style diaper for newborns).
- The scallops (spat or juveniles in net bags) are positioned over the covered gel packs and are covered with another layer of damp packing material. To track temperature changes, a maximum-minimum thermometer or disposable temperature logger can be placed among the scallops. Additional gel pack(s) can be placed on top of the contents for longer trips.

Figure 6. Wet tank for onboard holding of scallops.

- The lid is placed on the container and taped securely shut. It is important to put some mechanical pressure on the scallops to prevent gaping and dehydration. If Styrofoam is used, the box is then placed in its cardboard housing.

- The container is labeled clearly for shipment, including contact telephone numbers for sender and receiver.

Transport of scallop seed

Development of scallop farming enterprises in the Pacific Northwest area, as in some areas of Japan, is dependent on reliable and cost-effective access to scallop seed from hatchery (Pacific Northwest) or nursery (Japan) sources (Ventilla 1982, Ito 1991, Walker 1993). Two approaches to large-scale seed transport have been widely used in Japan for spat and juvenile scallops (Ventilla 1982).

1. The "oxygen" or "wet" method.
2. The "exposure" or "dry" method.

A slightly modified version of Ventilla's Table II (see original document) on spat and seed transport methods is reproduced here (Table 2).

The method above is an example of the "exposure" method, adapted for smaller, unrefrigerated shipments, including air cargo. Note that spat (>1 mm) or juveniles (3-9 mm) are usually placed in fine mesh or screen bags (e.g., pearl nets) for shipment by the "exposure" or "dry" method. This step controls densities and greatly increases efficiency in transferring the seed into seawater at the destination.

The general method with Styrofoam box containers was used (Heath and Dobie 2000, in press) to move juvenile *P. yessoensis* (3-8 mm size) from Island Scallops Ltd. hatchery on Vancouver Island to Prince Rupert and the Queen Charlotte Islands on British Columbia's north coast (9 h duration) for experimental growout trials. Survival was above 75% even though the multiple step transfer was done during hot summer weather in early July.

Transport of scallop larvae
Wet oxygen method

Competent or ready-to-set scallop larvae (260-280 µm size) for remote setting applications and small spat (0.3-1.0 mm) for nursery rearing can be successfully transported by the "wet" method with oxygenation. A convenient variation of the "oxygen" method of Ventilla (1982) is as follows (S. Scrase, Pacific Aqua Products Inc., pers. comm.).

- Equipment: one liter plastic pop bottles with optional air filler valve on screw caps, insulated plastic drink cooler with gel pack in lid, and an oxygen tank with regulator.

- Seawater chilled to 7-8°C, saturated with oxygen and containing 15 million larvae per liter is put in a bottle, capped, and injected with oxygen until bottle surface is taut (about 5 psi).

- Bottle is placed in drink cooler with frozen gel pack installed in lid.

- Container is shipped to destination, preferably as "carry-on" baggage if by air travel. If the trip is prolonged, every 2 hours, the bottles of larvae are gently rolled to resuspend settled larvae. Trip durations of over 20 hours can be accommodated using this method.

Dry method

A "dry" method for shipping scallop larvae and small spat (size ranges same as above) is also available and is similar to the method used for shipping eyed-larvae of oysters and other bivalve larvae (e.g., Donaldson 1991). The general procedure for preparing, packaging and shipping of bivalve larvae, including scallops, is given below.

- Larvae are collected by draining from culture tank with a siphon onto a screen (minimum 260 µm for competent Japanese scallop larvae) in a water bath to relieve stress from pressure.

Table 2. Spat and seed transport methods for *Patinopecten yessoensis*.

Stage	Transport method	Description of method	Shell size (mm)	Period of year (in Japan)	Duration of trip (h)	Survival rate (%)	Remarks
Spat	Oxygen method	Spat in polyethylene bag with oxygenated SW. Transport by freezer truck (2-5°C).	0.8-1.5	Up to Sept.	20	90	The smaller the spat the better. 2,000-4,000/bag with bags stacked in two layers. O_2 put into bag until it swells, then bag is sealed.
Spat	Exposure method	Spat put into pearl net or fish box and transport by freezer truck (2-5°C).	2-5	Nov.-Apr.	20-30	80-90	1,000-2,000 spat/box. Pack the spat in the evening and move at night. Pack fast and transfer fast. Cover in sacking soaked in SW to prevent "biting."
Juvenile to half-grown	Exposure method	Seed in pearl nets or fish boxes and transport by freezer truck (6-8°C).	5-9	Nov.-Mar.	20-40	80-90	Use wet sacking to prevent drying out and "biting." All handling to be done during cool periods.

After Ventlla 1982; SW=seawater.

- The larvae are then graded through a series of screens by vigorous washing with seawater from a hose.
- Once separated by size, the larvae are bundled in a setting group on a piece of screening material, blotted with paper towel to remove excess water, and weighed for a count of the larvae (by weight to number conversion for given size).
- When a sufficient number of larvae are grouped for the shipment, they can be wrapped (on piece of screen) in a seawater-dampened paper towel and put in a plastic bag.
- The bags of larvae are placed into an insulated box (e.g., small Styrofoam cooler) containing a frozen gel pack. The gel pack is insulated with paper packing so larvae bundle does not come in direct contact with gel ice.
- To track temperature changes, a maximum-minimum thermometer or disposable temperature logger can be placed near the bundle of larvae. Temperature should remain in range of 5-8°C. Additional gel packs can be placed on top of the contents for longer trips. Transport time should be within 24 hours for best larvae setting success.
- The lid is placed on the container and taped securely shut. The container is clearly labeled for shipment, including contact telephone numbers for sender and receiver.

SPECIAL PROCEDURES FOR HANDLING SCALLOP LARVAE AND SEED IN CULTURE
Larval and spat handling procedures in remote setting

Scallop remote setting is based on the observation that, after transport to a "remote" site (e.g., farm or nursery), a reasonably high percentage of scallop larvae (20-30%) can successfully metamorphose or "set" in collector units in natural seawater and survive to be viable juveniles (S. Scrase, Pacific Aqua Products Inc., pers. comm.). This process has many similarities to remote setting of Pacific oysters (Jones and Jones 1988, Roland and Broadley 1991), but with some notable differences. For example, scallop setting can be done in ocean waters at ambient temperature instead of in heated tanks of seawater, as in standard oyster remote setting.

Scallop setting is usually done in spring (April to June) in the Pacific Northwest as follows:

- At the shipping destination (e.g., remote setting site) the larvae are resuspended in a clean plastic bucket (10 to 20 L) of seawater from the site to acclimate them to ambient temperature.
- A floating remote scallop setting facility or enclosure (Fig. 7) simply consists of a rectangular perimeter float (5 m × 6 m) with a plastic tarpaulin suspended inside it to enclose a volume of ocean water. Inside the enclosure is an aeration system, which is simply an array of PVC tubing with small holes at regular intervals, connected to a compressed air supply. Also placed inside are hundreds of spat collectors, usually made of fine-meshed (2-3 mm) Japanese onion bags stuffed with Netlon, a synthetic mesh material with "memory" or old monofilament fish netting (original method attributed to Toyosaku, in Ventilla 1982).
- The amount of larvae added to the setting pond is adjusted to achieve an optimum spat density target of about 1,500 spat per collector (Ventilla 1982), based on the anticipated setting rate (e.g., 30%). For example, if 500 collector bags are used in a set at 30% settlement, then about 2.2 million larvae are added to the pond. Aeration is applied to distribute the larvae evenly throughout the volume for an even set in the collectors.
- After three to four days in the setting pond, when the larvae have had ample opportunity to swim into the collectors, set, and attach to the Netlon, the collector bags are moved during cool conditions (morning or evening) to the nursery longline. In this system, the collector bags are attached on droplines (10-15 nets per line) at intervals of about

Figure 7. Remote setting enclosure at scallop farm site.

Figure 8. Seed is placed in pearl net for growout or holding.

0.7 m for deployment below the thermocline and/or halocline (about 10-15 m) (Ventilla 1982).

Intermediate culture considerations

"Intermediate culture" or rearing of scallops, using the Japanese method (Ventilla 1982, Ito 1991), refers to the rearing stage involving pyramid-shaped pearl nets (35 cm × 35 cm, Fig. 8) following nursery rearing in seed collector bags. The last phase, final growout, can be done in many ways (e.g., cylindrical or "lantern" nets, larger mesh pearl nets, ear-hanging, or bottom sowing, among others).

In general, for best growth and survival of scallops, it is better to handle them as little as possible without jeopardizing them to predators, excessive fouling, or overcrowding. Conditions will vary from site to site with respect to growth rate and timing and severity of settlement of biofouling organisms (e.g., barnacles, mussels, tube worms) and predators (e.g., starfish, crabs, flatworms). Careful monitoring of the site and scallop stock will provide guidance on the appropriate timing of sorting and handling steps. Schedules developed for culture in Japan can only be used as general guides because growth rates and biotic communities are often quite different in the Pacific Northwest (Walker 1993).

Handling procedures for scallop seed during intermediate culture

A flow chart illustrating the handling steps for Japanese scallop culture in British Columbia is given in Fig. 9. Thinning or sorting is needed to reduce the culture density as the animals grow in order to control stress and minimize "biting" or conchiolin. The timing of sorting is usually determined by the scallop size. However, settlement of predators such as the bivalve-eating flatworm, *Pseudostylochus ostreophagus* (Quayle 1988), requires immediate attention to prevent heavy mortalities of seed in collector bags (S. Scrase, Pacific Aqua Products Inc., pers. comm.). Fortunately, the timely transfer of the seed to clean pearl nets is highly effective in controlling predation by juvenile flatworms.

The recommended procedure for handling scallop seed during sorting operations involves working quickly to minimize the time that seed is exposed—taking special care to avoid direct sunlight and wind exposure. The sequence for the first sort of seed from collectors is as follows.

- The subsurface longline with collector bags is brought to the surface, preferably during a cool period with high salinity (>26 ppt) present in surface waters. Check the salinity with a refractometer or salinometer.

- Collector bags are removed from droplines and moved to shaded area. The use of tarpaulin curtains around the sorting area works well in sunny weather. The contents of the collector bags are shaken and removed into sorting boxes positioned in a bench-height tank with flowing seawater. The scallop seed are generally still attached to the Netlon netting from the collector bag (Fig. 10) and, consequently, must be shaken off into the box where they collect on the screen at the bottom.

- When enough seed are removed from collectors, the box is lifted out of the tank and examined for unwanted items (e.g., predators) and treated accordingly.

- Clean seed is scooped with a suitable volumetric scoop (i.e., seed count is based on count per volume conversion for given seed size) and placed in pearl nets (Fig. 11) at the desired density (e.g., 60-80 seed per net for 1-2 mm seed).

- When a dropline of 15 nets (tied together in linear fashion) is loaded, it is tied onto the longline and deployed in the ocean.

The next sort (at a size of about 3 mm) is performed to reduce stocking densities (to 10 scallops per net) and to provide clean pearl nets with larger mesh for improved water flow. At this time, the growing scallops are also sorted for uniformity (similar sized seed grown together to reduce biting). The scallops

LAND OR OCEAN NURSERY
3-4 months
0.3 mm seed attached to netting in fine mesh bags

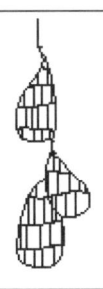

FIRST SORT
Seed removed from bags and sorted by size into pearl nets at 60-80 per net

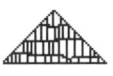

0.6-1.0 mm   1.0-1.6 mm   >1.6 mm

INTERMEDIATE GROWOUT AT FARM SITE ON LONGLINES
3-5 months

SUSPENDED GROWOUT
SECOND SORT
Seed sorted at 3 cm into pearl nets at 10 per net & 15 nets per drop or into lantern nets at 10 per layer

12-14 months

HARVEST
10-14 cm

Total: 19-24 mo.

Figure 9. Flow chart of phases in B.C. culture of Japanese scallops. Time from spawning to final harvest of 10-14 cm live scallops ranges from 19 to 24 months, depending on method and growing conditions

are then deployed for the final growout stage (up to 12-14 months if large scallops [12-14 cm] are to be grown; S. Scrase, Pacific Aqua Products Inc., pers. comm.). Large live Japanese scallops (12-14 cm) from British Columbia currently sell for about US $1.00 each at farmgate or landed value (Fig. 12).

PAPERWORK FOR INTERNATIONAL SHIPMENTS OF LIVE SCALLOPS

Timely arrival at international destinations with a perishable product often involves making several shipping connections and obtaining customs approval at the other end. When live scallops are to be shipped across national borders, make sure that you are aware of relevant trade and customs regulations. Do not assume anything! Some airport personnel are not well informed with proper handling and processing of live shellfish shipments. Difficulties with regulations may cause your scallops to be placed in unprotected or uncontrolled storage, or subject to temperature abuse. It is essential to arrange for the live shipment to be met at its destination by a competent representative to avoid this type of problem. It may be well worthwhile to use professional specialists, such as customs brokers, to prepare shipping documents that will satisfy all trade and health requirements at the foreign destination.

Figure 10. Seed on collector insert is shaken off into seed sorting boxes on vessel.

Figure 11. Seed is placed in pearl net for growout, holding, or transfer.

Figure 12. Two-year-old *P. yessoensis* shucked open to check meat condition.

Acknowledgments

The author thanks the following people for assistance in providing information on certain scallop handling techniques: Tom Harper of Unique Seafarms Ltd.; Rob Saunders and Barb Bunting of Island Scallops Ltd.; and Stephen Scrase of Pacific Aqua Products Inc.

References

Bernard, F.R. 1983. Catalogue of the living Bivalvia of the eastern Pacific Ocean: Bering Strait to Cape Horn. Can. Spec. Publ. Fish. Aquat. Sci. 61. 102 pp.

Blackbourn, J., S.M. Bower, and G.R. Meyer. 1998. *Perkinsus qugwadi* sp. nov. (incertae sedis), a pathogenic protozoan parasite of Japanese scallops, *Patinopecten yessoensis*, cultured in British Columbia, Canada. Can. J. Zool. 76:942-953.

Bourne, N. 1988. Scallop culture in British Columbia. In: S. Keller (ed.), Proceedings of the Fourth Alaska Aquaculture Conference. University of Alaska Sea Grant, AK-SG-88-04, Fairbanks, pp. 35-41.

Bourne, N. 1991. Fisheries and aquaculture: West coast of North America. In: S.E. Shumway (ed.), Scallops: Biology, ecology and aquaculture. Elsevier, Amsterdam, pp. 925-942.

Bourne, N.F., and R. Harbo. 1987. Size limits for pink and spiny scallops. In: Status of invertebrate fisheries off the Pacific coast of Canada (1985/86). Can. Tech. Rep. Fish. Aquat. Sci. 1576:113-122.

Bourne, N., C.A. Hodgson, and J.N.C. Whyte. 1989. A manual for scallop culture in British Columbia. Can. Tech. Rep. Fish. Aquat. Sci. 1694. 215 pp.

Bower, S.M., and G.R. Meyer. 1994. Causes of mortalities among cultured Japanese scallops, *Patinopecten yessoensis*, in British Columbia, Canada. In: N.F. Bourne, B.L. Bunting, and L.D. Townsend (eds.), Proceedings of the 9th International Pectinid Workshop, Nanaimo, B.C., Canada, April 22-27, 1993. Can. Tech. Rep. Fish. Aquat. Sci. 1994(1):85-94.

Bower, S.M, J. Blackbourn, and G.R. Meyer. 1998. Distribution, prevalence, and pathogenicity of the protozoan *Perkinsus qugwadi* in Japanese scallops, *Patinopecten yessoensis*, cultured in British Columbia, Canada. Canadian Journal of Zoology 76:954-959.

Bower, S.M., J. Blackbourn, G.R. Meyer, and D.W. Welch. 1999. Effect of *Perkinsus qugwadi* on various species and strains of scallops. Dis. Aquat. Org. 36:143-151.

Cross, S.F. 1994. Oceanographic conditions conducive to culture of the Japanese scallop, *Patinopecten yessoensis*, in British Columbia, Canada. In: Bourne, N.F., B.L. Bunting, and L.D. Townsend (eds.), Proceedings of the 9th International Pectinid Workshop, Nanaimo, B.C., Canada, April 22-27, 1993. Can. Tech. Rep. Fish. Aquat. Sci. 1994(2):9-14.

Cross, S.F., and B.C. Kingzett. 1992. Biophysical criteria for shellfish culture in British Columbia. British Columbia Ministry of Agriculture, Fisheries and Food, ISBN 0-7718-9332-9. 40 pp.

CSSP. 1995. Canadian Shellfish Sanitation Program: Manual of operations. Fisheries and Oceans Canada and Environment Canada, Ottawa.

Culver, C.S., J.B. Richards, and H.M. Page. 2000. Manipulation of the cementing process of the purple-hinge rock scallop, *Crassadoma gigantea*. Presentation at National Shellfisheries Association, Seattle, WA, March 19-23, 2000.

Donaldson, J. 1991. Setting procedures: Ordering, shipping, and handling larvae: View from the hatchery. In: T.Y. Nosho and K.K. Chew (eds.), Remote setting and nursery culture for shellfish growers: Workshop record. University of Washington Sea Grant Program, WSG-WO 91-02, Seattle, pp. 7-10.

FAO. 1999. FAO-STAT database: http://apps.fao.org/. Food and Agricultural Organization, Rome.

Grau, G. 1959. Pectinidae of the eastern Pacific. Univ. South. Calif. Publ. Alan Hancock Found. Pac. Series. 23. 208 pp.

Griffin, K.L., and M.L. Ward. 1992. Annual management report for the shellfish fisheries of the Eastern Aleutians area, 1991. In: Annual management report for the shellfish fisheries of the Westward Region, 1991. Alaska Dept. Fish and Game, Comm. Fish. Div., Reg. Inf. Rep. 4K92-9. Kodiak, pp. 109-126.

Harbo, R.M. 1997. Shells and shellfish of the Pacific Northwest. Harbour Publishing, Madiera Park, B.C. 270 pp.

Harbo, R., and K. Hobbs. 1997. Scallop dive and trawl fisheries. In: R.M. Harbo and K. Hobbs (eds.), Pacific commercial fishery updates for invertebrate resources (1994). Can. Manuscr. Rep. Fish. Aquat. Sci. 2369:37-43.

Heath, W.A. 1997. From harvest to market: Maintaining the quality and value of live Manila clams (*Tapes philippinarum*) In: B. Paust and J. Peters (eds.), Marketing and shipping live aquatic products. Northeast Regional Agricultural Engineering Service, NRAES-107, Ithaca. NY, pp. 180-185.

Heath, W.A., and S. Dobie. 2000. Shellfish production on British Columbia's North Coast: An industry in transition. Bull. Aquacul. Assoc. Canada 100(2):14-22.

Heath, W.A., and P.M. Gubbels. 1993. Estimated costs and returns for a scallop grow-out enterprise. British Columbia Ministry of Agriculture, Fisheries and Food, Aquaculture Industry Report 93-07. 24 pp.

Ito, H. 1991. Fisheries and aquaculture: Japan. In: S.E. Shumway (ed.), Scallops: Biology, ecology and aquaculture. Elsevier, Amsterdam, pp. 1017-1055.

Jones, G., and B. Jones. 1988. Advances in the remote setting of oyster larvae. British Columbia Ministry of Agriculture and Fisheries, ISBN 0-7718-8627-6, Victoria. 88 pp.

Kaiser, R.J. 1986. Characteristics of the Pacific weathervane scallop (*Pecten [Patinopecten] caurinus*, Gould 1850) fishery in Alaska, 1967-1981. Alaska Dept. Fish and Game, Comm. Fish. Div., Unpublished Report Cat. RUR-5J86-01.

Kelly, E.M. 1998. Determining economic feasibility of rock scallop *(Crassadoma gigantea)* aquaculture in Washington State. Presented at the Scallop Culture Symposium at Aquaculture '98, Las Vegas, World Aquaculture Society, Abstract.

Kingzett, B.C., and K.T. Pirquet. 1995. Towards quality assurance: An information manual for BC shellfish growers. British Columbia Ministry of Agriculture, Fisheries and Food, Aquaculture and Commercial Fisheries Branch. 89 pp.

Kruse, G.H. 1994. Fishery management plan for commercial scallop fisheries in Alaska. Alaska Dept. Fish and Game, Comm. Fish. Manage. Dev. Div., Draft Special Publication 5, Juneau.

Kruse, G.H., and S.M. Shirley. 1994. The Alaska scallop fishery and its management. In: N.F. Bourne, B.L. Bunting, and L.D. Townsend (eds.), Proceedings of the 9th International Pectinid Workshop, Nanaimo, B.C., Canada, April 22-27, 1993. Can. Tech. Rep. Fish. Aquat. Sci. 1994(2):170-175.

Lauzier, R.B., and G. Parker. 1999. A review of the biology and fisheries of the pink and spiny scallop. Canadian Stock Assessement Secretariat Research Document 99/153. 4pp.

Leighton, D.L. 1979. A growth profile for the rock scallop *Hinnites multirugosus* held at several depths off La Jolla, California. Mar. Biol. 51:229-232.

MacDonald, B.A., R.J. Thompson, and N.F. Bourne. 1991. Growth and reproductive energetics of three scallop species from British Columbia *(Chlamys hastata, Chlamys rubida,* and *Crassadoma gigantea)*. Can. J. Fish. Aquat. Sci. 48:215-221.

NSSP. 1993. National Shellfish Sanitation Program manual of operations. Part I, Sanitation of shellfish growing areas. Part II, Sanitation of the harvesting, processing and distribution of shellfish, 1993 revision. U.S. Food and Drug Administration, Center for Food Safety and Applied Nutrition, Office of Seafood, Washington, DC 20204.

Osborne, J. 2000. A new approach to shellfish aquaculture development in British Columbia: The Clayoquot Sound and Barkley Sound shellfish aquaculture steering committees. Bull. Aquacul. Assoc. Canada 100 (2):23-29.

Overaa, T. 2001. Live transport of the great scallop *(Pecten maximus)*. In: B.C. Paust and A.A. Rice (eds.), Marketing and shipping live aquatic products: Proceedings of the Second International Conference and Exhibition, November 1999, Seattle, WA. University of Alaska Sea Grant, AK-SG-01-03, Fairbanks. (This volume.)

Quayle, D.B. 1988. Pacific oyster culture in British Columbia. Can. Bull. Fish. Aquat. Sci. 218. 214 pp.

RaLonde, R. 1992. Shellfish aquaculture in Alaska: Its promise and constraints. In: Growing shellfish in Alaska. University of Alaska Marine Advisory Program, Anchorage. Alaska's Marine Resources 7(4):2-5.

Roland, W. and T.A. Broadley. 1990. A manual for producing oyster seed by remote setting. British Columbia, Ministry of Agriculture, Fisheries and Food, Aquaculture and Commercial Fisheries Branch, ISBN 0-7718-8918-6. 58 pp.

Saunders, R.G., and W.A. Heath. 1994. Recent developments in scallop farming in British Columbia. Bull. Aquacul. Assoc. Canada 94(3):3-7.

Shirley, S.M., and G.H. Kruse. 1995. Development of the fishery for weathervane scallops, *Patinopecten caurinus* (Gould, 1850), in Alaska. J. Shellfish Res. 14:71-78.

Sizemore, R.E., and L.Y. Palensky. 1993. Fisheries management implications of new growth and longevity data for pink *(Chlamys rubida)* and spiny scallops *(C. hastata)* from Puget Sound, Washington. J. Shellfish Res. 12:145-146.

Starr, R.M., and J.E. McCrae. 1983. Weathervane scallop *(Patinopecten caurinus)* investigations in Oregon, 1981-1983. Oregon Dept. Fish Wildlife Info. Rep. 83-10. 55 pp.

Stocker, M., and I. Perry (eds.). 2000. Report of the PSARC Invertebrate Subcommittee Meeting, Nov. 28-29, 2000. In: Canadian Stock Assessement Secretariat Proceedings Series 2000-26. 16 pp.

Ventilla, R.F. 1982. The scallop industry in Japan. Adv. Mar. Biol. 20:309-345.

Walker, T.A. 1993. Island scallops: Farming the Japanese scallop in British Columbia. Aquaculture Magazine, May/June, pp. 38-49.

Yamaha Fishery Journal. 1990. Scallop aquaculture: Solving the mystery of good and poor harvests. Yamaha Fishery Journal 34. 8 pp.

The Harvest and Culture of Live Freshwater Aquatic Invertebrates

Barry Thoele
Live Aquatics, Staples, Minnesota

INTRODUCTION

Freshwater aquatic invertebrates have been harvested or cultured in one form or another for decades. They have been used by small-scale fishing bait operations and cultivated and dried as additives to commercial fish food. More important, they are used by nature as food for a wide range of species from ducks to salamanders and fish. Aquatic invertebrates supply all the necessary essential vitamins and nutrients in forms that are readily digestible. It is interesting to note that some of these nutrients may be responsible for reduced mortalities as shown in studies done in Canada of the invertebrate *Gammarus lacustris* used as a supplement and as a main diet for rainbow trout.

The lakes throughout Minnesota have an abundance of invertebrates. Indeed, it is a common joke here that the mosquito is our state bird. By far the most popular species for commercial harvest and culture are the amphipods *Gammarus lacustris* and *Hyalella azteca*. In terms of culturing or farming these small shrimp-like animals, it has been my experience that nature has already created the best means of culture. Thus, my business goal has been to duplicate nature on a scale that would balance itself out when completely established or, at least, require only minimal manipulation on my part. Keep in mind that, although I have spent over ten years in the field studying the nature of these and other organisms, this study was accomplished with little laboratory work and with no access to sophisticated equipment other than a microscope and magnifying glass.

This extensive field study has persuaded me to develop a commercial venture involving the culture and harvesting of freshwater invertebrates. As pioneer harvesters of what may be a newly exploited resource, those involved need to understand the place and function of each of these species in a balanced ecosystem. For the purpose of this paper I will first identify the invertebrates and then move to harvest methods. Finally, I will discuss culturing and marketing possibilities.

SPECIES AND GROUPS UNDER CONSIDERATION

Crustaceans

    Amphipods

        Gammarus lacustris

        Hyalella azteca

    Branchiopods

        Daphnia magna

        Daphnia pulex

        Cladocera

    Copepods

        Cyclops

Insects (immature stages)

    Chaoborus americanus ("glassworms")

    Chironomids ("bloodworms")

Aquatic invertebrates are the foundation of the entire aquatic food chain. In some cases, invertebrates are responsible for the stable flow of plant food energy to the higher animal levels and thus provide a vital link that stabilizes the energy flow in active and healthy aquatic ecosystems. For example, by feeding on plankton (primarily photosynthetic algae), *Daphnia* populations are able to alter various water quality levels produced by photosynthesis and, in turn, provide a control to the population of algae, other plankters, and possibly vertebrates present in the system.

Gammarus are commonly considered to be grazers feeding on the plants, and, to some extent, on the phytoplankton. These important freshwater invertebrates also feed on bacteria and decomposing matter on the lake bottom and are, in turn, eaten by other aquatic invertebrates and vertebrates, including fish.

Chaoborus ("glassworms") are also predators of invertebrate populations, including *Daphnia* and copepods, and may be considered part of the planktonic community. They are, in turn, consumed at all stages of their development by higher invertebrates and vertebrates including, to a very large extent, fish. In our freshly dug ponds, *Chaoborus* was the first species to show up in the pond, even before there was food for them to eat.

Chironomids, on the other hand, are water filtering invertebrates that eat anything small enough to get caught in their web. This feeding apparatus is capable of straining bacteria and the smallest of invertebrates.

Each of these species, with the exception of *Daphnia* and the copepods, if given the opportunity, will also feed on higher organisms such as newly hatched fry. They are not predators of higher species by nature, but food supply and availability combined with the survival instinct can change this predisposition. For this reason the size of the invertebrate should be closely considered when choosing food for young fish.

Most of these species exist in one form or another in every corner of the world. However, care should be taken not to introduce a non-native species into natural ecosystems. Careless actions of this sort will have negative repercussions and could devastate the natural balance of the system. It is my position that, with the exception of freshwater bodies severely impacted by humans and various damaging land practices, most of these species will be present in a healthy ecosystem.

Harvesting selected species
Gammarus lacustris, Hyalella azteca (Amphipods, scuds, freshwater shrimp)

Amphipods typically live in shallows of natural lakes, although they are also found in rivers and streams throughout the world. A good *Gammarus* lake will likely have good assemblage of submerged vegetation consisting of "cabbage," milfoil, and coontail. *Gammarus* are not common in lakes with acid water unless there is a high concentration of calcium carbonate. Although one species of *Gammarus* does fairly well under these conditions, I will not deal with that species here because it is not as plentiful and more study is needed to establish proper handling techniques.

Gammarus thrive in lakes that have cattail borders. Some prairie pothole lakes are known to sustain enormous populations. In these situations, the only limiting factors on *Gammarus* populations is water depth and nearby agricultural practices, for example, pesticide and herbicide use. Winter anoxia, common to many northern lakes, is not a problem with *Gammarus* since this invertebrate is able to move to the underside of the ice and cling there. The organism is able to maintain this position, in some cases, for months at a time making only short forays for food. Food is very abundant at this time because most other organisms have died and gases created by decomposition on the bottom tend to float detrital material to the surface. Many of these lakes also have bottom accumulations of decomposing organic matter several feet thick which produce vast amounts of hydrogen sulfide gas. *Gammarus* has the ability to survive in these conditions, attesting to their adaptability to different water types.

Open water harvesting is difficult and should only be done when absolutely necessary. This is because *Gammarus* are only stable for harvesting when the water temperature is below 48°F (9°C). Mortalities increase exponentially with populations located in warmer water. This needs to be carefully considered when harvesting *Gammarus* for restocking projects. The only way I have found that ensures the survival of viable brood stock is to confine harvesting to the collection of overwintering adults. *Gammarus* species in Minnesota, and possibly elsewhere, overwinter as adults and, by the spring thaw, most have paired for mating or have mated. Then they wait for the ice to melt away from the shorelines and for the water to warm before the females molt and hatch the young.

For winter harvesting, I constructed a powered harvester fondly named an "ice boat" that consists of a 2.0-4.0 horsepower 12 or 24 volt electric motor, a graphite propeller, and a frame. The frame is constructed to act as a buoyant sled that can travel along the *underside* of the ice, using a 100 foot long flexible power cord and floating poly control ropes. Using this device, I have been able to harvest a circle approximately 200 feet in diameter by working in ever smaller concentric circles.

Nets constructed from nylon netting of various widths and sizes are towed behind the ice boat. *Gammarus* nets of up to ⅛ inch mesh were placed on rigid frames—fashioned somewhat after trawls used for harvesting ocean shrimp. The mouth of the under-ice net is variously sized to take advantage of different conditions under the ice. I found that 2 ft × 4 ft was the most manageable overall. Smaller and deeper nets pull through the water more easily. The best *Gammarus* net I use is 2 ft high × 4 ft wide × 8 ft diameter with the codend shaped in the form of a cone. This particular net configuration allows collected material to move to a collection bag that is emptied by simply emptying the collected organisms into a bucket or cooler. In the case of an exceptional catch, something that does happen, the collected organisms are scooped out of the trawl using a small mesh hand net and carefully placed in a bucket or cooler.

I use ½ inch copper pipe with soldered elbows on the corners to create a rigid frame for this drag. Two 12 ft brail or towing lines are added by tying a loop to the middle of the line and tying each end to a different corner. I found it easier to remove the net from the ice if I attached both ends of one line to one side of the net. A float consisting of closed-cell foam made for pipe insulation is affixed to the frame and floats the net against the ice and above vegetation. In some cases, kicker chains are added to the mouth of the net in order to gently disturb the *Gammarus* as the net is towed over vegetation. These chains consist of a 24 inch piece of ½ inch PVC (polyvinyl chloride) attached to the rear of the ice boat by a light nylon rope. At 4 inch intervals, pieces of very light steel or aluminum lamp chain 12 inches long are attached to the PVC. The objective is to drag the PVC in front of the net. The chain gently brushes against the *Gammarus*, causing them to swim upward, we hope into the net.

Once set in motion, the ice boat is designed to operate unattended in ever smaller concentric circles. Under normal working circumstances, a single set of 12 volt deep cycle lead acid batteries will furnish power for up to 8 hours of continuous operation. This is based on the use of batteries using latest technologies, primarily GNB (Gould National Batteries, Inc.) group 31, 205 amp, tournament deep cycle batteries. Five to ten circles is about average under normal conditions before the net needs to be emptied. If the net is full after the first ten circles, the next time allow fewer circles because the resulting compression at the bottom of a full net when emptying will raise mortalities and may damage the overall viability of the harvest.

All invertebrates will suffer immediate frostbite if exposed to subfreezing temperatures. Extreme care should be taken when handling any invertebrates out of the water under these conditions. If it is necessary to harvest product under extreme conditions, a portable enclosure can be placed over the harvest hole and insulated coolers should be used to transport the product to holding tanks, avoiding any direct exposure to the frigid air. If long duration transport is necessary following harvesting, oxygen can be used for aeration, but only coarse bubble diffusers should be used. I have transported product over the road during the winter for up to 24 hours with the use of oxygen. These shipments consisted of up to 35 gallons of water holding approximately 140 kg drained weight of product in two 120 gallon insulated holding tanks with suspension nets in the tanks to reduce compaction. *Gammarus* can easily be shipped FedEx (Federal Express) or UPS (United Parcel Service) second day air if they are provided with ample room to avoid asphyxiation caused by compaction within the shipping container.

As stated, I prefer under-ice harvest because it is far more efficient than other methods. From a single 2 ft × 3 ft hole cut through the ice, a variety of species can be harvested on any given pond. After the hole has been cut and all small chips of ice have been removed, the net is attached to the ice boat and the boat is passed through the hole. A small amount of power is applied to the boat to tighten the control ropes. The net is then passed under the ice, ensuring that the brail lines are straight and taut. When the entire assembly is floating under the ice, power is applied to the unit and one need only feed the power cord and the control rope through the hole as they are pulled by the unit. Once the rope is out to the desired length, a steady pull will turn the ice boat in the direction of the control rope. As the net is towed, the wash from the propeller pushes large amounts of water and suspended material including invertebrates through the net as it is being towed in a circle around the harvest hole.

The size of the net mesh will determine the size and type of resident invertebrates that are caught. In some cases, several different species of *Gammarus,* diving beetles, dragonflies, and several species of mayfly may be present and collected in a ⅛ inch mesh net. These will have to be sorted once they are brought to the storage facility or they can be transported directly to a restoration project site and introduced together as a balanced blend of organisms to reestablish the food chain.

As stated above, different size meshes are used to harvest different invertebrates. Location is also a factor when looking for specific species. For example, *Gammarus* can be found in many ponds where they are the predominant species. The same can be said for "glassworms" and *Daphnia*.

Daphnia

When harvesting *Daphnia* as the primary species, larger lakes or ponds are usually easier to harvest. The plankton in these water bodies tend to isolate themselves into dense aggregations, allowing for less sorting and less work overall. Nets are constructed for this species of very fine nylon mesh netting or cotton shear. The basic design is similar to the *Gammarus* net with one important exception—these micro-invertebrates do not tolerate desiccation or direct exposure to the atmosphere. To enable them to remain in the water at all times, a bucket is attached to the codend of the net. This water-filled bucket is simply removed from the hole in the ice and poured into a proper storage container. In this way compaction is also avoided. This is a factor to be considered when harvesting any aquatic invertebrate, as stress caused by compaction or pressure has shown to reduce the percentage of viable offspring and can raise mortalities in the adults.

Using this strategy, invertebrates can be transported directly to hauling tanks suspended in water and without exposure to subfreezing temperatures. This method can also be used for *Gammarus*, although I found it to be unnecessary. This general method will work for the harvest of most invertebrates with some minor alterations to accommodate organism size or distribution.

Portable enclosures currently available for use in the regional ice fishing industry are ideally suited for this type of harvesting and can greatly reduce the chance of exposure to subfreezing temperatures. Many are equipped with large deep sleds for ease of transport to and from the ice.

CULTURE TECHNIQUES

Each invertebrate has unique needs in terms of water chemistry, temperature, and food requirements. Each species is cultured in accordance with these needs. I have found the invertebrates under my study to be easy to maintain and culture in the short term. However, in order to culture them on a scale large enough to supply product to the aquaculture industry in quantities of 50-100 kg or more, it will be necessary to construct artificial ponds. These culture systems are actually artificial ecosystems including various types of vegetation. *Gammarus* could be stocked in this type of system, along with other invertebrates, for harvest in the fall and winter. Artificial systems of this sort can be a benefit to all aquaculture facilities, both as a source of high quality food for the fish and also as a possible additional profit center for the facility. Surplus invertebrates can be sold to other farming operations.

All of the species I have discussed exist in the wild in massive numbers and, when conditions are right, can be cultured at even higher densities. I have harvested from ponds with wild populations as high as 10,000 per cubic meter. Many ponds and lakes throughout Minnesota sustain populations that high. Aquaculture operations in Asia, particularly the producers of ornamental fish, have for years used culture ponds and rice paddies to grow food for the fish because no dry food was available or needed. Everything from *Moina* to "bloodworms" has been cultured without the use of sophisticated instruments to measure water chemistry.

I have researched the practice of fertilizing ponds to promote algae bloom in order to reduce water clarity. This is done to deprive unwanted bottom-dwelling weeds of sunlight, effectively eliminating them from the system. In this body of information, no reference was located pertaining to the resident invertebrate population other than to speak of their biological oxygen demand (BOD) within the system. The use of invertebrates to alter water chemistry, reduce algae densities, and control aquatic vegetation is only now being studied. Several companies have undertaken the not-so-small task of restoring the balance of diversity and ecology to systems that have been over-taxed by many years of unchanging aquaculture, agricultural, or other uses.

With a healthy aquatic ecosystem and a diverse forage base, we will all see better production in our ponds. With additional forage, the strain on any one part of the system will be lessened, providing a quicker rebound for harvested species and, in the end, better use of the resource.

Marketing and distribution

In the time that I have been involved with live aquatics, I have been contacted by companies as far away as Amsterdam, China, and Russia that are interested in purchasing product. Although the demand is clearly there, the costs involved with shipping to these locations may be prohibitive unless arrangements can be made to decrease the cost of airfreight. The on-site culturing for each specific product is also a possibility.

However, I have found shipping within the continental United States to be efficient and reliable, though a little on the expensive side. There are ways to overcome this obstacle and still provide reliable next day or two day shipping through the use of regional distributors and local shipping firms such as Spee Dee Delivery in St. Cloud, Minnesota. Through the effective use of available transport infrastructure, it is possible for an invertebrate distributor to cover as much as a five state area. Small regional shipping companies are able to deliver freight within a five state area for as little as $6.00 for a 15 inch × 11 inch × 12 inch container weighing 10 lb. This is the average size and weight of a package containing 2 kg of any product.

Regional distributors of invertebrate products could be established with minimal investment and space requirements. The bulk of the investment in a holding and packaging facility would be in tanks and refrigeration. With storage tanks consisting of recycled boxes with liners cut to fit from sheet polystyrene, space can be kept to a minimum. Storage boxes of this sort can be laid flat until needed and shipping containers take little time to construct. Currently I spend about two hours a week constructing shipping containers.

Purchasing ready-made shipping containers was investigated and discounted because our available dry storage area was insufficient to hold even a minimum order. These shipping containers varied in cost and size. Only a few of these containers were able to withstand the test specifications required by FedEx in order to comply with their current container strength standards. However, containers constructed at our facility fit tightly together and the use of 1.5 inch foam side walls create a rigid, nearly crush-proof insulated container. These shipping containers surpass FedEx standards and we have not had a single claim for damage.

All shipments are packed using a 1:2 ratio—that is ⅓ water to ⅔ pure oxygen. The water temperature at the time of packing is 42°F (6°C). This enables the distributor to ship 2 kg of *Gammarus* in 4 kg water using a 15 inch × 11 inch × 12 inch shipping container for up to two days of transport time without loss. As an added precaution, I use water saturated with oxygen when packing, though this is more a cautionary matter than a necessity.

Heat is the major enemy in this shipping process. Shipping is faultless within the cold weather months from October through May. Once the temperatures are consistently over 60°F (16°C) ambient air temperature, we use gel ice packs to avoid heating in the event of prolonged exposure to direct sunlight or the container being temporarily stored in a heated area. With these precautions, we can ship well into May.

Summer has been a stumbling block for shipping and handling many of these invertebrate species. As the abundance of invertebrates increases over the warm weather period, so do mortalities when the harvested product is handled. During the warm season, species such as *Gammarus* are no longer suitable for restoration projects. Because of their inability to survive cold tempering prior to shipping, these species do not show a lot of promise for warm water harvest and summer sales.

On the other hand, *Chaoborus* are produced in massive numbers throughout the warm water period and are harvestable in some cases even from shore. I personally have harvested them from the thermocline of lakes with a fine mesh trawl at all times of the year, though some sorting must be done to remove pupae and unwanted insects if they are harvested for aquarium culture.

Afterword

The information I have put together in this report is the culmination of years of painstaking field research and countless hours in college and public libraries. Little or no reference material was located specific to the large-scale collecting or culture. The techniques and inventions described are the product of years of hit-and-miss work and the application of a great deal of common sense. The ice boat is the accomplishment of my life and, as such, I hope that its additional uses and possibilities will benefit everyone.

Optimizing Waterless Shipping Conditions for *Macrobrachium rosenbergii*

John Kubaryk and Carol Harper
University of Puerto Rico, Mayaguez, Puerto Rico

INTRODUCTION

Our project is focused on the post-harvest holding and dry shipping of freshwater shrimp. The induction of hibernation permits Japanese marketers to ship Kuruma shrimp *(Penaeus japonicus)* live without water using chilled sawdust as the packaging material *(Yamaha Fisheries Journal* 1989, Korringa 1976). Only a certain type of sawdust is acceptable (Korringa 1976). Our research group in Puerto Rico is now in the process of developing similar strategies.

SHRIMP MARKETS

At the Marketing and Shipping Live Aquatic Products '96 conference, we reported that at some Japanese restaurants consumers were paying up to $200 per pound for live shrimp. Recent investigations on the Internet (www.sea-world.com, April 1998) indicate that Japanese markets were paying about 6.5 times more for live products than for frozen.

Since the 1996 conference, the University of Puerto Rico's Food and Agricultural Research Entrepreneurship Center (FARE) has been contacted by a New York broker about supplying 10,000 pounds per week of live freshwater shrimp *(Macrobrachium rosenbergii)*. With this information, the leadership of Puerto Rico's Science and Technology Board awarded our university group $398,000 to further develop "Waterless Shipping of Live Shrimp."

The economic implications are important. Shrimp are high-priced food products and standard commodities worldwide. However, the Puerto Rican market and those of other Central American countries are unable to support large aquaculture operations. Diverse export markets outside of the Caribbean region must be located for these products. Our goal is to overcome this limitation by developing practical methods for the live transport of regionally produced shrimp to the continental United States and other parts of the world. It is also our goal to develop strategies of shipping live product in the most economical way possible.

The shrimp market in the United States and elsewhere is very significant. It has been demonstrated that the growth in the U.S. food market is, for the most part, limited by population growth which is approximately 2% per year (Behne 1983). However, the trade imbalance for shrimp in the U.S. market exceeds this level of growth and is surpassed only by that for oil (NOAA 1990). With this marketing reality in mind, our group is attempting to develop processing and marketing strategies in order that this region might be able to supply continental United States and global markets with live shrimp. It is also our intent to use this work as the foundation for the expansion and increased viability of the Puerto Rican shrimp industry.

Our objective is to develop a practical shipping strategy to bring this product to the marketplace. The University of Puerto Rico owns a commercial shrimp farm consisting of 52 one-acre ponds. Currently, this farm is our main project. University leadership has requested that we patent a working handling and shipping system and also market the shrimp cultured at this farm.

RESEARCH TOPICS

One of our objectives is to educate graduate students. At present four students are funded by this project. One student, Amarilis, is involved with the correlation between temperature change and metabolic activity using HPLC techniques. Another student, Celida, will consider different metabolism rates as indicated by lactic acid changes during the transport of the animals. A recently enrolled student, Janneth, will be working on the development of a handling system to keep internal container temperature within plus or minus 1° of 15°C. Another new student, Belkis, is interested in working on the application of HACCP procedures to our system to ensure that all food safety regulations are satisfied.

Research has been and is currently being conducted in the following areas:

1. Development of strategies that can be used to optimize relative humidity conditions to minimize the weight of water necessary to guarantee 100% relative humidity conditions in a closed shipping container.

2. Determining the range of temperatures that induce reduced metabolism and concurrent cessation of movement without mortality.

3. Studying the effect of rapid versus slow cooling rates on the survival of shrimp placed in the desired states of movement cessation and low metabolic rate.

4. Determining the optimum initial and holding temperatures for use with live shrimp using the low weight shipping container strategy.

Environmental limits of aquatic animals

In nature, aquatic animals confront highly unpredictable environmental conditions. As they strive to survive and reproduce, animals such as the freshwater shrimp face various obstacles, including temporally or spatially limited food supplies and changing temperature and oxygen levels. Adaptations to extreme conditions, particularly in terms of temperature, pH, and water activity or salinity conditions, are present in many aquatic animals (Jaenicke 1981). Metabolic rate depression is used by both endotherms and ectoderms to survive harsh environmental conditions related to temperature and oxygen levels.

Temperature

Cold tolerance is of particular importance in our study of the freshwater shrimp. Temperatures below 14°C and above 35°C are generally reported to be lethal to *Macrobrachium* (New and Singholka 1985). It is apparent that induction of the desired state of low metabolism or chill coma will involve temperatures well above those that result in the formation of ice crystals in the animal. However, it is possible that even nonlethal temperatures in the so-called non-freeze range may result in injury or death of the shrimp. Shrimp handling strategies must consider a number of hazards. The commercial handling of this valuable product may unwittingly involve indirect chilling at depressed temperatures that the animals can endure for only a specific length of time. Holding the shrimp beyond this period of time in shipping containers will result in their injury or death. Likewise, direct chilling methods might be involved in which the drop to the desired holding temperature takes place too rapidly. We are attempting to develop remedies for these hazards.

Oxygen

Some aquatic invertebrates have the natural ability to survive periods of air exposure or emersion. Such exposure is present when *Macrobrachium* shrimp crawl out of ponds during periods of low dissolved oxygen (DO) or when they form burrows in flooded soils characterized by low oxygen levels. The shrimp can survive by reducing oxygen requirements and/or utilizing anaerobic energy metabolism. In general, most crustaceans and subtidal mollusks have a much lower tolerance for environmental anoxia than those occupying the intertidal zone. However, all can still be termed to be euryoic in that they have varying abilities to use oxygen when available and anaerobic metabolism when it is absent. However, the duration of time that even intertidal animals can survive emersion is limited. For example, the longest period of emersion that a particular tropical intertidal chiton has in its natural habitat is approximately six hours. However, when placed in an outdoor artificial aquarium, half of the test individuals were alive after 24-36 hours of air exposure (McMahon et al. 1991).

Also some aquatic invertebrates can moderate oxygen uptake by establishing a resting metabolic rate as a compensatory response to low oxygen availability. Many of these same animals, when even lower oxygen levels are encountered, can survive by causing their resting metabolic rate to be independent of oxygen availability (Herreid 1980). This latter level of oxygen adjustment is often referred to as the critical oxygen tension (P_c) and it has been reported that crustaceans from poorly oxygenated waters have a lower P_c than those from well-oxygenated waters (Felder 1979, Spotte 1983).

Rapid chilling vs. slow chilling

During anaerobic metabolism there is a reduction in overall metabolism in some invertebrates, such as bivalves, but not in others, such as crustaceans. The results from the series of studies that investigated the effects of rapid chilling were somewhat surprising. Shrimp that had been rapidly chilled to the final holding temperature of 27°C experienced better survival rates when reimmersed in room temperature water than the shrimp that were slow chilled to the same temperature. These shrimp were slow cooled from 27°C to 15°C in water chilled 1°C every 10 minutes, then removed and, following a holding period, put in room temperature water. The shrimp that were rapidly cooled were immediately placed in 15°C water and removed after movement stopped.

Recovery

The time required for the slow-chilled shrimp to return to normal levels of activity was much longer than the observed recovery time of the rapidly cooled shrimp, none of which died. One of the slow-cooled shrimp died. The rapidly cooled shrimp were also much more animate than the slow-cooled animals, none of which fully recovered. This type of response is also seen in insects where a cold-shock pretreatment improved survival at storage temperature through a process called the rapid cold-hardening response (Chen et al. 1987, Lee et al. 1987). Even though we did not look at energy stores of the shrimp used in this experiment, the fact that shrimp fed the day prior to pretreatment had significantly ($P < 0.05$) higher rates of survival, apparently corresponding with that found in insects. In insects, the larger reserves of stored energy found in cold-selected breeding lines and/or the use of these reserves at lower rates by resorting to low maintenance metabolic levels, may protect them against chilling injury compared to the control strain (Chen and Walker 1994).

These results also demonstrate that the stress associated with capture by seining and transportation to the packaging center was detrimental to the survival of the shrimp in a waterless environment. It is apparent that a recovery period is needed and that harvesting and local transport should be completed one day prior to packaging. After waterless shipping overnight at 15°C, of the animals that had been delivered to the shipping center 24 hours earlier and held overnight, 4 were alive and 8 were dead. The shrimp that were held at the seining location overnight before transport to the packaging area and then undergoing the same treatment had 2 survive and 11 die. The group consisting of animals seined and transported the same day they were packaged had no survivors.

Macrobrachium species are distributed throughout the tropical and subtropical areas of the world. Some species prefer clear water rivers, while the species under study in this project, *M. rosenbergii*, prefers extremely turbid waters (New and Singholka 1985). The species are highly adapted to these zones. For example, the freshwater crayfish, *Orconectes limosus*, inhabits the mud zone of polluted rivers. When it is removed from water and placed in an air environment, only a small drop in energy usage is observed. It would appear that during these periods of anoxia there is no corresponding drop in energy usage such as that found in other species such as bivalves (Gade 1983). Unlike the warm water *Macrobrachium,* the crayfish *Orconectes* has been successfully reared in ponds in the Finger Lakes region of New York (Bardach et al. 1972). A temperature of 14°C would be considered within their normal environmental range.

It is apparent that the reactions of these invertebrates to aerial exposure or emersion tend to vary. This might begin to explain why shrimp, when exposed to a specific aeration treatment during which they are bathed in a constant current of air, had the best survival versus that of shrimp placed in closed containers containing pure oxygen and compressed air. There is the possibility that carbon dioxide, a by-product of metabolism, accumulated in the sealed containers and overwhelmed the animals despite the presence of high oxygen concentrations in the containers. It should be noted that when chiton are immersed for a period of 17 hours, blood carbon dioxide levels peak at 12 hours, which also corresponded to a minimum blood pH value (McMahon et al. 1991). This could be due to what is known as the Bohr-Root effect. Regardless of the actual cause, the shrimp in our studies that have survived the storage interval do not exhibit sections of their gills clumped together or collapsed as has been observed in blue crabs exposed to air (DeFur et al. 1988).

Metabolic by-products

The metabolic by-products that are toxic and are, consequently, of primary concern to shippers of live animals are ammonia and carbon dioxide. For this reason, we have directed some of our attention to the use of zeolites. Our work was reported at the first live shipping conference. Zeolites are crystalline, hydrated alumino-silicates that have an amazing array of chemical and physical properties. These properties suggest that this mineral may become a standout among the various mineral amendments used in the agricultural industry, particularly as the development of new aquaculture technologies intensify (Mumpton and Fishman 1977). When dried at 300-400°C for a few hours to remove the water that fills the areas around the exchangeable cations, zeolites become capable of absorbing gases including carbon dioxide. In their normal state, zeolites are some of the most effective ion exchangers known to man and have also been used to remove ammonia from waste waters (Kliivi and Semmens 1980), to reduce noxious fumes of ammonia and hydrogen sulfide from poultry houses (Ernst 1968), and to remove ammonia from recirculation systems used in the production of aquatic animals for human consumption (Johnson and Sieburth 1974). In spite of their initial promise, it is surprising that we have to report that the addition of zeolite to the storage chambers did not initially improve shrimp survival.

HANDLING PROTOCOL

The handling protocol used in this project is straightforward. The day before the shrimp are to be packaged into the waterless shipping containers, they are seined, placed into transportation coolers provided with aerators, and transported to the packaging area. Several hours later the shrimp are fed their normal compounded feed and are then left overnight before undergoing the cold treatment and packaging on the following day. Ammonia production is minimal since they have been without food for some 16 hours.

Carbon dioxide buildup

The shrimp are next given a cool water pretreatment at 15°C for 15 minutes and are then placed into the storage containers. However, it became apparent that carbon dioxide, a by-product of respiration, accumulated in the storage containers and the zeolite was unable to deal with this buildup. This led us to try the use of carbon dioxide scavengers (Brody 1994). The addition of this strategy allowed us to significantly improve shrimp survival to approximately 95% after 21-22 hours of storage. Current results show that the use of carbon dioxide scavengers (calcium hydroxide and sodium hydroxide) with either treated (pre-dried) or untreated zeolite in high oxygen conditions result in better survival rates than in shipments involving only high oxygen conditions. In addition, high oxygen conditions have been shown to result in better survival rates than either aerated or compressed air conditions. Further tests will be run to determine the degree to which treated and untreated zeolite supplements enhance survival rates.

Shrimp behavior

Our laboratory study involved four basic handling steps: (1) cold treatment, (2) packaging in a waterless storage container, (3) storage over a precise interval, and (4) reimmersion in water at room temperature. Our various experiments indicated that three different types of behavior were exhibited by post-treatment shrimp. These behaviors are described below.

The shrimp *Macrobrachium,* as do all members of the order Decapoda, have five pairs of walking legs, which have allowed them to become highly adapted at crawling. They also have a large extended abdomen that provides them the capability of rapid backward swimming by flipping their tail—an important escape response. When placed directly in any of the pretreatment water baths for rapid cooling, the first reaction of the shrimp was to rapidly swim in any direction to escape the cold, even propelling themselves out of the bath. Even though the cooling bath contains seven inches of water with an additional five inches of freeboard, the ability of the shrimp to propel themselves a foot or more above the water surface was impressive. We refer to this temperature-induced behavior as propulsion-like. These short-term bursts of rapid tail flipping are also seen, but not to the same extreme, when the stored shrimp are revived by reimmersion.

Some of the pretreated shrimp are placed in waterless storage or shipping containers that are saturated with pure oxygen, held at 15°C for up to 15 hours, and then reimmersed in room temperature water. We found that these animals are much more aggressive than normal shrimp and refer to this pure oxygen induced behavior as cannibalistic.

The final state, sometimes called the zombie state, refers to the behavior of animals that have survived 24 hour storage periods. The criteria for determining actual survival are quite simple. The test animals should be capable of pumping water across their branchial chambers and to twitch and fan their abdomen when they are reimmersed in room temperature water. However, if after approximately two hours they are obviously dead or do not show any signs of returning to normal behavior, the shrimp are considered not to have survived.

Because the cold water pretreatment had such a dramatic effect on the shrimp, we concluded that anesthetizing the shrimp before subjecting them to this treatment might increase survival rates. It has long been known that nitrogen is an effective anesthetic for insects (Hooper 1970). We found that bubbling nitrogen through room temperature water for 15 minutes had no anesthetic effect on the shrimp.

Anesthesia

Indonesian clove oil is an effective anesthesia for use in the hatchery rearing of the rabbit fish, *Siganus argentes* (Tamaru et al. 1995). We tested the effect of different concentrations of eugenol (200-300 ppm), the active ingredient of clove oil. Initially we experienced difficulties placing this oil into solution. It is also caustic and disintegrated the polystyrene holding containers. The problem was solved by adding 3 g Tween 20 and 5 g Tween 60 to 9 g eugenol, then adding a sufficient amount of water to fill a 100 ml volumetric flask, and stirring the solution for 15 minutes. Even though the solution worked well as an anesthetic, it did not significantly increase survival when used as a pretreatment method. Shrimp survival was higher from just prechilling than from first anesthetizing the animals and then prechilling. A possible explanation for this is that clove oil may have an undesirable caustic effect on the crustaceans. Our research involving the development of optimal shipping methods for this commercially important species will continue.

NOTES ON PROCEDURES AND RESULTS

Approximately 35-50 minutes are needed to place the harvested shrimp into buckets, to rinse adhering mud, and to transfer the animals into unaerated containers of pond water at ambient temperature. Another 45 minutes is required to transport these shrimp to the university processing area. We quickly learned that, in order to obtain the best survival during the post-harvest holding period, the seining of the ponds and subsequent transport of the shrimp should occur in the morning of the day prior to stocking into the storage containers. Also, it is best to feed shrimp following harvest. This is somewhat surprising. However, feeding improves the survival rate even though this practice would tend to produce additional amounts of ammonia. Working with these basic steps, it is our intent to come up with a working system and to educate workers in the care and handling of these shrimp.

Rapid chilling yields higher survival rate

Upon arrival at the processing area, the shrimp are held in static tanks provided with aerators. The tropical *Macrobrachium* lives only within the temperature range of 13-31°C, and when the shrimp are placed in the temperature range of 15-17°C they go into a semi-comatose state in which there is little activity or movement. We tested what would happen if the temperature of the water was slowly lowered from the 25-27°C ambient temperature of the processing building, to 15°C over 30 minutes. We also investigated what might happen if we dumped the shrimp into water prechilled at 15°C. Much to our surprise, we found that the shrimp that were dumped into the prechilled water had much higher survival rates during the storage period.

Containers for storage and shipping

In waterless shipping there is no water in the storage and shipping containers, other than the water that comes with the shrimp. After the shrimp have been chilled to 15°C for 15 minutes, they are removed from the water bath using a colander and gently shaken off. They are then ready for packaging.

The storage containers have carbon dioxide scavengers consisting of calcium hydroxide and sodium hydroxide. For every 300 g of shrimp (individual size range 50-120 g), 1.5 g each of those two compounds is placed with the shrimp to absorb the carbon dioxide produced by the shrimp. After a series of trials using different gases, we now introduce a 100% oxygen atmosphere into the storage container. What we are doing right now is very low tech. Our methods and equipment will improve over time.

REVIEW OF CURRENT PROCEDURE

We place the shrimp into a comatose state (chilled to 15°C); place them in aluminum pie pans; introduce the scavengers; place each unit of shrimp into a plastic bag (currently a Ziploc bag); fill the bag with oxygen; and place these units into the storage container (currently a refrigerator maintained at 15°C). The use of this container as a commercial storage container has its limitations, primarily because the holding temperature fluctuates in the range of 14.5-16.5°C. An advanced environmental container is en route to our laboratory and we will begin using this new system soon.

Survival

We have been able to attain 100% survival following 22 hours of dry storage. These shrimp regain normal levels of activity and, within approximately two hours, they are looking for food.

We use a practical definition of survival. If a shrimp that has been held for the stipulated number of hours in the storage container, after being placed in water with aerators, is able to bite you after an hour—we consider this animal to have survived the handling process. A somewhat different determination must be made for shrimp held for longer periods of time.

After 30 hours of dry storage, the shrimp are still alive. When they are placed in the recovery tanks they are capable of moving water along their gills and they flip around, but they generally die after a short period of time. Danford and Uglow (2001) provide us with the idea that the shrimp, following the dry storage period, are attempting to dump large amounts of ammonia. Once our laboratory is properly set up, we will be able to use a recirculating system. We anticipate that the rapid removal of ammonia from the holding system will allow these shrimp to survive.

Other species

Another goal of our project is to develop a system of methodologies that can be adapted for use with other aquatic animals. This will undoubtedly be difficult because the various commercial species have different temperatures and atmosphere needs. However, we are in search of a basic procedure that can be used in this developing industry.

Anesthetizing

We have made a number of mistakes in the course of our project. For example, we thought that survival rates would be increased if we anesthetized the shrimp first and then put them to sleep gently by slowly decreasing water temperature.

The aquaculture literature mentions the use of clove oil as an anesthetic for fish. We investigated the of clove oil to our developing handling process. Clove oil presents several problems: (1) it is not miscible in water, (2) it is corrosive, (3) clove oil solution will burn through the Styrofoam. To make a long story short, after we found a way to place the oil into a workable solution at the correct parts per million dosage rate to put the test animals to sleep, it did not help a bit. We experienced a lower survival rate by using the anesthetic first than by not using it at all.

We also examined the use of another anesthetic that is described in the literature. Nitrogen is frequently used to anesthetize insect larvae. We bubbled nitrogen in a water bath to investigate its effect on freshwater shrimp. Nitrogen did not have any effect on the shrimp. It did not work as an anesthetic.

Oxygen

We also had problems involving air. Initially in our study we found that simple aeration worked best. This was accomplished by placing common tank aerators into our packages of dry shrimp. We flushed the packages with atmospheric air. Following later trials we found that the highest survival rates are achieved through the use of a 100% oxygen atmosphere. We also used commercial oxygen tablets commonly used in the aquarium trade. We did not observe enhanced survival through the use of these tablets.

Zeolites

Three years ago at the first live conference, I reported on the use of zeolites to neutralize ammonia. Initially we had a good success with this substance. However, since our initial trials, results have been inconsistent. Consequently, we have not been able to make a decision about the continued use of zeolites. Simply by listening to several of the reports given at this conference, we are gaining several ideas about why zeolites did not work to enhance survival.

Our work with zeolites needs to be carefully described. We heat treated zeolite samples at 300-400°C for 3-4 hours to remove water. It was our understanding that this procedure would enhance the ability of zeolite to trap ammonia and carbon dioxide. We have been wondering why this substance has not worked as well as we thought it should. We reported three years ago that zeolites seemed to be beneficial because it removes ammonia from the water.

We were using 12 g zeolite per 300-400 g shrimp. It is quite possible that the zeolite was functioning as expected.

The shrimp survived dry storage for a substantial period of time. However, the problem appears when the shrimp are placed into the recovery tanks. They simply do not come out of it if held beyond a certain number of hours. It is now obvious from previous conference reports that the freshwater shrimp were dumping large amounts of ammonia into the recovery water. The zeolite mixed in with the shrimp during dry storage may actually have helped pick up some of this released ammonia. Up to this time, we thought that our survival problems were just temperature related. We now realize that we need to look at ammonia buildup in the receiving water. Using an adequate recirculating system we should be able to increase survival from 22 hours to 30 hours and beyond.

Next step

In conclusion, our next step is to finish optimizing our handling and shipping procedure. We expect to complete this work by spring 2000 and then we will start building containers. Our next goal is to conduct actual shipments. We are now in the process of assembling a list of industry members at good receiving facilities who can participate with us on actual shipments. We hope to quickly work out the various logistical challenges including airline technicalities and other considerations. Please contact us if you wish to become a participant.

Acknowledgments

We would like to thank the Puerto Rican Industrial Development Company (PRIDCO) and the National Fisheries Institute for funding this research. PRIDCO is also funding the studies of four master's degree students at the University of Puerto Rico.

References

Bardach, J., J.H. Ryther, and W.O. McLarney. 1972. Aquaculture: The farming and husbandry of freshwater and marine organisms. Wiley Interscience, New York. 868 pp.

Behne, J.R. 1983. Growth in a non-growth industry—expanding our horizons. Food Technol. 37:22-24,27.

Brody, A.L. 1994. Internal package gas scavengers and emitters. In: A.L. Brody, (ed.), Modified atmosphere food packaging. Institute of Packaging Professionals, Herdon, VA, pp.19-30.

Chen, C.P., D.L. Denlinger, and R.E. Lee Jr. 1987. Cold-shock injury and rapid cold-hardening in the flesh fly, *Sarcophaga crassipalpis*. Physiol. Zool. 60:297-304.

Chen, C.P., and V.A. Walker. 1994. Cold-shock and chilling tolerance in drosophila. J. Insect Physiol. 40:661-669.

Danford, A.R. and R.F. Uglow. 2001. Physiological responses of blue crabs, *Callinectes* sp., to procedures used in the soft crab fishery in La Laguna de Terminos, Mexico. In: B.C. Paust and A.A. Rice (eds.), Marketing and shipping live aquatic products: Proceedings of the Second International Conference and Exhibition, November 1999, Seattle, WA. University of Alaska Sea Grant, AK-SG-01-03, Fairbanks. (This volume.)

DeFur, P.L., A. Pease, A. Siebelink, and S. Elfers. 1988. Respiratory responses to blue crabs, *Callinectes sapidus*, to emersion. Comp. Biochem. Physiol. 89A:97-101.

Ernst, R.A. 1968. The effects of ammonia on poultry. Feedstuffs 40:40.

Felder, D.L. 1979. Respiratory adaptations of the estuarine mud shrimp, *Callianassa jamaicense* (Schmitt, 1935) (Crustacea, Decapoda, Thalassinidae). Biol. Bull. 157:125-137.

Gade, G. 1983. Energy metabolism of arthropods and mollusks during environmental and functional anaerobiosis. J. Exp. Zool. 228:415-429.

Herreid, C.F. 1980. Hypoxia in invertebrates. Comp. Biochem. Physiol. 67A:311-320.

Hooper, G.H.S. 1970. The use of CO_2, N_2, and cold to immobilize adults of Mediterranean fruit flies. J. Econ. Entomol. 63:1962-1963.

Jaenicke, R. 1981. Enzymes under extremes of physical conditions. Annu. Rev. Biophys. Bioeng. 10:1-67.

Johnson, P.W., and J.M. Sieburth. 1974. Ammonia removal by selective ion exchange, a backup system for microbiological filters in a closed-system aquaculture. Aquaculture 4:61-67.

Kliivi, J.R., and M.J. Semmens. 1980. An evaluation of pretreated natural zeolites for ammonium removal. Water Res. 14:161-168.

Korringa, P. 1976. Farming penaeid shrimp in Japan. In: P. Korringa, Farming marine fishes and shrimps: A multidisciplinary treatise. Elsevier Scientific Publishing Co., Amsterdam, pp. 91-122.

Lee, R.E. Jr., C.P. Chen, and D.L. Denlinger. 1987. A rapid cold-hardening process in insects. Science 238:1415-1417.

McMahon, B.R., W.W. Burggren, A.W. Pinder, and M.G. Wheatly. 1991. Air exposure and physiological compensation in a tropical intertidal chiton, *Chiton stokesii* (Mollusca: Polyplacophora). Physiol. Zool. 64:728-747.

Mumpton, F.A., and P.H. Fishman. 1977. The application of natural zeolites in animal science and aquaculture. Anim. Sci. 45:1188-1203.

New, M.B., and S. Singholka. 1985. Freshwater prawn farming. FAO Fisheries Technical Paper 225, Rome. 118 pp.

NOAA. 1990. Fisheries of the United States. NOAA Current Fishery Statistics No. 8900. 111 pp.

Spotte, D.G. 1983. Oxygen consumption and the whole body lactate accumulation during progressive hypoxia in the tropical freshwater prawn, *Macrobrachium rosenbergii* (de Man). J. Exp. Zool. 226:19-27.

Tamaru, C.S., C. Carlstrom-Trick, and W.J. FitzGerald. 1995. Clove oil, Minyak cengkeh, a natural fish anesthetic. In: Sustainable Aquaculture 95 Proceedings. Pacon International, P.O. Box 11568, Honolulu, HI 96828.

Yamaha Fishery Journal. 1989. Prawn culture: Spread of technology sparks industrialization. Yamaha Fishery Journal 30. 8 pp.

Author biographies

John Kubaryk graduated from Auburn University in 1980 with a Ph.D. in fish and animal nutrition and was hired as an assistant professor in 1980 by the Department of Marine Sciences, University of Puerto Rico, as a seafood technologist. Over the past 18 years he has taught graduate classes and developed research programs in the areas of aquatic nutrition, water quality, and seafood technology. From June 1991 until March 1998 he was director of the Department of Marine Sciences.

Carol Harper graduated in 1991 from Colorado State University with a Ph.D. in agricultural engineering, specializing in food engineering. Her master's thesis from Oregon State University in 1985 was on the live shipment of Dungeness crab. After doing food safety research for the National Center for Food Safety and Technology in the Chicago office of the U.S. Food and Drug Administration for five years, she moved to Puerto Rico and is an associate professor in the Department of Agricultural Engineering. She is currently doing research and teaching graduate and undergraduate courses in the areas of food engineering, food packaging, and food safety.

Questions from the audience

QUESTION: If the storage temperature is 15°C, what is the temperature of the recovery water?

J. KUBARYK: The recovery water is at room temperature or 25-27°C.

QUESTION: Have you experimented slowly with warming the shrimp following dry storage?

J. KUBARYK: There seemed to be no difference when we brought them up slowly. However, after careful examination, we noticed that the shrimp actually came out of it better by warming them quickly.

QUESTION: Would the solubility of ammonia at a lower temperature be less drastic to the shrimp?

J. KUBARYK: We have not started looking at this question. Once we get the lab built, and it should be done by December 1999, we will start thinking about what we are going to do about ammonia loading and the holding system requirements needed for full recovery.

HARPER: I think a lot of our problem was that the zeolite did not make effective contact with the ammonia—the ammonia was around the gills of the shrimp while the zeolite was on the bottom of the container.

QUESTION: How effective are the carbon dioxide scavengers?

HARPER: The scavengers increased survival a lot. However, we have not measured anything yet. We are now just beginning experiments. The grad students will begin to work on this sort of question once we select areas of concentration. The students will take over topics that have the best potential of developing into full-scale research projects.

AUDIENCE COMMENT: Perhaps when you rewater the shrimp following the dry transport period, you may need to go through a two-phase program. The first step is to get them into water—providing them enough water to dump the ammonia that they have been sequestering over the transport period. Then, let us say within 20-30 minutes, transfer them into the fresh water in which you hope they will recover. In other words, get rid of the ammonia somehow so that you do not have to depend upon a biofilter to get the job done.

J. KUBARYK: I am a nutritionist by training. One of my graduate students and I are using an outdoor green water recirculating system for tilapia. We do not have any ammonia in this system. We actually have clear green water systems where we stock about 1,000 fish per cubic meter. We will look at your suggestion. We might be setting up a recirculating system in the lab based on what we have been doing outdoors. Of course, the problem with ammonia only came to light yesterday with several of the other talks.

QUESTION: Why are we considering the use of HACCP in this project?

HARPER: Granted—the product is still alive. It is not food yet, but that is going to come. HACCP is there for seafood and we must be able to guarantee that our product will be able to meet regulations. Do you absolutely need to use HACCP? No, you do not. This was clearly established at a recirculating aquaculture conference in Roanoke, Virginia, two years ago. Live products do not require a HACCP plan. The reason we are looking at the development of a HACCP plan is because we are using different chemicals. Even though the use of these products is generally regarded as safe, we are planning to investigate this topic quite carefully. Another reason for our interest in HACCP applications is that one of the graduate students has stated she would like to look into this matter.

Hazard analysis is routine when dealing with what will eventually become foodstuffs. For example, I know that beef industries in some countries are keeping a complete history so that authorities can trace the product and know where it is coming from. If there are any problems, they can quickly locate the source. I think this will eventually become true for the live seafood industry.

Keeping Baitfish Alive and Healthy in Holding Tanks: Tips for Retail Outlets

Hugh Thomforde
Lonoke Agriculture Center, University of Arkansas at Pine Bluff, Lonoke, Arkansas

Introduction

U.S. farmers produce $37 million per year in fathead minnows, golden shiners, white suckers, goldfish, and other species that are marketed as sport fishing live bait (1998 Census of Aquaculture, USDA-NASS). Many farmers absorb the cost of fish that die between farm and retail bait shops. Various types of mishandling can cause high mortalities. The best management practices recommended for use with baitfish live holding and transport involves the careful use of water quality maintenance methods and product handling strategies. This report summarizes management practices used to improve fish survival and increase profits.

Maintain dissolved oxygen

To add oxygen and remove accumulated carbon dioxide, constantly agitate the holding water. This can be done with a surface agitator or by bubbling air into the water using a blower system. If the fish are observed to be struggling against currents created by bubbles, reduce the air flow or move the air stones to create areas of quiet, yet well-oxygenated water.

The only way to ensure sufficient "air" in the holding water is to measure dissolved oxygen (DO). This measurement should be made at regular intervals when the tank is full of baitfish. Keep oxygen above 4 ppm (parts per million). To estimate oxygen conditions in the absence of a DO measuring instrument, stand back and watch the behavior of the baitfish. If the fish stay away from the surface and move together in schools, there is probably enough oxygen in the water. For new operations, the most economical and practical approach to DO management is to purchase a prepackaged aeration system specifically sized for the volume and depth of the particular tanks and the maximum pounds of fish to be held in these tanks.

Dechlorinate water

Tap water must be dechlorinated before it is brought in contact with fish. Water from most municipal supplies contains 0.5-2.0 ppm residual chlorine. Water containing no more than 2 ppm residual chlorine can be dechlorinated through the addition of 5 grams sodium thiosulfate per 100 gallons of city water. Commercial preparations for dechlorination are available from a variety of sources, including pet shops. Special care must be taken when using makeup water carrying residual chlorine concentrations above 2.0 ppm.

Keep fish cool

Retailers loose most of their baitfish stock during the hot summer months. The best strategy is to place the holding tanks in the coolest possible location, such as an air-conditioned room. Keep water temperature below approximately 65°F (18°C). When fish are cool they release ammonia more slowly and do not use quite as much oxygen. Fish held under these conditions are subject to lower levels of stress and, as a consequence, tend to experience lower mortality rates.

Prevent temperature shock

Major baitfish losses can be caused by temperature shock at the time of delivery to the retailer. A simple precaution can be used to reduce fish mortalities. Using a reasonably accurate thermometer, check the temperature of the holding water onboard the hauling truck and the water in your vats or tanks. The hauling water will typically be 55-60°F (13-16°C). The newly delivered baitfish should be acclimated or "tempered" by slowly changing their holding water temperature over a period of time. Temper fish by changing water temperature no more than 10°F (6°C) in 20 minutes. Do not attempt the final transfer of the baitfish until water in the retail facility is within a few degrees of the hauling water. If necessary, non-chlorinated ice can be used to cool water (Fig. 1). Remember that rapid temperature changes kill fish!

HOLD THE AMMONIA

Fish slowly release ammonia as part of their normal metabolic process. Even at low concentrations, ammonia is toxic to fish. If tanks are neglected and the concentration of ammonia is allowed to increase, it is inevitable that many baitfish will die. The easiest and most reliable way to remove ammonia is to regularly change the water. Drain the tank to approximately the ¼ volume level and then refill with new chlorine-free water. Frequent water exchanges reduce stress on the baitfish because the accumulating ammonia is diluted.

In general, the maximum safe level for un-ionized ammonia is about 0.1 ppm, or 2 ppm total ammonia nitrogen. The ammonia concentration should be measured just before changing the water, when this waste product is at its peak concentration. A variety of inexpensive test kits are available for the measurement of ammonia. Over a period of time during which ammonia levels are carefully monitored, retail operator experience is usually adequate to determine the frequency of holding water changes. If a retail facility does not have an ammonia test kit, change the baitfish holding water at least once a day.

DON'T FEED THE FISH

Feeding baitfish in vats will cause ammonia concentrations to increase greatly! If it becomes necessary to feed the baitfish, additional changes will be needed to flush a great deal more water through the tanks. Feed sparingly and only if the fish appear to be extremely thin. Watch them closely and make sure that the baitfish are actually eating the feed.

REPLACE LOST SALT

Because of the nature of the live transport and holding business, baitfish experience some level of handling stress. Salt can provide some relief for this stress. The general recommendation for most bait shop situations is to add 2 pounds of canning salt per 100 gallons holding water. This addition should be done

Figure 1. Fish haulers add ice to keep water around 55-60°F (13-16°C). Low temperature reduces fish metabolism and improves hauling conditions.

only once, when the baitfish are first received, to replace salts lost from handling stress. The careful application of salt also stimulates the release of mucus, which reduces susceptibility of baitfish to infections.

ROTATE STOCK

Even the smallest retail shop must have at least two tanks in order to allow for stock rotation and to control possible disease outbreaks (Fig. 2). In preparation for the arrival of a new batch of baitfish, one of these tanks should be drained and then allowed to dry. If the bottom of the tank cannot be dried completely, disinfect the tank by applying ¾ cup of household bleach per gallon of water and letting it stand for 5 minutes. When holding different sizes or species of baitfish in the same tank, separate them with dividers. In order to control disease, never mix batches of fish.

DON'T OVERCROWD FISH

Every holding tank has a specific carrying capacity or recommended maximum density of baitfish. As a general rule, fish density should not exceed more than a pound of fish per 4 gallons of water. Some retailers hold only one pound of baitfish per 10 gallons. The more baitfish held in a tank, the more that tank will need to be flushed to eliminate ammonia.

Remove dead fish

Dead fish spread disease, degrade water quality, and are unsightly. Check holding tanks several times daily, and remove dead fish.

Watch your water quality

Widespread baitfish mortalities can be a problem in this industry. If batch after batch of fish die in the tanks without explanation the water must be tested to determine a possible cause. In such cases, the supplier should be asked if similar problems are occurring at other bait shops on the delivery route. It is recommended that pH, oxygen, and ammonia levels be measured. The local Cooperative Extension agent may also be able to help. Low cost test kits are available for accurate and timely monitoring of water quality conditions.

Don't dispose of live bait into water systems

The intentional release of live baitfish in the wild is illegal in some areas and is not recommended. Bait shop customers must be encouraged to dispose of unused live baitfish away from aquatic areas.

Start out small

Before plunging into the live baitfish industry, first complete a pilot project. Conduct small-scale trials to avoid large financial losses later on. It is recommended that the retailer develop and maintain a notebook. This compact collection of records should include important phone numbers; daily records for each tank regarding water changes, temperatures, and other water quality observations; the number of fish added to the tank; and quantities removed live and dead. This notebook will assist the retailer in remembering the strategies that work and those that do not in a given situation.

Figure 2. Even the smallest retail shop must have at least two tanks. This allows you to rotate stock and to control disease.

Conclusion

Proper handling of baitfish requires a good understanding of the needs of individual baitfish species and water quality conditions required to keep them alive in holding tanks. Mishandling of baitfish will result in large financial losses. The careful adherence to the several handling strategies suggested in this report will significantly reduce the financial risks faced by those involved in the retailing of baitfish.

# What's New in Live Fish and Shellfish At-Sea Holding Systems: High Tech and Low Tech

Mick Kronman
National Fisherman Magazine, Santa Barbara, California

Abstract

During the past decade's boom in live seafood commerce, Pacific Coast fishermen have identified "stress points" encountered during the at-sea handling and holding of fish and shellfish. These harvesters have learned strategies to reduce the stress and increase the survivability of their catch. Maturing technology—both high-tech and low-tech—has assisted in this learning process. Some harvesters, for example, praise oxygen bubblers, air stones, titanium chillers, and high-flow, tube-in-shell evaporators. Others, meanwhile, opt for simpler high-volume water systems or pump-free designs that utilize a rocking sea or the forward motion of a boat to maintain their catch and minimize dead-loss.

Introduction

I think the most important lesson we can learn about what is going on with the development of at-sea live seafood holding systems is that HAACP, as a concept, a protocol, and a means of quality control, is now being embraced at the point of production—on the fishing boats themselves. Fishermen, especially Pacific Coast fishermen who have spent the last 10 years working with live seafood, have had enough time on the grounds to begin identifying where the stress points are on the live products they harvest and deliver.

The incentive for this application is obvious. California halibut fetches US $2.00 per pound fresh and $4.00 per pound live. Spot prawns that sell for $3.00 US a pound fresh are $8.00 a pound live. That is a terrific incentive for fishermen to upgrade their holding systems via the development of high tech or low tech methods, to reduce mortalities, and to deliver a live healthy product that remains vigorous for a long period of time.

Refrigeration

One of the stress points that the fishermen have identified is, of course, the problem of keeping water cold. Originally, for example, the literature suggested that 40°F (4°C) water was appropriate for the live holding of spot prawns and that a similar temperature was suitable for rockfish. However, what fishermen have discovered is that 34-35°F (1.1-1.7°C) is more appropriate. Holding water maintained within this narrow temperature range actually sends shrimp or rockfish into a state of semi-dormancy during which they excrete less waste, utilize less oxygen, and are easier to keep alive.

For this reason, more attention is being paid by the operators of both small and large harvesting boats to the most appropriate use of refrigeration systems. We are now seeing an increased use of titanium aboard these boats—titanium grid chillers and tanks, single pass titanium evaporators, and so on. The use of titanium avoids the occurrence of toxic copper ions leached from components in traditional refrigeration systems into the holding water. Also, considerable thought is being given to the most efficient use of these refrigeration systems.

During this time, fishermen have been working closely with manufacturers to incorporate into the mechanical systems aboard their vessels small refrigeration units that can accommodate the size of these vessels and their fisheries. One example of this type of progress is the advent of titanium grid chillers that are actually full immersion chillers that go directly into live tanks. In addition, single pass evaporators are used in concert with other water quality equipment in closed recirculating systems to recharge the holding water four to seven times a day. These systems remove waste materials while keeping the animals as cold as necessary.

We are seeing a ramped-up learning curve for fishermen in terms of refrigeration technology. Thanks to businesses like Aqua Logic and Integrated Marine Systems, fishermen now can purchase modular refrigeration systems that require no special expertise to install. These systems come almost prefabricated. All you have to do is hook up the inflow and outflow lines and you are ready to go. It is apparent that there is a general marriage occurring between the fishermen and manufacturers at this level.

Aeration

Harvesters in different fisheries have learned that grid aerators and air stones are one way to increase the amount of dissolved oxygen in a live holding system. In many fisheries it seems like you just cannot get too much oxygen to the fish. California's live sheepshead fishery is an example of this. I know that prawn fishermen in this region are also learning this same lesson. Some prawn live harvesters are even beginning to experiment with pure oxygen bubblers, not unlike the systems displayed at this conference by Point Four Systems.

There is some reticence among fishermen to move to a system using oxygen, a highly combustible material. Fishing boats generally do not have the controlled environments found at supermarkets and aquaculture facilities, but certainly some fishermen have them onboard and are experimenting with them successfully. With prawns, for example, you can see the change right onboard—just like in a supermarket—where oxygen is released into the live tank. The animals turn from a pale pinkish-white color to bright red almost instantly. So the incentive is there, although fishermen are very cautious about using compressed oxygen at sea. Many of these harvesters are looking forward to working with manufacturers to develop safe and easily maintainable onboard systems.

Fishermen are finding very successful low tech alternatives to the problem of aeration. Many fishermen have built venturis into their water pumping systems. This is quite often done by just plumbing a "T" off of the pressure side of the aeration pumps, or their water pumps, and drawing in ambient air by way of the venturi effect, creating a practical dissolved oxygen enhancement in their systems.

Another low tech solution that took fishermen ten years to understand is that finfish survive better in a round tank rather than in a square tank. So we are seeing a lot of retrofits to round tanks on commercial fishing boats in the finfish fishery along the Pacific Coast.

Filtering

Fishermen have also realized that filtering and removing waste like ammonia and other materials is very important—both in the finfish business and, of course, in prawn fisheries where the animals come up covered with silt and mud. In addition to turning over the onboard holding water three or four times a day through the introduction of seawater, fishermen are starting to think about using biofiltration when operating in situations where the flow-through strategy cannot be used. Biofilters like bead filters are used throughout the aquaculture industry, but have been a challenge for the commercial fishing industry because they are fairly bulky in size. But adaptations in the filters themselves are near—adaptations that may make them suitable for onboard use in the live fish industry. I am referring here to bead filters that serve both as a straining medium and as a medium for growing two kinds of bacteria that turn waste products first into nitrites and then into nitrates—turning toxic wastes into forms that are relatively harmless to the fish.

Enough advancements have been made with the design and use of bead filters, that fishermen are now for the first time considering importing this type of technology onto their vessels. They are beginning to take advantage of filtration methods present in land-based aquaculture and holding system operations. Much of this technology has been right there on the shoreline, but it is only now making the crossover into fishing industry.

Handling

The point of production or live harvesting is probably the most critical place where benefits to the landed product can accrue. All the work that the folks in this audience undertake to keep those animals alive in holding facilities and shipping facilities around the world can be greatly augmented by appropriate handling at sea. One of the things that the fishermen have learned is that the less you touch fish or shellfish with the human hands the better. It appears that the very handling of finfish with the human hand quite often removes the protective slime that fish have as a natural barrier against infection in the environment. Once you remove that slime, the fish becomes almost an instantaneous receptor to bacteria. These bacteria start the downward cycle—making it very difficult for the people holding or transporting the fish to keep them alive.

Live harvesting fishermen have developed such things as net systems to make possible the proper handling of the fish and venting devices to deflate gas bladders that have inflated when the fish are taken from depth to the surface. The bottom line theory is the less we touch these fish the better they will be. The same goes for shrimp.

The way many fishermen make use of their receiving tanks at sea is changing. Instead of leaving fish and shellfish in onboard tanks at night, for example, harvesters now often moor their animals by placing them back into the sea using specially designed holding pens and other structures. They are being very careful about how they design and deploy those receivers. If, for example, they place the harvested fish in barrels, they position these structures sideways to the sea. They have found that fish endure less stress if they can swim horizontally rather than if they are forced to mill about in a vertical column.

Also, wave motion has less of a jarring effect on a horizontally placed receiver than one held in the vertical position.

Fishermen also moor receiving barrels so that the sea is three-quarters of the way to the top of the barrels, reducing jarring and increasing water flow in the process. They use plastic, 55-gallon pickle barrels to which they add flotation and drill circulation holes so that buoyancy and water flow can be adequately controlled. Using this design strategy, waves can lap up the structure yet the barrels are not rocked about by the wave motion.

These are just a few of the practical methods fishermen are using to control the onboard environments in which harvested fish and shellfish are held. The photographs demonstrate some aspects of this technology and some of the means by which fishermen are trying to reduce stress loading on the animals. I want to thank the manufacturers including Aqua Logic for providing this material.

Holding systems illustrated

Titanium grid chillers measuring only 36 inches tall by about two inches thick are becoming more commonly used in regional live fisheries (not illustrated). These chillers fit quite nicely into the tank of a small fishing boat. You must remember that most of the boats that are delivering live fish along the Pacific Coast these days are in the range of 35-50 feet. They are often very well adapted to this type of fishery and also to this kind of technology. The chiller's titanium coils are tightly packed. Although titanium does not offer the thermal conductivity of copper, thin-wall construction incorporated into its design reduces this loss of efficiency to negligible levels. This is the kind of system that you will be seeing more often in boats within the above length range.

Shrimp-handling (Fig. 1): After the shrimp come aboard they are sorted on a 4 inch deep table filled with water. They then slide *untouched* into wire-mesh cages positioned on a transport table. These cages are then stacked in the harvesting vessel's refrigerated live tank. Once the shrimp are placed on the sorting table and are directed into the cages and placed in refrigerated seawater, they are not touched with human hands. The caged shrimp are ready for transport and they will not be touched again. Keep in mind the general theme at work here—the less touching the better.

Figure 2 provides an example of a biofiltration system that can be used onboard. The illustration is from a land-side facility, but it shows the loop in which biofilters can be incorporated. These filters have fairly large capacities; however, it will be challenging to get these units onto smaller fishing boats. Because of breakthroughs currently being made in biofiltration technology involving the modification of the beads and filter medium, it appears quite possible that this component of a recirculation system may be converted into a manageable size and placed on fishing boats within the next couple of years.

The use of this type of onboard system has considerable practical value. In lobsters that are held this way on land, biofiltration reduces mortality from approximately 15% down to 3%. Fishermen firmly

Figure 1. Stress reduction strategies aboard a shrimp vessel. Courtesy of Jon Chaiton, Inland Seafood Company, Atlanta, Georgia.

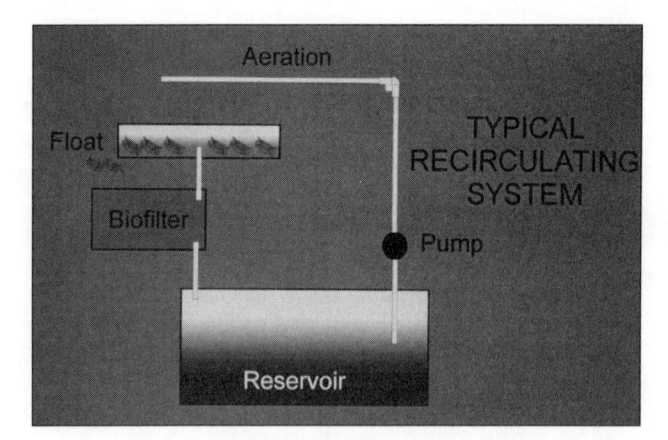

Figure 2. Small-scale biofiltration system.

The same user-friendly technology has been applied to the titanium tube-in-shell evaporator (Fig. 4). In this chilling unit, the refrigerant freon circulates through the tubes and seawater is pumped around the tubes. It is provided with a removable fiberglass shell that can be taken apart, cleaned, and reassembled with a series of O-rings. In this manner the seawater cooling chamber can be cleaned of various detritus, barnacles, and other growth to keep heat-exchange capacity of the unit at its greatest efficiency.

Figure 5 depicts a Santa Barbara, California, live ridgeback shrimp harvesting boat with a typical above-deck refrigeration system. The entire mechan-

believe that importing this type of technology on-board their harvesting boats will further reduce the level of mortality.

Figure 3 is an example of one of the small integrated refrigeration units that is typically seen on West Coast live boats these days. On the upper right side is a seawater inlet. The beauty of these systems is that they are fisherman-friendly. You are not required to have any special expertise or technical knowledge to install the units on a fishing vessel. It would take a day or, at the most, a day and a half to hook these units up and make them a part of the vessel's live holding system. In certain cases, some contract labor may be needed if you do not have the necessary understanding of the system and facilities or tools to get the job done in a timely manner.

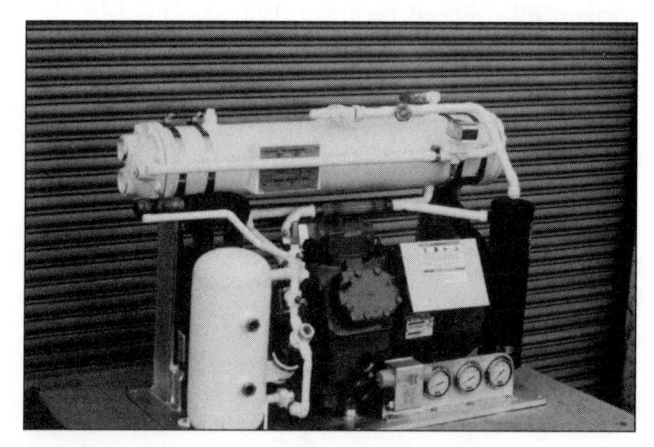

Figure 4. Titanium tube-in-shell evaporator.

ical system is not visible, but it shows how the shrimp are handled. The shrimp are handled in fairly high densities. They seem to be able to tolerate this treatment, even during day-fishing. However, these densities become less and less acceptable over time as the fisherman proceeds into a second or third day. This is particularly true with the more sensitive species, the spot prawn. It is necessary to thin these animals—to handle and live store them in lower densities. Fishermen are learning about acceptable densities relative to mortality levels by trial and error.

The fact must be remembered that those involved with the Pacific Coast live rockfish fishery make use of every type of fishing vessels—ranging from kayaks to 35-foot boats. Much of the technology used aboard these vessels is relatively basic and the solutions to mortality problems are low tech in nature. Figure 6 is a classic reflection of what is happening in live fish fisheries in California. It is a high-tech aluminum

Figure 3. Small integrated refrigeration unit intended for use of small harvesting vessels. Courtesy of Mark Burn, specialist in small-scale refrigeration systems, Integrated Marine Systems, Port Townsend, Washington.

Marketing and Shipping Live Aquatic Products

Figure 5. Refrigeration system aboard a California ridgeback shrimp harvesting vessel.

Figure 7. The rockfish are placed in a live tank and transferred to the holding tank on the mother ship.

skiff on the back of a commercial sea urchin dive boat. The skiff is used to live harvest rockfish during periodic seasonal sea urchin closures. The fish are placed in the skiff live tank and then transferred to the holding tank aboard the mother ship (Fig. 7), tiny as it might seem, and then transported to shore.

Figure 8 shows a low-tech, pumpless water circulation strategy that is gaining popularity in Pacific Coast live fish and shellfish fisheries. The intake device services the skiff's live tank in a pump-free fashion. When the boat is planing, water shoots through the forward-facing scoop, through a system of plumbing and valving, and aft to the tank. Through the use of this pumpless system, the fisherman can regulate the amount of water entering and exiting the tank.

Even when vessels employing this type of simple technology are at anchor in the evening, fishermen can adjust the water level in the tank with valves so that active circulation can be maintained with the sea much like in the case of a floating receiver. The regional harvesters have enjoyed great success at a very low cost using this low-tech means of keeping their animals alive. This is a relatively new water circulation strategy in the fleet, but one that has proved remarkably successful and the popularity of this design feature is sure to grow.

Figure 9 shows a crab shedding system on the U.S. East Coast. These systems are becoming more sophisticated all the time. Regional crabbers have managed to get off the water and move their shedding

Figure 6. Use of small catcher boats in the California live rockfish fishery.

Figure 8. This intake device services the skiff's live tank in a pumpless water system. Water shoots through the forward-facing scoop, through plumbing, and aft to the tank.

operations inland by 20-40 miles. To accomplish this move, various recirculation innovations have been used, including protein skimmers (Figs. 10-11). A skimmer makes use of air carefully pumped through the system—the bubbles binding to contaminants, creating a bubbly slurry that is skimmed out of the system. Live facility operators have been able to reduce blue crab mortalities from as high as 60% down to 15-10% or even lower. The product is peeler crabs destined for the soft-shell market. Once they have shed their old shells, they are ready to market.

Author biography

Mick Kronman is Pacific Bureau Chief at *National Fisherman Magazine*. He has been with *National Fisherman* for 17 years and also serves as a fisheries consultant.

Figure 9. A land-based live crab shedding system.

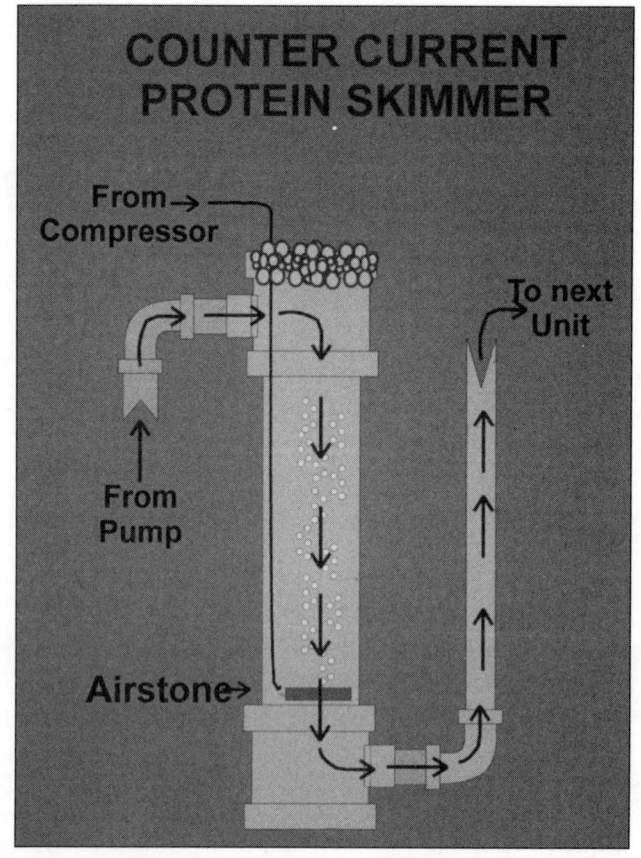

Figure 10. Counter-current protein skimmer.

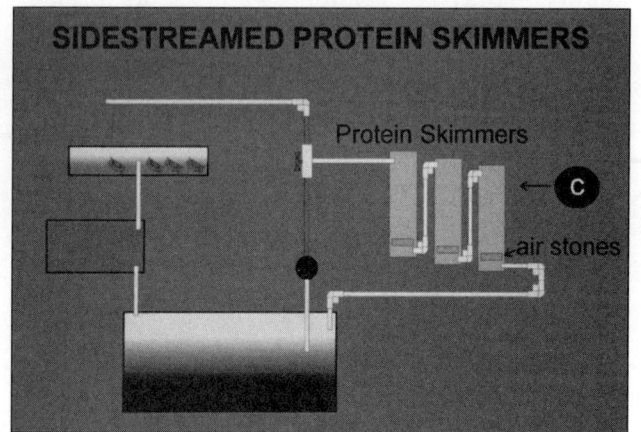

Figure 11. Sidestream protein skimmer.

Opportunity or Threat? Implications of the Live Halibut Fishery in British Columbia from the Harvester Perspective

Kim Mauriks
Dorcas Point Farms Inc. Nanoose Bay, British Columbia, Canada

Introduction

This report is a discussion on live marketing and its utility in the Pacific halibut fishery. Descriptions of the attitudes of halibut harvesters and the regulatory requirements of the International Pacific Halibut Commission (IPHC) are included. The main points of this review are as follows:

1. The Pacific halibut industry is an old and successful fishery that remains in very good condition. This stability predisposes this fishery to conservative management practices. Adaptation to change will probably be slow.

2. I am in the process of developing an innovation in which commercially captured Pacific halibut are live held in netpens, ongrown, and marketed during the off-season period. Although their number is steadily decreasing, some of my fellow harvesters believe that I will damage certain traditions underlying the stability of the fishery by pursuing this innovative strategy. I typically counter with the argument that I want to perpetuate these essential traditions and, in order to accomplish this goal, the management system must change a bit. I believe that if we want our children to have a chance to make a living from the sea, fishing and marketing procedures will have to change.

3. The fear of change among certain halibut harvesters and managers is a driving force behind the regulation of this fishery. These conservative practices need to be adjusted to allow the Pacific halibut fishery to adapt to changing world conditions.

Discussion

When our live holding project was described at the IPHC annual meeting in Seattle this year (1999), it immediately became an "international incident." These negative emotions were felt mainly by buyers who feared that a live holding strategy would take away their control over fishermen. Their main point appeared to be that "the sky will fall" if I continued my experimental program. These buyers were the main group lobbying Canadian fishery managers to stop these "illegal actions." Fortunately, a Canadian bureaucrat explained that my activities were not illegal and that the live holding of Pacific halibut was well within the bounds of the halibut treaty.

I showed a film the next day at the IPHC meeting and answered all their questions in a candid manner. I think that this information totally defused the remaining animosity. In the end the American and Canadian conference boards (fishermen's and other industry representatives who vote on industry initiatives and regulations at the IPHC meetings) voted not to change the dead fish regulation that disallows the landing of round (live fish are round) product, but not to hinder my project either. However, they were too apprehensive to "officially" endorse the project.

After the vote, fishermen told me that I should not take the vote to heart and that they truly applauded my efforts. One fellow actually stood up and spoke to the whole meeting, saying that my efforts were for the benefit of everyone and that I should be supported. So, all in all, management came along with me in the course of a couple of days. Fishing industry representatives from Alaska even asked for my phone number so they could contact me in the future for information.

The reasons for developing a practical halibut live holding strategy are quite simple. A question that should be asked is—why now? Bruce Leaman (director, International Pacific Halibut Commission) recently said, "I think everybody outside the industry that you mention this to will say, 'This is too logical. Why haven't you guys been doing this all along?' " The answer involves the traditional nature of the Pacific halibut fishery. This type of development has not come along because the region has had a very healthy fishery for 76 years. It is probably the best wild fishery in the world. For generations harvesters have just gone out, fished, and earned a very good living.

However, about ten years ago, our world started to turn upside down as the market began to change. It took awhile for this new information to sink in. The world market now has top quality cultured product available year-round—a range of products competing with our seasonal halibut product. If we do not meet this marketing challenge, members of the halibut industry will slowly lose their previously enjoyed market domination. This same thing has happened in the salmon industry. If we meet the quality and availability standards demanded in the changing marketplace, there is no reason wild Pacific halibut should be banished to second grade markets.

The title of this report includes the phrase "opportunity or threat." In order to get the most from this resource, we must send our product into the marketplace year-round and in the product form of highest quality. I have no doubt that a new generation of these innovative marketers will be able to satisfy all the concerns of the IPHC commissioners.

The halibut fishery has progressed toward a quota fishery that takes place eight months of the year. It is a highly managed fishery, particularly in Canada, where we have a full validation system. We account for every pound of halibut harvested, except for those caught in the sport fishery, which is not monitored to this same level of accuracy. To be sure, there may be a small degree of poaching. Pound for pound, however, the Pacific halibut fishery is probably the best-managed fishery in the world.

This careful management is the reason that we still have a fishery. It is the reason we will be able to handle all the data and sampling requirements originating from the commission. Live holding might actually provide opportunities for the collection of additional types of valuable data. For the first time, we will have a large volume of halibut being held captive. This will allow projects, such as an investigation into the nature of chalky halibut, which were never possible in the traditional fishery.

We will be able to handle all of the issues the director of the IPHC has brought up. During the course of the project, we will handle the international treaty concerns. I hope that I will not have to become a treaty expert before this is all done. I also hope that people will be logical about this issue. For example, a basic problem needs to be resolved right now. To stop us from bringing in live fish, managers are using a dead fish quality rule that was meant to force fishermen to dress their catch at sea, not later at the dock. We wish to exceed this quality standard. I suggest that we develop a workable set of live fish rules and begin to deal with this new marketing opportunity in a constructive manner.

The fact is that many fishermen do not want to see an end to their traditional way of doing business. It has worked for the better part of a century, so why change now? Most of our current problems with the industry stem from the word "tradition," and the resistance to our movement away from traditional forms of business. Most people do not like change. For many in the industry, the initiative to move to an individual quota fishery was a huge leap. A few years of experience now tells us that this new way of managing the fishery is working better than any of us could have imagined. I think the development of the live holding strategy is one of the final steps in the development of the Pacific halibut fishery.

Traditionally, commercial fisheries are supply driven. Simply stated, there are fish in the ocean, fishermen go out and catch them, and then they worry about selling them or hiring somebody else to sell them for later. Traditionally a fisherman would try to catch the fish as fast as possible. However, in this new marketing age, we must act more like farmers and become vertically integrated all the way from the fisherman on the fishing vessel to the consumer.

We will undoubtedly continue to fish using the same methods members of the industry have used for generations, but we need to build up an inventory strategy like any other production business. The question is—how are we planning to supply the expanding fresh market? At about the time Canada went into the quota system eight years ago, the market's capacity for fresh fish was 400,000 pounds a week. Beyond this, the entire fresh market system would become clogged. Now, just over two million pounds a week can be moved into the fresh market. This market sector has expanded in a major way and we must become clever in satisfying the demand.

I have had fishermen come up to me and say, "Oh, now you're going to compete with us in the frozen market during the winter. You're going to be selling and competing with our frozen product." My response is that, first, a prime fresh product is not competing with a frozen product. It is an entirely different product. We are dealing with different groups of consumers. I usually tell them that I am pulling my fish out of the regular market and, in a very minuscule way, expanding a previously underdeveloped market sector for you. I am pulling my product away from the traditional winter season frozen halibut market. I am expanding the market into the four months of the year in which fresh product is not available. I am further developing the fresh market. In the end, if we can produce a consistently high quality product, our efforts will increase the market for everybody.

The Canadian halibut quota in 1999 was 12.1 million pounds. My project did just under 1% of that quota this year, 104,000 pounds. One percent is the maximum level allowed per fishing vessel in the halibut fishery in Canada. The 104,000 pounds is most definitely not a market—it is nothing compared to a market that can handle two million pounds of fresh product a week. Potentially, we could take our entire Canadian quota, save it for later retail sale, and sell it into those four winter months and we still would not have enough product for the off-season. In addition, I am sure the market will keep on increasing. I estimate that the world market wants more than 71 million pounds. This demand will be satisfied. It will be coming from Chile, Norway, Iceland, and other fish farming countries in a big way.

As others at this conference have stated, we want to make sure we are able to maintain a solid grasp on our share of that market. By applying a more flexible approach to our fishery, in the future we will be in a better position to deal with halibut culture as it proliferates or deal with different product forms as they are developed. At the very least, we must attain the ability to compete with them on an even basis.

So, when dealing with and attempting to inform other harvesters, my biggest issue is to show them that this is not the end—the live holding marketing strategy is a part of the future. I want my kids to be able to fish. I think this innovation will allow our children to continue fishing and, simultaneously, open up a whole new world of market opportunities.

Are there other benefits associated with the way I market fresh halibut? When our fish is sold in Los Angeles or New York, I personally hear what that buyer thought about the fish. I quickly learn what I have to change in terms of fishing practices, holding practices, or in myriad other details. Before I began to direct market the halibut into the fresh market, the "game" was played out primarily between the fisherman and the local buyer. The questions are pretty much the same—are the halibut two days old or are they four days old? Every once in a while, the local buyer gets stuck with a few 10-day-old fish. Then he does the same thing to the wholesaler who, in turn, does the same thing to the retailer. In the end, the consumer ends up with what sometimes is a very poor fish. The fisherman rarely find out about this. Some harvesters really do not care about this type of information. My system is vertically integrated—we are directly connected to the marketplace and its end users. I think that this is one of the most important lessons the aquaculture industry has taught us.

Last year, the Pacific Halibut Council held a meeting to look at the marketing problems in the Pacific halibut industry. John Forrester, formerly of Stolt Seafarm, was present at this meeting. He was talking about our marketing problems and, more specifically, about a pivotal problem within the commercial industry. At the end of his presentation, Forrester said, "You guys have to get over your adversarial ways. You have to work together instead of always pointing your fingers at each other. And you must start looking at the whole marketing picture." At this point, everyone looked at each other and said, "Adversarial? Not me. We're fine." As soon as John left, though, the usual practice of blaming the "other" group or sector for the mounting problems continued.

Conclusion

I am happy to report that the International Pacific Halibut Commission, the Department of Fisheries and Oceans Canada, the Province of British Columbia, and the fishermen are getting behind this concept and are beginning to cooperate. The attitude that "If I cannot do it, neither will you!" seems to be fading for the first time. I believe they are able to see clearly the opportunities made possible by this new concept. Also for the first time, more than just a handful of harvesters thought it would be a good idea to allow fishermen to keep their halibut bycatch during the off-season if they have quota shares for it. In the past, nobody wanted to see others profit while they could not.

Marketing British Columbia halibut in this manner helps everybody by spreading the highest quality product over a longer period of availability. Fresh halibut will no longer be a seasonal product and can be made available year-round.

It will increase the overall marketability of all halibut product forms throughout the marketplace. Maybe, after the passage of a century, the industry is finally starting to mature.

Resource Management and Environmental Issues Concerning Live Halibut Landings

Bruce M. Leaman
International Pacific Halibut Commission, Seattle, Washington

Introduction

The product form at landing for Pacific halibut has traditionally been with gills and entrails removed. This form has been mandated by regulation of the International Pacific Halibut Commission (IPHC) since 1995. This regulation was introduced to avoid the quality problems associated with landings of round fish during the short, intense fisheries of the 1990s and to improve the opportunities for IPHC samplers to obtain otoliths. However, the issue of product form for halibut (e.g., whole, filleted, steaked, etc.) has never been significant for IPHC, rather it has been a market-driven issue. The mandate of IPHC has concerned primarily stock health, productivity, and accurate stock assessments.

Recently, an innovative approach to increasing the added-value of halibut has been introduced in British Columbia. Fish captured legally at sea under provisions of the normal commercial fishery are transported live to shore-based holding pens, for subsequent sale during the closed season for halibut fishing. The intent of the project is to gain a higher unit value through the sale of fresh, wild fish throughout the year. The holding operation permits quality, inventory, and delivery control of greater precision than during the regular halibut fishing season.

I would first like to profile the species and its fishery and then review some of the implications for halibut management, should the practice of live landing become a greater proportion of total halibut landings. The British Columbia live-fish operation raises a number of issues for IPHC. These issues can be grouped under the headings of fishing practices, holding practices, and regulatory issues.

Fishery background

The International Pacific Halibut Commission has been managing the Pacific halibut stock throughout its range since 1923 (Fig. 1). The IPHC was created at the request of the halibut industry to address the problems of resource depletion in the late 1910s. The present-day fishery is far-removed in character from those of previous times. Prior to 1991 in Canada and 1995 in the United States, the fishery was regulated primarily by controlling the fishing season length. With the introduction of advanced navigational technology and improved fishing gear in the 1980s, the season length for the halibut fishery had begun to shrink from several months per year, to only several days per year. This shortening occurred despite a steadily increasing stock size in the 1980s and 1990s. In Alaskan waters, by the early 1990s, the season was composed of a series of one-day openings, often with limits governed by vessel size. The fishery in British Columbia was only slightly longer.

These short, derby-style fisheries resulted in tremendous quality problems because vessels would set more gear than could be hauled in the 24-hour openings. Many of the harvested fish would not be dressed or iced for up to several days after capture. The movement to individual quota (IQ) management programs in the United States and Canada was largely in response to the quality and manageability problems created by these derby fisheries. The IQ programs allowed harvesters to set their own business plans and devote more time to fish quality. The season was extended to 245 days, from March 15 to November 15 annually. The fishery is presently in the 65-70 million pound range (net weight) and the average fish size in the catch is approximately 25 pounds.

The four-month closure of the fishery creates a gap in the supply of fresh, wild halibut to the market. The live-fish holding project in British Columbia is an attempt to fill this gap, but it raises a number of concerns for IPHC.

Fishing practices

The IPHC expends considerable effort to include all sources of mortality in its stock assessment. Not all fish caught at sea may be suitable for live holding and delivery to subsequent markets. Markets may pay a premium for fish of specific size ranges, condi-

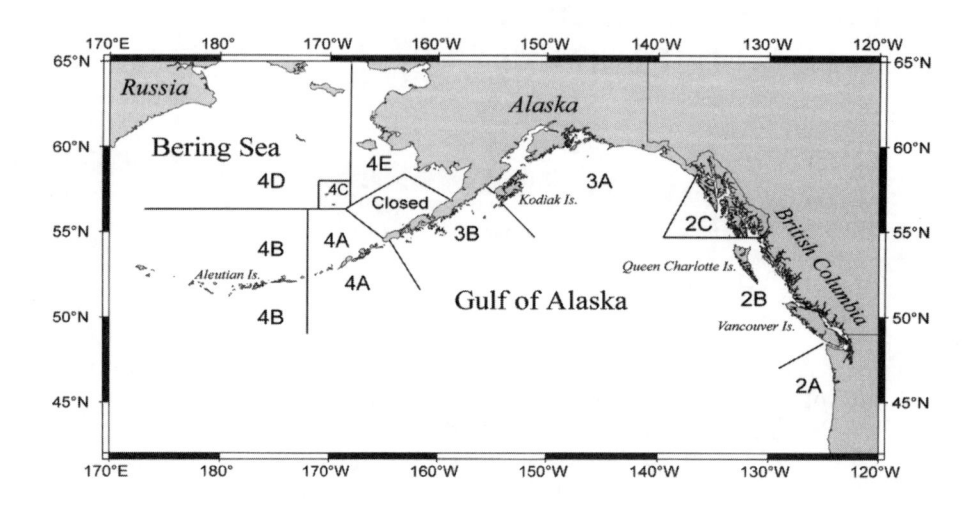

Figure 1. International Pacific Halibut Commission regulatory areas.

tion, or other features, which could introduce incentives to discard fish at sea that did not have appropriate characteristics for the markets being served. If such high-grading occurs at sea and is unrecorded, then an additional source of mortality which may not be accounted for correctly in the assessment is imposed on the stock. If this unrecorded discard mortality is large, the stock assessment model will not be capable of differentiating this increased mortality from lower recruitment. The net effect on estimated abundance will be the same, but the information used to estimate relationships of stock and recruitment, as well as to project future stock scenarios, will be incorrect. Significant bias between the commercial size limit and the fish retained for live fish operations may also introduce bias into the estimated selectivity for the commercial fishery.

The scale of the live fish operation in British Columbia is presently small (about 1% of the total quota) and the impact of the imperfect data capture or wasteful fishing operations would be almost undetectable in the stock assessment. However, the principle of responsible fishing operations and accurate data capture remains the same regardless of the scale of such fishing. Prudent oversight of operations is required.

HOLDING PRACTICES

The practice of holding halibut in pens is still in its infancy on the west coast of North America and much knowledge of optimal procedures remains to be acquired. Mortality of fish in holding pens is a cost to the operator, who has a clear incentive to minimize such mortality. The IPHC's prime concerns about holding practices relate to mortality in pens, potential disease issues, sampling, data integrity, and tracking of fish to the point of sale.

The issues of mortality of Pacific halibut in holding pens and data integrity are closely linked. In standard landings of halibut, fish are tracked from the vessel to point of initial sale, all fish must be unloaded from the vessel once unloading begins, and the totals are recorded on a sales slip and accounted for in the harvester's IQ records. If fish are unloaded by the harvester into pens owned by the harvester, then the requirements for documentation may not be met, since the fish would not yet be sold. A system of validation for removals and tracking of product to point of sale is clearly needed to ensure that total removals from the resource are accounted for. IPHC suggests that tagging and validation of fish at both input and output of pens would be required. Missing or loose tags would still have the corresponding fish counted as removals, and any fish found untagged would need to be released back to the wild.

Transmission of diseases from pen holding operations to wild fish is a concern for any operation open to the natural environment. The concern does not relate to new diseases, but rather to the amplification of existing diseases or parasites within the holding environment. Since the holding of wild halibut in pens is still in its infancy, the time is opportune to establish fish health protocols and the attendant monitoring and screening procedures. These protocols are necessary both to ensure the health of the penned fish and for assessing whether risks to wild stocks exist.

REGULATORY ISSUES

The primary regulatory issues for penned halibut concern sampling opportunities, monitoring of pen throughput, and validation. IPHC samples randomly from landings to obtain biological information on the catch and aging structures for input to the stock assessment process. The aging structures are otoliths that must be taken from the inside of the otic capsules of the halibut skulls. Normally, the intensity of such sampling is on the order of 1-5% of the total quota by area and introduces no constraint on commercial operations because fish are dead at the time of offloading. In the case of live offloads, fish would need to be killed to obtain the otoliths and the sampling would need to occur at input to the holding pens to preserve randomness in fish selection for sampling.

The preceding section noted the need for adequate validation of halibut throughput in holding pens. Validation of tag numbers and fish at both input and output can be time-consuming and expensive, particularly for remote locations where validation personnel must be transported from some distance. However, the absence of such validation would create an unacceptable risk to the integrity of the data capture for these removals. The regulations governing IQ offloading in Canada presently require full validation for each fish, which are subsequently tagged on the tail for marketing purposes. Offloads of U.S. IQ halibut must be processed through a registered buyer but are validated only at the level of total weight by area. Enforcement staff have expressed concern about the potential problems that would be created if holding pens and the associated registered buyers were distributed widely throughout Alaska, and fish could be offloaded directly to these pens. The additional costs of the necessary validation for such operations may introduce new economic constraints on the viability of halibut holding in some jurisdictions.

INTERNATIONAL MANAGEMENT

The Pacific halibut is managed jointly by the United States and Canada. Regulations passed by the International Pacific Halibut Commission at its annual meeting, and concurred with by the two governments, are to be incorporated into each country's domestic regulations. The derby fisheries noted above created significant quality problems in halibut because of the often substantial time that elapsed between capture and processing of the fish. Fish would be brought in, round and un-iced, simply because the vessel crew could not sacrifice the time required to process, at the expense of less time spent fishing. The regulation requiring dressing of fish (i.e., the gills and entrails removed) prior to offloading was introduced by IPHC, and adopted by the two countries, largely to address these quality problems, but also to facilitate biological sampling by IPHC staff.

The advent of IQ fisheries with their slower pace and extended season, in conjunction with the now-standard process of dressing and icing fish at sea, eliminated the quality problems of the derby fisheries. The regulation requiring dressing at sea remains in both the IPHC and U.S. regulations. Since 1999 the Canadian government has explicitly rejected this IPHC regulation, in order to permit legal offloading of live halibut to holding pens. While the issue of live fish offloads is minor and one for which adequate validation framework can be developed, IPHC would prefer to avoid having either country reject regulations adopted within the IPHC venue. Such selective adoption of regulations is not a sound course for a treaty-based organization, since it provides a poor precedent for successful implementation of regulations governing more difficult issues. It is therefore highly desirable for the two countries to resolve the acceptability of live fish holding within IPHC regulations.

SUMMARY

Live holding of Pacific halibut represents an innovative approach to increasing the added value of the catch. Regulatory and international management issues associated with this initiative should be resolved, and adequate monitoring and validation procedures should be implemented before the practice becomes widespread. Long-term risks of holding practices on the environment and interaction with wild halibut stocks should also be assessed. With adequate measures to safeguard data integrity for fisheries management, live holding of halibut for off-season sales could provide a year-round supply of fresh, wild halibut in the marketplace.

Sterling Pacific Halibut: A New Approach

Kim Mauriks
Dorcas Point Farms Inc., Nanoose Bay, British Columbia, Canada

Introduction

Traditionally, fresh Pacific halibut, *Hippoglossus stenolepis,* is available in the marketplace only on a seasonal basis. During the off-season, a frozen product is available in limited supply. As a commercial fisherman trying to obtain maximum value for my catch, I set up a project to develop methods for producing a consistent premium fresh product year-round. Halibut were captured by longline during the annual commercial fishery and transported in a live hold aboard the harvesting vessel to netpens for ongrowing and eventual marketing. In this way, enterprising halibut harvesters will be able to provide a freshly harvested or live product every day of the year. The initial market response has been very favorable. We are marketing the fish as Sterling Pacific Halibut because, in the aquaculture trade, sterling is the best.

Figure 1. The vessel used in this project is a 50-foot fiberglass longliner, the *Triple M II*.

The fishery

The vessel used in this project is a 50-foot fiberglass longliner, the *Triple M II* (Fig. 1). This vessel was built by our family in the 1960s. She was the second freezer boat on the coast and was converted for live holding in 1999. The live holding system consists of an 18 cubic meter tank equipped with a titanium chiller and an oxygen injection system. We found that this system could hold about 6,000 pounds of live fish. Over typical holding periods, mortalities could be kept at about 2%.

Harvesting trips are usually one to two days long. We fish within close proximity of the pens, somewhere between one to six hours travel time. The only modification to our normal longline gear is the use of barbless hooks. This makes for easy removal of the hook and, therefore, less damage and stress to the fish. We fished anywhere from 25 fathoms to 150 fathoms in depth. It is interesting to note that at shallower depths the fish were so lively that they were too hard to handle. Consequently, it worked out better to place fishing gear at deeper depths and harvest fish that were partially in shock. There did not appear to be any long-term ill effects associated with harvesting halibut from deeper depths.

The gear is soaked or fished for about two to four hours. This is enough time to get a sufficient number of fish on the hooks while minimizing their capture time and exposure to sea lice. We found that up to about two-meter seas were tolerable for the fish—any more than that and our mortalities would rise substantially.

When we begin hauling the longline, the first job is to record the bottom temperature with a temperature probe snapped to the groundline. This temperature is programmed into the refrigerated seawater (RSW) computer that controls water temperature in the vessel holding system. We keep the temperature in the hold at 0.5°C lower than that of the bottom water to calm the fish.

As the fish come aboard, they are placed on the examining table where the hook is removed and any adhering sea lice are rinsed off. The halibut are then measured and examined for injuries (Fig. 2). The length measurement is taken to determine if the fish is of legal size (32 inches/82 cm minimum) and to

Figure 2. As the fish come aboard they are examined for injuries.

determine the weight using length-weight tables. In this way, we calculate the amount of product so as to not overload the hold. The fish are then gently placed in the vessel holding tank.

OFFLOADING PROCEDURE

When we offload the halibut, the water in the hold is pumped down to about a three-foot depth so the crew can work properly. The fish are gently placed into a wet brailer in lots of about 10 fish or 250 pounds. This varies with the size of the fish. Large fish are lifted on their own so as not to harm the smaller ones. The brailer is of web design and is provided with a vinyl liner. This liner has a regular pattern of slots to allow water drainage. Ideally, we would like to retain the water around the halibut, but the quota validation system requires a weight measurement for management of the halibut fishery.

Once the weight is recorded, the fish are placed in a sorting tank (Fig. 3) where they are sorted for best use. Each fish is tagged with its own number so it can be followed through the holding and marketing process.

The fish are sorted into three groups:

1. The first group is intended for long-term rearing and later marketing. These fish must be in perfect shape, with clear eyes, normal skin coloration, and no significant injuries.

2. The second group is selected for placement in an acclimation-harvest pen. These fish have visible signs of stress or an injury. We harvest from this pen on a weekly basis and market the fish that we feel are not suitable for long-term rearing. The fish that have recovered from the stress associated with capture are then transferred to one of the long-term holding pens.

3. The third group is selected for immediate harvest. These are fish that we feel will not survive until the next scheduled harvest.

ONGROWING

The pen site we are using is in Quatsino Sound at the northwestern tip of Vancouver Island, British Columbia. The sound is sufficiently protected to allow for year-round live holding and off-season harvesting. We use four 15 m × 15 m × 20 m deep salmon pens that have been altered with a polyethylene frame to provide them with a flat bottom. The water temperatures at 20 m ranges between 8 and 12°C and the dissolved oxygen (DO) readings range from 6 to 10 ppm.

The fish are monitored daily with an underwater video camera to observe feeding and record the general condition of the fish. Divers are sent down regularly to remove any mortalities and inspect the integrity of the pens. This year we suffered an 8% loss due to mortality. We feel this mortality level was largely the result of two factors:

1. Inadequate feeding.

2. The external parasite (*Entobdella hippoglossi*).

Figure 3. The fish are placed in a sorting tank.

The live held halibut are fed a ration of specially formulated pellets. Since our fish are large and not accustomed to eating pellets, the Norwegian-style pellets did not work very well. We found that our fish prefer a large moist feed, such as chunks of salmon or squid. We were told that this response is normal and that the fish would eventually change over to the pellet diet. However, this changeover period proved to be unacceptable because the loss of growth potential is too great and the fish get in a weakened state that leads to other problems. Therefore, we will be experimenting with different feed types this year to maximize feeding response. We observed a very good response with a sausage-style feed and will develop it further this year.

Because of the above-mentioned diet problem, the halibut did not achieve any net gain in weight. The longest period some of the fish were held was 10 months. Some fish were obviously very well fed, but the majority were underfed. We ended up with a 2.8% net weight loss—the loss due to mortality was greater than our growth. We were not able to generate this figure until the pens were completely empty in March 2000. Another problem surfaced at this time. Unfortunately, the fish bit off the growth-monitoring identification tags from each other. The tags were more appealing than the pellets.

Because the fish were in a stressed state from capture and weak because of the lack of proper feed, they were more susceptible to parasites. *Entobdella hippoglossi* is a monogenean skin parasite that is present on the fish when they are captured. With the higher holding densities and higher water temperatures in the pens, the parasite has ideal growing and transmission conditions. In Norway, infestations of this parasite have resulted in loss of appetite and mortality. Our experience this year seems to confirm this. Feeding behavior and parasite infestation are closely linked. Improvements in either area will help overall. This coming season we will treat the fish for the parasite onboard before they are placed in the pens, thereby minimizing the introduction of the parasite into the holding system. We experimented this year with freshwater baths and were very encouraged by the results.

In addition to parasite and water temperature problems, our holding site is also subject to occasional harmful algal blooms. British Columbia is subject to these plankton blooms from late July to the middle of September. During the blooms, the halibut faired quite well in comparison to the salmon at a nearby farm. The salmon farm suffered considerable losses, while the halibut merely lost their appetites with very little immediate mortality. However, this also contributed to the feeding problem, which seems to be at the center of all our concerns.

HARVESTING

Being able to harvest halibut in order to take best advantage of market demand is what this project is all about. Presently we are removing between 2,500 to 5,000 pounds of halibut during each harvest. The bottom of the pen is raised to the surface to facilitate the removal of the fish and then lowered until the next harvest (Fig. 4). The fish are brailed into a stun tank containing slush and carbon dioxide, held there for about 5 minutes, and then bled. These processing steps are all contained within the hull of the transport vessel. The fish are then shipped in slush totes to the processing plant by ship and truck. The trip requires a total elapsed time of about 3 hours.

The key to our live inventory project is our ability to supply our customers with consistently high quality product throughout the year. This coming year we will explore the possibility of marketing the product live—i.e., transporting live fish directly to a final customer. So far, we have not had any requests for live halibut for the restaurant market. However, we have been approached by international aquarium wholesalers in need of live fish for display purposes.

Figure 4. The bottom of the pen is raised to the surface to facilitate the removal of the fish and then lowered until the next harvest.

Conclusion

The market cannot get enough of our product. However, before we can increase production to meet this demand we must be confident of our husbandry practices for maintaining the stock in the pens. Everything hinges on our ability to reduce the economic risk to an acceptable level by improving these husbandry techniques. Until we can count on a certain level of weight gain, we will be unable to make the infrastructure investments needed to increase our production. In order for the concept to be viable, growth must accompany the greater marketability. We are optimistic about our prospects.

Resource Management Issues in California's Commercial Nearshore Live/Premium Finfish Fishery

Christine Pattison
California Department of Fish and Game, Morro Bay, California

Introduction

The total number of fish in California's nearshore area is unknown. Therefore, fishery managers do not know how many fish can be safely harvested. Recent trends involving reduced landings strongly suggest resource overexploitation. Both commercial and recreational fisheries are utilizing this resource. Commercial and recreational fishers as well as resource managers agree that the harvest needs to be reduced to a sustainable level. However, no agreement has been reached on how to go about accomplishing this goal, nor on how the resource should be allocated among users.

Historically, commercial use of these nearshore resources has been minimal. Many commercial hook-and-line fishers who traditionally fished offshore have now switched to the more valuable nearshore live-fish fishery. This movement has been brought about by the more restrictive trip limits and quotas (Appendix 1) imposed by the Pacific Fishery Management Council (PFMC) and the California Department of Fish and Game (CDFG), and the significantly higher price paid per pound for live fish.

Currently, the nearshore fishery is managed by both the CDFG and the PFMC. Groups concerned about this fishery include sport fishing organizations, environmental groups, commercial passenger fishing vessel operators, recreational fishers, other resource users, managers, and the California Legislature. The intensity of fishing on the nearshore fishery stocks and concerns about the sustainability of these stocks have led to the passage of the Marine Life Management Act of 1998 (MLMA) and the Nearshore Fisheries Management Act of 1998 (NFMA). Both legislative acts significantly and fundamentally change the way California's marine resources are managed by transferring management authority for nearshore fisheries from the state legislature to the Fish and Game Commission (FGC).

The MLMA mandates that scientifically based fisheries management plans be used to manage California's fisheries. Long term sustainability is the goal of these plans. The CDFG is currently in the process of developing a nearshore fishery management plan with input from various user groups. Resource users providing input include members of the sport and commercial fishing industries, aquaculture industries, coastal and ocean tourism and recreation industries, marine conservation organizations, local governments, marine scientists, and the public.

The commercial nearshore live/premium fish fishery began in California in the mid-1980s and has increased substantially over the years. The fishery occurs over rocky habitat from the intertidal zone out to about 15 fathoms. In 1998, nearshore fish landings totaled 670 metric tons (417 tons in the form of live product) with an ex-vessel value of $3.3 million ($2.7 million for live product). The potentially high profit and low overhead of this unique fishery have caused a tremendous increase in the number of fishers—from 76 in 1989 to over 1,000 in 1999. All agree that there are too many fishers in the nearshore fishery, but again, cannot agree on how to reduce the numbers.

Several factors make it difficult for resource managers to monitor and collect biological samples from this nontraditional fishery. These include the large number of participants; numerous landings and landing sites; the time constraints imposed by the need to deliver live fish to the ultimate consumer as quickly as possible; language and cultural barriers; and uncooperative fishers and buyers. The industry needs to join resource managers in finding solutions. In short, the industry needs to be active in the management process.

Fishers need to become more conscientious stewards of the resource by staying within quotas and observing size and catch restrictions. This includes the returning of sublegal fish after proper hook removal and careful swim bladder deflation. The industry needs to promote and encourage conservation among fishers, buyers, and retailers in order for management plans to succeed. It is crucial that industry cooperate with biologists collecting fishery data. Biologists need accurate and reliable information to develop effective fishery management plans. With little biological knowledge, resource managers must take a more conservative approach and use more restrictive measures to manage the resource.

Resource management of California's commercial nearshore fishery

There is considerable concern for the status of California's nearshore fish stocks and the impact that the commercial live/premium fishery is having on these stocks. We do not know how many fish are in the nearshore environment, how many fish larvae are produced, or how many fish are ultimately recruited into the fishery. Certain types of fish mortality or removal, such as undocumented landings, mortalities as a result of catch and release fishing, natural mortalities (e.g., predation), and natural weather events, such as El Niño, have not been quantified. We also do not know the extent of mortalities due to loss of habitat (filling in of estuaries), habitat degradation, water quality changes, temperature changes, and pollution (e.g., runoff from urban areas). Due to the lack of knowledge regarding populations in the nearshore environment, resource managers must take a precautionary approach in setting allowable harvest levels.

The management goal is to establish a maximum sustainable yield (MSY), which is defined as the highest average yield over time that does not result in a continuing reduction in stock abundance. MSY takes into account fluctuations in abundance and environmental variability. Some of the basic fishery management tools used to achieve MSY include:

1. Limiting the harvest by quotas and size limits.

2. Limiting fishing efficiency by gear restrictions.

3. Limiting fishing effort by restricting number of fishers, areas open to the fishery, fishing time or season (Appendix 1).

The MLMA mandates the development of a nearshore fishery management plan by September 1, 2002, and provides for the FGC to adopt regulations implementing the plan. The FGC may also adopt interim management measures to regulate the take of nearshore fish stocks until a fishery management plan is adopted. Currently, the FGC is developing a restricted access (limited entry) program for the California nearshore fishery with a proposed control date between May 1, 1999 and December 31, 1999. It is also proposing a moratorium on the issuance of new Nearshore Fishery Permits after May 15, 2000. Regulations adopted by the commission may include, but are not limited to, establishing restricted access areas, requiring submittal of landing and permit information including logbooks, and regulating fishing seasons, areas, and gear. Interim harvest guidelines for individual fish species or species groups may also be established.

The MLMA established commercial size limits for ten nearshore species. Nearshore species were defined in the NFMA as:

- Rockfish (Sebastes).
- California sheephead (*Semicossyphus pulcher*).
- Greenlings (*Hexagrammos*).
- Cabezon (*Scopaenichthys marmoratus*).
- California scorpionfish (*Scorpaena guttata*).
- Other fish species found primarily in rocky reef or kelp habitat in nearshore waters may also be included.

The MLMA requires that all commercial fishing vessels be registered and requires the possession of a Nearshore Fishery Permit to take, possess, or land any of the ten nearshore species. In addition, federal regulations require that groundfish species for which there is a size limit must be sorted prior to weighing. This weight must be reported separately on the CDFG receipt (Appendix 1). All of these regulations are important management steps that, if enforced statewide, will help fishery biologists quantify landings and more accurately estimate, by species, the number and pounds of fish being removed from the nearshore ecosystem.

If any regulations are to be effective in protecting the nearshore fishes, it is essential that fishers and buyers be well informed about the following:

1. Concept of sustainable fisheries.

2. Identification of species.

3. Importance of size limits.

4. Importance of allowing more fish to reproduce before being harvested.

5. The basic biology of the nearshore fishes, especially the rockfishes, which are slow-growing, long-lived, and residential, and have irregular recruitment patterns.

Another critical element in the management of nearshore fish is rigorous enforcement of regulations and the verification of species composition in market categories with market sampling.

Recommendations for additional management measures:

1. Change the California Fish and Game Code from permissive to restrictive (e.g., nothing can be harvested unless it is specifically permitted).

2. Establish legal minimum size limit for brown rockfish (*Sebastes auriculatus*) of 12 inches TL. Sample length data from Morro Bay port complex for 1993 through 1998 indicates that 38% of the sampled fish were below 12 inches TL. Twelve inches is the length at which 50% of the females are mature. California Assembly Bill 1241 (California Assemblyman F. Keeley) included a legal minimum size limit of 12 inches TL for brown rockfish. However, California Senate Bill 1336 (California Senator M. Thompson) listed legal minimum size limits for the near shore with the exception of the brown rockfish. Due to the order in which the bills were signed by then Governor Pete Wilson, Senate Bill 1336 (California Senator M. Thompson), which did not include a minimum size limit for brown rockfish, took precedent over Assembly Bill 1241 list that included the brown rockfish.

3. Restrict commercial fishing gear to rod-and-reel in designated nearshore areas around major recreational ports. This will reduce the amount of commercial fishing effort in areas most frequented by recreational fishers.

4. Encourage fishers to use voluntary logbooks. Logbooks would provide biologists with crucial information on effort, gear, fishing location, species, and bycatch. This information is needed to describe and understand the nearshore fishery. Biologists theorize that as areas geographically close to ports are overfished, fishers move farther from ports into more remote areas and/or increase fishing effort to maintain catch levels. Information from logbooks would answer these questions.

CALIFORNIA'S COMMERCIAL NEARSHORE FISHERY

Preliminary 1998 commercial landings of nearshore live/premium fishes reported on CDFG market receipts were 670 tons (417 tons live) with an ex-vessel value of $3.3 million ($2.7 million live) (Table 1). The number of documented landings is approximately 40,000 annually. The number of undocumented landings is unknown, but it is suspected to be quite substantial. There are 1,200 miles of coastline in California, with nine major port complexes with a total of 110 other ports, and hundreds of additional locations where fish can be landed (launch ramps, boat slips, docks, piers, beaches, etc).

The principal goal of this nontraditional fishery is to deliver the fish, live and in a good condition, to the ultimate consumer in as timely a manner as possible. Trucks or vans equipped with aerated tanks are used to transport fish directly to fish markets, restaurants, and individuals. Many fishers deliver and sell their own catch. All these elements have complicated the required documentation of landings.

Ex-vessel prices ranged from $0.20 to $12.00 per pound, with an average price of $2.50 per pound. Prices vary with the species, condition, and size of the fish. Many fish do not survive the rigors of capture and transport and are sold dead, often at greatly reduced prices. Because of their decreased value, dead fish that were intended for the live-fish market may be discarded at sea, used as bait, discarded at the dock, sold to another market, given away, or taken home for personal use. These fish may not be reported on a landing receipt. Under current restrictive quotas, fishers cannot economically afford to have dead fish counted against their quota. Consequently, the tendency is for only the high priced live fish to be recorded on the receipt.

This fishery has increased substantially since 1988 and continues to supply California's Asian communities with live and premium quality fishes. Prior to 1988, the price per pound for line-caught rockfish ranged from $0.50 to $1.50. The impetus of this fishery is the unprecedented high price paid for live fish.

Another driving force behind the development of this fishery is the modest capital investment required to enter it. Vessels of the nearshore fishery range in size from 8 ft (kayak) to 67 ft. The predominate vessel is a 14-20 foot light aluminum skiff with an outboard engine. Larger vessels may serve as mother ships for several smaller skiffs. Some fishers rent or borrow vessels while others fish from shore. Before 1999, many kayaks and smaller boats were not registered with CDFG as commercial vessels. When landing records were summarized, unregistered boats were not distinguishable from one another. A further complication was that some fish-

Table 1. Annual landings in metric tons of top ten nearshore finfishes in California in 1998.[a]

Market category	California t	Value ($1,000s)	Northern California t	Central California t	Southern California t
Cabezon	152	1,067	31	121	<1
Black rockfish	84	103	66	18	<1
Gopher rockfish group[b]	67	395	4	63	<1
Bolina rockfish group[c]	62	270	3	59	<1
California sheephead	56	341	<1	1	55
California scorpionfish	45	168	0	<1	45
Blue rockfish	41	56	21	20	<1
Grass rockfish	35	369	5	31	0
Lingcod[d]	29	79	8	22	<1
Copper rockfish	22	60	15	6	<1
Subtotal	593	2,908	151	342	101
Other fishes	77	341	22	38	13
Total	670	3,249	175	381	114

[a] Preliminary 1998 CDFG market receipt landing data.
[b] Includes market category gopher rockfish.
[c] Includes market category brown rockfish.
[d] Only live landings. Landings January-July 1998.

ers used more than one boat during the calendar year. Fishers used multiple boats due to the fact that quota limits were placed on the boat rather than fisher. The use of additional vessels is also due to boat damage caused by fishing near the rocky shoreline.

In 1998, 802 fishers made at least one landing of nearshore fishes. However, the most active participants (landings of at least 500 kg during the year) numbered only 237 (Table 2). These active fishers landed 90% of the total statewide landings.

Nearshore fishes were caught with a variety of gear types including hook-and-line, trap, and net, as well as by divers. Hook-and-line gear was the reported method for 72% of statewide landings (Table 3). Hook-and-line gear included rod-and-reel; horizontal and vertical set lines; pipes (sticks) consisting of short (4-8 ft) sections of PVC pipe (rebar or cable) with up to 15 (typically 5) hooked leaders attached; and groundfish troll lines. Pipes are generally baited with frozen squid and fished (soaked) for 1-2 hours depending on how much gear is being used. Baited traps are often soaked for 24-48 hours. Fishers traveled farther from their home ports and explored more remote fishing grounds as the demand for live/premium fishes continued and the resources close to ports declined.

The nearshore fishery occurs year-round, but monthly landings are highly variable due to weather. Because the fishery occurs from the intertidal zone out to about 15 fathoms, but primarily less than 5 fathoms, it is very dependent upon good weather and ocean conditions that allow fishing close to the rocky shoreline.

California began sampling the commercial live/premium fishery in 1993. When fish are offloaded at markets, biologists collect information on species, length, and weight. Live fish landings were not identified as live in the landing records until 1994. Fish landings are recorded by market categories, not individual species. This is an important consideration when attempting to describe landings by species. A major goal of market sampling is to determine the species composition of the different market categories. From the combination of sample data and landing data, estimates are made of total pounds landed by species. Species composition along with length and weight information is used to monitor the fishery over time. Unfortunately, in many ports, biolo-

Table 2. Number of fishers landing nearshore finfishes in 1998.[a]

Number of fishers	Northern California	Central California	Southern California	California
< 50 kg (<110 lb)	323	58	198	80
50 to <500 kg (110 to <1,105 lb)	341	71	182	93
500 to <5,000 kg (1105 to <11,050 lb)	206	56	113	38
>5,000 kg (>11,050 lb)	31	8	19	4
Total	901	193	512	215

[a]Preliminary 1998 CDFG market receipt landing data.
Note: Some fishers operate in more than one area.

gists are unable to sample live fish landings because of time constraints, uncooperative fishermen and buyers, and cultural and language barriers.

Landings are reported in market categories that include specific (e.g., "cabezon") and nonspecific (e.g., "small rockfish") categories. Markets typically buy fish in groups based on value, not species. In 1998, CDFG sampling of market categories indicated that specific categories might contain from one to seven species while nonspecific categories may contain from three to twelve species. For example, market sampling in Morro Bay found the species composition of the market category designated as cabezon to include cabezon, grass rockfish (*Sebastes rastrelliger*), kelp greenling (*Hexagrammos decagrammus*), and copper rockfish (*Sebastes caurinus*).

Approximately one hundred different market categories of marine fishes were documented as landed live in 1998. Only twenty-nine categories are included here: eighteen rockfish, five targeted species, and six incidental categories. Four categories (red, unspecified, small rockfish groups, and lingcod, *Ophiodon elongatus*) included both nearshore and offshore catches. Only live fish were included from these four categories.

Landings of cabezon, black rockfish (*Sebastes melanops*), gopher rockfish (*Sebastes carnatus*) group, bolina rockfish group, California sheephead, and California scorpionfish categories dominated the harvest with 466 tons (304 tons live). These groups comprise 70% of statewide landings, and have an ex-vessel value of $2.3 million ($2.0 million live) (Table 1).

The regional distribution of the California fishery is as follows:

1. Northern California
   - Including the port complexes of Eureka and Fort Bragg.
   - Landings totaled 175 tons (61 tons live).
   - Produced 26% of statewide landings, with an ex-vessel value of $550,000 ($374,000 live).
   - Landings were dominated by black rockfish, cabezon, blue rockfish (*Sebastes mystinus*), copper rockfish, lingcod, China rockfish (*Sebastes nebulosus*), and vermilion rockfish (*Sebastes miniatus*) categories which accounted for 82% of the area's landings.
   - Line gear caught 97% of the landings.

2. Central California
   - Including the port complexes of Bodega Bay, San Francisco, Monterey Bay, and Morro Bay

Table 3. Percentage of annual landings of nearshore finfishes by gear type in 1998.[a]

Gear type	California	Northern California	Central California	Southern California
Line	72	97	80	34
Trap	22	<1	18	45
Net[b]	3	2	2	15
Dive	<1	0	0	5
Other	<1	<1	<1	1

[a]Preliminary 1998 CDFG market receipt landing data.
[b]Includes trawl and other net types.
Note: Some fishers may use more than one gear type during a trip

- Landings totaled 380 tons (280 tons live)
- Produced 57% of statewide landings, with an ex-vessel value of $2.2 million ($1.9 million live)
- Central California landings were dominated by cabezon, gopher rockfish group, bolina rockfish group, grass rockfish, lingcod, and blue rockfish categories, which accounted for 83% of the area's landings (Table 1).
- In terms of statewide statistics, the port of Morro Bay was number one in both landings (131 tons, 20% of total) and ex-vessel value ($973,000, 30% of total).
- Line gear caught 80% of the landings followed by trap gear at 18%.

3. Southern California
- Including the port complexes of Santa Barbara, Los Angeles, and San Diego.
- Landings totaled 114 tons (75 tons live).
- Produced 17% of statewide landings, with an ex-vessel value of $548,000 ($423,000 live).
- Landings were dominated by California sheephead, California scorpionfish, kelp greenling, and leopard shark (*Triakis semifasciata*) categories, which accounted for 95% of the area's landings Table 1.
- Trap gear caught 45% of the landings followed by line gear at 34% and net at 15%.

CONCLUSIONS

There are concerns about the status of the nearshore fish populations and a lack of knowledge about stock identification, abundance, and recruitment. Because of these issues, conservative approaches to interim management with substantially lower harvest levels are required. Currently, resource managers are compelled to severely limit individual fishers to reduce the harvest in the nearshore fish fishery. In addition to state regulations, federal groundfish regulations apply to most of the species targeted in the nearshore fishery.

In 1999, more restrictive harvest levels began impacting the nearshore fishers. In 2000, severe cuts were made in the rockfish and lingcod allowable catch levels. Both the commercial and recreational fisheries have closed periods (Appendix 1). The PFMC asked the governors of Washington, Oregon, and California to declare a state of disaster in the commercial groundfish fisheries. Such a proclamation could lead to federal disaster relief assistance pursuant to the provisions of the Magnuson Act. One of the main problems is excess fishing capacity. The FGC is currently considering several interim management measures, one of which is restricting access through a limited entry program.

As a biologist, my goal is to have a long-term sustainable harvest in both the commercial and recreational nearshore fisheries. I hope that is the goal of the industry, as well, and that scientists, resource managers, industry, and other groups can work together to achieve a healthy and sustainable nearshore fishery.

APPENDIX 1.
SUMMARY OF REGULATIONS AFFECTING THE NEARSHORE FISHERY

The groundfish fishery within state waters (0 to 3 nautical miles) is managed by the California Department of Fish and Game (CDFG) and in federal waters (3 to 200 nautical miles) by the National Marine Fisheries Service (NMFS) through recommendations made by the Pacific Fishery Management Council (PFMC). California adopts federal groundfish regulations. The *Sebastes* complex (rockfish), cabezon, greenlings, lingcod, and California scorpionfish are all considered groundfish. Both the state and federal regulations apply to vessels fishing and landing fish in California. In addition, federal regulations require that groundfish species for which there is a trip limit, size limit, or optimum yield must be sorted prior to weighing and the weight reported separately on the CDFG landing receipt. Open access fishery applies to vessels fishing without a Federal limited entry permit or permitted vessels using non-endorsement gear. The Commercial Fishery Harvest Guidelines are allocated between the Open Access Fishery and Limited Entry Fishery. The majority of nearshore fishes are harvested by line and trap gear in the open access fishery. Details of regulations are printed in the California Fish and Game Code and the Federal Register. To avoid repetition, if restrictions remained the same next year they are not listed in the following year. Only when restrictions changed are they listed.

1994

1. **Federal.** Effective January 1, 1994. Commercial Open Access Fishery: Limited to no more than 10,000 pounds of rockfish per trip and no more than 40,000 pounds per calendar month per vessel.

1995

2. **Federal.** Effective January 1, 1995. **Commercial Open Access Fishery:** Limited to 20,000 pounds of lingcod during any calendar month per vessel. Minimum size for lingcod is 22 inches total length (TL).

1996

3. **State.** Effective January 1, 1996. **Commercial:** Set lines limited to not more than 15 hooks per line and no more than 150 hooks per vessel in waters within one nautical mile of the main land shore.

1997

4. **Federal.** Effective October 1, 1997. **Commercial Open Access Fishery:** Limited to 15,000 pounds of lingcod during any calendar month per vessel.

1998

5. **Federal.** Effective January 1, 1998. **Commercial Open Access Fishery:** Limited to 1,000 pounds of lingcod during any two-month fishing period per vessel. Minimum size for lingcod is 24 inches TL.

6. **Federal.** Effective July 1, 1998. **Commercial Open Access Fishery:** Limited to no more than 10,000 pounds of rockfish per trip and 33,000 pounds per month per vessel.

7. **Federal.** Effective July 1, 1998. **Commercial Open Access Fishery:** Limited to 250 pounds of lingcod per month per vessel.

8. **Federal.** Effective August 1, 1998. **Commercial Open Access Fishery:** Lingcod may not be taken, retained, possessed, or landed.

9. **Federal.** Effective September 1, 1998. **Commercial Open Access Fishery:** Limited to no more than 33,000 pounds of rockfish.

10. **Federal.** Effective October 1, 1998. **Commercial Open Access Fishery:** Area north of 42°50′N (Cape Blanco) closed to take of rockfish. Area south of 42°50′N (Cape Blanco) limited to no more than 10,000 pounds of rockfish per trip and 33,000 pounds per month per vessel.

1999

11. **Federal.** Effective January 1, 1999. **Commercial Open Access Fishery:** Area north of 40°30′N (Cape Mendocino) limited to no more than 3,600 pounds of rockfish per month per vessel. Area south of 40°30′N (Cape Mendocino) limited to no more than 2,000 pounds of rockfish per month per vessel.

12. **State.** Effective January 1, 1999. **Commercial:** Minimum size limits for the following nearshore species: black-and-yellow rockfish (*Sebastes chrysomelas*) 10 inches TL, cabezon (*Scopaenichthys*

marmoratus) 14 inches TL, greenlings (genus *Hexagrammos*) 12 inches TL, California sheephead (*Semicossyphus pulcher*) 12 inches TL, China rockfish (*Sebastes nebulosus*) 12 inches TL, gopher rockfish (*Sebastes carnatus*) 10 inches TL, grass rockfish (*Sebastes rastrelliger*) 12 inches TL, kelp rockfish (*Sebastes atrovirens*) 10 inches TL, and the California scorpionfish (*Scorpaena guttata*) 10 inches TL. Possession of a Nearshore Fishery Permit is required to take, possess, or land any of the above mentioned ten species. Limits finfish traps to 50 traps per permittee and requires trap doors to be secured open at night. Requires all commercial fishing vessels to be commercially registered.

13. **Federal.** Effective April 1, 1999. **Commercial Open Access Fishery:** Area north of 40°30′N (Cape Mendocino) limited to no more than 12,000 pounds of rockfish per month per vessel.

14. **Federal.** Effective April 1, 1999. **Commercial Open Access Fishery:** Limited to 250 pounds of lingcod per month per vessel. Open season: April 1–November 30 only.

15. **Federal.** Effective October 1, 1999. **Commercial Open Access Fishery:** Area south of 40°30′N (Cape Mendocino) limited to no more than 500 pounds of rockfish per month per vessel.

16. **Federal.** Effective October 1, 1999. **Commercial Open Access Fishery:** No lingcod may be retained or landed.

2000

17. **Federal.** Effective January 1, 2000. **Commercial:** Rockfishes grouped into assemblages of Nearshore, Shelf, and Slope for management purposes.

18. **Federal.** Effective January 1, 2000. **Commercial Open Access Fishery:** Area south of 36°N (near Lopez Point) closed January through February to the commercial take or possession of nearshore rockfish. Area north of 36°N (near Lopez Point) north to 40°10′N (near Cape Mendocino) closed March through April to the commercial take or possession of nearshore rockfish.

19. **Federal.** Effective January 1, 2000. **Commercial Open Access Fishery:** No more than 550 pounds of nearshore rockfish may be landed during any 2-month cumulative period south of 40°10′N (near Cape Mendocino). No more than 1,000 pounds of rockfish may be landed during the 2-month cumulative periods north of 40°10′N (near Cape Mendocino).

20. **Federal.** Effective January 1, 2000. **Commercial Open Access Fishery:** No retention of lingcod.

21. **State.** Effective January 1, 2000. **Recreational:** Area south of 36°N (near Lopez Point) closed January through February to the take or possession of nearshore and shelf rockfish. Area north of 36°N (near Lopez Point) to 40°10′N (near Cape Mendocino) closed March through April to the recreational take or possession of near shore and shelf rockfish and lingcod. Rockfish bag limit of 10 fish. Minimum size limits for the following nearshore species: cabezon 14 inches TL, greenlings 12 inches TL, California scorpionfish 10 inches TL, and lingcod 26 inches TL.

Shipping Live Fish into British Columbia, Canada: Basic Regulatory Requirements

Dorothee Kieser
Department of Fisheries and Oceans, Pacific Biological Station, Nanaimo, British Columbia, Canada

Abstract

Wild stocks of fish are of great value to British Columbia. To protect these stocks, both federal and provincial agencies have developed regulations to minimize potential impacts associated with the importation and transfer of aquatic species. Import regulations for finfish, mollusks, and crustaceans destined for human consumption, ornamental trade, research and bioassays, and aquaculture are outlined.

Introduction

Current consumer interest and good shipping methods allow live aquatic species to be shipped globally, often into new areas. This has aided the formation of new industries associated with these transfers and has led to the availability of new species in the food market and aquarium trade. However, such activities need to be controlled to minimize negative environmental impacts on fish stocks in the receiving area. Many species are destined for strict containment (for human consumption or aquarium use), never to be released into natural fish habitat. Others are shipped to be used for aquaculture where they may be held in strict containment. Or they may be introduced directly to open waters, for instance beach culture of oysters or bait fish.

While levels of risk to fish habitat and organisms in that habitat vary with the introduced species and the destination, all transfers have the potential to have some impact in the receiving area. In some cases, it may not be the release of the purposely introduced species that is deleterious to native species, but rather the inadvertent release of disease agents or accompanying nuisance species.

To protect native species, importations of live fish into British Columbia and transfers within the province are controlled through the federal Fisheries Act, through provincial regulations under the Wildlife Act, and under the Aquaculture Regulations. In addition, species imported for human consumption are under the jurisdiction of the Fish Inspection Act administered by the Canadian Food Inspection Agency (CFIA) to address concerns for human health.

Regulatory control

The Fishery (General) Regulations under the Canadian Fisheries Act outline the license requirements for the release of fish into fish rearing facilities and into fish habitat (Table 1). In addition, the Fisheries Act contains the Pacific Fishery Regulations, 1993, which include a section on the prohibition of certain species from import into British Columbia (Table 2). All shipments of live salmonids must comply with the Fish Health Protection Regulations regardless of the use of the fish (human consumption, aquaculture, etc.). These regulations are described in more detail in the section on aquaculture below. A section of the Provincial Wildlife Act, specifically British Columbia Reg. 261/83, applies to freshwater finfish moved within the Province (Table 3). Also, the pertinent appendices of the Convention of International Trade in Endangered Species (CITES) Regulations apply to the importation of live fish into British Columbia. Fish imported live for human consumption must meet the conditions of the Fish Inspection Act.

Human consumption

All fish imported for human consumption must follow the Fish Inspection Act of the CFIA to ensure wholesomeness. In addition, certain species listed under Section 5 of the Pacific Fishery Regulations, 1993, are prohibited from import. Under special conditions, these species may be licensed if a risk assessment carried out on the proposed importation indicates that conditions of risk mitigation can reduce the risk to native stocks to an acceptable level. For instance tilapia imports will only be licensed if the fish come from a fish-health inspected facility, where no salmonid fish are present in the water supply, and only if the effluent water at the receiving

Table 1. Fishery (General) Regulations, under the Canadian Fisheries Act, pertaining to the transfer of live fish.

PART VIII
RELEASE OF LIVE FISH INTO FISH HABITAT AND TRANSFER OF LIVE FISH TO A FISH REARING FACILITY

54. In this Part, "licence" means a licence to release live fish into fish habitat or to transfer live fish to a fish rearing facility.

Release or Transfer of Fish

55. (1) Subject to subsection (2), no person shall, unless authorized to do so under a licence,
   (a) release live fish into any fish habitat; or
   (b) transfer any live fish to any fish rearing facility.
   (2) Subsection (1) does not apply in respect of fish that is immediately returned to the waters in which it was caught.

Licence to Release or Transfer Fish

56. The Minister may issue a licence if
   (a) the release or transfer of the fish would be in keeping with the proper management and control of fisheries;
   (b) the fish do not have any disease or disease agent that may be harmful to the protection and conservation of fish; and
   (c) the release or transfer of the fish will not have an adverse effect on the stock size of fish or the genetic characteristics of fish or fish stocks.

Licence Fee

57. There is no fee for a licence issued under this Part.

---

site is discharged into the municipal sewage system. These conditions are in place to minimize the potential transfer of fish disease agents to local stocks, especially salmonids, and to reduce the likelihood of tilapia entering British Columbia fish habitat.

If the finfish (other than salmonids) and invertebrate species are destined strictly for human consumption and are not listed in Table 2, they need to meet only the criteria set by CFIA to ensure there are no human health concerns. Examples of such transfers are the importation of live rockfish, geoduck, clams, mussels, and crabs. However, importers must keep in mind that the transfer of such fish and shellfish into fish habitat or fish rearing facilities is illegal. Companies wishing to import any live species for human consumption should contact the closest CFIA office for licensing requirements.

Live salmon, trout, char, and all other fish of the family Salmonidae may only be imported into Canada (or from one province to another) if an import permit has been obtained from a Local Fish Health Officer (LFHO) in the Region into which the fish will be shipped. Lists of contact addresses for LFHOs in different regions are available from the author. For more details on the salmonid import requirements, see the section on Aquaculture below.

ORNAMENTAL TRADE

Similar to the requirements in effect for fish imported for human consumption, the fish species listed under Section 5 of the Pacific Fishery Regulations, 1993, are prohibited from import for ornamental or aquarium holding. A license may be granted if risk mitigation conditions are in place. Such mitigation measures may include health testing requirements at the source, quarantine holding, and veterinary inspection in the recipient facility after arrival. One example is the importation of ornamental koi, which belong to the same genus as the carp (*Cyprinus*). Appendix 1 gives the requirements to obtain a license to import koi and other listed ornamental species. These requirements are intended to minimize the potential for the introduction of fish disease agents and parasites to native stocks. The need for these safeguards is demonstrated by the many examples in the scientific literature of fish pathogens being released into new areas through the transfer of live fish (Ganzhorn et al. 1992).

Table 2. Pacific Fishery Regulations, 1993, which prohibit the importation of species listed below.

GENERAL PROVISIONS
Import of Fish

5. No person shall bring into the Province any live fish of a species set out in Schedule VIII.

SCHEDULE VIII
(Section 5)
PROHIBITED IMPORT LIVE FISH

Column I Item	Common Name of Species	Column II Scientific Name of Species
1.	Bass, Bluegill, sunfish	*Acantharchus, Ambloplites, Centrarchus, Enneacanthus, Lepomis, Micropterus, Morone, Perca, Percina, Pomoxis,* and *Stizostedium*
2.	Blackfish (Sacramento)	*Orthodon*
3.	Bowfin	*Amia calva*
4.	Buffalo fish	*Ictiobus*
5.	Carp	*Catla, Cirrhina, Ctenopharyngodon, Cyprinus, Hypophthalmichthys, Labeo,* and *Mylopharyngodon*
6.	Catfish	*Clarias, Ictalurus,* and *Noturus*
7.	Drum (Sheepshead)	*Aplodinotus*
8.	Eel	*Anguilla*
9.	Minnow (Fathead)	*Pimephales*
10.	Gars	*Lepisosteus*
11.	Lamprey	*Ichthyomyzan, Lampetra,* and *Petromyzon*
12.	Pike	*Esox*
13.	Quillback and Carpsucker	*Carpiodes*
14.	Roach	*Leuciscus*
15.	Rudd	*Scardinius*
16.	Shad and Alewife	*Alosa* and *Dorosoma*
17.	Stickleback	*Apeltes, Culaea (Eucalia), Gasterosteus,* and *Pungitius*
18.	Sucker	*Catostomus, Cycleptus, Erimyzon, Hypenelium, Minytrema,* and *Moxostoma*
19.	Tilapia	*Tilapia*
20.	Moon snail	*Polinices*
21.	Oyster crab	*Pinnotheres*
22.	Oyster drill	*Thais, Ocenebra,* and *Urosalpinx*
23.	Rock lobster	*Jasus*

Table 3. Regulations pursuant to the British Columbia Wildlife Act to the transport, possession, and traffic in live fish.

Page 438   The British Columbia Gazette—Part II   July 26, 1983

B.C. Reg. 261/83, filed July 15, 1983, pursuant to the WILDLIFE ACT [Section 110(2)(h)(aa)]. Order in Council 1186, approved and ordered July 13, 1983.

On the recommendation of the undersigned, the Lieutenant Governor, by and with the advice and consent of the Executive Committee, orders that the following regulation is made:

FRESHWATER FISH REGULATION

Interpretation
1. In this regulation "fish" means a freshwater species of
    (a) Order *Petromyzoniformes* (lampreys), or
    (b) Class *Osteichthyes* (bony fishes)
        and their eggs and juvenile stages but does not include
    (c) goldfish, or
    (d) species of ornamental tropical fishes

Offences
2. A person commits an offence where he
    (a) has in possession,
    (b) transports, or
    (c) traffics in live fish unless authorized by a permit.—A.J. BRUMMET, *Minister of Environment*; W.R. BENNETT, *Presiding Member of the Executive Council*

Ornamental fish of tropical origin are exempted under the provincial Wildlife Act from the regulations on transport, traffic, and possession of finfish. However, they must still meet federal requirements (such as the Pacific Fishery Regulations).

BIOASSAYS AND RESEARCH

Conditions similar to importation of the ornamental species apply when fish are imported for bioassays and research. Fish species listed in Section 5 of the Pacific Fishery Regulations, 1993, are prohibited from import. Under certain conditions a license may be granted if on the basis of a risk assessment and mitigation steps, risks to native species are considered minimal.

For all of the intended uses listed above (human consumption, ornamental trade, and bioassays and research) only species listed Table 2 require a Fish Transplant/Import license. However, for aquaculture uses and if fish are to be transferred into fish habitat, the requirements listed below come into effect (see Table 1).

AQUACULTURE
Salmonids

The primary regulatory framework for all transfers of salmonids into Canada and between Canadian provinces is given in the Fish Health Protection Regulations (FHPR). In addition, British Columbia has developed policies which govern the importation of Atlantic salmon (*Salmo salar*) and all *Oncorhynchus* species.

The FHPR apply to all fish of the family Salmonidae and are designed "to prevent the spread of infectious diseases through inspection of production facilities' fish stocks, and to control the movement of infected fish. Compliance with these Regulations require that four consecutive satisfactory inspections over a period of not less than 18 months must be conducted at a facility prior to certification" (Department of Fisheries and Oceans 1984). Only fish certified under the FHPR are eligible for an import permit.

The federal policies that regulate the importation of Atlantic and Pacific salmon into British Columbia stipulate the following:

1. Only eggs are allowed to be imported. Fry or later life stages are not permitted. Because eggs can be surface-disinfected, this requirement significantly reduces the type and numbers of fish disease agents that can accompany the shipment.

2. The source facility must be FHPR certified. Certification assures that the source farm has been inspected for disease agents of concern a minimum of four times in the previous 18 months.

3. Quarantine holding is required. Eggs and resulting fry must be held in quarantine with strict effluent disinfection and discharge to ground for a minimum of 120 days after the fry have hatched. This ensures that fish pathogens discharged from the facility will not enter fish-bearing waters.

4. Post-importation health testing schedules must be followed. Fry must be tested for disease agents

of concern every 30 days throughout the quarantine holding period, and again prior to sea water entry.

Pacific oysters and Manila clams

Seed may only be imported from health certified sources to licensed aquaculture sites.

All other species of finfish, mollusks, and crustaceans

All importations of species of fish (finfish, mollusks, and crustaceans) which are to be used in aquaculture or to be transferred to fish-bearing waters and that are not covered by the above categories, must be approved by the Assistant Deputy Minister of Science. Import permits may be granted after an assessment of the health, genetic, and ecological risks and when risk management measures are in place to ensure minimal impact on fisheries resources, habitat, or aquaculture (Dextrase 1999). As an example, sources of interest for species such as geoducks, blackcod, etc., to be cultured in British Columbia would have a thorough review by the federal-provincial Fish Transplant Committee. To initiate the licensing process, the proponent should contact the committee at the author's address to obtain the most current information on the transplant review requirements.

CONCLUSION

Some members of industries handling live aquatic species consider these requirements very restrictive. However, given the monetary, social, and environmental values of the native stocks and the vast number of examples where both intentional and accidental introductions of new species or new genetic stocks have had profound effects on local ecosystems, great caution is necessary to assure that introductions do not negatively impact on the receiving ecosystem.

If you wish to import live fish species into British Columbia, please contact the author by mail, email (kieserd@pac.dfo-mpo.gc.ca), or by fax (250-756-7053) or telephone (250-756-7069) for further information on obtaining a license. A Web site on introductions and transfers is being prepared.

REFERENCES

Department of Fisheries and Oceans. 1984. Fish Health Protection Regulations: Manual of Compliance. Fish. Mar. Serv. Misc. Spec. Publ., revised. 43 pp.

Dextrase, A.J., and M.A. Coscarelli. 1999. Intentional introductions of nonindigenous freshwater organisms in North America. In: R. Claudi and J. Leach (eds.), Nonindigenous freshwater organisms: Vectors, biology, and impacts. Lewis Publishers, Washington, DC, pp. 61-98.

Ganzhorn, J., J.S. Rohovec, and J.L. Fryer. 1992. Dissemination of microbial pathogens through introductions and transfers of finfish. In: A. Rosenfield and R. Mann (eds.), Dispersal of living organisms into aquatic ecosystems. Maryland Sea Grant Publications, College Park, MD.

APPENDIX 1.
Fisheries and Oceans
Pêches et Océans

PROCEDURE FOR THE IMPORTATION OF RESTRICTED NON-FOOD FISH INTO BRITISH COLUMBIA

Koi carp and more than forty other genera of fish are listed in the B.C. (General) Fishery Regulations as prohibited from import into British Columbia. Special requirements must be met before permission can be granted to bring these fish, or their eggs, into the Province. Upon application for importation, the Fish Transplant Committee may recommend approval of such an importation if the conditions listed below can be met by the importer:

1. Fish must be destined for display only. *Fish destined for release into natural waters of the province will not be approved;*

2. The importer must provide an approved containment system (see Section I) for holding of the imported fish by this procedure;

3. Fish must be held in the approved containment system until written approval for transfer (see Section II) from that system is received from the Transplant Committee; and

4. In case of mortalities, the inspecting officer must be called to obtain a diagnosis. Mortalities may have to be sent to a diagnostic laboratory for evaluation.

I) Inspection of containment system:

a) Inspection of the containment system must be carried out by a member of the Fish Transplant Committee or designate ("approved inspector").

b) The containment system must be in an enclosure separate from all other fish. The system must consist of a self-contained tank or series of tanks whose effluent must be disinfected, discharged to ground or disposed of into municipal sewage.

c) No other fish may be present in the containment system.

d) Fish must be secure from predation and theft.

e) The inspection report must include a complete description of the system including volume of containers and effluent, method of effluent disposal, treatment of effluent or exchange water and postal address of its owner and the location of the containment system.

II) Inspection of fish and approval for transfer:

a) Fish must be inspected by an approved inspector within 48 hours of arrival and again after 21 days at the isolation facility. They may then be released for transfer to other units if the inspection results, and (where necessary) testing of mortalities is satisfactory. No live fish may be removed from the containment system until officially released in writing by a member of the Federal-Provincial Fish Transplant Committee (the only exception may be for the purposes of fish health testing, where the inspector requires live fish to be moved to a fish health laboratory).

b) If evidence of infectious disease development is present, or undiagnosed mortalities have occurred, the holding period in the containment system may be extended.

c) If any pathogen of concern is detected during the inspection or any fish-health testing, the fish will not be permitted to be transferred from the containment system and may have to be destroyed.

d) Approval for transfer will be considered only if both inspections were satisfactory.

e) Should two separate groups of imported fish be held in the same isolation enclosure, no fish may be removed from the enclosure until the final inspections on both groups have been satisfactory and written approval for transfer has been obtained.

f) If no inspection is carried out within 30 days of the importation of the fish, the imported fish and any fish sharing the water supply may be seized.

The costs of all inspections, diagnostic work, and any other costs associated with the importation must be borne by the applicant.

Please note that without approval from the Department of Fisheries and Oceans, it is illegal to release or transfer live fish into the natural (fish-bearing) waters of the province.

Resource Management Issues: Question and Answer Session

Bruce M. Leaman
International Pacific Halibut Commission, Seattle, Washington

Kim Mauriks
Dorcas Point Farms Inc., Nanoose Bay, British Columbia, Canada

Christine Pattison
California Department of Fish and Game, Morro Bay, California

QUESTION: (to K. Mauriks) I notice that you call your business Dorcas Point Farms. Do you market your fish as farm fish or as wild caught halibut?

K. MAURIKS: Dorcas Point just happens to be where I live. To work with government grants and to get farm sites and other things, we needed a name that portrayed what we were trying to do, so we just threw "Farms" in there. We are marketing the fish as "Sterling Pacific Halibut" because, in the aquaculture trade, sterling is the best. There has never been product trademarked as Sterling Pacific Halibut, so that is what we are marketing it as.

QUESTION: (to K. Mauriks) Earlier you said you just bled the fish when they go to market. Does that mean that you do not remove the gills and entrails?

K. MAURIKS: The IPHC regulation states that, at the dock, no fish can be landed with gills and entrails intact. This was enacted to force harvesters to dress at sea to raise the quality from when the derby fishery mentality was still active. We now have a quota fishery. What we do is live hold the fish in the netpens, then stun and bleed them, and send them off to a processing plant, because we cannot process the fish at the pen site. At this point, the gills and the entrails are removed in the seafood plant. Whatever product form is needed will come out of this plant.

QUESTION: (to K. Mauriks) I am interested in what you must do after you start feeding the fish. Does your operation fall under farmed fish regulation?

K. MAURIKS: Yes, it does. There are strict rules concerning what you can and cannot do on an aquaculture site. We are currently in a gray area. Are we farmers or are we fishermen? Are we ponding or pounding? There are a bunch of different names for it.

This live holding strategy is being done in other parts of the world with bluefin tuna and Atlantic cod on our East Coast, but not wild halibut. European farms are dealing with cultured halibut—we are dealing with wild halibut. I cannot ask anybody for help because nobody has had to deal with these problems before, for example, how to get feed to large wild fish in these kinds of densities.

They do not want us to use wet feed (primarily chunked chum salmon), because you can get into all sorts of water quality problems. However, these same managers realize that we are dealing with a wild fish and we have to get some suitable food into them—to tease them into eating. Basically, they just said, "Kim, we realize what you're trying to do here, but minimize your use of wet feed." We are going to be working with different forms of feed and expect that the quality will be going up.

QUESTION: (to K. Mauriks) Can you give me some reasons why you would be less likely to high grade halibut. [Note: "High grading" refers to the practice of selecting out certain fish size categories, usually fish of a larger size, and rejecting the remainder.]

K. MAURIKS: I did not have any reasons to high grade in the normal halibut fishery. Everything could be sold at such a good price. In the normal halibut fishery involving "dead product," commercial buyers sometimes pay a higher price for larger fish. This is probably the greatest incentive for fishermen to high grade and it probably does happen once in a while. This is a personal moral matter that you cannot dictate to people.

In our case, we are now getting such a good price. Also, the fishing is slower the way we are doing it. I am not going to release any that I do not have to release unless they are undersized. Every one is precious and we need a certain amount of cash flow.

So we kill the few that we bring in that are not perfect for the pen. These fish still go out on a one- or two-day fresh basis. It is still a very high quality product and the system is in place to move it to market. So, there is no reason for us to high grade the fish.

QUESTION: (to K. Mauriks) Have you made any observations on the frequency of chalky fish coming out of your netpens?

K. MAURIKS: We have been looking at this problem since day one with our halibut. The buyers have been trying to find out if there is anything that we can do in terms of selective fishing or fish handling methods to reduce or eliminate the problem. Nothing has jumped out of our data at this point. The occurrence of chalky halibut in our fish is random. I thought I had actually figured it out this year. We have had two fish out of 2,000 or so that were chalky. That is well below the industry standard. I thought that we must have been doing everything perfectly. Maybe it is the stunning and the bleeding, because we were doing these steps in the best manner possible.

And then, all of a sudden in early September, after we went through the peak of the water temperature in late August, we brought in a load of halibut that was 10% chalky—out of nowhere. We had not had chalky fish all summer and then, all of a sudden, we had chalky fish.

This chalkiness was in freshly caught fish. It was not from the pen-held fish. Consequently, I thought that we now have some chalkiness in the area. We were thinking then that perhaps the condition was dietary or had something to do with the environment.

We decided to take the next market order from fish that had been held in the pens. These fish had not been in the wild for two or three months. They were off the diet that wild fish would have been eating. They were getting a mixture of pellets and chum salmon. Unfortunately, we had the same 10% of chalky halibut.

Then the next harvest after this was a mix. But, again, we had it. Who knows—we got a fairly controlled experiment going on here and maybe we will find out what is going on with the fish. We are going start looking at meat samples because there might be something that we can do in a holding situation. If the fish are caught from the wild, there might be nothing that can be done to take care of this problem. Maybe we will come up with an answer that will help the industry.

B. LEAMAN: If I could make an additional comment on this matter. We did several experiments this year looking at various treatments: stunning, stunning and bleeding, just bleeding, and then no treatment. And then we did a lot of work on looking at temperatures of the fish, time on deck, temperature of the fish when they come out of the water, temperature when they went into the hold and so forth.

We have not been able to complete a detailed analysis of this time and temperature data. At this point, nothing gross jumps out as a mitigating factor to explain the occurrence of chalkiness. It could be that the predisposition to chalkiness is precapture in nature—whether it be exercise on the hook, whether it be temperature, or low oxygen—we are not sure.

You understand that the ultimate cause of this meat quality problem is low pH in the flesh—there is too much acidity. It appears to be very knife-edged when the fish become chalky, a sudden transition appears to be present. But the actual ultimate cause of this is not certain. As mentioned, it may be precapture or it may be temperature related or caused by low oxygen water. And it could be caused by what they are feeding on.

QUESTION: (to B. Leaman) Question concerning the distribution of chalkiness in individual fish.

B. LEAMAN: Most of the work that has been done so far suggests that chalkiness starts developing from the tail forward. Although I have talked to one buyer who said that he has observed chalkiness in the center part of the fillet, most other folks have seen it developing from the tail and the dorsal area forward into the center part of the fillet.

One of the projects that we are considering is some means of testing pH of the flesh at the time of capture. That might give us some indication about where we might direct future research on this problem. Then again this may be something that is an industry issue—more so than a IPHC issue.

FREDRIK SVERRE: We believe that the chalkiness is due to parasites similar to those present in your herring. We believe we can develop a vaccine against it. Maybe in the future we might be able to help wild fishery management and live holding to reduce the effects of the chalkiness.

QUESTION: (to K. Mauriks) Are you planning to move to the next step in the next couple of years to start adding cultured halibut to your pens?

K. MAURIKS: Yes, I am going to look at supplying cultured halibut in the future. In my view, this is something that is coming. For sure I do not want to have a smaller and smaller portion of the world's supply of halibut.

If it is possible, we will move in that direction. However, it is not a consistent process yet. But if it is going to be, I want to be a part of this movement and to do it right. This is partially why I am here right now. I am setting up the husbandry process, the marketing, and the whole infrastructure that will be needed. If, down the road a ways there develops the need for a cultured supply, we will hit the ground running and we already have the market.

QUESTION: (to K. Mauriks) If you are going to go ahead with the concept of working with cultured halibut, a number of questions become involved. Experience on the East Coast, with a range of fisheries that are now gradually moving toward the addition of cultured stock to a wild supply, is that it does impose very serious problems for the management of the existing fisheries. I do not think it really should do this, but it does.

There is a very considerable constraint on the proper development of the cultivated stock because of the management regulations for the existing wild stock. Is this something that you are beginning to address? You will soon run into problems with root stock supply, particularly with the type of regulations which will suddenly say you cannot trade in these halibut, even though you have owned them since they were very small because they are less than 25 pounds or whatever else it may be. Might this also be something that the IPHC will begin to address?

K. MAURIKS: To tell you the truth, I have been busy fishing. What you are referring to is a ways away. I have not looked at this.

B. LEAMAN: Some aspects of that are of fair concern to us and undersized fish (fish below the IPHC minimum legal size) in the marketplace is an important one right now. I just finished looking at the issue of how much western Pacific halibut of primarily Russian origin is being imported into North America. This really frustrates the ability of the enforcement folks who are trying to enforce a 32-inch size limit in North America when you have a different size limit or no size limit at all in Russia and fish are showing up in the domestic marketplace.

This really complicates the problem for enforcement. It is not insurmountable, but it is a significant problem right now. The same thing might occur if you do not have adequate tracking of the product coming out of an aquaculture operation. I do not think that this is insurmountable, either. I think that if we are going to move in some of these directions, then we need to do the planning right now to set up the kind of infrastructure, the kind of regulatory framework, and the monitoring framework necessary that will allow this kind of operation work . . . if this is the direction that we want to go.

COMMENT: A couple of comments in regard to development of this in the aquaculture industry. I have been involved with this form of development. Number one, it is quite possible to create a reasonable paper trail so that you can insure that undersized fish are coming from hatcheries and not from wild stocks. It is been done with several other species and it is not an insurmountable object.

Number two is that, along with this, no free government has enough police power to watch every dock, every roadway, every entry port. The best way to get compliance is to work with the people in the industry because ultimately they are going to be the best enforcement people.

COMMENT: In the United States this matter would be handled on a state by state level. The state governments are going to have to deal with this issue. Products they produce in their states are what they are concerned with—a good example would be abalone culture in California. Obviously, in California the farmers sell two and three inch abalone into markets all over the world that have been produced by aquaculture. Yet, prior to this, there was minimum size in the commercial harvest that prevented small abalone from entering the marketplace. I think that the state is going to have to be reasonable—as long as the product has been marked or tagged . . . that there is a paperwork trail to go along with the product that is, in fact, an aquaculture product.

Some states may still refuse to move in this direction. I can only guess that the State of Florida would, at some point in the future, perhaps ten years down the road, reject the proposal to support farmed spiny lobster because of the product's small size . . . because of the fact they could not tell if it was, in fact, harvested from the wild and short sized. But I think it is only a matter of time before they have to come around and work with us in order to get the aquaculture product and the wild-caught product into the marketplace.

QUESTION: I have a hot question that you may not want to answer. What kind of reaction do you expect from the Alaska fisheries managers concerning this plan?

B. LEAMAN: There are a number of concerns that have been expressed by the commissioners and they are generally reflecting the concerns of the constituents that they represent. Probably the biggest one is fear of aquaculture. People are simply afraid of losing their livelihood because of the loss of market to another form of product.

The second of the major objections in Alaska is enforcement for this type of business. This is why I am suggesting that—and this goes along the lines of a previous comment—no nation has enough police force to watch everything that might happen. This should not be the approach. It should be full validation and this may be the cost of doing business in this manner. The IPHC does not have a position pro or con on this matter. At this point, all we are saying is that here are the guidelines that we think are important for decent resource management.

The monitoring of removals and inputs and so forth is one of the key things that has made the IPHC work. We monitor all kinds of removals ranging from incidental mortality elsewhere, bycatch, and so forth. What we are talking about here is just simply another removal. You need to have the appropriate framework for monitoring this removal as well.

Some of the people in the enforcement groups in Alaska are, I think, approaching this development from the perspective that "this has to be enforced," as opposed to what kind of mechanism do we need to make sure this is monitored. There may be an issue here in terms of education or whatever. I am giving you the perspective of what I think might be coming from that group.

COMMENT: I would like to add one additional point to allow this group to better understand where halibut is coming from. At the moment halibut farming is growing at the same speed as the farmed salmon harvesting. In terms of halibut farming, we are now at the same level that the farmed salmon industry was several years ago. Today salmon farmers are producing 900,000 metric tons of salmon a year. In 25 to 30 years halibut farming may reach the same production level. We need to recognize that halibut is a superior fish compared to any other fish out there in the marketplace. If the demand is there, production will be there as well.

Therefore, it is my opinion that the Pacific halibut industry needs to adopt aquaculture into their overall production. This needs to be done in order to be part of the market expansion, to follow the growth of future market share or else we will be left behind. Also, this investment has to start while the market value of the fish is high so that we can afford to stay with it if the prices drop thirty years from now.

QUESTION: (to B. Leaman and C. Pattison) We have heard the description of the California situation in terms of live rockfish fisheries development. Concerning the Canadian live fishery situation, what is going on in Canada?

B. LEAMAN: This will be a short answer in terms of what is happening in the British Columbia live fishery. Keep in mind that I left this fishery a number of years ago. The resource status is quite poor in British Columbia. This probably has a lot to do with the nature of regulations that were not put into effect during the early development of these fisheries. It became a classic gold rush fishery, where the fishery got going and found itself on a roller coaster before there was any chance to even understand some of the biology behind these animals. Because they are rockfishes, they are extremely long-lived with low annual productivity.

The situation right now, concerning the live fish fishery, is that many folks are coming forward and saying that they have been discarding a lot of fish. And so mortality that was assessed through looking at just the removals seen at the dock was not necessarily the appropriate estimate for total removals. Again, I think that this is a monitoring issue.

QUESTION: (to C. Pattison) Have there been any proposals in California to do a similar sort of grow-out procedure for rockfish?

C. PATTISON: Are you interested in long-term holding or the actual culturing of rockfish? You are talking about long-term holding. The answer is no, not that I know of. Probably somebody has thought about it or looked into it—and may even be doing it. Again, I am not aware of it. But with these new quotas, the fisheries are greatly reduced. With this newly limited resource, I imagine that we will be seeing more and more of this development in the future. Members of the California live industry do very short-term holding right now, just a couple of days until the buyer comes to a location to offload. They are just using netted pens in bays.

The Live Reef Food Fish Trade in Hong Kong: Problems and Prospects

Yvonne Sadovy
The University of Hong Kong, Hong Kong, China

Abstract

The lucrative live reef fish trade, centered in Southeast Asia, has increased markedly since the early 1990s. Hong Kong is the major importer, accounting for about 60% of the total trade, currently estimated at about 50,000 metric tons annually. Traditionally, fishes came from the South China Sea. As demand grew, local sources became progressively depleted and importers sought live fish from more distant regions, now ranging from the Seychelles to Fiji. This expansion brought with it a new problem, that of ciguatoxic fishes, which caused an unprecedented number of cases of ciguatera in Hong Kong in 1998 and 1999, and seriously undermined public confidence in food fish. The trade has also been criticized for the extensive use of sodium cyanide to catch some species in some areas and for aggregation fishing.

This paper examines the diversity of fishes traded in Hong Kong, their value, and the many factors affecting prices. The major problems currently affecting the trade, over-exploitation, unsafe (ciguatoxic) fish, and destructive fishing methods, and possible solutions to such problems are explored and prospects for the trade evaluated.

Introduction

Although fish have long been kept alive until shortly before cooking in parts of Asia, the substantial international trade in live reef fishes for food that we see today only began to develop in the 1980s and has expanded particularly rapidly since the early 1990s. Today, the trade in all of Asia is worth an estimated US $600-700 million (about 50,000 metric tons of fish), with Hong Kong, the major importer, consuming and re-exporting to southern mainland China about 60% of the fishes in trade ($300-400 million US) (see review by Johannes and Reipen 1995, Chan 2001).

Although a wide range of marine invertebrates is also traded alive for food, tropical reef fish represent the major component in both value and volume (see Chan 2001). Live reef fish are also traded for ornamental purposes but this article is concerned only with the live reef fish trade (LRFT) for the purpose of consumption. While most fishes in trade are wild-caught at a marketable size, there is also a significant mariculture sector involving the wild capture of juveniles and sub-market-sized fish for culture (growout), which will be discussed.

Since Hong Kong is the major importer of live reef fish, I shall focus on Hong Kong's role in this trade. Economically, the trade is important to Hong Kong, exceeding by several times the total value of its entire traditional (dead/frozen) fish fishery (Lee and Sadovy 1998). It represents at least 10% of the value of all foodstuffs imported (in 1997 total foodstuffs—meat, dairy/eggs, seafood, vegetables, nuts—imported were valued at $6.01 billion US, Fong and Anderson 2000). The economic and biological factors that bear directly on the Hong Kong LRFT are therefore important to the local economy, and, as we shall see, also have repercussions far into the Indo-Pacific. Other countries with significant LRF businesses are Taiwan, Singapore, mainland China (largely through Hong Kong), and Chinese communities in Malaysia and Australia.

This extremely lucrative trade is experiencing several difficulties that go beyond the recent economic downturn in Southeast Asia and which need to be resolved for a safe and sustainable, high value fishery. In assessing problems and prospects, I focus on four areas: growth and expansion of the Hong Kong-based LRFT, composition and value of the Hong Kong trade, the problem of ciguatera (illness caused by natural fish poisoning), and the impact of the trade on fish stocks.

Profile of the Trade
Growth and expansion of the Hong Kong–based LRFT

The sale of fish, both freshwater and marine, kept alive until just before cooking, has long been popular in parts of Asia and particularly in southern China, among Cantonese Chinese. Fishes were originally caught locally, or raised in marine and freshwater culture (Johannes and Riepen 1995, Akimichi 1998).

By the late 1960s, marine fishes sold alive in Hong Kong were coming from sectors of the South China Sea ever more distant from Hong Kong, with the consequence that the public was exposed to a wide variety of fishes. The increasing wealth at the time stimulated the market for these desirable fishes, particularly for a range of grouper species, as well as for species in several other reef fish families, such as the humphead (also known as the Napoleon or Maori) wrasse (*Cheilinus undulatus*), for their fine texture and flavor. Growth in the trade, with animals originating far from Hong Kong, was made possible by high retail prices, which allowed for high transport costs, while improvements in transport times, vessels, and networks facilitated trade with areas formerly inaccessible.

International trade was originally conducted by sea in the Southeast Asia region, and, as demand increased and fish stocks became depleted, businesses moved farther into the islands of the South China Sea (Johannes and Riepen 1995). By the mid-1970s, the Philippines became a major source country and in the 1980s, businesses moved to Indonesia and the trade became so profitable that fishes were also transported by air. One business started working in Palau in 1984 with a large live fish vessel (vivier) (Johannes and Riepen 1995). In the 1990s, businesses moved farther east and west: to the Maldives in 1993 and the Marshall and Solomon islands by the mid-1990s. Today, trade is conducted as far away as Fiji to the east (Yeeting 1999), with at least one trial shipment coming out of the Seychelles (Bentley and Aumeeruddy 1999), to the west of Hong Kong. Viviers can be very large, with capacities attaining 30 metric tons.

The Hong Kong trade is based either on the collection of fish by fishers on Hong Kong vessels, or through the purchase of fish directly from fishers or middlemen in source countries. Capture methods include hook and line, fish trap, and cyanide, the latter particularly in Indonesia and the Philippines, the two major supply countries. Fishing may be carried out legally, sometimes under joint-venture arrangements, or illegally, by poaching (e.g., Johannes and Riepen 1995, Bentley 1999). In some cases, cyanide has evidently been introduced by middlemen or Hong Kong–based businesses. For some species, cyanide is the major collection method applied; its use is widely banned for fishing but it is evidently readily available throughout the region.

Live fish are also obtained through the process of growout (mariculture). This involves the capture of juveniles or small, sub-market sized adults, and their maintenance in floating cages or ponds until they attain marketable size. Growout occurs in source countries, and there is also an international trade in juveniles for growout in demand countries. Major source countries for grouper juveniles are the Philippines and Thailand. Hatchery rearing of grouper to supply juveniles for growout is successfully operated at commercial levels only in Taiwan.

Composition and value of the Hong Kong trade

About 40 species are involved in the LRFT with certain species and sizes of fish particularly highly valued. The most important fishes in terms of both volume and overall value are approximately 30 species of grouper (Serranidae), especially the tiger grouper (*Epinephelus fuscoguttatus*), the marbled (or flowery), grouper (*E. polyphekadion*), and low volumes of the highly valued giant grouper (*E. lanceolatus*) and high-finned grouper (*Cromileptes altivelis*). Other high value species, albeit traded in low volumes, are several wrasses (Labridae), with one species, the humphead wrasse, particularly highly prized. Other predominantly reef species that are traded include the snappers (Lutjanidae), particularly *Lutjanus argentimaculatus* (mangrove snapper), species of jack (Carangidae), grunt (Haemulidae), parrotfish (Scaridae), scorpionfish (Scorpaenidae), and the temperate water sea breams (Sparidae). The majority of these fishes are wild-caught either as market-size adults, or as juveniles or sub-market size adults that are then grown-out. A small proportion of the total trade in live reef fish is cultured from hatchery-reared juveniles, mainly two grouper species, *Epinephelus coioides* (green grouper) and *E. malabaricus* (malabar grouper). Preferred sizes range from 0.8-1.2 kg for single plate-serving size to banquet-size servings (Johannes and Riepen 1995).

The value per kilogram of fishes in Hong Kong's trade varies markedly depending on several factors, the most important of which are species, season/festivities, demand/supply, general economic situation, wild/cultured source and, for some species, absolute body size. An additional factor, ciguatera (fish poisoning), became evident in 1998 and is discussed in more detail below. Data on wholesale prices were obtained from informal interviews carried out at wholesale markets by the Agriculture, Fisheries and Conservation Department of the Hong Kong Special Administrative Region (AFCD-HKSAR) with independent advice to the author from a major industry participant, Patrick Chan of Brightfuture Ltd.

Imports of live reef fish are monitored in several ways in Hong Kong, none of them fully comprehensive (Sadovy 1998). Imports by air and on non–Hong Kong licensed vessels are collected through the submission of trade declarations at import and summarized by the Department of Census and Statistics. These data include weights and total values of shipments and, since 1997, also several details by species under the Harmonized Code system. Additional data on prices and species composition are collected on a voluntary basis by AFCD from wholesale markets. These data are estimated to represent the imports of about 50% of major fish traders in Hong Kong and half the total volume of live marine fish imported into Hong Kong by fishing vessels (AFCD, pers. comm.).

Data are presented for major imported species (Fig. 1) in terms of both wholesale price in $ HK per kg (US $ are pegged to the HK $ at a rate of US $1 = HK $7.8) and monthly, or multi-month, volumes traded from January 1997 to June 1999, inclusive. The collection of voluntary data began in January 1997 and was originally based on three-month totals, with monthly data from July 1998. The AFCD prices given in Fig. 1 should be taken as approximate and are used for illustrative and comparative purposes only; they may overestimate wholesale values by as much as 20% (P. Chan, Brightfuture, Hong Kong, pers. comm.). Mark-up from wholesale to retail is between 100% and 150%.

The price per kilogram and tonnage data indicate several trends. The highly variable monthly import volumes show a clear inverse relationship with price for most species. Volume imported depends on a number of factors, including available supply and various festivities such as Chinese New Year (January or February), winter solstice, and wedding banquets which cluster around auspicious dates. Prices also depend on species (particularly highly valued are the humphead wrasse, giant grouper, and coral trout, especially the leopard coral trout, *Plectropomus leopardus*, and the spotted coral trout, *P. maculatus*), either for their taste, their color (red is particularly auspicious), or for other intrinsic values such as medicinal importance. The regional economic downturn, starting with a sharp drop in the Hang Seng index in late 1997, generally dampened the retail market for expensive live reef fish.

Size within a species may be important. For example, smaller, plate-sized, humphead wrasse and giant grouper are worth more per kilogram than larger individuals which have to be carved up prior to sale (Lau and Parry-Jones 1999). Lower prices go to snappers and other reef fishes, as well as "cultured" fish, which fetch prices about 20% lower than wild-caught fish of the same species. This is likely a question of perception in most cases; taste-tests using the malabar grouper strongly suggest that most people cannot tell the difference (OmniTrak 1997). Prices have also dropped across the board since peaking in the mid-1990s (see Johannes and Riepen 1995), prior to the economic problems in the region, when some species fetched prices 3- to 4-fold higher.

An additional factor that caused significant price declines were two major incidents in Hong Kong, in 1998 and 1999, representing hundreds of cases of ciguatera. Ciguatera is a condition in humans, a food poisoning, caused by eating fish that harbor ciguatoxins. It is a natural phenomenon in certain reef species areas of the Indo-Pacific (and western tropical Atlantic) (see details below). The major incidents took place in early 1998 and early 1999, sending prices down by as much as 60% (P. Chan, Brightfuture, Hong Kong, pers. comm.) and undermining public confidence in fish (see Fig. 1 and prices for early 1998). The price decline applied to all fishes and not just those recognized to pose a greater risk; freshwater and cultured species, which do not normally pose any risk of ciguatera, were also avoided following these cases. The tiger grouper was one of the species implicated.

The problem of ciguatera and its impact on trade

Ciguatera (fish poisoning) is a serious health problem in the tropics and subtropics (Chan et al. 1992), one that is likely to grow with increasing international trade in reef fishes. Ciguatera has not historically been a problem in Southeast Asia (ciguatoxins are biotoxins not commonly reported from fishes in the northern South China Sea) and so the general public is largely naïve to ciguatera. However, with increasing numbers of live fish being brought into the region from known hotspots of ciguatoxic fishes in the western Pacific (e.g., Lewis 1986), ciguatera is expected to represent a significant problem in Hong Kong, and for other importing economies, as demand for live reef fish grows. A large proportion of the species in the local LRFT is potentially ciguatoxic (Lee and Sadovy 1998). Ciguatera

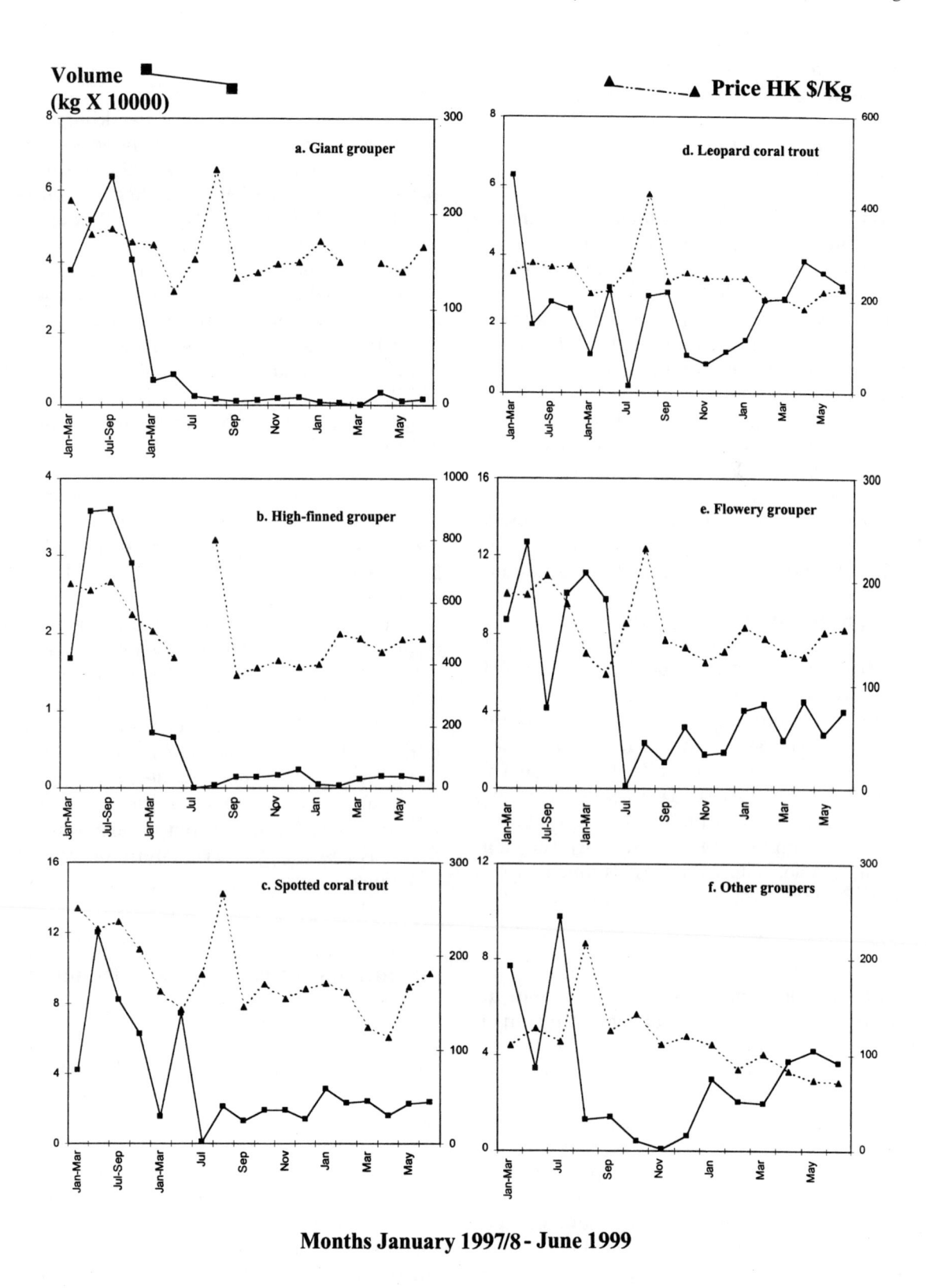

Figure 1. Weight (kg) and average wholesale prices (HK $) per kg of 12 categories of live reef fishes imported into Hong Kong by sea between January 1997 and June 1999 (except f, j, k, and l which run from January 1998). Data are provided three times a month (as originally collected) and then monthly. Prices were collected by interviews with fish traders at Aberdeen and Mong Kok wholesale markets. Values should only be used for illustrative and comparative purposes since they were not rigorously collected. Left axis is the weight × 10,000 kg (solid line and squares) and right axis is price (HK $) (dashed line and triangles). Prices for

**Volume
(kg X 10000)**   **Price HK $/Kg**

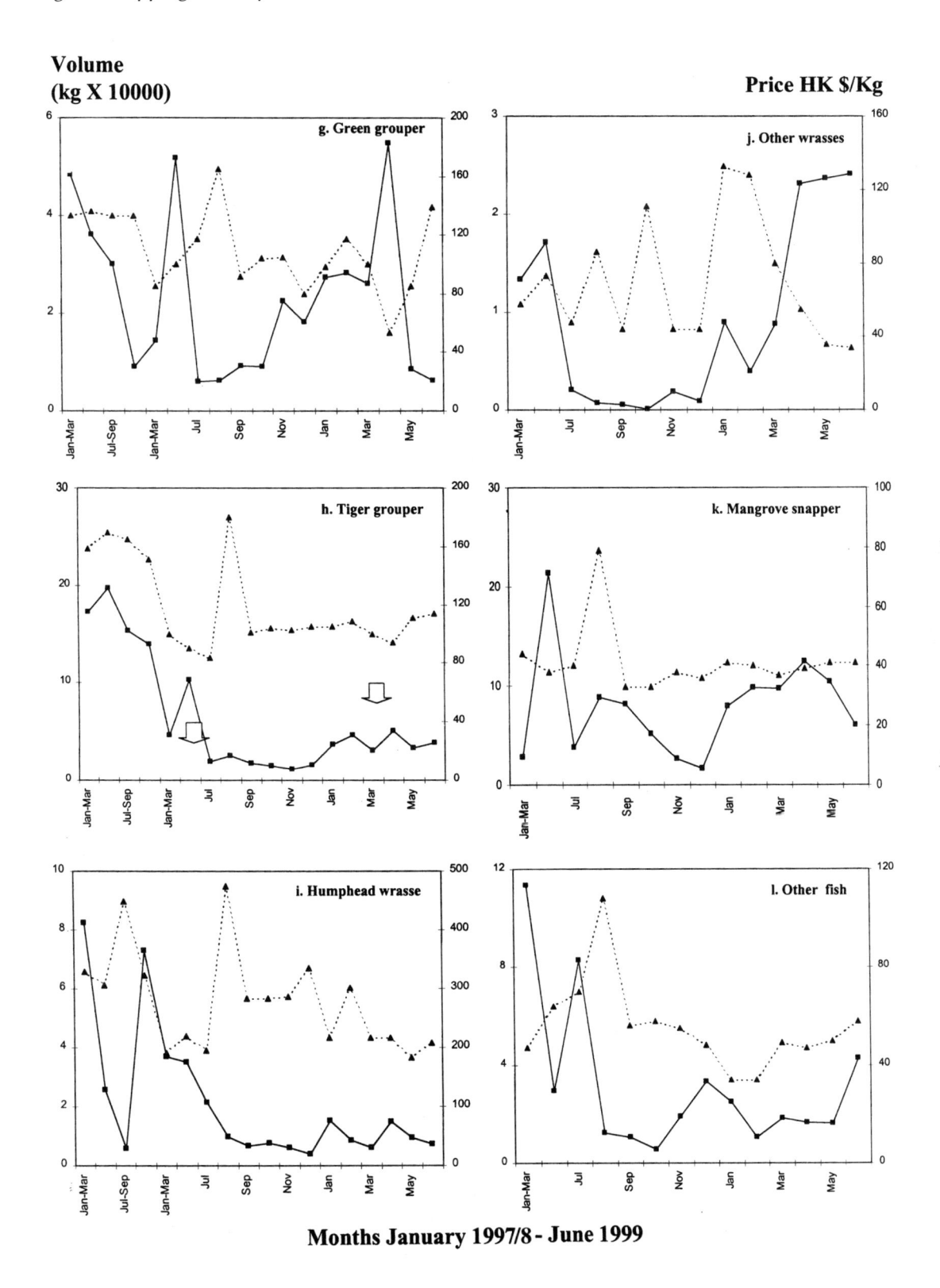

(Figures g. Green grouper, h. Tiger grouper, i. Humphead wrasse, j. Other wrasses, k. Mangrove snapper, l. Other fish)

Months January 1997/8 - June 1999

giant grouper and humphead wrasse vary markedly depending on size (smaller individuals fetch more per kilogram than larger ones). Prices are averages of small and large fish. The arrows for h., tiger grouper, approximately represent the periods in early 1998 and early 1999 when many cases of ciguatera were reported. The tiger grouper was the species implicated in some of the cases. Interviews were conducted by the Department of Agriculture, Fisheries and Conservation of the HKSAR.

causes diarrhea, nausea, vomiting, abdominal pain, loss of muscle coordination, hot and cold feeling reversal, and pain and itching. These symptoms may recur for as long as 6 months. Death occasionally occurs (U.S. Department of Health and Human Services 1999)

Available figures indicate a marked increase in confirmed ciguatera cases in Hong Kong from the 1980s into the 1990s. Although it was little known in Hong Kong prior to 1984, between 1984 and 1988 there were 23 cases of ciguatera poisoning reported affecting 182 people locally (Hong Kong Standard 27/5/88). In the last decade, the number of reported cases has increased from seven cases between 1988 and 1990, to more than 400 in 1998 (Hong Kong Department of Health) (Fig. 2). Doctors, however, believe that the actual number of cases is much higher and that most incidents are either unreported, or misdiagnosed as food poisoning (Chan et al. 1992).

Ciguatera is a significant health and resource problem in tropical areas because of its erratic, and often unpredictable, spatial and temporal distribution, although hotspots have been documented (Lewis 1986). It is particularly problematic for nations wishing to export fishes that risk bearing ciguatoxins (Dalzell 1992), and for places, like Hong Kong, that are naïve to the risk of ciguatera and without a monitoring program to tackle the issue. Moreover, based on conversations with the author, some importers themselves appear to be largely unaware of, or unconcerned about, the potential risks of importing ciguatoxic fishes. As one example, an importer knowingly brought a shipment of ciguatoxic fishes into Hong Kong (the fishes had been tested prior to arrival), and when requested by the government not to land them, diverted the shipment for sale in mainland China.

The increase in cases of ciguatera in Hong Kong in the late 1990s came about because of two factors. The first was the unwitting expansion of the trade into areas where ciguatoxic fishes are prevalent (Fig. 3). The second is that Hong Kong has no official measures to protect the public from ciguatoxic fishes imported live. This is, in part, because "live fish" is not considered to be food in Hong Kong and hence is not subject to rigorous monitoring or controls. Informal testing, of unknown accuracy, of imported fish is evidently carried out sporadically, but the government has no official means of preventing the sale of toxic live fish in Hong Kong. Moreover, the Hong Kong government seems unwilling to protect its public by monitoring for country of origin and prohibiting sale of fish imported from suspect areas, as is done elsewhere (Table 1). Although government posters are distributed with warnings, I have never seen one posted in any major retail area, with the exception of one on Lamma Island, western Hong Kong, which had had the warning removed, leaving attractive pictures of suspect species!

The impact of LRFT on fish stocks

The valuable LRFT has placed an unprecedented pressure on populations of certain larger reef fishes in Southeast Asia, and increasingly beyond, to satisfy a rapidly increasing demand. This pressure has led to probable overfishing of many species, and poses a threat to certain particularly vulnerable species. In many areas, it has also brought about the introduction of a fishing method that involves the use of the poison, sodium cyanide (e.g., Barber and Pratt 1997).

The expansion of the trade to areas far into the Pacific and Indian oceans has occurred largely because of depletions of populations of target species in Southeast Asia. Estimates of sustainable yield in this region suggest that current levels of exploitation are unsustainable (K.A. Warren-Rhodes, NASA-Ames Research Center, Moffett Field, CA, pers. comm.) and Hong Kong businessmen report having to move ever further in search of sufficient

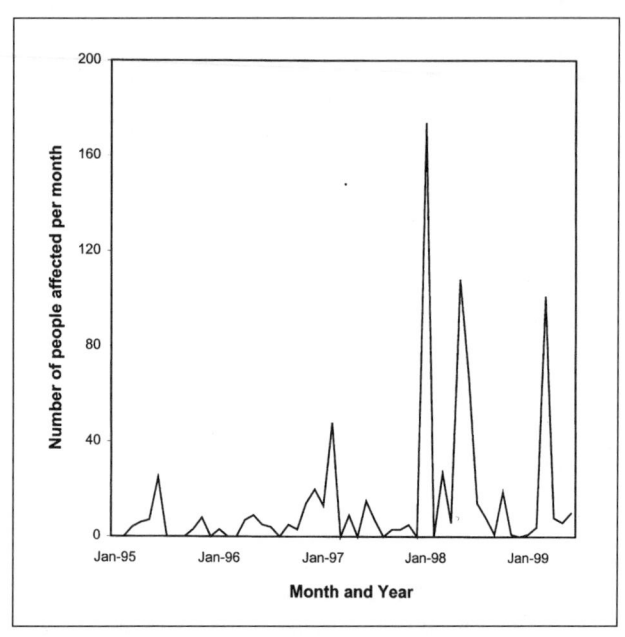

Figure 2. Number of people affected monthly by ciguatera between January 1995 and June 1999. Official figures of the Health Department of the HKSAR.

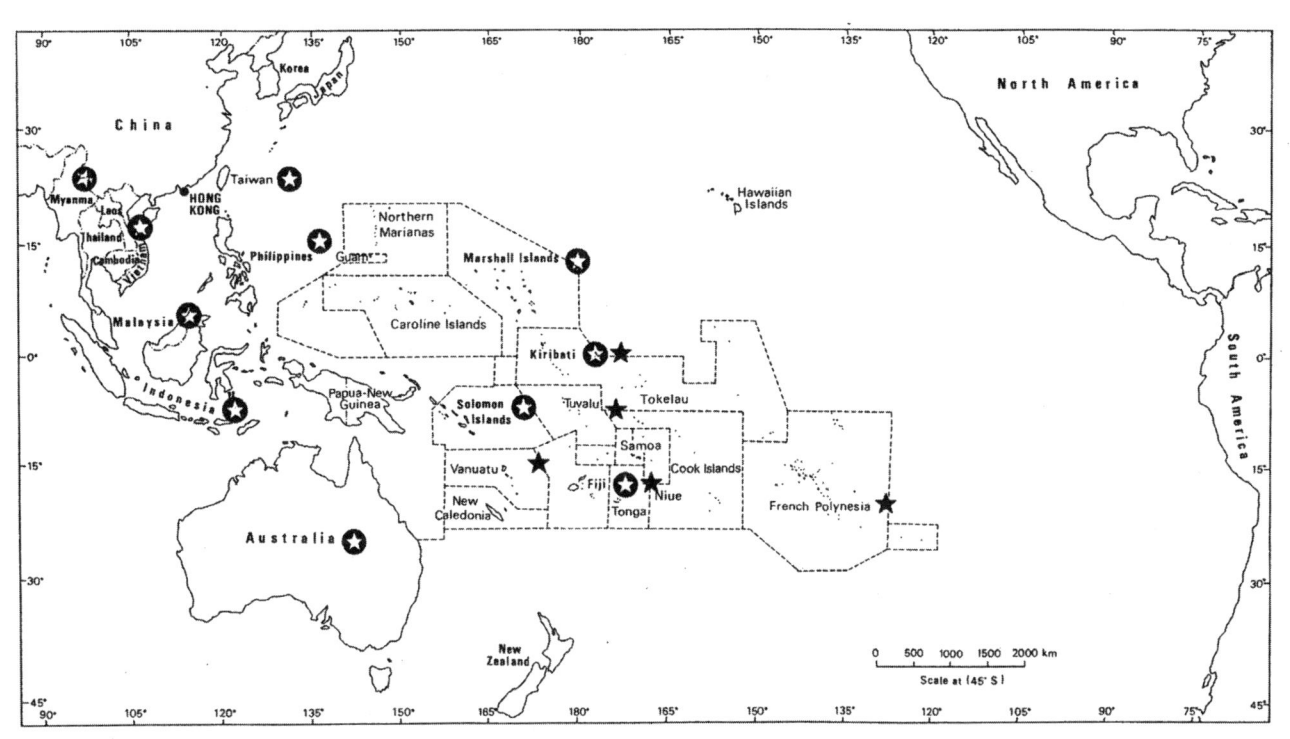

Figure 3. Map showing locations in the South China Sea and Pacific Ocean where the LRFT is conducted (white star in black circle). Black stars show general areas exploited by the LRFT where fishes can be ciguatoxic.

supplies. The types of larger reef fishes targeted cannot withstand heavy levels of exploitation because of their life histories which include long life, slow growth, and relatively low replacement rates. Concerns over sustainability caused Palau to cease participating in the LRFT in 1988, to recommence briefly in the early 1990s, while the Seychelles has decided to limit severely the number of businesses operating because of concerns over sustainability (Johannes and Riepen 1995, Bentley and Aumeeruddy 1999).

Apparent depletions are further exacerbated by several factors. Fishing approaches that target spawning aggregations, where catchability is high and where a large proportion of spawning animals can be removed in a short period (e.g., Johannes 1997, Johannes and Lam 1999, Rhodes 1999), are becoming increasingly common and are potentially damaging to stocks. The targeting of plate-size individuals means that, in several larger species (such as humphead wrasse, giant and tiger groupers), preferred trade sizes are in the juvenile size range. More recently, smaller fish have been particularly sought, possibly because they generally pose a lower threat of ciguatera, or are cheaper. Properly managed fisheries by and large eschew the taking of juveniles as being poor fishing practice with the potential for producing growth overfishing, and, ultimately, recruitment overfishing.

Another potential cause of overfishing is the wild-capture of juveniles and sub-market size adults for mariculture growout (Sadovy and Pet 1998). Millions of small juveniles are captured for growout and trade each year. It is unknown what volumes of extraction are sustainable but, in some areas, there are concerns that catches of juveniles are declining (pers. comm. during field visits to Philippines and Thailand). Moreover, the impacts of juvenile capture on future stock sizes may be significant in some areas. Concerns over limits to fry supply have led to bans on fry export, or export below certain sizes, in Vietnam, Malaysia, and China, although significant illegal export persists (Sadovy, unpubl. data).

There is also concern over the status of particularly vulnerable and valuable species included in the LRFT, in particular the humphead wrasse and the giant grouper. These species appear to be naturally uncommon, probably long-lived, and, given what we know of species with similar life history traits (Jennings et al. 1999), unlikely to be able to withstand current levels of exploitation. Wherever the

Table 1. Examples of regulations relating to ciguatera fish poisoning (CFP).

European Union:	Article 5, Directive 91/293/EEC prohibits marketing for human consumption poisonous fish . . . or fishery products containing biotoxin such as ciguatera toxins or muscle-paralyzing toxins.
USA:	HACCP Guidelines, preventive measures for naturally occurring toxins include making sure that incoming fish have not been caught in an area for which there is a CFP advisory or for which there is knowledge of a CFP problem.
Australia:	Applies HACCP guidelines (see USA); dead and live fish are treated similarly (Ross Marriott, Australia, June 9, 1998, pers. comm.) Sale of specified species prohibited.
Tahiti:	Sale of specified ciguatoxic species prohibited.
Puerto Rico:	Sale of specified ciguatoxic species prohibited.

humphead wrasse has been targeted, numbers have dropped rapidly, leading to enough concern to implement export prohibitions of the species, or of certain sizes of the species (Palawan in the Philippines, Indonesia, and Maldives). Moreover, concerns over overexploitation and resultant conservation status led to the inclusion of both species on the 1996 IUCN (International Union for the Conservation of Nature) Red List, a signal that wild populations may be seriously affected by current and projected levels of fishing pressure (Baillie and Groombridge 1996).

The use of sodium cyanide has probably elicited the most concern in the LRFT. Cyanide is a toxin that, ironically, has long been used to take live fish, first in the ornamental reef fish trade and, more recently, for food fishes. The toxin is widely used, especially in the Philippines and eastern Indonesia (Barber and Pratt 1997, Erdmann and Pet-Soede 1997). The concern over cyanide is that it can, under certain conditions, kill coral (Jones and Steven 1997) and could potentially damage the reef ecosystem itself, destroying the habitat that reef organisms depend upon. Its use is also known to result in wasteful bycatch in the form of nontarget organisms that cannot escape the poison and therefore die. The extent of such bycatch is unknown but, under circumstances where cyanide solution is applied and water circulation is low, it is likely to be substantial. It is a destructive fishing technique that is spreading with the LRFT. Its use cannot be condoned under any circumstances. In the Philippines, the International Marinelife Alliance (IMA) has established cyanide detection laboratories to certify fish as cyanide-free prior to export. Programs have been introduced in the Philippines by the Haribon Foundation, IMA, and others, to train fishers in hook and line fishing to reduce the increasingly entrenched dependence on cyanide.

CONCLUSIONS: PROBLEMS AND PROSPECTS

There are three major impediments to a safe, sustainable, and cyanide-free LRFT.

1. The impacts of the LRFT on wild stocks, and particularly on vulnerable species, need to be examined because fishing levels are evidently unsustainable. The targeting of spawning aggregations, because of their extreme vulnerability to fishing and history of extirpation following overfishing, should be strongly discouraged and/or regulated or, ideally, avoided. Source countries will have to consider implementing export quotas or introducing protected areas to safeguard local stocks. Particularly vulnerable species, such as the humphead wrasse and the giant grouper, may have to be phased out of the LRFT, if taken from the wild. The excessive take of juveniles or sub-market size adults from the wild for the purpose of growout also needs to be examined to determine sustainable levels of harvest. Wasteful bycatch taken by certain fishing techniques should also be reduced.

2. To ensure a safe food supply to importing economies, measures are needed to address the problem of ciguatoxic fishes. At present, given the absence of a reliable "dockside" method for detecting ciguatoxins or fail-safe laboratory procedures for the range of toxins involved, the most

practical approach would be to follow the initiative of other economies in dealing with this issue by avoiding the import of fish from areas where ciguatoxic fishes are commonly encountered. In Hong Kong, the government would have the necessary authority to prohibit the import and sale of contaminated or suspect live fish if this were classified as food.

3. The use of destructive fishing methods, especially the widespread application of cyanide, should be eliminated and is to be abhorred in any well-practiced fishery. Programs that involve cyanide detection, together with a commitment from the industry not to trade in fishes found to be, or suspected to have been, taken with cyanide are needed to tackle this problem. Destructive or wasteful fishing approaches, such as those sometimes used to take juveniles for growout (e.g., the bag or fyke net) should be identified and eliminated (e.g., Johannes and Ogburn 1999).

The long-term prospects of the LRFT depend on how the problems of overfishing, unsafe (ciguatoxic) fish, and destructive fishing are addressed. Solutions require not only action by source countries but also by demand centers, by the industry, and by regional intergovernmental organizations involved in marine resource use, such as APEC (Asia-Pacific Economic Cooperation). Possible measures for adoption include reciprocal agreements on cyanide-free certification, close monitoring of trade by species and source country (to avoid species/sources implicated in ciguatoxins), and an eco-labeling program (such as that proposed by the Marine Stewardship Council) which identifies fish captured and cultured sustainably. An evaluation of the role of mariculture in the LRFT is also needed to determine whether, if conducted properly, it can reduce pressure on wild stocks without causing additional problems of coastal pollution, increased pressures on wild fish stocks for feed, etc.

Current levels of exploitation for live reef fish are apparently unsustainable. If a well-managed mariculture industry cannot adequately substitute wild-caught fish to allow for a sustainable fishery sector, the result will ultimately and inevitably be fewer of the preferred live fish on the market. This means higher prices to the consumer. Given that these fish are part of a luxury food market, it is appropriate that consumers absorb the true costs of harvesting limited stocks of wild animals, costs currently being subsidized by lost future revenues from overfished stocks, often in impoverished areas, and environmental degradation.

Acknowledgments

I am grateful to the following who have helped me to prepare this manuscript or enabled me to attend the meeting in Seattle: Michelle Legault, Rachel Wong, Bob Johannes, Patrick Chan, Brian Paust, and John Peters.

References

Akimichi, T. 1998. Live grouper trade and ethno-networks in Southeast Asia. Proceedings APEC [Asia-Pacific Economic Cooperation] Workshop on the Impacts of Destructive Fishing Practices on the Marine Environment, December 1997, Hong Kong, pp. 240-248.

Baillie, J., and B. Groombridge. 1996. 1996 IUCN red list of threatened animals. IUCN (International Union for the Conservation of Nature), Gland, Switzerland.

Barber, C.V., and V.R. Pratt. 1997. Sullied seas: Strategies for combating cyanide fishing in Southeast Asia and beyond. World Resources Institute, Washington, DC.

Bentley, N. 1999. Fishing for solutions: Can the live trade in wild groupers and wrasses from Southeast Asia be managed? TRAFFIC Southeast Asia, Petaling Jaya, Malaysia.

Bentley, N., and R. Aumeeruddy. 1999. The live reef fishery in the Seychelles. Secretariat of the Pacific Community Live Reef Fish Information Bulletin 6:5-7.

Chan, P.S.W. 2001. Marketing aspects of the live seafood trade in Hong Kong and the People's Republic of China. In: B.C. Paust and A.A. Rice (eds.), Marketing and shipping live aquatic products: Proceedings of the Second International Conference and Exhibition, November 1999, Seattle, WA. University of Alaska Sea Grant, AK-SG-01-03, Fairbanks. (This volume.)

Chan, T.Y.K., A.Y.W. Chan, and J. Sham. 1992. The clinical features and management of ciguatera fish poisoning. J. Hong Kong Med. Assoc. 44(2):119-121.

Dalzell, P. 1992. Ciguatera fish poisoning and fisheries development in the South Pacific region. Bull. Soc. Path. Ex. 85:435-444.

Erdmann, M.V., and L. Pet-Soede. 1997. An overview of destructive fishing practices in Indonesia. Proceedings APEC Workshop on the Impacts of Destructive Fishing Practices on the Marine Environment, December 1997, Hong Kong, pp. 25-34.

Fong, Q.S.W., and J.L. Anderson. 2000. Assessment of the Hong Kong shark fin trade. INFOFISH International 1/2000:28-32.

Jennings, S., J.D. Reynolds, and V.C. Polunin. 1999. Predicting the vulnerability of tropical reef fishes to exploitation with phylogenies and life histories. Cons. Biol. 13:1466-1475.

Johannes, R.E. 1997. Grouper spawning aggregations need protection. Secretariat of the Pacific Community Live Reef Fish Information Bulletin 3:13-14.

Johannes, R.E., and M. Lam. 1999. The live reef food fish trade in the Solomon Islands. Secretariat of the Pacific Community Live Reef Fish Information Bulletin 5:8-15.

Johannes, R.E., and N.J. Ogburn. 1999. Collecting grouper seed for aquaculture in the Philippines. Secretariat of the Pacific Community Live Reef Fish Information Bulletin 6:35-48.

Johannes, R.E., and M. Riepen. 1995. Environmental, economic and social implications of the live reef fish trade in Asia and the western Pacific. Report to the Nature Conservancy and the South Pacific Forum Fisheries Agency, Oct. 1995, pp. 1-82.

Jones, R.J., and A.L. Steven. 1997. Effects of cyanide on corals in relation to cyanide fishing on reefs. Mar. Freshw. Res. 48:517-522.

Lau, P.P.F., and R. Parry-Jones. 1999. The Hong Kong trade in live reef fish for food. TRAFFIC East Asia and World Wide Fund for Nature, Hong Kong.

Lee, C., and Y. Sadovy. 1998. A taste for live fish: Hong Kong's role in the live reef fish trade. ICLARM Quarterly 21(2):38-42.

Lewis, N.D. 1986. Epidemiology and impact of ciguatera in the Pacific: A review. Mar. Fish. Rev. 48(4):6-13.

OmniTrak Group Inc. 1997. Summary on the taste test between the mariculture and the wild-caught malabar grouper. The Nature Conservancy. Available from OmniTrak HQ, 841 Bishop Street, Honolulu, HI, 96813.

Rhodes, K.L. 1999. Grouper aggregation protection in proactive Pohnpei. Secretariat of the Pacific Community Live Reef Fish Information Bulletin 6:14-15.

Sadovy, Y. 1998. The live reef fish trade: A role for importers in combating destructive fishing practices—example of Hong Kong, China. Proceedings APEC Workshop on the Impacts of Destructive Fishing Practices on the Marine Environment, December 1997, Hong Kong, pp. 200-207.

Sadovy, Y., and J. Pet. 1998. Wild collection of juveniles for grouper mariculture: Just another capture fishery? Secretariat of the Pacific Community Live Reef Fish Information Bulletin 4:36-39.

U.S. Department of Health and Human Services. 1999. U.S. Department of Health and Human Services food code, HACCP guidelines (Hazard Analysis Critical Control Point). Washington, DC.

Yeeting, B.M. 1999. Live reef fish developments in Fiji. Secretariat of the Pacific Community Live Reef Fish Information Bulletin 6:19-24.

Marketing Aspects of the Live Seafood Trade in Hong Kong and the People's Republic of China

Patrick S.W. Chan
Brightfuture Industries Limited, Kowloon, Hong Kong, China

Abstract

Hong Kong is the biggest live seafood market in Southeast Asia. As the economy of the People's Republic of China (PRC) has grown in the past few years, the demand for live seafood has increased tremendously. Although a small quantity of live seafood is imported into the PRC directly, the majority of this product is re-exported from Hong Kong because the latter is a free port and has no restraints on the importation of seafood. Consequently, in addition to the substantial local demand, Hong Kong serves as a gateway for live seafood going into the PRC market.

This report is a general review on the various types of live seafood products entering the Hong Kong and PRC markets. Also covered are air and sea transportation considerations, including product safety factors and Hong Kong import formalities and customs requirements.

Introduction

Hong Kong is one of the major live seafood markets in the world. Eating a wide variety of seafood including live seafood items is a tradition of the people living along the southeast coast of China. Over the past three decades, the restaurant industry in Hong Kong has improved the methods to cook seafood. This "eating culture" has been gradually accepted by the people inhabiting neighboring countries, particularly those with large Chinese populations including Taiwan, Singapore, Malaysia, and Thailand.

Following the adoption of the open door policy in the PRC, live seafood has also been introduced to this vast country—first to the Shenzhen Economic Zone which is located just next to Hong Kong. Now Hong Kong–style live seafood restaurants can be seen in Beijing, Shanghai, and the other big cities of the PRC, even in the distant province of Tibet. Because of the large market demand in the PRC, the quantity of seafood coming into Hong Kong, which has traditionally served as a gateway to the PRC, is enormous.

Types of Live Seafood for the Hong Kong Market

The major types of live seafood brought into Hong Kong include live reef fish, lobsters, mantis prawns, crabs, prawns, and shellfish

Live reef fish

The reef fish imported into Hong Kong are generally caught in the regions below 30° latitude in both in the Northern and Southern hemispheres. Generally, bottomfish found on coral reefs within these regions are acceptable to the Hong Kong live market. The highest-priced fish include highfin grouper and humphead wrasse, with current prices at about US $64.00 per kilogram. The medium priced fish include various types of coral trout and are priced at about $38.00 per kilogram. The low priced fish include various types of grouper and are priced at approximately $20.00 per kilogram. The industry estimates that about 30,000-35,000 tons of live reef fish are imported into Hong Kong each year, with about 50-55% of this amount being re-exported to the PRC.

Lobsters

Spiny lobsters from tropical regions and rock lobsters from south Australia are the most popular lobsters used by restaurants in Hong Kong and the PRC. Rock lobsters from south Australia occupy almost 55% of the total market for lobsters. The Australian lobster season is closed between May and October of each year. During this closure period, lobster supply decreases and prices go up. Some restaurants will switch over to using crayfish and lobsters from North America during this period.

Crayfish are cheaper compared to the typical market prices for spiny lobster. Also, crayfish are not very popular because the shell of the crayfish is hard and does not match up very well with the traditional Chinese cuisine. At present spiny lobsters shipped from Cuba, Florida, Mexico, New Zealand, Australia, Papua New Guinea, Indonesia, Philippines, Vietnam, Myanmar, India, and South Africa are imported to the Hong Kong market. In 1998 more than 9,000 tons of lobsters were imported into this market.

Mantis prawns

Giant mantis prawns are very popular in Hong Kong seafood restaurants. The prawns are caught in the wild and imported from Indonesia, Thailand, Vietnam, and Cambodia. The preferred size for this live product is over 30 cm, but those in the range of 20-30 cm are also acceptable.

Crabs

Mud crabs are imported from Pakistan and Sri Lanka because of their low price. The mud crabs originating from the PRC and Vietnam are also well liked by Hong Kong consumers because of the general consensus that they taste better. Dungeness crabs from Canada, king crabs from Australia, and snow crabs from Canada and Japan are also available in the Hong Kong market. From August to November of each year a large quantity of freshwater hairy crabs are imported from Zhejiang Province in the PRC. In the past, the hairy crabs were caught from the wild, but this species is now cultured because of the large demand. These cultured crabs are gradually becoming acceptable to the market. The success in the culture of hairy crabs points to a business opportunity for other countries with similar growing conditions. Individual crabs weighing 300 grams or more may reach US $50.00 per kilogram. The mud crab season is between September and November of each year.

Prawns

The trawlers operating from Hong Kong are able to provide a sufficient supply of prawns for the local market between late February and late October. These fishing operations are affected when the northeast monsoon begins to blow in the South China Sea. Christmas and the Chinese New Year are the best marketing periods for imported frozen prawns that are normally imported from Australia, United States, and Southeast Asia. In addition to wild prawns, cultured prawns, mainly in the form of black tiger prawns, are regularly imported from Thailand by air and from the PRC by land transport over the border. The price for cultured prawns is normally cheaper during the summer, as the mortality is higher. The price will pick up when the weather becomes cooler.

Shellfish

Live abalone is the most popular shellfish sold in the Hong Kong market. Most abalone is 4-5 cm in size and is imported mainly from Taiwanese abalone culture centers. Small quantities of a similar type of abalone are imported from the PRC. However, due to the growing market demand in the PRC, the majority of this abalone is sold locally. In addition to the cultured product, wild abalone of 20 cm size from South Africa is also acceptable in the Hong Kong market. Geoduck clams from the West Coast of Canada are welcomed in both Hong Kong and the PRC markets because the skin of this clam is white and looks cleaner than other species. The skin of clams from the U.S. East Coast is typically black and is not welcomed by the restaurants even though they taste the same. Other live shellfish, for example cultured scallops from Korea and razor clams from Scotland, are imported to Hong Kong, but the quantities are limited.

Other live seafood such as coconut crabs, snow crabs, and giant freshwater eels are also imported to Hong Kong. However, the total quantity is small.

TRANSPORT OF LIVE SEAFOOD BY SHIP

Live reef fish is the major single live seafood item for the Hong Kong market. About 30,000-35,000 tons of live reef fish are imported from overseas countries. The majority of this live fish is imported by ship. This quantity does not include the fish caught by the local fishermen in the reefs of the South China Sea. Countries now exporting live reef fish to Hong Kong include Indonesia, Malaysia, Philippines, Australia, Solomon Islands, Kiribati, Marshall Islands, India, Mayanmar, Thailand, Vietnam, the Maldives, Seychelles, and Fiji. In other words, live fish carriers are able to bring fish from countries as far as 6,000 nautical miles from Hong Kong in a single voyage of less than 25 days.

Currently, live fish traders use two types of live fish carriers. The first type is the traditional fishing vessel of Hong Kong. This design was first introduced from Scotland. The original design was a metal hull trawler operating in the North Sea and is capable of operating in rough sea conditions. Shipbuilders in Hong Kong followed this design and began to build the ship using timber instead of metal.

Almost 99% of Hong Kong fishermen use wooden fishing vessels because they can be exempted from obtaining proper qualification for navigation. This policy has been used by the local authorities because the majority of the fishermen are poorly educated and are unable to attend any training courses for navigation. Various types of local carriers and live holding vessels are also used in this industry (Fig. 1).

Apart from trawling, some of the vessels are built with live wells for fishermen involved in live fish operations. Initially the vessel was about 50-60 feet in length and with engine size of less than 300 horse power (HP). Now some vessels are built up to 120 feet in length with engine power of up to 1500 HP. A 120-foot live harvesting vessel is typically equipped with 30-40 live wells and holds about 20 tons of live fish (Fig. 2.)

Some traders now use metal hull live fish carriers (Figs. 3, 4). Some of these vessels are second-hand live fish carriers bought from Japan. Others are small cargo ships or tuna vessels converted to live fish carriers. Generally speaking, the live well capacity in a metal hull vessel is larger than that possible in a live carrier made from timber, as the latter type vessel requires more live well partitions to support the hull.

Both types of vessels share one thing in common—they use water inlets and outlets installed in the hulls. These through-hull facilities provide for good water circulation during sailing, the water flow each hour reaching ten times the tank holding capacity. All carriers are also equipped with strong pumping systems that are required to maintain water circulation when the vessel is stationary, such as when loading and discharging fish.

Although they are equipped with good pumping facilities, special attention must be paid to the following situations during loading and unloading live fish.

1. *Tide movements.* The oxygen content of the surface water will be lower during low tide, and exposure with the heated seawater from shallow areas is a high risk for the fish being loaded into the carrier.
2. *Air pressure.* Low air pressure will force the fish to move toward the surface of the water where the temperature is higher and where there is also less dissolved oxygen in the water.

Figure 1. A Taiwanese local fish carrier.

3. *Water temperature.* Fish will become more active when placed in warmer water. The oxygen consumption of fish may double or triple with every 10°C rise in temperature. This is particularly important to consider when the fish are under stress such as during loading and unloading. When the fish become scared, they tend to school tightly together in a small area of the live well. This may result in drastic drop in oxygen content in this small volume of water. Good water circulation is a proper solution for this problem and the transfer of fish to different live wells by rotation also can help. When the live wells are loaded at 70% of the full capacity, it is preferable to inject pure oxygen into the water through the use of diffusers.

The holding capacity of a particular live well depends on the characteristics of the reef fish. The average

Figure 2. A 120-foot live harvesting vessel is typically equipped with 30-40 live wells and holds about 20 tons of live fish.

Figure 3. Metal hull live fish carrier.

Figure 4. Live well in metal hull fish carrier.

holding ratio is between 8 to 14:1 (i.e., 8-14 tons of water for each 1,000 kg unit of fish). The size of fish is also an important factor to be considered when determining live well holding capacity because 20 tails of fish weighing 1 kg each will use more oxygen than one tail of fish weighing 20 kg. Snapper is a more active fish than grouper while the latter requires more floor space. The vessel officer supervising the loading of fish needs to be flexible and have good observation abilities. The success of each shipment of fish relies on the experience of the officer concerned and his timely and accurate actions.

Buyers from Hong Kong prefer to select and weigh the fish immediately before loading. This is certainly not a good arrangement as it is more stressful to the fish. However, this is an effective way to avoid the risk of weight loss, theft, and mortality by mishandling after weighing. No Hong Kong buyer has ever used a vacuum fish pump.

TRANSPORT OF LIVE SEAFOOD BY AIR

With an increasing amount of experience and improved skills and equipment, more and more live seafood is being transported by air, particularly those products with higher selling prices. Generally speaking, live fish is the most difficult live item to transport by air. However, skills and equipment have improved and presently the survival rate of live fish is very good, particularly if the total transportation time is less than 24 hours. All types of seafood face the same problem once they are transported by air, such as water quality changes. Once the fish are packed in the shipping container, there is hardly any chance to change the water, so the condition of the initial supply of water has to be maintained until the live products arrive in the buyer's hand. The following factors must be considered when delivering live seafood by air:

- Oxygen content of the water.
- Avoidance of carbon dioxide buildup.
- Avoidance of detrimental changes in pH level.
- Avoidance of detrimental changes of temperature.
- Buildup of fish discharges.
- Loss of fish surface mucus.

Some of these factors are interrelated. In other words, if a correct step is taken a few problems can be avoided. A well-equipped holding and packing center will improve the chance of success in the shipment of live products transported by air.

AIR TRANSPORT HOLDING AND PACKING CENTER

A good holding and packing center should have the following characteristics:

- Be located near the airport.

- Be located near the seaside or with good supply of seawater.
- Have access to a reliable power supply.
- Be equipped with holding pools furnished with chilling facilities.
- Have a packing area.
- Have loading and unloading areas for transport.

Once the fish are packed in a shipping container, the water therein provides only a limited amount of survival time for the fish. Every minute counts when packing live seafood for air transportation. An experienced operator knows how much time the packing team requires to pack one box, so the team will start packing with just enough time for them to finish their task and move the container to the airport in time for the flight. It is ideal for the packing center to be situated not more than a 30 minutes drive from the airport. Operating costs can be reduced if seawater can be pumped directly to the center. This also cuts down the cost of water for the holding facilities that are essential for all packing centers. An emergency supply of water will be needed to save lives if the condition of the water in the holding pools turns bad suddenly.

All live seafood items should be starved for at least 24 hours before they are packed to avoid the inevitable occurrence of vomiting of undigested food which will then pollute the holding water. This purging will lead to detrimental pH changes and kill the packed seafood. Live reef fish can be given a freshwater bath for 2-3 minutes when they are first delivered to the center. Fish will vomit the undigested food in freshwater and this bath also kills various kinds of worms and parasites attached to the body of the fish.

The temperature of the holding water should be in the range of 21-23°C. Because reef fish normally live in water within the temperature range of 24-30°C, a gradual reduction of this temperature in the holding pool will make the fish inactive and less stressed. Other types of seafood such as lobsters, mantis prawns, and crabs should be kept in separated holding pools with the same temperature. However, with shellfish, the freshwater bath should be avoided. The water in all holding pools should be well circulated. Water must be passed through a biofilter in order to neutralize ammonia content. Oxygen content can be improved by injection of air through the use of an air compressor and diffusers.

The temperature of water should be lowered a further 2-3°C prior to packing. This chilling process must be slow and be completed in about four hours. Packing water should be at the same temperature as that of the holding pool. An anesthetic agent will be used in the water if the fish are packed in polyethylene bags. The packing water should be able to cool the fish to near the pseudo-hibernation point. The anesthetic is an additional measure to ensure that the fish will not become too active when the water temperature warms during the transportation period. It must be noted that the use of anesthetics is not approved for food fish and seafood in most markets. Even if anesthetics are approved for food products, the purge period following delivery would probably be greater than the usual pre-purchase holding time. In spite of this, anesthetics are commonly used in Southeast Asia.

The Australian live fish exporters were the first to use a plastic bin to transport live fish by air to Hong Kong. This particular bin is insulated and able to hold about one ton of water. A battery-operated air pump is fitted in the upper compartment of the bin and injects air into the water by way of a diffuser. This shipping container is also provided with a simple skimmer. Each bin is able to hold about 240 kg of live fish and the survival rate is very good if the container can be delivered to the buyer within 24 hours. Because the water temperature can be well maintained in the bin, no anesthetic is used. However, the cost of returning the bins to the originating exporter is very costly.

Packing live fish in polyethylene bags and expanded polystyrene boxes requires a skillful working team. Fish are packed in a 1:3 or 4 fish-to-water ratio (1 kg fish to 3-4 kg of water), depending on the type of fish involved and the total transport time. During shipment, the fish are maintained in the stage of pseudo-hibernation. They are weighed and put inside the bag that is already positioned in the polystyrene box. The box is passed onto the second worker who is responsible for injecting pure oxygen into the bag and securing the bag with elastic bands. The box is then passed to the final worker who will check the packing, add coolant, and seal the polystyrene box with sealing tape. An experienced working team can complete one box in one minute.

Lobster must be held without food for several days prior to shipment. However, lobster will begin to digest their muscle tissue and build up waste if they are not given food for too long a period of time. During packing, the lobsters are cooled to the point where they become inactive—normally 17-18°C for tropical lobsters and 4-6°C for cold-water lobsters.

Lobsters can be placed in expanded polystyrene shipping containers with their tails banded and packed in layers separated by moist newspapers. Normally, no more than three layers of lobsters should be packed in one box. Wood shavings and polystyrene chips have been placed between lobsters with good result. It is also very common to see tropical lobsters rolled up in newspaper in order to control their movements. This method has proved to be quite successful. Other exporters roll the lobsters in dry sand, a practice that tends to calm the lobsters during transportation. Suppliers in tropical countries commonly apply this practice to small lobsters. Lobsters can survive up to 40 hours without water as long as they are kept in an environment with the relative humidity over 70% and the temperature maintained in the range of 16-18°C.

Mantis prawns also require similar control over food intake prior to shipment. The general practice is to lower the water temperature slowly until the prawns show sign of pseudo-hibernation. These prawns should be packed individually and placed inside a plastic cone to avoid body damage during transport. The prawns are oriented in a vertical position inside the polystyrene box. Packing them in layers is not recommended because their bodies are too soft to withstand the pressure. They can survive up to 24 hours if the humidity and temperature can be maintained within a certain range during the transport period.

With abalone, no food should be given for at least 2-3 days prior to export. The abalone are weighed and placed inside a plastic basket before returning to the water for the cooling process. This basket is then placed inside a plastic bag that is filled with pure oxygen before final sealing. Abalone can survive up to 36 hours in a cool and moist environment.

The majority of the live prawns shipped to Hong Kong are black tiger prawns. No food is given to the prawns for at least two days prior to harvest from the culture ponds. Prawns should be cooled to a temperature that achieves a state of lethargy. The chilling process must be carefully monitored and water temperature should not be depressed lower than 18°C or the prawns will be killed. About 6 kg of prawns are placed inside a polyethylene bag that is filled with pure oxygen. A cooling agent such as a gel pack must be used to maintain the temperature inside the polystyrene box.

Since the market prices of certain other types of shellfish and crayfish are quite low, it is not financially viable to transport them by expensive air service. Should there be any need for these products to be sent by air, the rules for air transportation have to be observed. The rate of successful deliveries relies on the experience of the exporter and updated information on weather, flight delays, and the cargo clearance time at the destination. Live seafood survive better at lower temperatures, so every effort must be made to ensure the packing temperature is maintained until the cargo is delivered to the buyer.

IMPORT FORMALITIES

Air cargo

Hong Kong is a free port and does not levy any customs tariffs or duties on imports. Hong Kong also does not maintain anti-dumping laws and countervailing duty laws. There are no value-added or general service taxes. However, the cargo-handling charge is about HK $1.4 per kilogram. A consignee can collect the cargo on production of the airway bills and a letter of authorization from the consignor or company stamps. Normally, a consignee will be appointed by a transportation company to withdraw cargo from the airport. The rental of a truck is normally between HK $500 and HK $900, depending on the capacity of the vehicle. If the live seafood is sent in polystyrene boxes, additional labor charges will be required for the loading and unloading of the boxes to the vehicle.

Airway bill

An airway bill must be prepared by the shipper's cargo handling agent. The original copy goes with the cargo and a photocopy is faxed to consignees who will be responsible for the withdrawal of the cargo from the Hong Kong airport.

Certificate of origin

A certificate of origin is not generally required. But check with the buyer since it may be needed in certain circumstances.

Import and export declaration

Import and export declaration must be made by the consignee within 14 days after the importation or exportation of any article other than cargo for transshipment, transit, or for exhibition purposes with a value less than HK$1,000. The information contained on the declaration is used primarily by the Census and Statistics Department to enforce the various regulations related to import and export declarations.

Customs inspection

Physical inspection of the goods at the airport will be conducted on a selective basis after the inspection of the airway bill. The customs hours for general cargo are Monday though Friday 0800 to 1500. However, live products and perishables can receive clearance outside of regular customs office hours.

Health certificate

Live marine fish are exempt and do not require a health certificate. However, a health certificate for chilled and frozen fish is required. All crayfish and shellfish require health certificates and the original copy must be attached to the cargo. The health certificate of the imported marine product must be issued by the competent authority in the country of origin stating that

- The marine product is processed and packed under hygienic conditions.
- The marine product does not contain any substance including biotoxins, contaminants like pesticides, trace metals, etc. in such amount as to be poisonous, harmful, or injurious to health.
- The marine product is fit for human consumption and is permitted to be sold as food in the country of origin.

For marine products coming from cholera infected regions, the following additional certification is also required:

- The marine product was not collected from areas where any cholera case has been reported.
- The marine product has been found to be free from the infection of cholera vibrios.

General information

The Hong Kong International Airport is about 50 km from the city. A very good highway network connects the airport to the city. Normally, it takes about 35-40 minutes to reach the urban areas. However, a total of 2-3 hours is usually needed for the transportation workers to clear the cargo and deliver the containers to the consignee. The air temperature could reach 35°C between mid-May to late September. Sufficient coolants must be used to maintain the proper packing temperature.

AUTHOR BIOGRAPHY

Mr. Chan has served as chairman of the Hong Kong Chamber of the Seafood Merchants Limited since 1998. The HK Chamber represents 95% of the live reef fish importers and wholesalers and 65% of the live seafood retailers in Hong Kong. The HK Chamber is a legally registered organization that represents the industry and voices the views of this diverse industry to the government and public. Since 1998, the Chamber has assisted both the Hong Kong Agriculture and Fishery and Health Departments to deal with food poisoning incidents relating to live reef fish containing ciguatera toxin. Mr. Chan is also General Manager of Brightfuture Industries Limited, one of the major live reef fish importers in Hong Kong. He has extensive experience in the live seafood industry and in-depth knowledge of seafood markets in Hong Kong and the People's Republic of China.

Wholesale and Retail Marketing Aspects of the Hong Kong Live Seafood Business

Patrick S.W. Chan
Brightfuture Industries Limited, Kowloon, Hong Kong, China

Abstract

Each year about 30,000-35,000 metric tons of live reef fish are imported into Hong Kong from the Philippines, Australia, the Maldives, Vietnam, Malaysia, and Thailand. Of this amount, 55-60% is re-exported to the PRC. Traditions in Hong Kong and the PRC each call for their own types and sizes of fish. Different importation methods are also required in each of these two markets.

In Hong Kong, a well-developed relationship and protocol exists between importers, who run live fish carriers, retailers, who hold fish for distribution to restaurants, and the seafood restaurants themselves. This relationship may be changing as some restaurant chains buy fish directly from wholesalers and as more overseas suppliers begin sending live fish by air.

Rules regarding importing live seafood to the PRC are also very complex. Import taxes and charges are levied by the PRC Central Government, as well as by other government departments. Different cities charge different rates and have different import clearance policies. Several alternative pathways into the country also exist, with varying levels of risk and legality. Foreign traders wishing to enter the PRC market may want to secure the help of Hong Kong agents.

Introduction

Among all the live seafood trading in Hong Kong, live reef fish has the largest share of the market. Each year about 30,000-35,000 metric tons of live reef fish are imported into Hong Kong, with a total wholesale value of US $490 million. Because of the constant demand from the People's Republic of China (PRC) market, about 55-60% of the live fish is re-exported to the PRC. The majority of this live fish is exported to the PRC through a special arrangement that requires paying only part of the full import duties. Since there are traditional differences between the two places, different types and sizes of fish are needed in these two markets. This report involves a broad discussion of the wholesale, retail, and exporting of live reef fish and other live seafood species in Hong Kong and adjacent territories.

Relationships Among Importers, Wholesalers, Retailers, and Restaurants

People normally find that the price paid for a live reef fish in a Hong Kong seafood restaurant is exceedingly high. This has created a wrong impression for members of the public and particularly the foreign suppliers of live fish. They may have a feeling that they were deceived by the Hong Kong buyers because their selling price is so low.

In fact, an imported live fish is required to go through several traders before it reaches the restaurant. A well-developed relationship among the importers, wholesalers, retailers, and seafood restaurants is clearly seen in live reef fish trading in Hong Kong. The operations of the importer and wholesaler require large amounts of capital. The annual business turnover of a major wholesaler in Hong Kong will reach US $25 million. One 15 metric ton shipment of live fish imported via ship may involve an expenditure of $250,000, an amount that is beyond the capability of most retailers and normally can be handled only by the wholesaler. Retailers buy fish from wholesalers and control market distributions. Seafood restaurants are the end users.

Live reef fish importers run one or more live fish carriers. Foreign agents are appointed who are responsible for the arrangement of adequate quantities of fish and the clearance to take or harvest fish in the country. Those substantial importers who own floating cage stations in Hong Kong also act as wholesalers, as they have sufficient facilities to hold such large quantities of live fish. Small importers sell their fish to the wholesaler and the latter sells the fish to the retailers after taking an 8-14% profit. Retailers hold their fish in their shops until they can be sold. The marketing officers of the retailing shops telephone the restaurants in their sales networks each morning to take orders. The fish is delivered to the restaurants that afternoon. As there is risk of mortality during the holding period, retailers normally take a profit of 25-35% and the restaurants then mark up an additional 100-150% profit.

This system has been maintained for many years, as importers and wholesalers like to sell their fish as quickly as possible to avoid loss from mortality. They are not interested in the sale of small quantities to restaurants, even though they can earn more. However, this situation has changed because operators with a chain of restaurants have bought fish directly from the wholesalers in the recent two or three years. This situation was not seen in the past and now restaurant operators have to take whatever means possible to cut operating costs.

As handling skills have improved over recent years, more and more overseas suppliers have begun to send live fish to Hong Kong by air. As the quantity in each shipment is small, a number of retailers have started importing live fish by air and do not rely completely on the wholesalers. At the moment the situation is chaotic and the identities of businesses serving as wholesalers and retailers are difficult to define. General speaking, the wholesalers with their sea importing capability are still taking the leading role in live reef fish trading in Hong Kong.

Countries from which live seafood is imported

About 50% of the live reef fish supply is imported from Indonesia, closely followed by the Philippines, Australia, Maldives, Vietnam, Malaysia, and Thailand. Live reef fish exports from Indonesia began in 1988. Most of the suppliers are Indonesian Chinese who normally set up their floating cage stations at suitable locations and mobilize fishermen in the nearby area to catch fish. Fish are bought from these fishermen and are held at the holding stations until they have enough quantity to notify the Hong Kong buyer to send a live fish carrier to collect the fish. This method of operation will continue in most of the regions in Indonesia, as there is no other means of transport to export the fish. However, in big cities like Jakarta and Bali, where international airports are available, suppliers operate their own live fish carriers and buy fish from fishermen from regions within a four or five day voyage. Their accumulations are periodically sent to Hong Kong by air. These suppliers also collect and export lobsters.

Suppliers from Cairns in Australia, Manila in the Philippines, Sabah of Malaysia, Vietnam, and Thailand rely heavily on air transportation and now more than 80% of the catches are sent to Hong Kong by air. It is apparent that air transportation has become increasingly important to live reef fish trading.

Almost all lobsters are sent to Hong Kong by air. Each year more than 9,000 metric tons of live lobsters are imported. The Australian lobsters comprise more than 50% of the market.

Payment and trading rules in Hong Kong

Wholesalers normally settle an account with the importers within one week after the sale. If the fish cannot be sold instantly the wholesaler is required to buy the fish at a price agreeable to both parties and the risk will then be transferred to the wholesaler. The relationship between the importer and wholesaler is close and it is not uncommon to see the wholesaler provide financial aid to the importer. This is seen particularly when the importer's live carrier or ship needs urgent repair or an additional deposit for future shipment of fish is needed.

Retailers are required to settle their bills within 10 to 14 days. However, because the economy has declined over the past two years, unsettled accounts have dragged on for 4-6 weeks. A discount of 3% is given to retailers to compensate them for the water on the fish during the process of fish weighing.

Retailers get higher profits from restaurants. However, the normal restaurant payment term is 30-45 days. The payment schedule from restaurants located in big hotels is even longer. In addition, restaurant operators periodically "force" retailers to subscribe to dinner coupon campaigns during special business promotions. Participation in this type of promotion may require several tens of thousands of HK dollars a year. Retailers also pay 3% of their total sales for the year as a commission to the restaurant staff. This commission normally comes due prior to the Chinese New Year.

It would appear that all the benefits go to restaurant operators. However, we must understand that Hong Kong is one of the most expensive places to live in the world and that businesses are required to pay very high employee salaries and premise rentals. Nevertheless, operating a restaurant is a very profitable business. In Hong Kong about 95% of restaurants are Chinese restaurants and most of them sell live seafood.

RE-EXPORT OF SEAFOOD TO THE PRC

An import tax of about 17% is paid for seafood exported from Hong Kong to the PRC. Additional charges are also levied by other government departments and, at present, different cities are charging different rates. The policy for import clearance of live seafood is also different from area to area. This situation is applied not only to seafood but also to all imported commodities, which is very confusing. However, organizations with strong backgrounds are given quotas to import various types of seafood at much lower tax rates. Some of these quotas are sold to seafood traders. Those who do not possess quotas must find other ways to import seafood.

In the past seven or eight years, a large amount of live seafood has been imported to the PRC via a small port of Yantian, which is located on the east border of the New Territories of Hong Kong. Sha Tau Kok is designated for the culture of fish and is located just adjacent to Yantian. The culture fishermen in Sha Tau Kok are allowed to sell their products in Yantian and a fishing cooperative was formed many years ago. The cooperative managed to obtain special approval from the authorities and, as a consequence, an import tax of only 3% is levied for all products from Sha Tau Kok.

The fishermen in Sha Tau Kok have made good use of this privilege and act as the transport agents for traders who wish to bring live seafood to Yantian. It is an open secret that much of this imported seafood is not cultured product, and bribes are offered to the officers concerned to facilitate the import clearance. This channel for importing seafood has become more and more difficult because the PRC Central Government has taken drastic action to eliminate smuggling activities. Recently several shipments of seafood were detained and heavy fines were imposed. However, live seafood import activities are still going on.

Following the opening of the new airport in Hong Kong, a new live seafood entry point was established in Shekou which is an economic industries zone adjacent to the western border of Hong Kong. A few Hong Kong transportation companies are now cooperating with the state owned organizations in this zone that have seafood import quotas needed to deliver seafood destined for traders in the PRC. Several fishing vessels are plying the waters between Shekou and Tung Chung, which is a port only a five minute drive from the Hong Kong airport. At present, a large quantity of live seafood imported by air is entering the PRC using this channel. The service charge placed on these imports covers custom clearance, import tax, and transportation service. Different types of seafood are required to pay different service charge rates. Nevertheless, this importation channel can save a lot of time and the service charge is cheaper than the normal import duty.

Shekou also provides the convenience for those marketers who wish to redistribute seafood to other big cities like Shanghai and Beijing. The Shenzhen airport is about a 25 minute drive from Shekou. Currently, some Hong Kong operators have set up holding centers in Shekou and are providing holding and repackaging services for live seafood traders in the PRC.

Starting in 1996, Australian lobster suppliers managed to send their products directly to the PRC without going through the traders in Hong Kong. They worked with operators who can readily make payments in foreign currency. However, following the implementation of a new policy from PRC Central Government in 1997, no foreign currencies are allowed to be remitted out of the country. The Chinese currency, the RMB, is not a hard currency and there is a control on removing RMB from the country. A large number of Australian marketers were hard hit by this new policy, and could not get their money back after sending their lobsters to the PRC.

In the past, seafood operators in big cities such as Beijing and Shanghai relied on local retailers to supply them with product from Yantian. A problem arose with these retailers because many of them, after securing a line of credit with the traders in Yantian, just ran away with the cargo. The chances of locating them was slim because they only operated with a truck and a hand phone. Many Hong Kong seafood operators set up shops in Yantian a few years ago and most of them have suffered huge losses from these unreliable clients. At the moment, operators in Yantian, most of whom are local people, are very cautious about selling their products. However, they are able to change the RMB into Hong Kong currency by way of the black market and, in this way, are still able to survive in the industry.

Table 1. Marketed fish species with common names and Hong Kong local names.

Scientific name	Common name	Local name
High priced fish		
Cheilinus undulatus	Humphead wrasse	So Mei
Cromileptes altivelis	High-finned grouper	Lo Shu Pan
Medium priced fish		
Plectropomus areolatus	Spotted coral trout	Sai Sing
Plectropomus leopardus	Red coral trout	Tung Sing
Low priced fish		
Epinephelus polyphekadion	Flowery grouper	Charm Pan
Epinephelus malabaricus	Green grouper	Ching Pan
Epinephelus bleekeri	Brownspotted grouper	Chi Ma Pan
Epinephelus fuscoguttatus	Tiger grouper	Lo Fu Pan

As can be seen, the live seafood trading situation in the PRC is very complicated. It is not advisable for foreign traders to sell their products directly to the PRC until the situation is clear. It will be much easier and safer if they gain the assistance of a Hong Kong agent or sell their products directly to Hong Kong traders.

MARKETED FISH SPECIES

Nine of the most common fish marketed live are listed in Table 1.

Preferred types of live reef fish for the Hong Kong and PRC markets

Red coral trout (Fig. 1) is the most commonly used medium priced fish in both Hong Kong and the PRC. Red color signifies "fortune" in the Chinese tradition. All Chinese hosts would like to present a red coral trout at dinner receptions celebrating weddings, birthdays, and other celebrations. At present, the red coral trout destined for the Hong Kong and PRC markets are captured from the wild and the taste of the fish is good.

The word "fish" has the same pronunciation as the Chinese word that represents "plentiful." This is a very important "sign" in the traditional agricultural society of China. At all dinner receptions, fish is a necessary item on the menu. If people cannot afford coral trout, then they can use green grouper (Ching Pan) (Fig. 2) as an alternative. Ching Pan is mostly supplied by aquaculture operators and, as a consequence, the supply is very steady. However, the situation in the PRC is different because people are inclined to use freshwater fish at their receptions if they cannot afford the expensive fish species.

Following the recent economic crisis in Southeast Asia, high priced fish are no longer so popular. So Mei (Fig. 3) and Lo Shu Pan (Fig. 4) are expensive because they taste good and their supply is limited. In the PRC, the fish that are served at a reception dinner indicate the importance of the guest. It also shows that the host is capable of affording the expensive fish. This has become a tradition in the commercial field in the PRC. Officials from state-owned organizations like to order expensive seafood at their social gatherings as the bills only go to their organizations. In fact, most of the people in the PRC are not able to afford these costly seafood meals. They just take the opportunity to enjoy themselves at the expense of their employer. Lately, this situation has been rectified following the implementation of an anti-corruption policy by the PRC Central Government. The situation in Hong Kong is different. Apart from social functions, people will order an expensive meal of fish after they have made some easy money like winning from horse racing or profit from the stock market.

Figure 1. *Plectropomus leopardus,* red coral trout (Tung Sing) are now the most popular fish in Hong Kong. Wholesale price is about US $38-40.00/ kg.

Figure 2. *Epinephelus malabaricus,* green grouper (Ching Pan) is purchased as an alternative to more favored fish.

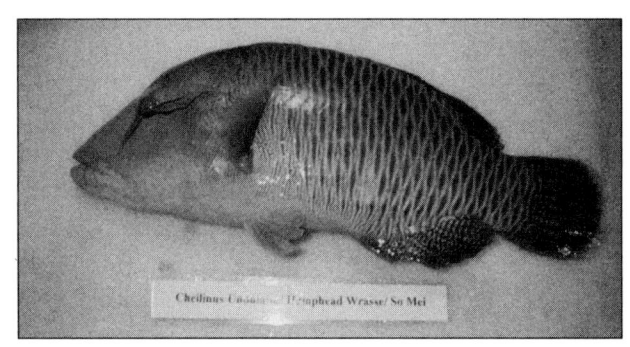

Figure 3. *Cheilinus undulatus,* humphead wrasse (So Mai).

Figure 4. *Cromileptes altivelis,* high-finned grouper (Lo Shu Pan) is an expensive fish.

QUESTIONS FROM THE AUDIENCE

J. CHAITON: Would you describe fish mortality problems observed along the route from supplier to wholesaler to retailer to restaurant? Also, what do you do with your dead fish?

P. CHAN: There are some mortalities. When becoming involved with this type of transportation, it is most important that you carefully determine fish condition. If fish condition is good, mortality will be lower. It is difficult to say what the average mortality might be because the condition of the fish can be so different.

Concerning the second question, because our trade is mainly for live fish, the price for the dead fish, provided they are in good condition, is only one fifth of the live fish price.

QUESTION: Are there any problems with the water quality in Hong Kong associated with keeping the fish alive?

P. CHAN: Hong Kong water is not very good because our pollution control is not well developed. Also there is rapid development in areas neighboring Hong Kong. In addition, water temperatures change rapidly. During the summer our water temperature can rise to about 31°C while in winter the water temperature can drop to about 15°C. For tropical fish, this is quite a big challenge. Consequently, we have to be very careful. In terms of live seafood wholesalers, when the fish arrive they want to sell it as soon as possible. However, once the fish arrives at the retail shop, because of their ability to use temperature controls, filter systems, and sterilizing systems, the fish will survive much better.

QUESTION: Concerning the red coral trout, is the meat white or red?

P. CHAN: The meat color is white.

An Overview of Irish Live Crustacean Fisheries

Ian Lawler
Irish Sea Fisheries Board, Dunlaughaire, Ireland

INTRODUCTION

This paper provides an overview of Irish live crustacean fisheries. Ireland is positioned in the North Atlantic with an extensive continental shelf area to the west. However, most of the live crustacean fisheries are in inshore waters, primarily within the six-mile limit, although some extend out to 12 miles. About 83% of the Irish fleet or approximately 1,700 vessels are inshore craft under 15 meters in length fishing up to 12 miles from the coast. The largest numbers of inshore vessels are found on the west coast of the country, particularly in areas like Galway and Mayo, because of the large number of sheltered inshore bays in the area. In these bays, much of the fishing is done using small vessels up to 5 m in length termed punts (or more traditionally, currachs) and powered by outboards. All Irish crustacean fisheries with the exception of crawfish use pots or creels. With the exception of shrimp pots they are typically D-shaped in cross section and constructed from plastic coated steel with a steel bar base and netted sides. The heavy base and D shape ensure that the pots right themselves no matter how they land on the seabed. The crabs or lobsters enter via two soft eye entrances on opposite sides of the pot attracted by a central bait bag. Variations include lighter homemade versions used by vessels without power haulers, constructed with timber bases and hoops of uPVC pipe (unplasticized polyvinyl chloride) and weighted with small amounts of concrete.

The average annual landings of the main crustacean species are:

- Brown crab—6,000-7,000 metric tons
- Lobster—500-700 metric tons
- Velvet crab—300 metric tons
- Shrimp—400-500 metric tons
- Spider crab—150 metric tons
- Crawfish—25 metric tons

Official statistics for landings by the inshore sector estimate the total value of the landed catch to be 30 million Irish pounds (35 million U.S. dollars). The breakdown of the catch is shown in Fig. 1. This chart includes mariculture production such as Pacific oysters (*Crassostrea gigas*), bottom cultured mussels, etc. The levels of brown crab landings by the inshore sector are probably underestimated. The offshore brown crab fishery is the only other significant contributor to crustacean landings.

SPECIES PROFILES
Brown crab

Brown crab (*Cancer pagurus*), while closely related to the Dungeness crab (*Cancer magister*) found on the North American west coast, is much more robustly built (Fig. 2). The majority, usually around 80%, of crab landed in the fishery are female. The Irish fishery has distinct offshore and inshore segments. The offshore sector is prosecuted by four purpose built vivier "supercrabbers" which have a total annual catch of about 3,500 metric tons. These vessels fish up to 60 miles offshore and in water depths

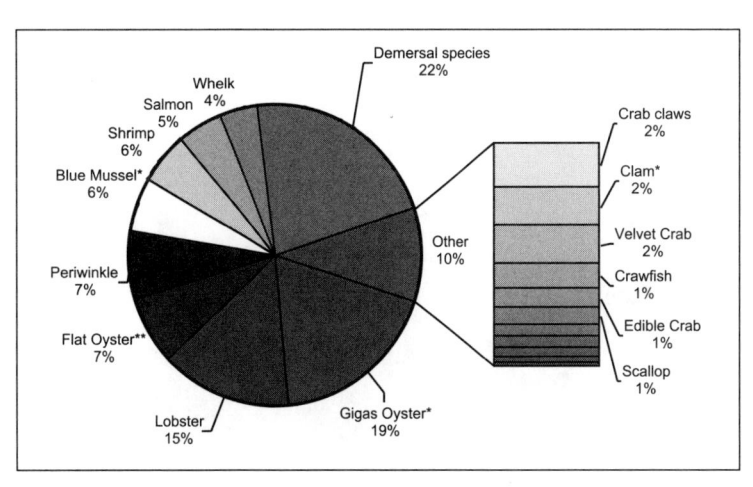

Figure 1. Composition of the fisheries catch in Ireland, including mariculture.

Figure 2. Brown crab (*Cancer pagurus*), Ireland's major crustacean fishery.

to 200 meters working up to 2,500 22-inch pots per boat. During the initial development of the fishery pots up to 36 inches were used. However, as the catches stabilized it was found that the smaller pots were easier to handle and store. They will haul about half of these pots (1,250 pots) per day in wind speeds up to force seven. These are very seaworthy vessels, 18 meters in length, built of steel with full shelterdecks and equipped with 30 cubic meter vivier tanks capable of holding 10 metric tons of crab. Figure 3 shows one of the vessels, the MFV *Peadair Elaine*. This vessel is equipped with a hydraulic hatch to close up the shelterdeck when fishing operations are not in progress, particularly during rough weather. In the photo the vessel is shooting, or deploying pots. The pots are shot at full speed—around nine knots—with pots going over the side every seven seconds. Figure 4 shows the "shooter"—the crewmember deploying the pots standing at the shooting table. Immediately on his left is a steel bar on which the eyesplices of the 2 fathom legs or branch lines are threaded. These are spaced at 14 fathom intervals on the mainline. The procedure commences with the marker buoy and weight at one end of the mainline being shot away, and the first branch line eyesplice is removed from the steel bar by the shooter. He then attaches a pot to the branch line by passing of a toggle of 25 mm uPVC plastic pipe attached to the pot by a short length of rope through the eyesplice. As the mainline runs out it then pulls the pot over the side, with the help of a shove to the pot from the shooter. As the shooter awaits the pot being pulled over the side he readies the next branch line by removing the eyesplice from the steel bar. Generally two crewmen keep the shooter supplied with baited pots. When he is shooting at full speed, the total elapsed shooting time is about seven seconds or less per pot. The advantage of this system is that, if the mainline becomes tangled, all that will happen is this steel bar will bend and the eyesplices are pulled off and over the side. When tangles occur the crew retreat to a safe distance until the tangle goes over the side and the vessel has slowed sufficiently to safely clear the problem.

Figure 5 is of the retrieval station with one crewmember on the stand wearing a safety harness. The pots are hauled to the surface using a slave hauler and then pulled aboard. Figure 6 is a close-up of the eyesplice and toggle. When vessels first tried out this system a concern was the strength of link. When tested it was found that 14 millimeter rope broke before the toggle. After the crabs are cleared

Figure 3. The MFV *Peadair Elaine*, one of four offshore supercrabber vessels built to fish brown crab off Ireland. The vessel is shooting (deploying) pots.

Figure 4. Crewmember deploying brown crab pots on the MFV *Peadair Elaine*.

Figure 5. Crewmember at crab pot retrieval station on the MFV *Peadair Elaine*. The pots are hauled to the surface using a slave hauler, and then pulled aboard.

Figure 6. Close-up of the eyesplice and toggle on the crab pot deploy-retrieval system, MFV *Peadair Elaine*.

prevents the crabs from damaging one another. The crabs are then placed in the vivier tank. Figure 8 shows crewmembers emptying the vivier tank. When it is full there is usually crab to a depth of four feet. On this occasion the total crab weight was over 10 tons. When landing the crab care has to be taken not to use containers with drainage holes that permit the tips of the crab legs to protrude, as when they are placed on the quay or in the vivier truck they can be broken off. During the course of transport the resultant blood loss can cause significant mortalities.

The majority of brown crab landed by the offshore fishery is shipped live to the north of France. The typical shipping procedure involves the use of simple vivier trucks equipped with water tanks and aeration systems. The total transport time to France is usually about 30 hours. This is about the maximum length of time that crab survive in the vivier trucks in current use. Recently, there has been a lot of interest in the use of airfreight to transport live crab to destinations farther afield.

In contrast to the offshore fishery, the inshore fishery is far more varied, using vessels ranging from punts with outboards to well-built GRP vessels of about 13 meters in length. The latter type of vessel can fish up to 1,000 pots; however, 200-400 is more usual.

The northwest coast has the largest inshore fishery just inshore of the area worked by the large supercrabbers. Elsewhere around the coast brown crab

from the pot, the bait bag is cleaned and rebaited. The bait is commonly frozen herring or mackerel, rejects from a processing line. It is important that old bait is removed, as it starts to repel crab if it is more than 48 hours old. The crabs are then nicked (Fig. 7). The French nicking method, in which the ligament underneath the dactylus of the claw is cut,

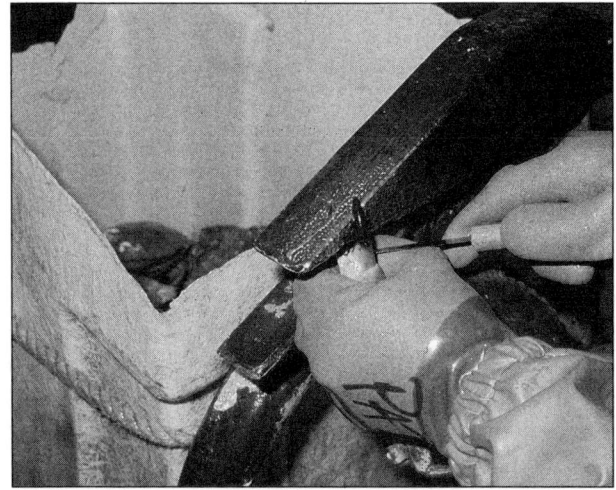

Figure 7. Brown crab (*Cancer pagurus*) during the nicking process. The French nicking method, in which the ligament underneath the dactylus of the claw is cut, prevents the crabs from damaging one another.

is mainly a bycatch of other fisheries such as the velvet crab or lobster. There is, however, a trend toward an all year fishery for crab among the larger inshore vessels. Figure 9 shows a traditional northwestern crab vessel, this one of a design derived from Norse origins which used to be very common along the northwest coast. This vessel is about 10.5 meters in length with 4 crew. Landings can be up to 150 40-kg boxes per day. In this area most of the inshore catch is processed. On the more modern GRP vessels in use, wells or vivier tanks are increasing in use.

Lobster

In common with the inshore crab fishery the European lobster (*Homarus gammarus*) (Fig. 10) fishery is worked by a varied fleet ranging from punts upward. The larger vessels usually fish about 900 pots, but 200-400 pots is average around the coast. This fishery tends to be seasonal and confined to the summer months from May to about October. This is because the lobsters are not very active and hence not easily caught during the winter. Due to overexploitation, lobster is no longer the major component of trap fisheries and is now a bycatch to brown crab and velvet crab in many areas. Because of this Irish fishermen became interested in the management techniques used in the Maine lobster industry and with the assistance of the Bord Iascaigh Mhara (BIM) made a number of visits to observe the fishery prior to introducing similar measures in Ireland, in particular the V-notching of female lobsters (Fig. 11). Backed by appropriate legislation prohibiting the landing and sale of V-notched lobsters and with the assistance of European funding, a number of regional V-notch programs have been instituted. These programs usually involve fishermen's cooperatives to which all fishermen make annual contributions. The funds are used, along with matching European PESCA Programme funds, to "buy back" berried female lobsters that are V-notched prior to release by an authorized person such as a fishery officer. It is estimated that 60,000 female lobsters have been notched and released since 1995. The V-notches appear to last through at least three molts, during which time it is hoped they breed a few times. In addition one local fishermen's group has funded the construction of a lobster hatchery and releases 20,000 juveniles per year, while other groups have purchased substantial numbers of juveniles from other hatcheries for release in their own areas. Given the recapture rates reported in studies elsewhere, the cost/benefit of this activity needs to be considered. Figure 12 is a 15 meter GRP lobster pot vessel fishing off the Aran Islands on the west coast. The vessel is equipped with twin-engines due to the nature of the coast being worked. This type of vessel is becoming increasingly popular for use by the larger, more year-round operators, fishing lobster and brown crab. More typical inshore fishing vessels are 8-12 meters in length.

After capture lobsters are generally held "dry" under damp sacking as most vessels do not have vivier tanks. In most instances, at the end of the day's fishing they are placed in a large floating box known as a keep pen. The lobsters are banded to keep them from damaging one another. They are retained in the floating pens until a large quantity buyer comes around with a vivier truck, or a sale can be arranged with a local buyer. Local buyers will hold the lobster in large holding ponds. The pond in Fig. 13 is typical flow-through lobster pond.

Velvet crab

The velvet crab, *Necora puber*, is a portunid crab typically of about 60-100 millimeters carapace width (Fig. 14). They are fished by many of the smaller inshore vessels, as velvet crab are very much an inshore species. The fishery is year-round in some areas, such as Galway, where large inshore sheltered bays are located. Velvet crab are generally exported live to Spain, though some are processed prior to export. They are typically tightly packed in orange crates to reduce their opportunities to fight and damage one another, and are shipped in standard vivier transports. They do not tolerate long exposures in air.

Shrimp

Shrimp, *Palaemon serratus* (Fig. 15), are generally fished by the smallest vessels in the fleet. The typical vessels are punts fishing 100 to 200 pots (Fig. 16). The shrimp pots are usually light plastic pots of French manufacture. This winter fishery extends from October to January. Much of the product is processed ashore, cooked, and exported in that fashion. However, a significant amount of the harvest is now exported to France in vivier trucks. Cylindrical pots are used, each weighing about two pounds. The shrimp are held alive by the fishermen, typically in pots with the entrance blocked by foam.

Marketing and Shipping Live Aquatic Products

Figure 8. A crewmember empties the vivier tank. When the tank is full the brown crab depth is four feet.

Figure 11. A V-notched female European lobster. A resource management program in Ireland marks berried females with the V-notch. Fishermen who catch the marked lobsters are reimbursed to return them to the sea to breed.

Figure 9. Traditional northwestern inshore crab vessel, of Norse design. This vessel is about 10.5 meters in length with four crew. Landings can be about 150 40-kg boxes per day.

Figure 12. A 15 meter GRP lobster pot vessel fishing off the Aran Islands, west coast of Ireland. The vessel is equipped with twin engines. This type of vessel is becoming increasingly popular for use by the larger, year-round operators, fishing lobster and brown crab.

Figure 10. European lobster *(Homarus gammarus)*. Due to overexploitation, lobster is no longer the major component of trap fisheries in Ireland, and is now a bycatch to brown crab and velvet crab in many areas.

Figure 13. Local buyers hold the lobster in large, flow-through holding ponds.

Figure 14. The velvet crab, *Necora puber*, is a portunid crab typically of about 60-100 millimeters carapace width.

Figure 15. The fishery for shrimp, *Palaemon serratus*, extends from October to January.

Figure 16. Shrimp are generally fished by the smallest vessels in the fleet. This punt can fish 100 to 200 pots.

Spider crab

Spider crab, *Maja squinado*, (Fig. 17) grow up to half a meter across the legs, and are mainly fished in the southwest of Ireland where they are most abundant. This species is usually harvested during a summer fishery from May to October. Spider crabs molt in July and August, interrupting the commercial fishery. The brown crab pots previously described are used in this fishery with one variation. The fishermen use a 10-inch plastic funnel located on the top of the pot to allow this rather large and gangly animal to enter the pot. This design is also suitable for spiny lobster or crawfish. Spider crabs are mainly exported live to Spain.

Crawfish

Last and probably least in terms of Irish crustacean landings is the crawfish, a spiny lobster, *Palinurus elephas* (Fig. 18). Along the west coast of the country this resource has been overfished by tangle netting. Landings have declined from 270 metric tons at the peak of trap fisheries in the 1960s, down to 180 metric tons with the introduction of tangle nets in the 1970s, to a current catch of 10-20 metric tons annually. As crawfish need a wide entrance to a trap they escape quite easily and typically traps have to be hauled twice a day. The introduction of tangle nets, which are hauled every two or three days, resulted in a large increase in catches which could not be sustained. Efforts are now being made to

Figure 17. Spider crab, *Maja squinado*, grow up to half a meter across the legs, and are mainly fished in the southwest of Ireland where they are most abundant.

Figure 18. The crayfish, *Palinurus elepha*, a spiny lobster, has been overfished by tangle netting along the west coast of Ireland.

restrict tangle netting for crawfish in Ireland. Irish crawfish are exported live to France and Spain.

CONCLUSIONS

In conclusion it may be seen from the above that crustaceans, particularly those for the live trade, are the lifeblood of much of the Irish inshore fleet. It is hoped that improved management measures, particularly for species such as lobster, will not only ensure the long term viability of the resource but improve the return in conjunction with appropriate infrastructural developments. The potential of other species such as Norway lobster or scampi (*Nephrops norvegicus*) which forms the basis of a valuable inshore potting fishery for the live market on the west coast of Scotland is currently being explored.

LITERATURE SOURCES

BIM. 1999. Irish inshore fisheries sector: Review and recommendations. BIM (Bord Iascaigh Mhara). Irish Sea Fisheries Board, Dublin.

Lawler, I., F. Nolan, and P. Waters. 1997. Capture, handling and storage of live prawns. BIM report. Irish Sea Fisheries Board, Dublin.

Pfeiffer, N., E. Magee, B. Ball, B. Munday, and I. Lawler. 1995. A review of shellfish potting activities on the west coast of Ireland. Report to DGXIV. Directorate General for Fisheries, European Commission, Brussels.

AUTHOR BIOGRAPHY

Ian Lawler graduated from Trinity College in Dublin, Ireland, with a Ph.D. in zoology in 1994. His thesis was on the growth and morphology of the scallop *Pecten maximus* around the Irish coast. He has worked on various projects, including the problem of ghost fishing, regional fisheries investigations, and shellfish pot fisheries. He now works for the Fisheries Development Division of Bord Iascaigh Mhara, the Irish Sea Fisheries Board, a semi-state development agency that promotes sustainable development of the sea fisheries sector. The Fisheries Development Division is pursuing new fishing opportunities, developing new technical conservation measures and inshore fisheries management, improving catch quality, and is involved with the restructuring and modernization of the fishing fleet.

The Construction of a Commercial Live Seafood Transshipment Facility: Review of General Specifications

Jon Chaiton
Emerald Partners, Marietta, Georgia

Introduction

This paper is about the construction of a commercial live seafood transshipment facility. I will describe a facility and some present general thoughts about what it takes to build one, including the major components. A separate paper provides a more detailed description of the components associated with such a facility. In this second report I also explain the function of these components, what their importance is, and when you should use them in different systems.

Description of Transshipment Facilities

Live seafood and other live aquatic products pass through a transshipment facility on their way to distant markets. This type of facility can be thought of as a fish or shellfish "hotel." The product is checked in, evaluated for quality, inventoried, and given a chance to recover from the rigors of the trip to the facility. Then, when the product has regained its strength and the market is ready, the product is repackaged and shipped to a domestic or international market destination. This destination could be a distributor, a wholesaler, or a restaurant.

Along the West Coast of the United States a lot of transshipment facilities have opened in the last ten years or so. In addition to transshipping, these businesses also often engage in the buying and selling of seafood, which is a separate business in itself. Figures 1-3 show some examples of holding tanks used as transshipment facilities.

Considerations When Designing a Live Seafood Transshipment Facility

One of the first planning items to consider prior to writing the necessary formal business plan for a live transshipment facility involves species selec-

Figure 1. Clam holding tanks in North Carolina. It's mostly an outdoor facility, although they have processing equipment indoors.

tion. Is the facility intended primarily for the holding of finfish or for shellfish? What are the biophysical or life-support requirements for each of the different species that will eventually be considered in the business plan?

Related to this decision concerning species selection is the sizing and capabilities of the facility. Prospective investors should develop a business plan with a long-term perspective. People often build facilities which, within a year, seem to be too small for their needs. So it is good to look ahead and build a facility that balances cost and capacity as well as a built-in capability to expand at a future date.

Several more subtle planning matters also need to be considered. If you are considering the construction of a transshipment facility, it is also important to remember that quarantine measures need to be built into the system. Chances are you will be receiving a mix of species from different suppliers, domestically or possibly even internationally, all bringing in the potential for different viruses, different pathogens, and different parasites. The proposed system must be able to separate these

Figure 2. A typical North Carolina crab shedding system. Note the lights strung over the top and the shallow trays where the crabs' molting schedule is monitored. These trays are typically made out of wood painted with epoxy or fiberglass resin.

animals and provide each group with an independent water supply.

The proposed facility must be able to accommodate certain handling strategies. For example, another author, Patrick Chan, mentions that you can give marine species a quick dip and they will regurgitate their stomach contents. This is a great prophylactic method for preventing transference of parasites into your system. We tend to dip the freshwater fish in salt water and the saltwater fish in freshwater to induce this preventive reaction. The active parasites on the fish, in the gill covers, and around the eyes do not like this salinity change and try to leave the environment. The proposed system, of course, will be preplanned to facilitate this strategy and to allow for the proper disposal of the cast-off parasites.

The size and type of the individual subsystems within a larger system need to be considered. Will the water have to be heated or chilled? Are you going to use freshwater, salt water, or brackish water? Are you planning to provide long-term holding or are you going to specialize with short-term holding only? For example, Kim Mauriks explained that he has a long-term holding pen and a short-term holding pen for his Pacific halibut. A number of additional decisions need to be made when dealing with the topic of subsystems—total plant volume and carrying capacity being major areas of concern.

THE BUSINESS PLAN

Once these various ideas and considerations have been well thought out, you need to start drafting a formal business plan. One of the most important lessons that a business plan can provide is to tell you which areas of the project have not been properly thought out. The investment in a transshipment facility should commence only after the business plan has been completed and found to be complete and accurate.

Generally speaking, your business plan should start out with a fact sheet or a corporate profile describing the proposed business. This can be done in outline form. A short introduction should follow explaining what you are trying to accomplish and the rationale behind the overall scheme. The business plan should include a management plan, a production plan, and a marketing plan—all of which are extremely important.

The management plan should identify the teams of people who are going to work with various sections of the proposed business activity—individuals who are involved in a hands-on manner. The goals and schedules for each team should be carefully established. Specifically state what kind of interactions people involved with the project should have in order to reduce opportunities for disputes later on in the planning process. A properly drafted management plan will help ensure that everyone involved in the planning process understands their role in the organization and its development.

The business plan should also include a financial plan that, in turn, will generate a variety of financial projections such as total return on investment.

Figure 3. This shows the sump for a swirl-separator at a lobster transshipment facility we built in Boothbay, Maine. A swirl separator is a centrifugal filter that operates passively. The pipes are the manifold distribution–water supply lines to the area where the bio towers are going to be.

You also need a section that deals with risks and opportunities. If it is your intent to write a business plan as part of an effort to seek investment from others, your prospective investors will want to know what the worst-case scenario could be and to learn about built-in contingency strategies. I am not saying you need to pound it home, but you need to let people know that you are aware of the down side of this business and have preformed recovery plans in mind. Even if you are not looking for money, if you are just writing the business plan for yourself, you need to recognize the risks associated with the project.

A construction plan, should new construction or renovations be needed, should also be incorporated into the business plan. The construction subsection within the business plan need not necessarily have blueprints per se, but carefully drawn schematics are often helpful.

FACILITY PLANNING

The first thing to consider when constructing a facility of this type is site selection. Site selection is very important because you're going to have to live with the site for quite a while, possibly very longterm. You will need to carefully consider water resources and the various options associated with water sources, water transport, and wastewater disposal. These and other site selection criteria will need to be carefully considered. Also, is this a new site or are you refurbishing an existing facility?

When determining prospective sites and your various construction options, consider how much money you have to work with. Is it better to get into a new facility that has been carefully designed with all your business needs in mind—at a higher cost? Or can you convert an existing structure into a reasonably functional facility—possibly at a lower cost?

Logistics and demographics also play an important role in site selection. Evaluate your access to domestic, local, and international markets. How far are you from the major airports? How far are you from the supply of products that you will be receiving? Are you on an island? You need to think in terms of number of hours to airports serviced by commercial carriers and distances to major trucking lines.

Another important category of items to be considered includes licenses, permits, and plans required by federal, state, county, and city governments for the construction and use of the proposed facility. A pressing issue that has become conspicuous over the past five to ten years is the matter of waste permits. Will you be allowed to release the effluent from the operation back into the sea or some other receiving water body after the water has passed through your closed or open system? You will need to obtain permits for whatever you do and this particular part of the permitting process can take months or years before everything is in order and the plant is operating. Obviously, all these things need to be done ahead of time because the government in your area will probably prohibit you from starting up the operation if you do not have a particular permit in place.

SCHEMATIC CONSIDERATIONS

Schematic considerations in the business plan encompass a variety of things. For example, when completing the construction sub-plan, you need to develop plans that carefully define product flow within the proposed plant. This includes such things as product arriving at and leaving your plant, your internal product handling, packaging and transport system, among others. How does the product get from the vessel that brings it to your plant into your holding water? Then how is the product moved out of the plant to another transport vessel or vehicle? Will it be processed or will it be repackaged and shipped out exactly the way it came in? You need to do a number of detailed flow charts showing how and where product will move through your facility. This is a very important consideration and must be properly completed. Otherwise you and your workers will be running into each other, or trying to move product in opposite directions and constantly knocking heads.

Your water supply system needs to be considered. Do you have a steady source of water supply from an inlet, a bay, or an ocean? Are you on well water or river water? If you are using water from a bay or inlet, you will need to determine if you will have access to this supply of water on a 24 hour basis or only at high tide.

You need to take a close look at the type of water recirculation system that will work best in the plant. Incidentally, the wastewater from this system may need to be pretreated, perhaps by initial chlorinating and then dechlorinating. The local municipal authorities will let you know about the type and extent of wastewater treatment that will be required.

The plant aeration system—compressors, blowers, and supply lines—also needs to be carefully considered. Are your holding tanks so deep that you will be required to use compressors instead of blowers? Incidentally, compressors typically have a lower volume of aeration as opposed to blowers. What kind of oxygenation system will be needed to support live product held at high loading densities?

You will also need to consider your water temperature control system. You may have to heat or chill water to accommodate the live holding of specific species. Again, the piping diagrams, blueprints, and the entire schematic of the temperature control system has to be laid out as a separate sub-plan within the formal business plan.

Cleaning systems are routinely overlooked and left out of the planning process for facility construction. Plans need to be completed not only for the cleaning and sanitation of the floor and handling equipment, but also for the interior of the pipes. The entire water transport system must be carefully considered. Pathogenic organisms such as *Vibrio* can easily build up anywhere in the system from the water intake to the outflow effluent. Unnoticed and unreachable contamination of this sort will cause tremendous problems down the road. Among other problems, your operation may become contaminated with *Pseudomonas,* which will exhibit itself as a pink, blotchy coloration on the sides of your tanks.

These things can be very difficult to eradicate once you get them. The proposed facility needs a carefully considered plan to address these issues. The water transport system can be designed so that you will be able to chlorinate sections of the piping on a regular basis—sterilizing and rinsing these sections out—and then reconnecting them to the recirculation system. If you choose to ignore these concerns, it will only be a matter of time before they come around and bite you back.

Electrical power supply is still another concern to be dealt with when planning a live-holding facility. Many kinds of power systems and backup power systems are available commercially. You may be considering a mobile system such as a vessel or a truck, or a static, land-based system. Your power system is critical to the integrity and continuous operation of the plant, so do not rely on a single source of power. If you need to, buy a standby generator and hook it up to your essential components, possibly a water pump or, more important, the aeration system. You can get away with not having water pumping capability for a period of time, if it is an emergency situation, but you always need to have that water aerated or oxygenated. Aeration is critical to the live holding function of the facility.

Each of the various systems mentioned above needs a separate plan and schematic, and probably a separate set of construction blueprints. I am often asked when it is necessary to use a blueprint, when to use schematics, and when the backs of napkins are good enough. Well, I think the back of a piece of scratch paper is a great place to start, but a considerable amount of additional thinking will be required. From this starting position you will develop schematics. Then, before beginning construction, you will need a set of blueprints.

You need to have blueprints because it is a good idea to have a licensed architectural engineer sign off on the construction documents. In doing so, these professionals assume some liability for the building and its proper operation. If an accident occurs—for example, a wall breeches or water floods out of a tank and injures somebody because the tank wall was not thick enough or was otherwise built improperly and did not have enough reinforcing steel—the liability often falls to the architectural engineer. This person stated that the wall in question should not have broken. Given the nature of this liability, engineers are not willing to sign off on poorly conceived plans. It is very important to think about this issue of liability.

CONSTRUCTION

Before you break ground there are many additional things to consider. Contact your municipality to determine if any pipelines, wires, or cables are near your building site. You need to look at all the plans and schematics that have been drawn out for the proposed facility and think of them in terms of tiers, starting with plant components at the deepest excavation level.

This deepest level probably includes water supply lines, water drain lines, and below-ground sumps that the holding tanks drain into (Fig. 3). Once these components are carefully examined, direct your attention to the ground level components of the overall system. Above ground considerations might include truck access, shelters of various types, and the structure or building that will cover the whole operation.

During component installation, you will need to pay close attention electrical connections. Electrical and certain mechanical connections need to be properly coded when a wet, washed down environment is involved. If you have open electrical receptacles, somebody is going to get shocked. If electrical system components are not grounded properly, again, somebody is going to receive an electrical shock. I suggest that you hire a fully licensed electrician familiar with wet application of electrical components for this type of work.

The need for professional design assistance can be clearly seen when working with concrete. In terms of concrete work, the use of fiberglass fiber is now extremely common. You can add fiber to a yard of concrete for about an additional five dollars per yard. In our immediate area, this supplement places the price for a cubic yard of concrete somewhere in the range of $80.00-$90.00 to the average builder.

The pounds per square inch (psi) rating of the concrete is important to consider. Walls can be made of 3,000 psi or 5,000 psi concrete, with or without fiber and steel. This decision should be made by the architect because inadequately designed concrete structures can crack, causing potential problems. It is very difficult to fix cracks in tanks once they have appeared. I am not saying that defects such as this cannot be repaired, but it can be quite costly. Incidentally, we do not cut expansion joints in tanks. Because concrete expands and contracts with temperature, an expansion joint is placed in the concrete where we expect or want a crack to occur. When holding tanks are designed we cannot allow cracks, so plenty of steel and other reinforcement are used to maintain the integrity of the tank or other component.

Other systems are involved in the construction of a live holding facility. Each of these systems will need to be carefully covered in the business plan.

FINAL THOUGHTS

Once construction has been completed on a particular section of the holding system, it is important to test this subsystem before starting operations. If you were working 16 feet underground laying in wastewater pipes, you will need to put temporary plugs in them and pneumatically test them using air pressure *before* they are buried under compacted soil and a layer of concrete. If a leak is discovered in a pipe that is 16 feet underground with a slab over it and a big tank on top of it, the situation can quickly become a mess.

Who should do the actual construction work? I am often asked how to determine if a general contractor should be called in for the job. In some cases the owner can be the general contractor and just hire subcontractors to do the job. This decision depends on your experience, your confidence, your money, and how you want the thing to come out based on your options. I would suggest that if you are not sure about something in the overall construction plan, for example, the placement of a particular component, do not guess. It would be wise to get professional help in that area. We all have an idea about how these systems work and how we want things to function, but building an entire system can be fairly overwhelming when you begin to look at all the different schematics and all the different processes involved. I think it is good to get as much help on the initial portion of the construction project as possible, so that once the facility is erected, it will work to your satisfaction.

Always remember to be prepared and have your contingency plans ready and well-practiced when emergency situations arise. A closed recirculating system that is full of product needs a 24-hour-a-day, seven-day-a-week baby-sitter. These systems require a tremendous amount of time. A tremendous inventory investment is also involved.

You are advised to stick with market-driven products. If you fill your plant with more speculative products that you hope to find markets for, you may end up with marketing failures and, as a consequence, not be able to see the full life expectancy of your plant. You will probably be out of business.

Finally, get professional help when you have questions about the construction and operation of a live holding facility.

An Insight into the Shanghai Market for Imported Live Seafood

Thomas Liu
Shanghai World Ocean Trading Co. Ltd., Shanghai, People's Republic of China

Summary

Eating imported live seafood such as lobsters, geoduck clams, and other species has become stylish among the Chinese people. These consumers are rather particular about their food and are also very concerned about "face-saving" while entertaining guests. You can now find many well-decorated seafood restaurants serving live seafood dishes in every big city in China, even in far inland regions such as Lhasa (the capital city of the Tibet Autonomous Region) and Urumqi (the capital city of the Xingjiang Autonomous Regions).

Essentially, this huge market fascinates marketers and other people engaged in the business. However, the live industry in the People's Republic of China (PRC) is experiencing some problems which come from Chinese central government policies that control the importation of live seafood. Also, the industry has been impacted by the Asian financial crisis. The following is a general survey dealing with the market for imported live seafood in Shanghai.

From curiosity to initial prosperity

During the time of Mao Zhedong, Chinese insisted on strict adherence to thrift. People never had additional desires beyond those in their lives. However, following China's reform process and opening to the outside world, since 1991 imported live seafood has been gradually introduced to consumers in mainland China. At first, foreign live seafood was transferred via boat from Hong Kong. Although this was an illegal practice because the items were not cleared through Chinese Customs, live seafood still successfully pushed into our market. However, this extended illegal dealing raised the concern of the Chinese government.

In late 1996, the Agriculture Department of the PRC approved a policy that permitted its affiliated companies to acquire tariff-free quotas for the importation of live seafood. However, these large state-run companies, such as Shanghai Fisheries General, Beijing Blue Water, Liaoning Pelagic Fisheries, and others, just sold their quotas and did not directly involve themselves with the deals. During 1997-1998, live seafood trading became more active. Beginning at this time, it became common for more than 20 containers of Australian live rock lobster (700 kg per container) to reach Shanghai on a daily basis.

Diverse foreign live seafood species in the Shanghai market

To this date, many kinds of live seafood from different nations have been introduced into the Shanghai market. In this metropolis you can find almost all the same foreign live seafoods as are available and popular in Hong Kong. This availability may be attributed to chefs working in the Shanghai seafood restaurants—most of them are "Hongkongese." They are bringing many popular seafood dishes into Shanghai and their cuisine is now spreading nationwide.

Foreign live seafood in our market range from high-valued fish from Indonesia and Australia to lobster from locations such as Australia, New Zealand, Indonesia, South Africa, Mexico, and the United States. Other popular products include crab from Canada, the United States, Australia, and Southeast Asian nations, shrimp from Thailand, geoduck clams from Canada and the United States, abalone from Australia and Taiwan, and oysters from Canada.

Among the various foreign live seafood suppliers, Australia and New Zealand have taken most of the lobster share; Canada and the United States overwhelm the geoduck clam share and also play an important role in crab supply. Table 1 shows the total amount of live seafood imported into the Shanghai market from January 1998 to July 1998. Table 2 shows seafood values, from trading companies with tariff-free quotas who sell to clients. Note that the statistics in Table 2 are conservative.

Table 1. Value of live seafood imports into Shanghai, January-July 1998.

Source	
Australia and New Zealand	US $45 million
Canada and the United States	US $18.3 million
Thailand	US $9.8 million

SHANGHAI CURRENTLY RANKS IN THE TOP POSITION IN THE CHINESE LIVE SEAFOOD MARKET

In the People's Republic of China there are three important live seafood markets—Shanghai, Yantian (a Shenzhen city very near to Hong Kong), and Beijing. Shanghai is the most influential and largest distribution center of imported live seafood. This position of prominence is due to several factors. Not only is Shanghai an international airline port, but the city is also located in the center of East China—the most developed area in China. Over 60% of all imported live seafood is consumed there. Shanghai has become a barometer for the whole seafood market. Yantian is a place that is used for the smuggling of seafood. Large amounts of smuggled live seafood are transferred from here to Shanghai. If the central government of the PRC issues good trade policies such as a tariff-free quota, Yantian will lose much of her former brilliance. The amount of total foreign live seafood imported directly into Beijing is far less than that imported to Shanghai.

The most famous live seafood markets in Shanghai are located in the Tongchuang Road area. Almost all of the top wholesalers from across the nation have set up shops there. It is very noisy and busy.

HOW TO IMPORT LIVE SEAFOOD INTO CHINA

There are three ways of importing live seafood into China.

The first way is the illegal way via Hong Kong. We order various goods, for example, lobsters, from foreign suppliers and hire a designated consignee in Hong Kong who has the means to ship the live product to Yantian by boat. After being placed in reconditioning tanks in Yantian for one day, the lobsters are then shipped to Shanghai via domestic airline. We have to pay 9.00 RMB per kg (based on the use of 700 kg lobster containers) to the consignee. The consignee is not responsible for the goods if they are confiscated by the customs authorities. So, this importation method is full of risks and greatly increases costs.

The second, legal, way to import live seafood involves paying taxes. The official tariffs in the PRC for imported live seafood are high. The tariff rate is 35% for lobsters and 30% for other products. In addition, our government imposes another 13% as an increment tax.

The third way to import live seafood is to buy tariff-free quota from one of the state-run companies. This strategy proved to be attractive to the market-

Table 2. Live seafood imported into Shanghai.

1998	Lobster (over 95% from Aust. and N.Z.)	Geoduck clams (from Canada and U.S.)	Crab (about 70% Dungeness from Canada and U.S.)	Shrimp (from Thailand)
Jan.	272	16.1	53.2	270
Feb.	200	11.2	36.4	190
Mar.	180	11.2	56.0	210
Apr.	172	14.0	53.0	210
May	219	15.0	61.6	167
June	212	14.0	70.0	97
July	250	19.6	102.0	2
Total	1,505	101.1	432.2	1,146

Units: metric tons

ers involved with live trade. Unfortunately, the policy did not last for very long and was suspended in April 1999.

Now let us make a close study of the costs involved in the importation of live products into the PRC, using as examples rock lobsters from Australia and New Zealand and geoduck clams from North America. At the time of this writing, the Chinese currency, the RMB, has a conversion ratio (RMB:$US) of 8.4:1.0. Table 3 shows added costs for live lobster in the Shanghai market.

It is clear why people take major risks to transfer Australian and New Zealand rock lobsters to the PRC via Hong Kong—profits can be substantial. Now rock lobster marketers from Australia and New Zealand are adopting similar strategies to ship product directly to the mainland. When deciding the most economical way of importing other kinds of products, consider the geoduck clam and tariffs ratified by Chinese Customs. Table 4 shows added costs for geoduck clams in the Shanghai market. Many live seafoods, such as geoduck clams, Dungeness crabs etc., are still directly shipped into Shanghai legally.

SEAFOOD MARKET CHAIN IN CHINA

Generally speaking, those who are directly involved in this business are private companies or other self owned operations. Some of these organizations are large enough to accept several whole containers of goods. Figure 1 is the sales flow chart or for typical transactions.

In order to better survive in this increasingly fierce market, trading companies and trading agents tend to be closely tied with foreign suppliers and top wholesalers. Indeed, some unhappy things, such as delaying payment or refusing to pay for a shipment based on false goods inspections, have occurred in our market. These cases are infrequent and will become fewer as our market gradually matures. Also, these problems may be avoided if you take the time to select an honest and responsible trading partner.

PROFIT

The profits associated with this type of business are often not as substantial as expected and are sometimes disappointing to the parties involved. The average margin of profit at the wholesale level was formerly 50%. Currently, the average profit margin is in the range of 1-5% and sometimes at a loss. Profit at the retail level is now about 3-8%. In spite of these constraints, the margin of profit for foreign (imported) live seafood dishes can be as high as 30-50%. The reasons for these moderate levels of profit are:

1. It is impossible to control the amount of foreign live seafood shipped into Shanghai. If whole salers cannot sell all the goods in their holding pools, it becomes necessary for them to cut the price to clean out stocks that are no longer fit to keep.

2. The demand for imported live seafoods that have already been marketed in Shanghai appears not to be increasing. Influenced by the Asian financial crisis, China's economy is also depressed.

Table 3. Added costs for live lobster in the Shanghai market.

Illegal way	Pay tax	Buy tariff-free quota
9.00 RMB/kg (charged by bold consignee)	Customs approved price for lobster—$25.00/kg	7.00 RMB/kg (charged by government)
7.00 RMB/kg domestic freight	Tariff: $25 × 35% = $8.75	
5% loss due to transportation	Increment tax: ($25 + $8.75) × 13% = $4.39	
Total: 9.00 RMB + 7.0 RMB + ($25 × 8.3 × 5%) = 26.40 RMB/kg	Total: ($8.75 + $4.39) × 8.3 = 109.0 RMB/kg	Total: 7.00 RMB/kg

RMB:$US = 8.4:1

Table 4. Added costs for geoduck clams in the Shanghai market.

Illegal way	Pay tax	Buy tariff-free quota
May charge 400 RMB/case (a few people monopolize)	Customs approved price for geoduck clams—$6.00/kg	7.00 RMB/kg (charged by government)
Does not include domestic freight	Tariff: [(40 lb × 0.454) × $6] × 30% = $32.70	
	Increment Tax: [(40 lb × 0.454) × $6 + $32.70] × 13% = $18.40	
Total (not including other loss) is far higher than 400 RMB	Total: ($32.70 + $18.40) × 8.3 = 424.10 RMB	Total: (40 lb × 0.454) × 7.00 RMB = 127.10 RMB

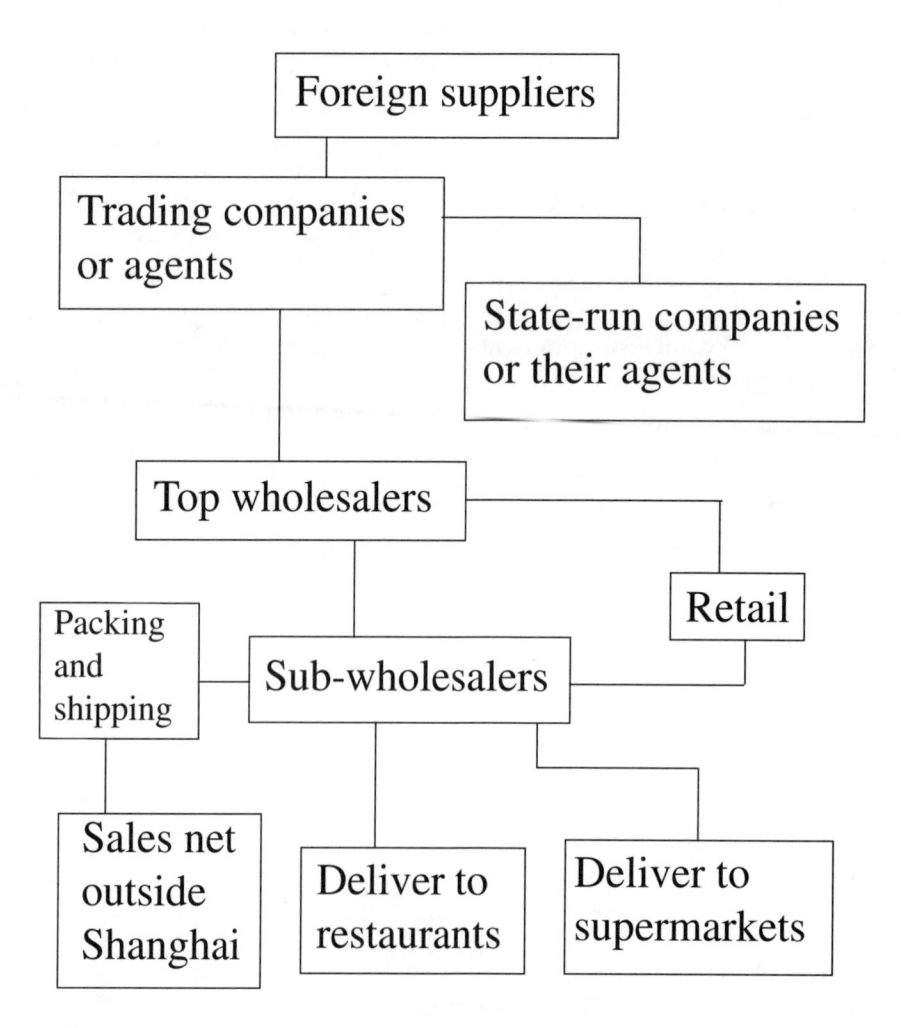

Figure 1. Seafood market chain, or sales flow chart, for typical transactions in China.

Table 5. Wholesale prices for geoduck clams and Dungeness crabs on the Shanghai market, 1998.

	Jan.	Feb.	Mar.	Apr.	May	June	July
Geoduck	4,430	4,050	3,850	3,530	3,250	3,200	3,150
Dungeness	1,600	1,680	1,705	1,350	1,310	1,280	1,160

RMB per 40 lb case.

3. The cost of importing live seafood has also sharply increased. Added cost factors include tariffs, other taxes, and fluctuating currency conversion rates. Consumers are not willing to bear all these extra fees.

Table 5 shows the wholesale prices of geoduck clams and Dungeness crabs in the Shanghai market during January to July 1998. Note that the prices are for class 1 geoduck clams. Class 2 geoduck are lower by 300-600 RMB per case. Importing costs include a 7.00 RMB per kg quota fee. The source of this data is a wholesaler specializing in the wholesale marketing of geoduck clams and Dungeness crab.

Summary

The live seafood trade provides an important enrichment to our traditional dishes. Without a doubt, the trade benefits both our consumers and our restaurant industry which, until recently, has lacked the supplement provided by live seafood.

However, in order to balance foreign monetary exchanges, our government has placed controls on this and other trades that do not strongly influence the basic necessary needs of our society. Fortunately, this control is likely to be only temporary. The probable short-term nature of these controls is due to the following developments:

1. China is now applying to become a member of the World Trade Organization (WTO). In order to abide by WTO trade standards, the tariff on live seafood must be dropped by a considerable amount.

2. China is now making plans for the development of diversified sources of seafood and supports the development of seafood culture strategies. However, it is difficult to culture many seafood species that are currently being imported because of the nature of our water resources.

3. China is now looking forward to a period of greater economic prosperity.

For these reasons, it is easy to insist that the live seafood trade must have a bright future in China. Foreign suppliers who are able to introduce into China new delicious live products at the right price, or who have developed new technologies to handle or culture live seafood, will find great benefits in our market.

The National Seafood Hazard Analysis Critical Control Point Program and the Live Seafood Industry

Donald Kramer
University of Alaska Marine Advisory Program, Anchorage, Alaska

Introduction

This report will give a basic understanding of the Hazard Analysis Critical Control Point (HACCP) approach to seafood safety control. We will discuss what HACCP means to live shippers and briefly cover the hazards associated with live fish, crustaceans, and mollusks.

Overview of the HACCP concept

First, I want to address issues raised in an editorial published recently in *Infofish International*. The issue focuses on the following quote from this editorial:

"For most industries and regulatory personnel, understanding of the concept of HACCP *per se* was a difficult task, compounded by diverse interpretations and expert opinion albeit confusing, on the subject. However, the dust is settling and most ambiguities have been cleared, thanks to a series of national and international initiatives." (Source: Editorial, Seafood quality and regulatory measures. *Infofish International*, 5/99:3)

HACCP should not be a difficult idea to convey. It is a very easy concept that can be explained in just a few minutes.

There are essentially two parts to HACCP. The first is the hazard analysis part which can also be described as the "do we have a problem?" part of the safety analysis. The second part of the program involves critical control points or the "how we are going to take care of our problems" part of the program.

Keep in mind that this is a very easy concept. In the case of seafood safety, you examine your product to determine if anything is there that will hurt or make your consumers sick. If a hazard is identified at a specific processing step, then you go to the second part and determine how you are going to take care of this problem. This is the basic nature of HACCP.

At the time HACCP was first announced by the Pillsbury Corp. and U.S. military laboratories, the major groups who helped initiate the program, we did not have the seven principles that now define this program. Later, when the National Science Foundation (U.S.) recommended that all food industries use HACCP as a way of controlling safety problems, a committee was formed that developed these seven guiding principles. I think they are excellent principles.

The first of these principles involves the "HA" segment of HACCP—hazard analysis. You conduct a hazard analysis. In the case of shipping a seafood product, you check to see if there is anything about the product that has the potential of causing people harm, making them sick, or killing them, which is, of course, the most serious thing that you could do.

The second part of the program involves what you do if you have one of these problems. Principles 2-7 outline how to take care of a problem. They are very logical and easy to apply to your situation. In this second step, you decide where in your processing sequence you can get rid of this hazard. Sometimes you find yourself dealing with a hazard that you cannot get rid of. The place to stop this type of problem is right at the start of the processing sequence. For example, you will not accept shellfish that contains a toxin that you cannot later get rid of, like paralytic shellfish poisoning. You just will not accept that batch of shellfish.

Often there will be some way to get rid of the hazard. You will choose a point in the production chain at which to accomplish this. It could be at the receiving end where you reject some raw product that contains something you cannot control, or it could be later in the process. In the case of pathogens, for example, you can cook them to death. There are many possible places in the production chain for a critical control point.

You also need to establish critical limits to ensure that the method of getting rid of that hazard actually does so. To determine if the critical limits are being met, you must monitor them. If these critical limits are not met, you then must take corrective action and verify that this corrective action is working. Finally, the regulatory people want to see records. This concludes the seven guiding HACCP principles.

The seven steps are very simple. However, this does not mean that you have just completed the entire HACCP training course, because we go into the principles in detail.

HACCP FOR SAFETY OR QUALITY ASSURANCE

Another issue raised by the same editorial in *Infofish International* is illustrated by the following quotation:

"Nearly 35 per cent of the world's catch ends up on the international market; as much as 50 per cent coming from developing countries. Aptly so, seafood industries in the developing world have been quick to adopt modern methods and approaches to quality assurance. In keeping with the developments in major markets, countries exporting fish and fishery products in Asia, Africa and Latin America have recognized Hazard Analysis Critical Control Point (HACCP) as the basis for their seafood quality assurance programs."

What does it mean when you say you have a HACCP program? To some people, it means they have a quality assurance program. To the U.S. regulatory people, it means that you have a food safety program. The U.S. Food and Drug Administration (FDA) seafood regulation zeros in on safety—this is the only area of concentration. Although there are some other provisions in the regulation related to sanitation, the HACCP part of the regulation focuses in on safe seafood. Likewise, the U.S. Department of Agriculture (USDA) red meat and poultry regulation focuses on safety. Future regulations pertaining to dairy products, fruit juices, eggs, and other food groups will probably also focus on safety. Food safety is the recurrent theme.

Guides published by the Seafood HACCP Alliance have been written with safety in mind. The HACCP Alliance's Encore HACCP Manual, a technical publication dealing with fresh and frozen finfish, cooked ready-to-eat crustaceans, and smoked fish, and the closely related topic of sanitation also focuses on safety. However, several other food inspection organizations in the United States and the world use HACCP to focus on topics in addition to safety. For example, the National Marine Fisheries Service uses HACCP to cover quality and economic fraud.

Other countries look at HACCP in various ways. For example, Canada has integrated HACCP with their quality management program. When this program first came out, there were 12 critical control points that processors were required to address. That system was re-engineered in 1997 and now has three parts. The first of these HACCP sections focuses on safety. In addition to part one, there is a prerequisite plan part dealing with plant environment and recall programs and the program element known as RAPP. RAPP stands for Regulatory Action Points Plan and essentially ensures that no tainted, decomposed, or unwholesome product is sent to market. The Canadian Quality Management Plan (CQMP) is now similar to the United States with regard to HACCP. The HACCP part of the CQMP now allows processors to identify the critical control points and use them for the processing of safe food.

In 1993, Chile developed a technical and administrative document titled "For regulating the HACCP-based quality assurance program." HACCP is being used a bit differently in Chile. It is used for food safety, but also as the basis for a quality assurance program.

Ireland provides another example concerning the interpretation of HACCP provisions. I have a quote from an Irish fish processor: "I would sum up HACCP as follows. Plant proud, production oriented, quality oriented, personnel oriented, customer satisfaction." I could go on with a dozen of these quotes and descriptions of other uses of HACCP. In these cases, HACCP is used as a way of solving a problem—a solution methodology.

You can use HACCP for other uses including protocols for the live handling of seafood species. The HACCP approach is simply a way of taking care of a problem. HACCP can be used in all kinds of problem solving efforts. However, when it is used to refer to something other than safety, please call it something else. U.S. regulatory people would like the term "critical control point" to be applied only to the topic of food safety. When you use the HACCP approach for quality assurance, call it a "quality assurance control point." not a "critical control point" (CCP). The term "critical" to regulators means that if you do not eliminate the hazard at this control point, somebody is going to get sick or be injured. Then they will probably sue you, something that the regulatory people will not like. They might react by shutting down your plant or placing an embargo on your product.

So, when you use CCP use it for a HACCP program for food safety. If you want to use the HACCP approach for quality assurance, do so. It is an excellent approach. Just call your control points "quality assurance control points."

Likewise, the seafood HACCP Alliance is publishing a manual, in which they will discuss sanitation control points. Although they discuss sanitation along with safety, I would advise you to keep your sanitation standard operating procedure (SSOP) as a separate document. Keep your quality assurance program as a separate program, as well. Your HACCP program should then be restricted to the topic of food safety.

Enforcement concerns

I have now taught parts of about 50 HACCP training courses. Chuck Crapo and I have been traveling all over Alaska in the effort to educate the industry about this program. In the course of this work, we have seen that the major difficulty is determining when a hazard is significant—when a hazard must be controlled. A hazard is significant when the regulatory people say that it must be considered significant. Significant means:

1. It is reasonably likely to happen.
2. It has the potential to make someone sick or to cause injury.

It is our hope that the regulators will allow seafood industry members to use their industry experience to determine when a hazard is truly significant. The regulatory agencies have stated that they will cooperate with industry with regard to this matter. FDA has published a guide intended to help processors and others put together HACCP plans. Among other things, this guide lists a broad range of hazards. We are finding that this guide is being used almost as part of the regulation. We hope that the regulatory people will accept that a perceived hazard is not significant if industry has adequate reasons to support this determination.

HACCP and the live
seafood industry

There appears to be the impression that live seafood does not fall under HACCP because it is not yet an actual food. The theory is that the harvesters and retailers are exempt if the product is kept alive from one link in the marketing chain to the next. Following this reasoning, HACCP does not have to be considered because the product is not yet a food—it is still a live animal. Members of the live industry should be advised that the regulators will probably make a decision very quickly regarding who in the chain is going to be responsible for the identification of significant hazards and the development of a HACCP plan.

What are the possible hazards? First, marine life sometimes comes with toxins. Alaska is, of course, very concerned about paralytic shellfish poison (PSP). In the case of live fish there is the potential for ciguatera contamination. Somebody somewhere along the marketing chain will have to make a decision as to whether the product is free of toxins.

All kinds of things can occur in the environment that can lead to contamination. Participants in states that have large agricultural industries have to worry about chemicals that get into rivers, lakes, and coastal areas. Furthermore, contaminants can be in the water, on the harvesting boat, on the transporting boat, or in the holding pond water. The unintentionally or deliberate addition of chemicals (for example to control disease) and pharmaceuticals might also be a problem.

A seafood processor who converts fish into a final product may occasionally add preservatives or nutritional additives. The seafood industry does not often do this, but certainly the cereal industry and others do. Many of the products that we eat are fortified with supplemental nutrients. Color may occasionally be added, as well. In live shipping, supplements may be added to prevent disease or reduce the activity of the fish. These need to be examined as potential hazards.

With some products, bacterial growth is a problem. One example in the marine environment is the group of microbial organisms known as vibrios. Vibrios can survive in temperatures as low as 41-46°F. If temperatures get high enough during your transportation scheme, vibrios can increase in the live product. This is certainly a consideration when dealing with bivalve mollusks. Raw molluskan shellfish are covered in the seafood HACCP regulation as a separate section. They are commonly transported live and the regulators want to make sure that they come from waters that are clean and free of pathogens. They have a very defined tagging procedure. A certain amount of identifying information must be placed on the tag which must remain with the product all the way through the transport chain whether or not they are transported live or in shucked form.

QUESTIONS FROM THE AUDIENCE

QUESTION: What are the relative roles of the U.S. Department of Commerce and the Food and Drug Administration regarding HACCP?

KRAMER: HACCP for seafood products is in the bailiwick of the FDA. They have the regulation and they enforce the regulation. The U.S. Department of Commerce does not have any responsibility for enforcing HACCP. However, the U.S. Department of Commerce has a voluntary program to do inspections and check your HACCP plan. Their program differs in that their version of HACCP covers more than just seafood safety—it covers quality and economic fraud. Foreign countries tend to like the Department of Commerce program because they have some assurance of quality as well as safety. As mentioned, this is not a regulatory function as with the FDA.

QUESTION: How do you determine when a risk or hazard is unacceptable? Do you have to show that it is unacceptable or do you show that it is acceptable?

KRAMER: That is a difficult question. There are different levels of acceptability. We allow the presence of *Vibrio vulnificus*. However, as many as eight to ten people die each year from *V. vulnificus*. But if one person dies from *Clostridium botulinum* it is considered a major problem. The seafood industry in Alaska had one botulism problem in the 1970s and another in the 1980s—problems that cost millions of dollars and caused companies to go bankrupt. Yet, we have other toxins and marine organisms that kill as many as half a dozen to a dozen people every year and we "accept" that.

You have to make the decision based on your best information. Nobody wants to cause someone to be ill, partly because you will probably be sued—an economic hardship. I do not think any food producer wants to make people sick or to have anybody die as a result of consuming their food product. You need to do your best to determine if this is likely to occur. I know that "likely to occur" is not a quantitative concept—it is a best guess based on past history, information present in the literature, information from CDC (Centers for Disease Control) and other agencies, and information from FDA. This often ends up being a compromise between the producer and the regulators. They have to come up with a solution as to whether something has to be controlled or not.

Restraints to Shipping Live Product: Lessons from the AquaSeed Corporation Experience

Per Heggelund
AquaSeed Corporation, Seattle, Washington

Summary

The Lacey Act is the U.S. federal law governing a broad range of commercial activities including the live shipment of fish and shellfish. This act, since its revision in 1981, regulates the shipment of all fish and wildlife, dead or alive, from egg to the adult life stage. Application of the Lacey Act can conflict with individual state laws. Consequently, complying with the dictates of this body of regulations can be confusing and frustrating for live shippers. As an owner of a private aquaculture operation that ships live product worldwide, I will present the problems associated with regulatory compliance from the shipper's point of view.

Introduction

In his contribution, Don Kramer made some interesting points related to the topics I cover in this paper. Dr. Kramer stressed human health issues associated with live shipping—specifically food safety issues. He also noted that there are no HACCP regulations covering fish as long as they are alive. However, we do have other regulations that have an important bearing on this industry. This other body of regulations relates to fish health. In fact, some of the concepts behind these fish health regulations are more stringent, at least in philosophy, than those that deal with human health issues.

Many, if not most, of the fish health regulations being referred to here are based on the principle of zero tolerance to a long list of bacteria and viruses. We do not often have this degree of stringency in human food health regulations. Consequently, as I will describe, there are anomalies in some of these regulations.

I reviewed a very similar topic a couple of years ago at this same conference. I learned that some of my listeners were frightened by the content of that presentation and thought that I might have been trying, in essence, to scare other producers away from the live shipping industry by providing a review of the heavy-handed regulation present in the industry. Today I will again present practical information about the nature of regulation in this industry. I am not trying to eliminate competition in the section of the industry in which AquaSeed operates. I wish only to present an objective interpretation of an important business planning concern.

I will describe the body of regulations, the Lacey Act, which comprises the most stringent portion of fish health regulations present in the live industry worldwide. My message is that you, as a member of this industry, must watch this regulatory "bar" or hurdle. Great caution will be needed, because I think this bar will be further elevated in the future. You will need to abide by the Lacey Act, something that may prove to be very difficult. As members of this sector of the live industry, we are excluded from many markets simply because we, as producers operating within the United States, cannot meet these regulations and, consequently, cannot conduct our business. I encourage you to look at the current mass of regulations and be certain that you do not fall into any of a number of traps as you develop new markets.

In this report I cover the fish health regulations that pertain specifically to salmonids—salmon and trout species in the United States and internationally. I am using salmonids as an example because this is the section of the live seafood industry that I am involved with and have been working in for the last 20 years.

Overview of the AquaSeed Corporation

I will start with a brief overview of what the AquaSeed Corporation attempts to do. AquaSeed Corporation is a breeder of Pacific salmon. We breed coho salmon and Donaldson steelhead. We have accumulated a 30-year history for the selective breeding of coho salmon. Our effort is based on a classical breeding program that we purchased from Campbell's Soup in 1991. Campbell's began developing this program in the early 1970s as a cooperative project with University of Washington Sea Grant. The breeding protocol was patterned after a similar program developed in the poultry industry. Since our acquisition of the program, AquaSeed has seen a salmonid growth rate that is five times faster than that of our stock when the start-up program was initiated in the 1970s.

We sell the eyed eggs, or embryos, of coho salmon and steelhead. We also sell a few fry and smolts, which are in the category of live fish. I have been working with these live products through AquaSeed for about 15 years. I have been involved in the salmon farming industry since 1980 and was involved in the importation of Norwegian salmon to the West Coast of North America in 1981. I believe that it was the first time this farmed Atlantic species was imported into the western United States.

Our company's headquarters are located in Seattle, Washington. Our production facility is located just south of Olympia in the small town of Rochester. It is in an inland location and has available fresh water that is totally pathogen free. We pump this water from wells at the rate of about 5,000 gallons a minute. Our main markets are Japan and Chile. We operate a marketing company in Chile and sell domestically in the United States, as well.

REVIEW OF THE LACEY ACT

With that background, I will now cover the U.S. federal laws that govern shipment of live seafood and shellfish. These laws govern AquaSeed's ability to ship and control associated certification procedures. I will also look at some of the pertinent state laws that are on the books. In the United States, we do not have a uniform federal law dealing with fish health specifically, so every state must have its own set of laws. The Lacey Act sits on top of these state laws and provides federal penalties for these laws.

The Lacey Act was the first fish and wildlife law that was signed in the United States with enactment around 1900. Originally, its purpose was to a remove wild game from commerce.

Like so many other pieces of legislation, the Lacey Act has been rewritten and various amendments have been made to it over the years. The last rewrite occurred in 1981, when Congress merged three other wildlife laws or acts into the Lacey Act. That is when fish became an official part of the Lacey Act.

Because the Lacey Act deals specifically with wild animals and birds, livestock is exempt from it. However, we do not have a definition for livestock that specifically includes fish. As a consequence, fish and mollusks are not exempt from the dictates of the Lacey Act. All fish and shellfish are included in the Lacey Act, whether we farm them or catch them in the wild. That is essentially our problem as farmers—we have been sucked into the Lacey Act in a way that makes some of us uncomfortable. We have witnessed at least three or four cases in which fish farmers, primarily trout farmers, have been sued and taken to court under the Lacey Act. In three of these cases, the resulting litigation has had a devastating effect on their business.

Even if you are in a business like ours where you are dealing with the eggs and fry from *farmed* animals that we have laboriously domesticated over the past 30 years, you will still be part of the Lacey Act. Somebody within the regulatory structure could pick up some aspect of your business and really make things difficult for you.

As can be seen, the Lacey Act is being used to federalize penalties if state or international laws are broken. Using an example from another session at this conference, the International Pacific Halibut Commission's international treaty could, technically, be enforced by the Lacey Act.

The Lacey Act is enforced by two agencies—the U.S. Fish and Wildlife Service under the Department of Interior, and the National Marine Fisheries Service under the Department of Commerce. They have dual responsibilities and both agencies are fully involved with the implementation of the Lacey Act. For example, the Lacey Act is often used to prosecute foreign fleets or fishing activities that break either international treaties or U.S. treaties and laws. The Lacey Act also gives teeth to the state regulations. If you do not comply with a state regulation, the federal government can prosecute you under the Lacey Act.

OUTLINE OF REGULATIONS GOVERNING EXPORTATION

I would like to review the export documentation needed in order to ship products such as those marketed by the AquaSeed Corporation. Again, these requirements specifically pertain to salmon and trout. As mentioned previously, in many cases these requirements are more stringent than those involved with the shipment of live mussel and other types of live seafood. The documentation process has become rather complicated. I am hoping that over time the government, working in a cooperative manner with industry, will be able to streamline the process. For example, we would like to use electronic documents. Currently we must complete the required documents entirely by hand and place a blue signature upon the completed forms. The entire process has become quite cumbersome.

Among other things, we are required to complete two forms for the State of Washington. The first form deals with all imports or transfers of live finfish within Washington and must be used whenever any products, not just salmonids, are moved through the State of Washington. The second form covers fish health regulations involving required tests for viruses and bacteria. The diseases that need to be tested for vary from species to species. It is a multiple-use form for the export, import, or transfer of product between facilities.

Several years ago, the state came up with a supplemental certificate to be completed by the shipper. If you are bringing product into the state, this certificate must be included with the shipment. We proposed to state workers and the Department of Fish and Wildlife that we just add a box to a form in current use and continue to use just one form. Little progress has been made.

In addition to the previously mentioned state transfer permit, an underlying certificate is required. It must be signed by a veterinarian who has tested the fish for the different diseases. Quite a few diseases must be screened. This is the third piece of paper from the State of Washington that we encounter when shipping salmon and trout.

There is very little uniformity in certificates used within states or between states. Forms originating from the State of Oregon are very different from those from Washington. If we intended to ship my product from Washington to Oregon, we would be obliged to use a transfer permit in the State of Washington, a health certificate, and Oregon's form, as well.

An additional form, this one federal, from the U.S. Fish and Wildlife Service is sometimes required. U.S. Fish and Wildlife Service is one of the agencies assigned the task of enforcing the Lacey Act. This document is a certificate that is directly linked to the Lacey Act. We have now been exempted from using this form when we export salmon products such as eyed salmon eggs. However, when we import from across the federal border, we need to complete this item.

Similar to the way the State of Washington deals with the non-native species, Maine requires a zebra mussel certificate. The supplier must sign this declaration. So, if you are working with farming operations in Maine, this export declaration must be completed in addition to the regular health certificates previously described.

INTERNATIONAL REGULATIONS

There are approximately 50 different fish health regulations in the United States that are currently active. Adherence to this body of regulations can be very confusing. In addition, every country in the world has its own set of regulations. Obviously, this does not simplify the process of conducting international business. The Office International des Epizooties (OIE), located in Paris, attempts to streamline international and national fish health regulations. This agency is now part of the World Trade Organization and is playing a bigger role than previously. These international workers are now in the process of developing what I would describe as fairly stringent regulations. These fish health regulations are beginning to mirror the regulations we are currently dealing with in terms of salmon and trout species.

CONCLUSION

Using history as a guide, I would say that the bar is gradually being raised for us—not just for salmon and trout, but for almost all live seafood. This concerns me because, in the long run, it will hamper international trade. This is a problem that our industry will be forced to deal with.

On the international level, I think that the best forum to address this concern is through the OIE. Unfortunately, this organization is currently little more than an academic technical organization without much input from the industry. There is no industry panel, for example, something that is needed to keep the developing body of regulations from becoming impractical.

The paperwork load encountered when complying with these regulations is horrendous. Also, the animal testing required by these same regulations is impractical. For example, all of the live fish and shellfish being tested have to be killed. Industry members cannot just take blood samples in a manner similar to what is done with livestock and, for that matter, humans. These are lethal samples and this sacrifice has become extremely costly for the industry. This is something that we are currently trying to change.

We are also trying to have our farm products redefined as livestock in the United States. The thought here is that if the industry can gain the livestock designation, our products would then be looked upon as farmed animals and would be out from under the Lacey Act. We have a petition in front of the U.S. Secretary of Agriculture requesting this redefinition. It has taken a long time and we still do not have this more appropriate designation.

I hope that changes like this will simplify our industry. We have an infant industry that is being overburdened with fish health regulations. There are far too many agencies involved and it is constraining the development of the live industry. It may come to pass that sectors of our industry will have to deal with separate regulations. For example, the livestock products such as farmed fish and shellfish would be regulated differently from fish that are used for enhancement. We may have to consider options such as this in order to develop a viable farmed fish and shellfish industry in the United States. We are simply not able to accomplish this important task under the present regulatory environment.

Questions from the Audience

QUESTION: What would you say are the most significant hazards posed by your product and how do you handle them to minimize those hazards in terms of fish health?

HEGGELUND: In terms of fish health? Well, right now, we have to do lethal sampling of all our fish and have them checked according to regulations that are established by recipient countries, in this case either Japan or Chile. We follow them to the teeth—you cannot afford not to.

QUESTION: What level of testing would you consider to be appropriate in order to handle what you consider to be the legitimate hazards that are associated with your product?

HEGGELUND: First of all, we have to go to the traditional livestock-type sampling, meaning nonlethal testing, where we take blood samples and then run statistical inferences on whatever diseases we are concerned with. We also have to recognize the fact that we can never have zero tolerance for any type of organism. It is impractical. We used to have zero tolerance provisions in the United States on human food with the Delaney Clause under the Food and Drug Act. However, this was removed about three years ago. We have to set tolerances that are realistic, rather than zero. Zero is not a realistic tolerance. Many of these items will have to be negotiated with the concerned parties, so I do not have a particular number to give you right now.

QUESTION: A comment concerning the previous answer. Even if you are sampling for vibrios or ISA (infectious salmon anemia), zero tolerance is not involved. Rather, what is involved is the statistical detection level technical limit using a sample of 150 fish. I am well aware of the situation on the East Coast where we found that a vaccine being used had statistically few, but nonetheless a few living organisms carried by the vaccine. The vaccine actually created the disease that it was meant to control. My point is that this problem was not detected using standard detection systems. Zero tolerance is only a statistical level of safety.

HEGGELUND: Yes. Disease testing is only as good as the methodology that is being used. People in the industry are extremely concerned about the new sensitive testing methods that are coming out, such as DNA probes. These new strategies can sample and detect fragments of a pathogen, rather than the whole viable pathogen. We feel that we do not need to detect the pathogen, rather we need to deal with the disease. These are fish and health disease regulations—not pathogen regulations. So we may have to look at changing the philosophy of these regulations, because they are impractical for us to live with. Also, we see the regulatory bar being raised. We are now looking for more bugs and, on top of that, we are getting methodology that is more sensitive. We see this as a problem.

QUESTION: How are the regulations here in the United States compared to Norway? Are the regulations more stringent there than here?

HEGGELUND: There is a total ban on salmon smolts and eyed eggs transported into Norway. The Norwegians do not accept them, period. We see the same situation in other countries, for example New Zealand and Australia. To some extent, part of Canada is also involved. To give you a specific example, we can transport a smolt from British Columbia to the State of Washington. We, however, cannot ship smolts into British Columbia. In terms of the regulations in Norway, a ban is about as strict as you can get. I have transported eyed eggs from Scandinavia into the State of Washington and other parts of the United States.

AUTHOR BIOGRAPHY

Per Heggelund, a native of Norway, came to the United States in 1965. He holds a B.S. from the University of Washington School of Fisheries. In addition, he holds an M.S. in food science and an M.B.A. in finance and international business. He held a faculty position at the University of Alaska as a seafood specialist and later worked with the National Food Processors Association in Seattle and Washington, D.C. In the early 1980s, he pioneered the importation of farmed salmon from Norway to the U.S. West Coast. Later he obtained federal permits to import eyed eggs to the Pacific Northwest.

Shipping Live Aquatic Products: Biological, Regulatory, and Environmental Considerations

John G. Nickum
U.S. Fish and Wildlife Service, Denver, Colorado

INTRODUCTION

This report is about the three Rs—risks, regulation, and romantic naturalism. Shipping live aquatic animals or plants from one part of the world to another part involves some risks to both the sending and the receiving ecosystems. In today's world—where there is risk, there is regulation, and, frequently, an emotional outcry to "save the ecosystem." Persons in the business of shipping live plants and animals must be aware of the regulations, should be aware of any risks associated with the movement of their products, and probably will benefit by being able to predict the responses of those individuals and groups who oppose transport of live products on the basis of wishing to preserve ecosystems in their "natural condition."

We hear frequent references to a "global economy" and the implications of international trade, multinational corporations, and instant communications from anywhere on earth. Increasingly, we also live in a "global ecosystem." News reports from New York earlier this fall were filled with alarm concerning "new" strain of encephalitis. Where did it come from? How did it get here? What effects will it have? Environmentalists are focused intensely on "native" species and "natural" ecosystems. Are these concerns valid? If so, to what extent? And what can and should be done? What is the manager, business or resource, to do?

Risks

Risks can be assessed systematically and, frequently quantitatively. However, "arguments from ignorance," in which claims based only on perceptions, or even fabrications, are made, must be identified and condemned for what they are. Risk assessments can be done at various levels, depending on subjective judgments as to the probable effects that could take place if the species being shipped were to become established in the receiving ecosystem. Risk assessment procedures are quite well established.

Regulations

Regulations concerning the shipment of live aquatic products have been imposed by federal governments, state governments, and local governments. For better or worse, it is the responsibility of the shipper to know these regulations. In the United States, import regulations are based primarily on the injurious wildlife provisions of the Lacey Act. However, the Lacey Act also provides support for state or local regulations pertaining to wildlife when transport across jurisdictional boundaries is involved. In most other nations, jurisdiction for regulating the import or export of live products rests with the national governments.

Romantic naturalism

Much of the argument against transport of live aquatic plants and animals is based on philosophies founded in "romantic naturalism." Is this how ecosystems really function? Should ecosystems be studied and evaluated as functional systems, or only as structural systems? Is nature perfect? In addition to the topics mentioned, specifically risks and regulations, the role and philosophical basis for such "environmental" concerns will be discussed.

REGULATORY CONCERNS

In terms of the regulations and related topics, I speak not so much as a regulator because I do not do that type of thing in my current position, but rather I speak as a senior scientist. If there is a motive that I might be carrying into this meeting, it would be the plea that we can bring a lot of this discussion about live commerce down to science. Frankly, we can make much of the regulatory discussion about the developing live industry a lot more scientific than it has been. I might add that in the process of work, we will be able to reduce a lot of the rhetoric and a lot of the emotions that are involved. Consequently, I am speaking more from this perspective than as a regulator.

Opinions expressed in this paper are those of the author, not necessarily those of the U.S. Fish and Wildlife Service.

Yes—I do have experience with this topic of live commerce. For several years I was responsible for the interpretation of Title 50 of the Lacey Act—injurious wildlife regulations. I think that this work is largely why I am at this conference. Again, however, I would like to make the statement that we as a group must try to move to a working position where we can be a little more scientific—a position where we actually do some of the science that we think we have already done. It will be to everyone's benefit if the industry can come from this rational base.

In this report, I comment on three different regulatory concerns, and then work into more detailed reviews of these topics in order to take a realistic look at some of the risks associated with the live trade. I will then talk about how this type of review can lead to regulation and then incorporate into a short discussion about this how we look at the environment.

Review of some basic realities

I would like to start with a simple fact. There are six billion people in this world at this time. In terms of world commercial trade, this singular fact has a tremendous influence on what is done in terms of the movement of products and also how things are done. Relative to live shipment and the live aquatic products industry, this can only mean that the markets are there—no question about it. The retail prices mentioned about live products in Hong Kong markets may be world highs. However, there are markets in other parts of the world where prices are nearly as high. In short, the markets are there and the movement of live products will occur.

I think we must deal with this reality. Now, in the course of the rapid development of this industry, can we also remain reasonable? I think the following is also an important fact. A point drawn from Chaiton's talk at this conference is the need for licensed engineers when a complex live holding system is designed and built. These people are in various ways accountable for the structure and function of the systems they develop. Now moving away from the construction of physical systems toward the development of management systems, there are no licensed professional resource biologists. The point is that the design of a physical system, such as a live holding facility, is a highly predictable process. A good architectural engineer will say that this physical system will work and it should work. As biologists, we are not willing to go out on that limb. We do not say that this system will or will not work.

So for biological systems the issue is what level of risk is acceptable. There is tremendous uncertainty in the biological world and a lot of the regulation governing this work reflects the uncertainty. In today's society, we want to have zero risk. This, of course, is impossible. However, we do make the attempt to establish regulations on the basis of zero risk, at least in a philosophical sense.

And the precautionary principle: The Lacey Act in perspective

Per Heggelund (AquaSeed Corporation, Seattle, Washington) mentioned the Lacey Act and some of the problems that come from this body of regulations. This act is acknowledged to be a risk reduction system, not as a risk elimination system. Yet, we do end up in the situation of wanting to have all of the risk eliminated, rather than just simply reduced. A question I like to ask sometimes with respect to this topic is "what do we know and how do we know it?" Within what limits do we know things?

Taking another look at this question from the HACCP perspective would be "is it likely to result in an unacceptable risk to the environment?" This is where a lot of the regulations start to come apart. Regulations tend to unravel when we put specific limits to such things as identifying unacceptable levels of risk, because of all the uncertainties.

I would make the suggestion that we need to try to move back to the point of knowing what the uncertainties are. We need to quantify the things about which we are certain and move in that direction. One of the things that I deplore in the literature describing the environmental world is the fact that so many scientists are speaking about environmental risk, but they are not speaking scientifically. There can be a huge difference between a scientist speaking generally and a scientist speaking scientifically. Try to keep this in mind. Always try to ask that question, within what limits do we know this? Having arrived at this point, I think we can start making some progress.

In any case, at this time in history there are live aquatic products moving from one part of the world to another. There will be some risks and where there is risk there is going to be regulation. Can this movement be an acceptable type of a risk in this global economy and this global ecosystem?

At this point, it might be good to ask is it really reasonable to think in terms of an environment that is perfect? I often hear the statement made that a particular ecosystem is the product of millions of years of evolution. Are the ecosystems out around us the products of millions of years of ecosystem—or of evolution? Well, I guess it depends on how you look at it. Some of the critters that are out there could be traced way back to the earliest times. But I think that if we went back say about 15,000 years we will see a very different environment around this area. At about that time there were continental ice sheets impacting the region and they drastically affected what was going on, particularly in northern latitudes. So the bottom line to this line of thought is that ecosystems are dynamic and we need to look at them as dynamic functional systems, not just as static structural systems.

When you try to explain the function of an ecosystem, to actually explain how an ecosystem works and to predict how it will work, it becomes a very difficult task. Going back to our earlier discussion about the certified architectural engineer, that job is simple in terms of explaining how the system to be built will work. The natural ecosystem, on the other hand, is very complex and we tend to lose the quantification for the thing we are attempting to understand.

And so, we then find it convenient to fall back on something that a lot of people in the environmental field call the "precautionary principle," which is "when in doubt don't take a chance." Do no harm. The problem, though, is what does it mean to not take a chance. What is "doing no harm"? Keeping it the way it was? Taking it back the way it was 300 years ago? I do not know the answer to these questions. There is a huge uncertainty here as far as I am concerned.

It is possible to look at these risks in a systematic manner. A series of risk analysis systems have been developed—the passive approach being one strategy. This and other approaches, in turn, can lead into decision support systems. A decision support system will tell you have checked all the different places where something could go wrong. You can incorporate into these systems the degree of certainty or uncertainty. Using this strategy, you can at least know that you have touched all the bases and come to understand the level of probability that something will go wrong.

You will then have to make a subjective judgment about the proposed project. Or, perhaps, you can resort to the wisdom of our Congress in Washington, D.C., allowing those folks to make the decisions for us. In this manner, we can find out whether a particular risk can be considered to be acceptable or not.

I would contend again that ecosystems are dynamic—they can accept some change. The reality is that they will accept some forms of change. Consequently, our job is to figure out how to predict this change and determine how to make it as beneficial as possible.

A document that contains some interesting items relative to what is and is not a substantial risk is the Congressional Research Service Report for Congress on Harmful Non-Native Species, dated September 15, 1999. At this point distribution has not been made to the general public. I volunteered to review it and thereby obtained a copy. It states that aquatic nuisance species are nonindigenous species. It says that something that is not in its natural place—it really cannot be a nuisance if it is in its natural place—is, in fact, a nuisance species. However, if we look at ecosystems from a functional standpoint, there are places, for example, in the Midwest where nonindigenous species such as black bullheads and yellow perch have clearly become aquatic nuisance species.

My argument is that native species can also become nuisances. We need to look at what is happening, what the effects might be, and try to quantify the situation as best we can before continuing into a project. At any rate, this report to Congress relative to non-native species does indicate that harm usually comes from the non-natives. The document also acknowledges that most of our food supply comes from non-native species. Many other products come from non-native species.

Some of these products come from controlled and managed ecosystems in which various functional aspects are quite predictable. For example, a cornfield in the middle of Iowa is a functional ecosystem. It is a carefully structured ecosystem and is tightly managed. It has a high input of energy, a high input of nutrients, and predictable output. There is an argument as to whether it is efficient or not, but it is an ecosystem.

Can we go to that extreme of extending this discussion to the aquatic world. Yes—some catfish ponds, carp ponds, and tilapia ponds do approach the level of a cornfield. But as you move out into the broader environment, more uncertainty is introduced. Looking at what is happening in this world, this particular document goes on to list the federal laws, acts of Congress, and then the rules and regulations that have developed to implement the necessary regulations. And, yes, the lead regulation is the Lacey Act—the first item reviewed. There are 13 other major regulatory items that also relate to the potential harm caused by nonindigenous species.

There is an interesting statement made relative to the Lacey Act that should be mentioned here. It states "moreover, grounds for exclusion (for preventing something from being imported) were expanded beyond the traditional harm to agriculture, horticulture and forestry interests to include harm to wildlife and wildlife resources." This has also been interpreted as including fisheries. Then the drafters of this document go on to make the statement that the inclusion of the above-mentioned extended grounds for exclusion could mean that nearly any non-native species could be considered for exclusion since most, perhaps all, ecologists would hold that the inclusion of any non-native species risks harm to wildlife resources.

The point is clearly made that if the movement of any non-native can be considered harmful, this action will become subject to Lacey Act action. I would say that this position is almost conventional wisdom among "environmentalists" at this point. However, I do not think that it is a conventional wisdom among "ecologists." Ecologists and environmentalists have concerns about the environment. Ecologists, however, are professional biologists who know the quantitative limits of what they do and do not know.

At any rate, the Lacey Act has two very different aspects to its structure that work together. One aspect is related to injurious wildlife. Anything that is interpreted as being potentially injurious to wildlife or wildlife resources can be excluded from entering the United States. The other aspect of the Lacey Act supports and defends various state and foreign laws. Any action that is a matter of a state regulation, a foreign regulation, a treaty, or whatever is supported by the Lacey Act.

The Lacey Act has the potential of elevating something that was a misdemeanor at the state level into a federal felony. If you violate a state regulation in the taking, transporting, possessing, selling, importing, and/or exporting of a fish and wildlife product, you have violated the Lacey Act. It is the Lacey Act violation that really has the potential of grabbing you, not the state regulation that was involved. It is this act of violating the state regulation that is a violation of the Lacey Act. When this unfortunate event occurs, you must proceed to uniform sentencing laws and the penalties can be quite severe. Consequently, you have to be very careful.

This is why Per Heggelund has to know all about 50 states in which his customers reside—each state has extremely different regulations. Here is an example of the complexities involved. I noticed the signature on the bottom of one of those transport forms—the signature of a highly respected veterinarian. Now the State of Illinois four or five years back absolutely rejected his signature because the state authorities did not think he was the right person to sign the document even though the veterinarian in question is an extremely well qualified professional person. This points out the differences from one state to another. To have shipped something into Illinois with his signature would have been a violation of state law, and the persons involved with the shipment could have been prosecuted under the Lacey Act. As far as I know, nothing ever happened in this particular situation, but you get into some really awkward situations under such regulations.

Incidentally, the Lacey Act dates back many years and is related to events that occurred in New York, Pennsylvania, and that general area. Shippers of wildlife product went back and forth across the border and literally thumbed their noses at management folks on the other side, saying, "Hey, I hunted deer in New York. I'm selling them in Pennsylvania. Isn't that tough." Well, the federal government provided the teeth behind the solution for this problem and the Lacey Act was born.

The question about the challenged veterinarian is a different situation from poached deer in Pennsylvania, but the laws and regulations are still very much in place. As pointed out by others attending this conference, the responsibility rests squarely with the person in charge of the movement as to whether this movement is legal.

THE THREE RS

A lot of what I have been talking about up to this point in the report relates more to the rhetoric involved in the regulation of this industry rather than the real science involved. I think that we need to fall back to another one of our "Rs." Recall that the three Rs being discussed in this report are risk, regulation, and romantic naturalism.

Romantic naturalism was a philosophy that was very much in vogue in the late 1700s and early 1800s. There has been a rebirth of this idea in recent years. Romantic naturalism states that anything that is natural is perfect and if anything is not natural, then it is really bad.

This is the reason for my recurrent plea for those involved to understand things as functional systems. What is the proper measure of the tolerance of these functional systems? Ecosystems can be very—let us add a fourth "R"—they can be very resilient. Resilience is part of the fabric of a natural ecosystem. If you really want to get a dose of what it means to be resilient, start reading some of the reports that paleontologists put out. They talk about blue-green algae and bacteria that have been on this planet for billions of years. Over this period, they have not changed much. However, they have tolerated enormous changes in the environment around them.

Now, I do not think that this would be an environment in which we would fit very well—that one back there during the earliest of times with the so-called prokaryotic critters. There is not much room for humans in that picture. So really what we should be talking about is what is the resilience or, putting it another way, what are the limits of the systems we have, in this day and age? Do we really want to push them to these limits? I would suggest probably not. Therefore, it becomes imperative for us to try to understand the nature of these functional systems and what their functional limits may be.

It is obvious that we are not going to have the luxury of maintaining an ecosystem structure exactly as it was 300 years ago, 3,000 years ago, or 30,000 years ago. This is because now there are six billion people in this world and this large population is clamoring for products from all over the world. They are going to move product and there are going to be changes.

ARGUMENTS FROM IGNORANCE

We are finding interesting changes. For example, something that has moved into many areas in the Great Plains is a grass known as crested wheat grass. It is very draught resistant, serves as a good soil cover, and provides a lot of forage. However, most of the growth of this grass is above ground, where most of the native grasses do their work below ground. Consequently, crested wheat grass lends itself to a different sod producing system. Is this a problem? We really do not know the answer to this question yet.

You can look at similar examples throughout all of the different species that have been moved around and their effects on these natural systems. We need to recognize the potential we have in the form of risk assessment systems and on decision support systems to check all the bases—to know what the relative certainties and uncertainties may be. We then simply proceed to make the best decisions possible.

We cannot afford to deal with what philosophers call arguments from ignorance. The precautionary principle is one such argument. I can easily make the argument that if Per Heggelund transports one of his Donaldson trout to Minnesota, it will cause irreparable damage to the aquatic ecosystems in Minnesota. Does he have to prove I am wrong? I suggest that since I made the statement that this transaction is damaging, then I need to prove that I am right.

However, in today's world, the argument for ignorance will often prevail. If a manager makes a statement that something might go wrong, that there could be a risk involved here, that the transfer may push this ecosystem beyond its functional limits (although this is usually not the argument), then the precautionary principle will be brought out and the transaction will not occur. The usual argument is that the transfer will change the structure of the ecosystem. For some people this means an irreversible change. The ecosystem will be changed forever and, clearly, if the structure has changed then the function of the system must also change. Let us try to know what our limits are and then productively work within those limits.

Finally, I would like to add to my "Rs" of risk, regulation, romantic naturalism and, more recently, resilience, another R without which I think all of our efforts tend to go down the tubes. Let us add a fifth R and call it respect for each other—respect for the work that we do and respect for the businesses we are in. Then we can start to move forward into these challenging areas of global commerce.

QUESTIONS FROM THE AUDIENCE

QUESTION: I am curious about the impact of the Lacey Act on commercially harvested live seafood as well as on farmed seafood, for example, live salmon, that is commercially harvested and shipped as live product or whatever.

J. NICKUM: In general, the regulations implementing the injurious wildlife part of the Lacey Act would say that if the product is harvested from the waters of North America and brought directly to port, this is not included in the section dealing with injurious wildlife. I do not think that language has changed.

However, if the same North American product was diverted to a Japanese ship and was initially transported to Japan and then came back again across the ocean, there would be the possibility of it being mixed in with all kinds of things from Asia. At this point, the shipment then would be subject to Lacey Act regulations. In general, commercial harvests from the surrounding waters of North America would not be included in the exclusions mentioned in the Lacey Act. The shipment in question might be subject to state regulation, and, if there was a violation of state regulation, then the penalty part of the Lacey Act would kick in.

QUESTION: When you say North America, does this also include Canada?

J. NICKUM: Normally Canada would be included within this broad zone. Our interpretation has been that you really cannot draw a line in the water—there are no magic barriers there.

QUESTION: If I could add, I think the terminology is if they are taken from the waters of North America, that they have to be landed in the United States to be exempt from Title 50 of the Act. So, if the product is taken in North American waters and landed in Canada, you will still have to have a Title 50 certificate to bring them to the United States.

QUESTION: Why have the states developed different sets of regulations?

J. NICKUM: A lot of the confusion over the matter of state regulations goes back to the fact that in the U.S. Constitution all rights and privileges not specifically reserved to the federal government are given to the states. Fish and wildlife matters, as a general rule, were not reserved to the federal government. Therefore, they are state domain and the states are extremely jealous over this management authority. So we have ended up with 50 different sets of wildlife and associated regulations with the exception of Migratory Bird Treaty Act, the Endangered Species Act, and a few other items of this type.

Author biography

John G. Nickum received his M.S. in zoology and botany from the University of South Dakota and his Ph.D. in zoology and microbiology from Southern Illinois University. He has served as the Regional Science Officer and Research Coordinator in Denver, Colorado, for the U.S. Fish and Wildlife Service since 1998.

Do Live Marine Products Serve as Pathways for the Introduction of Nonindigenous Species?

Annette M. Olson
University of Washington, Seattle, Washington

INTRODUCTION

Two kinds of nonindigenous species are associated with the trade in live products. One type is the live products themselves. The target product species fall under very high levels of scrutiny—for environmental safety and other kinds of regulations. Many times this scrutiny has been invited by the industry, in order to insure uniform standards across the industry.

Non-target or hitchhiking species, on the other hand, are pests, pathogens, and other species of unknown status that might come along with the product. They come in the packing material, the water, or the packaging. They may also be attached to or living in the target species, as with disease organisms. This suggests that, in addition to the product and its handling, the handling and disposal of packaging has potential for bringing these unintentional introductions.

I am focusing on these unintentional introductions because they're very difficult to get a handle on. It is a risk assessment approach that focuses on where the problems might be. We can take a systematic approach to understanding the risk, rather than painting the whole industry with the same brush. We can look at what particular products or practices might be a problem and then work on adapting to those. My risk assessment framework looks more at the institutional arrangements—what people are doing as they process a product.

Why are nonindigenous species a problem? Because they not only have regulatory and management practice implications for the industry, but also because a number of parts of the industry are affected by them. Pests affect the industry directly if they get into holding facilities, and can affect the products that you're working with. In oyster culture, a number of pests and pathogens can greatly increase the cost of doing business and decrease the value or quantity of yield of the product.

I have been doing research for the last few years on nonindigenous species. I've worked with people on the side of industry, government, and nongovernment organizations (NGOs)—people approaching the problem from many different perspectives. Scott Smith and I worked closely to bring to Washington state an awareness of exotic species and why they are a problem.

When I attended the live shipment conference several years ago, I was struck by the fact that not every product and not every process was the same in terms of the risk it might pose for introducing nonindigenous species. Unintentional introductions are particularly difficult to get a handle on, because, if you think of it in HACCP terms, the hazard analysis is made very complicated by not knowing where to look.

New products are often emerging, and are coming from new sources. Often the operators may be very small, and they may change the products that they ship throughout the year, or as markets emerge. Sometimes there are no strong industry associations with whom you can start.

I am interested in characterizing these diverse pathways. After this is done, we can target education in best management practices on portions of the industry where the risk actually lies, rather than developing very broad regulatory approaches that might apply to the whole industry and maybe not appropriately.

INVASION

An invasion of nonindigenous species begins with many species in a source region, which may be native to that region or non-native. Then there's a stage of transport in which live colonists arrive in the host region. This is the first big hurdle for anything that's hitchhiking along with a product, because it has to survive the transport, arrive alive, and be released into the host environment. So just that act of release, or of not releasing, is a major barrier to an invasion.

Even if live colonists are released into the environment, they may or may not become established. If they do establish, an invasion has occurred. Only if they have undesirable impacts, though, would we call them a nuisance species. Not all invaders are nuisance species.

Even intentional introductions, species that are intentionally introduced because they are intended to do some good, show a very low rate of success or establishment. Even when you handpick them to be introduced into your environment, they frequently just don't take. The area in which this is best known is in biocontrol, where people are bringing in insects to control other insects or pest plants. Something like 1% of the biocontrol introductions are actually successful.

Therefore, if it's just a random process, fewer and fewer species are present and capable, as you go through these stages of invasion, of becoming a nuisance species. Once they are alive and in the host environment, they can spread from any point in a secondary fashion. Sometimes the transport of products might be involved in spread, as well as in bringing them into a new host environment.

Methodology

I characterized the pathways in terms of the factors that affect the risk that a species is going to move from one stage to the next of the invasion. I identified three kinds of factors:

- Biology and ecology of the organisms.
- Human activities.
- Characteristics of the vectors themselves—the physical objects, like shipping crates and vessels, that are moved from place to place.

My focus is on the human activities, the transport stage. This is the stage in which one goes from a source environment to a host environment. We can break that stage down into smaller pieces:

- Harvesting in the source habitat
- Handling
- Packaging
- Shipping
- Marketing
- Use
- Waste disposal

These human activities are the factors that we can actually control to change the level of risk. We can do different things in harvesting, for example, or handle the products differently when we're marketing, or educate users to dispose of them differently.

The vectors that might be associated with these different activities are as follows:

- The equipment for harvest and processing.
- Packaging containers and media.
- Ballast in holding systems.
- Distribution in marketing facilities.
- Cartons.
- Coolers or vehicles that they're transported in.
- Disposal options that are available.

I mapped my research onto the sequence of activities. In the first scoping-type stage, I was learning from shippers, marketers, and users what was actually used in the Puget Sound region. Then I identified potentially risky products.

I surveyed marketers and users. If there was no market for use of a product in the host region, we said this pathway is provisionally closed. In other words, for the purposes of this hazard assessment, which we wanted to do quickly, we didn't want to spend lots of time and money trying to understand a pathway that's closed.

If this product or type of product had been used in the host region, we could have sampled shipments of that product to see whether they're carrying any hitchhikers. Then we could have surveyed suppliers to see whether there was anything about their practices that might have been contributing to the presence of hitchhikers. In all cases then, this initial scoping, which involved interacting with folks in the industry, was also directed back in terms of educational products toward the industry.

We didn't want to look at things that were already being addressed by existing nuisance species policy and management. We didn't want to look at shipping because ballast water studies are well under way. There's already oversight in the area of aquaculture and mariculture, so there wasn't a need for us to dig into that more. Public and private aquaria are, at least in our state, the target of an educational campaign, to inform people about nonindigenous species.

We chose to look at scientific specimens, live seafood, and live bait. Our study of live bait illustrates how the protocol of defining a pathway as provisionally closed might work.

RESULTS
Scientific specimens and live seafood

For our pilot study we ordered two shipments of scientific specimens. One was fucus, or rockweed, which is used in developmental biology studies. The other was mixed algae, which includes several seaweed species used in a biology lab class to teach how to identify algae. We also ordered three shipments of Maine lobster through contacts that we found over the Internet.

We went through these shipments, and classified the fauna and flora present in the shipments. In addition to the target taxa, which for animals were the lobsters, there were numerous nontarget taxa found in all these shipments. Most of them were isopods, some were amphipods, and a few were worms. We identified them to the lowest taxonomic level that we could, using a dissecting microscope, but we didn't identify any to species.

Among the flora, there were between three and six nontarget species. We didn't count diatoms but there were many diatom species. Overall, we found that there were 21 or 22 multicellular species in the scientific specimens, and between five and eleven species in the live seafood. These species were found largely in the packing material.

We determined that seaweeds themselves, because they're such a rich habitat for invertebrates, are a relatively high-risk product. Who ships seaweeds? It's mostly educational institutions. One of the first things that we chose to do with our research funding was to develop a brochure for the research education and testing community, the people who receive live products for educational research purposes. That brochure is produced by Washington Sea Grant.

One of the features of the brochure, which might be particularly useful for the industry, is a graphic that shows escape routes. These are the different ways "hitchhikers" could get out of your institution and into the environment. The graphic could be very easily tailored for the industry as an educational product.

Live bait

The third pathway that we looked at was live bait. There are several subpathways within it:

- Local bait shops that import bait for retail sale.
- Recreational users who increasingly can order directly from the Internet.
- Users who transport from out of state.
- Suppliers who stock bait vending machines.
- Possibly some other existing, but as yet unrecognized pathways.

For this portion, we had a two-phase study; in our pilot study, we did a telephone survey of local bait shops. We identified all of the local bait shops in the Seattle area using two different phone directories, called all of them, and made site visits to seven of them. We also called five suppliers, looking for the same pattern of nonindigenous species that occur in the seaweed packaging for bait marts.

First, we found that seven of the local bait shops sold or shipped live bait. We didn't ask whether the bait was from marine sources, but we visited all of those shops, and none of them had marine bait.

We called the suppliers, and found that none of them shipped live marine bait to Washington state. The same suppliers who were shipping live marine bait to the San Francisco Bay area were not shipping it to Washington state. Therefore, we regarded live bait as a provisionally closed pathway.

Subsequently, we did a much more extensive telephone survey of retailers in Washington's coastal counties. Since they are the only counties likely to contain shops selling live marine bait, you could say that we covered the whole state. First, we identified likely retailers of live bait, removing shops that were located inland. In Washington, the boundaries of several coastal counties run from Puget Sound up to the crest of the Cascades. We decided that shops in towns in the Cascades probably weren't carrying marine bait, so we removed them from our list.

That left us with 110 shops from which we drew a random sample. I can't exaggerate the importance of having a random sample when you're doing this kind of study, or you can severely compromise your results. However, we did a stratification, in which we made sure that we got at least two shops from each county. In one case, Skagit County, we couldn't do that.

We also resampled all of the shops from the pilot study, and administered a simple telephone questionnaire to 41 shops. We did not conduct any site visits or survey suppliers for this study. We had an excellent response rate, with only 22% of the people we called saying they didn't want to talk to us, or not answering the telephone.

A majority did not carry live bait at all. They were marine oriented and were carrying frozen bait. Those who carried live bait got it from a local source. Those who imported bait got it from Oregon, which were actually earthworms. No imported marine bait was being brought in. It looks to us like people do not ship live bait from Maine for use in marine waters in Washington. If I'm wrong, I want to hear about it.

Method Evaluation

For rapid identification of risks associated with a commercial pathway, a telephone survey of a random sample of retailers can be reliable. We got the same results from doing this very extensive survey as we did from a very limited one. Site visits to a subsample of the retailers and telephone surveys of suppliers can be used to test the reliability of those telephone survey results.

Constructing the list from which to draw the random sample is nontrivial. This is where I think that industry associations can be very helpful, because, when you're already organized, you have your mailing list of members, and can then draw randomly among those.

Finally, pilot studies can be particularly helpful in identifying flaws in the survey instrument. I mentioned that we forgot to ask whether the live bait was marine in our first telephone survey, which we corrected in our subsequent one.

Conclusion

This problem has some real dimensions. There are some real threats, both to the environment and to the industry from nonindigenous species. However, these threats don't need to be overblown. Sometimes the consequences can be very negative, but it is possible to find out where the problems are and handle them very reasonably in an educational context.

The other point is that the level of concern is rising, and the regulatory bar is being raised. Regulatory approaches have one very serious limit, though, and that is enforcement. The human resources to implement regulatory approaches are already stressed beyond their limits.

What we really need is education and self-education, so that people don't do the simple thing and toss the seaweed into Puget Sound, but do the equally simple thing of tossing it into the wastebasket and sending it to the landfill.

Questions from the Audience

QUESTION: I'm a little stumped as to why there's no live marine bait coming into Washington. Is it just that the local suppliers are adequate, or are there state regulations?

A. OLSON: There is a regulatory dimension to it, but that is not what is causing it. The permit process is triggered by a permit application. Since most state resources go toward regulating the aquaculture industry, bait shops don't submit permit applications. The regulation could probably technically apply to them, but the ability to actually implement that as a regulatory approach is pretty limited.

It was quite funny that when we went to these shops in our pilot study, and asked them if they had any live marine worms, they were puzzled. They said, "Why don't you go out and dig your own?" Therefore, I think that there is a tradition of private individual users harvesting their own bait. That could easily change, though.

So, I wouldn't say that this pathway is forever closed. In fact, I'm working with Washington Sea Grant to develop a brochure targeted to the bait shops on our original list. It will make them aware and ask them to inform their customers about the risk, because the real risk actually falls with the customers in the bait arena.

QUESTION: Were any of the bait shops exporting from Washington state?

A. OLSON: Yes, but we did not look at exports. We know that there's some export to Oregon and vice versa, but we weren't looking at that element, because of the nature of our funding. We were trying to assess risks for Puget Sound.

QUESTION: How many of the beasts that came on the algae scientific specimens were alive?

A. OLSON: We didn't count anything that wasn't alive.

QUESTION: Did you try putting them into, for example, an aquarium with Puget Sound water, to see what would actually take?

A. OLSON: No. We were trying to develop a rapid screening process, which would allow us to determine if something requires further inspection or not. Those types of questions would be very valid ones to follow up with research specimens.

However, because the research community has been a vector in the past, we decided that it was more important to inform them about the problem, than to spend a year trying to determine exactly how big the problem is.

Marketing and Shipping Live Aquatic Products
University of Alaska Sea Grant • AK-SG-01-03, 2001

Live Seafood: A Recipe for Biological and Regulatory Concern?

Todd W. Miller and John W. Chapman
Oregon State University, Hatfield Marine Science Center, Newport, Oregon

Eugene V. Coan
California Academy of Sciences, San Francisco, California

Abstract

The expanding live seafood market has created a significant and increasing potential for accidental introductions of live seafood species into northeast Pacific coastal waters. Of 36 marine and estuarine bivalve species available in western U.S. retail markets, only 13 are native to this region. Eleven of the 23 species that are nonindigenous to the northeast Pacific (nearly half of the total) were introduced intentionally. Measures to prevent such introductions are warranted. However, state legislative and resource agency efforts to manage nonindigenous species have been difficult to implement. Laws of this sort, for example, create uneven competition among production industries in different states. Efforts to reduce the risks of introduced species from the seafood trade are most likely to be effective at federal and international levels. Research, education, and cooperation should be emphasized, rather than rules and regulations.

Introduction

Introductions of marine and estuarine nonindigenous species from ballast water traffic (Carlton and Geller 1993, Cohen et al. 1995) and aquaculture practices (Carlton 1975, 1979; Rosenthal 1980; Mann 1983; Chew 1990) are attracting intense interest. Meanwhile, other mechanisms of introduction, such as the live seafood trade, which may also be important, have largely escaped attention. Shells of nonindigenous clams imported to the northeast Pacific as live seafood are found occasionally as the remains of bait fishing activities on river and ocean shores (e.g., Carlton 1975, Coan 1998, Chapman and Miller 1999). These shell remains are evidence that live seafood species can be transported into geographical areas where accidental or intentional introductions are possible (Chapman and Miller 1999).

Past introductions of nonindigenous species such as oysters and soft-shell clams for seafood markets demonstrate that accidental or intentional introductions of seafood species have occurred. Introduced species, once brought into a region, are unconstrained by political or economic boundaries and, therefore, become the concern of entire biogeographic regions. Many seafood species are exported outside of their natural ranges to areas where they do not yet have reproducing populations. The seafood trade may appear to be a minor mechanism for introduction of marine and estuarine species in comparison with the volumes of ballast water released by merchant marine traffic (Carlton and Geller 1993) or aquaculture (Mann 1983, Chew 1990), but the correlation is poor between the scale of the actual mechanism involved and the probability of introduction (Carlton 1999). Unauthorized introductions associated with seafood have occurred (McMahan 1982, Cohen et al. 1995, Cohen and Carlton 1997). The live seafood trade could be a vector for introducing species around the world.

We examined native and nonindigenous marine and estuarine bivalve species sold as live seafood on the West Coast of the United States for this analysis. Because introduced species are not affected by political boundaries, all coastal waters of the entire northeast Pacific are the geographical regions of concern.

Methods

Common bivalve seafood species of the northeast Pacific, documented in publications, personal observations, communications, or Internet postings are included in this survey. An introduced species is defined as a reproductive population that is established by human activity where it did not occur previously. The origins and introductions of bivalve species of the northeast Pacific markets are inferred from previously published records or using the criteria for introduced species summarized in Carlton (1979) and Chapman and Carlton (1991 and 1994).

Results

All 36 species surveyed (Tables 1 and 2) occur within marine or estuarine waters between the latitudes 30° and 60°N and are able survive in similar storage and shipping conditions. Twenty-three of these 36 seafood species are nonindigenous to the northeast Pacific (Table 2). Fourteen of the 23 nonindigenous species have disjointed distributions—they occur on opposite sides of continents or on different continents (Table 2, column 3). These 14 species thus appear to have been introduced. The ocean quahog may occur naturally in both Europe and eastern North America, but the remaining 13 species, 56.5%, appear to have been introduced somewhere in the world outside of their natural ranges.

Native species

Thirteen native northeast Pacific species that are harvested and sold only in the western United States (Table 1) are of little threat to northeast Pacific ecosystems. The smooth venus (Table 1), primarily a tropical species imported to the United States from western Mexico, lives in higher temperatures than occur in the more northern northeast Pacific waters where it is sold.

Low and high risk categories of nonindigenous species

The potential risks of introducing nonindigenous seafood species from retail markets (Table 2) are both consequential and variable in nature. Nonindigenous northeast Pacific seafood species can be classified into categories of risk (Table 2, column 4) including:

1. Species introduced in the past, from which harvests of local populations are made for local markets.

2. Species cultured to marketable size in local waters from introduced spat.

3. Species that have been introduced locally but are not harvested locally, the market source being foreign.

4. Imported species available only from foreign sources.

The magnitudes of ecological risk resulting from introducing these nonindigenous species into the

Table 1. Native marine bivalve mollusks available in northeast Pacific live seafood markets.

Native origin and species	Common name	Distribution
Western North America		
Chlamys hastata	Spiny scallop[a]	WNA[a,b,c]
Chlamys rubida	Reddish scallop,[a] pink scallop	WNA[a,b,c]
Clinocardium nuttallii	Nuttall cockle,[a] basket cockle	WNA[a,b,c]
Mytilus californianus	California mussel[a]	WNA[b,c]
Mytilus trossulus	Foolish mussel[a]	WNA[b,c] ENA[d]
Ostrea conchaphila	Olympia oyster[a]	WNA[b,c]
Panopea abrupta	Pacific geoduck[a]	WNA[b,c]
Patinopecten caurinus	Weathervane scallop[a]	WNA[a,b,c]
Protothaca staminea	Pacific littleneck[a]	WNA[a,b,c]
Saxidomus nuttalli	California butter clam[a]	WNA[a,b,c]
Siliqua patula	Pacific razor[a]	WNA[a,b,c]
Tresus capax	Fat gaper[a]	WNA[a,b,c]
Western Mexico		
Chione fluctifraga	Smooth venus[a]	MEX[b,e]

ENA=Eastern North America, WNA=Western North America, MEX=Mexico.
[a]Turgeon et al. 1998; [b]Harvest region; [c]Kozloff and Price 1997; [d]Brunel et al. 1998; [e]Abbott and Dance 1982.

Table 2. Scientific and common names of nonindigenous bivalve mollusks available live in seafood markets of the northeast Pacific.

Native origin and species	Common name	Distribution	Risk category
Eastern North America			
Arctica islandica	Ocean quahog[a]	ENA[a,b] EU[c]	4
Argopecten irradians	Bay scallop[a]	ENA[b,a] EA[d]	4
Cyrtodaria siliqua	Northern propellor clam[a]	ENA[b,a]	4
Crassostrea virginica	Eastern oyster,[a] Atlantic oyster	ENA[a,b] WNA[a,b]	1,2
Ensis directus	Atlantic jackknife[a]	ENA[a,b] EU[e]	4
Mercenaria mercenaria	Northern quahog,[a] bay quahog	ENA[a,b] WNA[a] EU[f]	3
Mya arenaria	Softshell,[a] Atlantic softshell	ENA[a,b] WNA[a] EU[g]	3
Mytilus edulis	Blue mussel,[a] Atlantic blue mussel	ENA[a,b] WNA[a] EU[h] CH[h]	3
Petricolaria pholadiformis	False angel wing[a]	ENA[a,b] WNA[a] EU[i]	3
Placopecten magellanicus	Sea scallop,[a] Atlantic sea scallop	ENA[a,b]	4
Spisula solidissima	Atlantic surf clam[a]	ENA[a,b]	4
Europe			
Ostrea edulis	Edible oyster,[a] flat oyster	ENA[b] EU[b,d] WNA[b,d]	2
Mytilus galloprovincialis	Mediterranean mussel[a]	WNA[b,j] EU[b,c] EA[k] WA[l]	1,2
South America			
Protothaca thaca	Chilean clam	AR[b,m]	4
Ostrea puelchana	Argentine oyster	AR[b,n,o]	4
East Asia			
Anadara granosa	Blood clam	EA[b,p]	4
Crassostrea gigas	Pacific oyster[a]	WA AU CH[b] EA EU J NZ MEX[b,d] WNA[b,d]	1,2
Crassostrea sikamea	Kumamoto oyster	AU J[b,q] WNA[b,q]	1,2
Mizuhopecten yessoensis	Japanese weathervane[a]	J[r] WNA[b,s]	1,2
Venerupis philipanarum	Japanese littleneck,[a] Manilla clam	EA EU[b,d] WNA[b,d]	1,2
New Zealand			
Chione stutchburyi	New Zealand cockle	NZ[b,t]	4
Paphies australis	Pipi clam	NZ[b,u]	4
Perna canaliculus	Green mussel	NZ[b,v]	4

AR=Argentina, AU=Australia, CH=Chile, EA=Eastern Asia, ENA=Eastern North America, EU=Europe, J=Japan, WA=Western Africa, MEX=Mexico, NZ=New Zealand, WNA=Western North America.

Risk categories: (1) species introduced in the past, from which harvests of local populations are made for local markets; (2) species cultured to marketable size in local waters from introduced spat; (3) species that have been introduced locally but are not harvested locally, the market source being foreign and; (4) imported species available only from foreign sources.

[a]Turgeon et al. 1998; [b]Harvest region; [c]Tebble 1966; [d]Chew 1990; [e]Essnik 1986; [f]Mann 1983; [g]Carlton 1975; [h]Seed 1992; [i]Coan 1997; [j]McDonald and Koehn 1988; [k]Lee and Morton 1985; [l]Hockey and van Erkom Schurink 1992; [m]Urban and Campos 1994; [n]Fernandez Castro and Bodoy 1987; [o]Arakawa 1990; [p]Yin et al. 1994; [q]Banks et al. 1994; [r]Chunde et al. 1995; [s]Saunders and Heath 1994; [t]Dobbinson et al. 1989; [u]Hooker and Creese 1995; [v]Siddall 1980.

northeast Pacific varies among habitats, categories, species, regions, and over time. Fully marine and estuarine species are unlikely to be successfully introduced into freshwater systems and freshwater species are of little risk in estuarine or marine systems. A species may be independently reproductive in particular bays or estuaries or specific latitudes, for instance, but require active culturing in others. A species may be successfully introduced for culture at one time, but later decline to unprofitable production rates because of, for example, environmental changes of one sort or another. Introduction of imported spat for culture to marketable size in coastal waters was widely practiced in the past (Barrett 1963) and then discontinued (Chew 1990).

The eastern oyster, the Pacific oyster, the Japanese littleneck clam (Chew 1990) and, recently, the Kumamoto oyster (Banks et al. 1994) (Table 2) were introduced into the northeast Pacific for commercial harvests and spawn naturally in some areas of Washington (risk category 1). However, each of these species must be raised from spat (risk category 2) to reach economical densities for commercial harvests. Previous methods of transplanting spat into local waters directly from their native regions were discontinued due to the great expenses required and the associated pest species that were unintentionally introduced with them (Carlton 1979, Chew 1990). The ecological effects of established populations of these risk category 1 and 2 species and their associated introduced species are poorly known, but could be substantial. Without climate or other environmental changes, or extensive human intervention, however, these species do not appear to be spreading further. Additional risks from these category 1 and 2 species, due to retail activities, may be small. Moreover, the recent spat grow-out methods from larvae produced in local laboratories and hatcheries prevent associations with other species. The risks of introducing associated pest species with category 2 species by recent culture methods are minor.

The ecological risk for category 3 species are also already occurring and unlikely to change due to retail activities. They are not cultivated locally for the retail market and it is unlikely that they will spread beyond their present distributions by accidental or unauthorized introductions. In the absence of environmental or climate changes that could cause these species to spread or proliferate, they also are less likely to produce greater ecological effects than those already present.

High risk category 4 species

The 12 risk category 4 nonindigenous species (Table 2) are the greatest concern for resource managers since they are not yet successfully introduced into the northeast Pacific. Of these species, two have been introduced beyond their native range and pose a serious and immediate risk of being introduced to the northeast Pacific. The Atlantic jackknife, *Ensis directus*, in particular, has successfully invaded and now dominates in benthic habitats in parts of northern Europe. The remaining 10 species are not known to be introduced outside of their natural range, and thus may pose less risk of being introduced to the coastal waters of the northeast Pacific.

The northeast Pacific may be disproportionately vulnerable to aquatic introductions. San Francisco Bay, California, is among the most intensely invaded aquatic environments in the world (Cohen et al. 1995) and the rate of invasions is increasing (Cohen and Carlton 1998). Seafood species may fit into the same pattern. Of 13 endemic northeast Pacific seafood species (Table 1), only *Mytilus trossulus* (7.6%) has been introduced to other regions in the world (Brunel et al. 1998). In contrast, 13 of the 23 (56.5%) imported species (Table 2) have been introduced to the northeast Pacific or elsewhere. Thus, the proportion of species imported to the northeast Pacific that have been introduced anywhere in the world is higher than the proportion of native northeast Pacific species that have been successfully exported.

Other mechanisms for introductions

The magnitude of present marine and estuarine introductions is just now being discovered and studied (Cohen and Carlton 1998, Eno et al. 1997, Geller et al. 1997, Carlton 1999). At the same time, global markets for live seafood are expanding. Nonindigenous marine species imported initially as food should be included in ongoing risk assessments reviewing other mechanisms for introduction.

The major vectors and processes that take place during invasions of aquatic ecosystems can be distinguished only from the patterns apparent in various documented global invasions. These global patterns, including dispersal, survival, and local extinctions of nonindigenous species, are all but unknown in marine and estuarine systems (Carlton 1999). Ballast-water traffic, fouling communities on hulls of seagoing ships, aquaculture activities, and fisheries and wildlife introductions are attracting substantial interest as vectors of aquatic introductions (e.g., Carlton 1979, Cohen et al. 1995, Eno et al. 1997, Smith 1998). However, they may not be the only mechanisms at work. Other possible vectors for introduction, including the seafood trade, should not be discounted as sources for major pest species (e.g., Cohen et al. 1995, Cohen and Carlton 1997). The absence of reported, unauthorized introductions of seafood species is not evidence that they do not occur.

The entire diversity of commercially available live marine and estuarine species capable of introduction into northeast Pacific waters is not included in Table 2. Not included are other major taxa transported around the world alive, including:

- Fish, crustaceans, and gastropods.
- Species available only to restaurants.
- The live bait trade.
- The aquarium and pet industry.
- Species listed only in customs records of live intercepts not sanctioned in U.S. commercial trade agreements.
- Species recorded in inter- and intra-state transport permits.
- Species potentially available for dispersal into northeast Pacific waters after introduction by any mechanism to Canada or Mexico.

Potential impacts of introduced seafood species

The benefits of accidentally introduced bivalves are unlikely to outweigh their economic, ecological, and social costs. The seafood industry depends on disease-free, sustainable fisheries. These fisheries are vulnerable to introduced pests, pathogens, competitors, predators, and species that alter ecosystem processes and fisheries production. Seafood is not frequently monitored for non-human parasites and pathogens for which native species may not have defenses (Bower et al. 1994). Introduced bivalves can alter the trophic dynamics and other critical processes of their new ecosystems (Rosenthal 1980, Griffiths et al. 1992, Kimmerer et al. 1994, Barber 1997, Thayer et al. 1997). The risks associated with the introduction of seafood species and their ultimate costs are likely to increase as global trade in live seafood increases.

Even a small fraction of nonindigenous species that prove to be harmful can produce large costs. The estimated annual cost associated with problems created by the introduced Asian freshwater clam, *Corbicula fluminea*, is $1 billion (Pimentel et al. 1999). The estimated annual costs of the introduced green crab, *Carcinus maenas*, in the United States is $44 million (Pimentel et al. 1999). Green crabs were probably introduced to the northeast Pacific coast by marine algae used to pack shipments of live lobsters from the northwest Atlantic (Cohen et al. 1995). Estimates of the annual economic costs associated with the Chinese mitten crab, *Eriocheir sinensis*, in California are not available but may be many millions. All three introductions are associated with the seafood trade (Carlton 1979, Cohen et al. 1995) and may have become established because of accidental or unauthorized releases into northeast Pacific waters.

Limiting the potential for seafood introductions: State level

The majority of nonindigenous seafood species available in northeast Pacific markets have already been introduced somewhere in the world. It is unnecessary to gather additional evidence in order to gain an understanding of the significant risks associated with further introductions. It is obvious that a critical need for action exist. Mandates by federal agencies under the Clean Water Act to require authorization or permits to import alien aquatic species into the United States, such as the Lacey Act, have not been enforced (Johnston 1999). Other than limitations from international trade agreements, live seafood imports are nearly unrestricted except for a few individual species (Horwath 1989). The legal liability for those responsible for successful introductions of seafood species is unclear. These circumstances may change as the new interagency Invasive Species Council, established by Executive Order 13112, becomes effective. Meanwhile, the states are responsible for their own protection (Charles Wahle, NOAA Invasive Species Coordinator, pers. comm., June 1999). This absence of federal rules places an unfair onus on the states to deal with a national and international problem. State laws and regulations are often resisted by industries because they create uneven interstate competitive advantages within industries.

The history of Oregon House Bill 3071 and Oregon Department of Fish and Game Administrative Rule 635-056 partially illustrates these problems. HB 3071 (located at gopher://gopher.leg.state.or.us:70/00/measure.dir/House_Measures/hb3000.dir/hb3071g.a) introduced by Representative Terry

Thompson of Newport to the 1999 Oregon State Legislature, contained provisions for the State Fish and Wildlife Commission, by rule, to establish and maintain a list of invasive, aquatic animal species that have the potential of harming native and anadromous fish runs in Oregon. The bill also outlawed the transport of live, invasive, aquatic animal species or introduction of species into the waters of the state except under a permit issued by the Oregon Department of Fish and Wildlife. The intent was to deter individuals from transporting unwanted aquatic "pests" as live bait, game fish, and live seafood species into the state (Terry Thompson, pers. comm., June 1999). HB 3071 was withdrawn after two amendments, introduced at the request of the Port of Portland and the Columbia River Steamship Operators Association, which excluded the shipping industry from the provisions of the bill and greatly increased the requirements for enforcement (Merriman 1999).

Oregon Administrative Rule 635-056-0000, designed "to regulate nonnative wildlife to protect native wildlife," classifies all non-native species as "Prohibited," "Controlled," or "Noncontrolled." No non-native seafood species presently has the "Noncontrolled" designation, a category that does not require a permit. For "Controlled" species, an importation permit may be required as set forth by the commission. For species that are not listed in this rule or pursuant to OAR 635-056-0140, no person may import, sell, exchange, or offer to purchase, sell, or exchange the species or any part thereof in Oregon until the species is classified. This prohibition is effective as of 1 January 2000, except for the zebra mussel, *Dreissena polymorpha*, and the mitten crab, *Eriocheir sinensis*, for which prohibition became effective on 1 January 1999. Species will be designated as "Noncontrolled," based on "scientific information" that the species presents a low risk of harm to native wildlife.

Limiting the potential for seafood introductions at federal and international levels

Federal rules and regulations on nonindigenous species are more likely to be passed and to be effective than state regulations due to the extensive scale of the problem. All benefits from actions at local levels could be lost without international cooperation from at least Mexico and Canada. This cooperation also may be more workable and effective through greater awareness and education than by rules and regulations. Stronger measures may prove difficult to implement.

ACKNOWLEDGMENTS

We thank James T. Carlton, Maritime Studies Program, Williams College, Mystic Seaport, CT; Charles Wahle, National Ocean and Atmosphere Agency, Washington, DC; and Anja Robinson, Department of Fisheries and Wildlife, Oregon State University, for comments and discussions of the manuscript and valuable references. This paper also greatly benefited from discussions and comments with Jim Golden and John Johnson, Oregon Department of Fish and Wildlife, on the seafood industry. Susan Gilmont and Janet Webster, Guin Library, OSU, are thanked for many difficult references found and delivered on short notice. We thank Representative Terry Thompson for providing us with the history of HB 3071. Jeff Daniels, president, Marinelli Seafood, Seattle, greatly assisted with the list. This paper was partially funded by Oregon Sea Grant NA36RG045, Project R/NIS-01-PD to JWC from the National Oceanic and Atmospheric Administration to the Oregon State University Sea Grant College Program and by appropriations made by the Oregon State Legislature. The views expressed here are those of the authors alone and do not necessarily reflect the views of NOAA, EPA, or any of their subagencies, the views of any private companies, or other individuals.

REFERENCES

Abbott, R.A., and S.P. Dance. 1982. Compendium of seashells. E.P. Dutton, Inc., New York.

Arakawa, K.Y. 1990. Commercially important species of oysters in the world. Mar. Behav. Physiol. 17:1-13.

Banks, M.A., D.J. McGoldrick, W. Borgeson, and D. Hedgecock. 1994. Gametic incompatibility and genetic divergence of Pacific and Kumamoto oysters, *Crassostrea gigas* and *Crassostrea sikamea*. Mar. Biol. 121:127-135.

Barber, B.J. 1997. Impacts of bivalve introductions on marine ecosystems: A review. In: M. Azeta, K. Takayanagi, M.P. McVey, P.K. Park, and B.J. Keller (eds.), Proceedings of the 25th UJNR aquaculture panel symposium. Bulletin of the National Research Institute of Aquaculture, Yokohama, Japan, Supplement 3, pp. 141-153.

Barrett, E.M. 1963. The California oyster industry. Calif. Dep. Fish Game Fish Bull. 123:1-103.

Bower, S.M., S.E. McGladdery, and I.M. Price. 1994. Synopsis of infectious diseases and parasites of commercially exploited shellfish. Ann. Rev. Fish Dis. 4:1-199.

Brunel, P., L. Bosse, and G. Lamarche. 1998. Catalogue of the marine invertebrates of the estuary and Gulf of Saint Lawrence. Can. Spec. Publ. Fish. Aquat. Sci. 126.

Carlton, J. T. 1975. Introduced intertidal invertebrates. In: R.I. Smith and J.T. Carlton (eds.), Light's manual: Intertidal invertebrates of the central California coast. 3rd edn. Univ. California Press, Berkeley, pp. 17-25.

Carlton, J.T. 1979. History, biogeography, and ecology of the introduced marine and estuarine invertebrates of the Pacific coast of North America. Ph.D. thesis, University of California, Davis.

Carlton, J.T. 1999. The scale and ecological consequences of biological invasions in the world's oceans. In: T. Sandlund et al. (eds.), Invasive species and biodiversity management. Kluwer Academic Publishers, The Netherlands, pp. 195-212.

Carlton, J.T., and J.B. Geller 1993. Ecological roulette: The global transport of nonindigenous marine organisms. Science 261:78-82.

Chapman J.W., and J.T. Carlton. 1991. A test of criteria for introduced species: The global invasion by the isopod *Synidotea laevidorsalis* (Miers, 1881). J. Crust. Biol. 11:386-400.

Chapman J.W., and J.T. Carlton. 1994. Predicted discoveries of the introduced isopod *Synidotea laevidorsalis* (Miers, 1881). J. Crust. Biol. 14:700-714.

Chapman, J.W., and T.W. Miller 1999. The odd northeast Pacific records of the bivalve *Arctica islandica* (Linnaeus, 1767): Bait remnants? The Festivus 31(5):55-57.

Chew, K.K. 1990. Global bivalve shellfish introductions. World Aquacult. 21(3):9-22.

Chunde, W., W. Yaoxian, and C. Suzhi. 1995. Some introduced molluscs in China. Sinozoologia 12:180-191.

Coan, E.V. 1997. Recent species of the genus *Petricola* in the eastern Pacific (Bivalvia: Veneroidea). The Veliger 40:298-340.

Coan, E.V. 1998. A bivalve oddity from an Oregon beach. The Festivus 30(3):40.

Cohen, A.N., and J.T. Carlton. 1997. Transoceanic transport mechanisms: The introduction of the Chinese mitten crab *Eriocheir sinensis* to California. Pac. Sci. 51:1-11.

Cohen, A.N., and J.T. Carlton. 1998. Accelerating invasion rates in a highly invaded estuary. Science 279:555-558.

Cohen, A.N., J.T. Carlton, and M. Fountain. 1995. Introduction, dispersal and potential impacts of the green crab *Carcinus maenas* in San Francisco Bay, California. Mar. Biol. 122:225-237.

Dobbinson, S.J., M.F. Barker, and J.B. Jillett 1989. Experimental shore level transplantation of the New Zealand cockle *Chione stutchburyi*. J. Shellfish Res. 8:197-212.

Eno, N.C., R.A. Clark, and W.G. Sanderson (eds.). 1997. Non-native marine species in British waters: A review and directory. Joint Nature Conservation Committee. Peterborough, U.K.

Essnik, K. 1986. Look out for *Ensis directus*. Bull. Estuar. Brackish Water Sci. Assoc. Lond. 45:22-23.

Fernandez Castro, N., and A. Bodoy. 1987. Growth of the oyster *Ostrea puelchana* (d'Orbigny) at two sites of potential cultivation in Argentina. Aquaculture 65:127-140.

Geller, J.B., E.D. Walton, E.D. Grosholz, and G.M. Ruiz. 1997. Cryptic invasions of the crab *Carcinus* detected by molecular phylogeography. Mol. Ecol. 6:901-906.

Griffiths, C.L., P.A.R. Hockey, C. Van Erkom, C. Schurink, and P.J. Le Roux. 1992. Marine invasive aliens on South African shores: Implications for community structure and trophic functioning. S. Afr. J. Mar. Sci. 12:713-722.

Hockey, P.A.R., and C. van Erkom Schurink. 1992. The invasive biology of the mussel *Mytilus galloprovincialis* on the southern African coast. Trans. R. Soc. S. Afr. 48:123-140.

Hooker, S.H., and R.G. Creese. 1995. The reproductive biology of pipi, *Paphies australis* (Gmelin, 1790) (Bivalvia: Mesodesmatidae). 2. Spatial patterns of the reproductive cycle. J. Shellfish Res. 14:17-24.

Horwath, J.L. 1989. Importation or shipment of injurious wildlife: Mitten crabs, U.S. Fed. Reg. 54(98):22286-22289

Johnston, C.N. 1999. Why ballast water discharges should be regulated under the Clean Water Act. In: J. Pederson (ed.), First National Conference on Marine Bioinvasions. Massachusetts Institute of Technology, Cambridge, p. 2.

Kimmerer, W.J., E. Gartside, and I.J. Orsi. 1994. Predation by an introduced clam as the likely cause of substantial declines in zooplankton in San Francisco Bay. Mar. Ecol. Prog. Ser. 113:81-93.

Kozloff, E.N. and L.H. Price. 1997. Phylum Mollusca: Class Bivalvia. In: E.N. Kozloff and L. H. Price (eds.), Marine invertebrates of the Pacific Northwest. Univ. Washington Press, Seattle, pp. 258-288.

Lee, S.E., and B. Morton. 1985. The introduction of the Mediterranean mussel *Mytilus galloprovincialis* into Hong Kong. Malacol. Rev. 18:107-109.

Mann, R. 1983. The role of introduced bivalve mollusc species in mariculture. J. World Maricult. Soc. 14:546-559.

McDonald, J.H., and R.K. Koehn 1988. The mussels *Mytilus galloprovincialis* and *M. trossulus* on the Pacific coast of North America. Mar. Biol. 99:111-118.

McMahon, R.F. 1982. The occurrence and spread of the introduced Asiatic freshwater clam, *Corbicula fluminea* (Muller), in North America: 1924-1982. Nautilus 96(4):134-141.

Merriman, E. 1999. Shipping industry kills invasive species bill. Capital Press, Salem Statesman Journal 30, May 21.

Miller, T.W. 1995. First record of the green crab, *Carcinus maenas*, in Humboldt Bay, California. Calif. Fish & Game 82:93-96.

Pimentel, D., L. Lach, R. Zuniga, and D. Morrison. 1999. Environmental and economic costs associated with non-indigenous species in the United States. Bio-Science, Draft copy www.news./cornell.edu/Jan99/species_costs.html.

Rosenthal, H. 1980. Implications of transplantations to aquaculture and ecosystems. Mar. Fish. Rev. 42:1-14.

Saunders, R.G., and W.A. Heath. 1994. New developments of scallop farming in British Columbia. Bull. Aquacult. Assoc. Can. 94-2:3-7.

Seed, R. 1992. Systematics, evolution, and distribution of mussels belonging to the genus *Mytilus*. Am. Malacol. Bull. 9:123-137.

Siddall, S.E. 1980. A clarification of the genus *Perna* (Mytilidae). Bull. Mar. Sci. 30:858-870.

Smith, S.S. 1998. Washington State aquatic nuisance species management plan. Washington Department of Fish and Wildlife, Olympia.

Tebble, N. 1966. British bivalve seashells. Alden Press, Osney Mead.

Thayer, S.A., R.C. Haas, R.D. Hunter, and R.H. Kushler. 1997. Zebra mussel *Dreissena polymorpha* effects on sediment, other zoobenthos, and the diet and growth of adult yellow perch (*Perca flavescens*) in pond enclosures. Can. J. Fish. Aquat. Sci. 54:1903-1915.

Turgeon, D.D., J.F. Quinn, A.E. Bogan, E.V. Coan, F.G. Hochberg, W.G. Lyons, P.M. Mikkelsen, R.J. Neves, C.F.E. Roper, G. Rosenberg, B. Roth, A. Scheltema, F.G. Thompson, M. Vecchione, and J.D. Williams. 1998. Common and scientific names for aquatic invertebrates from the United States and Canada: Mollusks. American Fisheries Society, Special Publication 26.

Urban, H.J., and B. Campos. 1994. Population dynamics of the bivalves *Gari solida*, *Semele solida* and *Protothaca thaca* from a small bay in Chile at 36 degrees S. Mar. Ecol. Prog. Ser. 115:93-102.

Yin, B., Y. Teng, and Y. Jiang. 1994. Studies on transportation and handling of the live *Arca granosa*. Shandong Fisheries/Qilu Yuye 11(2):6-8.

Review of Impacts of Aquatic Exotic Species: What's at Risk?

Paul Heimowitz
Oregon State University Extension Sea Grant, Oregon City, Oregon

Abstract

This paper summarizes the range of negative ecological, human health, and socioeconomic consequences caused by introductions of non-native aquatic species, and discusses examples from invasions by freshwater and marine plants and animals. Uncertainty about the scale, nature, and timing of impacts complicates efforts to predict whether a non-native species introduction will cause problems in a specific location. Therefore, a conservative policy approach should consider all relevant possibilities.

Introduction

Characterizing environmental risk involves analysis of the probability that an event will occur and the extent of any resulting injuries (Davies 1999). Therefore, when evaluating the risk posed by the shipping and marketing of live aquatic products, it is important to look at both potential introduction pathways and the potential effects if a species is introduced outside its native range. While introduction pathways can be analyzed within the limits of how a particular species is handled, it is important to take a comprehensive view of the potential impacts. Infamous last words of "this species can't breed, outcompete, etc. under these conditions" are not uncommon in episodes of non-native species invasions.

Although the biology of a plant or animal may be well understood in its native range, it is impossible to predict with 100% accuracy how that species will behave in a new environment with different stimuli (Ruiz et al. 1997). For example, a crab that typically does not prey on oysters in its native range may become a significant oyster predator at a new location under the right conditions. A species' rate of spread in one location may also be extremely different from how quickly the same species invades another region (Grosholz 1996).

This paper will examine all theoretical impacts of non-native species introductions linked to the marketing and transportation of live aquatic products, not just those that have already been experienced from this pathway. One consequence of the inherent uncertainty in invasion biology is a confusing interplay between references to "non-native" species versus "invasive" or "nuisance" species. Many non-native aquatic organisms, such as Pacific oysters (*Crassostrea gigas*) currently being cultured in the Pacific Northwest, are considered beneficial by the majority of society. In some cases, evidence exists that non-native aquatic plants and animals can benefit certain native species (OTA 1993). The scope of this paper is focused on the potential negative impacts from non-native species introductions, but a truly comprehensive risk assessment also needs to consider positive interactions.

Harmful effects from aquatic invasions can be divided into three main impact categories:

- Ecological
- Human health
- Socioeconomic

As with any classification, these distinctions often blend together, as it is becoming increasingly recognized that ecological effects inevitably mean human health and economic impacts. Therefore, many of the examples used in this paper to illustrate a specific impact can cross into other categories. It is important to keep this overlap and synergy in mind when attempting to gauge the summation of impacts from a particular non-native species introduction.

Ecological Impacts
Habitat alteration

Cumulatively, invasive species present a tremendous risk to ecological health and are cited as a major factor behind the listing of threatened and endangered species in the United States (Wilcove et al. 1998). Among ecological impacts, habitat alteration is a key problem caused by both invasive plants and animals. Because invasive species are difficult to eradicate, these changes are often long-term.

For example, a number of species of the Atlantic cordgrass *Spartina* have been established on the West Coast. *Spartina alterniflora* is one of the most troubling because it grows lower in the intertidal zone of estuaries and is capable of rapidly converting open mudflat habitats into monotypic meadows. Shellfish that require open mudflats, including commercially important species like the Pacific oyster, are displaced. Open mud feeding areas used by shorebirds are also reduced (Daehler and Strong 1996).

An invasive variety of the marine algae *Caulerpa taxifolia* has recently carpeted thousands of acres in the Mediterranean, drastically transforming benthic habitats (Goldschmid 1999). Non-native species can also significantly damage water quality in aquatic habitats. Common carp, *Cyprinus carpio,* are known to destroy vegetation and increase water turbidity and siltation to the detriment of native fish and wildlife (Fuller et al. 1999). Aquatic weed infestations can seriously reduce light penetration in rivers and lakes and, after they die off and decay, cause oxygen levels to plummet. Through food web connections, invasive species can create new opportunities for exposure to contaminants. Asian clams (*Potamocorbula amurensis*) in San Francisco Bay may be leading to harmful accumulation of trace elements like selenium in sturgeon and other bottom feeders (Thompson and Luoma 1999).

Predation

Although obviously not an issue with invasive plants, predation is another serious impact of non-native species introductions. Native prey species may have adapted defense mechanisms while co-evolving with native predators, but they are vulnerable to new predatory "tricks" when an invader arrives.

The European green crab is an example of a generalist predator that has successfully established itself on many foreign coasts. Green crabs consume a variety of prey, including bivalves, gastropods, worms, algae, barnacles, and other crabs. This species has been blamed for dramatic declines in the numbers of soft-shell clams *Mya arenaria* in the northeastern United States, and appears to be a major controlling force in the distribution of certain intertidal organisms (Cohen et al. 1995). Recently arrived to the west coast of North America, green crabs have raised concerns about impacts to native shellfish and commercial aquaculture operations.

At their extreme, predatory impacts from invasive species can lead to disappearance of native species. For example, introduced large-mouth and small-mouth bass have been linked to a number of local native fish and amphibian extirpations in the American Southwest (Fuller et al. 1999). Invasive species can also cause indirect predation effects. Large shells from veined rapa whelks (*Rapana venosa*) recently introduced to Chesapeake Bay have provided an opportunity for local hermit crabs to reach previously unrecorded sizes, potentially increasing their predatory impact on oyster spat (Harding and Mann 1999).

Competition

Invasive species can harm native plants and animals by competing for space, food, or other resources. By taking over large areas of benthic habitat in the Great Lakes, zebra mussels (*Dreissena polymorpha*) have led to significant declines in native mussels and may be affecting spawning success of species like lake trout. Achieving densities greater than 10,000 per square meter, zebra mussels play a major role in filtering phytoplankton from the water column. This can then limit feeding opportunities for zooplankton and other invertebrates. Similar trophic impacts have been experienced in San Francisco Bay due to the filter-feeding dominance of *Potamocorbula amurensis* (Ruiz et al. 1997). Where space, food, or some other critical factor limits the abundance of life within a particular community, the successful expansion of an invasive organism implies that other community members have less competitive advantage and may experience a decline.

Diseases

Another ecological impact from invasive aquatic species is the introduction of new diseases and pathogens to native and commercially valuable species. This has been a very important issue for shrimp aquaculture, where importation of non-native shrimp species has led to outbreaks of viral and bacterial infections. Beyond economic impacts to shrimp growers, these diseases have the potential of affecting native species. For example, in 1998 the Texas Parks and Wildlife Department reported the first occurrence of "white spot" disease in one native shrimp found near aquaculture facilities in Brownsville (Texas Agricultural Extension Service 1998). Citing another example, the Asian tapeworm

Bothriocephalus opsarichthydis was likely introduced to native fish in the United States by grass carp introduced from China (Fuller et al. 1999).

Hybridization

Finally, invasive species can alter ecological communities by hybridizing with natives. This is a less common, but potentially serious, impact. Hybridization can result in a loss of genetic purity and reduced reproduction for native species, which can be particularly serious when threatened or endangered populations are involved. For example, introduced brook trout *Salvelinus fontinalis* are known to hybridize with native bull trout, *Salvelinus confluentus,* and the resulting hybrids are generally sterile (Fuller et al. 1999). Escapes of farmed Atlantic salmon in Puget Sound have raised concerns about potential genetic impacts to Pacific salmon (Volpe 1999, Stenson 1998).

HUMAN HEALTH IMPACTS

In addition to the ecological implications of invasive species as disease agents, impacts to human health are another important issue. Although not directly related to the live aquatic products trade, cholera epidemics provide frightful illustrations of the fact that invasive species can be both invisible to the naked eye and deadly to people. In 1991, an epidemic of cholera hit South America, killing over 10,000 people and infecting over one million during the next 4 years. Although other factors were involved, contaminated ballast water discharged in Latin American ports has been pointed to as a likely source of that water-borne disease (Bright 1998). Studies in Chesapeake Bay have found occurrence of at least one form of the *Vibrio cholerae* bacteria in 100% of sampled ships coming from foreign ports (Rawlings et al. 1999).

Similarly, although human impacts from toxic red tides are not always linked to non-native species, the increased frequency of these events has been linked to global transportation of dinoflagellates and their cysts in ballast water (Hallergraeff and Bolch 1991).

The recent arrival of Chinese mitten crab (*Eriocheir sinensis*) to California has raised fears about human illness directly related to seafood consumption. The Chinese mitten crab has been reported to host the Oriental lung fluke (*Paragonimus westermani*), a flatworm that has infected many people in Asia and causes tuberculosis-like respiratory problems.

The lung fluke and its freshwater snail primary host species have not been detected in the recent California invasion of mitten crab, but potential infection pathways exist (Veldhuizen and Stanish 1999).

SOCIOECONOMIC IMPACTS

Socioeconomic costs go hand-in-hand with losses of natural resources. For example, the European green crab's fondness for shellfish has not only changed intertidal food webs, but also has economically damaged aquaculture operations on the Atlantic and Pacific coasts of North America. This invader has been assigned responsibility for major declines in commercial soft-shell clam production in New England and Canada. Its continuing impacts on commercial and native shellfish in the United States cost an estimated $44 million annually (Lafferty and Kuris 1996).

Extreme efforts to eradicate a non-native species can magnify the scope of impact. Efforts to eliminate infestation of a South African sabellid marine worm plaguing California abalone led to intentional destruction of commercial abalone stock in the 1990s, causing revenue losses that, in some cases, put aquaculture operations out of business (Culver et al. 1997).

Non-native species invasions and control efforts involve significant costs to recreation. Fast-growing, tangled mats of *Hydrilla* have become a major nuisance to anglers, swimmers, and boaters in certain states. Infestations of this aquatic weed in two lakes in Florida alone have cost approximately $10 million per year in recreational losses (Center et al. 1997). Whirling disease, caused by the non-native parasite *Myxobolus cerebralis*, has caused significant disruptions to recreational trout anglers—most recently to prized fisheries in the vicinity of Yellowstone National Park (Whirling Disease Foundation 1999). When invasive species reduce opportunities for viewing native plants and animals, fishing, boating, shellfish gathering, and other recreational activities, these social impacts cause economic ripples in the form of lost tourism dollars to affected communities.

Invasive species also generate substantial costs for control and facility maintenance and repair. Zebra mussels (*Dreissena polymorpha*) provide an infamous example. The ability of the zebra mussel to clog water intake pipes, shut down power plants, and transform freshwater habitats have led to damages and control costs estimated at as high as $5 billion per year (Pimentel et al. 1999). During the

1980s, expenses from similar impacts to nuclear power plants and other facilities caused by the Asian clam *Corbicula fluminea* were calculated at $1 billion annually (OTA 1993). An estimated $100 million is spent each year to manage aquatic weeds, the majority being non-native (OTA 1993). The recent invasion of Chinese mitten crab in California has disrupted commercial shrimp fisheries, increased operation costs of water diversion facilities, and raised concerns about bank and levee damage (Veldhuizen and Stanish 1999).

Finally, although measurement is difficult and a point of controversy, non-native species invasions involve a real cost to certain human aesthetic values. To some, there is a high value to maintaining the look and composition of aquatic ecosystems from one generation to the next. Any artificial changes to these natural areas, such as replacement of a dominant native fish with a non-native fish, damages that "existence" value. Contingent valuation studies, such as determining "willingness to pay" for preventing a non-native introduction, may have a role in future efforts to quantify these impacts (Randall 1987).

Conclusion

The above list represents a range of potential impacts from invasive species introductions. Most will not occur for a given species, and as noted previously, may stack up differently for a given species based on a particular set of environmental conditions. Many of the examples in this paper illustrate more severe consequences, but there are certainly many cases where impacts are less dramatic and, consequently, sometimes studied and reported less, as well.

Severity depends as much on the value assigned to the affected resources as it does on the site-specific behavior and population dynamics of an invader. For example, the economic impact of establishing a European green crab population in a highly invaded and polluted habitat with low commercial shellfish abundance will likely be much smaller than in a habitat rich with native shellfish and supporting commercial aquaculture operations. To further complicate risk characterization, there are often significant lag times between an invasion and the identification of resulting problems. From the Mediterranean fruit fly to many invasive weeds, non-native species may become locally established for decades before their extent and negative impacts reach a scale that attracts attention (Carey 1996). The Asian copepod *Pseudodiaptomus inopinus* has become very abundant in certain northwestern estuaries (Cordell and Morrison 1996). While this animal has certainly caused changes to food web dynamics and other aspects of the ecosystem, it is undetermined whether natural resources are being harmed or will be 20 years from now. The numbers of invasive species like *P. inopinus* with uncertain impacts typically outnumber those that are known to cause harm.

Repeating an earlier point, environmental risk evaluation involves analysis of the likelihood that an event will occur and the degree of any resulting injuries. There are at least some physical science principles that can help estimate the probabilities of failure for methods to contain shipments of live non-native species. But what does one do with all this uncertainty when trying to estimate the damages associated a non-native species invasion? Some ecologists have developed models and statistical rules to help narrow the range of possibilities, but most agree that such predictions are nearly impossible (Ruiz et al. 1997). Ultimately, it becomes a policy question. When reviewing an application to import a new live seafood product, should extreme, worst case possibilities of all applicable ecological, human health, and socioeconomic impacts be taken into account? Or should only documented impacts from the same species in the same geographic region be considered? Past experiences suggest that a conservative approach be followed.

References

Bright, C. 1998. Life out of bounds: Bioinvasion in a borderless world. W.W. Norton, New York

Carey, J.R. 1996. The incipient Mediterranean fruit fly population in California: Implications for invasion biology. Ecology 77:1690-1697.

Center, T.D., J.H. Frank, and F.A. Dray. 1997. Biological Control. In: D. Simberloff et al. (eds.), Strangers in paradise. Island Press, Washington, DC, pp. 245-266.

Cohen, A.N., J.T. Carlton, and M.C. Fountain. 1995. Introduction, dispersal, and potential impacts of the green crab *Carcinus maenas* in San Francisco Bay, California. Marine Biology 122:225-237.

Cordell, J.R., and S.M. Morrison. 1996. The invasive Asian copepod *Pseudodiaptomus inopinus* in Oregon, Washington, and British Columbia estuaries. Estuaries 19:629-638.

Culver, C.S., A.M. Kuris, and B. Beede. 1997. Identification and management of the exotic sabellid pest in California cultured abalone. California Sea Grant Publication T-041, La Jolla.

Daehler, C.C., and D.R. Strong. 1996. Status, prediction, and prevention of introduced cordgrass *Spartina* spp. invasions in Pacific estuaries, USA. Biol. Conserv. 78:51-58.

Davies, J.C. (ed.). 1999. Comparative risk analysis in the 1990's. In: Comparing environmental risks: Tools for setting government priorities. Resources for the Future, Washington, DC, pp. 4-19.

Fuller, P.L., L.G. Nico, and J.D. Williams. 1999. Non-indigenous fishes introduced into inland waters of the United States. American Fisheries Society Special Publication 27, Bethesda, MD.

Goldschmid, A. 1999. Essay about *Caulerpa taxifolia*. In: Marine biology I. Colloquial Meeting of Marine Biology I, Salzburg, May 6, 1999. University of Salzburg. http://www.sbg.ac.at/ipk/avstudio/pierofun/ct/caulerpa.htm.

Grosholz, E.D. 1996. Contrasting rates of spread for introduced species in terrestrial and marine systems. Ecology 77:1680-1686.

Haellegraeff, G.M., and C.J. Bolch. 1991. Transport of toxic dinoflagellate cysts via ships' ballast water. Mar. Pollut. Bull. 22:27-30.

Harding, J.M., and R. Mann. 1999. Habitat and prey preferences of veined rapa whelks (*Rapana venosa*) in the Chesapeake Bay: Direct and indirect trophic consequences. In: First National Conference on Marine Bioinvasions, Abstracts, January 24-27, 1999. Massachusetts Institute of Technology Sea Grant, Cambridge, MA.

Lafferty, K.D., and A.M. Kuris. 1996. Biological control of marine pests. Ecology 77:1989-2000.

OTA. 1993. Harmful non-indigenous species in the United States. Office of Technology Assessment, U.S. Congress, OTA-F-565, U.S. Government Printing Office, Washington, DC.

Pimentel, D., L. Lach, R. Zuniga, and D. Morrison. 1999. Environmental and economic costs associated with non-indigenous species in the United States. Cornell University, June 12 report. http:/www.news.cornell.edu/ releases/Jan99/ species_costs.html.

Randall, A. 1987. Resource economics: An economic approach to natural resource and environmental policy. John Wiley & Son, New York.

Rawlings, T.K., G.M. Ruiz, S. Schoenfeld, F.C. Dobbs, L.A. Drake, A. Huq, and R.R. Colwell. 1999. Ecology and ballast-mediated transfer of *Vibrio cholerae* O1 and O139. In: First National Conference on Marine Bioinvasions, Abstracts, January 24-27, 1999. Massachusetts Institute of Technology Sea Grant, Cambridge, MA.

Ruiz, G.M., J.T. Carlton, E.D. Grosholz, and A.H. Hines. 1997. Global invasions of marine and estuarine habitats by non-indigenous species: Mechanisms, extent, and consequences. Am. Zool. 37:621-632

Stenson, B. 1998. Net pen pollution threats get full hearing. In: Sound and Straits Newsletter, February. People for Puget Sound, Seattle, WA.

Texas Agricultural Extension Service. 1998. Exotic disease found in wild shrimp near Brownsville. Calhoun County Marine Advisory Newsletter, 5/98, Port Lavaca, TX.

Thompson, J., and S. Luoma. 1999. Food web and contaminant flow effects of an exotic bivalve in San Francisco Bay, California. In: First National Conference on Marine Bioinvasions, Abstracts, January 24-27, 1999. Massachusetts Institute of Technology Sea Grant, Cambridge, MA.

Veldhuizen, T.C., and S. Stanish. 1999. Overview of the life history, abundance, and impacts of the Chinese mitten crab, *Eriocheir sinensis*. California Department of Water Resources, Sacramento.

Volpe, J.P. 1999. Atlantic salmon (*Salmo salar*) in British Columbia and the biology of invasion. In: First National Conference on Marine Bioinvasions, Abstracts, January 24-27, 1999. Massachusetts Institute of Technology Sea Grant, Cambridge, MA.

Whirling Disease Foundation. 1999. Whirling disease found in Yellowstone National Park. Whirling Disease Foundation, Bozeman, MT. http://www.whirlingdisease.org/whirling/ynp.html.

Wilcove, D.S., D. Rothstein, J. Dubow, A. Phillips, and E. Losos. 1998. Quantifying threats to imperiled species in the United States. BioScience 48(8):607-615.

Impact of the Green Crab on the Washington State Shellfish Aquaculture Industry

Charlie Stephens
Kamilche Sea Farms, Shelton, Washington

Introduction

I operate a small shellfish farm on Totten Inlet in Puget Sound, Washington, and have been an active member in the Pacific Coast Shellfish Growers Association. The association has about 120 members in Washington, Oregon, California, Alaska, and British Columbia. This report provides information on exotic species, specifically one exotic species that is threatening the Washington shellfish industry—the green crab. I will provide some information about how our industry has dealt with the problem of the green crab as it has reared its ugly head along the West Coast.

Green crab and other exotics

The green crab has made its way around the world from its original home in Western Europe at least in part through human mediated pathways. This is not something that has just happened by natural means—humans have facilitated the movement of the green crab by transmitting it unwittingly. It is now present in South Africa, the East Coast of the United States, and along the West Coast of the United States where it was first sighted in 1989 in San Francisco Bay.

Since that time, the green crab made its way northward and is now pretty well established in most of the coastal embayments in California including northern California, Oregon, and Washington. A few years ago, it was noted in Washington's Willapa Bay. It now appears that the green crab is here to stay, although it is too early to say for sure.

Willapa Bay is a very important oyster growing region in Washington. Washington is the second most important oyster producing state in the United States. Consequently, many millions of dollars of cultured shellfish product in Willapa Bay are at risk due to the spread of this invasive crab species.

As far as we know, the shellfish industry is not responsible for the transmission of this species up the West Coast over the last few years. I think that most evidence points to the fact that the green crab has been spreading on its own. The green crab is able to reproduce and possibly its larval stages are spread by ocean currents. Fortunately, our industry cannot be fingered for that.

However, it is true that the activities of molluskan shellfish growers are a potential vector for the spread of this crab. There are plenty of examples from the past where those involved with oyster and shellfish culture have been guilty of accidental introductions. Probably the best example of this type of introduction is the oyster drill. The drill is a small gastropod that came over from Japan in shipments of Pacific oyster seed. These were brought over to the West Coast in great quantities. The drill has become firmly established in many bays in Puget Sound and has become a real pest. Many oyster growers expend a great amount of energy and money dealing with this species. Another introduction into this region was the Manila clam which was an accidental but, fortunately, has proved to be a more beneficial hitchhiker.

Members of the shellfish industry must adhere to some basic strategies to make sure that we are not the actual vectors facilitating the movement of these exotic species. We do not want to witness the green crab become the same sort of problem as is currently present with the oyster drill.

Preventing the spread of the green crab

Regional shellfish growers have taken steps to comply with regulations developed to prevent the spread of the green crab. These steps pertain to the shipment of seed oysters, clams, mussels, and geoduck, and to the shipping of mature product or shell stock. This is a difficult task because there are many shipments of both seed and shell stock oysters and other shellfish, up and down our coast between California, Oregon, Washington, and British Columbia. Movements to Alaska are not as pronounced.

The regulations are currently not being applied to the shipment of finished market-ready product from the grower to the retailer and to the ultimate consumer. This terminal portion of the market chain is not considered to be a realistic potential channel for the transmission of green crab. In the case of shipments of live finfish in tanks, this may become an issue.

The main prevention measure required for immature shellfish is a chemical dip of all seed shipped from green crab infested areas to growing areas, particularly those located in Washington that are currently free of green crab. This treatment involves a chlorine dip typically for one hour. Visual inspections, record keeping, and reporting activities are also required by regulation. As can be imagined, this adds considerably to the cost of seed shellfish.

The handling of shell stock involves equally stringent requirements. Growers have been required to install systems that completely separate shell stock originating from infected areas from shell stock that is grown and harvested from non-infected areas. The key requirement is the total separation of those two systems—cross-contamination does not occur.

For example, when oysters are harvested and moved from Humboldt Bay, which is now considered a green crab area, to Willapa Bay or to Puget Sound, they first have to be thoroughly washed at the harvest site. After the oysters are transported and unloaded at processing plants in the Puget Sound or Willapa Bay areas, the trucks used for the haul are pressure-washed and chemically treated, typically with a chlorine solution. All of the loading docks and tub containers have to be kept separate from other equipment. Even forklifts that are used for the movement of product from green crab infected areas have to be kept completely separate from the equipment that is designated for noninfected areas. This is also true for processing areas and storage facilities, such as the coolers.

In processing operations, the shucking line must be run completely separate from other product so that there can be no chance of product co-mingling at any step along the way. In actual practice, the processors often designate certain days of the week when they will shuck only product from areas that require these additional regulations.

This list of precautions continues after the product is shucked, processed, and packaged. Afterward, the plant has to be thoroughly cleaned of all shell and debris from raw product that originated from the infected areas. This debris must be collected and stored in a separate upland site so there is no chance of co-mingling. This also includes the wash material. Large volumes of fresh water are used in the washing of plants involved with the handling of shell stock and finished product. All of this washdown debris has to be channeled into a separate drain system and disposed of separately on an upland site. Finally, the floor drains need to be chemically treated following the completion of processing.

In addition to all of the above, a number of inspections and reports have to be done on a daily basis. These requirements include performing visual inspections, filling in charts, and reporting to the agencies involved with preventing the further spread of this animal. Also, the precautions that I have mentioned apply for any site. If an oyster shucking plant is located on the water, for example, right on a bay, the operator must comply with even stricter requirements. These stricter requirements include having screens on the floor drains where any wash water is going to flow. The facility operator also must have shields or fencing around the plant so that there is no chance of a renegade green crab making a desperate dash for open water.

Here is another example of how strict these containment strategies have become. The conveyor systems that bring product into the plants are typically open. However, when product is brought from Humboldt Bay or other green crab infected areas, those conveyors have to be completely enclosed. Green crabs are very wily and have good survival instincts. Empty shell leaving the plant following processing needs to go through a blast heat tunnel, so that it is effectively sterilized once it leaves the plant. That shell must also be disposed of in a separate upland site.

As you might expect, all of these additional steps add significantly to the cost of the product. There are not only additional capital costs associated with the physical facilities to meet these requirements, but also increased daily operational costs because many of the precautions are behavior and management items.

Although my company is not directly affected by these kinds of regulations and costs, I have talked to a number of my fellow shellfish growers to get an idea what the total dollar amount is when it comes to complying with these new regulations. I have come up with a very rough calculation from these interviews. Capital costs for these additions amount to about $75,000 at this point for our industry coastwide. The operating cost escalation is even more important—amounting to about $185,000 over the last couple of years. The capital costs are one-time costs, but the operating costs are going to go on for the foreseeable future.

Conclusion

The main message that I would like to give is that, although no one likes to have to deal with yet another regulation, members of the industry feel that these precautions are practical and that they are things we can live with. We have complied with the required regulations and feel that a good working relationship has been established with the agencies. Quite a bit of trust has been built, which is necessary for any regulation to be effective.

Effective compliance with these regulations will earn the industry two big payoffs.

1. We have a great deal of confidence that the shellfish industry is not contributing to the problem. If green crab are discovered somewhere in Puget Sound tomorrow, we have a great deal of confidence that it will not be our industry found responsible for the spread.
2. Perhaps even more important, we hope that an environmentally conscious public will perceive the shellfish industry as good stewards of a common natural resource. That is no small thing when we are marketing something to the general public.

Questions from the Audience

QUESTION: Are the oysters produced in potentially affected areas selling in the marketplace at reduced prices? The second part of the question is, the shellfish tags which accompany the product to the marketplace, do they denote that they are coming out of potentially infested waters?

C. STEPHENS: I do not know the answer to the first question. The second question is a good one. It makes me think that maybe we should pick up on it as a marketing advantage. All of our product has to be properly tagged anyway with warning labels and the whole nine yards. It might be to our advantage to put on those tags, "This product is guaranteed to be harvested and grown in a green crab-free area."

QUESTION: You mentioned the costs to your industry of avoiding the spread the green crab into new areas. What about in California where the green crab are already present? Are green crabs negatively affecting the California oyster industry?

C. STEPHENS: Yes, they are to some extent. However, the shellfish culturing activity in this particular region, for example, in Tomales Bay, is not nearly as extensive as it is in Oregon and Washington. So there is not the opportunity for the great economic loss of the type we would have here in Washington and Oregon.

But there has been predation by green crab on mostly young Pacific oysters that are grown in what we call rack-and-bag culture. Actually, it is now believed that rack-and-bag culture, although it is a great way to grow oysters, might also be the perfect environment for growing green crab. They can crawl into the bags, which are made of quarter- to half-inch mesh, at a small growth stage and then eat their way to nirvana. Nothing else can get at them while they are in the bags.

QUESTION: What is the extent of financial losses in the rack-and-bag operations?

C. STEPHENS: Just the last few years people have been seeing some economic impacts to their oysters in bags. I do not know the actual extent of these losses.

QUESTION: What would be the advantage of tagging your oysters as coming from a certified green crab-free area? It seems to me that this would convey no advantage in terms of product quality. However, it would put at a commercial disadvantage those people who do have green crab, not through any malpractice on their part but through random misfortune. It seems to me that there are no safety issues involved. There may be some environmental issues, but if your oysters are clean and properly washed, there is no reason why you would need to red flag them as green crab impacted. The only thing I can see in this tagging idea is that it would create concerns in those areas that happen to be affected by green crabs.

C. STEPHENS: Yes indeed. I think that comment was a little bit ill-advised on my part. I am affected by the fact that shellfish growers are currently painted as being bad guys in many ways. We are always looking for ways to promote ourselves as the good guys.

QUESTION: I am not convinced that it is, in fact, an ill-advised comment. You could relate this to the voluntary declaration systems that are in place and are used by some shellfish growers or suppliers. They receive added value because the marketplace perceives that there is added value to the product because it has been "declared" as basically being clean of some problem.

In the same light, you could potentially project this idea and say that these oysters are clean and parasite free, and, as a consequence, obtain value added in the marketplace. This would, in fact, promote the line of thinking in the customer base that follows the line, "If that's clean, what have I been eating this whole time?" I am sorry that this comment is necessary. It is all part of competition and as seafood suppliers, we should try to present the best seafood to the public.

C. STEPHENS: Right—there are many aspects to it.

QUESTION: Are there any signs of the green crab in British Columbia?

HEIMOWITZ: The green crab has already leapfrogged into the southern Vancouver Island area, probably by the larval dispersal with ocean currents. Those currents eventually come into Puget Sound and Strait of Georgia area, as well.

C. STEPHENS: It is not a forgone conclusion that, because we have green crab in our waters, our whole industry is suddenly going to collapse. We can take many steps.

ANITA COOK: I work with Washington State Fish and Wildlife. I am the Puget Sound coordinator for green crab monitoring. One comment I need to make is that we are not sure yet what is going to happen with this animal. Unusual events may be occurring in these impacted areas and no one knows what is required to develop established populations. At least in Washington, we are trying to monitor the problem and to keep the green population "pool" at the lowest possible size to discourage further green crab extensions. It appears that the green crab grows very rapidly, so they may also have a shorter life span. If you do not have one of these unusual ocean climate events during the periods when the adult green crab are present, then maybe they will not be able to continue their range extension.

Also worth noting here is the apparent fact that there was a sighting back in 1961 of green crab in Willapa Bay. This sighting is documented in Ricketts and Calvin [*Between Pacific Tides,* Fourth Edition, page 379]. This is a dependable sighting although we have not been able to gain further information—how many were present and so on. It is obvious that green crabs were present in Willapa Bay and disappeared later. Also, the red rock crab is capable of beating up on the green crab.

C. STEPHENS: In areas where the red rock crab and the green crab co-occur in California, the red rock crab is our best ally. It is hard for a shellfish grower to admit that the red rock crab can be an ally, but it really can be.

QUESTION: In my work, I found that other bivalves are much more at risk from green crab predation than oysters. I am wondering if oyster growers are essentially taking responsibility for all the other shellfish industries or is it more of a cooperative effort?

C. STEPHENS: I am not sure if I can speak for everyone, but I think most shellfish growers see molluskan shellfish—oysters, clams, mussels, and geoducks—as one industry.

QUESTION: Are all of these practices you are talking about used shellfish-industry-wide and not just for oysters?

C. STEPHENS: Yes. In fact, the permits that the State Department of Fish and Wildlife sign with individual companies are not specifically for oysters. These same practices also have to occur with clams, mussels, and geoducks. Right now the oyster is the main product that is being shipped north and south.

A New Direction for Monitoring Lobster Meat Yield, Using Advances in Acoustic Probing

R.J. Cawthorn and A. Battison
Atlantic Veterinary College, University of Prince Edward Island, Charlottetown, Prince Edward Island, Canada

J. Guigné, K. Klein, and Q. Liu
Guigné International Limited, Paradise, Newfoundland, Canada

A. MacKenzie, R. MacMillan, and D. Rainnie
Atlantic Veterinary College, University of Prince Edward Island, Charlottetown, Prince Edward Island, Canada

Introduction

The development of a seafood ultrasonic probe represents the integration of the principles of veterinary medicine with Smart Acoustics™ technology. The health approach was developed by the Lobster Science Centre, Atlantic Veterinary College, and the acoustics innovations were provided by Guigné International Limited (GIL). The purpose of the probe, initially developed for use with the American lobster *Homarus americanus*, is to determine lobster meat yields and lobster health on an instantaneous basis with a non-invasive acoustic approach.

Background to the Development of an Ultrasonic Probe

The genesis of the Lobster Ultrasonic (LU) Probe (patent pending) was twofold:

1. Researchers at the Atlantic Veterinary College were conducting nutritional research on lobster diets and needed an accurate, rapid method of determining meat yields.

2. Similarly, food scientists at the Prince Edward Island Food Technology Centre needed to determine meat yields for value-added processing in the lobster industry.

In addition, Clearwater Fine Foods Inc. (CFFI) of Bedford, Nova Scotia, one of the world's largest shippers of live lobsters, was interested in the potential of the ultrasonic lobster probe to aid handling and market decisions.

Initial funding for the "proof-of-concept" study was provided to GIL by the Industrial Research Assistance Program (National Research Council of Canada). Additional developement funds were provided by CFFI.

In Canada, annual landings of lobster total about 38,000 metric tons, with a landed value of CAN $420 million in 1998 (Fisheries and Oceans Canada). In the United States, the annual landings are about 28,000 metric tons. The economic impact of this traditional fishery is highly significant to the fishing communities of eastern North America.

The Atlantic Veterinary College has an excellent Aquatic Animal Facility, which facilitates research on crustaceans in a highly controlled environment. However, determining the health of marine species, especially crustaceans, can be difficult. The primary reason we focus on lobster health is that 10-15% of the value of the lobster is lost, for various reasons, after the lobster is trapped. Many infectious and non-infectious stressors affect lobster health. The triad of host-parasite-environment changes significantly *after* lobsters are caught. Recent losses in the Long Island Sound lobster fishery demonstrate the need for a crustacean health monitoring program. We anticipate that the LU Probe can be used by various sectors of the lobster fishery, including fishers, buyers, biologists, processors, exporters, and veterinarians, to develop a Lobster Health Surveillance Program.

DESCRIPTION OF THE ACOUSTIC PROBE

During development of the LU Probe, we noted that a lobster is composed of two different acoustic media —fluid (i.e., hemolymph) and solid (i.e., muscle = meat). The proportions of these vary, depending on the physiological status of the lobster. Several acoustic parameters were examined during the course of this research: attenuation, frequency, location, reproducibility, and velocity. We have determined that certain points on the crusher claws (Fig. 1) provide a highly reproducible signal for determining meat yields.

Our study included detailed dissections to determine the locations of internal structures (i.e., apodemes) (Fig. 2). We determined several biological and health parameters for each lobster: carapace length, sex, weight, hemocyte counts (two methods), differential hemocyte count, osmolality of hemolymph, hemolymph protein (two methods), and prophenoloxidase levels. Overall we accepted the null hypotheses that higher meat content in lobsters

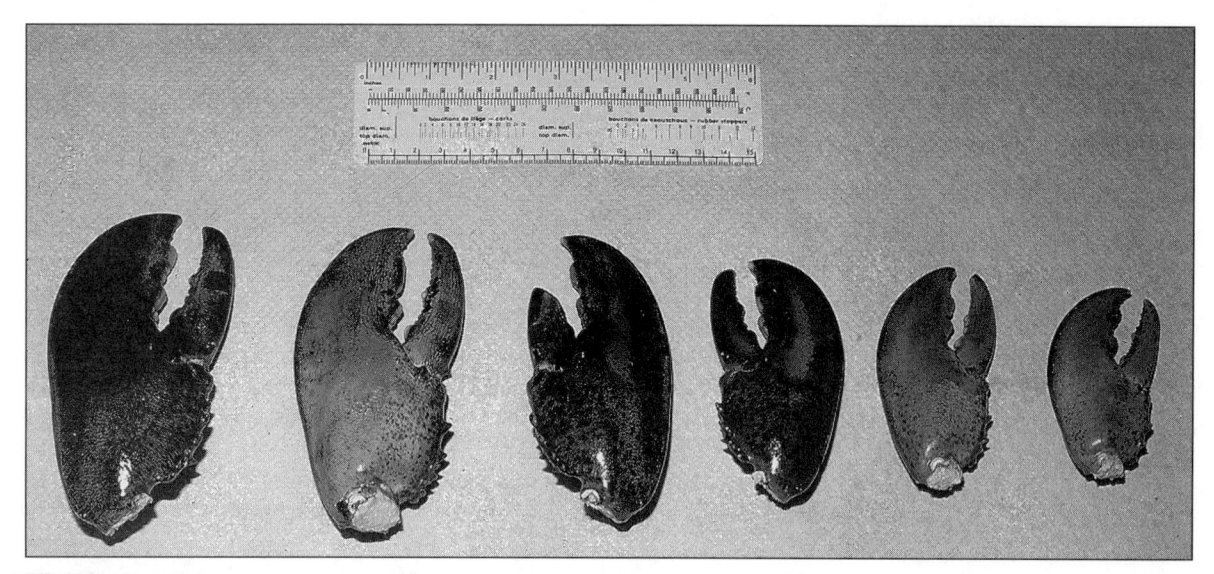

Figure 1. Range of lobster crusher claws used to determine optimum location of transducers for the LU Probe.

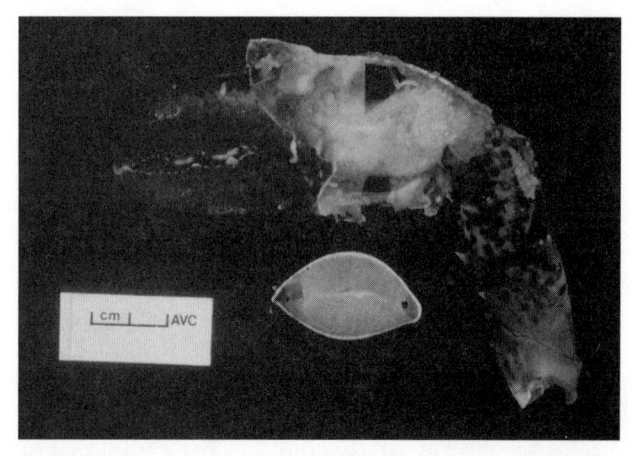

Figure 2. Dissection of lobster crusher claw to demonstrate location of apodeme. Arrow in (upper) claw points to white apodeme; in (lower) cross section, apodeme is the white horizontal structure.

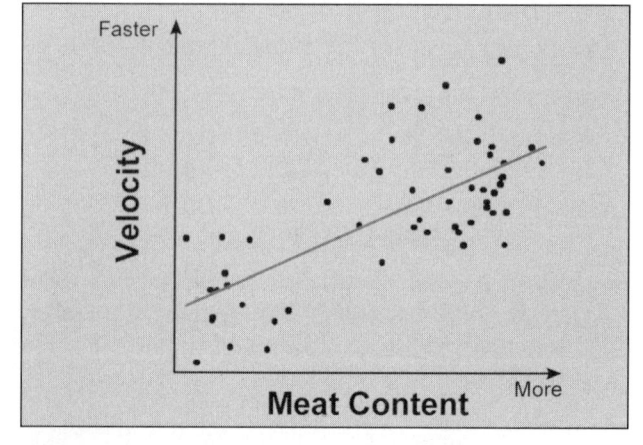

Figure 3. An example of an acoustic result, showing that velocity increases with increasing meat yield in the crusher claw of a lobster.

results in faster sound speeds (Fig. 3) and that higher meat yield results in more acoustic energy loss.

We now have a high degree of precision (accuracy) in determining meat yield in lobsters. The LU Probe system presently consists of a handheld measurement probe with signal generation and processing unit. Our prototype LU Probe test bed functioned very well (Figs. 4, 5).

The ultrasonic coupling gel facilitates acoustic transmission and reception and fills any gap between the flat face of the transducer and the curved shell of the lobster. The gel is water soluble and nontoxic.

Note that we have "ground-truthed" the acoustic signals by developing a freeze-drying methodology

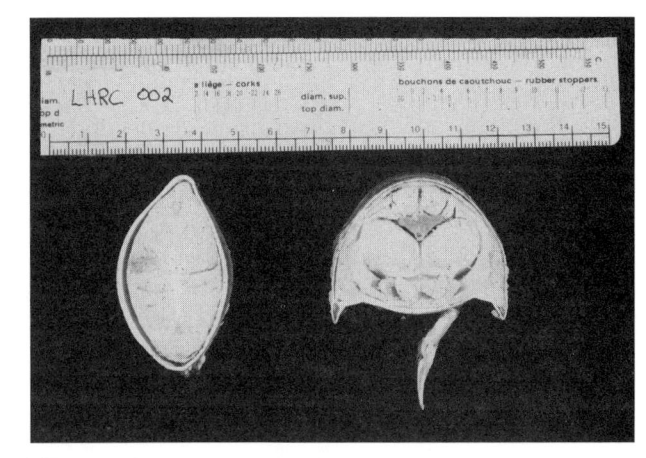

Figure 6. Freeze-dried lobster "I." Fully meated, hard shell lobster. High meat yield.

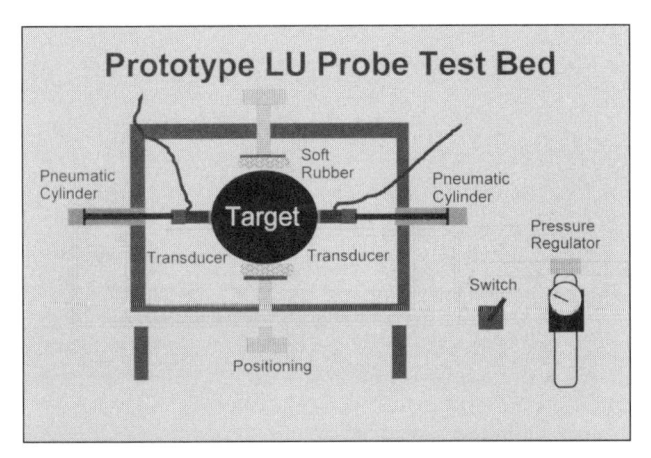

Figure 4. Prototype LU Probe test bed. Pneumatic cylinders, with use of pressure regulator, hold lobster in place.

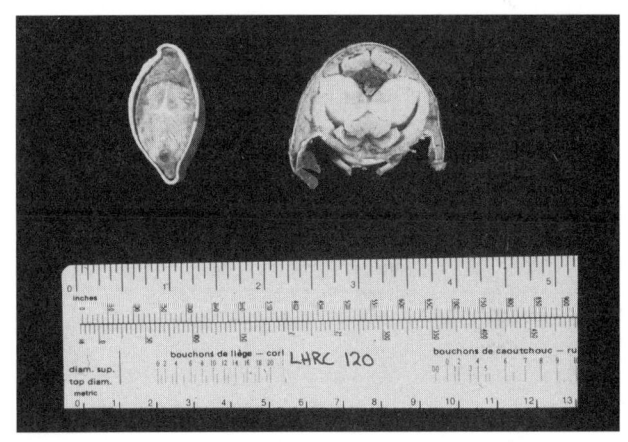

Figure 7. Freeze-dried lobster "II." Poorly meated, not quite hard shell lobster. Medium meat yield.

Figure 5. Live lobster in LU Probe test bed. Signal generation and processing unit is at the right side of the figure.

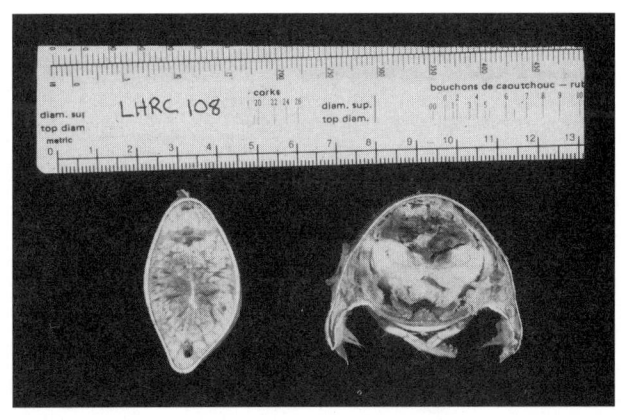

Figure 8. Freeze-dried lobster "III." Very poorly meated, soft shell lobster. Low meat yield.

(manuscript in preparation) to determine meat yield in lobsters (Figs. 6, 7, 8). Consequently there is complete integration between the acoustic approach and the health approach to determining meat yields.

Conclusion

We now recognize that there are correlations between acoustic signals and some health parameters, i.e., total hemolymph protein. We anticipate that we can develop a new paradigm of lobster health utilizing Smart Acoustics™ technology. Further applications include determining meat yield and health status of other species of lobsters, crabs, and shrimps. Perhaps we can use a similar acoustic innovation to determine the health status of various bivalves or the size of pearls in the cultured pearl oyster industry.

In summary, the LU Probe provides a cost-effective, instantaneous, noninvasive tool to determine meat yields in live lobsters. Eventually the LU Probe should be able to determine lobster health in a similar manner.

Using HACCP Principles and Physiological Studies to Improve Marketing Practices for Live Crustaceans

S. Gomez-Jimenez
Centro de Investigacion en Alimentacion y Desarrollo (CIAD), Hermosillo, Mexico

R.F. Uglow
University of Hull, Hull, U.K.

R. Pacheco-Aguilar
Centro de Investigacion en Alimentacion y Desarrollo (CIAD), Hermosillo, Mexico

L.O. Noriega-Orozco
CIAD-Guaymas Unit, Guaymas, Mexico

Abstract

When aquatic animals are removed from their natural environment they show a series of compensatory responses up to a point designated CL—the critical limit. Beyond this point there are pathological changes leading to overt disease or intrinsic quality loss. Many of the practices and methods used commonly throughout the shellfish live trade, worldwide, may impose serious stresses that, collectively, impair the animals' physiological compensatory responses.

The Hazard Analysis Critical Control Point (HACCP) system, widely used in the food industry, is shown to be an effective means of assuring consistently high product quality. HACCP involves identifying aspects of holding and distribution systems that are potentially harmful to the animals (as identified by their physiological performances) and then providing alternative procedures. Such a scheme offers obvious advantages over traditional quality control systems, based on visual inspections of product that may have deteriorated, i.e., prevention is better than cure.

Here, we give the results of a series of physiological studies on the responses of the spiny lobster, *Panulirus interruptus*, to several of the most common stressors it may encounter during its live marketing. The application of HACCP procedures to a particular case study where handling steps taking place between the point of capture and throughout the marketing chain is examined. Attention is drawn to those aspects of the chain of handling steps that were considered potentially harmful and to the establishment of the animals' tolerance limits to them.

Introduction

The HACCP (Hazard Analysis and Critical Control Point) methodology, was developed in the 1960s jointly by the Pillsbury Company and the U.S. Space Program (Leaper 1997). A high level of testing was implemented by the company to ensure that the food produced for the astronauts was safe. As this could not be achieved by finished product testing alone, the HACCP concept was initiated. HACCP is derived from "Failure Mode and Effect Analysis," an engineering system that looks at a product and all its components and manufacturing stages, and asks "What can go wrong within the total system?"

According to Huss (1993), traditional food quality control has been microbiological in nature and based on three principles:

1. Education and training.
2. Inspection of facilities and operations.
3. Microbiological testing.

He notes that these programs were aimed at improving the understanding of the causes and effects of microbial contamination in order to improve handling and ensure compliance with prescribed standards and procedures. In addition, there was a heavy reliance on post-process testing to determine if the process was in compliance with established criteria. Thus, this system was essentially a reactive one, with problems being discovered only after they had already occurred.

HACCP, by contrast, recognizes the fact that quality cannot be "inspected" into the product. Rather, the HACCP system attempts to analyze the particular product or process, to identify and quantify the potential hazards, and to take steps to ensure that the likelihood of their occurrence is reduced or eliminated and to document the whole process. Mortimore and Wallace (1994) summarize the HACCP process as follows:

1. Look at your process/product from start to finish.
2. Decide where hazards could occur.
3. Put in controls and monitor them.
4. Write it all down and keep records.
5. Ensure that it continues to work effectively.

The HACCP concept was first applied to low acidity canning products (Huss 1993). Since then, many governments have laid down new HACCP-based standards for the production and marketing of fishery products. Although the HACCP system was originally designed for use in food safety and has traditionally been used in this area, the HACCP principles are also applicable to other non-food goods (Mortimore and Wallace 1994).

The decision to apply the HACCP principles to live marketing procedures involving aquatic animals is due to the high mortalities that this specialized trade has been experiencing and the loss of intrinsic quality of the animals upon delivery to the marketplace. These events have caused great economic losses to some fisheries (Uglow et al. 1986, MacMullen 1986). It must be noted that reliable information from individual companies concerning mortality rates of species traditionally marketed in live form is difficult to obtain. However, a few available reports exist describing the high mortalities recorded during the live marketing of crustaceans including *Necora puber*, *Cancer pagurus*, and *Carcinus maenas* (Whyman et al. 1985, MacMullen 1986, Uglow et al. 1986, Hosie 1993).

The aim of the present study is to apply HACCP principles to a segment of the live marketing chain of the spiny lobster, *Panulirus interruptus*, in order to identify those steps that are critical to the quality and survival of the animals.

MATERIAL AND METHODS

There are 26 lobster fishing cooperatives in the Baja California, Mexico, currently catching the resource (Fig. 1). The entire marketing chain is very long and quite complex because each cooperative is free to sell its live product to any buyer, using either their own or the buyer's live holding and shipping system. To follow this complete chain from point of capture to final destination (Asian markets in most cases), and/or to follow each of the 26 marketing chains from these cooperatives, is beyond the scope of this study.

A cooperative located in Bahia Magdalena accepted an invitation to participate in this preliminary HACCP application study. A five-day visit was made to Bahia Magdalena (Magdalena Island) in January 1997. Also, a questionnaire was developed to collect information from fishermen and administrative managers of the lobster fishing cooperatives.

The seven principles of HACCP methodology can be expanded into fourteen basic steps (Campden Food and Drink Research Association 1992). Because of the core importance of these steps in the HACCP methodology, they will be described below with modifications to allow for applications involving live animals and their physiological responses to the identified handling procedures.

Step 1. Terms of reference

This first step in HACCP analysis provides the framework for the rest of the process. It outlines the scope of the plan and ensures that top management is firmly committed to the process. It allows those involved in the process, production, and line management, for example, to be informed and to gain their support, as this is crucial to the successful implementation of the HACCP plan. The relevant product or process is outlined here, as well as the hazard category.

Step 2. HACCP team selection

Kirby (1994) recommends that a multidisciplinary team be drawn up, incorporating management, quality assurance, and the production personnel involved in the particular process under consideration. This

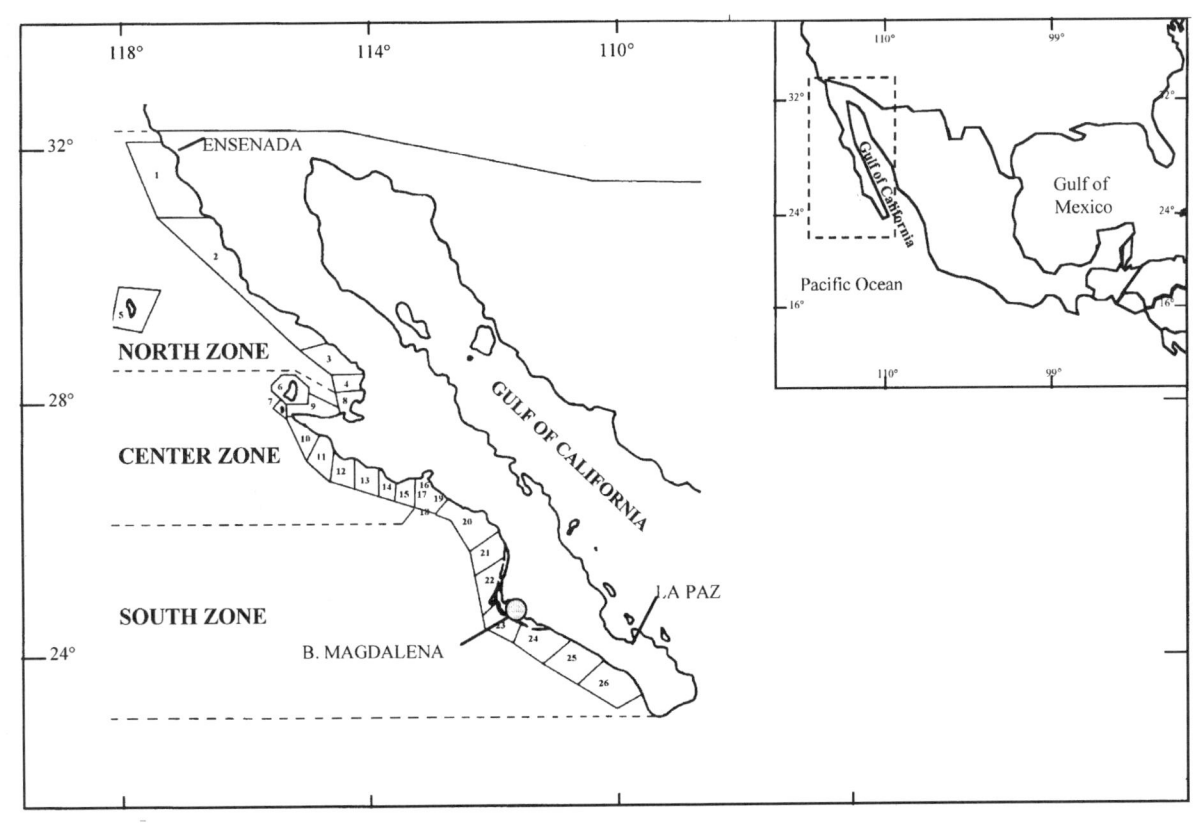

Figure 1. Cooperative fishing areas. The circle symbol shows where the study was performed.

is necessary as the support of all involved is crucial for the successful implementation of the system. In addition, a range of knowledge and skills is needed to develop a HACCP plan. It is important that the required resources, such as reference materials that affect the quality and mortality of the product, are available to the team. Access to field conditions and/or live-holding facilities is also important.

Step 3. Product description

At this stage, product composition, structure, method of handling, holding methods, and transporting conditions are described. This will be important when determining what hazards are involved and their severity. This exercise puts a clear picture of the product in the minds of the team and allows them to focus on the various activities involved in the process.

Step 4. End-use identification

This step allows the product to be categorized according to its associated risks category, when the main user and the handling methods are identified.

Step 5. Process flow diagram

The preparation of a process flow diagram, outlining all the steps that are involved in the particular process, is essential. This requires a degree of understanding and familiarity with the entire operation, and generally involves the production personnel. The process flow diagram serves to focus the study on the process and clearly shows all the relevant activities, including delays, as well as indicating the various process specifications, equipment, and materials.

Step 6. Verification on site

Once the process flow chart has been elaborated, its accuracy must be verified "on site." Any deviations should be noted and the necessary changes made to the diagram. The team should then confirm that the amended chart now accurately depicts the process. Records of the changes should be made.

Step 7. Listing of hazards and relevant control measures

This step involves the identification of all the conditions, connected to the process or product, that pose a threat to the intrinsic quality and mortality of the animal. Identification and rating as a potential hazard, or not, is done according to the likelihood of the occurrence of a hazard and the severity of its effect. This is done for every step of the process. Those hazards that are rated sufficiently likely to occur, and of sufficient severity, are then listed and the possible control measures are established.

Step 8: CCP determination

Once the various physiological, immunological, and other hazards have been identified and rated, their Critical Control Points can be determined using the CCP "decision tree" (Fig. 2).

Step 9: Establishment of critical limits (CL) for each CCP

A target level for each hazard that has been identified should be set. This level will be set in the minimum or maximum values that can be safely reached without causing loss of intrinsic quality or the death of the animal. Such limits may be a specified maximum or minimum temperature or a minimum recovery time after emersion. Other limit levels, such as maximum ambient ammonia in the holding tanks and maximum and minimum salinities, can also be set.

Step 10: Monitoring

Monitoring is critical, as it could mean the difference between an effective or failing program. Monitoring allows the process managers to determine if there is a loss of control or the potential for one, depending on how stable the observed values are relative to the CL. Thus corrective action can be taken before complete loss of control occurs. At this step it is necessary to establish when and how the monitoring will be done, and who will do it.

Step 11: Corrective action procedures

When the monitoring activities indicate noncompliance with the target levels, steps have to be taken to intervene and correct the problem. An action plan for this activity should be drawn up, indicating:

1. Actions to be taken immediately, who should be informed, and in what manner.

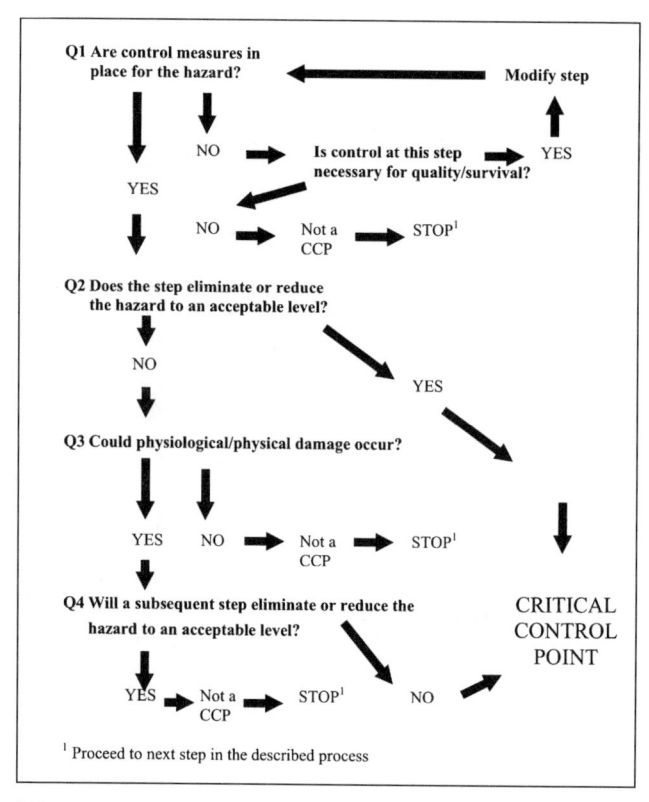

Figure 2. CCP decision tree. Answer the questions in sequence at each step for the identified hazard.

2. What will be done with the weak/dead animal.
3. Which steps will be taken to determine the source of the problem, in order to prevent a recurrence. (The emphasis here is on prevention—the key concept of HACCP.)
4. Who is responsible for making the relevant decisions.

Step 12: Verification procedures

This is to ensure that the system is working as intended. The verification procedures consist of checking that all the CCP are monitored and that all the data recorded are under the critical limits established. It is also important to include validation of the HACCP plan as part of the verification procedures.

Step 13: Documentation and record keeping

It is essential that all above activities and relevant collected data are properly documented. These records allow the management staff to spot and correct undesirable trends or patterns that may be vital to ensuring product quality and survival.

Step 14: Review of the HACCP plan

A periodic review of the HACCP plan may become necessary for a number of reasons.

1. Problems or complaints about the product.
2. Intrinsic quality or mortality risk related to the species.
3. New information on hazards or risks.

Thus the need for periodic review is clear, as this allows HACCP to be proactive in the management and control of the various hazards associated with the live marketing of crustaceans.

RESULTS

With this preliminary HACCP application, it was not possible for our team to complete all 14 steps of the HACCP methodology. Some of these steps are missing because their application at this stage was unrealistic because of the distances of the journeys involved and other logistical considerations.

The following results summarize this preliminary HACCP application dealing with the live marketing of crustaceans:

Application of step 1 (Terms of reference)

Although this step was carried out with some initial involvement of the management of the cooperative, it did not involve the fishermen in any great detail. Sporadically, some of these harvesters showed interest, but there was a noticeable lack of communication about this HACCP project between the two parties. In order for a HACCP program to be successful, it is necessary to develop a strategy that motivates the fishermen and assures their involvement and interest in the project. At this stage, this probably will require collaborative input from a sociologist or psychologist operating within the HACCP team.

The product details were summarized as follows: "Live animals that are required to go through a series of handling, holding, and transport procedures to reach the final market." The hazard category involves those hazards associated with their survival and the maintenance of their intrinsic quality.

Application of step 2 (HACCP team selection)

During this preliminary effort, a multidisciplinary team could not be drawn up because of the restrictions mentioned in step 1. However, a preliminary team was formed that was able to obtain information on the different processes involved and to access field conditions and/or live-holding facilities.

Application of step 3 (Product description)

The product is a live animal. It is a lobster with anatomical features, such as antennae, that are highly vulnerable to physical damage and which, when damaged along the chain, represent a site of blood loss that weakens the animal. In addition, other parts of its anatomy, such as appendages and carapace, are also fragile and damage or losses to these leads to an animal being weaker and thus a poor candidate for transport. Such animals will probably be rejected at the market because of their unattractive appearance and clear loss of intrinsic quality. Excessive handling procedures, such as repeated weighing, are considered a problem because they greatly increase the chance of physical damage. Additional hazards are those related to the distribution of the consigned animals, especially emersion and seawater quality variables such as ammonia, nitrite, oxygen levels, and salinity. When being consigned, emersion at high temperatures, especially at the beginning of the season (October), must be avoided as much as possible.

Application of step 4 (End-use identification)

The intended end-users of this product are general consumers and there are no particular risks associated with them.

Application of step 5 (Process flow diagram)

The live lobster flow chart is shown in Fig. 3. It shows all the significant handling steps, from point of capture to the point of first sale.

Application of step 6 (Verification on site)

The verification of the flow chart was carried out within a week following the first visit and no significant changes were made in that specific section of the market chain.

Applications of steps 7 and 8 (List of hazards and relevant control measures and CCP determination)

The data showing the identified hazards through the marketing chain, their ratings, and control measures are provided in Table 1.

Application of step 9 (Establishing critical limits (CL) for each CCP)

Table 2 shows the critical limits, monitoring, corrective actions, records, and verification procedures developed during the course of this project. In setting the critical limits, it was necessary to consult the relevant literature. Where possible, the critical limits used in this exercise are specific to *P. interruptus*. However, if data were not available, information dealing with other crustaceans was considered.

DISCUSSION

The reasons for the high mortalities that can still occur in this trade have been investigated by a number of authors (Uglow et al. 1986, Hosie 1993, Regnault 1994, Schmitt 1995, Whiteley 1995, Taylor and Waldron 1997, Jussila et al. 1997, Paterson et al. 1997) on several crustacean species, including *Nephrops norvegicus*, *Cancer pagurus*, *Necora puber*, *Panulirus cygnus,* and *Homarus gammarus*. The main conclusion drawn is that the accumulated stresses imposed on the animals throughout their marketing may act to weaken the animal or even cause its death.

The assured delivery of a consignment of lobsters in good condition and with a low mortality requires the diligent use of criteria capable of recognizing stress in lobsters and of procedures for reversing the effects of this stress at the successive stages in the market chain. This is where HACCP principles can have a positive impact on the improvement of quality and reduction of mortality rates in this industry. In this preliminary HACCP application, the preparation of the flow chart provided an opportunity to list in systematic order all the potential hazards involved in this particular section of the market chain. It also allowed the opportunity to establish and test control measures, some of which are spe-

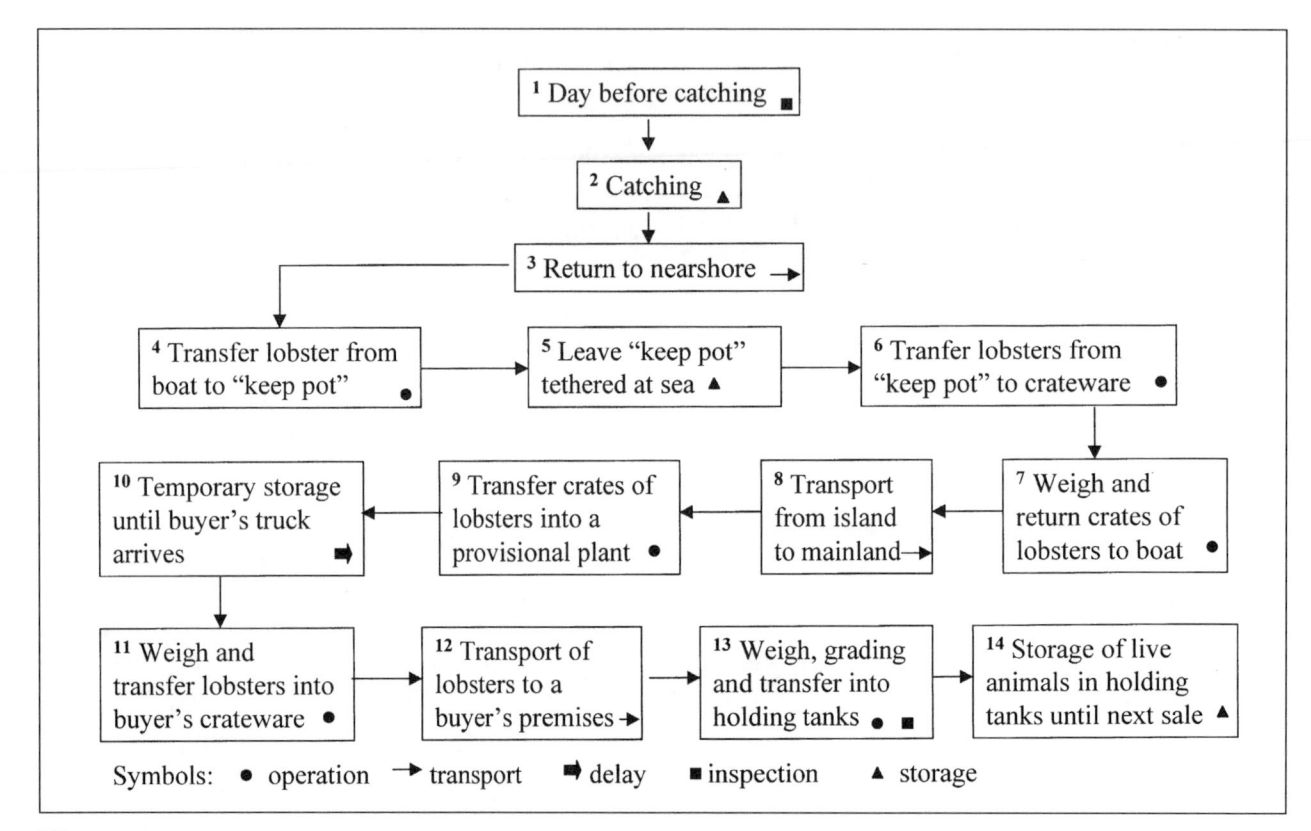

Figure 3. Live Lobster flow chart.

cies-specific, using the laboratory data reported in Gomez-Jimenez 1998.

It is not our contention that the application of HACCP methodology will solve all the problems faced by this industry. It is necessary to implement an intensive training program on the handling and other relevant techniques to all fishermen and decision-makers in the cooperatives in order to increase their awareness of the need for animal care. In this respect, the involvement of social specialists would be useful. Furthermore, more empirical research is still needed to establish the normal profile of conveniently measured stress indicators at each stage of handling in this Baja fishery, so that abnormal situations can be identified and remedied using HACCP principles.

The benefits of applying preventive approaches, such as HACCP, in the live crustacean trade may lead to an improvement in the overall intrinsic quality of the animals and a reduction in mortalities that will improve the prospects of profitable trade in the international market place.

Table 1. Risk analysis: identified hazards and their control measures.

Process step	Identified hazard	Is the identified hazard likely to occur? Yes/No	Justify the decision	Control measures
Product: Live spiny lobster				
1. Day before catching	None	—		
2. Catching period (Capture)	a. Temperature increase	Yes*	Direct sunlight increases body temperature, causes desiccation, and speeds up internal hypoxia.	Avoid direct sunlight on the animals. Use methods that maintain a high relative humidity (e.g. covering with wet sacking).
	b. Physical damage	Yes*	When catch is good the boat is full with lobsters on floor and this makes the transit onboard difficult.	Leave a free side to walk and allow catching practices.
3. Return to shore	None	—		
4. Transfer lobsters from boat to "keep pot"	a. Physical damage	No	Boats are small and therefore daily catch is not large enough to cause physical damage.	
5. Leave "keep pot" tethered at sea	a. Physical damage	Yes*	There is no uniformity in the "keep pot" and limbs can be eaten by fish.	Reduce the density and the duration inside the "keep pot." Redesign the "keep pot."
	b. Temperature increase	No	Because there is enough water circulation.	
6. Transfer lobsters from "keep pot" to crateware	a. Physical damage	Yes	Use of inadequate crateware.	Adequate crateware tailored to morphological features of the spiny lobsters.
7. Weigh and return crates of lobsters to boat	a. Temperature increase	Yes	Long queues to deliver the animals into the plant.	Avoid direct sunlight.

Marketing and Shipping Live Aquatic Products

8. Transport from island to mainland	a. Temperature increase and desiccation	No	Short time and the species is tolerant to these conditions.
9. Transfer crates of lobsters into a provisional plant	None	—	
10. Temporary storage, until buyer's truck arrives	a. High temperatures and low relative humidity	Yes**	Extreme conditions for the animals.	Reduce the storage time to the minimum or apply a time-temperature control.
11. Weigh and transfer lobsters into buyer's crateware	a. Physical damage	Yes*	At the end of the procedure, it is possible to observe many lost appendages.	To avoid transfer from one crateware system into another.
12. Transport of lobsters to a buyer's premises	a. Emersion	No	The temperature during transport is low and time is short.	
13. Weigh, grade, and transfer lobsters into holding tanks	a. Physical damage	Yes*	Excessive handling and at the end of the procedure many appendages can be lost.	To avoid transfer from one crateware system into another.
14. Storage of live animals in holding tanks until next sale	a. Physical damage	Yes**	Densely packed animals induced antagonistic behavior.	Avoid dense packing when kept in water.
	b. High ambient ammonia levels	Yes**	Excretion of animals.	Control of ammonia levels and utilize an appropriate system for removing ammonia from the water.
	c. Low oxygen concentration	Yes**	Inadequate air system and quick removal of oxygen from stressed animals.	Control of dissolved oxygen.
	d. Salinity changes	Yes**	Use of freshwater ice to cool down seawater temperature and evaporation.	Control of salinity.
	e. Temperature changes and cooling rate	Yes**	High temperature increases metabolic rate. During abrupt transfer to low temperatures the animal may automize some or all of its limbs as a shock reaction.	Control of water temperature and appropriate cooling rate for the species prior to packing.

* These hazards can be eliminated in the future through an intensive training at the fisherman level in order to establish good handling practices for live animals.
** These were the CCP identified and their critical limits are set in Table 2.

Table 2. Critical limits, monitoring, corrective actions, records, and verification procedures for live spiny lobster.

CCP no.	Process step	Identified hazard	Control measures	Critical limit
1	10. Temporary storage, until buyer's truck arrives	High temperature and low relative humidity	Reduce the storage time to the minimum or	No longer than 2 h or
			Apply time-temperature control	8-14°C for 12 h
2a	14. Storage of live animals in holding tanks	Physical damage	Avoid dense packing when kept in water	No more than 30 kg/m² for short term storage reduce to 5-10 kg/m² for longer-term
2b	14. Storage of live animals in holding tanks	High ambient ammonia levels	Control of ammonia levels	No higher than 6 mg/L
2c	14. Storage of live animals in holding tanks	Low oxygen concentration	Control of dissolved oxygen	No less than 85 % saturation
2d	14. Storage of live animals in holding tanks	Salinity changes	Control of salinity	No lower than 32 ppt No higher than 38 ppt
2e	14. Storage of live animals in holding tanks.	Temperature changes and cooling rate	Control of water temperature and appropriate cooling rate prior to packing	Water temperature: 12-14°C

Cooling rate: 0.6 to 1.0°C/hour |

Monitoring What, how, when (frequency)	Corrective actions	Records	Verification
Time (h): checking entrance time.	Temporary return of lobsters into "keep pot" and then into the sea, until the sale is made or	Storage form	Every sale
Time-temperature: checking entrance time and temperature in the storage room every h. Monitoring should be made using an ambient thermometer and checking the entrance time and date, every time a load of lobster is put into the storage room.	Transfer lobsters to a controlled temperature storage room (8-14°C) for 12 h.	Storage form	Every sale
Total weight of lobsters that are placed in each tank. Weight of lobsters when they are placed in the tanks.	Transfer the excess lobster's weight into another tank or a provisional container.	Tank monitoring form	For every consignment received
Measuring water ammonia levels twice an hour during the first 4 h after a new load of lobsters is put into the system, and thereafter continue monitoring every 8 h. Using a commercial kit	Partial change of water and review of the biological filters.	Tank monitoring form	Daily
Measuring water oxygen concentration every h during the first 4 h after a new load of lobsters is put into the system, and thereafter continue monitoring every 8 h. Using an oxygen electrode.	Add temporary large air diffuser until safe level is reached. Check the aeration system. Amend the water: biomass ratio.	Tank monitoring form	Daily
Measuring salinity levels every 6 h during summer and twice a day at other seasons using a portable refractometer.	At low levels: adjust the salinity by adding commercial salts for artificial seawater. At high levels: adjust the salinity adding fresh water.	Tank monitoring form	Daily
Checking water temperature every 6 h using a clearly visible thermometer.	Adjust the thermostat of the cooling system and review the origin of the failure.	Tank monitoring form	Daily
When starting the cooling rate, measure water temperature every 15 min and calculate the cooling rate.	Adjust the thermostat of the cooling system and review the origin of the failure.	Cooling rate form	For every shipment

Acknowledgments

We thank the cooperatives from Northwest Mexico for allowing access to their premises and supplying us with lobsters for the physiological studies. We are grateful to Armando Vega and Jeronimo Espinoza from CRIP-La Paz for logistical and technical support, and to CONACYT-Mexico and CVCP-Hull for financial support.

References

Campden Food and Drink Research Association. 1992. A practical guide to HACCP implementation. Campden Food and Drink Research Association Technical Manual 38. Gloucestershire, UK.

Gomez-Jimenez, S. 1998. Some physiological and immunological responses of the spiny lobster, *Panulirus interruptus* (Randall, 1840), to practices used in its live marketing in the Baja California fishery. Ph.D. thesis. Univerisity of Hull, UK.

Hosie, D.A. 1993. Aspects of the physiology of decapod crustaceans with particular reference to the live marketing of *Cancer pagurus* and *Necora puber*. Ph.D. thesis, University of Hull, UK.

Huss, H.H. 1993. Assurance of seafood quality. Technological Laboratory, Ministry of Fisheries, Denmark.

Jussila, J., J. Jago, E. Tsvetnenko, B. Dunstan, and L.H. Evans. 1997. Total and differential haemocyte counts in western rock lobsters (*Panulirus cignus* George) under post-harvest stress. Mar. Freshwater Res. 48:863-867.

Kirby, R. 1994. HACCP in practice. Food Control. 5(4):230-236.

Leaper, S. (ed.). 1997. HACCP: A practical guide. Campden and Chorleywood Food Research Association (CCFRA), Gloucestershire, UK.

MacMullen, P.H. 1986. An assessment of damage and mortality of the brown crab during vivier transport. Sea Fish Industry Authority Tech. Rep. 294. UK.

Mortimore, S., and C. Wallace. 1994. HACCP: A practical approach. Chapman & Hall, London.

Paterson, B.D., S.G. Grauf, and A.S. Ross. 1997. Haemolymph chemistry of tropical rock lobsters (*Panulirus ornatus*) brought onto a mother ship from a catching dinghy in Torres Strait. Mar. Freshwater Res. 48:835-838.

Regnault, M. 1994. Effect of air exposure on ammonia excretion and ammonia content of branchial water of the crab *Cancer pagurus*. J. Exp. Zool. 268:208-217.

Schmitt, A.S.C. 1995. Aspects of the physiology of some crustaceans species with particular reference to their live marketing. Ph.D. thesis, University of Hull, UK.

Taylor, H.H., and F.M. Waldron. 1997. Respiratory responses to air-exposure in the southern rock lobster, *Jasus edwardsii* (Hutton) (Decapoda: Palinuridae). Mar. Freshwater Res. 48:889-897.

Uglow, R.F., D.A. Hosie, I.T. Johnson, and P.H. MacMullen. 1986. Live handling and transport of crustacean shellfish: An investigation of mortalities. Sea Fish Industry Authority Tech. Rep. 280, UK.

Whiteley, M.N. 1995. The physiological basis of the ability of the lobster, *Homarus gammarus* (L.), to survive out of water and its commercial exploitation. Ph.D. thesis. University of Birmingham, UK.

Whyman, S., R.F. Uglow, and P.H. MacMullen. 1985. A study of the mortality rates of the velvet crab during holding and transport. Sea Fish Industry Authority Tech. Rep. 259, UK.

Live Seafood Holding Systems: Review of Systems and Components

John Chaiton
Emerald Partners, Marietta, Georgia

Introduction

This report focuses on live seafood shipping components and systems. While there are many types of live holding systems, certain components and practices are similar for all applications—from mobile systems for boats or trucks, to static systems inside a land-based plant. The ultimate goal for all of these systems is the same—whether you are shipping by air, by sea, or land, you want to get your product to market alive.

Shipping containers

First, the obvious fact is that live product must somehow be contained in a bag, a box, or a tank to protect it from the outside environment and to allow for at least some control over the interior environment of this container. One type of commonly used container is the one-way tank or box that is typically discarded at the other end of the market chain. Most often the containers are in the form of Styrofoam boxes. Another option is a reusable tank or box. Each different type of shipping container has its pros and cons. Obviously, the reusable type needs to be sent back and this necessity can add tremendously to the cost of getting the product to market. Those involved in the industry are only too aware of the complicated logistics involved in getting the containers back for reuse.

The product can be shipped while held in a small pool of water or, in some cases, without any water at all. We call this latter method "dry," although it includes small quantities of water. The maintenance of high levels of relative humidity coupled with carefully controlled internal temperature are critical considerations.

In order to be successful in this business, a number of complexities need to be confronted. For example, sourcing the seafood products and needed equipment is important. If you are thinking about bringing a product from a distant source, and a product of equal or better quality is available from a shorter distance, you need to look in that direction. You must remain informed about supply and market conditions and everything else in between. The longer the animals are in transit, the harder it is on them. From the time the animals are removed from the water to the time they get to the kitchen, the animals are undergoing stress. It is the cumulative effect of this stress that will ultimately kill the animals. Of course, if severe enough, the stress at any one of the steps along the marketing chain could also be lethal. Financial risk in the live business can be severe.

Holding tanks

There will be holding tanks onboard the fishing vessels and at the holding facilities. The type, shape, material, and size of the holding tanks varies depending on the application.

Holding tanks need to be built of materials that are not toxic to the animals. A variety of technical issues is involved. For example, fiberglass by itself is not even waterproof. It needs to have a final gel coat to create the waterproofing layer. In addition to being nontoxic and able to hold water, the material used in the construction of a holding tank also needs to be durable and easily washable. Smooth surfaces are important when it comes to maintenance, cleaning, and sanitation.

The size and number of tanks in a proposed facility will depend on the volume of live product that is anticipated. However, the shape of that tank can vary. If you have live fish that typically like to swim in one direction, as opposed to remaining quietly at or near the bottom, you probably will need round tanks. Many people put fish in rectangular tanks because they fit nicely into most spaces and have traditionally been used for live holding of fish. But the shape of the holding tank should depend on the nature of the fish and how it behaves in the tank.

The size and number of holding tanks and associated water supply considerations will depend on your operation. Consider how long you are planning to hold the products when making this determination. You may want to have a smaller, perhaps differently shaped, receiving tank to temporarily hold products before they go into your system for longer term holding. If you will be receiving numerous small shipments from different suppliers, the use of several small units, instead of a single large holding tank, can help reduce cross-contamination. Disease prevention is the positive outcome for this strategy; however, several small tanks will cost more on a cost-per-pound basis to operate rather than one larger unit.

Water pumps

The type of water pumps needed depends on the application. If you will be pulling water from a well, a specific type of pump will be needed. A recirculation system will require a different type of pump. For example, if your holding operation is onboard a truck, a 12 volt pump might be needed.

The typical water pump consists of a motor and a pump. Water should not contact any part of the motor, but it will contact the pump, which should contain no corrosive or toxic metals. Some pumps have non–stainless steel washers and bolts that will rust in a saltwater environment. This is why we use titanium components, for example, in chillers. Certain types of stainless steel will not last long in salt water.

The type of motors used in a pumping system needs to fit your application. For example, when hauling live seafood, if you have a small generator onboard your truck, you can use 110 volt electric current. However, you should have a backup pump that is powered by the available 12 volt system, or 24 volt for diesel trucks. Backup systems are necessary in case there is a problem with the generator and you need to circulate water. Backup systems for water pumping and aeration are essential, whether on a truck, on a vessel, or in a land-based or static plant.

Water pumping can use a variety of power sources. You can use hydraulic and pneumatic systems. Hydraulic systems involve fluid movement to convey power and pneumatic systems involve air or gas movement. You can use air compressors to drive pumps. Hydraulic pumps are great, but remember, oil and water do not mix. If you are using hydraulics or considering using this type of system, make sure you maintain the system so that no hydraulic fluid leaks in or around any of your holding tanks.

There is also something to be said for a newly applied mobile power source for auxiliary pumps—solar power backup systems. Some live haulers have solar panels fastened to their trucks which, in turn, feed electric power to storage batteries used for backup power support, should there be a problem.

You might also consider the use of inverters, which convert DC electrical power to AC and run off of a battery. This will allow you to run an electric pump off the battery serving the engine of the vehicle. Inverters are not very expensive and are highly recommended for backup use.

Filters

Water filters are very important to the overall operation of a live holding system. A filtration system can include mechanical, chemical, and biological filtration and combinations thereof. The size, use, care, and application of these filters will determine whether your product gets to market in great shape or dies before it ever gets the chance to be delivered. The financial aspects of your proposed business will dictate how you will deal with this component in the holding system. You cannot afford to skimp on filtration. I feel that you need to over-filter in order to provide for at least a small margin of safety. Frequently you will be advised by a consultant or make the determination based on your own calculations that you need a certain amount of filter surface area to handle a particular product biomass. If you determine that a small additional financial investment will double the potential size of your biological filter, I say why not make this investment? You do not want biological filtration capacity to be a limiting factor in your system.

Mechanical filtration

Figure 1 shows various particle sizes (in microns) that can be removed with different types of filtration. Mechanical filtration uses a mechanical method to remove particles. The first method is known as coarse screening. Typically, it is possible to remove particles down to 100 microns with coarse filtration. The problem is that the finer mechanical filters will quickly become saturated with particles and require more cleaning and backwashing. If you are busy running your operation, as I imagine everyone is, you do not have time to backwash fine particulate filters several times a day.

Another type of filtration is sedimentation. Using this filtering strategy, the effluent from the tank is

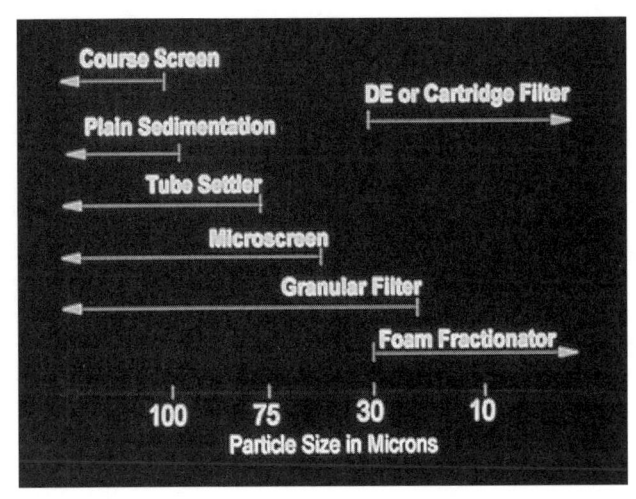

Figure 1. Particle sizes removed using various filtration methods.

Biological filtration and nitrogen

The nitrogen cycle (Fig. 2) can be thought of in simple terms. Animals excrete ammonia, which is converted to nitrite by a type of bacteria known as *Nitrosomonas*. Nitrite is then converted to nitrate by *Nitrobacter* bacteria. It is important to remember that ammonia is highly toxic. Nitrite is probably even more toxic while nitrate is far less toxic. Each species that rotates though the holding facility has a different tolerance to these compounds. For example, Maine lobster has a much stronger tolerance to nitrate than most fish species.

Given a properly working biological filter, the water ammonia level will spike when product is added to the holding tank and then will decline with time. Then there will be a spike in nitrite, which will also eventually drop. As nitrite drops, nitrate increases.

Only two things cause the nitrate level to go down. One is through water exchange. This can be accomplished by simply draining some of the old water and adding new water to bring the tank up to its full working volume. In this case, if the nitrate level is 200 mg per liter, and 50% of the water is replaced, theoretically the nitrate level should drop to approximately 100 mg per liter.

moved through a place of quiescence where the water moves very slowly and is not agitated. Some people even use the holding tank itself as a settling tank, a strategy that I do not encourage because I like to keep the water moving in the holding tanks. In a settling tank, the particulate matter with heavier specific gravity will rain out and land on the bottom of the tank. Later, after a substantial amount of sediment has built up, it can be removed by vacuuming.

Another type of filter, known as a tube settler, typically works down to particle size of about 75 microns. Related granular filters work very well. A bead filter, which uses grains instead of a screen to remove particulate material from the effluent, is a type of granular filter. The fluid travels through a granular bed and can remove particles down to about 20 microns.

Foam fractionation, an important part of any closed recirculation system, is used to remove minute particles of 30 microns or less. A foam fractionator, or protein skimmer, is a cylindrical tube. Water enters at the top of this tube and comes out the bottom and air enters at the bottom and comes out the top. This crosscurrent creates a foam of proteins at the top of the unit. There is typically an upside-down funnel at the top of the unit in which the foam builds up. The foam bubbles out the top of the funnel, spills down over the sides and drains into a collection vessel. This removes very fine solids and decreases the biological load for the nitrifying bacteria.

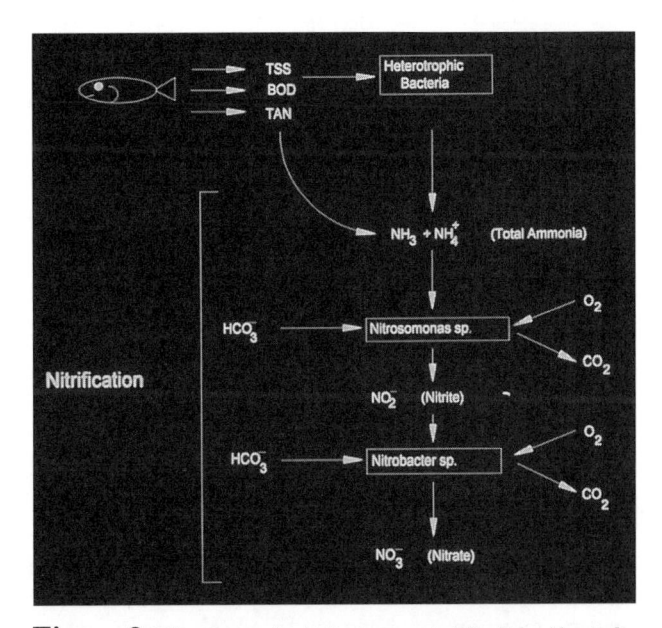

Figure 2. Nitrogen cycle. At the top are total solids. Also indicated are the biological oxygen demand (BOD), total ammonium nitrate (TAN), and other components that make up ammonia load.

It is important to note that sufficient water exchange may occur just in the daily operation of a holding facility. The water that is spilled on the floor when the animals are placed in and taken out of the tanks is replaced with what is called makeup water. This daily replacement with makeup water may be sufficient to control the gradual nitrate accumulation in the system.

The other method for removing nitrate is called denitrification. In this process, nitrate is converted back to nitrite and then released as nitrogen gas. People in the ornamental or aquarium trade are experts at this. Also, large aquaculture facilities in Israel use denitrification on a commercial basis.

Denitrification involves a series of anaerobic reactions. It is a bit tricky because, if the system is not working properly, nitrate is converted back to nitrite, which is 20 times more toxic than nitrate. This can lead to mortalities. Advances have been made in making the denitrifying process less risky. Dr. Phillip Lee in Texas has designed a component system that uses a computer controlled real-time reaction. I believe that this system is currently on the market. This component is simply plugged into the side of a tank and denitrifies the water by converting the nitrate to nitrite and then to nitrogen gas which is released to the atmosphere. Depending on the size of the operation, this may be a cost effective strategy for the reduction of nitrate. Denitrification provides for better water quality, and decreases the costs associated with having available large volumes of makeup water. Whether the cost is in the synthetic sea salt needed to make seawater or in buying or otherwise obtaining high quality water, there is a cost to replacement of holding water.

Bead filters

Bead filters function as both biological and mechanical filters. They work through straining, settling, interception, and adsorption. Straining involves the direct capture of large particles as they pass into small openings between the beads. Settling is the sinking of suspended solids onto the surface of the beads. When small particles fall directly onto the surface of a bead, they are captured and adsorbed onto the sticky biofilm. This is a very important part of this system component, because this biologically active layer or biofilm is distributed throughout the unit.

The filtering capacity of a bead filter depends on the size of the unit. In a typical live holding system, 100% of the water traveling through the handling

Figure 3. Motorized bead filters.

system does not have to be filtered or chilled on each pass. If you attempted this type of water processing, your chiller and filter systems would have to be relatively large. Biofilter units are expensive. The filter system on the left in Fig. 3, a BF (biofilter) 100, probably costs US $20,000-25,000 before installation. It is equipped with a 3 horsepower motor on top that needs electrical connections, starters, etc. There is also a cost associated with just moving it around. It is about 14 feet tall. Components such as these can take a lot of room and can be expensive to purchase and maintain.

Once you realize that there is no real practical reason to run all the water through the filter or chiller, you may then realize that you can use something like the third model. This is an example of a mechanical filter that also operates as a biological filter.

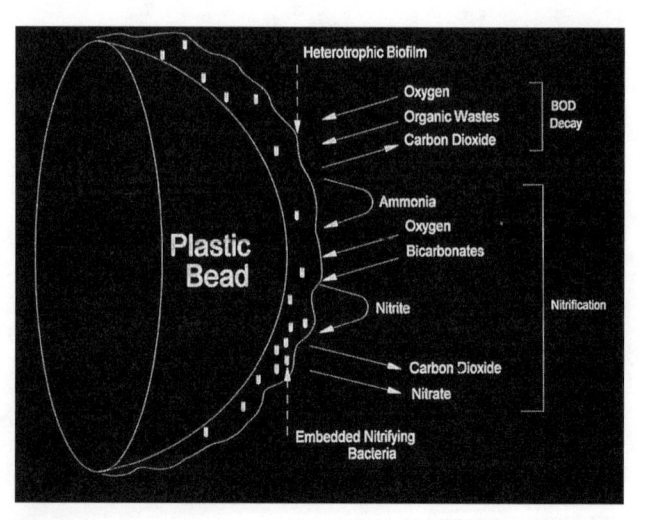

Figure 4. Nitrogen cycle on the surface of a filter bead.

The beads provide a fair amount of surface area (Fig. 4). The amount of surface area within a filter is a function of total volume, bead size, porosity, and bead shape. The more surface area within a filter, the more sites available for the adhesion of nitrifying bacteria. When nitrifying bacteria attach to the available surfaces, they begin converting ammonia to nitrite, and nitrite to nitrate, resulting in better water quality.

However, you should not entirely rely on one of these units to provide you with sufficient surface area to denitrify the holding water in the system. Make sure your biofilter is more than adequate. Use this unit as a mechanical particulate filter with an added bonus—it accomplishes denitrification as well.

Smaller versions of non-motorized bead filters would work quite well onboard a vessel because they can be tucked in the corner of a deck and fastened down. They work very well as a particulate filter—a capability that can be useful in many marine applications. For example, shrimp tend to regurgitate gut contents when put under stress and this will causes a lot of mucus and particulate matter to get into the holding water. Bead filters are good for straining out some of this debris, mucus, and slime. Furthermore, bead filters can be cleaned easily.

In addition, if you are planning to be more than 20 hours in transit, you will be able take advantage of some of the biological nitrification that bead filters are capable of performing. If you are hauling fish or shellfish for only a few hours, there will not be the need to convert ammonia to nitrite, and nitrite to nitrate. Bead filters need more than a few hours to accomplish this conversion and, in some cases, they will need days to significantly reduce accumulated nitrate levels.

The biofilm or bacteria associated with the proper action of bead filters must be kept active. If you are contemplating a live product journey of 24 hours or longer and need a properly conditioned filter, you can plug a small bead filter or another kind of biofilter into the static holding system in the holding facility and circulate water on a separate loop through that filter. This will keep the bacteria inside the filter fully activated and ready to consume ammonia and nitrite. Then, when it is time to pick up or deliver your product, you can plug this small, portable biofilter into the system on the truck or boat. The biofilter will already be charged up and ready to go without a 30 day conditioning period. This preconditioning strategy will help on long hauls.

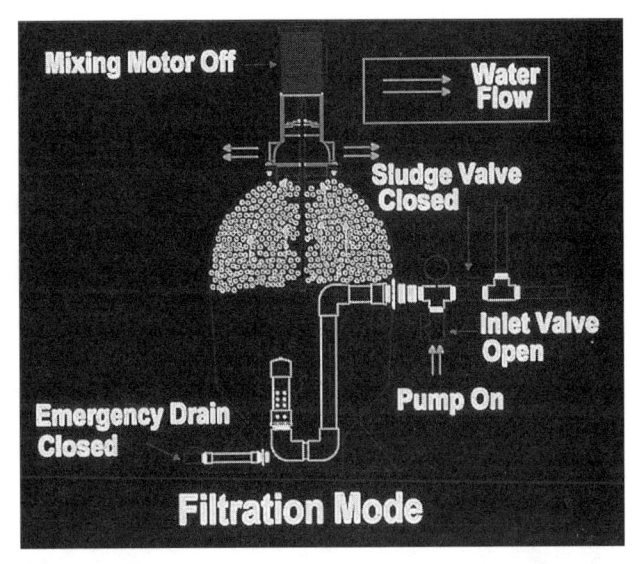

Figure 5. Bead filter backwash schematic, showing the bead bed in the upper half. Water enters from the pipe on the right side, goes through a U-pipe, passes up through the beads, and exits above.

A small porthole is normally built into the side of a bead filter. This allows you to observe the condition of the beads. When the beads are clean, they are very white. After use, the beads may become brown or encrusted with particles and a bed of sludge may accumulate in the bottom layer of the beads.

Cleaning a bead filter by backwashing

Some bead filters are designed to be backwashed (Fig. 5), and cleaning this type of filter can be accomplished quite easily. The unit needing cleaning is first isolated from the live holding system. The valves are closed so the water does not flow into and out of the unit. The motor, on top, is turned on. The motor has a stainless steel shaft that runs down the center of the unit and is equipped with two or three propellers along its length that mix up the beads. Some care must be taken not to overmix the beads. During this period of mechanical agitation, each bead is scraping against the next. If you scrape them too much, it is possible to remove all the biofilm—the nitrifying bacteria. This could virtually "kill" your filter, requiring an extensive period of reconditioning before it regains its previous biofiltering capacity. Therefore, turn on the agitation motor for perhaps 15 seconds. The washing process does not take long once the propellers start agitating the beads. You can observe the progress of the washing cycle through the porthole window.

When the motor is shut off, the beads float to the top of the cone and the debris falls to the bottom of

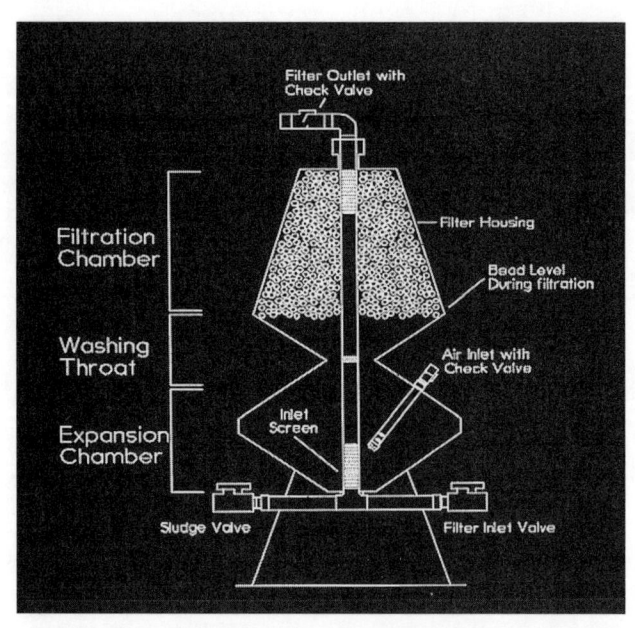

Figure 6. A bead filter that is cleaned by bubble-washing.

the unit. Depending on the species involved and the length of service since the last washing, the entire bottom part of the bead chamber may now be filled with sediment. After you understand how a bead filter works, you can then easily switch a few valves to flush or pull the sediment out of the collecting cone through a siphon.

Bubble washing a bead filter

Another type of bead filter can be cleaned by bubble washing (Fig. 6). In order to mix or agitate the beads, which are in the upper chamber, air enters from the bottom of the unit and passes up through the restricted neck. Then you open a release valve and it pulls the beads with it. The action of the air moving up through the beads and the water flowing down scrubs the beads just the right amount. During bubble washing, the water that has become saturated with sediment is lost. These bead filters can concentrate large amounts of sediment, and the waste material can be carried away with a single washing. This is good because there are costs associated with water, even if it is just the electricity used to pump it into the live holding facility.

Biotower filters

In a biotower, which is a large cylindrical vessel, air and water are pumped in from the bottom and water is drained out at the top. In order for this unit to operate properly, it is very important to have adequate aeration. If the filter is not functioning properly, there will be water movement channeling and anaerobic areas within the filter.

PARTICLE SIZE

In live holding water, the number of particles that are five to ten microns is substantial relative to the number of larger particles in the water. That is, the size of most of the particulate matter that needs to be removed from the holding water is tiny. Using a combination of protein skimmers and biofilm adhesion in biological filters, it is possible to remove virtually all contaminants. If you have a separate loop for the biological filter in which only a percentage of the water passes through the filter at one time, this cleaning result will not occur in the first pass, but eventually the waste particles will all be removed.

If a large percentage or possibly all of your holding water is going through a biological filter at once—fantastic. Waste particles will be removed faster and the bacteria will convert ammonia to nitrite and nitrate faster. It is simply a matter of what you can afford.

A higher percentage of bigger particles (50-100 microns) are removed at each pass of water through a filter. Since the majority of the particles are tiny, it is good to put as much water through your biological filter as possible. Again, the degree and intensity of filtration is dependent on cost. I would recommend that you put all of the holding water through a biofilter. Depending on conditions, it may be quite expensive to put all of your water through a particulate filter. To save money, you can use a branch of the biofilter to filter out the particulate matter.

Water and system sterilizers

A few words need to be mentioned about water sterilization. The addition of a sterilizing component to your overall system can be a good idea because it will reduce the risk of disease. If you are going to use an ultraviolet (UV) or ozone sterilizer in your water system, some care must be taken to make sure that this component is going to be effective. If you are using UV equipment, make sure that the UV bulbs have been properly maintained.

Chemicals can be useful clean water systems when there is no live product in the system. You also need to clean out the intake and effluent lines to kill any vibrios that may be growing on the surface of the pipes. The ability to accomplish this cleaning and sterilizing task needs to be built into the live holding system.

TEMPERATURE AND SALINITY CONTROL

As in the case of particulate removal or protein skimming, you do not need to heat or chill 100% of the water with each pass through the system. Also, heating or chilling can run as a separate loop. With proper attention to the efficient use of valving, you can use the same pumps that power your filtration system to drive holding water through a chiller or heater.

OXYGENATION

Two main types of hardware are used to aerate or oxygenate the holding water—blowers and compressors. Which method is better depends on the depth of the water in the holding system. This comes down to a question about air volume vs. air pressure. The desired results will dictate which equipment is best to use.

Diffusers are a very important part of the oxygenation process. The smaller the bubbles placed in the tanks the better the exchange of oxygen molecules with the water. Many people carry oxygen tanks that they get from welding companies on board their boats or trucks. These live carriers bleed oxygen from the tanks through either diffusers or needle valves into the main flow of water. With the addition of metering and flow devices, it is possible to monitor the amount of oxygen going into the water.

Figure 7 provides an example of a mechanical oxygenator or aerator. There are also oxygen generators on the market, which are air filters that sieve out the nitrogen molecules and the few carbon dioxide molecules that are present in atmospheric air. Using this type of equipment, it is possible to produce gas at the 92% oxygen level. One kilowatt hour of electric power will provide you with about one cubic meter of oxygen.

STRIPPING TOWERS

Stripping towers, also known as packed towers, remove carbon dioxide from the holding water. Towers of this sort are typically only needed in static systems. If you are thinking about holding a good

Figure 7. A mechanical oxygenator/aerator.

amount of product for a long period of time, it will probably be necessary to strip the carbon dioxide out of the system. As part of the normal respiratory process, fish are removing oxygen from the water and producing carbon dioxide.

A stripping tower should be placed after the biological filter and just before the treated water return to the holding tank. The water going into the holding tank will have less carbon dioxide in it. The stripping tower will help maintain pH levels as well.

A stripping tower can operate under pressure or passively, through gravity, in which case the water comes in the top and goes out the bottom. Towers can be provided with what are known as bioballs that scatter and fragment water movement. Towers can also have a fractionation plate in which the holding water blows against a flat surface or a cone to make the water spray. This will also help in the removal of accumulated carbon dioxide.

POWER

You always need to have backup sources for all the power systems in the proposed facility pneumatic, hydraulic, or electrical power provided by generators, batteries, or the sun. Backup system must be kept ready for immediate use during times of emergency. If you do not have frequent need to use any of your backup power systems, turn the backup equipment on once a month to make sure that the machinery is still in good working order. In terms of several power systems, it is possible to purchase automatic switchover controls for immediate access to backup power. Automatic switchover controls can also start and stop backup generators automatically each month to test the readiness of your system.

Disease control and cross-contamination prevention

Cross-contamination can be a real problem in a live holding facility. If you are in the process of designing a system with different live holding tanks for different products transported from different locations, you need to practice important prophylactic measures in order that you do not cross-contaminate one tank with the contents from another tank.

If a pathogen, like a parasite or virus, has become embedded in one holding tank, whether it is in a filter or in the pipes supplying water to a tank, you must ensure that it is not transferred to any other tank. The biological and financial consequences of cross-contamination can be devastating. In addition to the partitioning of plumbing and other water handling components, attention must be given to the development of handling protocols. For example, you cannot use a dip net in one tank and then walk over and use the same dip net in a different tank. You need to make sure to clean and sanitize that dip net first. Ideally, the dip net should be designated for use only in a particular tank.

It is always a good idea to clean and give a sanitizing dip to cage systems used to transport live fish or shrimp. Preventive measures should be used both when the cages come into your plant and before they are used again. Disease control is an imperative when dealing with live aquatic animals.

Helpful information

Always have available basic spare parts for all components in your system, particularly for critical components. If you do not have an impeller or certain type of seal sitting on the shelf, when a pump fails you will not be able to immediately fix the item. If you need that specific tank or series of tanks for product holding, you are in trouble. Carefully maintain an inventory of needed supplies so that you will be able keep your facility in full operation and stay on top of problems.

When operating a live holding system, you have legal, moral, and financial responsibilities to everyone and to yourself. If you think that there is the potential for a human health hazard in your system, you need to address it. HACCP procedures (Hazard Analysis Critical Control Point) provide a very convenient procedure for reviewing product quality and plant operation, and also for managing a live facility over the long term. Remember to keep good records and log books. A paper trail is very important to the successful operation of a business, especially when a problem occurs.

You need to know how your holding and transport system affects the price and marketability of your range of live products. The condition of the product upon arrival at the marketplace has everything to do with how much money you are going to make or lose in the transaction. There is no in between—if you are not making money, then you are losing money.

Finally, delayed stress syndrome is the culmination of various forms of stress that have impacted a product from time of harvest to the time it gets to the market. This syndrome is an important cause of product mortality. Examine every possible way to decrease, if only slightly, each stress point along the way. Look at each step in the transport chain and ask questions such as: How can we handle the product less? How can we keep the rate of metabolism down? How can we keep the ammonia out of the system? Not only will a clear focus on stress reduction help the animals that pass through your live holding system, but will also benefit your business clients. Customer satisfaction affects price and marketability and will go a long way to sustain your business enterprise.

PARTICIPANTS

Charles M. Adams
Institute of Food and Agricultural Sciences
University of Florida
P.O. Box 110240
Gainesville, Florida 32611-0240

Harry Ako
College of Tropical Agriculture and Human Resources
Honolulu, Hawaii

Arnt Amble
SINTEF Fisheries and Aquaculture
N-7465 Trondheim
Norway
arnt.amble@fish.sintef.no

Rich Bailey
University of Hawaii
Honolulu, Hawaii

A. Battison
Atlantic Veterinary College
University of Prince Edward Island
Charlottetown, Prince Edward Island
Canada C1A 4P3

Christopher Brown
Hawaii Institute of Marine Biology
Kaneohe, Hawaii

R.J. Cawthorn
Atlantic Veterinary College
University of Prince Edward Island
Charlottetown, Prince Edward Island
Canada C1A 4P3

Jon Chaiton
Emerald Partners
355 Nottingham Dr.
Marietta, Georgia 30066
Pooch@mindspring.com

Patrick S.W. Chan
Brightfuture Industries Limited
2/F, Kwun Ton Wholesale Fish Market
10 Tung Yuen St.
Yau Tong
Kowloon, Hong Kong
Bil@powernethk.com

John W. Chapman
Department of Fisheries and Wildlife
Oregon State University
Hatfield Marine Science Center
Newport, Oregon 97365-5296
john.chapman@hmsc.orst.edu

Eugene V. Coan
California Academy of Sciences
Department of Invertebrate Zoology
San Francisco, California 94118-4599

Brian Cole
University of Hawaii
Kaneohe, Hawaii

Stephen E. Crawford
International Marine Resources
130 Water St.
Eastport, Maine 04631

Angela R. Danford
University of Hull
Department of Biological Sciences
Hull, U.K. HU6 7RX
A.R.Danford@biosci.hull.ac.uk

Robert L. Degner
Institute of Food and Agricultural Sciences
University of Florida
P.O. Box 110240
Gainesville, Florida 32611-0240

John Garland
Clearwater Fine Foods Inc.
757 Bedford Hwy.
Bedford, Nova Scotia
Canada B4A 3Z7
Jgarland@cffi.com

S. Gomez-Jimenez
Centro de Investigacion en Alimentacion y
    Desarrollo (CIAD)
Apdo. Postal No. 1753
C.P. 83000
Hermosillo, Sonora
Mexico
S.Gomez@cascabel.ciad.mx

J. Guigné
Guigné International Limited
685 St. Thomas Line
Paradise, Newfoundland
Canada A1L 1C1

Carol Harper
Department of Agricultural Engineering
University of Puerto Rico
P.O. Box 9030
Mayaguez, Puerto Rico 00681-9030
c_harper@rumac.upr.clu.edu

Bill Harrower
Finfish Extension Biologist
British Columbia Ministry of Fisheries
2500 Cliffe Avenue
Courtenay, British Columbia
Canada V9N 5M6
Bill.Harrower@gems9.gov.bc.ca

William A. Heath
British Columbia Ministry of Fisheries
2500 Cliffe Ave.
Courtenay, British Columbia
Canada V9N 5M6
Bill.Heath@gems8.gov.bc.ca

Per Heggelund
AquaSeed Corporation
4530 Union Bay Pl. NE # 100
Seattle, Washington 98105
Pero@aquaseed.com

Paul Heimowitz
Oregon State University Extension Sea Grant
200 Warner-Milne Rd.
Oregon City, Oregon 97045
Paul.heimowitz@orst.edu

George Iwama
Professor, Faculty of Agricultural Science
University of British Columbia
208-2357 Main Mall
Vancouver, British Columbia
Canada V6T 1Z4
giwama@interchange.ubc.ca

Dorothee Kieser
Department of Fisheries and Oceans
Pacific Biological Station
Nanaimo, British Columbia
Canada V9R 5K6
KieserD@pac.dfo-mpo.gc.ca

K. Klein
Guigné International Limited
685 St. Thomas Line
Paradise, Newfoundland
Canada A1L 1C1

Donald Kramer
University of Alaska Marine Advisory Program
2221 E. Northern Lights Blvd.
Anchorage, AK 99508-4140

Mick Kronman
National Fisherman Magazine
P.O. Box 40214
Santa Barbara, California 93140
mkronman@aol.com

John Kubaryk
Department of Marine Sciences
Food Science and Technology Program
University of Puerto Rico
P.O. Box 9013
Mayaguez, Puerto Rico 00681-9013
j_kubaryk@rumac.upr.clu.edu

Sherry L. Larkin,
Institute of Food and Agricultural Sciences
University of Florida
P.O. Box 110240
Gainesville, Florida 32611-0240
Slarkin@ufl.edu

Ian Lawler
Irish Sea Fisheries Board
P.O. Box 12, Crofton Road
Dublin, Ireland
lawler@bim.ie

Bruce M. Leaman
International Pacific Halibut Commission
P.O. Box 95009
Seattle, Washington 98195
bruce@iphc.washington.edu

Donna J. Lee,
Institute of Food and Agricultural Sciences
University of Florida
P.O. Box 110240
Gainesville, Florida 32611-0240

Thomas Liu
Shanghai World Ocean Trading Co. Ltd.
30 Gao An Rood # 103
Shanghai
People's Republic of China 200030

Q. Liu
Guigné International Limited
685 St. Thomas Line
Paradise, Newfoundland
Canada A1L 1C1

A. MacKenzie
Atlantic Veterinary College
University of Prince Edward Island
Charlottetown, Prince Edward Island
Canada C1A 4P3

R. MacMillan
Atlantic Veterinary College
University of Prince Edward Island
Charlottetown, Prince Edward Island
Canada C1A 4P3

Kim Mauriks
Dorcas Point Farms Inc.
1429 Dorcas Point Road,
Nanoose Bay, British Columbia
Canada V9P 9B4
dorcaspt@nanaimo.ark.com

Todd W. Miller
Department of Fisheries and Wildlife
Oregon State University
Hatfield Marine Science Center
Newport, Oregon 97365-5296
todd.miller@hmsc.orst.edu

J. Walter Milon
Institute of Food and Agricultural Sciences
University of Florida
P.O. Box 110240
Gainesville, Florida 32611-0240

John G. Nickum
U.S. Fish and Wildlife Service
P.O. Box 25486
Denver, Colorado 80225-0486
john_nickum@fws.gov

L.O. Noriega-Orozco
CIAD-Guaymas Unit
P.O. Box 284 C.P. 85400
Guaymas, Sonora, Mexico

Lucía Ocampo V.
Centro de Investigaciones Biológicas
  del Noroeste (CIBNOR)
P.O. Box 128
La Paz, Mexico
locampo@cibnor.mx

Paul G. Olin
University of California Sea Grant
2604 Ventura Avenue
Santa Rosa, California 95403
pgolin@ucdavis.edu

Annette M. Olson
School of Marine Affairs
University of Washington
P.O. Box 355685
Seattle, Washington 98105-6715
olsonam@u.washington.edu

Toril Overaa
PB 59
6707 Raudeberg
Norway
sigbjon@frisurf.no

R. Pacheco-Aguilar
Centro de Investigacion en Alimentacion
  y Desarrollo (CIAD)
Apdo. Postal No. 1753
C.P. 83000
Hermosillo, Sonora
Mexico

Christine Pattison
California Department of Fish and Game
Ocean Fisheries Research
213 Beach Street
Morro Bay, California 93442
cpattiso@dfg2.ca.gov

Hans-Peder Pedersen
Capella Technologies
Esteustadvien 157
7049 Trondheim
Norway
HPP@captech.no

D. Rainnie
Atlantic Veterinary College
University of Prince Edward Island
Charlottetown, Prince Edward Island
Canada C1A 4P3

Bernard E. Rollin
Department of Philosophy
Colorado State University
Fort Collins, Colorado 80523-0015

Carlos Rosas
Lab. De Biologia Marine Experimental
Universidad Nacional Autónoma de México
Apdo. Post 69 Ciudad del Carmen
Campeche, Mexico
crv@hp.fciencias.unam.mx

Yvonne Sadovy
Department of Ecology and Biodiversity
University of Hong Kong
Pok Fu Lam Road
Hong Kong, China
yjsadovy@hkusua.hku.hk

David J. Scarratt
Hatchery International
2695 Highway 201, RR #3
Bridgetown, Nova Scotia
Canada B0S 1C0
scarratt@ns.sympatico.ca

John Seccombe
Aquahort Ltd.
52 Maraetai Heights Road
Maraetai Beach 1705
Auckland, New Zealand
Jseccombe@clear.net.nz

Charlie Stephens
Kamilche Sea Farms
SE 2741 Bloomfield Road
Shelton, Washington 98584
KamilcheSF@aol.com

Clyde S. Tamaru
Hawaii Sea Grant College Program
University of Hawaii
2525 Correa Road, HIG 205
Honolulu, Hawaii 96822
ctamaru@hawaii.edu

Barry Thoele
Live Aquatics
Route 1, Box 240
Staples, Minnesota 56479
Liveaqua@brainerd.net

Thea Thomas
P.O. Box 1566
Cordova, Alaska 99574
thea@gci.net

Hugh Thomforde
University of Arkansas at Pine Bluff
Lonoke Agriculture Center
P.O. Box 357
Lonoke, Arkansas 72086
hthomforde@uaex.edu

R.F. Uglow
Dept of Biological Sciences
University of Hull
Hull, U.K. HU67RX
R.F.Uglow@biosci.hull.ac.uk

Craig A. Watson
Tropical Aquaculture Laboratory
University of Florida
1408 24th Street S.E.
Ruskin, Florida 33570
caw@gnv.ifas.ufl.edu

INDEX

A

A New Direction for Monitoring Lobster Meat Yield, Using Advances in Acoustic Probing, 267-270
AALAC. *See* American Association for Accreditation of Laboratory Animal Care
abalone. *See also* California; shellfish
　culture in California, 179, 259
　exports to Hong Kong, 194, 198, 221
acoustic probing
　A New Direction for Monitoring Lobster Meat Yield, Using Advances in Acoustic Probing, 267-270
　description, 268-270
Adams, Charles M., 63
adrenaline, relation to stress, 20
aeration. *See also* oxygen; water quality
　at-sea holding tank, 146
　in baitfish tank, 141
　in-plant, 217-218
Aerococcus viridans, 10
aesthetics
　handler considerations, 109
　marketplace considerations, 102, 103
agriculture. *See also* aquaculture
　animal rights and, 36-37
air bladder
　deflation, 163
　grouper, 57-58
　rupture of, 46, 50
　venting, 146
　air pressure, effect on captive fish, 195
　air transport. *See also* emersion effects; transport
　in general, 10, 59-60, 73-74
　　for SE Asia market, 196-198, 202
　IATA standards, 61
　for kelp, 101, 102
　for lobster, 57
　for ornamentals, 73-74, 87, 88, 93
　stress effects, 39
Ako, Harry, 73
Alaska. *See also* British Columbia; Canada
　halibut fishery, 180
　Handling and Shipping of Live Northeast Pacific Scallops: Larvae to Adults, 111-124
　Norton Sound, 99
　paralytic shellfish poisoning, 227, 229
　Prince William Sound, 99
　Shipping and Handling the Marine Algae *Macrocystis* in Alaska, 99-103
algae. *See also* algal blooms; plants; seaweed
　aquaculture, 90
　as bivalve food, 105
　invasive, *Caulerpa taxifolia,* 258
　in ponds, 128
　Shipping and Handling the Marine Algae *Macrocystis* in Alaska, 99-103
　toxic algae testing costs, 106
algal blooms, in farms, 161

Amble, Arnt, 45
American Association for Accreditation of Laboratory Animal Care (AALAC), 43
American Quarter Horse Association, 35
Ammolock, 91
ammonia. *See also* biofilter; carbon dioxide; nitrate
　discussed, 3, 10, 91, 142
　pH levels and, 58
　in recirculation system, 52
　relation to oxygen consumption, 24, 81
　zeolite use, 80, 133-134, 138
ammonia efflux. *See also* waste
　Atlantic cod, 50
　as indicator of stress, 2, 3, 4, 5, 6, 12-13, 14-15, 28
　scallops, 108
　shrimp, 133, 136-137
An Overview of Irish Live Crustacean Fisheries, 207-213
anesthetic. *See also* clove oil; sedatives
　clove oil, 61
　local, 28
　for reef fish, 197
　for shrimp, 134-135, 136
anemones
　Florida harvest, 63
　Florida live harvest, 67
angelfish, Florida live harvest, 66
Animal Ethics and the Live Aquatic Animal Trade, 35-44
Animal Liberation (Singer), 36
animal rights
　Animal Ethics and the Live Aquatic Animal Trade, 35-44
　Animal Rights Advocacy, Public Perception, and the Trade in Live Animals, 27-33
　anti-cruelty ethic, 36-37
　corporate response to, 41
　livestock showing industry, 42
　New Zealand, 60
　public perceptions of, 36
Animal Rights Advocacy, Public Perception, and the Trade in Live Animals, 27-33
animal rights organizations (AROs), 29
animal testing, 35
Animal Welfare Act, 42
antibiotics. *See also* bacteria; disease
　cautions with, 80
aquaculture industry. *See also* farming; mariculture
　British Columbia, import of fish for, 174-175
　China, 203
　crab, 194
　Impact of the Green Crab on the Washington State Shell fish Aquaculture Industry, 263-266
　Japan, 114
　list of suppliers, 84-86
　prawns, 194
　reef fish, grouper, 184
　releases into environment, 249, 252-253
Aquaculture Regulations (Canada), 171
aquarium market, 61, 87. *See also* ornamental fishery
AquaSeed Corporation, overview, 231-232
Aquatic Farm Act of 1988, 112
Aristotle, 37
AROs. *See* animal rights organizations

Ascophyllum nodosum scorpioides, Live Rockweed (*Ascophyllum*) used as a Shipping Medium for the Live Transport of Marine Baitworms from Maine, 95-97
Asia. *See also* China; Hong Kong; *specific countries*
    lobster imports, 57
    ornamental production, 89
    pond techniques, 128
Asia boxes, 76
Asian Americans
    animal rights issues, 27-33, 41
    demand for product, 165
Asian clam (*Corbicula fluminea*), 260
Asian clam (*Potamocorbula amurensis*), 258
Asian copepod (*Pseudodiaptomus inopinus*), 260
Asian tapeworm (*Bothriocephalus opsarichthydis*), 259
Atlantic cod. *See also* cod
    aquaculture, 177
Atlantic jackknife (*Ensis directus*), 252
Atlantic salmon. *See also* salmon
    escape from farms, 259
Audubon Society, 30
Australia. *See also* New Zealand
    animal rights activism, 35
    exports to SE Asia, 194, 201, 202, 221, 223
    holding and transport facilities, 60
    import restrictions, 234
    live reef fish imports, 183
    lobster exports, 193
Austropotamobius pallipes, emersion effects, 14

B

Baby Fay incident, 36
bacteria. *See also* disease; pathogens
    in biofilter, 146
    fish vulnerability to, 146
    immunity to antibiotics, 80
    Nitrobacter, 285
    Nitrosomonas, 285
    UV control of, 53, 54-55, 288
    Vibrio contamination, 218, 224, 229-230, 259, 289
bag limits, for live ornamentals, 70
Bailey, Rich, 73
baitfish industry, 79-80
    disposal concerns, 96, 143, 249
    invertebrates, 125
    Keeping Baitfish Alive and Healthy in Holding Tanks: Tips for Retail Outlets, 141-143
    Live Rockweed (*Ascophyllum*) used as a Shipping Medium for the Live Transport of Marine Baitworms from Maine, 95-97
    non-target species in packing material, 245-246
ballast water. *See also* disease; pathogens
    organisms in, 244, 249, 252, 259
Barton, Dr. Bruce, 20
bass, as introduced species, 258
Battison, A., 267
Bay of Fundy, lobster, 51
Baynes Sound, 114
bead filter. *See also* biofilter; filtering
    cleaning, 287-288
    discussed, 286-288
    preconditioning, 287

bear hunting, 35
Beijing Blue Water, 221
Belgium, imports, 106
Billingsgate Market, 52
BIM. *See* Bord Iascaigh Mhara
bioassay, fish imports for, 174
biocontrol, 244
biofilter. *See also* filtering
    ammonia removal, 52, 54, 197
    at-sea system, 146, 147
    conditioning, 56
    operation, 285-286
    as system component, 54, 58
biotechnology, and ethics 39-40
biotower filter, 288. *See also* filtering
biotoxin monitoring. *See also* disease
    scallop fishery, 113
black market
    China, 201, 203, 221, 222
    in live ornamentals, 70
    live reef fish, 189
black rockfish, 167
Black Sea, alien invertebrates in, 96
blackcod. *See also* cod
    import into British Columbia, 175
blood glucose
    relation to cortisol, 20-21
    stress indicators, 28
    temperature-dependence, 12
blood lactate, during emersion, 12, 14
blood protein levels, during emersion, 12, 15
blood urate levels, during emersion, 12, 14
bloodworm, 128. *See also Glycera dibranchiata*
blue cod. *See also* cod
    live handling, 57, 60
blue crab (*Callinectes* sp.). *See also Callinectes sapidus*
    air exposure and dehydration effects, 5-6
    animal interactions and handling, 4
    characteristics, 2
    mortality reduction, 150
    Physiological Responses of Blue Crabs (*Callinectes* sp.) to Procedures Used in the Soft Crab Fishery in La Laguna de Terminos, Mexico, 1-8
    responses to stress, 1-8
    water quality and salinity effects, 4-5
blue rockfish, 167, 168. *See also* rockfish
blueprints, for commercial facility, 218
Bodega Bay. *See also* California
    rockfish landings, 167
The Body Shop, 35
Bohr-Root effect, 133
bolina rockfish, 167, 168
Bord Iascaigh Mhara (BIM), 210
Borneo, 90
boxes
    Asia boxes, 76
    Florida boxes, 75-76
    Hawaii boxes, 76
    for shipping, 75
boycotts, 30, 31, 38-39
Brett, Dr. Roland, 19

brill, 60
British Columbia. *See also* Alaska; Canada
    green crab introduction, 266
    Handling and Shipping of Live Northeast Pacific
        Scallops: Larvae to Adults, 111-124
    Opportunity or Threat? Implications of the Live Halibut
        Fishery in British Columbia from the Harvester
        Perspective, 151-153
    Patinopecten yessoensis culture, 114-115
    Resource Management and Environmental Issues
        Concerning Live Halibut Landings, 155-157
    salmon transport, 20
    Shipping Live Fish into British Columbia, Canada:
        Basic Regulatory Requirements, 171-176
        aquaculture, 174-175
        bioassays and research, 174
        ornamental trade, 172-174
    Sterling Pacific Halibut: A New Approach, 159-162
brook trout (*Salvelinus fontinalis*). *See also* trout
    hybridization, 259
Brown, Christopher, 73
brown crab (*Cancer pagurus*). *See also* crab
    holding and transport, 1
    Irish landings, 207
        French nicking method, 209
    marketing, 272, 276
    nitrogen metabolism, 10
    species profile, 207-210
bull trout, hybridization, 259
bullfight, 41
business plan, for commercial facility, 216-217
butterflyfish, 70

C

cabezon. *See also* rockfish
    California fishery, 164, 167, 168
calcium hydroxide, 135
California. *See also* San Francisco
    AB 1241 (Keeley), 165
    abalone culture, 179
    animal rights controversy, 30-31, 38-39
    at-sea holding systems, 145-150
    commercial nearshore fishery, 165-168
    exotic introductions, 95, 96, 97, 252, 258, 260, 263, 265
    Fish and Game Commission, 30, 31
    green crab introduction, 263, 265
    groundfish industry regulations, 169
    herring sac roe fishery, 100
    horse slaughter legislation, 35
    ornamental production, 89
    Resource Management Issues in California's Commercial
        Nearshore Live/Premium Finfish Fishery,
        163-170
    rockfish fishery, 148-149, 163-170, 180
        closed periods, 168-169
    SB 1336 (Thompson), 165
    scallop culture, 113
    wild animal harvesting, 31
California Department of Fish and Game (CDFG), 163, 169
California Fish and Game Commission, 163
California scorpionfish, 164, 167
California sheephead, 146, 164, 167

Callinectes danae, 1, 2
Callinectes rathbunae, 1, 2
Callinectes sapidus. *See also* blue crab
    Mexican fishery, 2
    oxygen consumption during emersion, 10
    United States fishery, 2
Cambodia, exports to SE Asia, 194
Campbell's Soup, 231-232
Canada. *See also* Alaska; British Columbia
    A New Direction for Monitoring Lobster Meat Yield,
        Using Advances in Acoustic Probing, 267-270
    animal rights activism, 35
    bear hunting, 35
    eastern, Short-Term Holding and Live Transport
        of Aquatic Animals: An Overview of Problems
        and Some Historic Solutions, 51-56
    exports
        to Hong Kong, 194
        to SE Asia, 221
    HACCP integration, 228
        Canadian Quality Management Plan, 228
        Regulatory Action Points Plan (RAPP), 228
    halibut quota, 153
    Handling and Shipping of Live Northeast Pacific
        Scallops: Larvae to Adults, 111-124
    import restrictions, 234
    imports
        from US, 64
        quarantine requirements, 174
    Lacey Act application to, 242
    mussel storage, 54
    Shipping Live Fish into British Columbia, Canada:
        Basic Regulatory Requirements, 171-176
Canadian Food Inspection Agency (CFIA), 171
Canadian Quality Management Plan (CQMP), 228
Canadian Shellfish Sanitation Program (CSSP), 115, 116
Carassius auratus, transport, 80
carbon dioxide. *See also* ammonia; oxygen
    accumulation, 54, 55-56, 82, 108
        shrimp, 133, 134
    scavenging, 135, 138
    stripping towers, 289
Caribbean, exports to US, 64
carp (*Cyprinus carpio*)
    environmental impacts, 258, 259
    ponds, 239
    temperature requirements, 92
    transport, 39
catch and release program, 39
catfish pond, 239
cattle industry, 37, 39, 43, 139
    castration, 43-44
    inspection and safety, 228
Caulerpa taxifolia, 258
Cawthorn, R.J., 267
CDC. *See* Centers for Disease Control
CDFG. *See* California Department of Fish and Game
Centers for Disease Control (CDC), 230
CFIA. *See* Canadian Food Inspection Agency
Chaiton, John, 215, 238, 283
chalky fish syndrome. *See also* disease; parasites
    halibut, 178-179

Chan, Patrick, 193, 201, 216
Chaoborus sp., harvesting and culture, 126, 129
Chapman, John W., 249
char, importation into British Columbia, 172
Cheilinus undulatus. See wrasse
Chesapeake Bay
    Callinectes sapidus fishery, 2
    invertebrate co-shipment, 96
chicken industry, 37
Chile
    exports to, 153, 234
    HACCP implementation, 228
China, 129. *See also* Hong Kong; Taiwan
    An Insight into the Shanghai Market for Imported Live Seafood, 221-225
        how to import live seafood, 222-223
        market chain, 223
        profit, 223-225
    Beijing Blue Water, 221
    exports to Hong Kong, 194
    fish export ban, 189
    imports
        Beijing, 203
        live reef fish, 183, 188, 201, 203-204
        port of Yantian, 203, 222
        Sha Tau Kok, 203
        Shanghai, 203
        Shekou entry point, 203
        tax rates, 203
    Liaoning Pelagic Fisheries, 221
    Marketing Aspects of the Live Seafood Trade in Hong Kong and the People's Republic of China, 193-199
    Shanghai Fisheries General, 221
China rockfish, 167
Chinatown. *See also* Asian Americans; San Francisco
animal rights controversy, 27-33
Chinese Consolidated Benevolent Association, 31
Chinese mitten crab (*Eriocheir sinensis*), exotic introduction, 253, 254, 259, 260
chironomids, harvesting and culture, 126
chiton, blood chemistry, 133
Chlamys rubida, background, 112-113
chlorine, 79-80. *See also* water quality
chlorine dip, to prevent pathogens, 264
cholera, 199
CIBNOR, Experimental Shrimp Farm, 23
ciguatera. *See also* disease
    in live reef fish, 183, 184, 185-188, 190-191
ciliates, 10
CITES. *See* Convention of International Trade in Endangered Species
clams
    British Columbia import regulations, 175
    import into British Columbia, 172
    introduced, 253
Clayoquot Sound, 114
Clean Water Act, 253

cleansing. *See also* filtering
    in-plant sanitation, 218, 228
    for infection prevention, 142, 264, 290
    shellfish, 116
    water and system sterilizers, 288-289
Clearwater Fine Foods, 267
Clearwater Lobsters, 10, 55
Clearwater Seafoods, 52
clove oil. *See also* anesthetics
    as anesthetic, 135, 136
    clown fish, culture and harvest, 63
    clown loach. *See also* ornamental fisheries
    handling steps, 90-92
Coan, Eugene V., 249
cod
    aquaculture, 177
    California fishery, 167
    Holding Tank System for Reconditioning Transport of Live Cod Recently Captured in Deep Water, 45-50
    live handling, 57
    Cohen, Dr. Andy, 96
    coho salmon. *See also* salmon
    aquaculture, 231-232
Cole, Brian, 73
Colorado
    animal research, 39, 40
    fishery, 39
    steel-jawed trap, 35
Columbia, ornamental production, 89
Columbia River Steamship Operators Association, 254
comb jelly, depredations, 96
concrete, for commercial facility, 219
Congiopodus leucopaecilus, live handling, 57
Constraints to Shipping Live Product: Lessons from the AquaSeed Corporation Experience, 231-235
The Construction of a Commercial Live Seafood Transshipment Facility: Review of General Specifications, 215-219
Convention of International Trade in Endangered Species (CITES), 171
copper rockfish, 167. *See also* rockfish
coral trout (*Plectropomus leopardus*). *See also* reef fish
harvest, 185, 193, 204, 205
cordgrass (*Spartina* sp.). *See also* plants
non-native establishment, 258
cortisol
    in egg, 21-22
    relation to stress, 20, 28, 49
Corydoras sp.
    pH requirements, 91
    transport, 80
Costa Rica, ornamental production, 89
CQMP. *See* Canadian Quality Management Plan
crab
    crab shedding system, 149-150
    cultured, 194
    dismemberment, 39
    export to SE Asia, 194, 221
    Florida live harvest, 63, 66-67
    import into British Columbia, 172
    introduced species, 253

Crangon crangon, stress-induced changes in, 4
Crassadoma gigantea. *See also* scallop
    background, 113-114
Crassostrea gigas. *See* oysters
Crawford, Stephen E., 95
crayfish (*Palinurus elephas*). *See also* lobster
    emersion effects, 14, 133
    exports to SE Asia, 193-194
    Ireland, 207
    Irish landings, 207
    species profile, 212-213
crested wheat grass, 241
cross-tolerance. *See also* stress
    cold shock, 22
    heat shock, 21
crustaceans. *See also* shellfish
    An Overview of Irish Live Crustacean Fisheries, 207-213
    British Columbia import regulations, 175
    carbon dioxide levels, 55-56
CSSP. *See* Canadian Shellfish Sanitation Program
Cuba, exports to SE Asia, 194
curio market, compared to live market, 70
customs broker, 121
cyanide, use in reef fishery, 183, 184, 188, 190, 191
Czech Republic, ornamental production, 89

D

damselfish, Florida live harvest, 66
Danford, Angela, 1, 9, 54
Daphnia sp., harvesting and culture, 125, 128
Deep Cove Fisheries, 57, 58, 61
Degner, Robert L., 63
diatoms, 245
dinoflagellates, 259
discus fish, temperature requirements, 92
disease. *See also* antibiotics; bacteria; biotoxin monitoring; ciguatera; invertebrates; parasites
    at growout, 114
    chalky fish syndrome, 178-179
    infectious salmon anemia, 234
    paralytic shellfish poisoning, 227, 229
    potential for, 215, 229
    prevention procedures, 216, 264, 290
    Pseudomonas, 218
    testing for, 233
        lethal testing, 233-234
    unintentional release of, 171-172
    Vibrio, 218, 229-230, 234, 289
diving beetle, 127
Dixon Entrance, 112
Do Live Marine Products Serve as Pathways for the Introduction of Nonindigenous Species?, 243-247
dog. *See also* animal rights
    laboratory, 40, 41-42
domestic animals. *See also* animal rights
    "Bill of Rights" for, 35
    as companion animals, 36
Dorcas Point Farms, 177
dragonfly nymph, 127
Drouin, Hélène, 54, 55

Dungeness crab (*Cancer magister*). *See also* crab
    harvest for SE Asia, 194, 223

E

education. *See also* research
    for handlers, 106
    importance of, 109, 246
eel, export to Hong Kong, 194
Effect of Long-Haul International Transport on Lobster Hemolymph Constituents and Nitrogen Metabolism, 9-18
electrical supply, for commercial facility, 218-219, 289
emersion effects
    Callinectes sp., 5-6
    Homarus americanus, 12-15
enforcement
    HACCP, 229
    Lacey Act, 233
    in live trade, 179-180
    recreational harvesting, 71
Entobdella hippoglossi. *See also* halibut; parasites
    effect on halibut, 160-161
environment. *See also* sustainability
    considerations about, 109, 171, 229
    ecosystem considerations, 238-241
    habitat alteration, 257-258
    live animal trade effect on, 31
    Live Seafood: A Recipe for Biological and Regulatory Concern?, 249-256
    Resource Management and Environmental Issues Concerning Live Halibut Landings, 155-157
    Review of Impacts of Aquatic Exotic Species: What's at Risk?, 257-261
    Shipping Live Aquatic Products: Biological, Regulatory, and Environmental Considerations, 237-242
Epinephelus
    coioides, harvest, 184
    malabaricus, harvest, 184
ethics
    anti-cruelty ethic, 36-37
    biotechnology and, 39-40
    handler considerations, 109
Eureka, rockfish landings, 167
Europe. *See also specific countries*
    animal rights activism, 35
    lobster imports, 57
    North American shipments to, 53
    Norway bivalve exports to, 105
    ornamental production, 89
exotic species, Review of Impacts of Aquatic Exotic Species: What's at Risk?, 257-261

F

facilities
    The Construction of a Commercial Live Seafood Transshipment Facility: Review of General Specifications, 215-219
    planning for, 217

Farfantepenaeus californiensis, Critical Oxygen Point in Yellowleg Shrimp (*Farfantepenaeus californiensis*): A Potential Species for the Live Seafood Trade, 23-25
farming, 61. *See also* aquaculture industry
    amphipods, 125
    based on fleet-harvested fish, 45-46
    live ornamentals, 88, 90
    mariculture, 92
    pen rearing as, 177
    scallops, 106, 111-112
fathead minnow, 141
FDA. *See* Food and Drug Administration
feeding
    additives and supplements, 229
    effect on water quality, 177
    live fish, 60
    recommendations against, 142, 197
    relation to recovery, 133, 135
    in transport, 50, 78, 198
FHPR. *See* Fish Health Protection Regulations
Fiji, reef fishery, 183, 184, 194
filtering. *See also* biofilter; cleansing; water quality
    at-sea holding tank, 146
    bead filters, 286-288
    biofilters, 285-286
    biotower filter, 288
    in general, 284
    granular filter, 285
    mechanical filter, 284-285
    protein skimmer, 56, 285
    tube settler filter, 285
    water and system sterilizers, 288-289
fish
    British Columbia import regulations, 175
    observing, 59
    pain affecting, 28, 31, 39, 42
    Physiological Stress Response in Fish, 19-22
    stress
        cellular stress response, 21
        confinement stress, 21
        cross-tolerance, 21
        field measurement, 21
        generalized stress response, 19-20
        measuring responses, 20-21
        measuring responses primary, secondary, tertiary responses, 20
        sensitivity, 39
fish food, 125. *See also* feeding
Fish Health Protection Regulations (FHPR) (British Columbia), 174
Fish Inspection Act (Canada), 171
Fisheries Act (Canada), 171
fishing, catch and release program, 39
fishing industry. *See also* animal rights
    attitude toward product, 52
    proactive role for, 39-40, 60, 61
    public perception of, 30, 31-32, 39
fishing vessel
    California rockfish fishery, 148-149, 165-166
    halibut fishery, 159
    Irish fishery, 207-208, 211, 212
    live transport by, 194-196

flatworm, 114, 259
    predation by, 120
Florida. *See also* ornamental fisheries
    animal rights activism, 42-43
    commercial collection in, 65-68
        saltwater products license, 67-68
    exports to SE Asia, 194
    live organism harvesting, 63
        angelfish, 66
        damselfish, 66
        surgeonfish, 66
    live ornamentals
        De Soto County, 88
        in general, 63-71, 87-89
        Hillsborough County, 88, 89
        stock status, 70
    spiny lobster farming, 180
Florida boxes, 75-76
Florida Department of Environmental Protection, 63
Florida Fish and Wildlife Conservation Commission, 65
Florida Marine Research Institute (FMRI), 65
Florida Sea Grant College Program, 63
Florida's Ornamental Marine Life Industry, 63-71
flounder
    live handling, 57
    live transport, 49
flow charts, 217
Floyd, Ruth, 91
Flynn, Sheridan, 55
FMRI. *See* Florida Marine Research Institute
food chain, exotic species in, 258
Food and Drug Act, Delaney Clause, 234
Food and Drug Administration (FDA), 228
Fort Bragg. *See also* California
    rockfish landings, 167
France. *See also* Europe
    imports from UK, 209, 210, 213
    scallop imports, 106
freshwater clam (*Corbicula fluminea*). *See also* clam
    costs, 253
freshwater dip. *See also* disease
    for regurgitation and parasite removal, 216
freshwater species, The Harvest and Culture of Live Freshwater Aquatic Invertebrates, 125-129
fucus. *See also* packing material; seaweed
    as packing material, 245
furanace, 80

G

gaffkemia. *See Aerococcus viridans*
Gammarus sp., harvest and culture, 125-129
Garland, John, 9
gas bladder. *See* air bladder
Gaskel, George, 39
geoduck
    exports to Hong Kong/China, 194, 221, 223, 225
    import into British Columbia, 172, 175
giant grouper (*Epinephelus lanceolatus*). *See also* grouper
    harvest for SE Asia trade, 184, 185, 189-190
gluconeogenesis, 20

Glycera dibranchiata, Live Rockweed (*Ascophyllum*) used as a Shipping Medium for the Live Transport of Marine Baitworms from Maine, 95-97
glycogenolysis, 20
golden shiner, 141
goldfish, 141
Gomez-Jimenez, S., 271
Goodall, Jane, 36
gopher rockfish, 168
gorgonians, Florida live harvest, 67
grass rockfish, 167, 168. *See also* rockfish
Great Lakes, zebra mussel introduction, 96
green crab (*Carcinus maenas*). *See also* crab
    dessication, 14
    Impact of the Green Crab on the Washington State Shellfish Aquaculture Industry, 263-266
    as introduced species, 96, 253, 259
    metabolism during emersion, 10
    preventing spread of, 263-265
greenlings, 164, 167
groundfish industry regulations. *See also* rockfish
    California, 169
grouper. *See also specific species*
    air bladder problems, 57-58
    harvest for SE Asia trade, 184-185, 193, 196, 204
    live handling, 57-58
growout. *See also* aquaculture; farming
    reef fishery, 184
Guigné International Limited, 267
Guigné, J., 267
Gulf Coast. *See also* Florida; Mexico
    Callinectes sapidus fishery, 2
Gulf Stream, 105

H

habitat alteration, 257-258. *See also* environment
HACCP. *See* Hazard Analysis Critical Control Point
hairy crab. *See also* crab
    harvest for SE Asia, 194
Haiti, exports to US, 64
halibut. *See also* halibut fishery
    live vs. fresh price, 145
    Opportunity or Threat? Implications of the Live Halibut Fishery in British Columbia from the Harvester Perspective, 151-153
    otolith samples, 155, 157
    Resource Management and Environmental Issues Concerning Live Halibut Landings, 155-157
    Sterling Pacific Halibut: A New Approach, 159-162
halibut fishery
    aquaculture, 177, 180
    background, 155
    chalky fish syndrome, 178-179
    feeding, 160-161
    fishing practices, 155-156, 159-160
    harvesting, 161
    holding practices, 156-157, 177-178
    international management, 157
    offloading procedure, 160
    regulatory issues, 157

Halifax, 9
    Sea Hive Corporation, 52
handling
    avoiding touching fish, 146-147
    by buyer, 196
    general recommendations, 146-147
    Live Fish Handling Strategies from Boat to Retail Establishment, 57-61
    lobster, compared to fish, 58-59
    scallops, quality control and mortality, 108
    stress-induced changes, 4, 9, 14-15
Haribon Foundation, 190
Harper, Carol, 131
The Harvest and Culture of Live Freshwater Aquatic Invertebrates, 125-129
Hawaii
    ornamental production, 89
    Shipping Practices in the Ornamental Fish Industry, 73-86
Hawaii boxes, 76
hazard analysis. *See also* safety
    The National Seafood Hazard Analysis Critical Control Point Program and the Live Seafood Industry, 227-230
    Using HACCP Principles and Physiological Studies to Improve Marketing Practices for Live Crustaceans, 271-282
Hazard Analysis Critical Control Point (HACCP), 231, 238, 243, 290
    overview, 139, 145, 227-228
heat shock, to reduce subsequent stress, 21
heat shock protein (HSP). *See also* temperature
    relation to stress, 21
Heath, William A., 111
Heggelund, Per, 231, 238, 240, 241
Heimowitz, Paul, 257
hemolymph constituents
    Effect of Long-Haul International Transport on Lobster Hemolymph Constituents and Nitrogen Metabolism, 9-18
    hemolymph changes, 12, 14-15
hermit crab. *See also* crab
    Florida live harvest, 67
    predation by, 258
herring
    sac roe fishery, 100, 103
    spawn-on-kelp fishery, 99-103
    prices, 102
Hexagrammos. *See* greenlings
high-finned grouper (*Cromileptes altivelis*). *See also* grouper
    harvest for SE Asia trade, 184, 193
Hippoglossus stenolepis. See halibut
HOBO Temperature Logger, 11
holding. *See also* transport
    Keeping Baitfish Alive and Healthy in Holding Tanks: Tips for Retail Outlets, 141-143
    Live Seafood Holding Systems: Review of Systems and Components, 283-290
        filtering, 284-285
        holding tanks, 283-284
        shipping containers, 283
        water pumps, 284

holding *(continued)*
    lobster, small-scale land-based, 53-54
    mussels, 54
    Short-Term Holding and Live Transport of Aquatic Animals: An Overview of Problems and Some Historic Solutions, 51-56
    What's New in Live Fish and Shellfish At-Sea Holding Systems: High Tech and Low Tech, 145-150
holding tank. *See also* pens; pound; reconditioning
    at-sea, 145-150, 194-196
    construction features, 58
    discussed, 283-284
    disease transmission from, 156-157
    disinfection, 142
    fish densities in, 45, 46-48, 76-78, 80, 142, 148
        reef fish, 195-196
    Holding Tank System for Reconditioning Transport of Live Cod Recently Captured in Deep Water, 45-50
    mortality, 156-157
    round vs. square, 49, 146, 147, 283
    use with pens, 147
Homarus americanus. See lobster
Hong Kong. *See also* China
    import formalities, 198-199
    imports, 60
        crabs, 194
        live reef fish, 193
        lobster, 193-194
        mantis prawns, 194
        prawns, 194
        shellfish, 194
    Live Reef Food Fish Trade in Hong Kong: Problems and Prospects, 183-192
        composition and value of trade, 184-185
        impact on fish stocks, 188-190
        payment and trading rules, 202-203
        problems and prospects, 190-191
        re-export to PRC, 203-204
        relationships among importers, wholesalers, restaurants, 201-202
        species preferences, 204
        trade profile, 183-184, 201, 238
    Marketing Aspects of the Live Seafood Trade in Hong Kong and the People's Republic of China, 193-199
    ornamental production, 89
    Wholesale and Retail Marketing Aspects of the Hong Kong Live Seafood Business, 201-205
The Horse Whisperer, 36
HSP. *See* heat shock protein
HSP-70, 21
Hull, U.K., air transport of lobster, 9-18
Humboldt Bay, 264
humidity, during emersion, 14, 51, 53
humphead wrasse, harvest for SE Asia trade, 184, 185, 189-190, 193
Hyalella azteca, harvest and culture, 125-129
Hydrilla, 259
hyperglycemia, during emersion, 11, 15

I

IATA standards, air transport, 61
"ice boat," 126-129
Iceland, exports to, 153
ignorance, arguments from, 241
IMA. *See* International Marinelife Alliance
immune system, stress effects on, 20
Impact of the Green Crab on the Washington State Shellfish Aquaculture Industry, 263-266
India
    exports to SE Asia, 194
    ornamental production, 89
Indonesia. *See also* Asia
    exports to SE Asia, 194, 202, 221
    exports to US, 64
    ornamental production, 89
    reef fishery, 184
Industrial Research Assistance Program (Canada), 267
infectious salmon anemia (ISA), 234. *See also* disease
Infofish International, 227, 228
International Marinelife Alliance (IMA), 190
International Pacific Halibut Commission (IPHC), 151, 155
international shipments, scallops, paperwork requirements, 121
Internet, 30
Invasive Species Council, 253
invertebrates. *See also* disease; parasites
    damage to kelp by, 100
    harvest as ornamentals, 65, 68, 69
    The Harvest and Culture of Live Freshwater Aquatic Invertebrates, 125-129
    pain experienced by, 42
        animal rights activism, 32
    removal
        from bivalves, 116
        from fish, 159
    unintentional transport and release, 95-97, 171, 245
investment, 106
IPHC. *See* International Pacific Halibut Commission
Ireland. *See also* Europe; United Kingdom
    An Overview of Irish Live Crustacean Fisheries, 207-213
    HACCP implementation, 228
Island Scallops Ltd., 114
Italy. *See also* Europe
    imports, 106
Iwama, George, 19

J

jack, harvest for SE Asia trade, 184
Japan. *See also* Asia
    exports to Hong Kong, 194
    Optimizing Waterless Shipping Conditions for *Macrobrachium rosenbergii*, 131-139
    Patinopecten (Mizuhopecten) yessoensis, 114-115
    US exports to, 64, 234
        spawn-on-kelp market, 99-103
Jasus edwardsii, emersion effects, 15

K

kanamycin, 80
Karl Wilhelm, 47
Keeping Baitfish Alive and Healthy in Holding Tanks: Tips for Retail Outlets, 141-143
kelp greenling, 167
Kieser, Dorothee, 171
Kiribati, exports to SE Asia, 194
Klein, K., 267
koi carp. *See also* carp
    temperature requirements, 92
Kolbe, Ed, 55
Korea. *See also* Asia
    exports to Hong Kong, 194
Kramer, Donald, 227, 231
Kronman, Mick, 145
Kubaryk, John, 131

L

Lacey Act, 231, 253. *See also* regulation
    interpretation, 237, 238, 240, 241-242
    review of, 232
lake trout. *See also* trout
    depredations on, 258
Laminaria, 99, 102
Larkin, Sherry, 63, 90
Lawler, Ian, 207
Leaman, Bruce, 151, 155, 177
Lee, Donna J., 63
Lee, Dr. Phillip, 286
Levenes' test, 11
light, in fish handling, 92, 93
Lilliefor's test, 11
lingcod, 167, 168. *See also* cod
Litopenaeus vannamei postlarvae, temperature and Pcr correlation, 24
Littorina saxatilis, 96
Liu, Q., 267
Liu, Thomas, 221
Live Ornamental Fish (LOF) code (HTS 030110), 63
Live Reef Food Fish Trade in Hong Kong: Problems and Prospects, 183-192
live rock. *See also* Florida
    culture and harvest, 63
    discussed, 90
    Florida live harvest, 66, 67
    regulations, 65
live sand
    discussed, 90
    Florida live harvest, 67
    regulations, 65
Live Seafood: A Recipe for Biological and Regulatory Concern?, 249-256
Live Seafood Holding Systems: Review of Systems and Components, 283-290
live transport. *See also* transport
    vs. processing, 109
livestock showing industry, 42

Lo Shu Pan, 204
lobster crate, 51
lobster (*Homarus gammarus*). *See also* crayfish; spiny lobster (*Panulirus interruptus*)
    A New Direction for Monitoring Lobster Meat Yield, Using Advances in Acoustic Probing, 267-270
    animal rights concerns, 39, 40
    Effect of Long-Haul International Transport on Lobster Hemolymph Constituents and Nitrogen Metabolism, 9-18
    exports to SE Asia, 193, 197-198, 202, 221
    handling, compared to fish, 58-59
    holding systems, 52
        biofiltration for, 147-148
        small-scale land-based, 53-54
    Irish landings, 207
        V-notching of female lobster, 210
    quality control, 61
    Short-Term Holding and Live Transport of Aquatic Animals: An Overview of Problems and Some Historic Solutions, 51-56
    species profile, 210
    transport, 39, 52-53
Lobster Science Center, 267
Long Island Sound, lobster fishery, 267
Lutjanus argentimaculatus, harvest for SE Asia trade, 184

M

McCleese, Dr. Don, 55
McIntyre Bay, 112
MacKenzie, A., 267
MacMillan, R., 267
Macrobrachium rosenbergii, Optimizing Waterless Shipping Conditions for *Macrobrachium rosenbergii,* 131-139
Macrocystis. See also seaweed
    Shipping and Handling the Marine Algae *Macrocystis* in Alaska, 99-103
Maine. *See also* lobster
    Live Rockweed (*Ascophyllum*) used as a Shipping Medium for the Live Transport of Marine Baitworms from Maine, 95-97, 245-246
    zebra mussel certificate, 233
Maine Department of Marine Resources, 97
Malaysia
    exports to Hong Kong, 194, 201, 202
    fish export ban, 189
    live reef fish imports, 183
    ornamental production, 89
Maldives
    exports to SE Asia, 194, 201, 202
    reef fish exports, 184
management, Resource Management Issues in California's Commercial Nearshore Live/Premium Finfish Fishery, 163-170
Manila clam. *See also* clam
    introduction, 263
mantis prawns. *See also* prawns
    harvest for SE Asia trade, 194, 198
Mao Zhedong, 221
marbled grouper (*Epinephelus polyphekadion*). *See also* grouper
    harvest for SE Asia trade, 184

mariculture. *See also* aquaculture industry; farming
    China, 225
    farming, 92
    oysters, 207
Marine Information System, 65
Marine Life Management Act of 1998 (MLMA), 163
marketing, 106, 152, 217, 219
    in general, 60
    Using HACCP Principles and Physiological Studies to Improve Marketing Practices for Live Crustaceans, 271-282
Marketing Aspects of the Live Seafood Trade in Hong Kong and the People's Republic of China, 193-199
Marshall Islands
    exports to SE Asia, 194
    reef fishery, 184
Mauriks, Kim, 151, 177, 216
mayfly nymph, 127
media, 41, 42
Mediterranean, exotic algae introduction, 258
metabolism. *See also* nitrogen metabolism
    effect on of handling stress, 4
    relation to oxygen capacity and temperature, 24, 56
    temperature effects on, 195
Mexico
    blue crab (*Callinectes* sp.) fishery
        Ciudad Del Carmen, Campeche fishery, 2
        responses to stress, 1-8
    Critical Oxygen Point in Yellowleg Shrimp (*Farfantepenaeus californiensis*): A Potential Species for the Live Seafood Trade, 23-25
    exports to China, 221
    exports to SE Asia, 194
    ornamental production, 89
    Using HACCP Principles and Physiological Studies to Improve Marketing Practices for Live Crustaceans, 271-282
MFV *Peadair Elaine*, 208
Miller, Todd W., 249
Milon, J. Walter, 63
Minnesota, 241
    The Harvest and Culture of Live Freshwater Aquatic Invertebrates, 125-129
MLMA. Marine Life Management Act of 1998
Moina, 128
mollusks. *See also* shellfish
    British Columbia import regulations, 175
monitoring
    A New Direction for Monitoring Lobster Meat Yield, Using Advances in Acoustic Probing, 267-270
    biotoxin monitoring, 113
monk fish, live handling, 57, 60, 61
Monterey Bay. *See also* California
    rockfish landings, 167
Monterey Bay Aquarium, 30
Morro Bay. *See also* California
    rockfish fishery, 165, 167, 168
Moynihan, Daniel Patrick, 29
MS-222. *See* tricane methane sulfonate
mud crab. *See also* crab
    harvest for SE Asia, 194

mudflats, cordgrass invasion, 258
mussels. *See also* shellfish
    holding and transport, 54
    import into British Columbia, 172
    Norway, 105
    shipment procedure, 53, 54
Myanmar, exports to SE Asia, 194
Mytilus trossulus, introductions, 252
Myxobolus cerebralis, 259

N

Napoleon, harvest for SE Asia trade, 184
National Cattlemen's Association, 35
National Institutes of Health, 35, 43
National Marine Fisheries Service (NMFS), 169
National Science Foundation (NSF), 227
National Shellfish Sanitation Program (NSSP), 54, 115, 116
The National Seafood Hazard Analysis Critical Control Point Program and the Live Seafood Industry, 227-230
Nature, 39
Nearshore Fisheries Management Act of 1998 (NFMA), 163
Nereis virens, Live Rockweed (*Ascophyllum*) used as a Shipping Medium for the Live Transport of Marine Baitworms from Maine, 95-97
net, stress effect on fish, 20
New York, crayfish culture, 133
New York State Department of Environmental Conservation, 38
New York Times, 35
New Zealand. *See also* Australia
    animal rights activism, 35
    "Code of Compliance for Export," 58
    exports to SE Asia, 194, 221, 223
    import restrictions, 234
    lobster exports, 57
NFMA. *See* Nearshore Fisheries Management Act of 1998
Nickum, John G., 237
nitrate. *See also* ammonia
    denitrification, 286
    toxic accumulations, 58
Nitrobacter, 285
nitrogen
    as anesthetic, 134-135, 136
    biofilter function and, 285-286
nitrogen metabolism. *See also* ammonia; metabolism
    Effect of Long-Haul International Transport on Lobster Hemolymph Constituents and Nitrogen Metabolism, 9-18
Nitrosomonas, 285
NMFS. *See* National Marine Fisheries Service
non-native species, unintentional introduction, 95-97, 126
Noriega-Orozco, L.O., 271
Norway. *See also* Europe
    exports to, 153
    Live Transport of the Great Scallop (*Pecten maximus*), 105-109
    salmon import restrictions, 234, 235
Norway lobster, 213

Nova Scotia. *See also* Canada
    A New Direction for Monitoring Lobster Meat Yield, Using Advances in Acoustic Probing, 267-270
    air transport of lobster, 9-18
    lobster holding and transport, 51-56
    mussel storage, 54
NSF. *See* National Science Foundation
NSSP. *See* National Shellfish Sanitation Program

O

Ocampo, Lucía V., 23
ocean quahog, 250
Office International des Epizooties (OIE), 233
OIE. *See* Office International des Epizooties
Okhotsk Sea, 114
Olin, Paul G., 27
Olson, Annette M., 243
Opportunity or Threat? Implications of the Live Halibut Fishery in British Columbia from the Harvester Perspective, 151-153
Orconectes limosus, emersion, 133
Oregon
    Administrative Rule 635-056, 253-254
    bait use, 246
    exotic introductions, 263
    HB 3071, 253
    import regulations, 233
Oregon Department of Fish and Wildlife, 254
Oriental lung fluke (*Paragonimus westermani*), introduction, 259
Ornamental Fish Industry, 87-93
ornamental fishery. *See also* Florida
    British Columbia import regulations, 172-174
    Florida's Ornamental Marine Life Industry, 63-71
    live reef fish, 183
    Ornamental Fish Industry, 87-93
        Florida's ornamental aquaculture industry, 87-89
        handling steps, 90-92
        other international sources, 89
        wild harvesting, 89-90
    Shipping Practices in the Ornamental Fish Industry, 73-86
        fish pack density, 76-78
        freight considerations, 73-74
        packing procedures, 78-79
        receiving fish, 80-82
        shipping additives, 79-80
        shipping bags, 74-75
        shipping boxes, 75-76
otolith samples, halibut, 155
Overaa, Toril, 105
oxygen. *See also* aeration; oxygen consumption; recirculation
    supplemental, 56, 58, 93, 129, 136
        aeration, 141, 143, 289
        aggression stimulation, 134
        at-sea mechanisms, 146
        injection, 159
        oxygen bubblers, 146
        in transit, 73, 83, 91

oxygen consumption
    conformity and regulation, 24
    critical oxygen point establishment, 23
    Critical Oxygen Point in Yellowleg Shrimp (*Farfantepenaeus californiensis*): A Potential Species for the Live Seafood Trade, 23-25
    during emersion, 9-10, 132
    relation to temperature, 108
oxygen supply, relation to mortality, 45, 46-47
oyster drill. *See also* pathogens
    introduction and establishment, 263
oysters (*Crassostrea gigas*)
    British Columbia import regulations, 175
    culture, 207, 257, 265
    export to China, 221
    farmed with scallops, 113
    non-native, 252
    Norway, 105
    transport, 51, 53

P

Pacheco-Aguilar, R., 271
Pacific Coast Shellfish Growers Association, 263
Pacific Fishery Management Council (PFMC), 163, 169
packing material. *See also* seaweed
    alternatives to seaweed, 97, 111, 198
    chilled sawdust, 131
    Do Live Marine Products Serve as Pathways for the Introduction of Nonindigenous Species?, 243-247
    dry sand, 198
    invertebrate inhabitants, 95, 96-97, 245
    newspaper, 198
    qualities required of, 116
pain. *See also* animal rights
    anti-cruelty ethic, 36-37
    in fish, 28, 31, 39, 42
pair bonding, in ornamental fish, 90
Pakistan, exports to SE Asia, 194
Palaemon serratus. *See* shrimp
Palau, reef fish exports, 184
Papua New Guinea, exports to SE Asia, 194
paralytic shellfish poisoning, 227, 229. *See also* disease
parasites. *See also* disease; invertebrates; pathogens
    ciliates, 10
    conditions required by, 107
    detecting, 78, 82, 159, 160-161
    flatworm, 114, 120
    oyster drill, 263
    Perkinsus qugwadi, 114
    preventing transference of, 215-216
    resistance to, 114
    treatments, 78
parrotfish, harvest for SE Asia trade, 184
pathogens. *See also* bacteria; disease; parasites
    in ballast water, 244, 249, 252, 259
    destroying, 227, 264
    Do Live Marine Products Serve as Pathways for the Introduction of Nonindigenous Species?, 243-247
    in ornamental fishery, 90-91
    oyster drill, 263

Patinopecten
    caurinus, background, 111-112, 114
    (Mizuhopecten) yessoensis, background, 114-115
Pattison, Christine, 163, 177
Pecten maximus, Live Transport of the Great Scallop *(Pecten maximus),* 105-109
Pedersen, Hans-Peder, 45
pens. *See also* holding tank; pounds
    disease transmission from, 156-157
    halibut fishery, 160-161
    lobster, 210
    processing plants and, 177
People for the Ethical Treatment of Animals (PETA), 27, 29, 30, 32, 39, 42
Perkinsus qugwadi, scallop resistence to, 114
permits
    imports into Canada, 172, 175
    live ornamental harvesting, 65
        saltwater products license (FL), 67-68
    Nearshore Fishery Permit (CA), 164
    saltwater products license (SPL), 67
    Washington shellfish industry, 266
    for waste discharge, 217
Pet Industry Joint Advisory Council, 63
Pet Products News Buying Guide, 68
PETA. *See* People for the Ethical Treatment of Animals
PFMC. *See* Pacific Fishery Management Council
pH
    ammonia and, 58, 81
    buffering, 58, 79
    factors affecting, 54, 82, 91, 197
    relation to halibut chalkiness, 178
    relation to oxygen consumption, 24
    phenicol, 80
Philippines. *See also* Asia
    exports to SE Asia, 194, 201, 202
    reef fishery, 184, 190
Physiological Responses of Blue Crabs *(Callinectes* sp.) to Procedures Used in the Soft Crab Fishery in La Laguna de Terminos, Mexico, 1-8
Pickering, Alan, 21
Pillsbury Corp., 227, 271
plankton bloom. *See* algal blooms
plants. *See also* algae
    Florida harvest, 63, 70, 87-88
    invasive species, 258, 259, 260
    Live Rockweed *(Ascophyllum)* used as a Shipping Medium for the Live Transport of Marine Baitworms from Maine, 95-97
plastic bags. *See also* transport
    ammonia-permeable, 92
    shipping with, 74-75
poaching, reef fishery, 184
Point Four Systems, 146
polystyrene bins, 59, 61
ponds, 239. *See also* aquaculture
    crayfish, 133
    Florida live ornamentals, 88
    for invertebrate culture, 128
Port of Portland, 254
pot, for live catch, 58

pounds, Shipping and Handling the Marine Algae *Macrocystis* in Alaska, 99-103
prawns. *See also* shrimp; spot prawn
    export to SE Asia, 194, 198
Prince Edward Island. *See also* Canada
    mussel storage, 54
processing, vs. live organism trade, 109, 152-153
protein skimmer, 56, 285. *See also* filtering
Pseudomonas. See also disease
    contamination, 218
public health concerns. *See also* hazard analysis; safety
    live food industry, 31
Puerto Rico, Optimizing Waterless Shipping Conditions for *Macrobrachium rosenbergii,* 131-139
Puget Sound. *See also* Washington
    exotic introductions, 263
    salmon farming, 259
purging. *See also* water quality
    in transport, 59, 197

Q

Qualicum Bay, 114
quality assurance, with HACCP, 228-229
quality control, achieving, 31, 61, 108-109
quality indicators, scallops, 107
quarantine requirements, 174, 215
Quatsino Sound, halibut fishery, 160
Queen Charlotte Islands, 112
queen conch, awareness campaign about, 71
quinaldine, 79-80
quota system, in halibut fishery, 152

R

rabbit fish, 135
rainbow trout. *See also* trout
    toxicant exposure, 21
Rainnie, D., 267
RAPP. *See* Regulatory Action Points Plan
recirculation. *See also* aeration; oxygen; water quality
    ammonia buildup, 52, 139, 197
    ocean-going container, 52-53
    small-scale land-based, 53-54, 217
    through-hull facilities for, 195
reconditioning. *See also* holding tank
    Holding Tank System for Reconditioning Transport of Live Cod Recently Captured in Deep Water, 45-50
    scallops, 108
record keeping
    hazard analysis and, 228, 274-275
    proactive recommendations for, 139, 165
    tagging, 229-230
recreational harvesting, live ornamentals, 65, 70-71
red rock crab, 266. *See also* crab
Red Sea, ornamental fish exports, 64
red tide, 259
reef environment, erosion effects on, 19-20
reef fishery
    cyanide use, 183, 184, 188, 190, 191

record keeping *(continued)*
  exports to Hong Kong, 183-192, 193, 194
  growout, 184, 191
  Live Reef Food Fish Trade in Hong Kong: Problems and Prospects, 183-192
    composition and value of trade, 184-185
    impact on fish stocks, 188-190
    problems and prospects, 190-191
    trade profile, 183-184
refrigeration. *See also* temperature control
  at-sea holding system, 145-146
regulations. *See also* Lacey Act
  animal rights activism affecting, 35
  Constraints to Shipping Live Product: Lessons from the AquaSeed Corporation Experience, 231-235
  for export, 232-233, 234
  in live ornamental trade, 70
  Live Seafood: A Recipe for Biological and Regulatory Concern?, 249-256
  Shipping Live Aquatic Products: Biological, Regulatory, and Environmental Considerations, 237-242
  Shipping Live Fish into British Columbia, Canada: Basic Regulatory Requirements, 171-176
Regulatory Action Points Plan (RAPP), 228
reproductive system, stress affecting, 20, 21
research. *See also* education
  animal rights and, 35, 37, 43
  fish imports for, 174, 245, 247
  Using HACCP Principles and Physiological Studies to Improve Marketing Practices for Live Crustaceans, 271-282
Research Council of Norway, 46
Resource Management and Environmental Issues Concerning Live Halibut Landings, 155-157
Resource Management Issues: Question and Answer Session, 177-181
Resource Management Issues in California's Commercial Nearshore Live/Premium Finfish Fishery, 163-170
restaurants. *See also* retailing
  An Insight into the Shanghai Market for Imported Live Seafood, 221-225
  holding and display systems, 53-54
  Hong Kong, relationships among wholesalers and restaurants, 201-202
  marketing procedures, 60
restoration, invertebrate species for, 127-128
retailing. *See also* restaurants
  Keeping Baitfish Alive and Healthy in Holding Tanks: Tips for Retail Outlets, 141-143
  Live Fish Handling Strategies from Boat to Retail Establishment, 57-61
Review of Impacts of Aquatic Exotic Species: What's at Risk?, 257-261
Ricketts and Calvin, 266
risk. *See also* safety
  of introduced species, 250-252
  in live seafood industry, 237, 239, 240
  Review of Impacts of Aquatic Exotic Species: What's at Risk?, 257-261
rock lobster. *See Jasus edwardsii*
  harvest for China trade, 193, 221, 223
rock wool, for packing material, 18

rockfish, 164, 165
  California, 148-149, 164-168
  import into British Columbia, 172
Rofan, Bob, 92
Rollin, Bernard E., 35
romantic naturalism, 237, 240-241
Rosas, Carlos, 1
Royal Society for the Prevention of Cruelty to Animals (RSPCA), 39
RSPCA. *See* Royal Society for the Prevention of Cruelty to Animals
Russia, 129
  halibut exports, 179

S

Sadovy, Yvonne, 183
safety. *See also* hazard analysis; risk
  Live Seafood: A Recipe for Biological and Regulatory Concern?, 249-256
  Live Seafood Holding Systems: Review of Systems and Components, 283-290
  The National Seafood Hazard Analysis Critical Control Point Program and the Live Seafood Industry, 227-230
  Shipping Live Aquatic Products: Biological, Regulatory, and Environmental Considerations, 237-242
salinity. *See also* salt
  relation to ammonia efflux, 4-5
  relation to oxygen capacity and temperature, 24
salinity difference, stress related to, *Callinectes* sp., 4-5
salmon
  aquaculture, AquaSeed Corp., 231-232
  disease, infectious salmon anemia, 234
  importation into British Columbia, 171, 172
    for aquaculture, 174-175
  smolt, 20
  transport, stress effects, 20, 21
salmonella, 31
salt. *See also* salinity
  adding to fish water, 21, 78, 79, 82, 91-92, 142
saltwater products license (SPL), 67. *See also* permits
  marine life endorsement (MLE), 67, 69
San Francisco. *See also* California
  animal rights controversy, 27-33, 38-39
  rockfish landings, 167
San Francisco Bay, alien introductions, 95, 96, 97, 252, 258, 263
San Francisco Estuary Institute, 96
sand dollar, Florida harvest, 63
sandworm. *See Nereis virens*
Santa Barbara. *See also* California
  shrimp harvest, 148-149
scallops. *See also* spiny scallop *(Chlamys hastata)*
  cultured, 194
  Handling and Shipping of Live Northeast Pacific Scallops: Larvae to Adults, 111-124
  harvesting practices, 115-116
    farmed Japanese, 116
    live mature, 115
    spiny and pink, 115-116
  larvae, transport, 117-119

scallops *(continued)*
    larvae and spat, handling, 119-120
    Live Transport of the Great Scallop *(Pecten maximus)*, 105-109
    mechanical shucking, 112, 113
    recommended handling practices for live mature scallops, 115-116
        gaping, 115
    seed
        handling, 120-121
        transport, 117
    transport, 53
        air transport, 116-117
        larvae, 117-119
        paperwork requirements, 121
        seed, 117
scampi *(Nephrops norvegicus)*, 213
    mortality, 276
    nitrogen metabolism, 10
Scarratt, David J., 51
Scopaenichthys marmoratus. See cabezon
Scorpaena guttata. See scorpionfish
scorpionfish, harvest for SE Asia trade, 184
Scotland. *See also* United Kingdom
    exports to Hong Kong, 194
SDS, exposure to fish, 21
sea bream, harvest for SE Asia trade, 184
sea conditions, effect on fish, 49, 147, 159
Sea Hive Corporation, 52, 55
Sea of Japan, 114
sea perch, live handling, 57, 60
sea urchin, packaging, 51-52
seahorse, in ornamental trade, 64
seasickness, fish susceptibility to, 49
seaweed. *See also* algae; packing material
    Live Rockweed *(Ascophyllum)* used as a Shipping Medium for the Live Transport of Marine Baitworms from Maine, 95-97
    as packing material, 18, 51, 52
        invertebrates found in, 95, 96-97, 245, 253
Sebastes rastrelliger, 167. *See also* rockfish
Seccombe, John, 57
sedatives. *See also* anesthetic
    for shipping, 79-80
Selye, Hans, 19
Semicossyphus pulcher. See sheephead
Seward, 112
Seychelles, reef fishery, 183, 184, 194
Sha Tau Kok, 203
Shanghai. *See also* China
    An Insight into the Shanghai Market for Imported Live Seafood, 221-225
Shanghai Fisheries General, 221
shark, 58
Shekou entry point, 203
shell market, compared to live market, 70
shellfish. *See also* crustaceans
    An Overview of Irish Live Crustacean Fisheries, 207-213
    British Columbia import regulations, 175
    effects of stress upon, 3
    export to SE Asia, 194

shellfish *(continued)*
    holding and transporting practices, 1, 197
    pain experienced by, 39
    Using HACCP Principles and Physiological Studies to Improve Marketing Practices for Live Crustaceans, 271-282
    What's New in Live Fish and Shellfish At-Sea Holding Systems: High Tech and Low Tech, 145-150
shipping. *See* transport
shipping containers, 283. *See also* holding
Shipping Live Aquatic Products: Biological, Regulatory, and Environmental Considerations, 237-242
shrimp
    Critical Oxygen Point in Yellowleg Shrimp *(Farfantepenaeus californiensis)*: A Potential Species for the Live Seafood Trade, 23-25
    disease associated with, 258
    export to SE Asia, 221
    holding systems, 147-150
    Irish landings, 207
    Optimizing Waterless Shipping Conditions for *Macrobrachium rosenbergii*, 131-139
    species profile, 210
    stress-induced changes in, 4, 287
    "white spot" disease, 258
Siganus argentes (rabbit fish), 135
Singapore. *See also* China; Hong Kong
    exports to US, 64
    live reef fish imports, 183
    ornamental production, 89
Singer, Peter, 36
skate, 60
Smith, Scott, 243
smooth venus, 250
snails, Florida live harvest, 63, 66, 67
snapper, harvest for SE Asia trade, 184, 185, 196
So Mei, 204
Society for the Prevention of Cruelty to Animals (SPCA), animal rights controversy, 31
sodium hydroxide, 135
soft-shell crab *(Mya arenaria). See also* crab
    green crab predation, 258, 259
sole, 60
Solomon Islands, reef fishery, 184
South Africa, exports to SE Asia, 194, 221
South America
    exports to China, 221
    ornamental production, 89
South China Sea, reef fishery, 183
southern pigfish, live handling, 57, 60
Spain. *See also* Europe
    animal rights activism, 41
    imports, 106
        from UK, 212, 213
Spanish hogfish, 70
Spee Dee Delivery, 129
spider crab *(Maja squinado). See also* crab
    Irish landings, 207
    species profile, 212

spiny lobster (*Panulirus interruptus*). *See also* lobster
    dessication, 14
    farming, Florida, 180
    HACCP principles for, 271-272
    harvest for SE Asia trade, 193, 194
    nitrogen metabolism, 10
spiny scallop (*Chlamys hastata*). *See also* scallop
    background, 112-113
    harvesting, 115-116
SPL. *See* saltwater products license
spot prawn. *See also* prawns
    handling and tank densities, 148
    live vs. fresh price, 145
Sri Lanka. *See also* Asia
    exports to SE Asia, 194
    ornamental production, 89
stacking, in transport, 61
starfish, Florida live harvest, 63, 67
state law, Lacey Act support for, 240-242
steel-jawed trap, 35, 38
steelhead, aquaculture, 231
Stephens, Charlie, 263
Sterling Pacific Halibut: A New Approach, 159-162
Sterling Pacific Halibut, 177
Strait of Georgia, scallops, 112, 113, 114
stress
    blue crab (*Callinectes* sp.) fishery, responses to stress, 1-8
    causes
        capture, 133
        high fish density, 46, 142
        pH, 82
        temperature, 46
    cross-tolerance
        cold shock, 22
        heat shock, 21
    defining, 19
    effect on quality, 107
    fish
        cellular stress response, 21
        confinement stress, 21
        cross-tolerance, 21
        field measurement, 21
        generalized stress response, 19-20
        measuring responses, 20-21
        sensitivity, 39
    harvest-induced, 115
    indicators
        ammonia efflux, 2
        regurgitation, 59
    Physiological Stress Response in Fish, 19-22
    as precursor to mortality, 3
    scallops, 107
stripping towers, carbon dioxide, 289
"Structure and Competitiveness of Florida's Tropical Ornamental Marine Species Industry," 68
sulfa-based drugs, 80
Sumatra, 90
Sundnes, Gunnar, 46
surgeonfish, Florida live harvest, 66
survival, definition, 136

sustainability. *See also* environment
    Alaska scallops, 112
    concerns about, 27, 29-30
    Irish crustacean fishery, 212-213
    reef fishery, 188-190, 191
        IUCN Red List, 190
    wild harvesting, 89-90
Sweden, "Bill of Rights" for farm animals, 35
swim bladder. *See* air bladder
swine industry, 39, 41
swordfish, boycotts, 30

T

tagging programs, shellfish, 265-266
Taiwan. *See also* China; Hong Kong
    exports to China, 221
    live reef fish imports, 183
Tamaru, Clyde S., 73
Tampa International Airport, 88, 89
temperature control
    Aquahort Heat'n'Chill pump, 59
    at-sea chiller systems, 147-148, 159
    with freshwater ice, 106
    in holding facility, 61, 218, 289
    refrigeration, 145-146
    tracking, 119
    in transit, 18, 52, 59, 79, 83
temperature effects
    baitfish, 141
    invertebrates, 126, 127, 129
    metabolism, 195, 197
    mortality, 39, 56, 126
    ornamental fish, 81, 92
    parasites, 107
    Pcr, 24
    semi-dormancy, 145
    shrimp, 132-133, 135
        propulsion-like behavior, 134
    stress, 46
temperature monitoring, HOBO Temperature Logger, 11
temperature shock, preventing, 141-142
tetracycline, 80
Texas, ornamental production, 89
Texas Parks and Wildlife, 258
Thailand. *See also* Asia
    exports to SE Asia, 194, 201, 202, 221
    exports to US, 64
    ornamental production, 89
    reef fishery, 184
"The care and handling of lobsters" (McCleese/Wilder), 55-56
Thoele, Barry, 125
Thomas, Thea, 99
Thomforde, Hugh, 141
Thompson, Terry, 253-254
Tibet, 193, 221
tiger barbs, 80
tiger grouper (*Epinephelus fuscoguttatus*). *See also* grouper
    harvest for SE Asia trade, 184
tiger prawn. *See also* prawns
    culture and harvest, 194, 198

tilapia
    British Columbia import regulations, 171-172
    stress reactions, 22
Tobago, exports to US, 64
Todgham, Ann, 21
Tomales Bay, 265. *See also* California
Totten Inlet, 263
transport. *See also* air transport; holding; transshipment
    Constraints to Shipping Live Product: Lessons from the AquaSeed Corporation Experience, 231-235
    dry, 283
        scallops, 107-108
    Holding Tank System for Reconditioning Transport of Live Cod Recently Captured in Deep Water, 45-50
    home-made shipping containers, 129
    Live Fish Handling Strategies from Boat to Retail Establishment, 57-61
    live transport by ship, 194-196
    live transport vs. processing, 109
    lobster transportation systems, 52-53
    mussels, 54
    ornamentals
        boxes, 75-76
        fish pack density, 76-78, 80, 142, 195-196
        in general, 74
        plastic bags, 74-75, 197
    packing material inhabitants, 95, 96-97
    polystyrene bins, 59, 61, 197
    shipping additives, 79-80
    Shipping Live Aquatic Products: Biological, Regulatory, and Environmental Considerations, 237-242
    Short-Term Holding and Live Transport of Aquatic Animals: An Overview of Problems and Some Historic Solutions, 51-56
    stress-related effects, 39, 60
transshipment
    The Construction of a Commercial Live Seafood Transshipment Facility: Review of General Specifications, 215-219
        business plan, 216-217
        facility planning, 217
trawling, for live catch, 58
tricane methane sulfonate (MS-222), 79-80
Trinidad, exports to US, 64
Triple M II, 159
tropical fish. *See also* ornamental fishery
    Florida production, 63-64
trout
    brown, confinement stress, 21
    disease affecting, 259
    hybridization, 259
    importation into British Columbia, 172
    rainbow, fish food and additives, 125
trumpeter, live handling, 57
tuna
    aquaculture, 177
    boycotts, 30
turtles, 38

U

UFAW. *See* Universities Federation for Animal Welfare
Uglow, Roger F., 1, 9, 271
ultraviolet (UV), for bacteria control, 53, 54-55, 288
United Kingdom. *See also* Ireland
    An Overview of Irish Live Crustacean Fisheries, 207-213
    animal rights activism, 32, 39, 41
    exports
        to Europe, 106
        to Hong Kong, 194
    quality control, 61
United States
    animal rights activism, 35
    baitfish industry, 141
    Callinectes sapidus fishery, 2
    exports to SE Asia, 193-194, 221
    National Shellfish Sanitation Program, 115
    net imports of live ornamental marine life, 63
    trade in live ornamentals, 64-65
    wholesaler survey, 68-69
United States Department of Agriculture (USDA), animal cruelty issues, 38
    Universities Federation for Animal Welfare (UFAW), 39
    University of Florida, Ruskin facility, 87
    University of Puerto Rico, Food and Agricultural Research Entrepreneurship Center, 131
U.S. Customs, 64
U.S. Department of Agriculture (USDA), 228, 230
U.S. Department of Commerce, 230
U.S. Fish and Wildlife Service
    Lacey Act enforcement, 233
    ornamental fish oversight, 64
U.S. International Trade Commission, 63
USDA. *See* U.S. Department of Agriculture
Using HACCP Principles and Physiological Studies to Improve Marketing Practices for Live Crustaceans, 271-282
UV. *See* ultraviolet

V

Vancouver Island, 114. *See also* Canada
    green crab introduction, 266
veal, 40
veined rapa whelk (*Rapana venosa*), impact on Chesapeake Bay, 258
velvet crab (*Necora puber*). *See also* crab
    holding and transport, 1, 14
    Irish landings, 207
    marketing, 272, 276
    metabolism during emersion, 10
    species profile, 210
Venezuela, ornamental production, 89
vermilion rockfish, 167. *See also* rockfish
Vibrio contamination, 218, 224, 229-230, 259, 289. *See also* bacteria; disease
Vietnam
    exports to SE Asia, 194, 201, 202
    fish export ban, 189
Vijayan, Matt, 21

W

Walgren, Congressman, 43
Washington
    bait use, 246
    hazardous waste program, 43
    Impact of the Green Crab on the Washington State Shellfish Aquaculture Industry, 263-266
    import regulations, 233
    scallop fishery, 113
waste. *See also* ammonia efflux
    in herring sac roe fishery, 100, 103
waste discharge
    disease prevention and, 264
    permits, 217
water
    adequate supplies of, 217
    for cleansing shellfish, 116
    makeup water, 286
water pumps. *See also* holding tank
    discussed, 284
water quality. *See also* aeration; filtering; recirculation
    dechlorination, 141
    feed type affecting, 177
    invertebrates affecting, 128
    for ornamental fish transport, 91
    pollution affecting, 205
    stabilizers, 79-80
    stress related to, 4-5
    tests, 143
Watson, Craig A., 87
weathervane scallop. *See Patinopecten caurinus*
Wetlok boxes, 102
whales, 36
What's New in Live Fish and Shellfish At-Sea Holding Systems: High Tech and Low Tech, 145-150
When Elephants Weep, 36
white sucker, 141
Wholesale and Retail Marketing Aspects of the Hong Kong Live Seafood Business, 201-205
wild harvesting, ornamental fishery, 89-90, 92
Wilder, Dr., 55-56
wildlife, live animal trade effect on, 31
Wildlife Act (Canada), 171
Willapa Bay. *See also* Washington
    green crab introduction, 263-264, 266
World Trade Organization (WTO), 225
wormweed. *See also* seaweed
    Live Rockweed (*Ascophyllum*) used as a Shipping Medium for the Live Transport of Marine Baitworms from Maine, 95-97
wrasse, harvest for SE Asia trade, 184, 185, 189-190, 193
WTO. *See* World Trade Organization
Wyoming, fishery, 39

Y

Yantian, 203, 222
yellowleg shrimp. *See Farfantepenaeus californiensis*
Yellowstone National Park, 259

Z

zebra mussel (*Dreissena polymorpha*)
    exotic introduction, 96, 254, 258, 259
    Maine certificate, 233
zeolite. *See also* ammonia; carbon dioxide
    gas absorption, 80, 91, 133-134, 136-137, 138
    use in transport, 80, 91, 133